Frommer's®

S0-CFF-494

Greek Islands
4th Edition

by John S. Bowman & Sherry Marker

with cruise coverage by Rebecca Tobin

WILEY

Wiley Publishing, Inc.

Published by:

Wiley Publishing, Inc.
111 River St.
Hoboken, NJ 07030-5774

ISBN-13: 978-0-7645-9832-6
ISBN-10: 0-7645-9832-5

Editor: Naomi Black
Production Editor: Bethany J. André
Cartographer: Roberta Stockwell
Photo Editor: Richard Fox
Production by Wiley Indianapolis Composition Services

Front cover photo: Cyclades, Santorini: Church at sunset, sea beyond
Back cover photo: The Parthenon, Athens

For information on our other products and services or to obtain technical support, please contact our Customer Care Department within the U.S. at 800/762-2974, outside the U.S. at 317/572-3993 or fax 317/572-4002.

Wiley also publishes its books in a variety of electronic formats. Some content that appears in print may not be available in electronic formats.

Manufactured in the United States of America

5   4   3   2   1

Contents

9   The Dodecanese   312

by John S. Bowman

10   The Northeastern Aegean Islands   360

by John S. Bowman

11   The Sporades   391

by John S. Bowman

12   The Ionian Islands   416

by John S. Bowman

Appendix A: Greece in Depth   438

Appendix B: The Greek Language   446

Appendix C: Useful Toll-Free Numbers & Websites   454

Index   457

List of Maps

An Invitation to the Reader

In researching this book, we discovered many wonderful places—hotels, restaurants, shops, and more. We're sure you'll find others. Please tell us about them, so we can share the information with your fellow travelers in upcoming editions. If you were disappointed with a recommendation, we'd love to know that, too. Please write to:

Frommer's Greek Islands, 4th Edition
Wiley Publishing, Inc. • 111 River St. • Hoboken, NJ 07030-5774

An Additional Note

Please be advised that travel information is subject to change at any time—and this is especially true of prices. We therefore suggest that you write or call ahead for confirmation when making your travel plans. The authors, editors, and publisher cannot be held responsible for the experiences of readers while traveling. Your safety is important to us, however, so we encourage you to stay alert and be aware of your surroundings. Keep a close eye on cameras, purses, and wallets, all favorite targets of thieves and pickpockets.

About the Authors

John S. Bowman has been a freelance writer and editor for more than 35 years. He specializes in nonfiction ranging from archaeology to zoology, baseball to biography. He first visited Greece in 1956 and has traveled and lived there over the years. He is the author of numerous guides to various regions in Greece. He currently resides in Northampton, Massachusetts.

Sherry Marker majored in classical Greek at Harvard, studied archaeology at the American School of Classical Studies in Athens, and did graduate work in ancient history at the University of California at Berkeley. The author of a number of guides to Greece, she has also written for the *New York Times, Travel + Leisure,* and *Hampshire Life.* When not in Greece, she lives in Massachusetts.

Rebecca Tobin has been writing about the travel business for the past 5 years, and about cruising for the past 3, as an editor and reporter for industry newspaper *Travel Weekly.* She has sampled food, fun, and deck chairs on more than 35 cruise ships. When she's not on the high seas, Rebecca is a landlubber in New York.

Other Great Guides for Your Trip:

Frommer's Greece
Frommer's Europe
Frommer's Europe from $85 a Day
Frommer's European Cruises & Ports of Call
Frommer's Gay & Lesbian Europe

Frommer's Star Ratings, Icons & Abbreviations

Every hotel, restaurant, and attraction listing in this guide has been ranked for quality, value, service, amenities, and special features using a **star-rating system.** In country, state, and regional guides, we also rate towns and regions to help you narrow down your choices and budget your time accordingly. Hotels and restaurants are rated on a scale of zero (recommended) to three stars (exceptional). Attractions, shopping, nightlife, towns, and regions are rated according to the following scale: zero stars (recommended), one star (highly recommended), two stars (very highly recommended), and three stars (must-see).

In addition to the star-rating system, we also use **seven feature icons** that point you to the great deals, in-the-know advice, and unique experiences that separate travelers from tourists. Throughout the book, look for:

Finds	Special finds—those places only insiders know about
Fun Fact	Fun facts—details that make travelers more informed and their trips more fun
Kids	Best bets for kids and advice for the whole family
Moments	Special moments—those experiences that memories are made of
Overrated	Places or experiences not worth your time or money
Tips	Insider tips—great ways to save time and money
Value	Great values—where to get the best deals

The following **abbreviations** are used for credit cards:

AE	American Express	DISC	Discover	V	Visa
DC	Diners Club	MC	MasterCard		

Frommers.com

Now that you have the guidebook to a great trip, visit our website at **www.frommers.com** for travel information on more than 3,000 destinations. With features updated regularly, we give you instant access to the most current trip-planning information available. At Frommers.com, you'll also find the best prices on airfares, accommodations, and car rentals—and you can even book travel online through our travel booking partners. At Frommers.com, you'll also find the following:

- Online updates to our most popular guidebooks
- Vacation sweepstakes and contest giveaways
- Newsletter highlighting the hottest travel trends
- Online travel message boards with featured travel discussions

What's New in the Greek Islands

PLANNING YOUR TRIP Since the last edition of this guide, the Olympic Games have come and gone in Greece. It appears to have created a sparkling new image of this country—a Greece that can deliver on both aesthetics and logistics (albeit it without a day to spare!). The opening and closing ceremonies truly dazzled the world and undoubtedly will lead to ever more tourists. And Greece got in the bargain an **improved transportation infrastructure:** a new airport, an extended Metro system, a surface trolley from central Athens to the coast, a circumferential highway to help drivers avoid central Athens, and a dramatic new bridge across the Gulf of Corinth.

The only downside: all the publicity about preparedness and security concerns. Nothing happened, and everything worked. That summer of 2004, Greek hotels in particular experienced drastic losses in clientele and profits. This threw the pricing structure of hotels into turmoil—the normal increases that accompany inflation can't be counted on for several years as the hotels try to regain their equilibrium. So, more than ever, we caution you to be flexible about the prices provided in this book. We can only say that for every hotel room more expensive than what we report, there will be another hotel room that's cheaper.

Booking Online By now most travelers are aware of the many online sites for making travel plans and reservations. Many offer discounts as well as reservations. But we must stress: Read the small print about cancellation policies—they can be pretty unforgiving! In our experience, it is often better to search the discount websites for prices but then to deal directly with the hotels. This holds true for airlines also. They often meet or even beat the so-called discount outfits, and the ticket purchased directly from the airline will get you better service if there are any problems along the way.

GETTING THERE Those who follow the tourist reports in the news may be aware that Olympic Airways has been operating in bankruptcy for several years and has been put up for sale. As we go to press, the winning bidder has not been announced but it appears that an existing European airline will take over and maintain pretty much the same service. Meanwhile, Olympic Airways continues to provide both direct flights from North America and almost all of its internal flights.

One of the bidders for the Olympic franchise, however, is the Greek airline, Aegean Airlines, which in the last few years has become a major competitor with Olympic Airways, especially for domestic service in Greece. It was awarded the European Regions Airline Association "Gold Award Airline of the Year" for 2004–05. The award recognizes Aegean Airlines' achievements not only in its operations—finances, electronic ticketing, and so on—but also in its good customer service and on-time performance. The ERAA has about 230 member airlines, so this award represents a significant achievement.

TRAVEL AGENCIES There is no shortage of travel agencies prepared to arrange your trip to and within Greece. A brand-new one is aiming at the high-end market. A young Greek man, Christos Stergiou, whose family runs a hotel and restaurant on the island of Patmos, started TrueGreece. Christos earned his undergraduate and graduate degrees (MBA from Stanford) in the U.S. and so brings a special combination of experience and awareness to the travel business. **TrueGreece** (www.truegreece.com) offers several "package" tours that include Athens and two islands. They will also customize itineraries, including those for honeymooners.

In addition to the finer hotels and restaurants to which TrueGreece takes its clients, it provides native-born, English-speaking escorts who provide a more intimate view of the locales visited. Also, it limits its groups to 16.

Another agency, the well-established **Windmills Travel,** with offices in Athens, Tinos, and Mykonos, has updated and expanded its website (www.windmills.gr), which now covers most questions travelers might have about Greece. The website includes a photo album for almost all of Greece. For information on short- and long-term island rentals, contact Windmill's Tinos manager, Sharon Turner (sharon@thn.forthnet.gr.).

Greece is beginning to embrace **ecotourism.** Much of the country is relatively unspoiled, and entrepreneurs are steadily offering more and more environmentally friendly activities. One of the least well known is Milia, a once-abandoned village in the mountains of western Crete. Starting in the 1980s, two local families began restoring buildings and converting the village into an eco-hideaway. They grow most of their own vegetables, raise animals, and even generate their solar electricity. Nature lovers should check www.milia.gr to learn about visiting.

ATHENS Where to Stay Grande Bretagne Hotel, Syntagma Square (© 210/333-0000; www.grandebretagne. gr); and **Hilton Hotel,** 46 Leoforos Vas. Sofias (© 210/728-1000; www.hilton. com), were extensively redecorated and renovated for the Athens 2004 Olympic Games. The Grande Bretagne now boasts two pools, and the Hilton redid its outdoor pool. Both hotels have high-speed Internet connections in all rooms, as well as their own spas and exercise facilities. A new boutique hotel, **Hotel Eridanus (Iridanos)** © 210/520-5360), has opened next to the newly relocated Varoulko's restaurant (see below) in the once down-at-the-heels Gazi district. What had been a gasworks is now an area bursting with boutiques, galleries, restaurants, and chic little hotels. **The Fresh Hotel** (© 210/524-8511), a less-expensive newcomer a few blocks away from the Iridanos at 26 Sofokleus, is home to the popular Athenian bar, Orange.

Where to Dine Another sign of the "reclaiming" of the Gazi district is the arrival of **Varoulko,** Greece's best fish restaurant, now at 80 Piraios (© 210/522-8400). A new menu at the new location offers sweetbreads, goat stew, and a spicy tripe soup along with its famous seafood dishes. If you haven't been to Athens for a few years, you'll be pleased to discover that **Aegli** (© 210/336-9363), the longtime favorite just off Syntagma Square in the National Garden, is back beside the Zappion Building, serving gourmet meals and snacks. Aegli offers some compensation for the closing of another long-time Athenian favorite just off Syntagma Square: Zonar's. See chapter 5.

Seeing the Sights Exploring Athens is easier than ever thanks to the new Metro system—and pleasanter than ever thanks to the pedestrianized walks linking the major archaeological sites. If you stop in at the main Metro station in Syntagma Square, you can get a map of the system. The Greek National Tourism Organization (EOT) at 2 Amerikis sometimes has maps of the **"Archaeological Park,"** which stretches from Hadrian's Gate past the Acropolis and Ancient Agora to the Kerameikos. As you explore Athens, on foot and by Metro, be sure to take in the two new museums in the Acropolis and Syntagma Metro stations, which display antiquities found during the Metro excavations. See chapter 5.

And save time to take in Athens's astonishing variety of small museums: If you only have time for one, go to **Benaki Museum of Islamic Art,** Agio Asomaton & Dipylou, Psirri (✆ **210/367-1000;** www.benaki.gr.). This was Greece's first museum of Islamic art. Just a block away, **The Museum of Traditional Pottery,** 4–6 Melidoni, Kerameikos (✆ **210/331-8491**), has a permanent collection and special exhibits of traditional and contemporary Greek pottery.

In nearby Plaka, **Frissiras Museum,** 3–7 Moni Asteriou, Plaka (✆ **210/323-4678**), is Athens's first museum to concentrate on 20th-century European art. The new **Pierides Museum of Ancient Cypriot Art,** 34–35 Kastorias, Votanikos (✆ **210/348-0000,** www.athinais,com.gr), does just what it says and records the art and politics of Cyprus.

THE SARONIC GULF ISLANDS At press time, **Hellas Flying Dolphins** had absorbed both Minoan Flying Dolphins and Ceres Flying Dolphins. There most certainly will be changes in nomenclature and service by the time you arrive, so do double-check all island boat information before you travel. It is a good idea to keep in mind that the recent proliferation of high-speed Flying Dolphin service to these islands has made it increasingly important to have both transportation and hotel reservations in summer. Check these websites for current info: www.saronicnet.com and www.magicaljourneys.com. See chapter 6.

CRETE The company that operates the **high-speed catamarans,** Hellas Flying Dolphins, has now instituted service between Piraeus and Chania, Crete (www.hellenicseaways.,gr). The catamaran rides are not cheap, but there's a wide range of options. The cheapest trip is 41€ ($53) one-way, 70€ ($91) round-trip. It cuts the trip time down to about 5 hours (compared to the regular ferry service time of about 12 hr). They promise daily service each way, but you arrive back in Piraeus at 1:15am.

Horseback riding is a relatively new activity on Crete. Most of the riding centers offer group rides or lessons—they do not seem geared for individual rentals (but you can ask). Generally, these outfits offer everything from half-day rides to week-long "packages" (hotel, meals, and so on). Look for **Zoraida's** at Georgiopolis, near Chania, on the Internet at www.zoraida.georgioupoli.net. **Odysseia Stables,** at Avdou, is located in the mountains southeast of Iraklion (www.horseriding.gr).

A more ambitious outfit is the **Therapeutic Holidays Camp** run by a British organization. Located at Karteros Beach (some 5km/3 miles east of Iraklion), it offers horseback riding as therapy for individuals with mental or physical disabilities. See www.therapeutic-holidays.org. This will cost you, but service is professional. In addition to riding, therapies include work-based activities such as bread-baking and gardening.

Also new on Crete as of 2005 is **ThalassoKosmos (Sea World),** essentially an elaborate aquarium with outdoor seawater tanks located at the old U.S. Air Force station at Gouves, about 16km (10 miles) along the coast east of Iraklion. It boasts 4,000 marine organisms and many opportunities for viewing them. Whether this experience contributes to people's reasons to go to Crete remains to be seen, but it is a worthy venture and has the support of the Hellenic Center of Marine Research, along with the Institutes of Marine Biology and Fish Farming.

Where to Stay   Greek hotels are constantly renovating and updating, but one of the more impressive makeovers within recent years is that of the **Lato Boutique Hotel** in Iraklion (www.lato.gr). In recognition of this transformation, the Lato has now been accepted into the international chain known as Boutique Hotels. Hotels in this association are not luxury hotels in the sense of opulent decor or extravagant amenities, but they must maintain high standards in their service as well as provide pleasing environments. See chapter 7.

THE DODECANESE   The proprietor of the S. Nikolis Hotel in Rhodes, which we have long recommended, has now opened a new hotel (close to the S. Nikolis), **Hippodamou Hammam**. It is in an old Turkish mansion, completely restored in a style that captures Greek and Turkish traditions. The word "hammam" refers to a Turkish bath, and this hotel does provide its guests with an authentic steam bath. It also has a small Internet cafe with wi-fi. The 10 rooms, each decorated in an individual style and some with antiques, range from 80€ to 150€ ($104–$195), continental breakfast included. For more information, go to www.s-nikolis.gr and contact the proprietor as indicated there.

1

The Best of the Greek Islands

From Santorini's dramatic caldera to the reconstructed palace of Knossos on Crete, the Greek Islands are spectacular. There aren't many places in the world where the forces of nature have come together with the ancient sites and architectural treasures to create such dramatic results.

It can be bewildering to plan your trip with so many options vying for your attention. Take us along and we'll do the work for you. We've traveled the country extensively and chosen the very best that Greece has to offer. We've explored the archaeological sites, visited the museums, inspected the hotels, reviewed the tavernas and ouzeries, and scoped out the beaches. Here's what we consider the best of the best.

1 The Best of Ancient Greece

- **The Acropolis** (Athens): No matter how many photographs you've seen, nothing can prepare you for watching the light change the marble of the buildings, still standing after thousands of years, from honey to rose to deep red to stark white. If the crowds get you down, remember how crowded the Acropolis was during religious festivals in antiquity. See p. 154.

- **Palace of Knossos** (Crete): A seemingly unending maze of rooms and levels and stairways and corridors and frescoed walls—this is the Minoan Palace of Knossos. It can be packed at peak hours, but it still exerts its power if you enter in the spirit of the labyrinth. King Minos ruled over the richest and most powerful of Minoan cities and, according to legend, his daughter Ariadne helped Theseus kill the Minotaur in the labyrinth and escape. See p. 197.

- **Akrotiri** (Cyclades): Santorini is undoubtedly one of the most spectacular islands in the world. The site of Akrotiri offers a unique glimpse into the life of a Minoan city, frozen in time by a volcanic eruption 3,600 years ago. Be sure to find out if this site, which closed to the public in 2004, has reopened.

- **Delos** (Cyclades): This tiny isle, just 3.2km (2 miles) offshore of Mykonos, was considered by the ancient Greeks to be both the geographical and spiritual center of the Cyclades; many considered this the holiest sanctuary in all of Greece. The extensive remains here testify to the island's former splendor. From Mount Kinthos (really just a hill, but the island's highest point), you can see many of the Cyclades most days; on a very clear day, you can see the entire archipelago. The 3 hours allotted by excursion boats from Mykonos or Tinos are hardly sufficient to explore this vast archaeological treasure. See chapter 8.

Greece

BULGARIA

Drama
Xanthi
THRACE
Kavala
Komotini
TURKEY
Alexandroupolis
Sea of Marmara

Thasos

Samothraki

Mt. Athos

Limnos

EUROPE

Aegean Sea

GREECE

Alonissos
SPORADES
Lesvos
(Mitilini)

Skyros
NORTHEASTERN
AEGEAN ISLANDS
TURKEY

Kimi
EVVIA

Izmir

Karystos
Hios

Andros
Samos
Sounion
Kea
Tinos
Ikaria
Siros
Mykonos
Patmos
Delos
Naxos
Paros
Serifos
Donoussa
Kalimnos
Antiparos
Sifnos
CYCLADES
Kos
Milos
Ios
Amorgos
Folegandros
Simi
Anafi
DODECANESE
Santorini

To Crete
(approx. 60 miles
from mainland)
↓

Rhodes

Mountain 🔺

Karpathos

2 The Best of Byzantine Greece

- **Church of Panayia Kera** (Kritsa, Crete): If Byzantine art seems a bit stilted and remote, this striking chapel in the foothills of eastern Crete will reward you with its unexpected intimacy. The 14th- and 15th-century frescoes are not only stunning but depict all the familiar Biblical stories. See p. 227.

- **Nea Moni** (Hios, Northeastern Aegean): Once home to 1,000 monks, this 12th-century monastery high in the interior mountains of Hios is now quietly inhabited by one elderly but sprightly nun and two friendly monks. Try to catch one of the excellent tours sometimes offered by the monks. The mosaics in the cathedral dome are works of extraordinary power and beauty; even in the half-obscurity of the nave, they radiate a brilliant gold. Check out the small museum, and take some time to explore the extensive monastery grounds. See p. 372.

- **A Profusion of Byzantine Churches in the Cyclades:** The fertile countryside of the island of Naxos is dotted by well-preserved Byzantine chapels. Parikia, the capital of Paros, has the Byzantine-era cathedral of Panayia Ekatondapiliani. Santorini boasts the 11th- to 12th-century church of the Panagia in the hamlet of Gonias Episkopi. See chapter 8.

3 The Best Beaches

- **Plaka** (Naxos, Cyclades): Naxos has the longest stretches of sea sand in the Cyclades, and Plaka is the most beautiful and pristine beach on the island. On its 5km (3-mile) stretch of mostly undeveloped shoreline, you can easily imagine yourself as Robinson Crusoe alone on his island (bending the plot to include a few sunbathing Fridays). If you need abundant amenities and a more active social scene, you can always head north to Ayia Anna or Ayios Prokopios. See p. 278.

- **Paradise** (Mykonos, Cyclades): Paradise is the quintessential party beach, known for wild revelry that continues through the night. An extensive complex built on the beach includes a bar, taverna, changing rooms, and souvenir shops. This is a place to see and be seen, a place to show off muscles laboriously acquired during the long winter months. See p. 285.

- **Lalaria Beach** (Skiathos, Sporades): This gleaming, white-pebble beach boasts vivid aquamarine water and white limestone cliffs with natural arches cut into them by the elements. Lalaria is not nearly as popular nor as accessible as Skiathos's famous Koukounaries, which is one of the reasons it's still gorgeous and pristine. See p. 396.

- **Megalo Seitani** (Samos, Northeastern Aegean): Megalo Seitani and its neighbor, Micro Seitani, are situated on the mountainous and remote northwest coast of Samos. There aren't any roads to this part of the island, so the only ways to reach the beaches are by a short boat ride or a rather long (and beautiful) hike. You won't regret taking the trouble, since both beaches are superb: Micro Seitani's crescent of pebbles in a rocky cove, and Megalo Seitani's expanse of pristine sand. See p. 366.

- **Vroulidia** (Hios, Northeastern Aegean): White sand, a cliff-rimmed cove, and a remote location at the southern tip of the island of Hios combine to make this one of the most exquisite small beaches in the northeastern Aegean. The rocky coast conceals many cove beaches similar to this one, and they rarely become crowded. See p. 376.

4 The Best Scenic Villages & Towns

- **Chania** (Crete): Radiating from its handsome harbor and backdropped by the White Mountains, Chania has managed to hold on to much of its Venetian-Renaissance and later Turkish heritage. Wander the old town's narrow lanes, filled with a heady mix of colorful local culture, and enjoy its charming hotels, excellent restaurants, interesting shops, and swinging nightspots. See p. 205.

- **Hora** (Folegandros, Cyclades): In this town huddled at the edge of a cliff, one square spills into the next, its green and blue paving slates outlined in brilliant white. On a steep hill overlooking the town is the ornate church of Kimisis Theotokou, often illuminated at night. The church's icon of the Virgin is paraded through the streets of Hora with great ceremony and revelry every Easter Sunday. Mercifully free of vehicular traffic, Hora is one of the most beautiful and least spoiled villages in the Cyclades. See p. 250.

- **Yialos** (Simi, Dodecanese): The entirety of Yialos, the main port of the tiny, rugged island of Simi, has been declared a protected architectural treasure, and for good reason. This pristine port with its extraordinary array of neoclassical mansions is a large part of why Simi is known as "the jewel of the Dodecanese." See p. 336.

- **Ermoupolis** (Siros, Cyclades): In the 19th century, this was the busiest port in the Cyclades. Today, it is still a hub for island travel and retains an astonishing number of handsome neoclassical governmental buildings, ship sheds and factories, and elegant town houses. Walk uphill from the harbor to Ano Siros (upper Siros) and you'll find an old *kastro* (fortress) and a miniature whitewashed Cycladic village. See p. 306.

- **Skopelos Town** (Skopelos, Sporades): The amazingly well-preserved Skopelos, a traditional whitewashed island port town, is adorned everywhere with pots of flowering plants. It offers some fairly sophisticated diversions, several excellent restaurants, a couple good hotels, and lots of shopping. See p. 404.

- **Corfu Town** (Corfu, Ionian Islands): With its Esplanade framed by a 19th-century palace and the arcaded Liston, its old town a Venice-like warren of structures practically untouched for several centuries, its massive Venetian fortresses, and all this enclosing a lively population and constant visitors, here is urban Greece at its most appealing. See p. 418.

- **Piryi & Mesta** (Hios, Northeastern Aegean): These two small towns, in the pastoral southern hills of Hios, are marvelous creations of the medieval imagination. Connected by their physical proximity and a shared history, each is quirkily unique and a delight to explore. In Piryi, every available surface is covered with elaborate geometric black-and-white decorations known as *Ksisti,* a technique that reaches extraordinary levels of virtuosity in the town square. Mesta has preserved its medieval urban fabric and conceals two fine churches within its maze of narrow streets. See p. 375.

5 The Best Museums

- **National Archaeological Museum** (Athens): This stunning collection, which reopened after a major renovation in 2004, has it all: superb red- and black-figured vases, bronze statues, Mycenaean gold, marble reliefs of gods and goddesses, and the hauntingly beautiful frescoes from Akrotiri, the Minoan site on the island of Santorini. See p. 162.
- **Museum of Greek Popular Musical Instruments** (Athens): Life-size photos of musicians beside their actual instruments and recordings of traditional Greek music make this one of the country's most charming museums. On our last visit, an elderly Greek gentleman listened to some music, transcribed it, stepped into the courtyard, and played it on his own violin! See p. 168.
- **Archaeological Museum of Iraklion** (Crete): Few museums in the world can boast of holding virtually all the important remains of a major culture. This museum can do just that with its Minoan collection, including superb frescoes from Knossos, elegant bronze and stone figurines, and exquisite gold jewelry. The museum also contains Neolithic, Archaic Greek, and Roman finds from throughout Crete. See p. 196.
- **Archaeological Museum of Chania** (Crete): Let's hear it for a truly engaging provincial museum, not one full of masterworks but rather of representative works from thousands of years, a collection that lets us see how many people experienced their different worlds. All this, in a former Italian-Renaissance church that feels like a special place. See p. 206.

6 The Best Resorts & Hotels

- **Andromeda Hotel** (Athens; © 210/643-7302): The city's first serious "boutique" hotel, located on a wonderfully quiet side street, the classy Andromeda offers charm, comfort, and a reassuringly helpful staff. See p. 144.
- **Grande Bretagne** (Athens; © 210/333-0000): Back for a return engagement and better than ever, Athens's premiere hotel still overlooks the best view in town if you have the right room: Syntagma Square, the Houses of Parliament and, in case you wondered, the Acropolis. See p. 142.
- **Atlantis Hotel** (Iraklion, Crete; © 2810/229-103): There are many more luxurious hotels in Greece, but few can beat the Atlantis's urban attractions: a central location, modern facilities, and views over a busy harbor. You can swim in the pool, work out in the fitness center, send e-mail via your laptop, and then within minutes enjoy a fine meal or visit a museum. See p. 199.
- **Doma** (Chania, Crete; © 28210/51-772): A former neoclassical mansion east of downtown, the Doma has been converted into a comfortable

and charming hotel, furnished with the proprietor's family heirlooms. Although it's not for those seeking the most luxurious amenities, its atmosphere appeals to many. See p. 210.

- **Astra Apartments** (Santorini, Cyclades; © **22860/23-641**): This small hotel with handsomely appointed apartments looks like a miniature whitewashed village—and has spectacular views over Santorini's famous caldera. The sunsets here are not to be believed, the staff is incredibly helpful, and the village of Imerovigli itself offers an escape from the touristic madness that overwhelms the island each summer. If you decide to get married here, you have but to speak to the manager, George Karayiannis (before you arrive, unless you want to tie the knot on a return visit). See p. 243.

- **Anemomilos Apartments** (Folegandros, Cyclades; © **22860/41-309**) and **Castro Hotel** (Folegandros, Cyclades; © **22860/41-230**): The small island of Folegandros has two of the nicest hotels in the Cyclades, both with terrific cliff-top locations. The Anemomilos has all the creature comforts, traditional decor, and a good location (it's just out of town), with a delicious pool and sea views that stretch forever. The Castro, built into the walls of the 12th-century

Venetian castle that encircles the village, has lots of character and the necessary modern comforts. See p. 252.

- **Rodos Palace** (Rhodes, Dodecanese; © **22410/25-222**): The largest five-star hotel in Greece and possibly in the entire Mediterranean, this "palace" was decorated by the famed designer of the movies *Ben Hur* and *Quo Vadis*. Located in Iksia, just outside Rhodes city, it offers all the amenities imaginable, including a family center—a resort within a resort designed to provide the ultimate holiday for travelers with children. See p. 325.

- **Hotel Nireus** (Simi, Dodecanese; © **22410/72-400**): Perfect island, perfect location, unpretentious, and tasteful. The views from the sea-facing rooms, framed by the fluid swirls of the wrought-iron balcony, define the spell of this little gem of an island. You'll never regret one more night on Simi, and here's the place to spend it. See p. 339.

- **White Rocks Hotel & Bungalows** (Kefalonia, Ionian Islands; © **26710/ 28-332**): For those who appreciate understated elegance, a shady retreat from all that sunshine, a private beach, and quiet but attentive service, this hotel, located a couple of miles outside Argostoli, can be paradise. See p. 433.

7 The Best Restaurants

- **Daphne's** (Athens; © **210/322-7971**): As well as Pompeiian-style wall frescoes and one of the nicest gardens in Athens, Daphne's offers consistently delicious food. It makes you wonder why other Greek restaurants can't make supposedly simple dishes like eggplant salad or yogurt with

quince taste this distinctive. Added to all this are strolling musicians—and the owners and staff are so delightful that you hate to leave, even when you can't eat another prawn with toasted almonds. See p. 147.

- **Vlassis** (Athens; © **210/646-3060**): This small restaurant with a very loyal following (ranging from prominent ambassadors to struggling artists) serves traditional *(paradisiako)* Greek cooking at its very best. A tempting choice if you have only one night in Athens—but be sure to make a reservation. See p. 154.

- **Varoulko** (Athens; 𝒞 **210/522-8400;** www.varoulko.gr): In its new Athens location, with a menu that adds tasty meat dishes to its signature seafood, Varoulko continues to win plaudits. Everything here is so good that many Athenians believe chef/owner Lefteris Lazarou serves not only the finest seafood in Athens, but some of the best food in all of Greece. See p. 153.

- **Nykterida** (Chania, Crete; 𝒞 **28210/64-215**): We're not saying that the location may influence your taste buds here, but the spectacular views from this restaurant high above Chania and Soudha Bay can definitely make you feel as if you're eating a meal like few others in Greece. See p. 211.

- **Selene** (Santorini, Cyclades; 𝒞 **22860/22-249**): The best restaurant on an island with lots of good places to eat,

Selene is one of the finest restaurants in all Greece. The reason: Owners George and Evelyn Hatzyiannakis constantly experiment with local produce to turn out their own innovative versions of traditional dishes. Inside, the dining room is elegant, while the terrace has a wonderful view over the caldera. See p. 247.

- **Petrino** (Kos, Dodecanese; 𝒞 **22420/27-251**): When royalty come to Kos, this is where they dine. Housed in an exquisitely restored, two-story, century-old stone *(petrino)* private residence, this is hands-down the most elegant taverna in Kos, with cuisine to match. This is what Greek home cooking would be if your mother were part divine. See p. 347.

- **Venetian Well** (Corfu, Ionian Islands; 𝒞 **26610/44-761**): A bit severe in its setting at the edge of a small enclosed square in Corfu town, with no attempt at the picturesque, this restaurant gets by on its more esoteric, international, and delicate menu. It's for those seeking a break from the standard Greek scene. See p. 426.

8 The Best Nightlife

- **Theater Under the Stars** (Athens): If you can, take in a performance of whatever is on at Herodes Atticus Theater in Athens. You'll be sitting where people have sat for thousands of years to enjoy a play beneath Greece's magical night sky. See chapter 5.

- **Mykonos** (Cyclades): Mykonos isn't the only island town in Greece with nightlife that continues through the morning, but it was the first and still offers the most abundant, varied scene in the Aegean. Year-round, the town's narrow, labyrinthine streets play host to a remarkably diverse crowd—Mykonos's unlimited ability

to reinvent itself has assured it of continued popularity. Spring and fall tend to be more sober and sophisticated, while the 3 months of summer are reserved for unrestrained revelry. See chapter 8.

- **Rhodes** (Dodecanese): From cafes to casinos, Rhodes has not only the reputation but also the stuff to back it up. A good nightlife scene is ultimately a matter of who shows up—and this, too, is where Rhodes stands out. It's the place to be seen, and if nobody seems to be looking, you can always watch. See chapter 9.

- **Skiathos** (Sporades): With as many as 50,000 foreigners packing this tiny island during the high season, the many nightspots in Skiathos town are often jammed with the mostly younger set. If you don't like the music at one club, cross the street. See chapter 11.

- **Corfu** (Ionian Islands): If raucous nightspots are what you look for on a holiday, Corfu offers probably the largest concentration in Greece. Most of these are beach resorts frequented by young foreigners. More sedate locales can be found in Corfu town. Put simply, Corfu hosts a variety of music, dancing, and "socializing" opportunities. See chapter 12.

2

Planning Your Trip to the Greek Islands

by John S. Bowman

Before any trip, most of us like to do a bit of advance planning. When should I go? What is this trip going to cost me? Will there be a special holiday when I visit? What practical advice might I appreciate? We'll answer these and other questions for you in this chapter.

1 The Regions in Brief

Greece is a land of sea and mountains. Over a fifth of the Greek landmass is islands, numbering several thousand if you count every floating crag—and nowhere in Greece will you find yourself more than 96km (60 miles) from the sea. It should come as no surprise that the sea has shaped the Greek imagination, as well as its history.

Mainland Greece is a great vertebrate, with the Pindos range reaching from north to south, and continuing, like a tail, through the Peloponnese. The highest of its peaks is Mount Olympus, the seat of the gods, nearly 3,000m (10,000 ft.) above sea level. Eighty percent of the Greek mainland is mountainous, which you will rapidly discover whether you make your way on foot or on wheels.

ATHENS Whether you arrive by sea or by air, chances are you'll debark in Athens. The city is not always pleasant and is sometimes exhausting, yet it's invaluable. Its **archaeological sites** and its **museums** alone warrant a couple of days of exploration. Between visits to the sites, a stroll in the **National Garden** will prove reviving. Then, after dark as the

city cools, the old streets of the **Plaka** district at the foot of the Acropolis offer you chances to stroll, shop, and have dinner with an Acropolis view. The central square, pedestrianized side streets, and residential streets of **Kolonaki** are where fashionable Athenians head to see and be seen—and to do some serious shopping. **Piraeus,** as in antiquity, serves as the port of Athens and the jumping-off point to most of the islands.

Athens is also a great base for day trips and overnight excursions, whether to the Temple of Poseidon at **Cape Sounion,** the forested slopes of **Mount Hymettus (Imittos),** the Monastery of **Kaisariani (Kessariani),** the Byzantine Monastery of **Daphni,** the legendary plains of **Marathon,** or the ruins of **Eleusis,** place of ancient mysteries.

THE SARONIC GULF ISLANDS Cupped between Attica and the Peloponnese, in the sheltering Saronic Gulf, these islands offer both proximity and retreat for Athenians who, like their visitors, long for calming waters and cooler breezes. In high season, the accessibility of these islands on any given day, especially on weekends, can be their downfall. Choose carefully your day and island, or you may be part of the crowd you're trying to avoid.

Aegina, so close to Athens it can be a daily commute, is the most besieged island, yet it possesses character and charm. The main port town of Aegina is picturesque and pleasant, while across the island to the east, set atop a pine-crested hill, stands the remarkably preserved Temple of Aphaia, a Doric gem. **Poros,** next island in line proceeding south, is convenient to both Athens and the Peloponnese. Its beaches and lively port are a draw, with the picturesque rubble of an ancient, scenically situated temple thrown in. Still farther south lies vehicle-free **Hydra,** remarkable for its natural beauty and handsome stone mansions built by sea captains. The port of Hydra has a lot to offer and knows it, all of which is reflected in the prices. It's a great place for pleasant strolls, views, and a swim off the rocks. **Spetses,** the furthest of these islands from Athens, offers glades of pine trees and fine beaches—and a great many hotels catering to package holiday tours from Europe.

CRETE The largest of the Greek islands, birthplace of the painter El Greco, possesses a landscape so diverse, concentrated, and enchanting that no description is likely to do it justice. Especially if you rent a car and do your own exploring, a week will pass like a day. More or less circling the island on the national highway (don't imagine an interstate), you'll drive a ring of inviting ports like **Iraklion,** the capital; **Chania; Rethymnon;** and **Ayios Nikolaos.** Venturing into the heartland of Crete—not far, since Crete's width ranges from 12 to 56km (7½-35 miles)—with a little imagination, you'll find the legendary palaces of the Minoans: **Knossos, Phaestos,** and **Ayia Triadha,** to mention

only a few. This is not to say that Crete is without classical sites, Byzantine monasteries, Venetian structures, and Turkish remains. It's Greece, after all. For the energetic, the **Gorge of Samaria** calls out, as does the sea.

When night falls, try the culinary delights that Crete has been known for for thousands of years: its wines, fresh goat cheese, and olives, all local and all part of Crete's spell.

THE CYCLADES In antiquity, the *Cyclades*—the "encirclers" or "circling islands"—had at their center the small island of **Delos,** where mythology tells us that Apollo and his sister Artemis were born. Declared a sanctuary where both birth and death were prohibited, Delos was an important spiritual, cultural, and commercial hub of the Aegean. Today, its extensive remains remind visitors of its former importance. It's easy to make a day trip here from **Mykonos,** whose white, cubelike houses and narrow, twisting streets began to attract first a trickle and then a flood of visitors in the 1960s. Today, almost every cruise ship puts in at Mykonos for at least a few hours, so that visitors can take in the proliferation of cafes, restaurants, and shops. Those who spend a few days here can stay in boutique hotels, sip martinis in sophisticated bars—or head inland to visit the island's less-visited villages.

Paros (sometimes called "the poor man's Mykonos"), is the transport hub of the Cyclades, with a gentle landscape, appealing villages, good beaches, and opportunities for windsurfing. From here you can get to **Tinos,** home to perhaps the most revered of all Greek Orthodox churches; **Naxos,** whose fertile valleys and high mountains lure hikers and campers; **Folegandros,** much of whose capital Hora is built within the walls of a medieval *kastro* (castle); and **Santorini,** which some believe to be the lost Atlantis.

On Santorini you'll find a black lava beach, the impressive remains of the Minoan settlement at Akrotiri, chic restaurants, boutique hotels—and the most spectacular sunsets in all of Greece.

THE DODECANESE This string of islands, named "the 12" despite the fact that they number more than that, nearly embrace the Turkish shoreline. Except for Rhodes and Kos, all of the Dodecanese are deforested, bare bones exposed to sun and sea. But what bones! Far to the north lies **Patmos** (already in the 5th century nicknamed "the Jerusalem of the Aegean"), a holy island where the Book of Revelation is said to have been penned and where the Monastery of St. John still dominates the land. Far to the south basks **Rhodes,** "City of the Sun," with more than 300 days of sunshine per year. For obvious reasons, it's the most touristed of the islands. Rhodes has it all: history and resorts, ruins and nightlife. There's even peace and quiet—we'll tell you where to find it.

Between these two lie an array of possibilities, from the uncompromised traditional charm of tiny **Simi** to the ruins and well-known beaches of **Kos.** And with

Turkey so close, you may want to consider an easily arranged side trip.

THE SPORADES Whether by air, ferry, or hydrofoil, the Sporades, strewn north and east of the island of Evvia (Euboea), are readily accessible from the mainland and offer verdant forest landscapes, gold-sand beaches, and crystalline waters. That's the good news. The bad news is that they are no secret. **Skiathos** is the most popular. **Skopelos,** whose lovely port is one of the most striking in Greece, is more rugged and remote than Skiathos, with more trails and fewer nightclubs. Relatively far-off **Skyros** is well worth a visit, offering underwater fishing and diving, sandy beaches, and luminously clear waters.

THE IONIAN ISLANDS Across centuries, these islands have been the apple of more than one empire's eye. Lush, temperate, blessed with ample rain and sun, and tended like architectural gardens, they are splendid. **Corfu,** the most noted and ornamented, is a gem, and is sought after accordingly. **Ithaka** is as yet somewhat out of the tourist loop, but needs no introduction for readers of the *Odyssey.* With adjustments for the nearly 3,000

⌐Tips Greece on the Web

Anyone with access to the Web can obtain a fair amount of information about Greece. Remember that these sources cannot necessarily be counted on for the most up-to-date, definitive, or complete information. We advise you to use computer searches as *supplements only,* and then check out specific "facts" on which you are going to base your travel plans. Websites are continually being changed and added, but among the most useful for broad-based searches are:

- www.frommers.com
- www.greekembassy.org
- www.gtp.gr
- www.phantis.com
- www.perseus.tufts.edu

Security in Greece: Red Alert

Inevitably and understandably, travelers might be concerned about the threat of terrorists in Greece. As for Al-Qaeda or Islamic militants, there has never been any indication that they have a presence, let alone an agenda, in Greece. For one thing, Greece is pro-Palestinian, and militant Muslims have no desire to offend. This is not to say that there might not be angry and anti-American Middle Easterners in Greece. In fact, many Greeks oppose U.S. foreign policies—most particularly, the war in Iraq. But in all locales where tourists are apt to be, you will find at least formal politeness. In conclusion, the potential threat from terrorists in Greece is no greater than in any place in the world today. If you remain concerned, governmental travel warnings for both security and health threats are posted by http://travel.state.gov for Americans; www.voyage.gc.ca for Canadians; www.fco.gov.uk for the British; and www.dfat.gov.au for Australians.

years that have elapsed, Homer's descriptions of the island still hold their own. If you can do without name recognition, **Kefalonia,** relatively inconspicuous and unspoiled, has a lot to offer: picturesque traditional villages, steep rocks plunging into the sea, fine beaches, and excellent local wine.

THE NORTHEASTERN AEGEAN ISLANDS The four major islands comprising this group form Europe's traditional sea border with the East. Beyond their strategic and thus richly historic location, they offer a taste of Greece that is less compromised by tourism and more deeply influenced by nearby Asia Minor and modern Turkey. **Samos,** unique among the islands in the extent to which it is covered with trees, produces excellent local wine. Its important archaeological sites and opportunities for outdoor activities make it a congenial and interesting destination, and it is an ideal place from which to enter and explore the northwestern Turkish coast. **Hios** is unspoiled and welcoming, offering isolated and spectacular beaches, as well as the stunning monastery of Nea Moni and some of Greece's most striking village architecture. The remaining islands of **Lesvos** and **Limnos,** for various reasons not major tourist destinations, have their ways of inviting and rewarding those who explore them.

2 Visitor Information

The **Greek National Tourism Organization (GNTO,** or **EOT** in Greece—and increasingly referred to as the Hellenic Tourism Organization) has offices throughout the world that can provide you with information concerning all aspects of travel to and in Greece. Look for them at **www.gnto.gr** or contact one of the following GNTO offices:

UNITED STATES   Olympic Tower, 645 Fifth Ave., 5th Floor, New York, NY 10022 (© **212/421-5777;** fax 212/ 826-6940).

AUSTRALIA & NEW ZEALAND   51 Pitt St., Sydney, NSW 2000 (© **02/ 241-1663;** fax 02/235-2174).

CANADA   1300 Bay St., Toronto, ON M5R 3K8 (© **416/968-2220;** fax

416/968-6533); 1170 Place du Frères André, Montreal, H3B 3C6 (© **514/ 871-1535;** fax 514/871-1498).

UNITED KINGDOM & IRELAND 4 Conduit St., London W1S 2DJ (© **0207/ 734-5997;** fax 0207/287-1369).

For the latest information on security issues, health risks, and similar issues in the U.S., you can call, fax, or send a

self-addressed, stamped envelope to the **Overseas Citizens Emergency Center,** Department of State, Room 4811, Washington, DC 20520 (© **202/647-5225;** www.travel.state.gov); ask for Consular Information Sheets. You can also get the latest information by contacting any U.S. embassy, consulate, or passport office.

3 Entry Requirements & Customs

ENTRY REQUIREMENTS

For information on how to get a passport, go to the "Fast Facts: Greece" section of this chapter—the websites listed provide downloadable passport applications as well as the current fees for processing passport applications. For an up-to-date country-by-country listing of passport requirements around the world, go to the "Foreign Entry Requirement" Web page of the U.S. State Department at **http:// travel.state.gov**.

For entry into Greece, citizens of Australia, Canada, New Zealand, South Africa, the United States, and almost all other non-E.U. countries are required to have a **valid passport,** which is stamped upon entry and exit, for stays up to 90 days. All U.S. citizens, even infants, must have a valid passport, but Canadian children under 16 may travel without a passport if accompanied by either parent. Longer stays must be arranged with the **Bureau of Aliens,** 173 Leoforos Alexandras, 11522 Athens (© **210/770-5711**).

Citizens of the United Kingdom and other members of the European Union are required to have only a valid passport for entry into Greece, and it is no longer stamped upon entry; you may stay an unlimited period (although you should inquire about this at a Greek consulate or at your embassy in Greece). Children under 16 from E.U. countries may travel without a passport if accompanied by

either parent. All E.U. citizens should check the requirements for non-E.U. countries through which you might travel to get to Greece.

CUSTOMS
WHAT YOU CAN BRING INTO GREECE

Passengers from North America arriving in Athens aboard international flights are generally not searched, and if you have nothing to declare, continue through the green lane. (Because of the continuing threat of terrorism, baggage is X-rayed before boarding of domestic flights.) However, citizens of the United States, Canada, Australia, New Zealand, and other non-E.U. countries do face a few common-sensical restrictions on what you can bring into Greece. Clearly, no narcotics: Greece is *very* tough on drug users! No explosives or weapons—although upon application, a sportsman might be able to bring in a legitimate hunting weapon. Only medications for amounts properly prescribed for your own use are allowed. Plants with soil are not. Dogs and cats can be brought in, but they must have proof of recent rabies and other health shots. No parrots are allowed.

You are allowed to bring into Greece duty-free personal belongings including clothes, camping gear, and most sports equipment. (Certain watersports equipment, such as windsurfers, can be brought in only if a Greek citizen residing

Tips Passport Savvy

Allow plenty of time before your trip to apply for a passport. In the United States, processing normally takes 3 weeks but can take longer during busy periods (especially spring). And keep in mind that if you need a passport in a hurry, you'll pay a higher processing fee. When traveling, safeguard your passport in an inconspicuous, inaccessible place like a money belt and keep a copy of the critical pages with your passport number in a separate place. If you lose your passport, visit the nearest consulate of your native country as soon as possible for a replacement. Meanwhile, keep a record of your passport's number in a separate part of your luggage.

in Greece guarantees they will be re-exported.) If you are traveling with your own scuba tank, you must have it sealed upon entry; it will be unsealed at recognized scuba locales. Visitors from outside the European Union are allowed up to 10 kilos of food and beverage, 200 cigarettes, 50 cigars, 250 grams of tobacco, 1 liter of distilled alcohol or 2 liters of wine, 50 grams of perfume, 500 grams of coffee, and 100 grams of tea.

You may bring two cameras with 10 rolls of film each, a movie or video camera, a portable radio, a phonograph or tape recorder, a typewriter, and a laptop computer. These will probably not be inspected, but in some cases they can be written into your passport, so you'd better have them when you leave! In fact, it is unlikely that you will be stopped at entry points, but if you are, and it is discovered that you are carrying much more than $1,000 in cash, this might be written in your passport. You will then be expected to produce receipts if you intend to leave without the same amount. Entering with your own car or other motor vehicle requires a fair amount of paperwork: Check with Greek embassy or consular authorities before setting out.

There are presently no restrictions on the amount of traveler's checks you may carry upon either arrival or departure, although technically, amounts over

$1,000 should be declared. If you plan to leave the country with more than $1,000 in bank notes (or its equivalent in other currency), technically you must declare at least that sum upon entry. No more than 1,000€ ($1,300) per traveler may be imported or exported.

U.K. citizens and those of other E.U. nations are relatively free from most of these restrictions, but you still must comply with some, such as those pertaining to drugs, firearms, certain plants, some animals, and scuba tanks. There are also restrictions on young people importing alcohol and tobacco. Even large sums of currency or unusual amounts of electronic equipment might warrant notice. Basically, you are allowed to bring in what is reasonable for personal use but not for engagement in a business.

WHAT YOU CAN TAKE OUT OF GREECE

Greek antiquities are strictly protected by law. No genuine antiquities may be taken out of Greece without prior special permission from the **Archaeological Service,** 3 Polignotou, Athens. Also, you must be able to explain how you acquired any genuinely old objects—in particular, icons or religious articles. A dealer or shopkeeper must provide you with an export certificate for any object dating from before 1830.

Remember to keep all receipts for major purchases in order to clear Customs on your return home.

Returning **U.S. citizens** who have been away for at least 48 hours are allowed to bring back, once every 30 days, $800 worth of merchandise duty-free. You'll be charged a flat rate of duty on the next $1,000 worth of purchases. Any dollar amount beyond that is dutiable at whatever rates apply. On mailed gifts, the duty-free limit is $200. Be sure to have your receipts or purchases handy to expedite the declaration process. *Note:* If you owe duty, you are required to pay it upon your arrival in the United States, either by cash, personal check, government check, traveler's check, or money order. In some locations you may pay by Visa or MasterCard.

To avoid having to pay duty on foreign-made personal items you owned before you left on your trip, bring along a bill of sale, an insurance policy, a jeweler's appraisal, or purchase receipts. You can register items readily identifiable by a permanently affixed serial number or marking—think laptop computers, cameras, and CD players—with Customs before you leave. Take the items to the nearest Customs office or register them with Customs at the airport from which you're departing. You'll receive, at no cost, a Certificate of Registration, which allows duty-free entry for the life of the item.

With some exceptions, you cannot bring fresh fruits and vegetables into the United States. For specifics on what you can bring back, download the invaluable free pamphlet *Know Before You Go* online at **www.cbp.gov**. (Click on "Travel," and then click on "Know Before You Go Online Brochure.") Or request the pamphlet from the **U.S. Customs & Border Protection (CBP),** 1300 Pennsylvania Ave. NW, Washington, DC 20229 (© 877/287-8667).

For a clear summary of **Canadian** rules, write for the booklet *I Declare,* issued by the **Canada Customs and Revenue Agency** (© **800/461-9999** in Canada, or 204/983-3500; www.ccra-adrc.gc.ca). Canada allows its citizens a C$750 exemption, and you're allowed to bring back duty-free 1 carton of cigarettes, 1 can of tobacco, 40 imperial ounces of liquor, and 50 cigars. In addition, you're allowed to mail gifts to Canada valued at less than C$60 a day, provided they're unsolicited and don't contain alcohol or tobacco. (Write on the package, "Unsolicited gift, under $60 value.") All valuables should be declared on Form Y-38 before your departure from Canada, including serial numbers of valuables you already own, such as expensive foreign cameras. *Note:* The C$750 exemption can only be used once a year and only after an absence of 7 days.

Citizens of the U.K. who are **returning from a European Union (E.U.) country** will go through a separate Customs Exit (called the "Blue Exit") especially for E.U. travelers. In essence, there is no limit on what you can bring back from an E.U. country, as long as the items are for personal use (this includes gifts), and as long as you have already paid the necessary duty and tax. However, Customs law sets guidance levels. If you bring in more than these levels, you may be asked to prove that the goods are for your own use. Guidance levels on goods bought in the E.U. for your own use are 3,200 cigarettes, 200 cigars, 400 cigarillos, 3 kilograms of smoking tobacco, 10 liters of spirits, 90 liters of wine, 20 liters of fortified wine (such as port or sherry), and 110 liters of beer.

The duty-free allowance in **Australia** is A$400 or, for those under 18, A$200. Citizens can bring in 250 cigarettes or 250 grams of loose tobacco, and 1,125 milliliters of alcohol. If you're returning with valuables you already own, such as foreign-made cameras, you should file Form B263. A helpful brochure available from Australian consulates or Customs offices is *Know Before You Go.* For more information, call the **Australian Customs Service** at ✆ **1300/363-263;** or go to www.customs.gov.au.

The duty-free allowance for **New Zealand** is NZ$700. Citizens over 17 can bring in 200 cigarettes, 50 cigars, or 250 grams of tobacco (or a mixture of all three if their combined weight doesn't exceed 250g); plus 4.5 liters of wine and beer, or 1.125 liters of liquor. New Zealand currency does not carry import or export restrictions. Fill out a certificate of export, listing the valuables you are taking out of the country; that way, you can bring them back without paying duty. Most questions are answered in a free pamphlet available at New Zealand consulates and Customs offices: *New Zealand Customs Guide for Travellers, Notice no. 4.* For more information, contact **New Zealand Customs,** The Customhouse, 17–21 Whitmore St., Box 2218, Wellington (✆ **04/473-6099** or 0800/428-786; www.customs.govt.nz).

4 Money

Greece is no longer the bargain country it once was, although it remains considerably cheaper than many major nations with advanced economies. Certainly for most visitors, the hotels and restaurants will be cheaper than in major cities such as New York or London. That said, you will be spending money day in and day out, so it is important to understand the ins and outs of how to handle your money.

CURRENCY

The currency in Greece is the **euro** (pronounced *evro* in Greek), abbreviated "Eu" and symbolized by €. (Anyone possessing the old drachma currency can try to exchange it in branches of the National Bank of Greece.)

The euro € comes in 7 paper notes and 8 coins. The notes are in different sizes and colors. They are in the following denominations: 5, 10, 20, 50, 100, 200, and 500. (Considering that each euro is worth over $1, those last bills are quite pricey!) Six of the coins are officially "cents"—but in Greece they have become referred to as *lepta,* the old Greek name for sums smaller than the drachma. They come in different sizes and their value is: 1, 2, 5, 10, 20, and 50. There are also 1€ and 2€ coins.

Although one side of the coins differs in each of the member E.U. nations, all coins and bills are legal tender in all countries using the euro.

It's a good idea to exchange at least some money—just enough to cover airport incidentals and transportation to your hotel—before you leave home, so you can avoid lines at airport ATMs (automated teller machines). You can

---

Tips **Small Change**

When you change money, ask for some small bills or loose change. Petty cash will come in handy for tipping and public transportation. Consider keeping the change separate from your larger bills, so that it's readily accessible and you'll be less of a target for theft (by constantly revealing where on your person you are keeping your money).

Regarding the Euro

When the euro was introduced, the U.S. dollar and the euro were about par ($1 equaled approximately 1€). As this book went to press, however, 1€ was worth approximately US$1.30. For up-to-the-minute exchange rates between the euro and the dollar, check the currency converter website **www.xe.com/ucc** each day when in Greece.

exchange money at your local American Express or Thomas Cook office or at your bank. If you're far away from a bank with currency-exchange services, American Express offers traveler's checks and foreign currency, though with a $15 order fee plus shipping costs, at www.american express.com or ℂ **800/807-6233.**

ATMs

The easiest and best way to get cash away from home is from an ATM. **Cirrus** (ℂ **800/424-7787;** www.mastercard.com) and **PLUS** (ℂ **800/843-7587;** www.visa. com) networks span the globe; look at the back of your bank card to see which network you're on, then call or check online for ATM locations at your destination. If your bank, credit, or debit card is affiliated with one of the major international credit cards (such as MasterCard or Visa), you should not have any trouble getting money in Greece; if in doubt, ask your bank or credit card company if your card will be acceptable in Greece. *Tip:* Greek ATMs use only numeric PINs (Personal Identification Numbers), so you must know how to convert letters to numerals (see your familiar ATM). Also, most Greek ATMs accept only a 4-digit PIN—you might have to change yours before you go.

In commercial centers, airports, all cities and larger towns, and most tourist centers, you will find at least a couple of machines accepting a wide range of cards. Smaller towns will often have only one ATM—and it may not accept your card. **Commercial Bank (Emboriki Trapeza)** services PLUS and Visa; **Credit Bank**

(Trapeza Pisteos) accepts Visa and American Express; **National Bank (Ethiniki Trapeza)** takes Cirrus and MasterCard/Access.

Transaction fees are usually built into the exchange rate you get; in any case, exchange rates are usually based on the wholesale rates of the major banks, so you may actually save money by withdrawing larger sums and paying your bills in cash. However, just as at home, there is usually a limit on how much you can withdraw in a single day; find out what it is before departure. Note, too, that the sums withdrawn are designated on the ATM screen in euros—not other currencies. Also keep in mind that many banks impose a fee every time a card is used at a different bank's ATM, and that fee can be higher for international transactions (up to $5 or more) than for domestic ones (where they're rarely more than $2). On top of this, the bank from which you withdraw cash may charge its own fee. To compare banks' ATM fees within the U.S., use www.bankrate.com. For international withdrawal fees, ask your bank.

CURRENCY-EXCHANGE OFFICES

Private and commercial foreign-exchange offices are found in major cities, larger towns, and centers of tourism throughout Greece. They are generally competitive, but their rates vary, so shop around if you must use one.

TRAVELER'S CHECKS

Traveler's checks are something of an anachronism from the days before the

ATM made cash accessible at any time. Traveler's checks used to be the only sound alternative to traveling with dangerously large amounts of cash. They were as reliable as currency but, unlike cash, they could be replaced if lost or stolen.

It should also be said that although in Greece today most hotels and shops still accept traveler's checks, many no longer do, and in any case they usually charge a small commission or give a poor exchange rate. Do not expect any Greek operations to cash your traveler's checks, however, unless you are paying for their services or goods.

You can get traveler's checks at almost any bank. **American Express** offers denominations of $20, $50, $100, $500, and (for cardholders only) $1,000. You'll pay a service charge ranging from 1% to 4%. If your bank charges more, you can call the check issuers about more competitive rates. Some organizations sell traveler's checks at reduced rates; the Automobile Association of America, for example, sells American Express checks in several currencies without commission or fee to AAA members. You can also get American Express traveler's checks over the phone by calling ℂ **800/221-7282;** Amex gold and platinum cardholders who use this number are exempt from the 1% fee.

Visa offers traveler's checks at Citibank locations nationwide, as well as at several other banks. The service charge ranges between 1.5% and 2%; checks come in denominations of $20, $50, $100, $500,

and $1,000. In the U.S. or Canada, call **Visa/Interpayment Services** at ℂ **800/732-1322** for information (ℂ **800/453-4284** from most other countries), which also sells Visa checks issued by Barclays Bank and Bank of America. **MasterCard** also offers traveler's checks. Call ℂ **800/223-9920** for a location near you. When abroad, contact the local operator and ask to place a collect call to 33/318-550 in the U.K. or 609/987-7300 in the U.S. **Citicorp** (ℂ **800/645-6556** in the U.S. and Canada; elsewhere, ℂ **813/623-1709** collect in the U.S.) also issues traveler's checks. Most British banks can issue their account holders a **Eurocheque** card and checkbook, which can be used at most cash machines and at Greek banks for an annual fee and a 2% charge.

Foreign-currency traveler's checks are useful if you're traveling to one country or to the euro zone; they're accepted at locations such as bed-and-breakfasts where dollar checks may not be accepted, and they minimize the amount of math you have to do at your destination. You'll pay the rate of exchange at the time of your purchase, so it's a good idea to monitor the rate; also, most companies charge a transaction fee per order and a shipping fee if you order online. **American Express, Visa, MasterCard,** and **Thomas Cook** all offer checks in euros. If you choose to carry traveler's checks, be sure to keep a record of their serial numbers separate from your checks in the event that they are stolen or lost. You'll get a refund faster if you know the numbers.

(*Tips* **Credit Cards in Greece**

Credit cards are effectively required for renting a car these days. In Greece, they are accepted in the better hotels and at most shops. *Note:* Even many of the better restaurants in major cities do *not* accept credit cards, and certainly most restaurants and smaller hotels in Greece do not accept them. Also, some hotels that require a credit card number when you make advance reservations will demand payment in cash; inquire beforehand if this will be the case.

CREDIT & DEBIT CARDS

Visa is the most widely accepted card, and MasterCard is usually accepted where you see signs for Access or Eurocard. Diners Club is also increasingly recognized. American Express is less frequently accepted because it charges a higher commission and is more protective of the cardholder in disagreements.

Credit cards are a safe way to carry money, they provide a convenient record of all your expenses, and they generally offer good exchange rates. You can also withdraw cash advances from your credit cards at banks or ATMs, provided you know your PIN. If you've forgotten yours, or didn't even know you had one, call the number on the back of your credit card and ask the bank to send it to you. It usually takes 5 to 7 business days, though some banks will provide the number over the phone if you tell them your mother's maiden name or some other personal information. Your credit card company will likely charge a commission (1% or 2%) on every foreign purchase you make, but you may be getting a good deal with credit cards when you factor in things like ATM fees and higher traveler's check exchange rates.

Keep in mind that credit card companies try to protect themselves from theft by limiting the funds someone can withdraw outside their home country, so call your credit card company before you leave home. And remember: If you use your charge card to obtain cash, you are borrowing money and presumably going to pay very high interest. It might be better to use your bank's debit card, which means you are taking cash out of your bank account.

For tips and telephone numbers to call if your wallet is stolen or lost, go to "Lost & Found" in the "Fast Facts: Greece" section later in this chapter.

EMERGENCY CASH   In an emergency, you can arrange to send money from home to a Greek bank. Telex transfers from the United Kingdom usually take at least 3 days and sometimes up to a week, with a charge of about 3%. Bank drafts are more expensive but potentially faster if you are in Athens. From Canada and the United States, money can be wired by **Western Union** (© **800/325-6000**) or **MoneyGram** (© **800/543-4080**). In Greece, call Western Union in the United States (© **001-314/298-2313**) to learn the location of an office. For MoneyGram, call the head office in Athens (© **01/322-0005**). For a fee (4%–10%, depending on the sum involved), money can be available in minutes at an agent for Western Union or MoneyGram.

Tips Dear Visa: I'm Off to Mykonos!

There are increasing reports of American travelers abroad who discover that their credit cards are invalidated after their first purchase: An automated security system "kicks in" to protect you on the assumption that your card has been stolen. To be sure this won't happen, call your credit card company or the bank that issued it and inform them of your impending trip. Even if you don't call your credit card company in advance, you can always call the card's toll-free emergency number (see "Fast Facts: Greece," later in this chapter) if a charge is refused—a good reason to carry the phone number with you. But perhaps the most important lesson is to carry more than one card on your trip. If one card doesn't work for any number of reasons, you'll have a backup.

5 When to Go

WEATHER Greece has a generally mild climate, though in the mountainous northern interior the winters are rather harsh and summers brief. Southern Greece enjoys a relatively mild winter, with temperatures averaging around 55° to 60°F (13°–16°C) in Athens. Summers are generally hot and dry, with daytime temperatures rising to 85° to 95°F (30°–35°C), usually cooled by prevailing north winds *(meltemi),* especially on the islands, which often cool appreciably in the evenings. And at some point in most summers, usually July, the temperature will rise to over 100°F (38°C).

For weather forecasts for major cities in Greece, try **www.weather.com.**

The best time to visit is **late April to mid-June,** when the wildflowers are in bloom and before summer arrives in force with hordes of tourists, higher prices, overbooked facilities, and strained services. **Orthodox Easter Week**—which takes place close to but not exactly concurrent with Easter in Western countries—sometimes falls in this period. It is a particularly exciting time to be in Greece, and most Greeks celebrate the special week. Many of the island resorts crank up for the season. However, so many Greeks living abroad return for this holiday that international flights and hotels are usually more expensive. Many museums and sites are closed for several of the days. So unless you can be on the ground well before or after Easter Week, we advise you not to go then, especially if this will be your first visit to Greece.

Average Monthly Temperatures & Precipitation

		Jan	Feb	Mar	Apr	May	June	July	Aug	Sept	Oct	Nov	Dec
Athens	Temp °F	52	54	58	65	74	86	92	92	82	72	63	56
	Temp °C	12	13	15	19	24	30	33	33	28	23	18	14
	Precip. (in.)	2.4	2.0	1.3	0.9	0.8	0.2	0.1	0.2	1.1	2.0	2.9	4.1
Crete	Temp °F	52	54	57	62	68	74	78	78	75	69	63	58
	Temp °C	13	13	14	17	20	24	26	26	24	21	18	15
	Precip. (in.)	2.4	2.0	1.3	0.9	0.8	0.2	0.1	0.2	1.1	2.0	2.9	4.1

If you possibly can, avoid traveling in **July and August** (especially around Aug 15). The crowds from Europe overwhelm facilities. In overcrowded southern Greece and the islands, midday temperatures are too high for much except beach and water activities. We strongly recommend that you not go unless you have firm reservations and enjoy close encounters with masses of fellow tourists and footloose students. Of course, the higher elevations remain cooler and less crowded, a plus for hikers, bikers, and those who don't demand sophisticated pleasures.

By **mid-September,** temperatures begin to fall and crowds thin, but it can still be hot. The weather remains generally calm and balmy well into October. If you can't get to Greece in the spring, and beaches are not your primary goal, this is a fine time to visit.

By **late October,** ferry service and flights are cutting back and most facilities on the islands begin to close for the winter, but the cooler fall atmosphere makes Athens and the mainland all the more pleasant. If you have the time, visit the islands first, then return for a tour of the mainland archaeological sites.

Winter (Nov–Mar) is not the time to visit Greece unless you want to join the Greeks for skiing in the mountains.

Tips **Two Holidays to Stay Put**

Greece observes a number of holidays during which museums, sites, government offices, banks, and such are closed. But during the days around Easter (a fluctuating holiday) and August 15, not only do many places shut down, but internal transportation is overwhelmed by Greeks returning to their home towns and villages. So although it is great to be in Greece to observe these occasions, do not plan to do much moving around.

However, some hotels and many good tavernas stay open, prices are at their lowest, and the southern mainland and Crete remain inviting, especially for those interested in archaeology and authentic local culture.

HOLIDAYS The legal national holidays of Greece are: **New Year's Day,** January 1; **Epiphany** (Baptism of Christ), January 6; **Clean Monday (Kathari Deftera),** day before Shrove Tuesday, 41 days before Easter (which in Greece may come in late Mar to late Apr; every few years it coincides with Easter Sunday in Western countries); **Independence Day,** March 25; **Good Friday to Easter,** including the Monday after Easter Sunday; **May Day** (Labor Day), May 1; **Whitmonday** (Holy Spirit Monday), day after Whitsunday (Pentecost), the seventh Sunday after Easter; **Assumption of the Virgin,** August 15; **Ochi Day,** October 28; **Christmas,** December 25 and 26.

On these holidays, government offices, banks, post offices, most stores, and many restaurants are closed; a few museums and attractions may remain open on several of the lesser holidays. But if you are intent on seeing a specific museum or site, be sure to find out before you leave home whether the place will be open. Meanwhile, visitors are often included in the celebration. Consult the "Greece Calendar of Events," below, if you are in the planning stage. If you are already in Greece, ask at your hotel or find one of the current English-language publications, such as the *Athens News,* the *Kathimerini* insert in the *International Herald Tribune,* the weekly brochure *Athens Today,* or the *Athenscope* section of the weekly *Hellenic Times.*

GREECE CALENDAR OF EVENTS

January

Feast of St. Basil (Ayios Vassilios). St. Basil is the Greek equivalent of Santa Claus. The holiday is marked by the exchange of gifts and a special cake, *vassilopita,* made with a coin in it; the person who gets the piece with the coin will have good luck. January 1.

Epiphany (Baptism of Christ). Baptismal fonts and water are blessed. A priest may throw a cross into the harbor and young men will try to recover it; the finder wins a special blessing. Children, who have been kept good during Christmas with threats of the *kalikantzari* (goblins), are allowed on the 12th day to help chase them away. January 6.

Gynecocracy (Gynaikokratia, Rule of Women). In some villages in Thrace, the women take over the cafes while the men stay home and do the housework. January 8.

February

Carnival (Karnavali). Be ready for parades, marching bands, costumes, drinking, dancing, and general loosening of inhibitions, depending on the locale. Some scholars say the name comes from the Latin for "farewell meat," while others hold that it comes from "car naval," the chariots celebrating the ancient sea god Poseidon (Saturn, to the Romans). The city of Patras shows its support of the latter theory with its famous chariot parade and wild Saturnalia, private parties, and public celebrations. Masked revels are widely held in Macedonia. On the island of Skyros, the pagan "Goat Dance" is performed, reminding us of the primitive Dionysiac nature of the festivities. Crete has its own colorful versions, while in the Ionian islands, festivities are more Italian. In Athens, people bop each other on their heads with plastic hammers. Celebrations last the 3 weeks before the beginning of Lent.

March

Independence Day and the Feast of the Annunciation. The two holidays are celebrated simultaneously with military parades, especially in Athens. The religious celebration is particularly important on the islands of Tinos and Hydra and in churches or monasteries named *Evanyelismos* (Bringer of Good News) or *Evanyelistria* (the feminine form of the name). March 25.

April

Sound-and-Light Performances. These begin on the Acropolis in Athens and in the Old Town on Rhodes. Nightly through October.

Procession of St. Spyridon (Ayios Spyridon). On Palm Sunday, the procession is held in Corfu town. St. Spyridon's remains are also paraded through the streets of Corfu town on Holy Saturday, August 1, and on the first Sunday in November.

Feast of St. George (Ayios Yioryios). The feast day of the patron saint of shepherds is an important rural celebration with dancing and feasting. Arachova, near Delphi, is famous for its festivities. The island of Skyros also gives its patron saint a big party on April 23. (If the 23rd comes before Easter, the celebration is postponed until the Mon after Easter.)

May

May Day. On this important urban holiday, families have picnics in the country and pick wildflowers, which are woven into wreaths and hung from balconies and over doorways. May Day

Holy Week Celebrations

Orthodox Easter, a time of extraordinary festivities in Greece, usually falls one or more weeks after Easter in the West—inquire ahead! The Good Friday exodus from Athens is truly amazing, and you can remain and enjoy the deserted city or—if you're fortunate and have made reservations, because Greeks take up most of the travel facilities—you can be among the celebrants in any town or village. Holy Week is usually marked by impressive solemn services and processions; serious feasting on roasted lamb, the traditional *margaritsa* soup, and homemade wine. Dancing takes place, often in traditional costumes. In a unique celebration on Patmos, the Last Supper is reenacted at the Monastery of St. John the Divine. *Tip:* Tourists must dress appropriately during this special time. Shorts, miniskirts, and sleeveless shirts will not only offend Greeks but will prohibit your entry to religious sites.

is still celebrated by Greek Communists and socialists as a working-class holiday. May 1.

Folk-Dance Performances. Dances begin in the amphitheater on Filopappos Hill in Athens and continue to September. Among the most regular and popular groups is the Dora Stratou Dance Troupe.

Hippocratic Oath. Ritual recitations of the oath by the citizens of Kos honor their favorite son, Hippocrates. Young girls in ancient dress, playing flutes, accompany a young boy in procession until he stops and recites in Greek the timeless oath of physicians everywhere. May through September.

Sound-and-Light Shows. The shows begin in Corfu town and continue to the end of September.

Feast of St. Constantine (Ayios Konstandinos). The first Orthodox emperor, Constantine, and his mother, **St. Helen (Ayia Eleni),** are honored, most interestingly, by fire-walking rituals *(anastenaria)* in four villages in Macedonian Greece: Ayia Eleni, Ayios Petros, Langada, and Meliki. It's a big party night for everyone named Costa and Eleni. (Name-days, rather than birthdays, are celebrated in Greece.) The anniversary of the Ionian reunion with Greece is also celebrated, mainly in Corfu. May 21.

June

Athens Festival. Featured are superb productions of ancient drama, opera, orchestra performances, ballet, modern dance, and popular entertainers. The festival takes place in the handsome Odeum of Herodes Atticus, on the southwest side of the Acropolis. June to early October.

Folk-Dance Performances. The site of these performances is the theater in the Old Town of Rhodes.

Wine Festival. This festival is held annually at Daphni, about 10km (7 miles) west of Athens; wine festivals are also held on Rhodes and elsewhere.

Simi Festival. The 4-month feast features concerts, theater, storytelling, and dance, starring acclaimed Greek and international artists. With its epicenter on the tiny island of Simi, the events spill over onto seven neighboring islands: Astypalea, Halki, Kastellorizo, Karpathos, Kassos, Nissiros, and Tilos. June through September.

Lycabettus Theater. A variety of performances is presented at the amphitheater on Mount Likavitos (Lycabettus) overlooking Athens. Mid-June to late August.

Miaoulia. This celebration on Hydra honors Hydriot Admiral Miaoulis, who set much of the Turkish fleet on fire by ramming them with explosives-filled fireboats. Weekend in mid-June.

Aegean Festival. In the harbor of Skiathos town, the Bourtzi Cultural Center presents ancient drama, modern dance, folk music and folk dance, concerts, and art exhibits. June through September.

International Classical Musical Festival. This annual festival takes place at Nafplion, in the Peloponnese. One week in June or July.

Midsummer Eve. The now-dried wreaths of flowers picked on May Day are burned to drive away witches, in a version of pagan ceremonies now associated with the birth of John the Baptist on June 24, Midsummer Day. June 23 to 24.

The Feast of the Holy Apostles (Ayii Apostoli, Petros, and Pavlos). Another important name-day. June 29.

Navy Week. The celebration takes place throughout Greece. In Volos, the voyage of the Argonauts is reenacted. On Hydra, the exploits of Adm. Andreas Miaoulis, naval hero of the War of Independence, are celebrated. Fishermen at Plomari on Lesvos stage a festival. End of June and beginning of July.

July

Puppet Festival. Hydra's annual festival has drawn puppeteers from countries as far away as Togo and Brazil. Early July.

Dodoni Festival. Classical dramas are presented at the ancient theater of Dodoni, south of Ioannina. For information, call © **26510/20-090.** July through September.

Epidaurus Festival. Performances of classical Greek drama take place in the famous amphitheater. For information, contact the **Greek Festival Office,** 4 Stadiou (© **210/322-1459** or 210/322-3111 to 3119, ext. 137). July to early September.

International Folklore Festival. At Naoussa, in Northern Greece, both amateur and professional dance companies gather from all over the world. For information, call © **23320/20-211** or e-mail cioff@nao.forthnet.gr.

Northern Greece National Theater. Classical drama is performed in the amphitheaters in Phillipi and on the island of Thasos. You will be able to see these productions without the hassles of Athens performances. For information, call © **2510/223-504.** July and August.

Hippokrateia Festival. Art, music, and theater come to the medieval castle of the Knights of St. John, in the main harbor of Kos. July and August.

Kalamata International Dance Festival. In Kalamata, in the southern Peloponnese, performances are given by prestigious dance companies from all over the world. Summer.

Dionysia Wine Festival. This is not a major event, but it's fun if you happen to find yourself on the island of Naxos. For information, call © **22850/22-923.** Mid-July.

Wine Festival at Rethymnon, Crete. Rethymnon hosts a wine festival as well as a **Renaissance Festival.** There are now wine festivals and arts festivals all over Greece, but among the more engaging are those held in Rethymnon. Sample the wines, then sample the Renaissance theatrical and musical performances. Mid-July to early September.

Feast of Ayia Marina. The feast of the protector of crops is widely celebrated in rural areas. July 17.

Feast of the Prophet Elijah (Profitis Elias). The prophet's feast day is celebrated in the hilltop shrines formerly sacred to the sun god Helios. The most famous shrine is on Mount Taygetos, near Sparta. July 18 to 20.

Feast of Ayia Paraskevi. The succession of Saint Days continues to be celebrated at the height of summer, when agricultural work is put on hold. July 26.

August

Feast of the Transfiguration (Metamorphosi). This feast day is observed in the numerous churches and monasteries of that name, though they aren't much for parties. August 6.

Aeschylia Festival of Ancient Drama. Classical dramas are staged at the archaeological site of Eleusis, home of the ancient Mysteries and birthplace of Aeschylus, west of Athens. August to mid-September.

Feast of the Assumption of the Virgin (Apokimisis tis Panayias). On this important day of religious pilgrimage, many come home to visit, so rooms are particularly hard to find. The holiday reaches monumental proportions in Tinos; thousands of people descend on the small port town to participate in an all-night vigil at the cathedral of Panayia Evanyelistria, in the procession of the town's miraculous icon, and in the requiem for the soldiers who died aboard the Greek battleship *Elli* on this day in 1940. August 15.

Epirotika Festival. Ioannina presents theatrical performances, concerts, and exhibitions. August to early September.

Olympus Festival. Cultural events take place in the Frankish Castle of Platamonas, near Mount Olympus. August.

Santorini Festival of Classical Music. International musicians and singers give outdoor performances for 2 weeks. End of August.

September
Feast of the Birth of the Virgin (Yenisis tis Panayias). Another major festival, especially on Spetses, the anniversary of the Battle of the Straits of Spetses is celebrated with a reenactment in the harbor, fireworks, and an all-night bash. September 8.

Feast of the Exaltation of the Cross (Ipsosi to Stavrou). This marks the end of summer's stretch of feasts, and even Stavros has had enough for a while. September 14.

October
Ochi Day. General Metaxa's negative reply (*ochi* is Greek for "no") to Mussolini's demands in 1940 conveniently extends the party with patriotic outpourings, including parades, folk music and folk dancing, and general festivity. October 28.

November
Feast of the Archangels Gabriel and Michael (Gavriel and Mihail). Ceremonies are held in the many churches named for the two archangels. November 8.

Feast of St. Andrew (Ayios Andreas). The patron saint of Patras provides another reason for a party in this swinging city. November 30.

December
Feast of St. Nikolaos (Ayios Nikolaos). This St. Nick is the patron saint of sailors. Numerous processions head down to the sea and to the many chapels dedicated to him. December 6.

Christmas. The day after Christmas honors the Gathering Around the Holy Family (Synaksis tis Panayias). December 25 and 26.

New Year's Eve. Children sing Christmas carols (*kalanda*) outdoors while their elders play cards, talk, smoke, eat, and imbibe. December 31.

6 Travel Insurance

Greece presents no special problems when it comes to insurable "incidents," but it should be noted that most Greeks do not carry very much insurance so you will not be able to collect much if you are in an accident. Check your existing homeowner's, medical, and automobile insurance policies as well as your credit card coverage before you buy travel insurance. You may already be covered for lost luggage, cancelled tickets, or medical expenses. If you are prepaying for your trip or taking a flight that has cancellation penalties, consider cancellation insurance. The cost of travel insurance varies widely, depending on the cost and length of your trip, your age, your health, and the type of trip you're taking. Expect to pay between 5% and 8% of the vacation itself.

TRIP-CANCELLATION INSURANCE

Trip-cancellation insurance helps you get your money reimbursed if you have to back out of a trip, if you have to return home early, or if your travel supplier goes bankrupt. Allowed reasons for cancellation can range from sickness to natural disasters to the State Department declaring your destination unsafe for travel (since the time you made your booking). Insurers usually won't cover vague fears, though, as many travelers discovered who tried to cancel their trips in October 2001 because they were wary of flying. In this unstable world, trip-cancellation insurance is a good buy if you're getting tickets well in advance—who knows what the state of the world, or of your airline, will be in 9 months? Insurance policy details vary, so read the fine print—and especially make sure that your airline or cruise line is on the list of carriers covered in case of bankruptcy.

A good resource is **"Travel Guard Alerts,"** a list of companies considered high-risk by Travel Guard International (see website below). Protect yourself further by paying for the insurance with a credit card—by law, you can get your money back on goods and services not received if you report the loss within 60 days after the charge is listed on your credit card statement.

Note: Many tour operators, particularly those offering trips to remote or high-risk areas, include insurance in the cost of the trip or can arrange insurance policies through a partnering provider, a convenient and often cost-effective way for the traveler to obtain insurance. Make sure the tour company is a reputable one,

however: Some experts suggest you avoid buying insurance from the tour or cruise company you're traveling with, saying it's better to buy from a "third party" insurer than to put all your money in one place.

For information, contact one of the following recommended insurers: **Access America** (© 866/307-3982; www.accessamerica.com); **Travel Guard International** (© 800/826-1300; www.travelguard.com); **Travel Insured International** (© 800/243-3174; www.travelinsured.com); or **Travelex Insurance Services** (© 800/228-9792; www.travelex-insurance.com).

MEDICAL INSURANCE Citizens of the U.K. and other E.U. nations will know your rights when traveling in other E.U. countries; if in doubt, check with the appropriate authorities. For non-E.U. nationals, most health plans (including HMOs, Medicare, and Medicaid) do not provide coverage, and the ones that do often require you to pay for services upfront and file the proper paperwork (for reimbursement) when you get home. In a worst-case scenario, there's the high cost of emergency evacuation. As a safety net, you may want to buy travel medical insurance.

If you require additional medical insurance, try **MEDEX Assistance** (© 800/537-2029; outside the U.S. and Canada, © 410/453-6300; www.medexassist.com) or **Travel Assistance International** (© 800/821-2828; www.travelassistance.com). For general information on Travel Assistance International's services, call the company's Worldwide Assistance Services, Inc., at © 800/777-8710. Other companies that can provide insurance and

---

Tips Quick ID

Tie a colorful ribbon or piece of yarn around your luggage handle, or slap a distinctive sticker on the side of your bag. This makes it less likely that someone will mistakenly appropriate it. And if your luggage gets lost, it will be easier to find.

Avoiding "Economy Class Syndrome"

Deep vein thrombosis, or as it's know in the world of flying, "economy-class syndrome," is a blood clot that develops in a deep vein. It's a potentially deadly condition that can be caused by sitting in cramped conditions—such as an airplane cabin—for too long. During a flight (especially a long-haul flight), get up, walk around, and stretch your legs every 60 to 90 minutes to keep your blood flowing. Other preventative measures include frequent flexing of the legs while sitting, drinking lots of water, and avoiding alcohol and sleeping pills. If you have a history of deep vein thrombosis, heart disease, or any other condition that puts you at high risk, some experts recommend wearing compression stockings or taking anticoagulants when you fly. Always ask your physician about the best course for you. Symptoms of deep vein thrombosis include leg pain or swelling, or even shortness of breath.

further information are: **Travel Guard International** (✆ 800/782-5151); **Travel Insured International** (✆ 800/243-3174); **International Medical Group** (✆ 800/628-4664; insurance@imglobal.com); **Assurance Health** (✆ 800/989-2345; www.buyinternationaltravel.com); **Wallach and Co.** (✆ 800/237-6615; www.wallach.com).

LOST-LUGGAGE INSURANCE On domestic flights, checked baggage is covered up to $2,500 per ticketed passenger. On international flights (including U.S. portions of international trips), baggage coverage is limited to approximately $9.07 per pound, up to approximately $635 per checked bag. If you plan to check items more valuable than the standard liability, see if your valuables are covered by your homeowner's policy, get baggage insurance as part of your comprehensive travel-insurance package, or buy Travel Guard's "BagTrak" product. Don't buy insurance at the airport, as it's usually overpriced. Be sure to take any valuables or irreplaceable items with you in your carry-on luggage, because many valuables (including books, money, and electronics) aren't covered by airline policies.

If your luggage is lost, immediately file a lost-luggage claim at the airport, detailing the luggage contents. For most airlines, you must report delayed, damaged, or lost baggage within 4 hours of arrival. The airlines are required to deliver luggage, once found, directly to your house or destination free of charge.

7 Health & Safety

GENERAL AVAILABILITY OF HEALTH CARE

There are no immunization requirements for getting into Greece, though it's always a good idea to have polio, tetanus, and typhoid covered when traveling anywhere. In Greece, modern hospitals, clinics, and pharmacies are to be found everywhere, and personnel, equipment, and supplies ensure excellent treatment.

Dental care is also widely available. Most doctors in Greece can speak English or some other European language.

You should bring along a sufficient quantity of any prescription medication you are taking and keep it in your carry-on luggage. Just in case, ask your doctor to write you new prescriptions, using the generic—not the brand—names.

COMMON AILMENTS   Diarrhea is no more a problem in Greece than it might be anytime you change diet and water supplies, but yes, occasionally visitors do experience it. Common over-the-counter preventatives and cures are available in Greek pharmacies, but if you are concerned, bring your own. (Cola soft drinks are said to help those with digestive difficulties from too much olive oil in their food.) If you expect to be taking sea trips and are inclined to get seasick, bring a preventative. Allergy sufferers should carry antihistamines, especially in the spring.

SUN   Between mid-June and September, too much exposure to the sun during midday could well lead to sunstroke or heatstroke. Sunscreen and a hat are strongly advised.

DIETARY RED FLAGS   Nothing in the Greek diet requires any special warning. Greece's natural water is excellent, although these days you will usually be served—and charged for—bottled water. Milk is pasteurized, though refrigeration is sometimes not the best, especially in out-of-the-way places. Vegetarians should find the Greek menu especially varied, as so many vegetables, grains, and fruits are available; all except vegans will also enjoy the seafood and yogurt. Greece, however, is not able to serve kosher meals.

BUGS, BITES & OTHER WILDLIFE CONCERNS   There is no particular risk of poisonous bites, although mosquitoes can occasionally be a nuisance: You might well travel with some "bug-off" substance. Dogs, by the way, should not present a danger of rabies, but you are strongly advised not to reach out and touch the dogs that roam around Greece.

WHAT TO DO IF YOU GET SICK AWAY FROM HOME

If you suffer from a chronic illness, consult your doctor about your travel plans before your departure. For conditions like epilepsy, diabetes, or heart problems, wear a **MedicAlert** identification tag (**www.medicalert.org**), which will immediately alert doctors to your condition and give them access to your records through MedicAlert's 24-hour hot line. Before setting off, contact **MedicAlert** (from within North America, ℂ **888/633-4298;** from abroad, **USA Code + 209/668-3333**). If you have special concerns, before heading abroad you might check out the United States Centers for Disease Control and Prevention (ℂ **800/311-3435;** www.cdc.gov/travel or www.istm.org) for advice on health and medical situations in foreign lands.

Pack **prescription medications** in your carry-on luggage, and carry prescription medications in their original containers, with pharmacy labels—otherwise they won't make it through airport security. (Even pills with codeine that are sold over the counter in Canada might be questioned.) Also bring along copies of your prescriptions in case you lose your pills or run out. Don't forget an extra pair of contact lenses or prescription glasses. Carry the generic names of prescription medicines, in case a local pharmacist is unfamiliar with the brand name.

Any foreign embassy or consulate can provide a list of area doctors who speak English. If you get sick, consider asking your hotel front desk to recommend a local doctor—even his or her own. You can also try the emergency room at a local hospital. In addition, many hospitals have walk-in clinics for emergency cases that are not life-threatening; you may not get immediate attention, but you won't pay the high price of an emergency room visit. For major cities in Greece, the phone numbers and addresses for hospitals or medical centers are given in the relevant "Fast Facts" section in each destination chapter. In an emergency, call a first-aid center (© 166), the nearest hospital (© 106), or the tourist police (© 171).

Emergency treatment is usually given free of charge in state hospitals, but be warned that only basic needs are met. The care in outpatient clinics, which are usually open mornings (8am–noon), is often somewhat better; you can find them next to most major hospitals, on some islands, and occasionally in rural areas, usually indicated by prominent signs.

One of the best sources for travelers with medical problems is the **International Association for Medical Assistance for Travelers (IAMAT).** Not only does it have a list of English-speaking doctors (who agree to reasonable fees) in some 120 cities abroad, it puts out specialized publications on diseases such as malaria. It can be reached in the United States at 417 Center St., Lewiston, NY 14092 (© **716/754-4883**); and in Canada at 40 Regal Rd., Guelph, ON N1K 1B5 (© **519/836-0102**). You can also write the office at 57 Voirets, 1212 Grand-Lancy, Geneva, Switzerland; or browse **www.iamat.org**.

Travelmed claims that, given enough warning, it can provide almost anyplace in Greece with everything from accessible transportation and wheelchairs to oxygen and dressings (© **800/878-3627** in the U.S; 702/454-6628 from abroad; www.travelmedintl.com).

Greeks have national medical insurance. Citizens of other E.U. nations should inquire before leaving, but your policies will probably cover treatment in Greece. Non-E.U. travelers should check your health plan to see if it provides appropriate coverage; you may want to buy **travel medical insurance** instead. (See the section on insurance, above.) Bring your insurance ID card with you when you travel. Although you will receive emergency care with no questions asked, make sure you have coverage at home.

STAYING SAFE

Greece is undeniably exposed to earthquakes, but there are few known instances of tourists being injured or killed in one of these. Of far more potential danger are automobile accidents: Greece has one of the worst vehicle accident rates in Europe. You should exercise great caution when driving over unfamiliar, often winding, and often poorly maintained roads. This holds true especially when you're driving at night. As for those who insist on renting motorbikes or similar vehicles, at the very least wear a helmet.

Crime directed at tourists was traditionally unheard of in Greece but in more recent years there are occasional reports of cars broken into, pickpockets, pursesnatchers, and the like. (Ask yourself whether it is necessary to travel with irreplaceable valuables like jewelry.) Normal precautions are called for. For instance, if you have hand luggage containing truly expensive items, whether jewelry or cameras, never hand it to an individual unless you are absolutely sure it will be safe with him or her. Tourists who report crimes to the local police will probably feel that you are not being taken all that seriously, but it is more likely that the Greek police have realized there is little they can do without solid identification of the culprits. As for the other side of the coin— police being exceptionally hard on foreigners, say, when enforcing traffic violations—although there is the rare reported incident, it does not seem to be widespread. (Drugs, however, are a different story: Greeks are *very* hard on anyone caught with them!)

DEALING WITH DISCRIMINATION

There is no denying that many Greeks are opposed to American foreign policies in recent years, but they almost never direct this at individual travelers.

That said, if you get to speaking with Greeks who dislike American policies, they will not be bashful about expressing their opinions and challenging yours. The special issues raised by the recent emergence of terrorism and the war in Iraq have been discussed above.

African Americans and other people of color should not experience treatment in Greece differing from treatment of anyone else, unless it is curiosity from people not accustomed to seeing strangers—in particular, you may be stared at.

8 Specialized Travel Resources

TRAVELERS WITH DISABILITIES

Increasingly, people with physical disabilities who travel abroad will find more options and resources out there than ever before. That said, few concessions exist for travelers with disabilities in Greece. Steep steps, uneven pavements, almost no cuts at curbstones, few ramps, narrow walks, slick stone, and traffic congestion can cause problems. Archaeological sites are, by their very nature, difficult to navigate, and crowded public transportation can be all but impossible.

The new airport and the new Athens Metro system are, however, wheelchair accessible, and thanks to the 2004 Olympics, an elevator now can take wheelchair-bound individuals to the top of the Acropolis; but even this requires that the wheelchair be pushed up a path. More modern and private facilities are only now beginning to provide ramps, but little else has been done. (Hotels that advertise "disability friendly" may mean nothing more than handrails in the bathtub!) That said, foreigners in wheelchairs—accompanied by companions—are becoming a more common sight in Greece. Several travel agencies now offer customized tours and itineraries for travelers with disabilities, but none as yet offer such services for Greece.

Perhaps the best online source of free travel information for people with disabilities is **Access-Able Travel Source** (℃ 303/232-2979; www.access-able. com). **New Directions** (℃ 805/967-2841; www.newdirectionstravel.com) will

discuss the possibilities of arranging tours for people with developmental disabilities. Organizations that offer assistance to travelers with disabilities include Philadelphia's **Moss Rehab Hospital** (℃ 800/2255-6677; www.mossresourcenet.org), which provides a library of accessible-travel resources online; **Society for Accessible Travel and Hospitality** (℃ 212/447-7284; www.sath.org; annual membership fees: $45 adults, $30 seniors and students), which offers a wealth of travel resources for all types of disabilities and informed recommendations on destinations, access guides, travel agents, tour operators, vehicle rentals, and companion services; and **American Foundation for the Blind** (℃ 800/232-5463; www.afb. org), a referral source for the blind or visually impaired that includes information on traveling with Seeing Eye dogs.

For more information specifically targeted to travelers with disabilities, check out the quarterly magazine *Emerging Horizons* ($14.95 per year, $19.95 outside the U.S.; www.emerginghorizons. com); **Twin Peaks Press** (℃ 360/694-2462; twinpeak@pacifier.com), offering travel-related books for travelers with special needs; and *Open World* magazine, published by the Society for Accessible Travel and Hospitality (see above; $13 per year, $21 outside the U.S.).

GAY & LESBIAN TRAVELERS

Greece—or at least parts of Greece—has a long tradition of being tolerant of homosexual men and in recent years these locales, at least, have extended this tolerance to lesbians. But it should be said: Although Greeks in Athens, Piraeus, and perhaps a few other major cities may not care one way or the other, Greeks in small towns and villages—indeed, most Greeks—do not appreciate flagrant displays of dress or behavior. Among the best-known hangouts for gays and lesbians are Mykonos and Chania, Crete, but many gays and lesbians travel all over Greece.

The **International Gay and Lesbian Travel Association** (IGLTA; ☎ **800/ 448-8550** or 954/776-2626; www.iglta. org) is the trade association for the gay and lesbian travel industry, and offers an online directory of gay- and lesbian-friendly travel businesses; go to their website and click on "Members."

Many agencies offer tours and travel itineraries specifically for gay and lesbian travelers. **Above and Beyond Tours** (☎ **800/397-2681;** www.abovebeyond tours.com) is one such. **Now, Voyager** (☎ **800/255-6951;** www.nowvoyager. com) is a well-known San Francisco–based gay-owned and -operated travel service. **Olivia Cruises & Resorts** (☎ **800/631-6277;** www.olivia.com) charters entire resorts and ships for exclusive lesbian vacations and offers smaller group experiences for both gay and lesbian travelers.

The following travel guides are available at most travel bookstores and gay and lesbian bookstores, or you can order them from **Giovanni's Room** bookstore, 345 S. 12th St., Philadelphia, PA 19107 (☎ **215/923-2960;** www.giovannisroom. com): *Frommer's Gay & Lesbian Europe* (www.frommers.com), an excellent travel resource; *Spartacus International Gay Guide* (www.spartacusworld. com) and *Odysseus* ([tel **800/57-5344**), both good, annual English-language guidebooks focused on gay men; the *Damron* guides (www.damron.com), with separate, annual books for gays and

lesbians; and *Gay Travel A to Z: The World of Gay & Lesbian Travel Options at Your Fingertips* by Marianne Ferrari (☎ **602/863-2408;** www.ferrari guides.com), a good gay and lesbian guidebook series.

Another helpful source is *Our World,* a magazine designed specifically for gay and lesbian travelers (10 issues yearly, $12), at 1104 N. Nova Rd., Suite 251, Daytona Beach, FL 32117 (☎ **386/441-5367;** www.ourworldmagazine.com). Not only is it full of ads for travel agencies and facilities that accommodate gays and lesbians, it carries firsthand accounts of visits to locales around the world.

In Athens, information about the **Hellenic Homosexual Liberation Movement (EOK)** can be found at 31 Apostolou Pavlou, Thisio/Athens. The *Greek Gay Guide,* published by Kraximo Press, P.O. Box 4228, 10210 Athens (☎ **210/362-5249**), can be purchased at some kiosks.

SENIOR TRAVEL

Greece does not offer too many discounts for seniors. Some museums and archaeological sites offer discounts for those 60 and over, but the practice is unpredictable, and in general these are restricted to citizens of an E.U. nation. *Tip:* We've heard reports of car rental agencies in Europe that will not rent to people over a certain age—usually 75 but as young as 70. Inquire beforehand.

For general information before you go, visit the U.S. Department of State website at http://travel.state.gov for information specifically for older Americans.

Try mentioning the fact that you're a senior when you make your travel reservations. Although almost all major U.S. airlines have cancelled their senior discount and coupon-book programs, many hotels continue to offer discounts for seniors.

Members of **AARP** (formerly known as the American Association of Retired Persons), 601 E St. NW, Washington, DC 20049 (© **888/687-2277**; www.aarp.org), get discounts on hotels, airfares, and car rentals. AARP offers members a wide range of benefits, including *AARP: The Magazine* and a monthly newsletter. Anyone over 50 can join.

Many reliable agencies and organizations target the 50-plus market. **Elderhostel** (© **877/426-8056**; www.elderhostel. org) arranges study programs for those ages 55 and over (and a spouse or companion of any age) in the U.S. and in more than 80 countries around the world. Most courses last 5 to 7 days in the U.S. (2–4 weeks abroad), and many include airfare, accommodations in university dormitories or modest inns, meals, and tuition. In Greece, groups typically settle in one area for a week or so, with excursions that focus on getting to know the history and culture. **ElderTreks** (© **800/741-7956**; www.eldertreks.com) offers small-group tours to off-the-beaten-path or adventure-travel locations, restricted to travelers 50 and older. Britons might prefer to deal with **Saga Holidays** (Saga Building, Folkestone, Kent CT20 1AZ; © **0800/ 096-0084**; www.saga.co.uk), which offers all-inclusive tours in Greece for those ages 50 and older.

We can recommend several publications offering travel resources and discounts for seniors. An annual subscription to the quarterly magazine *Travel 50 & Beyond* (www.travel50andbeyond.com) costs $14. *101 Tips for Mature Travelers,* available from Grand Circle Travel (© **800/221-2610**; www.gct.com), specializes in travel for seniors. **Vantage Travel** (© **800/322-6677**; www.vantage travel.com), which arranges tours for seniors, offers a free booklet, *151 Travel Tips for Mature Travelers.* One of the better guides for older travelers is *Unbelievably*

Good Deals and Great Adventures That You Absolutely Can't Get Unless You're Over 50 (McGraw-Hill, 2003) by Joan Rattner Heilman.

FAMILY TRAVEL

If you have enough trouble getting your kids out of the house in the morning, dragging them thousands of miles away may seem an insurmountable challenge. But family travel can be immensely rewarding, giving you new ways of seeing the world through smaller pairs of eyes.

How to Take Great Trips with Your Kids (Harvard Common Press) was published in 1983, but it is packed with good, still relevant general advice that can apply to travel anywhere.

Set goals for your family for your travels in Greece. The whole family can head for the beaches. At the other extreme, however, think twice about taking younger kids along on a full-day exploration of museums and archaeological sites. Travel with infants and very young children—say up to about age 5—can work; most children ages 6 to 16 become restless at historical sites. If you're lucky, your children may tune into history at some point in their teens.

There are the occasional "kid-friendly" distractions in Greece: playgrounds all over the place; waterparks here and there; and zoos. Greeks boys now play pickup basketball even in small towns—if your kids go for that, it's a great way to be quickly accepted. The kid-friendly icons throughout the book indicate places we feel might appeal to young people.

Most hotels allow children under 6 a free bed or cot in your room, and reduced prices for children under about 12. Some museums have children's prices, but by and large, Greece is not set up to offer reductions at every turn.

As for passport requirements for children, see "Entry Requirements," earlier in this chapter (or go to the State Department's website, www.travel.state.gov). If you are traveling with children other than your own, you must be sure you have full identification as well as notarized authorization from their parents.

Familyhostel (© **800/733-9753;** www.learn.unh.edu/familyhostel) takes the whole family, including kids ages 8 to 15, on moderately priced domestic and international learning vacations. Lectures, field trips, and sightseeing are guided by a team of academics.

Recommended family-travel Internet sites are **Family Travel Forum** (www.familytravelforum.com), a comprehensive site that offers customized trip-planning; **Family Travel Network** (www.family travelnetwork.com), an award-winning site that offers travel features, deals, and tips; **Traveling Internationally with Your Kids** (www.travelwithyourkids. com), a comprehensive site offering sound advice for long-distance and international travel with children; and **Family Travel Files** (www.thefamilytravelfiles.com), which offers an online magazine and a directory of off-the-beaten-path tours and tour operators for families.

To locate those accommodations, restaurants, and attractions that are particularly kid-friendly, look for the "Kids" icon throughout this guide.

FEMALE TRAVELERS

Women traveling in Greece will not run into any situations particularly different from those encountered by men. Exception: When visiting monasteries and some churches, women will be held to stricter dress codes and may even be denied entry.

That said, young women—especially singles or small groups—may well find Greek males coming on to them, especially at beaches, clubs, and other tourist locales. But our informants tell us that, in general, Greek males (a) do not attempt any physical contact; and (b) respect "No." One tactic said to work for women is to say, "I'm a Greek-American." The other advice is not to leave well-attended locales with someone you don't really know. Women should also be aware that some cafes and even restaurants are effectively male-only haunts; the males will not appreciate attempts by foreign women to enter these places.

Women Welcome Women World Wide (www.womenwelcomewomen.org. uk) works to foster international friendships by enabling women of different countries to visit one another. (Men can come along on the trips; they just can't join the club.) The big, active organization has more than 3,500 members from all walks of life in some 70 countries.

Check out the award-winning website **Journeywoman** (www.journeywoman. com), a "real life" women's travel information network where you can sign up for a free e-mail newsletter and get advice on everything from etiquette to dress to safety; or try the travel guide *Safety and Security for Women Who Travel,* by Sheila Swan Laufer and Peter Laufer (Travelers' Tales, 1998), offering common-sense advice and tips on safe travel.

STUDENT TRAVEL

In Greece, students with proper identification (ISIC and IYC cards) are given reduced entrance fees to archaeological sites and museums, as well as discounts on admission to most artistic events, theatrical performances, and festivals. So you'd be wise to arm yourself with an **International Student Identity Card (ISIC),** which offers substantial savings on rail passes, plane tickets, and entrance fees. It also provides you with basic health and life insurance and a 24-hour help line The card is available for $22 from **STA Travel** (© **800/781-4040;** www.sta.com or www.statravel.com), the biggest student travel agency in the world.

Frommers.com: The Complete Travel Resource

For an excellent travel-planning resource, we highly recommend Frommers.com (www.frommers.com), voted Best Travel Site by *PC Magazine*. We're a little biased, of course, but we guarantee that you'll find the travel tips, reviews, monthly vacation giveaways, bookstore, and online-booking capabilities indispensable. Among the special features are our popular **Destinations** section, where you'll get expert travel tips, hotel and dining recommendations, and advice on the sights to see for more than 3,500 destinations around the globe; **Frommers.com Newsletter**, with the latest deals, travel trends, and money-saving secrets; our **Community** area featuring **Message Boards**, where Frommer's readers post queries and share advice (sometimes our authors show up to answer questions); and our **Photo Center**, where you can post and share vacation tips. When your research is done, the **Online Reservations System** (www.frommers.com/book_a_trip) takes you to Frommer's preferred online partners for booking your vacation at affordable prices.

If you're no longer a student but are still under 26, you can get an **International Youth Travel Card (IYTC)** for the same price, also from STA Travel, which entitles you to some discounts (but not on museum admissions). *Note:* In 2002, STA Travel bought competitors Council Travel and USIT Campus after they went bankrupt. It still operates some offices under the Council name, but it's owned by STA. **Travel CUTS** (© **800/667-2887** or 416/614-2887; www.travelcuts.com) offers similar services for both Canadian and U.S. residents.

Irish students may prefer to turn to **USIT** (© **01/602-1904;** www.usitnow.ie), an Ireland-based specialist in student, youth, and independent travel.

In the United States, one of the major organizations for arranging overseas study for college-age students is the **Council on International Education Exchange,** or **CIEE** (© **800/407-8839;** www.ciee.org).

A Hostelling International membership can save students money in some 5,000 hostels in 70 countries, where sex-segregated, dormitory-style sleeping quarters cost about $15 to $35 per night. In the United States, membership is available through **Hostelling International–American Youth Hostels,** 8401 Colesville Rd., Silver Spring, MD 20910 (© **301/495-1240;** www.hiayh.org). A 1-year membership is free for ages 17 and under; $28 for ages 18 to 54; $18 for ages 55 and over.

In Greece, an International Guest Card can be obtained at the **Greek Association of Youth Hostels (OESE),** in Athens at 11 Botassi near Kaningos Square, behind Omonia (© **210/330-2340**).

9 Planning Your Trip Online

SURFING FOR AIRFARES

The "big three" online travel agencies, **Expedia.com, Travelocity.com,** and **Orbitz.com** sell most of the air tickets bought on the Internet. (Canadian travelers should try Expedia.ca and Travelocity.ca; U.K. residents can go for Expedia.co.uk and Opodo.co.uk). Each has different business deals with the airlines and may offer different fares for the same flights, so it's wise to shop around. Expedia and Travelocity will send you **e-mail notification** when a cheap fare to your favorite destination becomes available. Of the smaller travel agency websites, **SideStep** (www.sidestep.com) has gotten the best reviews from Frommer's authors. It's a browser add-on that purports to "search 140 sites at once," but in reality it beats competitors' fares as often as other sites do.

Also remember to check **airline websites,** especially those for European low-fare carriers such as Ryanair, whose fares are often misreported or missing from travel agency websites. Even with major airlines, you can often shave a few bucks from a fare by booking directly through the airline and avoiding a travel agency's transaction fee. But you'll get these discounts only by **booking online:** Most airlines now offer online-only fares that even their phone agents know nothing about, although many people insist that, after you have done your research with these discount sites, you can often get at least the same price by dealing directly with the airlines—and thereby get a ticket with better guarantees.

For the websites of airlines that fly to and from your destination, refer to "Getting There," p. 44.

Great **last-minute deals** are available through free weekly e-mail services provided directly by the airlines. Most of these are announced on Tuesday or Wednesday and must be purchased online. Most are only valid for travel that weekend, but some can be booked weeks or months in advance. For last-minute trips in Europe, **www. lastminute.com** often has better air-and-hotel package deals than the major-label sites. A website listing numerous bargain sites and airlines around the world is **www.itravelnet.com**.

If you're willing to give up some control over your flight details, use what is called an "**opaque**" **fare service** like **Priceline** (www.priceline.com; www.priceline.co.uk for Europeans) or its smaller competitor, **Hotwire** (www.hotwire.com). Both offer rock-bottom prices in exchange for travel on a "mystery airline" at a mysterious time of day, often with a mysterious change of planes en route. Your chances of getting a 6am or 11pm flight or going with an obscure airline are fairly high. Hotwire tells you prices before you buy; Priceline usually has better deals than Hotwire, but you have to play their "name our price" game. Priceline and Hotwire are great for flights within North America and between the U.S. and Europe. *Note:* In 2004 Priceline added a non-opaque service to its roster. You now have the option to pick exact flights, times, and airlines from a list of offers—or opt to bid on opaque fares as before. For much more about airfares and savvy air-travel tips and advice, pick up a copy of *Frommer's Fly Safe, Fly Smart* (Wiley Publishing, Inc.).

SURFING FOR HOTELS

Shopping online for hotels is generally done one of two ways: by booking through the hotel's own website, or by booking through an independent agency (or fare-service agency like Priceline; see above). These Internet hotel agencies have multiplied in mind-boggling numbers of late, competing for the business of millions of consumers surfing for accommodations around the world. This competitiveness can be a boon to consumers who have the patience and time to shop and compare the online sites for good deals—but shop you must, for prices can vary considerably from site to site. And keep in mind that hotels at the top of a site's listing may be there for no other reason than that they paid money to get the placement.

Of the "big three" sites, **Expedia** offers a long list of special deals and "virtual tours" or photos of available rooms so you can see what you're paying for (a feature that helps counter the claims that the best rooms are often held back from bargain booking websites). **Travelocity** posts unvarnished customer reviews and ranks its properties according to the AAA rating system. Also especially strong for hotels in Greece is **www.dilos.com**. An excellent free program, **TravelAxe** (www.travelaxe. net), can help you search hotel sites in only a few Greek cities, but it conveniently lists the total room prices, including taxes and service charges. It should be noted that the independent online agencies have to fax or e-mail reservation requests to the hotel, and these can get misplaced in the shuffle. More than once, travelers have arrived at a hotel only to be told that they have no reservation. In any case, it's a good idea to get a **confirmation number** and make a **printout** of any online booking transaction.

In the opaque website category, **Priceline** and **Hotwire** are even better for hotels than for airfares; with both, you're allowed to pick the neighborhood and quality level of your hotel before offering up your money. Priceline's hotel service is much better at getting five-star lodging for three-star prices than at finding anything at the bottom of the scale. On the downside, many hotels stick Priceline guests in their least desirable rooms. For both Priceline and Hotwire, you pay upfront, and the fee is nonrefundable. *Note:* Some hotels do not provide loyalty program credits or points or other frequent-stay amenities when you book a room through opaque online services.

SURFING FOR RENTAL CARS

For booking rental cars online, the best deals are usually found at rental-car company websites, although all the major online travel agencies also offer rental-car reservations services. Priceline and Hotwire work well for rental cars, too; the only "mystery" is which major rental company you get, and for most travelers the difference between Hertz, Avis, and Budget is negligible.

10 The 21st-Century Traveler

INTERNET ACCESS AWAY FROM HOME

Travelers have any number of ways to check e-mail and access the Internet on the road. Of course, using a laptop, PDA (personal digital assistant), or electronic organizer with modem gives you the most flexibility. If you don't have a computer, you can access your e-mail and office computer from cybercafes. These can now be found throughout Greece in any good-sized city.

WITHOUT YOUR OWN COMPUTER

It's hard nowadays to find a city that *doesn't* have a few cybercafes. Although there's no definitive directory for cybercafes—these are independent businesses, after all—two places to start looking are **www.world66.com** and **www.cybercafe. com**. Be forewarned, though, that these sites are woefully incomplete and out-of-date. Aside from formal cybercafes, some **youth hostels** nowadays have at least one computer on which you can access the Internet. Avoid **hotel business centers** unless you're willing to pay exorbitant rates.

Most major airports now have **Internet kiosks** scattered throughout their waiting areas. These kiosks, which you'll also see in shopping malls, hotel lobbies, and tourist information offices around the world, give you basic Web access for a per-minute fee that's usually higher than cybercafe prices. The kiosks' clunkiness and high price mean they should be avoided whenever possible.

To retrieve your e-mail, ask your **Internet Service Provider (ISP)** if it has a Web-based interface tied to your existing e-mail account. If your ISP doesn't have such an interface, you can use the free **mail2web** service (www.mail2web.com) to view and reply to your home e-mail. For more flexibility, you may want to open a free, Web-based e-mail account with **Yahoo! Mail,** at http://mail.yahoo.com. (Microsoft's Hotmail is another popular option, but Hotmail has severe spam problems.) Your home ISP may be able to forward your e-mail to the Web-based account automatically.

If you need to access files on your office computer, look into a service called **GoToMyPC** (www.gotomypc.com). The service provides a Web-based interface that allows you to access and manipulate a distant PC from anywhere—even from a cybercafe—provided your "target" PC is on and has an always-on connection to the Internet (such as with Road Runner cable). The service offers top-quality security, but if you're worried about hackers, use your own laptop rather than a cybercafe computer to access the GoToMyPC system.

WITH YOUR OWN COMPUTER

Wi-fi (wireless fidelity) is the buzzword in computer access. More and more hotels, cafes, and retailers are signing on as wireless "hot spots" from where you can get high-speed connection without cable wires, networking hardware, or a phone line (see below). You can get wi-fi connection one of several ways. Many laptops sold in the last year have built-in wi-fi capability (an 802.11b wireless Ethernet connection). Mac owners have their own networking technology, Apple AirPort. For those with older computers, an 802.11b **wi-fi card** (around $50) can be plugged into your laptop. You sign up for wireless access service much as you do

cellphone service, through a plan offered by one of several commercial companies that have made wireless service available in airports, hotel lobbies, and coffee shops, primarily in the U.S. (followed by the U.K. and Japan).

If wi-fi is not available at your destination, most business-class hotels throughout the world offer dataports for laptop modems, and a few thousand hotels in the U.S. and Europe now offer free high-speed Internet access using an Ethernet network cable. You can bring your own cables, but most hotels rent them for around $10. **Contact your hotel in advance** to see what your options are.

In addition, major Internet Service Providers (ISPs) have **local access numbers** around the world, allowing you to go online by placing a local call. Check your ISP's website or call its toll-free number and ask how you can use your current account away from home, and how much it will cost.

Wherever you go, bring a **connection kit** of the right power and phone adapters, a transformer (for Greece's 220 volts), a spare phone cord, and a spare Ethernet network cable—or find out whether your hotel supplies them to guests.

USING A CELLPHONE OUTSIDE THE U.S.

The three letters that define much of the world's **wireless capabilities** are GSM (Global System for Mobiles), a big, seamless network that makes for easy cross-border cellphone use throughout Europe and dozens of other countries worldwide. In the U.S., T-Mobile, Cingular/AT&T Wireless use this quasi-universal system; in Canada, Microcell and some PCS Rogers customers are GSM, and all Europeans and most Australians use GSM.

If your cellphone (*kineto,* in Greek) is on a GSM system, and you have a world-capable multiband phone such as many

Sony Ericsson, Motorola, or Samsung models, you can make and receive calls across civilized areas on much of the globe, from Andorra to Uganda. Call your wireless operator and ask for "international roaming" to be activated on your account. Unfortunately, per-minute charges can be high—usually $1 to $1.50 in western Europe and Greece.

That's why it's important to buy an "unlocked" world phone from the get-go. Many cellphone operators sell "locked" phones that restrict you from using any other removable computer memory phone chip (called a **SIM card**) card other than the ones they supply. Having an unlocked phone allows you to install a cheap, prepaid SIM card (found at a local retailer) in your destination country. (Show your phone to the salesperson; not all phones work on all networks.) You'll get a local phone number—and much, much lower calling rates. Getting an already locked phone unlocked can be a complicated process, but it can be done; call your cellular operator and say you'll be going abroad for several months and want to use the phone with a local provider.

For many, **renting** a cellphone is a good idea. While you can rent a phone from several sites in Greece—the airport, OTE, and cellphone stores in Athens and several major cities—we suggest renting the phone before you leave home. That way you can give relatives and business associates your new number, make sure the phone works, and take the phone wherever you go—especially helpful for overseas trips through several countries, where local phone-rental agencies often bill in local currency and may not let you take the phone to another country.

Cellphone rental isn't cheap. You'll usually pay US$40 to US$50 per week, plus airtime fees of at least a dollar a minute. If you're traveling to Europe, though, local rental companies often offer free incoming calls within their home country, which can save you big bucks. The bottom line: Shop around.

Two good wireless rental companies are **InTouch USA** (☎ **800/872-7626;** www.intouchglobal.com) and **RoadPost** (☎ **888/290-1606** or 905/272-5665; www.roadpost.com). Give them your itinerary, and they'll tell you what wireless products you need. Both support wireless phones in Greece—and both Roadpost and InTouch support BlackBerry.

For trips of more than a few weeks spent in one country, **buying a cellphone** becomes economically attractive, as many nations have cheap, no-questions-asked prepaid phone systems. Once you arrive at your destination, stop by a local cellphone store and get the cheapest package; you'll probably pay less than $100 for a phone and a starter calling card. Local calls may be as low as 10¢ per minute, and in many countries incoming calls are free.

True wilderness adventurers, or those heading to less-developed countries, should consider renting a **satellite phone ("satphone"),** which are different from cellphones in that they connect to satellites rather than ground-based towers. A satphone is more costly than a cellphone but works where there's no cellular signal and no towers. You can rent satellite phones from **RoadPost** (see above). InTouch USA (see above) offers a wider range of satphones but at higher rates. Per-minute call charges can be even cheaper than roaming charges with a regular cellphone, but the phone itself is more expensive (up to $150 per week), and depending on the service you choose, people calling you may incur high long-distance charges. As of this writing, satphones were so expensive, don't even think about buying one.

11 Getting There

BY PLANE

The vast majority of travelers reach Greece by plane, and most of them arrive at the new Athens airport—officially Eleftherios Venizelos International Airport, sometimes referred to by its new location as the Spata airport.

FROM NORTH AMERICA

UNITED STATES   At press time, only two regularly scheduled airlines offer direct, nonstop flights from the States to Athens: Olympic and Delta. **Olympic Airways** (✆ 800/223-1226; www.olympic-airways.gr) offers nonstop service daily from New York and twice weekly from Montreal and Toronto. Olympic will make arrangements to have your luggage transferred from other airlines arriving at New York for your connection. Also, if you fly Olympic transatlantic, it offers reduced fares to all its destinations within Greece. **Delta Air Lines** (✆ 800/241-4141; www.delta.com) offers service from throughout the United States, with all flights connecting to their nonstop Athens flights at JFK in New York (and in Atlanta during the summer).

All the other airlines make stops at some major European airport, where a change of planes is usually required **Alitalia** (✆ 800/223-5730; www.alitalia.com) offers flights from JFK that go to Greece via Rome. **British Airways** (✆ 800/247-9297; www.british-airways.com) has service to Athens from a number of major U.S. cities, all stopping in London (most at Heathrow, but some at Gatwick). **Lufthansa** (✆ 800/645-3880; www.lufthansa.com) provides superior service to Athens, Thessaloniki, and Crete from 10 U.S. cities, via Frankfurt. **Northwest/KLM Royal Dutch Airlines** (✆ 800/447-4747; www.klm.nl) has superior service from 10 major cities in the United States to Athens, with all

flights stopping in Amsterdam. **Swiss International Airlines** (✆ 877/359-7947; www.swiss.com) offers excellent service from Boston as well as New York, with all flights connecting to Athens at Zurich. **Virgin Atlantic Airways** (✆ 800/862-8621; www.virgin-atlantic.com) offers flights via London, with daily flights from Los Angeles and the New York area, and less frequent service from several other cities.

CANADA   In addition to the various airlines flying out of the United States, Canadians have a number of choices. **Olympic Airways** (✆ 800/223-1226; www.olympic-airways.gr) offers the only direct flights from Canada to Athens—two flights a week from Montreal and Toronto. **Air Canada** (✆ 888/247-2262; www.aircanada.ca) flies from Calgary, Montreal, Toronto, and Vancouver to various airports in Europe, with connections on Olympic to Athens. **Air France** (✆ 800/237-2747; www.airfrance.com), **British Airways** (✆ 800/247-9297; www.british-airways.com), **CSA Czech Airlines** (✆ 800/223-2365; www.csa.cz), **Iberia** (✆ 800/772-4642; www.iberia.com), **KLM Royal Dutch Airlines** (✆ 800/447-4747; www.klm.nl), **Lufthansa** (✆ 800/645-3880; www.lufthansa.com), **Swiss International Airlines** (✆ 877/359-7947; www.swiss.com), and **TAP Air Portugal** (✆ 800/221-7370; www.tap-airportugal.pt) all offer at least one flight per week from Calgary, Montreal, Toronto, or Vancouver via other European cities to Athens.

FROM EUROPE

IRELAND   **Aer Lingus** (✆ 01/836-5000 in Dublin; www.aerlingus.ie) and **British Airways** (✆ 0345/222-111 in Belfast; www.british-airways.com) both fly to Athens via London's Heathrow. Less-expensive charters operate in the summer from Belfast and Dublin to Athens, less frequently to Corfu, Crete, Mykonos, and Rhodes. Contact any major travel agency for details. Students should contact **USIT,** at Aston Quay, Dublin 2 (✆ **01/602-1904**), or at Fountain Centre, College Street, Belfast (✆ **02890//327-111**).

UNITED KINGDOM British Airways (✆ **0845/773-3377;** www.ba.com), **Olympic Airways** (✆ **0870/606-0460;** www.olympic-airways.gr), and **Virgin Atlantic Airways** (✆ **0870/380-2007;** www.virgin-atlantic.com) offer several flights daily from London's Heathrow Airport. For the smaller companies offering no-frill flights, contact **EasyJet** ✆ **0870/600-0000;** www.easyjet.com). Or consider the pass sold by **Europebyair** (in North America, ✆ **888/321-4737;** www.europebyair.com), which allows one-way flights for $99 between many European cities, including the most popular destinations in Greece. Several of the eastern European airlines, such as **CSA Czech Airlines** (✆ **0870/4443-747;** www.czechairlines.co.uk), have offered cheaper alternatives, but in recent years the status of some has been in doubt; make inquiries at the time you are prepared to book. There are also connecting flights to Athens and to Thessaloniki via various airlines from Aberdeen, Belfast, Birmingham, Bristol, Edinburgh, Glasgow, Leeds, Liverpool, Newcastle, and Southampton, as well as flights to Athens and the major islands from Birmingham, Cardiff, Gatwick, Glasgow, Luton, and Manchester.

FROM AUSTRALIA & NEW ZEALAND

AUSTRALIA Service to Athens is offered daily from Perth and Sydney and several times weekly from Brisbane and Melbourne by **Alitalia** (✆ **02/247-1308** in Sydney; www.alitalia.com), via Bangkok and Rome; **KLM Royal Dutch Airlines** (✆ **800/505-747** throughout Australia; www.klm.nl), via Singapore and Amsterdam; **Lufthansa** (✆ **02/367-3800** in Sydney; www.lufthansa.com), via Frankfurt; and **Olympic Airways** (✆ **02/251-2204** in Sydney; www.olympic-airways.gr), via Bangkok.

Generally, the lowest fares are offered by **Aeroflot** (✆ **02/233-7148** in Sydney; www.aeroflot.org), which provides weekly service from Sydney via Moscow; and by **Thai Airways** (✆ **02/844-0900** in Sydney; www.thaiair.com), which flies from Brisbane, Melbourne, Perth, and Sydney to Greece via Bangkok. **British Airways** (✆ **02/258-3000** in Sydney; www.british-airways.com) and **Qantas Airways** (✆ **02/957-0111** in Sydney; www.qantas.com) have regular service to London; the "Global Explorer Pass" allows you to make up to six stopovers wherever the two airlines fly, except in South America.

NEW ZEALAND   Air New Zealand is the first choice (✆ **0800/737-000;** www.airnewzealand.com). Other possibilities, which often involve stopovers and airline changes, include: **Singapore Airlines** (✆ **09/303-2506** in Auckland; www.singaporeair.com), with service via Singapore; **Thai Airways** (✆ **09/377-3886** in Auckland; www.thaiair.com), with service via Bangkok; **Qantas Airways** (✆ **09/303-3209** in Auckland; www.qantas.com); **Lufthansa** (✆ **09/303-1529** in Auckland); **British Airways** (✆ **09/367-7500** in Auckland; www.british-airways.com); and **Alitalia** (✆ **09/379-4457** in Auckland; www.alitalia.com).

FROM SOUTH AFRICA

Olympic Airways (✆ **11/880-1614;** www.olympic-airways.gr) offers the only direct flights from Johannesburg to Athens—about three times a week, each way. **Air France** (✆ **01/880-8040;** www.airfrance.com), **Alitalia** (✆ **01/880-9254;**

www.alitalia.com), **British Airways** (© **01/975-3931;** www.british-airways.com), and **Ethiopian Airlines** (© **01/616-7624;** www.ethiopianairlines.com) also offer occasional flights to and from Johannesburg, with connections via other foreign cities.

GETTING THROUGH THE AIRPORT

Citizens of the U.S., U.K., and other nations should be well briefed on your own nation's security policies and practices before setting out for Greece. Greece has upgraded its security at airports, but it is relatively uncomplicated compared to security at U.S. airports. Still, you should plan to arrive at the airport at least **1 hour** before a domestic flight and at least **2 hours** before an international flight. If you must show up late, tell an airline employee and you'll probably be whisked to the front of the line—but be forewarned: Many Greeks habitually show up late, so you will not find this an automatic advantage.

As a foreign traveler in Greece, you will have a passport; as backup, you might also want to bring a **current, government-issued photo ID** such as a driver's license. If you have an e-ticket, print out the **official confirmation page;** you must show your confirmation at the security checkpoint, and your ID at the ticket counter or the gate. (Non-E.U. children need passports even for domestic flights.)

Speed up security by **not wearing metal objects** such as big belt buckles or clanky earrings. If you have metallic body parts, a note from your doctor can prevent a long chat with the security screeners. Keep in mind that only **ticketed passengers** are allowed past security, except for those escorting passengers with disabilities or children.

The new security regulations have stabilized **what you can carry on** and **what you can't.** The general rule is that sharp objects are out, nail clippers are okay. Bring food in your carry-on rather than checking it, as explosive-detection machines used on checked luggage have been known to mistake food (especially chocolate, for some reason) for bombs.

Travelers in Greece are allowed one carry-on bag, plus a "personal item" such as a purse, briefcase, or laptop bag. Carry-on hoarders can stuff all sorts of things into a laptop bag; as long as it has a laptop in it, it's considered a personal item. In general, though, Greek domestic flights have lower limits on the weight of free luggage allowed, so you might on occasion be expected to pay a surcharge if you check in an unusual amount.

Airport screeners may decide that your checked luggage must be searched by hand. You can now purchase luggage

---

Tips Don't Stow It—Ship It

If ease of travel is your main concern and if money is no object, you can ship your luggage and sports equipment with one of the growing number of luggage-service companies that pick up, track, and deliver your luggage (often through couriers such as Federal Express) with minimum hassle for you. Traveling luggage-free may be ultra-convenient, but it's not cheap: One-way overnight shipping can cost from $100 to $200, depending on what you're sending. Still, for some people, especially the elderly or the infirm, it's a sensible solution to lugging heavy baggage. Specialists in door-to-door luggage delivery are **Virtual Bellhop** (www.virtualbellhop.com); **SkyCap International** (www.skycapinternational.com); **Luggage Express** (www.usxpluggageexpress.com); and **Sports Express** (www.sportsexpress.com).

Travel in the Age of Bankruptcy

Airlines these days can go bankrupt, so protect yourself by **buying your tickets with a credit card.** The Fair Credit Billing Act guarantees that you can get your money back from the credit card company if a travel supplier goes under (and if you request the refund within 60 days of the bankruptcy). **Travel insurance** can also help, but make sure it covers "carrier default" for your specific travel provider. And be aware that if a U.S. airline goes bust mid-trip, a 2001 federal law requires that other carriers take you to your destination (albeit on a space-available basis) for a fee of no more than $25, provided you rebook within 60 days of the cancellation.

locks that allow screeners to open and re-lock a checked bag if hand-searching is necessary. Look for Travel Sentry certified locks at luggage or travel shops and at Brookstone stores. (You can also buy them online at www.brookstone.com.) These locks, approved by the TSA, can be opened by luggage inspectors with a special code or key. For more information on the locks, visit www.travelsentry.org. If you use a lock other than a TSA-approved one, it will be cut from your suitcase if a TSA agent has to hand-search your luggage.

LONG-HAUL FLIGHTS: HOW TO STAY COMFORTABLE

Long flights can be trying; stuffy air and cramped seats can make you feel as if you're being sent parcel post in a small box. But with a little advance planning, you can make an otherwise unpleasant experience almost bearable.

- Your choice of airline and airplane will definitely affect your legroom. Find more details at www.seatguru.com, which has extensive details about almost every seat on six major U.S. airlines. For international airlines, the research firm Skytrax has posted a list of average seat pitches at **www.airlinequality.com.** And if you are concerned about meals, check out **www.airlinemeals.com** for the types of meals (with photos) you'll likely be served on airlines.

- Emergency-exit seats and bulkhead seats typically have the most legroom. Emergency-exit seats are usually held back for assignment the day of a flight (to ensure that the seat is filled by someone able-bodied); it's worth getting to the ticket counter early to snag one of these spots for a long flight. Many passengers find that bulkhead seating (the row facing the wall at the front of the cabin) offers more legroom, but keep in mind that bulkheads are where airlines often put baby bassinets, so you may be sitting next to an infant.

- To have two seats for yourself in a three-seat row, try for an aisle seat in a center section toward the back of coach. If you're traveling with a companion, book an aisle and a window seat. Middle seats are usually booked last, so chances are good you'll end up with three seats to yourselves. And in the event that a third passenger is assigned the middle seat, he or she will probably be more than happy to trade for a window or an aisle.

- Ask about entertainment options. Many airlines offer seatback video systems where you get to choose your movies or play video games—but only on some of their planes. (Boeing 777s are your best bet.)

Flying with Film & Video

Never pack film—exposed or unexposed—in checked bags, as the new, more powerful scanners in U.S. airports can fog film. The film you carry with you can be damaged by scanners as well. X-ray damage is cumulative; the faster the film, and the more times you put it through a scanner, the more likely the damage. Film under 800 ASA is usually safe for up to five scans. If you are told that your film must go through additional scans, U.S. regulations permit you to demand hand inspection. In international airports, you're at the mercy of airport officials. On international flights, store your film in transparent baggies, so you can remove it easily before you go through scanners. Keep in mind that airports are not the only places where your camera may be scanned: Highly trafficked attractions are X-raying visitors' bags with increasing frequency.

Most photo-supply stores sell protective pouches designed to block damaging X-rays. The pouches fit both film and loaded cameras. They should protect your film in checked baggage, but they also may raise alarms and result in a hand inspection.

You'll have little to worry about if you travel with a **digital camera.** Unlike film, which is sensitive to light, the digital camera and storage cards are not affected by airport X-rays, according to Nikon. Still, if you plan to travel extensively, you may want to play it safe and hand-carry your digital equipment or ask that it be inspected by hand.

Scanners of carry-ons will not damage **videotape** in video cameras, but the magnetic fields emitted by the walk-through security gateways and hand-held inspection wands will. Always place your loaded camcorder on the screening conveyor belt or have it hand-inspected. Be sure your batteries are charged, as you may be required to turn on the device to ensure that it is what it appears to be.

- To sleep, avoid the last row of any section or a row in front of an emergency exit, as these seats are the least likely to recline. Avoid seats near highly trafficked toilet areas. Avoid seats in the back of many jets—these can be narrower than those in the rest of coach class. You also may want to reserve a window seat so that you can rest your head and avoid being bumped in the aisle.
- Get up, walk around, and stretch every 60 to 90 minutes to keep your blood flowing. This helps avoid **deep vein thrombosis,** or "economy-class syndrome," a potentially deadly condition that can be caused by sitting in cramped conditions for too long. Other preventative measures include drinking lots of water and avoiding alcohol (see next bullet). See the box, "Avoiding 'Economy Class Syndrome,'" under "Health & Safety," p. 32.
- Drink water before, during, and after your flight to combat the lack of humidity in airplane cabins—which can be drier than the Sahara. Bring a

bottle of water on board. Avoid alcohol, which will dehydrate you.

- If you're flying with kids, don't forget to carry on toys, books, pacifiers, and chewing gum to relieve their ear pressure buildup during ascent and descent. Let each child pack his or her own backpack with favorite toys.

GETTING THERE BY SHIP

Most people who travel by ship to Greece from foreign ports come from Italy, although there is occasional service from Cyprus, Egypt, Israel, and Turkey. Brindisi to Patras is the most common ferry crossing, about a 10-hour voyage, with as many as seven departures a day in summer. There is also regular service, twice a day in summer, from Ancona and Bari, once daily from Otranto, and two or three times a week from Trieste or Venice. Most ferries stop at Corfu or Igoumenitsa, often at both; in summer, an occasional ship will also stop at Kefalonia.

If you want to learn more about the ferry services between Greece and foreign ports, the best website is Paleologos Agency's **www.ferries.gr**. Britons might try the London-based agency **Viamare Travel,** Graphic House, 2 Sumatra Rd., London NW6 1PU (② **0870/410-6040;** www.viamare.com). The new **Superfast Ferries Line,** 157 Leoforos Alkyonidon, 16673 Athens (② **210/969-1100;** www. superfast.com), offers service between Ancona and Patras (17 hr.), or between Ancona and Igoumenitsa (15 hr.); also between Bari and Patras (12 hr.) or between Bari and Igoumenitsa (8 hr.). Not all these so-called superfast ferries actually save that much time if you take into consideration boarding and debarking. In addition, their fares are almost twice as much as those of regular ferries.

On the regular ferries, one-way fares during high season from Brindisi to Patras at press time cost from about 50€

($65) for a tourist-class deck chair to about 150€ ($195) for an inside double cabin. Vehicles cost at least another 75€ to 150€ ($98–$195). *Note:* The lines usually offer considerable discounts on round-trip/return tickets. Fares to Igoumenitsa are considerably cheaper, but are by no means a better value unless your destination is nearby. Because of the number of shipping lines involved and the variations in schedules, we're not able to provide more concrete details. Consult a travel agent about the possibilities, book well ahead of time in summer, and reconfirm with the shipping line on the day of departure.

DRIVING YOUR OWN VEHICLE

To bring your own vehicle into Greece, valid registration papers, an international third-party insurance certificate, and a driver's license are required. Valid American and E.U. licenses are accepted in Greece. A free entry card allows you to keep your car in the country up to 4 months, after which another 8 months can be arranged without you paying import duty. Check with your own car insurance company to make sure you are fully covered.

CAR FERRIES   Car ferry service is available on most larger ferries. There's regular service from Piraeus to Aegina and to Poros in the Saronic Gulf; most of the Cyclades; Chania and Iraklion on Crete; Hios; Kos; Lesvos; Rhodes; and Samos. For the Cyclades, crossing is shorter and less expensive from Rafina, an hour east of Athens. From Patras, there's daily service to Corfu, Ithaka, and Kefalonia. The Sporades have service from Ayios Konstandinos, Kimi, and Volos (and then among the several islands). The short car ferry across the Gulf of Corinth from Rio to Antirio can save a lot of driving for those traveling between the northwest and the Peloponnese or Athens. There's also service between many

Street Names

The Greek word for "street" is *odos* and the word for "avenue" is *leoforos*, often abbreviated *Leof.*, usually applied to major thoroughfares. In practice, Greeks seldom employ either of those words—they just use the name. Also, Greeks customarily write the numbers after rather than before the street name. But in the interest of simplifying things, we provide the numbers before the names and drop the word "Odos" (as Greeks do). *Leoforos*, however, we retain as an indication of a major thoroughfare. By the way, *plateia*—think "place" or "plaza"—is Greek for "square," and usually means a large public square, such as Syntagma (Constitution) Square in Athens. Sometimes, however, a *plateia* may be little more than a wide area where important streets meet.

of the islands, even between Crete and Rhodes, as well as car-crossing to and from Turkey between Hios and Çesme; Lesvos and Dikeli; and Samos and Kusadasi. (If you intend to continue on with your vehicle to Turkey or if you're coming into Greece with a car, —long before setting off for either country—make sure you have all the necessary paperwork.)

GETTING THERE BY TRAIN

In the late 1990s, train service from western Europe was disrupted by the trouble in the Balkans. Even when running, the trains tend to be slow and also uncomfortable in the summer. But a Eurailpass is valid for connections all the way to Athens or Istanbul and includes the ferry service from Italy. Endless types of passes are now offered—long stays, short stays, and combinations with airlines, among others. Note that North Americans must purchase your Eurailpasses before you arrive in Europe. For information, see **www.raileurope.com**, or in the U.S. call ✆ **800/438-7245.**

12 Group Tours

Escorted tours are structured group tours, with a group leader. The price usually includes everything from airfare to hotels, meals, tours, admission costs, and local transportation. Two of the major organizers of such tours in Greece are **Homeric Tours** (✆ **800/223-5570;** www.homeric tours.com) and **Tourlite International** (✆ **800/272-7600;** www.tourlite.com). All tours fall into the "moderate" category in pricing and accommodations, and both companies carry the risk of all charter flights—that is, delays. Both offer some variety—often these tours provide local guides, and often they include short cruises as part of the entire stay. A more upscale agency is **TrueGreece** (in North America, ✆ **800/817-7098;** in Greece, ✆ 210/806-2619; www.truegreece.com), which offers small groups more intimate escorted tours to selected destinations.

Many people derive a certain ease and security from escorted trips. Escorted tours—whether by bus, motorcoach, train, or boat—let travelers sit back and enjoy the trip without having to spend lots of time behind the wheel or worrying about details. All the details are taken care of; you know your costs upfront; and there are few surprises. Escorted tours can take you to the maximum number of sights in the minimum amount of time with the least amount of hassle—you don't have to sweat over the plotting and planning of a vacation schedule. Escorted tours are particularly convenient for people with limited mobility. They can also be a great way to make new friends.

On the downside, an escorted tour often requires a big deposit upfront, and lodging and dining choices are predetermined. You'll get little opportunity for serendipitous interactions with locals. The tours can be jam-packed with activities, leaving you little time for individual sightseeing, whim, or adventure—plus they often focus only on the heavily touristed sites, so you miss out on the lesser-known gems.

Before you invest in an escorted tour, ask about the **cancellation policy:** Is a deposit required? Can the company cancel the trip if they don't get enough people? Do you get a refund if the company cancels? If *you* cancel? How late can you cancel if you are unable to go? When do you pay in full? *Note:* If you choose an escorted tour, think strongly about purchasing trip-cancellation insurance, especially if the tour operator asks you to pay upfront. See the section on "Travel Insurance," earlier in this chapter.

You'll also want to get a complete **schedule** of the trip to find out how much sightseeing is planned each day and whether enough time has been allotted for relaxation or solo wandering.

The **size** of the group is also important to know upfront. Generally, the smaller the group, the more flexible the itinerary, and the less time you'll spend waiting for people to get on and off the bus. Find out the **demographics** of the group as well. What is the age range? What is the gender breakdown? Is this a trip for couples or singles?

Discuss what is included in the **price.** You may have to pay for transportation to and from the airport. A box lunch may be included with an excursion, but drinks might cost extra. Tips may not be included. Find out if you will be charged if you opt out of certain activities or meals.

Before you invest in a package tour, get some answers. Ask about the **accommodation choices** and prices for each. Then look up the hotels' reviews in a Frommer's guide and check their rates online for your specific dates of travel. You'll also want to find out what **type of room** you get. If you need a certain type of room, ask for it; don't take whatever is thrown your way. Request a nonsmoking room, a quiet room, a room with a view, or whatever kind of room you fancy.

Finally, if you plan to travel alone, you'll need to know if a **single supplement** will be charged and if the company can match you up with a roommate.

13 Special-Interest Trips

ACTIVE TRAVELERS

Increasing numbers of travelers of all ages are seeking more active ways to experience Greece. We advise you to investigate closely what an activity involves—the level of difficulty, for example.

BICYCLING   More and more tourists are traveling in Greece by bicycle. For information, contact the **Hellenic Cycling Association,** National Velodrome, Marousi-Athens 15123 (© **210/689-3403**).

Trekking Hellas, 7 Filellinon, 10557 Athens (© **210/331-0323;** www.trekking.gr), can also assist you in arranging mountain-biking trips. But Greece is not the place to learn how to tour on a bicycle. Greek drivers have little experience in accommodating bicyclists, road shoulders in Greece are often nonexistent and even at best are not generous, and roads are not especially well maintained.

In the United States, **Classic Adventures,** Box 143, Hamlin, NY 14464

(© 800/777-8090; www.classicadventures.com), has been around since 1979. It often offers bicycle tours in Greece, such as a 12-day tour of Crete; or an 11-day coastal excursion that includes Corinth, Epidaurus, Mycenae, Olympia, and the island of Zakinthos. They offer a significant discount if you sign on before January 15.

Mountain bikes are better suited for Greek terrain. You can bring your own along by train (for a small fee) or by plane (free, though not easy). You can take your bicycle with you on Greek ferries and on trains, usually at no extra cost. You should also bring along spare parts, as they are rarely available outside the major cities.

If you insist on trying a bicycle in Greece, you can rent an old bike for very little at most major resorts, and good mountain bikes are increasingly available. On Crete, mountain bikes are available for rent in Iraklion at **Creta Travel Bureau,** 20–22 Epimenidou (© 2810/227-002), which also has offices in Rethymnon and Ayios Nikolaos. In Chania, try **Athanasakis Tours,** 25 Halidon (© 28210/44-965). On Paros, the **Mountain Bike Club,** near the post office in Parikia (©/fax 22840/23-778), rents good mountain bikes. On Rhodes, they are available at **Mike's Motor Club,** 23 Kazouli (© 22410/37-420). Kos is well suited to cycling, and bicycles are widely available for rent there.

CAMPING   Greece offers a wide variety of camping facilities throughout the country. Rough or freelance camping—setting up your camp on apparently unoccupied land—is forbidden by law but may be overlooked by local authorities. The **Greek National Tourism Organization** should have further information on its many licensed facilities, as well as a very informative booklet, *Camping in Greece,* published by the **Panhellenic Camping Association,** 102 Solonos, 10680 Athens (© 210/362-1560).

DIVING   Scuba diving is currently restricted throughout most of Greece because of potential harm to sunken antiquities and the environment. That said, many locales now allow diving under supervision by accredited "schools." On the mainland, these may be found along the coast of Attica, off the Peloponnese peninsula, and off Halkidiki and a few other places in the north. There is also limited diving off the islands of Corfu, Crete, Hydra, Kalimnos, Kefalonia, Mykonos, Paros, Rhodes, Santorini, Skiathos, and Zakinthos.

To single out a few at the more popular locales, on Corfu there is **Calypso Scuba Divers,** Ayios Gordis (© 26610/53-101); on Rhodes, the **Dive Med Center,** 5 Dragoumi, Rhodes town (© 22410/33-654); on Crete, **Paradise Dive Center,** 51 Giamboudaki, Rethymnon (©/fax 28310/53-258); and on Mykonos, **Lucky Scuba Divers,** Ornos Beach (© 22890/22-813). Even if you are qualified, you must dive under supervision. Above all, you are forbidden to photograph, let alone remove, anything that might possibly be regarded as an antiquity.

For more information, contact the **Organization of Underwater Activities** (© 210/982-3840) or the **Union of Greek Diving Centers** (© 210/922-9532). If you're a serious underwater explorer, contact the **Department of Underwater Archaeology,** 4 Al Soutsou, 10671 Athens (© 210/360-3662).

Snorkeling, however, is permitted, and the unusually clear waters make it a special pleasure. Simple equipment is widely available for rent or for sale.

FISHING   Opportunities for fishing abound. Contact **Amateur Anglers and Maritime Sports Club,** Akti Moutsopoulou, 18537 Piraeus (© 210/451-5731).

GOLF   There are relatively few golf courses in Greece, although several more are in the planning stages. Those now in existence are in Glifada (along the coast outside Athens), Halkidiki, Corfu, Crete (Elounda), and Rhodes. Any travel agent can supply the details.

HIKING   Greece offers endless opportunities for hiking, trekking, and walking. Greeks themselves are now showing interest in walking for pleasure, and there are a number of well-mapped and even signed walking routes.

Probably the best and most up-to-date source of information on nature-oriented tours or groups are the ads in magazines geared toward people with these interests—*Audubon Magazine,* for instance, for birders. But you need not sign up for special (and expensive!) tours to enjoy Greece's wildlife. Bring your own binoculars, and buy one of the many illustrated handbooks such as *Wildflowers of Greece,* by George Sfikas (Efstathiadis Books, Athens); or *Birds of Europe,* by Bertel Brun (McGraw-Hill).

In Greece, we recommend **Trekking Hellas,** in Athens at 7 Filellinon (© 210/ 331-0323), and in Thessaloniki at 71 Tsimiski (© 2310/222-128), for either guided tours or for help in planning your private trek. Other Greek travel agencies specializing in nature tours include: **Adrenaline Team,** 2 Kornarou and 28 Hermou, 10563 Athens (© 210/331-1777); **Athenogenes,** 18 Plateia Kolonaki, 10673 Athens (© 210/361-4829); and **Ey-Zhn,** 132 Leoforos Syngrou, 17671 Athens (© 210/921-6285). In the Sporades, try **Ikos Travel,** Patitiri, 37005 Alonissos (facing the quay; © 24240/65-320).

In the United States, **Appalachian Mountain Club,** 5 Joy St., Boston, MA 02108 (© 617/523-0636; www.amcbston.org), often organizes hiking tours in Greece. **Classic Adventures,** Box 143, Hamlin, NY 14464 (© 800/777-8090; www.classicadventures.com), sometimes offers hiking tours in regions of Greece. **Mountain Travel-Sobek,** 1266 66th St., Emeryville, CA 94608 (© 800/687-6235; www.mtsobek.com), sometimes conducts summer hikes and kayaking trips in the Greek mountains. **Country Walkers,** P.O. Box 180, Waterbury, VT 05676 (© 800/464-9255; www.countrywalkers. com), is another company that conducts occasional walking tours through regions of Greece. **Ecogreece,** P.O. Box 2614, Rancho Palo Verdes, CA 90275 (© 877/838-7748; www.ecogreece.com), conducts tours in Greece centered around activities such as sailing, hiking, diving, or riding.

Birders and nature lovers should contact the **Hellenic Ornithological Society,** 24 Vassiliou Irakleiou, 10682 Athens (© 210/822-7937; www.ornithologiki, gr). **Questers Worldwide Nature Tours,** 381 Park Ave. S., Suite 1201, New York, NY 10016 (© 800/468-8668; www. questers.com), sometimes offers nature tours in Greece. Also specializing in walking tours is **Alternative Travel Group,** 69–71 Banbury Rd., Oxford, OX2 6PJ England (© 44/1865-315678, or 800/527-5997 in the U.S; www.atg-oxford.co.uk); and **Naturetrek,** Cheriton, Alresford, Hants, England, S024 0NG (© 1982/733-051; www.nature-trek.co.uk).

HORSEBACK RIDING   You can go horseback riding in Greece at a fair number of places. Near Athens you'll find the **Athletic Riding Club** of Ekali (© 210/ 813-5576), and the **Hellenic Riding Club** in Maroussi (© 210/681-2506). Call for directions and reservations. Good facilities are also located on the islands of Corfu, Crete, Rhodes, and Skiathos, with smaller stables elsewhere (inquire at local travel agencies).

As for extended trips through various regions of Greece on horseback, several companies specialize in these. In North

America, try **Equitours,** Box 807, Dubois, WY 82513 (© **800/545-0019** or 307/455-3363); or **Hidden Trails,** 202–380 W. 1st Ave., Vancouver, BC V58 377 (© **888-987-2457;** www.hiddentrails.com). In Europe, try **Equitour,** based in Switzerland (© **0041/61-303-3108;** www.equitour.com).

MOUNTAINEERING   If you're interested in more strenuous trekking and mountain-climbing, contact the **Hellenic Federation of Mountaineering & Climbing,** 5 Milioni, 10673 Athens (© **210/364-5904**).

SPELUNKING   If you don't know what the word refers to, then don't do it. It refers to exploring caves, which are fragile environments that can be harmed easily. Visitors can fall prey to hypothermia if you go exploring without a guide. There are numerous caves in Greece and numerous individuals skilled in exploring them. For details, contact the **Hellenic Speleological Society,** 32 Sina, Athens (© **210/361-7824**).

WATERSPORTS   Watersports of various kinds are available at most major resort areas, and we mention the more important facilities in the relevant chapters that follow. **Parasailing** is possible at the larger resorts in summer. Although some of these facilities are limited to patrons of hotels and resorts, in many places they are available to anyone willing to pay.

Water-skiing facilities are widely available; there are several schools at Vouliagmeni, south of Athens, and usually at least one on each of the major islands. Contact the **Hellenic Water-Ski Federation,** Leoforos Poseidonos, 16777 Glyfada (© **210/894-7413**).

Windsurfing is becoming more popular in Greece, and boards are widely available for rent. The many coves and small bays along Greece's convoluted coastline are ideal for beginners. Instruction is available at reasonable prices. The best conditions and facilities are found on the islands of Corfu, Crete, Lefkada, Lesvos, Naxos, Paros, Samos, and Zakinthos. Contact the **Hellenic Wind-Surfing Association,** 7 Filellinon, 10557 Athens (© **210/323-0068**), for details about the many excellent schools in Greece.

EXTENDING THE MIND

ARCHAEOLOGICAL DIGS   The **American School of Classical Studies at Athens,** 6–8 Charlton St., Princeton, NJ 08540 (© **609/683-0800;** www.ascsa.edu.gr), often sponsors tours in Greece and adjacent Mediterranean lands guided by archaeologists and historians. **Archaeological Tours,** 271 Madison Ave., Suite 904, New York, NY 10016 (© **866/740-5130;** www.archaeologicaltrs.com), offers tours led by expert guides; typical tours might be to classical Greek sites or to Cyprus, Crete, and Santorini. **Free-Gate Tourism,** 585 Stewart Ave., Suite 310, Garden City, NY 11530 (© **888/373-3428;** www.freegatetours.com), also specializes in guided trips in Greece.

ART Group International Study Tours, 494 Eighth Ave., New York, NY 10001 (© **800/833-2111;** www.groupist.com), offers studies in the architecture, art, and culture of Greece, led by professionals. Especially attractive are the **Aegean Workshops** run by Harry Danos, a Greek-American architect and watercolorist. In spring and autumn, he leads groups to various regions of Greece, where he provides instruction in drawing and watercolor painting (and also ends up teaching the language). To learn more, call © **860/739-0378** mid-May through October, or © **239/455-2623** from November to mid-May. You can also e-mail hkdanos@webtv.net.

Athens Center for the Creative Arts, 48 Archimidou, Pangrati, 11636 Athens

(© 210/701-2268), offers summer programs. **Hellas Art Club** on the island of Hydra, at the Leto Hotel, 18040 Hydra (© **22980/53-385**), offers classes in painting, ceramics, music, theater, photography, Greek dancing, and cooking. And the American-run **Island Center for the Arts** conducts classes in painting, photography, artist's books, and Greek culture on Skopelos between June and September (© **617/623-6538;** info@ islandcenter.org).

MODERN GREEK Formal educational institutions and private language institutes throughout the English-speaking world offer many courses. There are also decent courses on tape for self-study. Be sure it is modern Greek you study—not classical Greek! If you are already in Greece, **Athens Center for the Creative Arts,** 48 Archimidou, Pangrati, 11636 Athens (© **210/701-2268**), is highly recommended. **School of Modern Greek Language of Aristotle University in Thessaloniki** also offers summer courses (www.auth.gr/smg). For basic vocabulary and phrases, see **appendix B** in this book.

PERSONAL GROWTH Skyros Center, which can be contacted in the United Kingdom at 92 Prince of Wales Rd., London NW5 3NE (© **020/7267-4424;** www.skyros.com), offers "personal growth" vacations on the island of Skyros, with courses in fitness, holistic health, creative writing, and handicrafts.

COOKING Rosemary Barron, an American food expert based in San Francisco, has for many years run a cooking school, Kandra Kitchen—usually on Santorini—in which participants learn how to prepare Greek foods. For more information, try her website, **www. rosemarybarronsgreece.com**.

14 Getting Around Greece

BY PLANE

Compared to the cheaper classes on ships and ferries, air travel within Greece can be expensive, but we recommend it for those pressed for time and/or heading for more distant destinations (even if the planes don't always hold strictly to their schedules). Until the late 1990s, **Olympic Airways** (© **210/966-6666;** www.olympicairlines.com) maintained a monopoly on domestic air travel and thus had little incentive to improve service. In the end, it declared bankruptcy and was placed under new management, which has steadily improved service. Better computerized booking has reduced the number of last-minute discoveries that you don't have a seat. Delayed flights are still common, although the quality of the service, which was criticized for some years, is reportedly better. (Olympic's domestic flight attendants tend to be more helpful than their international counterparts.) Also, Olympic has one of the best safety records of any major airline.

Book as far ahead of time as possible (especially in summer), reconfirm your booking before leaving for the airport, and arrive at the airport at least an hour before departure; the scene at a check-in counter can be quite hectic.

Olympic Airways has a number of offices in Athens, though most travel agents sell tickets as well. It offers **mainland** service to Aktaion Preveza, Alexandroupolis, Ioannina, Kalamata, Kavala, Kastoria, Kozani, and Thessaloniki. As for **islands,** Olympic services Astipalea, Chios, Corfu (Kerkira), Crete (Iraklion, Chania, Sitia), Ikaria, Karpathos, Kassos, Kastellorizo, Kefalonia, Kithira, Kos, Leros, Limnos, Milos, Mitilini (Lesvos), Mykonos, Naxos, Paros, Rhodes, Samos,

Santorini (Thira), Siros, Skiathos, Skyros, and Zakinthos. All of Olympic's domestic flights leave from the new international airport at Spata. Most flights are to or from Athens, although during the summer there may be some inter-island service. The baggage allowance is 15 kilos (33 lb.) per passenger, except with a connecting international flight; even the domestic flights generally ignore the weight limit unless you are way over. Smoking is prohibited on all domestic flights.

A round-trip ticket costs double the one-way fare. Sample round-trip fares (including taxes) at this writing are: Athens-Corfu, Rhodes, Thessaloniki, 220€ ($286); Athens-Iraklion, Chania, 204€ ($265); Athens-Ioannina, 196€ ($255); Athens-Santorini, 202€ ($263); Athens-Mykonos, 190€ ($247); Athens-Samos, 160€ ($208); Athens-Skiathos, 107€ ($139); Athens-Syros, 141€ ($183). As you can see, even the shorter trips, such as to Mykonos or Santorini, are not especially cheap, but there's no denying that for those with limited time, air travel is the best way to go. Ask, too, if Olympic still offers reduced fares for trips Monday through Thursday and trips that include a Saturday-night stay.

Over the years, several small private airlines have tried to compete with Olympic, but only one has survived to provide a real alternative: **Aegean Airlines.** From abroad, dial the code for Greece, then © 210/626-1000; within Greece, dial © 801/112-0000. You can also check www.aegeanair.com, which allows you to order e-tickets online. They offer service at somewhat reduced prices between Athens and the major destinations in Greece, including Alexandropoulis, Chania, Chios, Corfu, Ioannina, Iraklion, Kavala, Kos Mitilini, Mykonos, Patras, Rhodes, Santorini, and Thessaloniki. (They also offer direct flights to Rome, Milan, several major German cities, and Cyprus.) Foreign travel agents

may not be aware of Aegean Airlines, so check out their website. People who have been flying Aegean report being extremely satisfied with the airline's service, which they found reliable, safe, and hospitable.

Note: Most Greek domestic tickets are nonrefundable, and changing your flight can cost you up to 30% within 24 hours of departure and 50% within 12 hours.

BY BOAT

BY FERRY   Ferries are the most common, cheapest, and generally most "authentic" way to visit the islands, though the slow roll of a ferry can be authentically stomach-churning. A wide variety of vessels sail Greek waters—some huge, sleek, and new, with comfortable TV lounges, discos, and good restaurants; some old and ill-kept, but pleasant enough if you stay on deck.

The new Flying Dolphin hydrofoils also serve all the major islands. Undoubtedly faster, they cost almost twice as much as regular ferries, and their schedules are often interrupted by weather conditions. (Never rely on a tight connection between a hydrofoil and, say, an airplane flight.) Ferries, too, often don't hold exactly to their schedules, but they can be fun if you enjoy opportunities to meet people. Drinks and snacks are almost always sold, but the prices and selection are not that good, so you may want to bring along your own.

The map of Greece offered by the Greek National Tourism Organization (EOT), which indicates the common boat routes, is very useful in planning your sea travels. Once you've learned what is possible, you can turn your attention to what is available. Remember that the summer schedule is the fullest, spring and fall bring reduced service, and winter schedules are skeletal.

There are dozens of shipping companies, each with its own schedule—which,

Greek Ferry Routes

by the way, are regulated by the government. Your travel agent might have a copy of the monthly schedule, *Greek Travel Pages,* or you can search online at **www.gtp.gr** or **www.allgreekferies.com**. But it's best to go straight to an official information office, a travel agency, or the port authority as soon as you arrive at the place that you intend to leave via ferry.

Photos can give you some idea of the ships, but remember that any photo displayed was probably taken when the ship was new, no matter when it was reproduced, and it is unlikely that anyone will be able (or willing) to tell you its actual age. The bigger ferries offer greater

stability during rough weather. Except in summer, you can usually depend on getting aboard a ferry by showing up about an hour before scheduled departure—inter-island boats sometimes depart before their scheduled times—and purchasing a ticket from a dockside agent or aboard the ship itself, though this is often more expensive.

Your best bet is to buy a ticket from an agent ahead of time. In Athens, we recommend **Galaxy Travel,** 35 Voulis, near Syntagma Square (© **210/322-5960;** www.galaxytravel.gr); and **Alkyon Travel,** 97 Akademias, near Kanigos Square (© **210/383-2545**). During the high

Early Season Ferries

In the early weeks of the tourist season, from April to early May, boat service is altogether unpredictable. Boat schedules, at the best of times, are tentative—but during this time, they are wish lists, nothing more. Our best advice is that you wait until you get to Greece, then go to a major travel agency and ask for help.

season, both agencies keep long hours Monday through Saturday.

Note: Different travel agencies sell tickets to different lines—this is usually the policy of the line itself—and one agent might not know or bother to find out what else is offered. However, if you press reputable agencies like those above, they will at least tell you the options. The port authority is the most reliable source of information, and the shipping company itself or its agents usually offer better prices and may have tickets when other agents have exhausted their allotment. It often pays to compare vessels and prices.

First class usually means roomy air-conditioned cabins and its own lounge; on some routes it costs almost as much as flying. However, on longer overnight hauls, you're on a comfortable floating hotel and thus save the cost of lodging. Second class means smaller cabins (which you will probably have to share with strangers) and its own lounge. The tourist-class fare entitles you to a seat on the deck or in a lounge. (Tourists usually head for the deck, while Greeks stay inside, watch TV, and smoke copiously.) Hold onto your ticket; crews conduct ticket-control sweeps.

Note: Those taking a ferry to Turkey from one of the Dodecanese islands must submit passport and payment to an agent the day before departure.

We include more details on service and schedules in the relevant chapters that follow, as well as suggested travel agencies

and sources of local information. To give you some sense of the fares, here are examples for first-class travel from Piraeus at press time (compare with airfares during this same time, p. 55): to Crete (Iraklion), 80€ ($104); Kos, 110€ ($143); Mitilini (Lesvos), 80€ ($104); Mykonos, 60€ ($78); Naxos, 65€ ($85); Rhodes, 130€ ($169); Santorini, 65€ ($85). A small embarkation tax may be added.

BY HYDROFOIL Hydrofoils (often referred to by the principal line's trade name, Flying Dolphins, or by Greeks as *to flying*) are nearly twice as fast as ferries, and have comfortable airline-style seats. Their stops are much shorter, and they are less likely to cause seasickness. Although they cost nearly twice as much as ferries, are frequently fully booked in summer, can be quite bumpy during rough weather, and give little or no view of the passing scenery, they're the best choice if your time is limited. Everyone should ride one of these sleek little crafts at least once.

There is regular hydrofoil service to nearly all the major islands, with new schedules appearing often. Longer trips over open sea, such as between Santorini and Iraklion, Crete, may make them well worth the extra expense. (Smoking is prohibited, and actually less likely to be indulged in, possibly because the cabins seem so much like those of an aircraft.) The forward compartment offers better views but is also bumpy.

The Flying Dolphins are now operated by **Hellas Flying Dolphins,** Akti Kondyli and 2 Aitolikou, 18545 Piraeus (© **210/419-9100;** www.dolphins.gr). The service from Zea Marina in Piraeus to the Saronic Gulf islands and the Peloponnese is especially good. (The fare to Spetses is about 35€/$46, compared to about 18€/$23 for tourist-class ferry service.) Flying Dolphin service in the Sporades is recommended for its speed and regularity. There is also service from Rafina, on the east coast of Attika, to several of the Cyclades islands.

BY SAILBOAT & YACHT Many more tourists are choosing to explore Greece by sailboat or yacht. There are numerous facilities and options for both. Experienced sailors interested in renting a boat in Greece can contact the **Hellenic Professional and Bareboat Yacht Owners' Association,** A8–A9 Zea Marina, 18536 Piraeus (© **210/452-6335**). Consider signing up for one of the flotillas—a group of 12 or more boats sailing as a group led by a boat crewed by experienced sailors; the largest of such organizations is **Sunsail,** 980 Awald Rd., Annapolis, MD 21403 (© **888/350-3568;** www.sunsail.com). However, travel agencies should be able to put you in touch with one of these organizations.

At the other extreme, those who want to charter a yacht with anything from a basic skipper to a full crew should first contact the **Hellenic Professional Yacht Owners' Association** (listed above), or **Ghiolman Yachts,** 7 Filellinon, 10557 Athens (© **210/323-0330;** www.ghiolman.com). If you feel competent enough to make your own arrangements, contact **Valef Yachts Ltd.,** P.O. Box 391, Ambler, PA 19002 (© **215/641-1624;** www.valefyachts.com). In Greece, you can contact one of these associations or try a private agency such as **Alpha Yachting,** 67 Leoforos Possidonos, 16674 Glyfada (© **210/968-0486;** www.alphayachting.com). Also try **Aris Drivas Yachting,** 147 Neorion, Piraeus (© **210/411-3194**).

BY CAR

Driving in Greece is a bit of an adventure, but it's the best way to see the country at your own pace. *Note:* Greece has one of the highest accident rates in Europe, probably due somewhat to treacherous roads, mountain terrain, and poor maintenance of older cars as much as to reckless driving—although Greeks are certainly aggressive drivers. Athens is a particularly intimidating place in which to drive at first, and parking spaces are practically nonexistent in the center of town. (White arrows on blue markers sometimes indicated the main routes in and out of cities.) Accidents must be reported to the police for insurance claims.

The **Greek Automobile Touring Club (ELPA),** 395 Mesoyion, Athens 11527 (© **210/779-1615**), with offices in most cities, can help you with all matters relating to your car, issue **International Driver's Licenses,** and provide **maps and information** (© **174,** 24 hr. daily). ELPA's emergency road service number is © **104.** Though the service provided by the able ELPA mechanics is free for light repairs, definitely give a generous tip.

The price of gasoline fluctuates considerably from week to week and from service station to service station, but it remains consistently expensive: 1.20€ ($1.56) a liter, which works out to about $5.90 for an American gallon. There is no shortage of gasoline stations in all cities, good-sized towns, and major touristic centers, but if you are setting off for an excursion into one of the more remote mountain areas or to an isolated beach, yes, fill up on gas before setting out.

CAR RENTALS   There are many rental cars, and almost as much variation in prices. Many cars have a standard shift; if you must have an automatic, make sure in advance that one is available. You are strongly advised to make your reservation before leaving home and well in advance. Always ask if the quoted price includes insurance; many credit cards make the collision-damage waiver unnecessary, but you will find that most rental agencies automatically include this in their rates. You can sometimes save by booking at home before you leave; this is especially advisable in summer. If you are shopping around, let the agents see the number of competitors' brochures you're carrying.

Most companies require that the renter be at least 21 years old (25 for some car models). An occasional company won't rent to anyone older than 70 or 75. Definitely inquire beforehand! You must possess a valid Australian, Canadian, E.U.-nation, U.S., or International Driver's License. You must also have a major credit card (or be prepared to leave a large cash deposit).

The major car rental companies in Athens are **Avis** (© 210/322-4951), **Budget** (© 210/349-8700), **Hertz** (© 210/922-0102), **National** (© 210/349-3400), and **AutoEurope** (© 00800/11574-0300 toll-free from Greece), all with additional offices in major cities, at most airports, and on most islands. Smaller local companies usually have lower rates, but their vehicles are often older and not as well maintained. If you prefer to combine your car rental with your other travel arrangements, we recommend **Galaxy Travel,** 35 Voulis, near Syntagma Square (© 210/322-2091; www.galaxy travel.gr). It's open Monday through Saturday during the tourist season.

Rental rates vary widely—definitely inquire around. In high season, the cheaper daily rates will be about 55€ ($72) for a compact and 100€ ($130) for a full-size; weekly rates might run 350€ ($455) for a compact and 500€ ($650) for a full-size. In low season, rates are often negotiable in Greece in person. And be prepared for the addition of about 18% in VAT taxes plus 2% in municipal taxes to the quoted price. (There's often a surcharge for pickup and drop-off at airports.)

Note: You must have written permission from the car rental agency to take your rental car on a ferry or into a foreign country.

DRIVING RULES   In Greece, you drive on the right, pass on the left, and yield right-of-way to vehicles approaching from the right except where otherwise posted. Greece has adopted international

---

Warning

Legally, all non-E.U. drivers in Greece are required to carry an International Driver's License. In practice, most car rental agencies will rent to Americans and other non-E.U. drivers carrying their national driver's licenses. (One major exception is on the island of Hios.) This is fine so long as you don't get involved in an accident—especially one involving personal injury. Then you could discover that your insurance is voided on a technicality. Meanwhile, you run the risk of an individual policeman insisting that you must have the international license. Obtain one before leaving home (from the national automobile association) or from the Greek Automobile Touring Club (see above).

Greek law also requires that travelers have a motorcycle license to rent mopeds and other motorized cycles (see below).

road signs, though many Greeks apparently haven't learned what they mean yet. The maximum speed limit is 100kmph (65 mph) on open roads, and 50kmph (30 mph) in town, unless otherwise posted. Seat belts are required. The police have become stricter in recent years, especially with foreigners in rental cars; alcohol tests can be given and fines imposed on the spot. (If you feel you have been stopped or treated unfairly, get the officer's name and report him at the nearest tourist police station.) Honking is illegal in Athens, but you can hear that law broken by tarrying at a traffic signal.

PARKING   Parking a car has become a serious challenge in the cities and towns of Greece. The better hotels provide parking, either on their premises or by arrangement with a nearby lot. Greece has few public parking garages or lots. Follow the blue signs with the white P and you may be lucky enough to find a space. Most Greek city streets have restricted parking of one kind or another. In some cities, signs—usually yellow, and with the directions in English as well as in Greek—will indicate that you can park along the street but must purchase a ticket from the nearest kiosk. Otherwise, be prepared to park fairly far from your base or destination. If you lock the car and remove valuables from sight, you should not have to worry about a break-in.

BY TRAIN

Greek trains are generally slow but are inexpensive and fairly pleasant. The **Hellenic State Railway (OSE)** also offers bus service from stations adjacent to major train terminals. (Bus service is faster, but second-class train fare is nearly 50% cheaper, and trains offer more comfortable and scenic rides.) If you are interested in special arrangements involving rail passes for Greece (sometimes in combination with Olympic Airlines flights within Greece), check out **www.rail europe.com** or call © **888/382-7245** (in the U.S. only).

For information and tickets in Athens, visit the **OSE office** at 1–3 Karolou (© **210/522-4563**), or at 6 Sina (© **210/ 362-4402**), both near Omonia Square.

Purchase your ticket and reserve a seat ahead of time, as a 50% surcharge is added to tickets purchased on the train, and some lines are packed, especially in summer. A first-class ticket may be worth the extra cost, as seats are more comfortable and less crowded. There is sleeper service on the Athens–Thessaloniki run. Though the costly sleepers are a good value, you must be prepared to share a compartment with three to five others. Express service (6 hr.) runs twice a day, at 7am and 1pm.

Trains to Northern Greece (Alexandroupolis, Florina, Kalambaka, Lamia, Larissa, Thessaloniki, Volos, and other towns) leave from the Larissa station (Stathmos Larissis). **Trains to the Peloponnese** (Argos, Corinth, Patras) leave from the Peloponnese station (Stathmos Peloponnisou). Take trolley no. 1 or 5 from Syntagma Square to either station.

The Peloponnese circuit from Corinth to Patras, Pirgos (near Olympia), Tripolis, and Argos is one way to experience this scenic region, though the Athens–Patras stretch is often crowded. The spectacular spur between Diakofto and Kalavrita is particularly recommended for train enthusiasts.

BY BUS

Public buses are inexpensive but often overcrowded. Local bus lines vary from place to place, but on most islands the bus stop is in a central location with a posted schedule. Destinations are usually displayed on the front of the bus, but you might have to ask. The conductor will collect your fare after departure.

Note that in Athens and other large cities, a bus ticket *must* be purchased before *and* validated after boarding. Kiosks usually offer bus tickets as well as schedules. Tickets cost about .5€ (65¢).

Note: Save your ticket in case an "inspector" comes aboard. If you don't have a ticket, the fine can be 20€ ($26).

Greece has an extensive **long-distance bus service (KTEL),** an association of regional operators with green-and-yellow buses that leave from convenient central stations. For information about the long-distance-bus offices, contact the KTEL office in Athens (© 210/512-4910).

In Athens, most buses heading to destinations within **Attica** leave from the Mavromate terminal, north of the National Archaeological Museum. Most buses to **Central Greece** leave from 260 Liossion, 5km (3 miles) north of Omonia Square (take local bus no. 024 from Leoforos Amalias in front of the entrance to the National Garden and tell the driver your destination). Most buses to the **Peloponnese, Western, and Northern Greece** leave from the long-distance bus terminal at 100 Kifissou, 4km (2½ miles) northeast of Omonia Square. To get to the long-distance bus terminal, take local bus no. 051 from the stop located 2 blocks west of Omonia, near the big church of Ayios Konstandinos, at Zinonos and Menandrou.

Express buses between major cities, usually air-conditioned, can be booked through travel agencies. Make sure that your destination is understood—you wouldn't be the first to see a bit more of Greece than bargained for—and determine the bus's schedule and comforts before purchasing your ticket. Many buses are not air-conditioned, take torturous routes, and make frequent stops. (NO SMOKING signs are generally disregarded by drivers and conductors, as well as by many older male passengers.)

Organized and guided **bus tours** are widely available. Some of them will pick you up at your hotel; ask the hotel staff or any travel agent in Athens. We especially recommend **CHAT Tours** (www.chatours. com), the oldest and probably most experienced provider of a wide selection of bus tours led by highly articulate guides. Almost any travel agent can book a CHAT tour, but if you want to deal with the company directly, contact its office at 214 Bedford Rd., Toronto, Ontario M5R 2K9 (© **800/268-1180**). In Athens, the CHAT office is at 9 Xenofontos, 10557 Athens (© **210/323-0827**). Then there is the longtime favorite, **American Express,** with offices all over North America and Europe; the Athens office (© **210/325-4690**) is located at 31 Panepistimiou, right on the corner of Syntagma Square.

Note: Readers have complained that some bus groups are so large they feel removed from the leader; inquire about group size if this concerns you. Also, you should know that most if not all commercial bus tours stop at shops along the way as well as at the destinations; this is an accepted practice, appreciated by some travelers, annoying to others. You are not obliged to buy anything.

BY TAXI

Taxis are one of the most convenient means of getting about in Greece. They can also be the most exasperating, although there have been improvements in recent years. For instance, you no longer have to fight for a cab at most airports; just find the line. Cab fare is considerably lower in Athens than in London, New York, or Toronto. There is probably no greater percentage of cheats among Greece's cab drivers than in all major cities around the world—and many Greek taxi drivers are good-natured, helpful, and informative. Language and cultural difficulties, however, can make it easier for

Taxi Tips

- Taxi rates are in constant (upwards!) flux, so we will provide the rates as we go to press. First, though, check to see that the little window next to the euro display on the meter is "1" and not "2"—which is the setting for midnight-to-6am or outside-the-city-limits rates (which are about double the regular rate). If that's not the case, reach over and indicate that you notice.

- Then check that the meter starts at no more than .85€ ($1.10) as you set off—that is the maximum starting rate. Drivers have been known to start with a much higher number already registered; or they leave the meter off, then try to extort a much larger fare from you. Even if you don't speak a word of Greek besides "taxi," point at the meter and say "meter." The rate per kilometer has been about .30€ (40¢) within the city during daylight hours, and about .56€ (30¢) outside city limits or at night. The minimum fare for any trip is 1.75€ ($2.30).

- For a group of tourists, a driver may insist that each person pay the full metered fare. Pay only your proportion of the fare if all of you have the same destination. Pairs or groups of tourists should have a designated arguer; the others can write down names and numbers, stick with the luggage, or look for help—from a policeman, maitre d', or desk clerk.

- Late at night, especially at airports, ferry stops, and bus and railroad stations, a driver may refuse to use his meter and demand an exorbitant fare. Smile, shake your head, and look for another cab; if none are available, start writing down the driver's license number and he will probably relent.

- Legal surcharges include: 3€ ($3.90) from and to the main Athens airport; .90€ ($1.20) pickup at other airports, ports, bus terminals, or train terminals; .35€ (45¢) per piece of luggage over 10 kilos (22 lb)). (Road tolls are charged to the passengers—for example, you will pay 2€ ($2.60) for the new road from the airport to Athens.)

- A driver may say that your hotel is full, but that he knows a better and cheaper one. Laugh, and insist you'll take your chances at your hotel.

- A driver may want to let you off where it's most convenient for him. Be cooperative if it's easier and quicker for you to cross a busy avenue than for him to get you to the other side, but you don't have to get out of the cab until you're ready.

If things are obviously not going well for you, conspicuously write down the driver's name and number and by all means report him to the **tourist police** (ⓒ **171**) if he has the nerve to call your bluff. One of the best countertactics is to simply reach for the door latch and open the door slightly; he won't want to risk damaging it. (Two passengers can each open a door.)

Our final advice: Don't sweat the small change. So the driver is charging you 13€ ($17) for a ride you have been told should be about 10€ ($13); are you prepared to go to court for 3€ ($3.90)? Any difference above 5€ ($6.50) probably should be questioned—but it may have to do with traffic delays when the meter ticks at the rate of 7.25€ ($9.40) per hour. Most cabbies are honest—just be aware of the possibilities. And be sure to reward good service with a tip.

Warning

Although mopeds are the vehicle of choice in Greece, especially on the islands, be aware that there is a Greek law (prompted by a huge number of accidents) requiring that anyone driving a moped must have a motorcycle license. Agencies offering moped rentals rarely tell tourists this because very few tourists have motorcycle licenses. This makes for a whirlwind of troubles if an accident occurs and you are not a licensed motorcycle driver. You will not be covered by insurance and will have broken the law. Check with your own auto and/or medical insurance plan to see if you are covered for such an eventuality.

them to gouge you, and some drivers do take advantage of this.

The converse is also true: Language gaps can lead to genuine misunderstandings. Legitimate surcharges do apply—for heavy luggage, for rides from midnight to 6am (almost twice the regular rate!), for rides on holidays, and for rides from and to airports. Ask to see the official rate sheet that the driver is required to carry.

Get your hotel desk to help you hail or book a taxi. Radio cabs cost 2.50€ ($3.25) extra, but you'll have some leverage. Restaurants and businesses can also help you call or hail a cab, negotiate a fare, and make sure your destination is understood. Using a card from your hotel, write down your destination (or learn to pronounce it). Be willing to share a cab with other passengers picked up on the way, especially during rush hour; think of it as your contribution to better efficiency and less pollution. Be aware that you pay only your proportion of the shared fare.

Always have at least a vague idea of your destination as indicated by a map, so that you don't end up going to Plaka from Syntagma by way of Kolonaki. (There are, however, several ways of getting to Plaka from Syntagma.) Don't be bothered by bullying or bluster; counter with your own bluff, showing your self-confidence by keeping your cool. See also "Taxi Tips," above.

BY MOPED, MOTORBIKE & MOTORCYCLE

There seems to be no end to the number of mopeds, motorbikes, motorcycles, and related vehicles available for rent in Greece. They can be an inexpensive way to get around, especially in the islands, but they are not recommended for everyone: Greek hospitals admit scores of tourists injured on mopeds or motorbikes every summer, and there are a number of fatalities. Roads are often poorly paved and without shoulders; loose gravel or stones are another common problem. Meanwhile, as of 2000, Greek law requires that all renters of mopeds and motorcycles be licensed to operate such vehicles; it remains to be seen how this will be enforced. In any case, make sure you have insurance and that the machine is in good working condition before you take it. Helmets are required by law and strongly recommended, although you will rarely see Greeks wearing them.

You might wish that the larger motorbikes and motorcycles were forbidden on all the islands, as Greek youths seem to delight in punching holes in the mufflers and tearing around at all hours. (Some islands are wisely banning them from certain areas and restricting the hours of their use, as they are the single most common cause of complaints from tourists and residents alike.) The motorcycles rented to tourists are usually a bit quieter, but they are more expensive and at least as dangerous; strictly speaking, a special license is required to rent one.

BY BICYCLE

Bicycles are not nearly as common in Greece as they are throughout most of Europe, since they are not well suited to Greek terrain or temperament and would be downright dangerous in traffic. In less hectic towns and in the countryside, however, a bicycle might be fine for short distances. Older bikes are usually available for rent at modest prices in most resort areas, and good mountain bikes are increasingly available. (See "Active Travelers," earlier, for more information.)

15 Tips on Accommodations

Greece now offers a full spectrum of accommodations ranging from the extravagant to the basic. Within a given locale, of course, not all options are available, but most readers will find something that appeals to you.

Hotels used to be required to publicize a grading system imposed by the Greek government. Some classes still exist, with limits placed on prices depending on facilities (such as public areas, pools, and in-room amenities), but basically it is a market economy: Hotels know better than to ask for too much because competitors will undercut them. Frommer's rating system of stars and icons for special features takes care of all such differences.

International travelers will be familiar with some of the major chains—the Hilton, Best Western. A number of Greek chains, such as Louis and Chandris, also offer accommodations. These latter tend to be upscale hotels. However, most Greek hotels are independent lodgings run by hands-on owners.

SAVING ON YOUR HOTEL ROOM

The **rack rate** is the maximum rate that a hotel charges for a room. Hardly anybody pays full rate, however, except in high season or holidays. To lower the cost of your room:

- **Ask about special rates or other discounts.** Always ask whether a room less expensive than the first one quoted is available, or whether any special rates apply to you. You may qualify for corporate, student, military, senior, or other discounts. Find out the hotel policy on children—do kids stay free in the room or is there a special rate?

- **Dial direct.** When booking a room in a chain hotel, you'll often get a better deal by calling the individual hotel's reservations desk rather than the chain's main number.

- **Book online.** Many hotels offer Internet-only discounts, or supply

---

(*Tips* **Hotel Bathrooms**

The bathrooms in all the newer and higher-grade Greek hotels are now practically "state of the art," but travelers might appreciate knowing a few things in advance. Few hotels provide washcloths and many don't offer generously sized towels. Also, some midprice hotels provide only cramped showers. As it happens, the two things in generous supply are slippery marble and glass shower doors: Be very careful getting in and out of tubs or showers.

Tips   Booking a Room

Try to make reservations by fax so that you have a written record of the room and price agreed upon. Be aware that a double room in Greece does not always mean a room with a double bed, but a room with twin beds. Double beds in Greece are called "matrimonial beds," and rooms with such beds are often designated "honeymoon rooms." This can lead to misunderstandings.

Note that in a few instances—usually at the most expensive hotels—the prices quoted are per person. Note, too, that room prices, no matter what people say officially, are often negotiable, especially at the edges of the season. Because of Greek law and EOT regulations, hotel keepers are often reluctant to provide rates far in advance and often quote prices higher than their actual rates. When you bargain, don't cite our prices, which may be too high, but ask instead for the best current rate. Actual off-season prices may be as much as 25% lower than the lowest rate given to us for this book.

rooms to Priceline, Hotwire, or Expedia at rates much lower than the ones you can get through the hotel itself. Shop around. And if you have special needs—a quiet room, a room with a view—call the hotel directly and make your needs known after you've booked online.

- **Remember the law of supply and demand.** Resort hotels are most crowded and therefore most expensive on weekends, so discounts are usually available for midweek stays. Business hotels in downtown locations are busiest during the week, so you can expect big discounts on weekends. Many hotels have high-season and low-season rates, so booking the day after high season ends can mean big discounts.

- **Look into group or long-stay discounts.** If you are with a large group, you should be able to negotiate a bargain rate, since the hotel can then guarantee occupancy in a number of rooms. Likewise, if you're planning a long stay (at least 5 days), you might qualify for a discount. As a general rule, expect 1 night free after a 7-night stay.

- **Avoid excess charges and hidden costs.** When you book a room, ask whether the hotel charges for parking. Use your own cellphone, pay phones, or prepaid phone cards instead of dialing direct from hotel phones, which usually have exorbitant rates. And don't be tempted by the room's minibar offerings: Most hotels charge through the nose for water, soda, and snacks. Finally, ask about local taxes and service charges, which can increase the cost of a room by 15% or more.

- Consider the pros and cons of **all-inclusive** resorts and hotels. The term "all-inclusive" means different things at different hotels. Many all-inclusive hotels will include three meals daily, sports equipment, spa entry, and other amenities; others may include all or most drinks. In general, you'll save money going the "all-inclusive" way—as long as you use the facilities provided. The downside is that your choices are limited and you're stuck eating and playing in one place for the duration of your vacation.

- Carefully consider your hotel's meal plan. If you enjoy eating out and sampling the local cuisine, it makes sense to choose the **Continental Plan (CP),** which includes breakfast only, or the **European Plan (EP),** which doesn't include any meals and allows you maximum flexibility. If you're more interested in saving money, opt for the **Modified American Plan (MAP),** which includes breakfast and one meal; or opt for the **American Plan (AP),** which includes three meals. If you must choose the MAP, see if you can get a free lunch at your hotel if you decide to have dinner out.

- **Book an efficiency.** A room with a kitchenette allows you to shop for groceries and cook your own meals. This is a big money-saver, especially for families on long stays.

LANDING THE BEST ROOM

Somebody has to get the best room in the house. It might as well be you. Although it is unlikely that the average visitor to Greece will be staying at a hotel with a "frequent-guest," program, inquire if you think it might be a possibility. Always ask about a corner room. They're often larger and quieter, with more windows and light, and they often cost the same as standard rooms. When you make your reservation, ask if the hotel is renovating; if it is, request a room away from the construction. Ask about nonsmoking rooms; rooms with views; rooms with twin, queen- or king-size beds. If you're a light sleeper, request a quiet room away from vending machines, elevators, restaurants, bars, and discos. Ask for one of the rooms

that have been most recently renovated or redecorated.

If you aren't happy with your room when you arrive, ask for another. If another room is available, most lodgings will be willing to accommodate you.

In resort areas, particularly in warm climates, ask the following questions before you book a room:

- What's the view like? Cost-conscious travelers may be willing to pay less for a back room facing the parking lot, especially if you don't plan to spend much time in your room.
- Does the room have air-conditioning or ceiling fans? Do the windows open?
- Is there nighttime entertainment? If there is, and the party's alfresco, you may want to find out when showtime is over.
- What's included in the price? Your room may be moderately priced, but if you're charged for beach chairs, towels, sports equipment, and other amenities, you could end up spending more than you bargained for.
- How far is the room from the beach and other amenities? If it's far, is there transportation to and from the beach, and is it free?

Rentals (Apartments & Houses) An increasingly popular way to experience Greece is to rent an apartment or a house; the advantages include freedom from the formalities of a hotel, often a more desirable location, and a kitchen that allows you to avoid the costs and occasional crush of restaurants. Such rentals do not come cheap, but if you calculate what

---

Tips **Dial E for Easy**

For quick directions on how to call Greece, see the "Telephone" listing in the "Fast Facts" section at the end of this chapter; or check out the "Telephone Tips" on the inside front cover of this book.

two or more people might pay for a decent hotel, not to mention all the meals eaten out, a rental can turn out to be a good deal. (Cost per person per day in a really nice apartment runs about 100€/$130; a fancier villa with two bedrooms might cost about 200€/$260 per person per day.) Any full-service travel agency in your home country or in Greece should be able to put you in touch with an agency specializing in such rentals.

The fact is that the British dominate this field in Greece, both in terms of experience and sheer numbers of offerings. So via the Internet, anyone can now see what's offered and contact such outfits as **Abercrombie & Kent,** Ambrose Street, Cheltenham, Gloucestershire GL50 3LG (© **0845/0700-610;** www.villa-rentals.com); **Simply Travel Ltd.,** 12–442 Wood St., Kingston-Upon-Thames KT1 ISG (© **0870/166-4979;** www.simplytravel.co.uk); or **Pure Crete,** 79 George St., Croydon, Surrey CRO

1LD (© **020/8760-0879;** www.pure-crete.com). Among those in the United States are **Villas International,** 4830 Redwood Hwy., San Rafael, CA 94903 (© **800/221-2260;** www.villasintl.com); and **Villas and Apartments Abroad,** 183 Madison Ave., Suite 201, New York, NY 10016 (© **212/213-6435;** www.vaanyc.com). In Canada, try **Grecian Holidays,** 75 The Donaway W., Don Mills, Ontario M3C 2E9 (© **800/268-6786;** www.grecianholidays.com). For those interested in investigating further on the Web, try **www.crete.tournet.gr,** **www.vacation homes.com,** or **www.villavacations.com**.

Another option is to rent a traditional house in one of about 12 relatively rural or remote villages or settlements throughout Greece. These small traditional houses have been restored by the Greek National Tourism Organization (GNTO or EOT); to learn more about this possibility, contact the GNTO office nearest you. (See "Visitor Information," earlier in this chapter, or go to **www.gnto.gr**.)

16 Tips on Dining

A description of Greek food and the dining "experience" can fill an entire book. Here, we've focused on distinctive highlights of dining in Greece. Greek meals, for instance, usually start off with appetizers known as *mezedes*—small plates of hot and cold selections shared from the center of the table. A notable aspect of restaurants in Greece is that you can make a meal out of as little or as much as you want from any section of the menu—all *mezedes,* if you wish.

Another distinction of Greek restaurants is that you can order at almost any hour of the day. Not in every little village and not in the more stylish restaurants, but many will start serving meal courses by late morning and on through the day to late at night. Greeks eat their evening meal quite late—usually not before 8pm—but restaurants are prepared to accommodate foreigners who like to sit down as early as 5:30pm. Room rates at most hotels now include satisfying buffet

Tips Greek Siesta

The combination of hot climate, heavy lunches, and plain old tradition means that most Greeks take siestas. So keep siesta hours, about 2 to 5pm, in mind when planning your own day. Even in Athens, you should be considerate about contacting friends or acquaintances at home during these hours.

breakfasts. If you miss the buffet, a quick walk outside should take you to at least one cafe that can come up with the basics. Don't expect fresh orange juice, though. And if you have definite preferences for tea—especially herbal—consider bringing your own teabags.

Most restaurants now have a "cover charge" that includes the table setting and a small basket of bread. It used to be that Greek waiters brought ice-cold pitchers of fresh water to each table without being asked to, but this custom has pretty much vanished. If you request "natural water," they will bring tap water to your table, but if you ask simply for "water," you will be brought bottled water—and charged for it. (By Greek law, they are supposed to open the sealed top in your presence.)

17 Recommended Books, Films & Music

BOOKS It seems only proper to begin with **Homer,** who though reputedly blind, will open your eyes to a Greece that is timeless. The *Iliad* and the *Odyssey* remain *the* imaginative gateways to Greece. Of the many fine translations, we favor those of Richmond Lattimore (Perennial, 1999). And lest you have any doubts that Homer was describing the same landscape you'll be seeing, you might want to read, as a companion to the epics, John V. Luce's *Celebrating Homer's Landscapes* (Yale Univ. Press, 1998).

For a glimpse into **ancient Greek history,** read the reporters who were there at the time; it is still exciting. *The History* by Herodotus and Thucydides's *Peloponnesian War* hold their own as consummate storytelling and will place you firmly in classical Greece. Among many fine translations, the most accessible are those of Aubrey de Selincourt (Penguin, 2003). *A Basic Survey of Greek Art* is a good resource by John Boardman (Thames & Hudson, 4th rev. edition, 1996).

If you plan to attend any of the country's drama festivals, you will want to become familiar in advance with the play(s) you will see and perhaps bring along your favorite translation. For the tragedies, try those translated by David Grene and Richmond Lattimore (University of Chicago Press, 1991); for the comedies of Aristophanes, look for the translations by Paul Roche (Plume Books, 1984).

To be enlightened on the **Byzantine period,** you'd do well to start with Steven Runciman's *Byzantine Civilization* (North American Library, 2000) and Robin Cormack's *Byzantine Art* (Oxford Univ. Press, 2000). For an insider's account of scandal and splendor at the court of Justinian, pick up *The Secret History* of Procopius, translated by G. A. Williamson (Penguin, 1982). To put all this in quick perspective, as well as to follow the full sweep of Greek history to the present decade, *A Traveller's History of Greece,* by Boatswain and Nicolson (Interlink, 4th rev. ed., 2000), is a pocket-sized, helpful book.

In the **modern period,** Nikos Kazantzakis is the author who most appeals to foreigners. His *Zorba the Greek* (Touchstone, 1998) and *The Greek Passion* (Touchstone, 1959) are guaranteed to deliver you to Greece before your plane lands. Of the many travel books by foreigners, one still regarded as the most insightful is Henry Miller's *Colossus of Maroussi* (New Directions, 1975). And before taking on one of Lawrence Durrell's complete books about Greece, try the *Lawrence Durrell Travel Reader* (Carroll & Graf, 2004). For beach reading, John Fowles's *The Magus* (Laurel, 1985) is engaging. In a more serious vein concerning recent Greece, Nicholas Gage's *Eleni* (Ballantine, 1996) and Louis de Bernières's *Captain Corelli's Mandolin*

(Vintage, 1995) are both extremely captivating.

FILMS   Of the many films made in and about Greece, several come to mind, all more or less readily available on video or DVD. The films of Michael Cacoyannis—from his Euripides trilogy, including *Trojan Women* and *Iphigenia,* to his famed *Zorba the Greek*—are essential viewing. So too is Costa-Gavras's *Z,* a gripping political thriller inspired by the assassination of Grigorios Lambrakis in 1963. The film version of Nicholas Gage's *Eleni* manages to be nearly as disturbing as the book. There is no avoiding—and no reason to avoid—*Never on Sunday* and *Captain Corelli's Mandolin.* Finally, for a good laugh and to enjoy the Greek scenery, Jacqueline Bisset and Irene Papas team up to confront *High Season* on the island of Rhodes. The even sillier *Summer Lovers* (1982) is set on Santorini. And don't forget, 007 has "done" Greece *(For Your Eyes Only),* as did Gregory Peck in *The Guns of Navarone.*

MUSIC   There is no denying that most non-Greeks have not been exposed to much Greek music (Yanni doesn't count!). But Greece has a long and distinguished—and beautiful—musical tradition that will repay those with inquisitive musical tastes. (Where recordings are available online, their labels and numbers are given here. Recordings of others are probably to be found only in Greece.) Each region— indeed, many an island— has its own variation of trraditional folk music. The most complete collection is issued by the Greek Society for the Dissemination of National Music—over 30 CDs under its SDNM label. More easily acquired is Legacy's *Authentic Greek Folk Songs and Dances* (no. 318). If you want to focus on two especially strong regional traditions, Lyra Records (no. 0168) has a

fine selection of Cretan and Dodecanese folk music. The more recent *rembetika* music emerged at the time of the American jazz, to which it is often compared. Without intimate knowledge of the language, you lose the lyrics, but the emotion comes through. Lyra has a fine four-CD anthology (nos. 4635–4637 and 4644). Rounder Select (no. 1079) offers another option. Easydisc presents *The Athenians: Greek Songs, Dances and Rembetika* (no. 369019). For those who like the twangy-metallic sound of *bouzoukia* music, Rounder Select (no. 1139) offers one of its masters, Markos Vamvakaris.

Often drawing on folk music, *rembetika,* or *bouzoukia,* a more sophisticated "classical" music emerged by the 1950s. The two practitioners of *entekhno* (artistic) best known to the world at large are Manos Hatzidhakis and Mikis Theodorakis. The former is famed for his music for the film *Never on Sunday,* but would prefer to be known for more serious work such as his songs (try Columbia GCX 107). Theodorakis is also best known abroad for his music for the movie *Zorba,* but his masterwork is *To Axion Esti* (EMI Iterntionln no. 463759). Yannis Markopoulos, George Tsontakis, Stavros Xylouris, Nikolas Labrinakos, and Christos Hatzis are other contemporary "high art" Greek musicians whose works are worth seeking out. And Iannis Xenakis's demanding compositions have become part of the modern avant-garde repertory. You might start with his orchestral and chamber music on ColLegno (no. 20504).

Greece, of course, has its homegrown pop music, but it has been greatly influenced by international trends, including rock and, more recently, rap. One Greek pop star has an international following— Nana Mouskouri.

FAST FACTS: Greek Islands

American Express Amex maintains an extensive network of offices and agents throughout Greece. The Athens office prominently overlooks Syntagma Square. We indicate the locations of these offices and agencies throughout this book, as well as describe the various travel arrangements and financial services offered by American Express.

Appropriate Attire Dress—or undress!—codes have been greatly relaxed at Greek beach resorts in recent years, but Greeks remain uncomfortable with beachwear or slovenly garb in villages and cities. Women are expected to cover their arms and upper legs before entering monasteries and churches. Some priests and monks are stricter than others and may flatly bar men as well as women if they feel that the men are not dressed suitably.

ATMs See "Money," earlier in this chapter.

Banks Banks are open to the public Monday through Thursday from 8am to 2pm, Friday from 8am to 1:30pm. Some banks have additional hours for foreign-currency exchange. All banks are closed on the long list of Greek holidays. (See "When to Go," earlier in this chapter.)

Business Hours Greek business and office hours take some getting used to, especially in the afternoon, when most English-speaking people are accustomed to getting things done in high gear. Compounding the problem is that it is virtually impossible to pin down the precise hours of opening. We can start by saying that almost all stores and services are closed on Sunday—except, of course, tourist-oriented shops and services. On Monday, Wednesday, and Saturday, hours are usually 9am to 3pm; Tuesday, Thursday, and Friday, 9am to 2pm and 5 to 7pm. The afternoon siesta is generally observed from 3 to 5pm, though many tourist-oriented businesses have a minimal crew on duty during naptime, and they may keep extended hours, often from 8am to 10pm. (In fact, in tourist centers, shops may be open at all kinds of hours.) Most government offices are open Monday through Friday only, from 8am to 3pm. Call ahead to check the hours of businesses you *must* deal with, and try not to disturb Greek friends during siesta hours. *Final advice:* Anything you really need to accomplish in a government office, business, or store should be done on weekdays between about 9am and 1pm.

Car Rentals See "Getting Around Greece," earlier in this chapter.

Climate See "When to Go," earlier in this chapter.

Climate Control Almost all Greek hotels recommended in this guide now promise air-conditioning in the hot season and heating in the colder months. The equipment is indeed there, but you should be aware that—except in the most expensive hotels—neither will necessarily be as adequate as you might like.

Crime Crimes against tourists are not a significant concern in Greece. Athens is probably the safest capital in Europe. Pocket-picking and purse-snatching may be slightly on the rise, especially in heavily touristed areas, but breaking into cars remains rare. Tourists, however, are conspicuous and much more likely to carry valuables, so take normal precautions—lock the car, don't leave cameras and such gear visible, and so on. Young women should observe the obvious precautions in dealing with men in isolated locales.

Currency See "Money," earlier in this chapter.

Customs See "Entry Requirements & Customs" earlier in this chapter.

Dentists & Doctors Ask your embassy or consulate in a major city (or ask your hotel's management) to direct you to a dentist or doctor who speaks either English or some other common European language.

Driving Rules See "By Car," earlier in this chapter.

Drugs Greek authorities and laws are extremely tough when it comes to finding foreigners with drugs—starting with marijuana. Do *not* attempt to bring any illicit drugs into or out of Greece.

Drugstores These are called *pharmikon* in Greek; aside from the obvious indications in windows and interiors, they are identified by a green cross. For minor medical problems, go first to the nearest **pharmacy**. Pharmacists usually speak English, and many medications can be dispensed without prescription. In the larger cities, if it is closed, there should be a sign in the window directing you to the nearest open one. Newspapers also list the pharmacies that are open late or all night.

Electricity Electric current in Greece is 220 volts AC, alternating at 50 cycles. (Some larger hotels have 110-volt low-wattage outlets for electric shavers, but they aren't good for hair dryers and most other appliances.) Electrical outlets require Continental-type plugs with two round prongs. U.S. travelers will need an adapter plug *and* a transformer/converter, unless their appliances are dual-voltage. (Such transformers can be bought in stores like Radio Shack.) Laptop computer users will want to check their requirements; a transformer may be necessary, and surge protectors are recommended.

Embassies & Consulates See "Fast Facts: Athens" in chapter 5 for a list of embassies and consulates. United Kingdom citizens can get emergency aid by calling ℂ **210/727-2600** during the day; at night, try ℂ **210/723-7727**. United States citizens can get emergency aid by calling ℂ **210/721-2951** during the day; at night, try ℂ **210/729-4301**.

Emergencies Since 2001, almost all countries in Europe, including Greece, have adopted **112** as an all-purpose toll-free number for emergencies. In addition, the traditional numbers can be used throughout Greece. For the regular **police,** call ℂ **100;** for **tourist police,** call ℂ **171.** For **fire,** call ℂ **199.** For **medical emergencies** and/or first aid and/or an ambulance, call ℂ **166.** For **hospitals,** call ℂ **106.** For **automobile emergencies,** put out a triangular danger sign and call ℂ **104** or **154.** Embassies, consulates, and many hotels can recommend an English-speaking **doctor.**

Etiquette Greeks generally observe the same practices with which most of us are familiar, but there are a few special variations. When you are introduced to a Greek for the first time, a handshake is normal. When you get to know

Greeks fairly well, the kiss on both cheeks is the accepted greeting. By the way, when Greeks meet small children, they tend to pinch them on the cheeks or pat them. And Greeks wave goodbye with the back of the hand—to hold up the open palm is to give the "evil eye"! Either wave sideways or in a little circle, but always with the palm turned away. And Greeks do not put a priority on punctuality, so do not be offended if they do not show up until well after the appointed time.

Here are three books that discuss some situations you might encounter as you make your way around Greece:

- *The Global Etiquette Guide To Europe* (Wiley Publishing, Inc.)
- *Kiss, Bow or Shake Hands: How to Do Business in 60 Countries* (Adams Media)
- *Culture Shock: Greece!* (Graphic Arts Center Publishing Co.)

Faxes Almost all hotels in the higher categories, many telephone offices, some post offices, and some travel agencies will send and receive faxes locally and internationally for you at set fees. But don't forget: Sending a fax is the equivalent of making a phone call, so you must be prepared to pay for that plus the extra service of the fax machine.

Gifts If you are invited to a Greek's home for a meal or social event, flowers or chocolates are appropriate gifts.

Guides You may prefer to employ local guides to take you and/or a small circle of fellow travelers to visit sites or cities. Professional guides in Greece are thoroughly trained, and the fees they charge are well regulated. Most reputable travel agencies can arrange for such guides. You can also contact the **Union of Official Guides**, 9A Apollonos, 10557 Athens (*©* **210/322-9705**). Our only caution is that as good as these official guides are, they are trained to produce a stream of facts, not make small talk.

Haggling Greek merchants resent foreigners who try to haggle over prices. In general, the marked price is the cost of the item. That said, some "games" can be played. Hesitate, consult with your companions with the appropriate expressions of regret, set the object down—with thanks!—and head for the exit. You may well be offered a lower price. But that is the merchant's prerogative, and all depends upon the manner in which this behavior is conducted. If you come across as demanding or disapproving, you can forget any further negotiating.

Holidays See "When to Go," earlier in this chapter.

Information See "Visitor Information," earlier in this chapter.

Language Language is usually not a problem for English speakers in Greece, as so much of the population has lived abroad, where English is the primary language. Young people learn it in school, from Anglo-American–dominated pop culture, and in special classes meant to prepare them for the contemporary world of business. Many television programs are also broadcast in their original languages, and American prime-time soaps are very popular, nearly inescapable. Even advertisements have an increasingly high English content.

Don't let all this keep you from trying to pick up at least a few words of Greek; your effort will be rewarded by your hosts, who realize how difficult their language is for foreigners and will patiently help you improve your pronunciation and usage. Look for books and audio courses on learning Greek, including **Berlitz's Greek for Travelers, Passport's Conversational Greek in 7 Days,** and **Teach Yourself Greek Complete Course** (book and CD pack). Appendix B, "The Greek Language," can give you some basics.

Laptops Increasing numbers of travelers are taking their laptops with them, whether it's to keep up with work assignments, write personal messages, or stay in touch with the outside world via the Internet. Since Greece operates on 220 volts, you must make sure that your computer has a built-in capacity to handle this voltage. If not, take a transformer and probably a surge protector (see "Electricity," above). That will take care of the computer for all non-modem functions, but if you want to access the Internet, considerably more is involved. See "Internet Access Away from Home" in section 10, above.

Laundry & Dry Cleaning All cities and towns of any size will have both laundry and dry-cleaning establishments. Many travelers prefer to make arrangements through their hotel desks; this is fine, but be prepared to pay heavily for even the smallest bundle. (Then again, everything, including socks, will have been ironed!) If you are more ambitious (or frugal), you can seek out one of the laundries listed in the "Fast Facts" sections of major cities in the destination chapters. Most laundry places are attended; so if you want, you can leave your laundry to be picked up later. Be sure you are in agreement as to the time it will be ready, especially if you must leave town. A medium-size bag of laundry may cost about 15€ ($20), washed, dried, and neatly folded.

Legal Aid If you need legal assistance, contact your own or another English-speaking embassy or consulate.

Liquor Laws The minimum age for being served alcohol in public locales is 18. Wine and beer are generally available in eating places but not in all coffeehouses or dessert cafes. Alcoholic beverages are sold in food stores as well as liquor stores. Although a certain amount of high spirits is appreciated, Greeks do *not* appreciate public drunkenness. The resort centers where mobs of young foreigners party every night are tolerated as necessary for the tourist trade, but the behavior wins no respect for foreigners.

Lost & Found Be sure to contact all of your credit card companies the minute you discover your wallet has been lost or stolen, and file a report at the nearest police precinct. Your credit card company or insurer may require a police report number or record of the loss. Most credit card companies have an emergency toll-free number to call if your card is lost or stolen; they may be able to wire you a cash advance immediately or deliver an emergency credit card in a day or two. From Greece, Visa's U.S. emergency number is ✆ **001-800-11-638-0304**; within North America, it's ✆ **800/847-2911.** American Express cardholders and traveler's check holders call ✆ **001-336/393-1111**; within North America call ✆ **800/992-3404.** MasterCard holders call ✆ **001-800/11-887-0303**;

within North America call ✆ **800/307-7309.** For other credit cards, call the toll-free number directory at ✆ **800/555-1212.**

If you need emergency cash over the weekend when banks and American Express offices are closed, you can have money wired to you via **Western Union** (✆ **800/325-6000;** www.westernunion.com).

Identity theft or fraud are potential consequences of losing your wallet, especially if you've lost your driver's license along with your cash and credit cards. Notify the major credit-reporting bureaus immediately; placing a fraud alert on your records may protect you against liability for criminal activity. The three major U.S. credit-reporting agencies are **Equifax** (✆ **888/766-0008;** www.equifax.com), **Experian** (✆ **888/397-3742;** www.experian.com), and **TransUnion** (✆ **800/680-7289;** www.transunion.com). Finally, if you've lost all forms of photo ID, call your airline and explain the situation; they might allow you to board the plane if you have a copy of your passport or birth certificate and a copy of the police report you've filed.

Mail The mail service of Greece is reliable—but slow. (Postcards usually arrive weeks after you have arrived home.) You can receive mail addressed to you c/o Poste Restante, General Post Office, City (or Town), Island (or Province), Greece. You will need your passport to collect this mail. Many hotels will accept, hold, and even forward mail for you also; ask first. American Express clients can receive mail at any Amex office in Athens, Corfu, Iraklion, Mykonos, Patras, Rhodes, Santorini, Skiathos, and Thessaloniki, for a nominal fee and with proper identification. If you are in a particular hurry, try FedEx or one of the other major international private carriers; travel agencies can direct you to these.

Postage rates have been going up in Greece, as they are elsewhere. At press time, a postcard or a letter under 20 grams (about .7 oz.) cost .65€ (85¢) to North America and Europe; 20 to 50 grams (up to 1.75 oz.), 1.15€ ($1.50); 50 to 100 grams (3.5 oz.) 1.60€ ($2.10). Rates for packages depend on size as well as weight, but are reasonable. *Note:* Do not wrap or seal any package—you must be prepared to show the contents to a postal clerk.

Maps See "By Car," earlier in this chapter.

Newspapers & Magazines All cities, large towns, and major tourist centers have at least one shop or kiosk that carries a selection of foreign-language publications; most of these are flown or shipped in on the very day of publication. English-language readers have a wide selection, including most of the British papers *(Daily Telegraph, Financial Times, Guardian, Independent, Times),* the *International Herald Tribune* (with its English-language insert of the well-known Athens newspaper, *Kathimerini*), and *USA Today.* A decent (and cheaper!) alternative is the English-language paper published in Athens, *Athens News,* widely available throughout Greece.

Passports **For Residents of the United States:** If you are applying for your first passport, you must go in person to one of 6,000 passport desks across the country (most convenient are those in post offices). Passports can be renewed by downloading the appropriate form on the website of the U.S. Information

Center, **http://travel.state.gov**. For general information, call the **National Passport Information Center** (© 877/487-2778); or go to the State Department section of the U.S. Information Center website (above).

For Residents of Canada: Passport applications are available at travel agencies throughout Canada or from the central **Passport Office,** Department of Foreign Affairs and International Trade, Ottawa, ON K1A 0G3 (© 800/567-6868; www.dfait-maeci.gc.ca/passport).

For Residents of the United Kingdom: To pick up an application for a standard 10-year passport (5-year passport for children under 16), visit your nearest passport office, major post office, or travel agency. You can also contact the **United Kingdom Passport Service** at © 0870/521-0410; or search its website at www.ukpa.gov.uk.

For Residents of Ireland: You can apply for a 10-year passport at the **Passport Office,** Setanta Centre, Molesworth Street, Dublin 2 (© 01/671-1633; www.irlgov.ie/iveagh). Those under age 18 and over 65 must apply for a 12€ ($16) 3-year passport. You can also apply at 1A S. Mall, Cork (© 021/272-525); or at most main post offices.

For Residents of Australia: You can pick up an application from your local post office or any branch of **Passports Australia,** but you must schedule an interview at the passport office to present your application materials. Call the **Australian Passport Information Service** at © 131-232, or visit the government website at www.passports.gov.au.

For Residents of New Zealand: You can pick up a passport application at any **New Zealand Passports Office** or download it from their website. Contact the Passports Office at © 0800/225-050 in New Zealand or © 04/474-8100; or go to www.passports.govt.nz.

Pets See "Customs," above.

Pharmacies See "Drugstores," above.

Photocopying In most Greek cities, the bookstores offer commercial photocopying services.

Photography In several locales around Greece, photographing military or police installations is forbidden. These locales are posted and you are expected to observe the law. Cameras, film, accessories, and photo developing (including express service) are widely available, though slightly more expensive, in Greece.

Police To report a crime or medical emergency, or for information or other assistance, first contact the local **tourist police** (telephone numbers are under "Fast Facts" in the destination chapters that follow), where an English-speaking officer is more likely to be found. If there is no tourist police officer available (© 171), contact the **local police** at © 100.

Radio & Television The Greek ERT 1 radio station has weather and news in English at 7:40am. The BBC World Service can be picked up on short-wave frequencies, often at 9.140, 15.07, and 12.09 Mhz; on FM it is usually at 107.1. Antenna TV, CNN, Eurochannel, and other cable networks are widely available. Many better hotels offer cable television.

Reservations Only the rare expensive restaurant in Athens and a few resorts expect advance reservations. During the height of the tourist season, however, anyone with a tight schedule should definitely secure reservations; they are required at hotels, airlines, ship lines, and major festival performances.

Restrooms Public restrooms are generally available in any good-sized Greek town, and though they are sometimes rather crude, they usually do work. (Old-fashioned stand-up/squat facilities are still found.) Carry tissue or toilet paper with you at all times. In some places—even modern restaurants and hotels—you are told not to flush the paper down the toilet, but to use the receptacles provided. In an emergency, you can ask to use the facilities of a restaurant or shop. However, near major attractions, the facilities are denied to all but customers, because traffic is too heavy. If you use any such facilities, respect its sponsor and give an attendant a tip.

Safety See "Health & Safety," earlier in this chapter.

Smoking Greeks continue to be among the most persistent smokers. Smoking is prohibited on all domestic flights, in certain areas or types of ships, and in some public buildings (such as post offices), but except on airplanes, many Greeks—and some foreigners—feel free to puff away at will. (The airport in Athens is practically a cancer culture lab.) Hotels are only beginning to claim that they have set aside rooms or even floors for nonsmokers, so ask about them, if it matters to you. If you are really bothered by smoke while eating, about all you can do is position yourself as best as possible—and then be prepared to move if it gets really bad.

Taxes & Service Charges Unless otherwise noted, all hotel prices include a service charge of usually 12%, a 6% value-added tax (VAT), and a 4.5% community tax. In most restaurants, a 13% service charge, an 8% VAT, and some kind of municipal tax (in Athens it is 5%) are included in the prices and final bill. (By the way, don't confuse any of these charges with a standard "cover charge" that may be .50 to 1€ ($.65-$1.30) per place setting. Also see "Tipping," below.) A VAT of 18% is added to rental-car rates.

All purchases include a VAT of anywhere from 4% to 18%. If you have purchased an item that costs 100€ ($130) or more and are a citizen of a non–European Union nation, you can get most of this refunded (provided you export it within 90 days of purchase). It's easiest to shop at stores that display the sign TAX-FREE FOR TOURISTS. However, any store should be able to provide you with a Tax-Free Check Form, which you complete in the store. If you use your charge card, the receipt will list the VAT separately from the cost of the item. As you are leaving the country, present a copy of this form to the refund desk (usually at the Customs office). Be prepared to show both the goods and the receipt as proof of purchase. Also be prepared to wait a fair amount of time before you get the refund. (In fact, the process at the airport seems designed to discourage you from trying to obtain the refund.)

Telephone In the old days, most foreigners went to the offices of the **Telecommunications Organization of Greece** (**OTE**, pronounced *oh*-tay, or **Organismos Tilepikinonion tis Ellados**) to place most of their phone calls, especially overseas.

But because phone cards are now so widespread throughout Greece, this is no longer necessary, once you get the hang of using them. You must first purchase a phone card at an OTE office or at most kiosks. (If you expect to make any phone calls while in Greece, buy one at the airport's OTE office upon arrival.) The cards come in various denominations, from 3€ ($3.90) to 25€ ($33). The more costly the card, the cheaper the units.

The cost of a call with a phone card varies greatly depending on local, domestic, and international rates. A local call of up to 3 minutes to a fixed phone costs about .09€ (10¢), which is 3 units from a phone card; for each minute beyond that, it costs another .06€ (10¢) or 2 units off the card (so that a 10-min. local call costs 17 units or .51€/$.66).

By the way, all calls, even to the house next door, cost Greeks something, so if you use someone's telephone even for a local call, offer to pay the charges.

In larger cities and larger towns, kiosks have telephones from which you can make local calls for .10€ (13¢) for 3 minutes. (In remote areas, you can make long-distance calls from these phones.) A few of the older public pay phones that required coins are still around, but it's better to buy a phone card. If you must use an older pay phone, deposit the required coin and listen for a dial tone, an irregular beep. A regular beep indicates that the line is busy.

Note: As of November 2002, *all* phone numbers in Greece have 10 digits. All (except for mobile phones—see below) also precede the city/area code with a 2 and end that with a 0. For example, since the Athens city code was originally 1, it is now 210, followed by a 7-digit number, but all other numbers in Greece are code, then 5 or 6 digits. In all cases, even if you are calling someone in the same building, you must dial all 10 digits.

Calling a mobile (cell) phone in Greece requires substituting a 6 for the 2 that precedes the area code.

Long-distance calls, both domestic and international, can be quite expensive in Greece, especially at hotels, which may add a surcharge of up to 100%, unless you have a telephone credit card from a major long-distance provider such as AT&T, MCI, or Sprint.

If you prefer to make your call from an OTE office, these are centrally and conveniently located. (Local office locations are given under "Essentials" for the destinations in the chapters that follow.) At OTE offices, a clerk will assign you a booth with a metered phone. You can pay with a phone card, international credit card, or cash. Collect calls take much longer. To call Greece from the United States or Canada:

1. Dial the international access code 011.
2. Dial the country code 30.
3. Dial the city/area code which now always begins with 2 and ends with 0, and follow it with the rest of the number. So the entire number you'd dial would be 011-30 + area code + number.

If you are calling Greece from other countries, dial one of the following international access codes. From the United Kingdom, Ireland, and New Zealand, **00**; from Australia, **0011**. Then follow steps 2 through 3 above.

To make international calls from Greece, the easiest and cheapest way is to call your long-distance service provider before leaving home to determine the access number that you must dial in Greece. The principal access codes in Greece are: **AT&T**, ✆ **00800-1311; MCI**, ✆ **00800-1211;** and **Sprint**, ✆ **00800-1411.** Most companies also offer a voice-mail service in case the number you call is busy or there's no answer.

If you must use the Greek phone system to make a direct call abroad—whether using an OTE office, a phone that takes cards, or a phone that takes coins—dial the country code plus the area code (omitting the initial zero, if any), then dial the number. Some country codes are: **Australia**, 0061; **Canada**, 001; **Ireland**, 00353; **New Zealand**, 0064; **United Kingdom**, 0044; and **United States**, 001. Note that if you are going to put all the charges on your phone card (that is, not on your long-distance provider), you will be charged at a high rate per minute (at least 3 €/$3.90 to North America), so you should not make a call unless your phone card's remaining value can cover it.

For operator assistance: Dial **131** if you're making an international call. Dial **169** if you want to call a number in Greece.

Toll-free numbers: Numbers beginning with 080 within Greece are toll-free, but calling a 1-800 number in the U.S. from Greece will probably not be accepted. If it is accepted, it will cost the same as an overseas call.

Time The European 24-hour clock is officially used to measure time, so on schedules you'll see noon as 1200, 3:30pm as 1530, and 11pm as 2300. In informal conversation, however, Greeks express time much as we do—though noon may mean anywhere from noon to 3pm, afternoon is 3 to 7pm, and evening is 7pm to midnight.

Time Zone Greece is 2 hours ahead of Greenwich Mean Time. In reference to North American time zones, it's 7 hours ahead of Eastern Standard Time, 8 hours ahead of Central Standard Time, 9 hours ahead of Mountain Standard Time, and 10 hours ahead of Pacific Standard Time. Note that Greece does observe daylight saving time, although it may not start and stop on the same days as in North America.

Tipping Restaurant bills, including the VAT and any local taxes, include a 10% to 15% service charge. Nevertheless, it's customary to leave an additional 5% to 10% for the waiter, especially if he or she has provided special service. Certainly round off on larger bills; even on small bills, leave change up to the nearest 1€ ($1.30). Good taxi service merits a tip of 5% to 10%. (Greeks rarely tip taxi drivers, but tourists are expected to.) Hotel chambermaids should be left about 2€ ($2.60) per night per couple. Bellhops and doormen should be tipped 1€ ($1.30) to 5€ ($6.50), depending on the services they provide.

Useful Phone Numbers The phone numbers for **U.S. Department of State Overseas Citizens Services** (such as travel advisories and medical emergencies) are as follows. From abroad, ✆ **001-317/472-2328.** From North America, during East Coast daylight hours, ✆ **888/407-4747.** For 24-hour service, ✆ **202-647-4000.**

The **U.S. Passport Agency** can be reached at ✆ **877/487-2778.**

The **International Traveler's Hot Line for U.S. Centers for Disease Control** is ✆ **877/394-8747.**

Water   The public drinking water in Greece is safe to drink, although it can be slightly brackish in some locales near the sea. For that reason, many people prefer the bottled water commonly available at restaurants, hotels, cafes, food stores, and kiosks, but don't expect all brands to be especially bubbly. The days when Greek restaurants automatically served glasses of cold fresh water are gone; you are now usually made to feel that you must order bottled water, at which point you will have to choose between natural or carbonated (*metalliko*), and domestic or imported. Cafes, however, tend to provide a glass of natural water.

3

Suggested Greek Islands Itineraries

Greece is such a small country—its total area is about the state of Alabama's—that you might think it's possible to see much of it in a relatively short visit. Not so. Its mountainous terrain makes distances deceptive. Many desirable destinations are located on islands, requiring you many hours of travel back and forth. And so many destinations are desirable. But with special planning, you can get the most out of whatever limited time you have.

The itineraries laid out here require from 8 to 16 days on the ground in Greece. (In addition, plan on spending the better part of a day to get to Greece and another day to return home.) The itineraries mix modes of transportation: You'll take buses, trains, cars, ships, and planes. Greek public transportation—intercity buses and trains—is now fairly comfortable and reliable. It's also a great way to meet locals. Schedules, however, often meet the needs of workers, not tourists. Although isolating, driving a car provides you with the greatest flexibility. Thousands of travelers choose this option, but make sure you feel comfortable driving a rented car in Greece.

When choosing your jaunt, you have to balance cost with time. Some islands are served only by ship; others, by ship and plane. Because these itineraries include islands, they work best in the summer—May through September. In the off season, the weather is not dependable, many hotels and restaurants close, and airline and ferry schedules to some of these places become extremely limited. The converse of that also applies: The closer to high season you intend to travel, the more imperative it is to make reservations in advance.

All of the itineraries below end up in Athens and, in theory, you have 24 hours of leeway to allow for any unanticipated travel delays—weather, accidents, strikes. We must admit, though, that Greece keeps its own schedule. On any given day, a museum or archaeological site may be closed without notice. Call in advance to make sure that a destination will be open while you're traveling, and double-check your reservations, especially during special occasions such as Greek Easter week. We strongly advise you to avoid Greek Orthodox Easter; much of Greece shuts down and accommodations and transportation are on overload.

You can also sign up for one of the standard cruises that stop at several of the major islands and occasionally put into the mainland; as these last about 7 days, this would mean sailing off on your first day in Greece and then having only the last day for Athens. (Such cruises are described in detail in chapter 4.) Another alternative is to sign up for one of the bus tours—from 3 to 7 days—that visit the major mainland sites. Use the itineraries below, though, if you want to set your own pace and choose what you see. *Kalo taxidi* (have a good trip)!

1 The Greek Islands in 1 Week

Ideally, everyone should have a whole summer for Greece. But let's face it—most people leave home on a Friday evening and then fly back to work the next Sunday. That's 8 full days on the ground. We've included two weekends, but any 8 days will work. This itinerary is for you if you're interested in sampling the distinctive "historical" Greece. Mold this to your needs. You can always drop a museum or site and take time to relax on a beach. However, this particular itinerary involves a fair amount of moving about and checking in and out of hotels. Maximum Greek Islands in a minimum of time.

Day ❶: Athens & the Acropolis

Arrive in Athens and get settled in your hotel. Then, walk to the **Acropolis** ✸✸✸ (p. 154) to see the Parthenon, arguably the world's number-one destination. Make time for the Acropolis Museum (art-course sculptures!) while at the top or at the **Theater of Dionysos** ✸ (ground zero of Greek drama!) at its base. For a modest dinner, head to **Platanos Taverna** ✸✸ (p. 148) or another of the restaurants in the Plaka. (p. 147).

Day ❷: Athens & Santorini

Check out the gold masks, jewelry, sculptures, and other highlights at the **National Archaeological Museum** ✸✸✸ (p. 158). Then head to the **Ancient Agora** ✸✸ (p. 159) to experience the more down-to-earth ancient Athens. Imagine the individuals' lives when you visit the ancient **Kerameikos Cemetery** ✸ (p. 159). Any cafe nearby will do for a cool drink. Then hit the museum trail again (p. 161). Plan to lunch at **Oraia Ellada** in the Plaka (p. 150). Explore Syntagma Square (p. 137). Take the evening flight or overnight ferry to Santorini. Get a taxi to Oia and, after checking in at a hotel there, try **Skala** for dinner (p. 248).

Days ❸ & ❹: Santorini & Folegandros

You must see **Ancient Akrotiri** ✸✸✸ (p. 234). Spend the rest of the day at Kamari beach, with no end of cafes for snacks. Lunch on the beach at **Camille Stephani** ✸ (p. 248). Later, take in the restored mansion as you dine formally at **Restaurant-Bar 1800** ✸ (p. 248) in Oia. On Day 4, look for the ancient cave houses hollowed into the solidified ash (p. 238) before taking the 2-hr.-plus ferry ride to **Folegandros**. Get a taxi or bus to **Hora** ✸, Folegandros's capital. It's one of the most beautiful Cycladic villages and it's largely built inside the walls of a 12th-century Venetian castle. Cars—and motorcycles—are banned from Hora. It's easy to laze away the rest of the day at one of the cafes or restaurants in the perfect little *plateia* (square) shaded by almond trees. End the day with a swim at **Angali** beach before dinner. Then settle into your room at the very charming **Anemomilos Apartments** ✸✸ with its spectacular view out to sea or at the **Castro Hotel** ✸✸, built into a Venetian castle.

Days ❺ & ❻: Crete

Fly via Athens or take the ferry directly to **Iraklion, Crete** (p. 193). Go where the archaeologists do, and have lunch at the **Ionia** (p. 202). Then visit the **Palace of the Knossos** ✸✸✸ (p. 197), and the **Archaeological Museum** ✸✸✸ (p. 196). After a siesta, take the walking tour of Iraklion (p. 197) before treating yourself to the artichokes and aubergines at the **Kyriakos** ✸ (p. 201). Spend Day 6 back at the sites or touring **Chania** ✸✸ (go by rental car, public transportation, or escorted tour), with its relatively intact Venetian-Turkish old town (p. 205), or **Phaestos** ✸✸, the second most ambitious

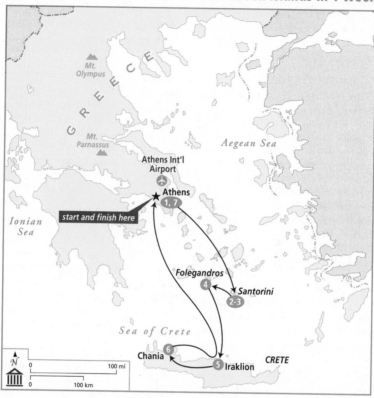

Minoan palace (p. 204). Expect to be on the road for 5 hours roundtrip for each. Eat lunch along the harbor at Chania or at the restaurant at Phaestos. By early evening, return to Iraklion for the shrimp in tomato sauce at **Giovanni** (p. 202).

Day ❼: Athens & the Temple of Poseidon

Take an early morning flight back to Athens. If you're up to another excursion,

continue on to the Temple of Poseidon at **Sounion** (p. 177). Stay for sunset before heading back to Athens for a nouvelle Greek dinner at **Daphne's** ★★★ (p. 147). If you still have the energy, top off your visit with a little late-night culture (see "Athens After Dark," p. 164).

Day ❽: Flight Home

Go to the airport, and fly home.

2 The Greek Islands in 2 Weeks

Two weeks is enough time to really taste the different flavors of the Greek Islands. You'll visit the must-see ancient monuments (the Acropolis in Athens, the Palace of the Knossos in Crete, and Akrotiri, nicknamed the "Pompeii of Greece"); the famous Mykonos, with its snow-white houses and trendy all-night bars; or the volcanic Santorini, with its amazing harbor and sheer cliffs. You'll also see less-famous places that we hope you'll fall in love with as you discover them. We're going to show you how to see all this and leave time for making some discoveries of your own. If you have the time and the energy, take our suggestions for the little, off-the-beaten-track spots near the more well-known places.

Day ❶: Athens & the Archaeological Parkway

Settle into your hotel, then go for a get-acquainted walk along **The Archaeological Park** ★★★, which runs from **Syntagma Square** around the **Acropolis** ★★★, past the **Agora** ★★, and into the **Plaka** ★★, the heart of old—and touristy—Athens (p. 154). Do what the Athenians do and stop for cappuccino, pastries, cheese, or yogurt at **Oraia Ellada** ★★ (p. 150), a shop with a restaurant, in the Plaka, with a drop-dead Acropolis view. Browse through the old and new Greek folk art before continuing your walk. (If you get really tired, hop the Metro back to your hotel.) For lunch, sit under the plane tree as you enjoy roast lamb at the **Platanos Taverna** ★★ (p. 148). Feeling revived? Stop in the little **Museum of Popular Greek Musical Instruments** ★★ (p. 168), just a few feet away, listen to Greek music and enjoy the peaceful garden there. The slumbering tortoises there may remind you it's siesta time. Go to your hotel for a nap before you head out again for a nighttime stroll back to the Acropolis (even if it's closed) and dinner. **Neon** ★ serves Greek cafeteria-style fast food in Syntagma Square (p. 150). Point to what you want and leave your phrase book in your pocket.

Day ❷: Museums & Mount Likavitos

Visit the **National Archaeological Museum** ★★★ to see art-course sculptures, gold, and other incredible artifacts (p. 158). Then head to the Acropolis, but first grab a snack at one of the kiosks on the slopes. Spend the rest of the day enjoying Athens's sprawling **National Garden** (p. 168), watching Greek families. Then have dinner at nearby **Aegli** ★★ (p. 149). Or ride the cable car up Mount Likavitos (p. 168) before dinner at **To Kafeneio** ★★ (p. 151). Located in Kolonaki, the restaurant near the mountain is a great place to enjoy the bustle of Athens's most fashionable neighborhood.

Day ❸: Mykonos & Paradise

By plane or ship, go to Mykonos. Settle into your hotel, then take a bus to one of the beaches outside town—**Paradise** ★ (p. 286) attracts partiers who love loud beach-bar music with their sun and sand, while **Ornos** is a quieter beach preferred by families (p. 286). Get a snack for lunch on the beach. Back in town, get lost in the town's winding streets; end up at **Le Caprice** in "Little Venice" for a dry martini and good people-watching (p. 294). Before dinner, walk to Mykonos's famous three waterside **windmills** to take in the view back across the harbor. You'll see Little Venice's bars, perched vertiginously over the sea. The fish is fresh at **Kounelas** ★ on the harbor (p. 293), where you'll vie for a table with locals.

Day ❹: Delos & Mykonos

Take an early excursion boat from Mykonos to **Delos** ★★★ (p. 295) and spend several hours admiring the acres of marble ruins. There's a little snack bar by the museum, but you'll probably do better bringing your own food from Mykonos and picnicking in a patch of shade cast by the ancient monuments. When you get back to Mykonos, tarry in its excellent shops, which include some of the best jewelers in Greece. Be sure to stop at the LALAoUNIS shop here

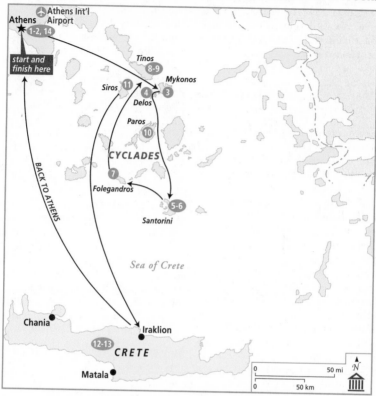

The map shows: Athens Int'l Airport, Athens (start and finish here, 1-2, 14), Tinos (8-9), Mykonos, Siros (11), Delos (4, 3), Paros (10), CYCLADES, Folegandros (7), Santorini (5-6), BACK TO ATHENS, Sea of Crete, Chania, Iraklion, CRETE (12-13), Matala. Scale: 0 – 50 mi / 0 – 50 km. N.

(p. 288). For dinner, sample the *mezedes* (appetizers) and grilled fish (or meat) at the **Sea Satin Market** ✦, past the windmills at Kato Myli, overlooking the sea (p. 294).

Day ❺: Santorini & Akrotiri

Head to **Santorini** next, by plane or ship (p. 231). We like going by ship, sailing into the deep harbor with its high cliffs, streaked with lava from the volcanic eruption that tore the island in half around 1450 B.C. This is one of the world's great travel experiences. Then, check into your hotel and rent a car or sign up for a tour and go to the ancient site of **Akrotiri** ✦✦✦, often called the "Pompeii of Greece" (p. 234). Then take

in the **Boutari Winery,** where your tour includes enough snacks and samples of local wines for a light lunch (p. 235). In the evening, do what everyone does in Fira, Santorini's capital: Wander down the narrow streets before having drinks and dinner. For an inventive, memorable meal in a beautiful setting, make reservations at one of the best restaurants in all of Greece: **Selene** ✦✦✦ (p. 247).

Day ❻: Ancient Thira & Kamari

Explore the island by car, tour, or the excellent local bus system. See the dramatic clifftop site of **Ancient Thira** ✦✦ (p. 235) before heading down to the famous black-sand beach at **Kamari** for a swim and lunch at the **Camille Stephani** ✦ taverna, a long-time favorite (p. 248). Back in Fira, see the fantastic reproductions of the beautiful Minoan wall paintings of Akrotiri in the **Thira Foundation** ☆ (p. 236). If you're here in season, watch the sun set from the village of **Imerovigli** (p. 242). Try **Katina's** ☆ or **Captain Dimitri's** ☆, two excellent fish places in Ammoudi, the minuscule port of little Ia (p. 247).

Day ⑦: Folegandros

Take the ferry from bustling Santorini to the little island of **Folegandros** (p. 249), one of the last "undiscovered" Cycladic islands. Explore the capital town of **Hora,** much of which is built into the walls of a Venetian fortress (p. 250). Swim at Livadaki or Ambeli beach (p. 251) before relaxing over dinner at one of the little tavernas clustered around the main square in Hora (p. 252). Stay either in the **Castro Hotel** (p. 252), built into the walls of the Venetian castle, or in the **Anemomilos** (p. 252), just outside town, with its own swimming pool and a drop-dead view out to sea.

Day ⑧: Folegandros to Tinos

Catch a ferry from Folegandros to **Tinos** (p. 298). Some days, this may involve changing ferries at Santorini, Sifnos, or Mykonos; you'll experience the hustle and bustle of the harbor front. While at sea, laze the day away watching the islands come and go on the horizon. Bring a picnic with you: the food on most island boats is as undistinguished as the scenery is beautiful! When you arrive at Tinos, if you want to be in the heart of things, stay at the harbor-front **Oceanis Hotel** (p. 303). If you want to be on the beach, get a room at the **Tinos Beach Hotel** (p. 304), just outside Tinos town. If you arrive late on Tinos, don't worry: the waterfront restaurants and cafes stay open almost all night (p. 304).

Day ⑨: Exploring Tinos

Head uphill in the cool and quiet of the morning to the **Cathedral of the Panagia Evangelistria** (p. 300). You may encounter a family bringing a baby to be baptized at this important shrine. Be sure to take in the cluster of small museums in the Cathedral precincts before strolling back downhill to stop in the **Archaeological Museum** (p. 300). Then, head out into the lush Tinian countryside, to take in some of its sparkling white villages with their bubbling springs and ornate **dovecotes** (p. 298). **Pirgos** (p. 302) is one of the loveliest villages, and lunch at one of the cafes on its shaded square is memorable (p. 302). If you want lunch by the sea, keep going to the beach at Panormos (p. 302), as yet undeveloped, but not for long. In the evening, explore the shops in Tinos town before eating a seriously good meal at **Metaxi Mas** (p. 304) or **Palaia Pallada** (p. 305). Most tourists on Tinos are Greek, and they know and love their food.

Day ⑩: Paros

There are frequent boats from Tinos to **Paros** (p. 259) and it's easy to sail over to spend a few hours or a full day on Paros, whose profusion of shops, boutiques, and restaurants have earned it the nickname of the "poor man's Mykonos." The island's capitol, **Parikia,** has its own handsome fortress, a lovingly restored Byzantine church, the **Ekatondapiliani,** which according to local legend has 100 doors (p. 263). If you're here in June, be sure to take in the **Valley of the Petaloudes** (Butterflies) (p. 263), an easy excursion by bus or car from Parikia. Then, catch a ferry back to Tinos for the night.

Day ⑪: Tinos to Siros

Take the ferry to **Siros** (p. 306), to experience an island unlike the other

Cyclades. Yes, Siros has some of the typical shining white, cubelike Cycladic houses, especially in **Ano Siros,** the oldest part of Siros's capitol, **Ermoupolis** (p. 308). Ermoupolis also has the most handsome city hall in the Cyclades—and an opera house modeled on Milan's La Scala! This was the most important and prosperous Cycladic island in the 19th century, and you can learn all about the shipbuilding that made Siros famous around the world at Ermoupolis's superb **Industrial Museum** (p. 307). That said, you may find it so pleasant to watch the world go by from one of the cafes or tavernas in Ermoupolis's main square, the spacious Plateia Miaoulis, that you don't budge for hours.

Day ⑫: Siros to Crete

Take the inter-island ferry from Siros to Crete (depending on the day of the week, you may have to take it on day 11) and on arriving at **Iraklion,** go straight from the dock to the **Lato Boutique Hotel** 🔆 (p. 200). Head either for the great Minoan **Palace of Knossos** 🔆🔆🔆 (p. 197) or the **Archaeological Museum** 🔆🔆🔆 (p. 196): opinions differ as to whether the one is best viewed before the other but they definitely complement each other. (Both stay open fairly late in high season.) Get away from the crowds by walking down to the harbor or out around the great **Venetian**

walls 🔆 (p. 197); if you are up for it, take our complete "stroll around the city" (p. 197). Have a refreshing drink on the Lion Fountain Square, but take your meals at the **Pantheon** (p. 202) for an "indigenous" experience or **Loukoulos** 🔆 for something more cosmopolitan (p. 202).

Day ⑬: Crete

Rent a car for the day or sign on with a tourist agency excursion. Archaeological buffs will appreciate **Phaestos** 🔆🔆 (p. 204), the second great Minoan Palace; include stops at **Gortyna** 🔆 (with its extraordinary Law Code) (p. 204) and, if time, **Matala** 🔆, with its seaside caves (p. 204). Bring a picnic for your midday meal. But city types might head along the coast to **Rethymnon** and/or **Chania** (reachable by frequent public transport), both with Old Towns filled with Venetian and Turkish structures (and lots of shops). If you've chosen the latter, plan to eat at **The Well of the Turk in Chania** 🔆 (p. 212) or the **Cava d'Oro** 🔆 in Rethymnon (p. 220) before heading back to Iraklion. Those taking the other trip will be ready for a final meal in Iraklion; choose between the basic **Ippocampus** (p. 203) or the more formal **Kyriakos** 🔆 (p. 201)

Day ⑭: To Athens

Fly back to Athens. End your trip with a final stroll beneath the Acropolis.

3 The Greek Islands with a Family

This itinerary works well for kids between 7 and 15 years old. We tried to balance the adults' reasons for coming all the way to Greece (seeing unique sites) with the children's desires (swimming in hotel pools). As for food? The varied Greek menu should provide something for everyone's taste. And for better or worse, fast food is increasingly available all over Greece. Heat, especially in high season, should be a concern for travelers of all ages. Stay out of the midday sun, especially on the beach. Most forms of transportation offer reduced rates for kids under 12, as do most hotels, museums, and archaeological sites. We also recognized that children usually wilt faster while traveling than adults do.

Days ❶ & ❷: Athens

After you arrive in Athens, settle in to off-set jet lag. Cool off by getting a day pass to the Hilton hotel pool (p. 144). By late afternoon, stroll over to the **Acropolis** ★★★ (p. 154). Before and after dinner at **Taverna Sigalas** (p. 149), walk around the **Plaka/Monasteraki** district (p. 137). On Day 2, visit the **National Archaeological Museum** ★★★ (p. 162)—forget the vases and go straight to the gold objects and the statues! Have lunch at the museum's outdoor cafe, or head to the **National Garden** with its cool paths, small zoo, and outdoor dining (p. 168). Later, take in the changing of the guard at the **Tomb Of the Unknown Soldier** on **Syntagma Square**. If no one in your family group is flagging, check out **Attica Zoological Park** ★★ (p. 168), which is open until 7pm, or the multimedia **Hellenic Cosmos Museum** (p. 168) and its interactive exhibits (hours vary). After a rest at your hotel, ride the cable-car up Mount Likavitos. And treat yourself to a traditional Greek dinner at the **Rhodia** ★ (p. 151).

Day ❸: Crete

Take a morning flight to **Iraklion**. Hit the lovely beach soon after checking into the **Xenia-Helios Hotel** ★ (p. 201); it's right out the door. The kids can also play basketball, tennis, or Ping-Pong here. Dine at the hotel or, if you are up to it, go into Iraklion for an early dinner at **Ippocampus** (p. 203). The kids should love the fried zucchini and potato slices. You'll like the seafood.

Day ❹: Knossos & Water City

Your hotel can arrange for you to visit the Minoan **Palace of Knossos** ★★★ (p. 197), one of the great archaeological sites of the world. Kids will appreciate the sheer complexity of the site. Reward them with time back at the hotel's beach or a visit to **Water City**, a waterpark at Kokkini Hani. That night, try dinner at the **Pantheon** (p. 202) in Iraklion's famous "Dirty Alley"—no longer "dirty" but still atmospheric.

Day ❺: Matala

In a rental car, drive to the caves and bluff-enclosed cove beach at **Matala** ★, once a major hippie destination (p. 204). Hang out here and be sure to bring a picnic lunch!

Day ❻: Santorini

Take the ferry to Santorini (a 5-hr trip). Check in at a hotel at **Kamari,** if you prefer a beach (p. 246); or at **Oia,** if you prefer a spectacular view (p. 244). In the evening, dine on the terrace overlooking the caldera at **Koukoumavlos** ★★ (p. 246) in Fira town. Try the yogurt panna cotta with pistachios, honey, and sour cherries for dessert.

Day ❼ & ❽: Akrotiri & Fira

On Day 7, visit the unique excavated ancient city (nicknamed the "Minoan Pompeii") at **Akrotiri** ★★★: Even jaded kids will be impressed by the three-story, 3,500-year-old houses (p. 234). Then snorkel (or relax) by the beach at **Kamari** (p. 239) or take in the sights of **Fira** town (p. 241). For Day 8, wake up in time to take the excursion to the volcanic islet in the caldera—it will probably be your only chance ever to walk on an emerging volcano (p. 239)! You should also have time to take the cable car from Fira town down to the shore and then come back up by donkey (p. 239) before flying to Athens in the early evening.

Day ❾: Flight Home

Take a taxi to the airport, and fly home.

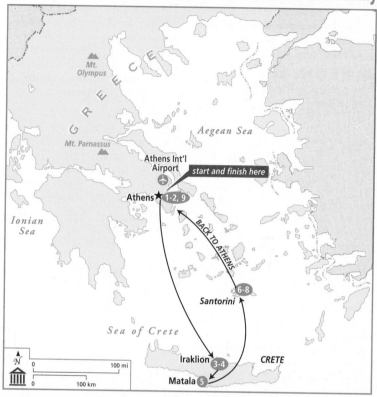

start and finish here

BACK TO ATHENS

4 In the Footsteps of the Apostle Paul

This itinerary is connected to early Western history. Not just for Christians, the trip follows the path of an ancient traveler. The Apostle Paul visited a number of Greek sites that are linked to the New Testament and the earliest years of Christianity. Paul visited territories belonging to modern Greece on at least three different journeys— and most of the places still bear the same names. These visits are accounted for in the Book of Acts in the Bible; we recommend reading the section beforehand and also taking along a copy of the New Testament. Due to the exigencies of modern travel and time, we can't plot a trip that follows Paul's exact itinerary, just highlights.

Days ❶ & ❷: Athens

Spend as in **Day 1** and the Athens part of **Day 2** in "The Greek Islands in 1 Week," earlier in this chapter. Include a walk to the hill opposite the Acropolis known as the **Pnyx** (p. 158); this was the meeting place of the Aereopagus (the Athenian Assembly), which Paul addressed on his first journey to Greece. Also, when you visit the **Ancient Agora** 🎯🎯 (p. 159), try to imagine Paul conversing with the people of Athens here.

Days ❸ & ❹: Rhodes & Lindos
Fly from Athens to **Rhodes** 🎯🎯 (p. 314). The **Old Town** of Rhodes is the oldest inhabited medieval town in Europe (p. 318). Don't miss the **Street of the Knights** 🎯🎯, a 600m-long (1,968-ft.) cobblestone street from the early 16th century. Take up Paul's journey by spending the day at picturesque **Lindos** (p. 330), where Paul is said to have landed. Explore the **Acropolis** 🎯 and the Byzantine **Church of the Panagia** 🎯 (p. 331). Lunch at **Mavriko** 🎯 (p. 333) for a French twist on Greek food. Back in Rhodes, try for a garden table at the **Romeo** 🎯 restaurant (p. 328).

Day ❺ & ❻: Patmos
On **Day 5**, set out for **Patmos** (p. 350), either by ferry direct from Rhodes or plane to Kos and then a ferry from there. At the port town Skala, check in to either the **Skala** or the **Blue Bay** 🎯 (p. 354). After dinner at **Grigoris Grill** (p. 356) or **Pantelis** (p. 356), you can wander through town. Patmos has 30-plus churches. Nothing remains on Patmos to testify to Paul's visit, but a must-see for Christians is the **Cave of the Apocalypse** 🎯, where John the Divine is said to have written the Book of Revelation (p. 352). Everyone will want to visit the nearby **Monastery of St. John** 🎯, built to withstand pirates (ca. 1090). It contains frescoes from the 12th century (p. 353). While at the monastery, lunch at the **Vagelis** restaurant (p. 356) and take in the view. In the evening, dine at the restaurant in the **Skala Hotel** (p. 354).

Day ❼: Patmos to Crete
You'll spend a long day returning to Rhodes by ferry and then flying on to

Iraklion, Crete (p. 193). (During high season occasional direct flights run from Rhodes to Crete; otherwise you'll have to go through Athens.) There is no shortage of hotels or restaurants in Iraklion—try the **Lato Boutique Hotel** 🎯 (p. 200) and **Loukoulos** 🎯 for dinner (p. 202).

Day ❽: Iraklion
To fully explore Crete would take many weeks, what with its Minoan, Roman, Byzantine, Venetian, Turkish, and 19th-century remains. Your hotel can arrange for you to visit the Minoan **Palace of Knossos** 🎯🎯🎯 (p. 197), one of the great archaeological sites of the world. And don't miss the **Archaeological Museum** 🎯🎯🎯 (p. 196). You can lunch at one of the many tavernas across from the entrance to Knossos and try **Ippocampus** or **Kyriakos** 🎯 (p. 201) for your evening meal.

Day ❾: Gortyna
Travelers focused on following Paul will definitely want to rent a car and take a day trip to visit **Gortyna**. There you'll see the ruins of the **Basilica of Ayios Titos** (p. 204); in the New Testament, this is the "Titus" appointed by Paul to head the Christian community of Crete (and still the patron saint of the island). The palace of **Phaestos** 🎯🎯 and the caves and beach at **Matala** 🎯 are definitely worth detours (p. 204). You can lunch at Phaestos itself or at one of the many restaurants at Matala.

Day ❿: Chania
In your rental car, travel to Chania (p. 205). Savor the stuffed crab at **Antigone** 🎯 (p. 211), along the harbor of Chania. Stop at the **Archaeological Museum** 🎯, which is in a 16th-century Venetian Catholic church and gives a peek at the many different cultures—from Neolithic through early Christians—who inhabited the area.

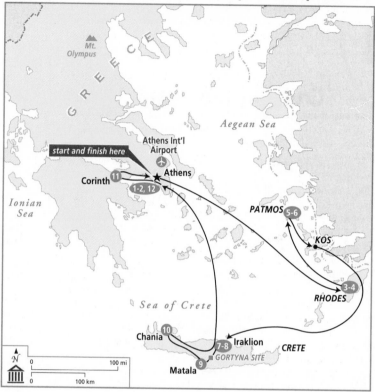

Days ⓫ & ⓬: Athens and Ancient Corinth

Fly back to the Athens airport in time to go to **Corinth** (ask at your hotel for info). **Ancient Corinth** is one of the major sites of ancient Greece, with numerous Roman remains that date from the time of Paul's visit. In particular, ask to see the Roman bema, or rostrum, said to be on the site where the Roman governor Gallio defended Paul. In addition to the link to Paul, the area stands on its own with a 6th-century **Temple of Apollo** and wide, marble-paved roads. Eat lunch at one of the many restaurants adjacent to the site. In the evening, treat yourself to dinner at **Daphne's** ★★★ (p. 147).

Days ⓭: Flight Home

Take a taxi to the airport, and fly home.

4

Cruising the Greek Islands

by Rebecca Tobin

The dramatic approach into the beautiful bowl-shaped harbor of Santorini, a partially submerged crater of an ancient volcano whose steep parched slopes are crowned by a whitewashed village, is what cruising the Greek islands is all about. Drop-dead gorgeous scenery. Plus, of course, ancient historic sites and lots of local culture, all without the hassle of deciphering ferry schedules and changing hotel rooms. You get on the ship, you unpack once, and the ship goes with you as your floating hotel. It's your familiar retreat after a long day of touring or a place to kick back and bask in the Greek sun. Greece is practically tailor-made for cruising. Among the most beautiful regions to cruise in all the world, the seas are relatively calm and the islands are individual in character, offering travelers a satisfying mix of local culture, stunning scenery, and ancient and medieval ruins to explore.

Most Greek island itineraries highlight the region's history with optional guided **shore excursions** that take in the major sights, spicing up the vacation brew with other, less history-minded excursions such as visits to beaches, meals at local restaurants, and fishing or sailing excursions.

Of course, you can choose to get off the ship at each port of call and head off on your own to explore the sights, hit the beach, or check out the local color at the nearest taverna. Solo is often the best way to go.

Cruising in the Greek islands has changed somewhat in the past couple of years. Royal Olympic Cruises (also known as Royal Olympia Cruises), which had made Greek cruises a specialty and was a strong presence in the region as well as in the U.S., stopped its cruise operations in early 2005; its ships have been auctioned off to other cruise companies. Festival Cruises, which marketed under the First European Cruises name in the U.S., shut its doors in 2004.

But there are still plenty of cruise lines, and vacations, to choose from. Another company, Louis Hellenic Cruises, last year stepped in and filled the void left by Royal Olympic by starting 3-, 4- and 7-night cruises in the islands. MSC Cruises snapped up several former Festival vessels. And the good news is that Greek island cruising seems to be stronger than ever. After the September 11, 2001, terrorist attacks and during the Iraq war, many cruise lines cut back on their eastern Mediterranean—and their entire European—itineraries, but that trend has been reversing ever since. Other companies are continuing to build on their previous offerings and add new ports.

1 Choosing the Right Cruise for You

In choosing your cruise, you need to think about what you want to see and at what level of comfort you want to see it.

We recommend you first decide **what you want to see.** Are you looking to visit the most popular islands—Mykonos, Santorini, and Rhodes—or are you interested in places off the beaten path? Whichever it is, you'll want to make sure the itinerary you choose allows you enough time to experience the place or places that really take your fancy. Some ships visit a port and spend the full day, while others visit two ports in 1 day, which limits your sightseeing time in each.

In the past, Greek law was designed so that only Greek-flagged ships could cruise between Greek ports, meaning that foreign-flagged vessels had to visit en route between other European ports, usually in Italy or Turkey. This law officially changed in 1999, but many Greek islands cruises maintain a similar routing, either beginning or ending their itineraries elsewhere. You'll have to consider embarkation and disembarkation points in making your decision. Do you mind flying to Venice or Istanbul to catch your ship?

Greece is also visited by ships as part of European itineraries where Greece is not the sole focus, but only one of several countries visited.

Next, consider **how long you want to spend cruising the islands**—3 days, a week, 2 weeks? If you have the time, you may want to consider a **cruisetour,** which combines a cruise to the islands with a guided tour of important sights on the mainland. This is made easy in Greece by the fact that some lines offer cruises of only 3 or 4 days, which you can combine with a land tour into a 1-week vacation, and 1-week cruises you can combine with a land tour to make a 2-week vacation.

Also consider **when you want to cruise.** While Greece has traditionally been a summer destination, the season has been stretched in recent years, and some lines now offer cruises here virtually year-round. While most of the action on the islands still takes place in the warmer months, late April through October, traveling at other times has its own special charms, including the fact it allows you to avoid the tourist crush (although some visitor facilities may be closed in the off season) and the hottest months (in July and Aug, temperatures can reach 100°F/38°C). For the record, August is the month the islands are most crowded with European vacationers (expect beaches, bars, and discos to be packed). April and November are the rainiest months. May and October are relatively problem-free, making them particularly nice times to sail in Greece.

You'll also want to think about **what you want out of the cruise experience.** Is the purpose of your cruise to see as much as you can of the islands, or to relax by the ship's pool? And what level of comfort, entertainment, on-board activities, and so forth do you require? Some ships spend a day or more at sea, meaning they don't visit a port at all that day, and while some experienced cruisers enjoy those days the most, treasuring the opportunity they offer for real relaxation, they won't do you much good if your goal is seeing as much of Greece as you can.

CHOOSING YOUR SHIP

Ships cruising the Greek islands range from small yacht-type vessels carrying fewer than 50 passengers, to traditional midsize ships, to resortlike 2,000-plus passenger megaships. Which you choose has a lot to do with your personality and vacation goals.

MEGASHIPS & LARGE SHIPS   Cruises aboard these vessels focus as much on on-board activities as they do on their destination. The ships are floating resorts—sometimes glitzy—offering American-style luxury and amenities along with attentive service. In a recent brochure, Holland America Line unabashedly stated that "when asked which European city he liked best, one guest replied 'My Holland America ship—that was my favorite city.'" We think that says it all.

These ships, which tend to be newer, feature Las Vegas–style shows, lavish casinos, big spas and gyms, plenty of bars and restaurants, extravagant meals, and lots of day-time activities. You or your children can take part in games, contests, cooking lessons, wine tastings, and sports tournaments—although generally few ethnic Greek activities are offered.

CLASSIC & MIDSIZE SHIPS   Ships in this category include older, classic vessels as well as some newer ships. Destination is more a focus than on the bigger ships, and itineraries may be very busy, with the ship visiting an island a day, or sometimes two. This leaves little time for on-board daytime activities, although some will be offered. In the Greek market, some of these ships feature Greek crews and cuisine, and service tends to be a big area of focus. Because these ships are often sold heavily in the Euro-pean markets, you'll likely hear many languages spoken onboard. The ships offer a variety of bars and lounges, at least one swimming pool and a small casino, a spa and gym, and plenty of open deck space. Entertainment is generally offered in a main show lounge; some ships have cinemas featuring recently released films.

SMALL SHIPS & YACHTS   Small ships and yachts tend to offer a more relaxed pace and may seek itineraries that focus on smaller, alternative ports, which they can get into because of their small size and shallow draft (the amount of ship that rides beneath the waterline). They may offer "soft adventure" cruise experiences focused on nature- and outdoor-oriented activities; or they may offer an experience more like that of a luxury yacht. Some of the ships feature Greek crews and Greek cuisine. On these small ships, there will typically be more interaction with fellow passengers than on larger ships—partially because there will be less entertainment, and because there may or may not be a swimming pool, casino, spa, or gym. Both cabins and public rooms range from small and serviceable to large and luxurious, depending on which ship you choose. Some ships are fully engine-powered while others are sailing vessels (even though these sails are typically more for show than for power).

In addition to the small ships we mention in depth later in this chapter, you may want to look into even smaller yachts, especially if you're seeking a charter or a truly private yachtlike experience. Several U.S. tour operators sell packages that include casual and elegant yachts from the Greece-based **Zeus Group,** such as *Panorama, Diogenis V.,* and *Viking Star,* which each carry around 40 to 50 guests.

2 Calculating the Cost

Cruises in the Greek islands range from 3 nights to 2 weeks, with prices per day rang-ing from around 115€ to more than 769€ ($150–$1,000) per person, double occu-pancy. These days, you're still almost always going to get a rate that's substantially **less than brochure prices.** Like new-car sticker prices, brochure rates are notoriously inflated. You can get a good price, as well as a shot at the best cabins on the ship, if you book early; alternatively, you might be able to get a good price if you wait until the last minute, when the lines are trying to top-up their sailings (unlike a hotel, cruise ships almost always sail full). Travel agencies and Web-based cruise-only agencies offer the best and "real" prices (see "Booking Your Cruise," below). Depending on demand, you may snag a two-for-one deal or free airfare or hotel stays. No matter what price you end up paying, rates include three meals a day (with a couple of exceptions, which we've noted in the ship reviews later), accommodations, on-board activities and entertainment and, if you book your airfare through the cruise line, a transfer from the airport to the ship. Some rates even include airfare (the inclusion of airfare is more common on European cruises than Caribbean cruises), and in rare cases the fare may include tips, shore excursions, and/or pre- and/or post-cruise hotel stays. Some cruises are packaged as cruisetours, meaning they include both hotel stays and land tours. Rarely included in the price are alcoholic beverages; almost never included are charges for spa and beauty treatments, Internet access, and shore excursions. Port charges, taxes, and other fees are usually, but not always, included in the cruise fare. We've noted exceptions below.

Cruise prices are based on two people sharing a cabin. Most lines have special **single supplement** prices for solo passengers wishing to have a cabin to themselves, usually ranging from 150% to 200% of the per-person rate. The "supplement," in this case, goes to the cruise line as their compensation for not getting two passenger fares for the cabin. At the opposite end, most lines offer highly discounted rates for a third or fourth person sharing a cabin with two full-fare passengers.

Seniors may be able to get extra savings on your cruise. Some lines will take 5% off the top for those 55 and over, and the senior rate applies even if the second person in the cabin is younger. Membership in groups such as AARP is not required, but such membership may bring additional savings.

If your package does not include **airfare,** you should consider booking air transportation through the cruise line. While the rates offered by the lines may or may not be as low as you can find on your own, booking through the line allows the cruise company to keep track of you if, for instance, your flight is delayed. In this case, the ship may be able to wait for you, and if it can't wait, it will arrange transportation for you to the next port of call. The cruise lines also negotiate special deals with hotels at port cities if you want to come in a few days before your cruise or stay after it.

3 Booking Your Cruise

Today, practically everybody has a website, and the difference between so-called **Web-based cruise sellers** and more **traditional travel agencies** is that the former rely on their sites for most of their actual bookings, while the latter use theirs as glorified advertising space to promote their offerings, doing most of their actual business in person or over the phone. As far as cruise prices go, there's no absolutely quantifiable difference between the real live travel agents and Internet-based cruise sellers. Sometimes you'll get the best price on the Web, and sometimes you'll get it through an agent—especially in the current market, where prices offered to agents and sites tend to be very similar across the board. Some agencies, online or off, get better prices from certain cruise lines because they sell a high volume of that line's product. On the other hand, some lines tout a "level playing field"—everybody gets the same price—and don't allow agents to advertise discounted rates.

In deciding how to book your cruise, consider your level of experience as a cruiser and as an Internet user. Most websites give you a menu of ships and itineraries to select from, plus a basic search capability that takes into account only destination, price, length of trip, and date, without consideration of the type of cruise experience each line offers. If you've cruised before and know exactly what you want, no problem. If, on the other hand, you have limited experience with cruising and with booking on the Web, it may be better to go through a traditional agent, who can help you wade through the choices and answer your questions, from which cabins have their views obstructed by lifeboats to information on dining and tuxedo rentals. No matter which way you wind up booking your cruise, you may want to first check out the cruise-line websites and browse the Internet for ship reviews, virtual tours, chats, and industry news.

To find an agent, rely on referrals from trusted friends and colleagues. Some agents really know the business—they travel themselves to sample what they sell—while others are not much more than order-takers. Start looking as soon as you can, which can result in early-booking rates and the best cabin choices.

CHOOSING A CABIN

One of your biggest decisions is what type of cabin you need. Will you be happy with a slightly cramped space without a window (the most budget-minded choice); a cabin with a private veranda; or a suite with a separate dining room, hot tub, and all the goodies?

Obviously, price will determine your choice. If you don't plan to spend time in your cabin except to sleep, shower, and change clothes, an **inside cabin** (that is, one without a porthole or window) might do just fine. If you get claustrophobic, however; or if you insist on sunshine first thing in the morning; or if you intend to hole up in your cabin for extended periods, pay a bit more and take an **outside cabin**—or even better, one with a **private balcony.**

When you book your cabin, you generally will not be choosing a specific cabin number but rather a cabin category, within which all units have the same amenities. With this in mind, one concern if you do go the window route is **obstructed views.** This isn't an issue with newer ships, since the lifeboats now are housed on the decks containing the public spaces like restaurants and lounges; the passenger cabins are either above or below those decks. But check to make sure none of the cabins in the category you've selected have windows that directly face lifeboats or other objects that may block your view of the clear blue sea. You can determine this by looking at a diagram of the ship (included in the cruise brochure) or by consulting with your travel agent.

Most ships offer cabins for two with private bathroom and shower, and twin beds that may be convertible to a queen-size. (Bathtubs are considered a luxury on most ships, and are offered only in the most expensive cabins.) Other variations are cabins with bunk beds (referred to in the brochures as "upper and lower berths"), cabins designed for three or four people, and connecting cabins for families.

Cabin amenities vary by line, and often include TVs (with a closed system of programmed movies and features), VCRs or DVD players, hair dryers, safes, and mini-refrigerators. If any of these are must-haves, let your agent know.

Usually the higher on the ship the cabin is located, the more expensive it is. But upper decks also tend to be rockier in rough seas than the middle or lower parts of the ship, a factor to consider if you're prone to seasickness.

The **size of a cabin** is determined by square feet. Keep in mind that ship cabins are generally smaller than the equivalent hotel rooms you'd find on land. As a rough guide, 11 sq. m (120 sq. ft.) is low-end and cramped, 17 sq. m (180 sq. ft.) is midrange and fairly roomy, and 23 sq. m (250 sq. ft.) and larger is suite-size and very comfortable.

If noise bothers you, pick a cabin far from the engine room and nowhere near the disco.

CHOOSING A MEALTIME

Because most ship dining rooms are not large enough to accommodate all passengers at one dinner seating (exceptions include many of the upscale lines), times and tables are assigned. When you book your trip, you will also indicate your preferred mealtime. Early, or "main," seating is usually at 6 or 6:30pm, late seating at 8 or 8:30pm. Lines catering to a majority of European clientele may offer seatings an hour or so later than these.

There are advantages to both times. **Early seating** is usually less crowded, and the preferred time for families and older passengers who want to get to bed early. Food items are fresher (they don't have to sit in warmers), but the waiters know that the second wave is coming, so they may be rushed. Early diners get first dibs on nighttime entertainment venues, and might be hungry enough in a few hours to take advantage of the midnight buffet. **Late seating** allows time for a nap or late spa appointment before dinner. Service is slower paced, and you can linger with after-dinner drinks, then catch the late show at 10pm.

When choosing a mealtime, you also need to consider **table size** (on most ships, you can request to be at a table for 2, 4, 8, 10, or 12) and whether you want to sit at a **smoking or nonsmoking table**—a particularly important factor in Europe, where smoking is quite popular (though most dining rooms are completely nonsmoking). It's tough to snag a table for two since they're usually in great demand.

Ships in the smaller and upscale categories have **open seating** arrangements, which means you can dine at any hour the restaurant is open. You also choose your dinner partners, or you can ask the maitre d' to sit you with other guests.

Many ships now also have one or two restaurants separate—in location, cuisine, and atmosphere—from the main dining room. These so-called **specialty restaurants** or **alternative restaurants** are open-seating, so you can choose your dinner time and dining companions. If you'd like to try an evening or two at these restaurants, make reservations in advance and ask if a separate cover charge applies.

On most ships, **breakfast** and **lunch** are open seating, but you may be requested to eat at an assigned time. (Early means breakfast at 7 or 8am, lunch at noon; late, breakfast at 8:30 or 9am, lunch at 1:30pm.) On ships with buffet restaurants, you can choose to have both meals there, at any time during open hours.

Inform the cruise line at the time you make your reservations if you have any **special dietary requests.** Some lines offer kosher menus; all will have vegetarian, low-fat, low-salt, and sugar-free options available.

DEPOSITS, CANCELLATIONS & EXTRAS

After you've made your decision as to which ship you will vacation on, you will be required to put down a deposit if you're booking 2 or more months in advance (with the remaining fare usually paid no later than 2 months in advance of your departure date); or you must pay the entire fare if you're booking within 60 or 70 days of your sailing date.

Cruise lines have varying policies regarding cancellations, and it's important to look at the fine print in the line's brochure to make sure you understand the policy. Most lines allow you to cancel for a full refund on your deposit and payment any time up to about 70 days before the sailing, after which you have to pay a penalty. If you cancel at the last minute, you likely will lose the entire fare you paid.

An agent will discuss with you optional **airline arrangements** offered by the lines, **transfers** from the airport to the pier, and any pre- or post-cruise **hotel or tour programs** (this kind of information is not always as easy to assess on a website without talking to a live agent). Some lines also let you purchase **shore excursions** in advance (for more on shore excursions, see the section later in this chapter). And you may also be able to pre-book certain on-board spa services.

If you are not booking airfare through the cruise line, make sure to allow several hours between the plane's arrival and the time you must board the ship. To reduce anxiety, it may be best to fly in the day before and spend the night in a hotel.

4 Cruise Preparation Practicalities

About 1 month before your cruise and no later than 1 week before, you should receive your **cruise documents,** including your airline tickets (if you purchased them from the cruise line), a boarding document with your cabin number and sometimes dining choices on it, boarding forms to fill out, luggage tags, and your prearranged bus-transfer vouchers and hotel vouchers (if applicable).

There will also be information about **shore excursions** and additional material detailing things you need to know before you sail. Most lines also list excursions on their websites and allow you to book shore excursions in advance of your sailing online (or via fax), which will give you first dibs at popular offerings that may sell out later.

Read all of this pre-trip information carefully. Make sure your cabin category and dining preferences are what you requested, and that your airline flight and arrival times are what you were told. If there are problems, call your agent immediately. Make sure there is enough time so you can arrive at the port no later than an hour before departure time.

You will be required to have a passport for your trip (see chapter 2 for more on this). If you are flying into Istanbul, you will also be required to have a Turkish visa, which can be obtained at Istanbul airport once you arrive.

Confirm your flight 3 days before departure. Also, before you leave for the airport, tie the tags provided by the cruise line onto your luggage and fill in your boarding cards. This will save you time when you arrive at the ship.

CASH MATTERS

You already paid for a good portion of your vacation when you paid for your cruise, but you will still need a credit card or traveler's checks to handle your **on-board expenses** (such as bar drinks, dry cleaning and laundry, e-mail, massage and other spa services, beauty-parlor services, photos taken by the ship's photographer, babysitting, wine at dinner, and souvenirs) as well as **shore excursions** and **tips** (see below for more on tipping). Expect to spend anywhere from 192€ to 385€ ($250–$500) per person or even more for the "extras" on a weeklong cruise, depending on how much you drink, shop, and buy shore excursions.

Some ships (but not all) will take a personal check for on-board expenses. If you want to pay in cash or by traveler's check, you will be asked to leave a deposit. Some ships have ATMs if you need to get cash while aboard, and some (but not all) offer currency-exchange services.

We suggest you keep careful track of your on-board expenses to avoid an unpleasant surprise at the end of your cruise. Some ships make this particularly easy by offering interactive TVs in cabins: By pushing the right buttons, you can check your account from the comfort of your stateroom. On other ships, you can get this information at the purser's office or guest-relations desk.

You will want to have some cash in hand when going ashore for expenses, including taxis, snacks or meals, drinks, small purchases, and tips for guides.

PACKING

Generally, ships describe their **daily recommended attire** as casual, informal, and formal, prompting many people to think they'll have to bring a steamer trunk full of clothes just to get through the trip. Not true; you can probably get along with about half of what you think you need. Also, almost all ships offer laundry and dry-cleaning services, and some have coin-operated self-serve laundries aboard, so you have the option of packing less and having your clothes cleaned midway through your trip.

During the day, the on-board style is casual, but keep in mind some ships do not allow swimsuits or tank tops in the dining room. Expect two formal dinners and two informal nights during a 5- to 7-day cruise, with the rest casual. There will usually be proportionally more formal nights on longer cruises.

The daily bulletin delivered to your cabin each day will advise you of the proper dress code for the evening. **Formal** means a tux or dark suit with tie for men; and a cocktail dress, long dress, gown, or dressy pantsuit for women. **Informal** is a jacket, tie, and dress slacks or a light suit for men (jeans are frowned upon); and a dress, skirt with blouse, or pants outfit for women. **Casual** means different things to different people. Typically it means a sports shirt or open dress shirt with slacks for men; women can wear skirts, dresses, or pants outfits. Though jeans and shorts are usually frowned upon, many people do wear them to dinner on casual nights.

Check your cruise documents to determine the number of formal nights (if any) during your cruise. Men who don't own a tuxedo might be able to rent one in advance through the cruise line's preferred supplier (who delivers the tux right to the ship). Information on this service often is sent with your cruise documents. Also, some cruises offer **theme nights,** so you may want to check your cruise documents to see if there are any you'll want to bring special clothes for. (For instance, "Greek Night" means everyone wears blue and white—the Greek national colors.)

If you want to bring the crown jewels, be careful. If you're not wearing them, leave them either in your in-room safe (if there is one) or with the purser.

In general, for Greece you're best off packing loose and comfortable cotton or other lightweight fabrics. You'll also want to pack a swimsuit, a sun hat, sunglasses, and plenty of sunscreen—the Greek sun can be intense. Obviously, you should adjust your wardrobe depending on when you plan to travel. Even if you're traveling in August, though, you should bring a sweater, as you'll be in and out of air-conditioning. And don't forget an umbrella.

For shore excursions, comfortable walking shoes are a must, as some involve walking on stone or marble. Also, some tours may visit religious sites that have a "no shorts or bare shoulders" policy, so it's best to bring something to cover up with. (If you're taking the tour through the cruise line, you'll be advised of this before you go.)

If you plan on bringing your own hair dryer, electric razor, curling iron, or other electrical device, check out the ship's electric current in advance. An adapter may be required.

5 Embarkation

Check-in is usually 2 to 3 hours before sailing. You will not be able to board the ship before the scheduled embarkation time. You have up until a half-hour (on some ships it's 1 hr.) before boarding.

At check-in, your boarding documents will be checked and your passport will likely be taken for immigration processing. You will get it back sometime during the cruise. (Make a photocopy and carry that as backup.) Depending on the cruise line, you may establish your **on-board credit account** at this point by presenting a major credit card or making a deposit in cash or traveler's checks. On other ships you need to go to the purser's office onboard to establish your account.

You may be given your **dining-room table assignment** in advance of your sailing (on your tickets) or as you check in, or find a card with your table number waiting for you in your stateroom. If you do not receive an assignment by the time you get to your stateroom, you will be directed to a maitre d's desk. This is also the place to make any changes if your assignment does not meet with your approval.

Once you're aboard, a crew member will show you to your cabin and will probably offer to carry your hand luggage. No tip is required for this service, though feel free to slip the steward a few bucks if you're feeling generous.

In your cabin, you will find a **daily program** detailing the day's events, mealtimes, and so forth, as well as important information on the ship's **safety procedures** and possibly its **deck plan**. Deck plans and directional signs are posted around the ship, generally at main stairways and elevators.

Tip: If you plan to use the ship's **spa services,** it's best to stop by as soon as you board the ship to make appointments so you can get your preferred times. (The best times, particularly the slots during the days at sea, go fast, and some popular treatments sell out.) Ditto dropping by the **shore excursions desk** if you plan to purchase an excursion.

Note: The ship's casino and shops are always closed when the ship is in port, and the fresh- or saltwater swimming pool(s) will be tarped.

Some lines offer **escorted tours** of the public rooms to get you acquainted with the ship. Check the daily program in your cabin for details.

LIFEBOAT/SAFETY DRILL

Ships are required by law to conduct safety drills the first day out. Most do this either right before the ship sails or shortly thereafter. At the start of the drill, the ship will broadcast its emergency signal. You will then be required to return to your cabin (if you're not there), grab your **life jacket** (which you're shown as soon as you arrive in your cabin), and report to your assigned muster station—outside along the promenade deck, or in a lounge or other public room. A notice on the back of your cabin door will list the procedures and advise you as to your assigned **muster station** and how to get there. You will also find directions to the muster station in the hallway. You will be alerted as to the time of the drill in both the daily program and in repeated

Tips   Dealing with Seasickness

If you suffer from seasickness, plan on packing **Bonine** or **Dramamine** in case your ship encounters rough seas. Keep in mind that with both these medications, it is recommended you not drink alcohol; Dramamine in particular can make you drowsy. Both can be bought over the counter. Ships stock supplies onboard, either at the purser's office or at the medical center. (In both cases, the medication will probably be free.)

An option is the **Transderm patch,** available by prescription only, which goes behind your ear and time-releases medication. The patch can be worn for up to 3 days, but comes with all sorts of side-effect warnings. Some people have had success in curbing seasickness with **ginger capsules** available at health-food stores. If you prefer not to ingest anything, you might try the **acupressure wristbands** available at most pharmacies. When set in the proper spot on the wrist, they effectively ease seasickness, although if the seas are particularly rough they may have to be supplemented with medication.

public announcements (and probably by your cabin steward as well). If you hide out in your cabin to avoid the drill, you'll likely get a knock by the cabin steward reminding you to please join the others.

If you're **traveling with children,** make sure your cabin is equipped with special children's life jackets. If not, alert your steward.

6 End-of-Cruise Procedures

Your shipboard account will close in the wee hours before departure, but prior to that time you will receive a preliminary bill in your cabin. If you are settling your account with your credit card, you don't have to do anything except make sure all the charges are correct. If there is a problem, report it to the purser's office.

If you are paying by cash or traveler's check, you will be asked to settle your account either during the day or night before you leave the ship. This will require a trip to the purser's office. A final invoice will be delivered to your room before departure.

TIPS

You will typically find tipping suggestions in your cabin on the last day of your cruise. These are only suggestions, but since service personnel make most (or all) of their salaries through tips, we don't recommend tipping less—unless, of course, bad service warrants it. (On some very upscale lines, acceptance of tips is strictly forbidden.)

Many cruise lines now **automatically add gratuities** to your shipboard account; and other lines will add gratuities to your bill on a request basis. It typically adds up to about 7.70€ ($10) per person, per day. This takes a little of the personal touch out of tipping, but then again, you don't have to worry about running around with envelopes of cash on the last night of your vacation. Check with your cruise line to see if they offer automatic tipping. If you prefer to tip the crew in person or in cash, your ship should be able to cancel the automatic tips. There's also nothing wrong with tipping your cabin steward or waiter on top of the automatic tips.

If you do decide to tip the crew on your own, the cruise line will provide suggested minimums. Generally, each passenger should usually tip his or her cabin steward and waiter about 2.70€ ($3.50) per day each, and the assistant waiter about 1.55€ ($2). That minimum comes to about 48€ ($63) for a 7-day cruise. You are, of course, free to tip more. On some European ships, the suggested minimums are even less. The reason: Europeans aren't as used to tipping as Americans. On some ships you are encouraged to tip the maitre d' and head waiter. You may also encounter cases where tips are pooled: you hand over a suggested amount and it's up to the crew to divide it among themselves. Bar bills often automatically include a 15% tip, but if the wine steward, for instance, has served you exceptionally well, you can slip him or her a bill, too. If you have spa or beauty treatments, you can tip that person at the time of the service (you can even do so on your shipboard charge account).

Don't tip the captain or other officers. They're professional, salaried employees.

The porters who carry your bags at the pier will expect a tip.

PACKING UP

Because of the number of bags being handled, big ships require guests to pack the night before departure and leave their bags in the hallway, usually by midnight. (Be sure they're tagged with the cruise line's luggage tags, which are color-coded to indicate deck number and disembarkation order.) The bags will be picked up overnight and removed from the ship before passengers are allowed to disembark. (Don't pack bottles or other breakables; luggage is often thrown from bin to bin as it's being offloaded.) You'll see them again in the cruise terminal, where they'll most likely be arranged by deck number. *Reminder:* When you're packing that last night, be sure to leave at least one extra change of clothing, as well as necessary toiletries, in the cabin with you.

Pack all your purchases in one suitcase. This way you can easily retrieve them if you're stopped at Customs.

7 The Cruise Lines & Their Ships

In this section, we describe the ships offering Greek islands cruises. Later in the chapter, we describe ships that visit Greece as parts of longer itineraries.

The lines are listed alphabetically. Rates are 2006 **brochure prices per person,** unless otherwise noted. Brochures usually include two sets of rates: The rack rate, which is usually inflated, and a discounted rate (which can be almost half off), whether for booking early or for taking advantage of a two-for-one promotion. Most lines offer special savings for third and fourth passengers sharing a cabin, and some have special rates for children. The **itineraries** we list are also for the 2006 season, unless otherwise noted. Both prices and itineraries are subject to change.

We've listed the **sizes of ships** in two ways: **passenger capacity** and **gross registered tons (GRTs).** Rather than describing actual tonnage, the latter is a measure of interior space used to produce revenue on a vessel. One GRT = 100 cubic feet of enclosed, revenue-generating space.

Note that **Piraeus,** mentioned below as an embarkation and disembarkation point, is the port city for Athens.

COSTA CRUISE LINES

World Trade Center, 80 SW 8th St., Miami, FL 33130-3097. © **800/462-6782**. www.costacruises.com.

This Italian line traces its origins back to 1860 and the Italian olive-oil business. Today, Carnival Corporation, parent of Carnival Cruise Lines, is the owner. Onboard, Italy shows through in nearly everything Costa offers, from the food (which can be disappointing), to the Italian design of the vessels, to the Italian-speaking crew (although they are not all from Italy), to the mostly Italian entertainers. The Italian experience is presented in a casual, warm, and humorous manner. You'll feel like you're part of one big Italian family.

The line's ships represent one of the newer fleets in the industry, sporting blue-and-yellow smokestacks emblazoned with a huge letter *C.* And the fleet is growing: Costa has added one new ship for the past 3 years, and another, its largest, is on the way in 2006. They are popular in the U.S./Caribbean market but are not designed strictly for a North American audience, and therein lies their charm. In Europe, the ships attract a good share of Italian and French passengers, so don't be surprised if your tablemates speak limited English.

Entertainment includes puppet and marionette shows, mimes, and acrobats. Opera singers sometimes come aboard to entertain. The line also offers an activities program for kids and teens.

CostaClassica (built in 1991; 1,300 passengers; 54,000 GRTs) offers spacious public rooms done in contemporary Italian design, with Italian marble and original artwork, including sculptures, paintings, murals, wall hangings, and handcrafted furnishings. The ship's 446 cabins average almost 19 sq. m (200 sq. ft.) each (that's big by industry standards). Ten spacious suites have verandas. *CostaRomantica* (built in 1993; 1,308 passengers; 53,000 GRTs) is a sister ship to the *Classica.*

CostaMediterranea (built in 2002; 2,112 passengers; 84,000 GRTs) is one of the line's newer ships, and boasts a large number of cabins with private verandas (nearly 65% of the ship's outside cabins have them). The ship has a *palazzi* theme, with rooms named and themed after famous Italian palaces. Ristorante degli Argentieri, for example, is designed after a home in Sicily.

CostaFortuna (built in 2004; 2,720 passengers; 105,000 GRTs) is cruising to Greece during the winter season. The ship is another new, modern cruise vessel that counts among its attributes balconies; multiple bars, lounges, and eateries; swimming pools; a large kids' play area; and a themed decor—in this case, the great Italian ocean liners of yore. Check out the miniature fleet of Costa ships affixed to the ceiling of the bar in *Fortuna's* atrium.

ITINERARIES & RATES

COSTA VICTORIA   **Seven-day round-trip Venice** cruise visits Bari (Italy), Katakolon, Santorini, Mykonos, Rhodes, and Dubrovnik (Croatia). Mondays, April through November. **Rates:** from 807€ ($1,049).

COSTA CLASSICA   **Seven-day round-trip from Venice** cruise calls at Ancona (Italy), Athens, Iraklion, Corfu, and Korcula (Croatia). May through September. **Rates:** from 830€ ($1,079).

COSTA FORTUNA   **Ten- and eleven-day Savona (Italy) round-trip** cruise visits Naples (Italy), Alexandria (Egypt), Limassol (Cyprus), Rhodes, Athens, Katakolon, and Maramis (Turkey). January through April. **Rates:** from 1,045€ ($1,359).

COSTA MEDITERRANEA   **Seven-day Venice round-trip** cruise calls at Greece and Turkey: Bari (Italy), Katakolon, Izmir (Turkey), Istanbul, and Dubrovnik (Croatia). May through September. **Rates:** from 915€ ($1,189).

CRYSTAL CRUISES
2049 Century Park E., Suite 1400, Los Angeles, CA 90067. © **310/785-9300**. www.crystalcruises.com.

Crystal's ships offer a cultured, elegant atmosphere and unobtrusive service. Food and wine play a big role: Crystal teamed up with noted Japanese chef Nobu Matsuhisa (of *Nobu* restaurant fame) to design the menus in the ship's Japanese restaurants. In 2004, Crystal launched its own proprietary wine label, C Wines. It also has invested heavily in education and enrichment. Passengers can begin learning a foreign language, take piano lessons, or pick up a new recipe or two while at sea. This operator offers luxury, but on a slightly larger and less-inclusive scale than lines like Silversea and Seabourn—alcohol, for example, is an a la carte purchase, but sodas are complimentary.

Crystal Symphony (built in 1997; 940 passengers; 51,004 GRTs) received a 9.2-million€ ($12-million) face-lift in 2004 and looks younger than its 9 years. Particular attention was paid to the spa, which was enlarged and redesigned to follow *feng shui* principles. Also upgraded: the dining room, the Internet cafe, and all cabins, where new window treatments, bedspreads, carpets, and flatscreen TVs were installed.

Crystal Serenity (built in 2003; 1,080 passengers; 68,000 GRTs), features up-to-date modern design and amenities. Places to relax are the Trident pool grill (comfy chairs), the Palm Court for high tea, and the line's signature Avenue Saloon. Cabins are spacious; the ship's upper-level penthouse suites (especially the top-of-the-line Crystal Penthouses) are top-notch.

In December 2005, the line transferred *Crystal Harmony,* a sister ship to *Crystal Symphony,* to its sister line, NYK Cruises.

ITINERARY & RATES
CRYSTAL SYMPHONY   **Seven-day Athens-to-Venice** cruise calls at Mykonos, Kusadasi (Turkey), Rhodes, and Santorini. May 18. **Rates:** from 1,535€ ($1,995); 4,769€ ($6,200) penthouse suite. The same itinerary in reverse departs Athens July 19. **Rates:** from 1,838€ ($2,390); 5,819€ ($7,565) penthouse. **Twelve-day Venice-to-Athens** cruise calls at Katakolon, Santorini, Samos, Kusadasi, Istanbul (Turkey), and Athens. June 18. **Rates:** from 2,612€ ($3,395); from 8,904€ ($11,575) penthouse suite. **Twelve-day Athens-to-Venice** cruise calls at Istanbul, Kusadasi (Turkey), Rhodes, Santorini, and Split (Croatia). July 26. **Rates:** from 3,069€ ($3,990); from 9,500€ ($12,350) penthouse.

CRYSTAL SERENITY   **Eleven-day Rome** cruise calls at Sorrento, Tripoli (Libya), Alexandria (Egypt), and Kusadasi (Turkey). It visits Santorini and Athens as well. October 13. **Rates:** from 2,731€ ($3,550); 7,912€ ($10,285) penthouse.

LOUIS HELLENIC CRUISES
5–7 Kanari St., 18537 Piraeus, Greece. www.louiscruises.com.

The Louis Group has been in the passenger shipping business for 70 years, but this Cyprus-based company got into cruising in earnest in 1986 when it purchased *Princesa Marissa* and set up Louis Cruise Lines. In late 2004, Louis started another cruise division called Louis Hellenic Cruises and dedicated 3 of its 12-plus ships to the Greek islands, quickly filling a gap left by the demise of Royal Olympic Cruises.

The *Perla* (built in 1968; 780 passengers; 16,710 GRTs) will be joined in 2006 by the *Serenade* (built 1967; 672 passengers, 14,173 GRTs). Think of the Louis experience this way: "Three-star ships, four-star service, five-star destinations." Louis's fleet consists of older, more classic-style vessels. It charters several of them to European cruise lines and then operates the rest out of Cyprus, Piraeus, Genoa, and Marseille. The ships aren't as flashy or as new as the ones used by the major U.S.-based cruise lines, so you won't find state-of-the art amenities, balconies, and multiple dining venues onboard Louis.

If, however, you're looking for a Greek experience both on the ship and off, you're in the right place. Few other cruise lines advertise that its ships' musicians play the *bouzouki,* a Greek instrument that looks like a guitar. Although Louis Hellenic is designed, to a degree, to appeal to an American market, Greek officers and an international group of passengers contribute to the European flavor onboard. The line also attracted former crew and ground operators from Royal Olympic. The itineraries are extremely port intensive, and the ships will sometimes visit more than one island in a day—which is why *Perla* makes four calls on a 3-day cruise.

Louis Hellenic is the only cruise line to offer 3-, 4- and 7-day itineraries in Greece, which means you can package a shorter cruise with a land vacation, or change to a higher grade: Cruise to Mykonos, stay there for a few days, and then pick up the next Louis sailing. Or cruise out of Athens to Santorini, disembark, and fly back at a later date.

With the formation of Louis Hellenic, the line has been making a bigger push into the U.S. market than ever before, but its strategy here is to sell through tour operators. It currently does not deal directly with individual passengers or with travel agents—although agents can work through tour operators. Many of the tour operators who specialize in or sell Greece vacations now use Louis in lieu of Royal Olympic.

ITINERARY & RATES

PERLA   **Three-day Athens round-trip** cruises call at Mykonos, Rhodes, Patmos, and Kusadasi. Fridays, March 10 through November 10. **Rates:** from319€ to 396€ ($415–$515), depending on the season. **Four-day Athens round-trip** cruises call at Mykonos, Kusadasi (Turkey), Patmos, Rhodes, Iraklion, and Santorini. Mondays from March 13 through November 13. **Rates:** from 492€ to 611€ ($640–$795).

SERENADE   **Seven-day Athens round-trip** cruises call at Istanbul (Turkey), Mykonos, Patmos, Rhodes, Iraklion, and Santorini. Fridays from April 7 through October 27. **Rates:** from 818€ to 968€ ($1,065–$1,260).

MSC CRUISES

6750 N. Andrews Ave., Fort Lauderdale, FL 33309. ✆ **800/666-9333.** www.msccruises.com.

This Swiss/Italian line, a subsidiary of shipping giant Mediterranean Shipping Co., offers "classic Italian cruising" on a combination of older ships that aren't the fanciest afloat but do offer good value for your money, as well as an increasing roster of newer ships, including some of the vessels that the line purchased from now-defunct Festival Cruises. The line has been growing at a rapid pace with an eye to becoming a major player in the U.S. market. This year MSC brings on yet another new ship, the *Musica* (built in 2006; 2,550 passengers; 89,000 GRTs), which will be the lines' largest to date. In addition to one 12-day cruise that calls in several Greek ports, *Musica* will call at Katakolon on its 7-day itineraries.

Most of the vessels are midsize and have been updated with comfortable, modern decor. The newest ships are more sophisticated than splashy.

The *Armonia* (built in 2001; 1,500 passengers; 58,600 GRTs) is indicative of most of MSC's current fleet. The ships aren't filled with balconies or alternative restaurants, but they are simply and elegantly decorated and have a lot of spacious public rooms for a ship of this size. The *Melody* (built in 1982; 1,250 passengers; 35,143 GRTs) is the largest of MSC Cruises' older fleet. The layout might be considered unusual by some—a case in point is the Mercury Theater, which is in the center of the ship and surrounded by cabins—but it has a good amount of deck space, including a dedicated kids' pool.

Without flashy attributes to draw passengers to their cruises, MSC has been focusing attention on its service and playing up its Italian ambience, as well as trying to "Americanize" the trips. One example: The dining staff is taught to ask Americans if they want coffee at the close of their meals. Still, most passengers, especially during the Europe-based cruises, will be European. You can expect about 20% of the passengers onboard to be North American. Itineraries are port-intensive, and the on-board experience friendly and fun.

ITINERARY & RATES

ARMONIA **Seven-day round-trip Venice** cruise calls at Bari (Italy), Santorini, Mykonos, Athens, Corfu, and Dubrovnik (Croatia). Sundays May 21 through October 22. **Rates:** from 883€ ($1,150). **Eleven-day round-trip Venice** calls at Split (Croatia), Corfu, Athens, Port Said (Egypt), Limassol (Cyprus), Rhodes, Kotor (Yugoslavia). October 29. **Rates:** from 1,229€ ($1,600).

MELODY **Eleven-day round-trip Genoa** cruise calls at Civitavecchia and Messina (Italy), Athens, Rhodes, Limassol (Cyprus), Iraklion, and Naples (Italy). March 22. **Rates:** from 1,137€ ($1,480). **Ten-day round-trip Genoa** cruise calls at Gabes (Tunisia), Tripoli (Libya), Benghazi (Libya), Santorini, Athens, Salerno and Civitavecchia (Italy). April 25. Rates: from 807€ ($1,050). **Eleven-day round-trip Genoa** cruise calls at Naples and Catania (Italy), Istanbul, Yalta (Ukraine), Athens, Argostoli, Leghorn (Italy). May 5, September 9, October 1. **Rates:** from 1,056€ ($1,375).

MUSICA **Eleven-day round-trip Venice-to-Genoa** cruise calls at Split (Croatia), Athens, Rhodes, Iraklion, Tunis (Tunisia), Palma (Majorca), Barcelona (Spain), and Marseille (France). October 28. **Rates:** from 1,268€ ($1,650).

NORWEGIAN CRUISE LINE

7665 Corporate Center Dr., Miami, FL 33126. © (800) 327-7030. www.ncl.com.

Most mega-cruise lines operate with two dinner seatings at set times each night. Not so Norwegian Cruise Line: This quasi-maverick company pushed the envelope a few years ago with a concept called Freestyle Dining. Eat in a different restaurant every night (or the same one; it's up to you) at whatever time you get hungry. Plus, NCL doesn't "do" formal nights, so you can dress casually every night—unless you're really dying to wear a tux (in which case, go right ahead). Its new ships were built for Freestyle Dining, which means they have nine or ten different eateries onboard. NCL packs in all the other cruise-y diversions, too: Big spas, swimming pools, balcony cabins, theater, casino. Its newest ship, *Norwegian Jewel* (built in 2005; 2,376 passengers; 92,000 GRTs), has Japanese and Chinese restaurants, a steakhouse, and a tapas bar, among others. *Jewel* will sail NCL's Europe program, which includes a handful of Greek Isles cruises.

Just a few years ago, the NCL fleet primarily consisted of mid-size vessels, but the line has been undergoing a transformation in recent years. The goal is to retire its older ships, and the line is bringing in a new ship each year. The line's newest ship, *Norwegian Jewel* (built in 2005; 2,376 passengers), will sail NCL's Europe program in 2006, and it's as modern as they come. The ship has Chinese and Japanese restaurants, a steakhouse, and a tapas bar, among others. One bar has three private karaoke rooms, each decorated in a different color and style.

And unlike its shiny white brethren, NCL has taken to painting its ships' hulls with images that match the ships' names. Jewel is no exception: Pictures of colorful jewels adorn the boat's exterior.

ITINERARY & RATES

NORWEGIAN JEWEL   **Twelve-day Istanbul-to-Athens** cruise calls at Izmir (Turkey), Mykonos, Santorini, Iraklion, Alexandria (Egypt), Corfu, Katakolon. September 15. Rates: from 1,777€ ($2,313). **Twelve-day Athens-to-Istanbul** cruise calls at Katakolon, Corfu, Alexandria (Egypt), Iraklion, Santorini, Mykonos, Izmir (Turkey). September 27. Rates: 1,739€ ($2,263).

OCEANIA CRUISES

8120 NW 53rd St., Miami, FL 33166. (C) **800/531-5658.** www.oceaniacruises.com.

This cruise line has grown quickly since its 2003 debut. It now boasts three ships, and there's talk about bringing on a fourth. The vessels, all from the former Renaissance Cruises fleet, are identical in layout, and their sizes, at 680 passengers each, make them small, cozy, and intimate, but able to stock a lot of amenities like multiple restaurants and big spas. Oceania straddles the line between the small luxury players and the larger though less pricey premium cruise lines. It tries to offer a reasonably priced yet intimate, casual, upscale experience.

Regatta, Insignia, and *Nautica* (built 1998–2000; 680 passengers; 30,277 GRTs) each boast a comfortable, cozy ambience. The emphasis is on casual, so you won't need to dress up (or even bring a tie or fancy dress). The cabins are spacious, and many of the outside ones have nice-size balconies. Public rooms, too, are of the big-but-not-too-big mold, and there are nice touches throughout the ships like teak decks and DVD players in the cabins. Two restaurants, the Polo steakhouse and Toscana Italian trattoria, are fine complements to the main restaurant and very much in demand. At the buffet restaurant you can dine alfresco and take advantage of great aft views.

ITINERARY & RATES

INSIGNIA   **Ten-day Rome-to-Athens** cruise calls at Florence, Positano, Sorrento, Taormina (Italy), Valletta (Malta), Santorini, Rhodes, Delos, and Mykonos. April 21. **Rates:** from 1,884€ ($2,449). **Ten-day Athens-to-Rome** cruise calls at Delos, Mykonos, Rhodes, Santorini, Valletta (Malta), Taormina, Sorrento, Positano, Florence (Italy). May 1, September 20. **Rates:** from 1,968€ to 2,384€ ($2,559–$3,099). **Ten-day Rome-to-Athens** cruise calls at Florence, Positano, Sorrento, Taormina (Italy), Valletta (Malta), Santorini, Rhodes, Delos, and Mykonos. September 30. **Rates:** from 2,384€ ($3,099).

NAUTICA   **Ten-day Athens-to-Rome** cruise calls at Delos, Mykonos, Rhodes, Santorini, Valletta (Malta), Taormina, Sorrento, Positano, and Florence (Italy). May 29.

Rates: from 1,968€ ($2,599). **Twelve-day Athens-to-Istanbul** cruise calls at Dubrovnik (Croatia), Corfu, Katakolon, Santorini, Delos, Mykonos, Rhodes, and Kusadasi (Turkey). May 5, August 21. **Rates:** from 2,227€ ($2,895). **Twelve-day Istanbul-to-Athens** cruise calls at Kusadasi (Turkey), Rhodes, Delos, Mykonos, Santorini, Katakolon, Corfu, Dubrovnik (Croatia). May 17, June 20, September 2. **Rates:** from 2,227€ ($2,895). **Twelve-day Rome-to-Istanbul** cruise calls at Florence (Italy), Bonifacio (Corsica), Positano (Italy), Athens, Delos, Mykonos, Santorini, Rhodes, and Kusadasi (Turkey). June 8. **Rates:** from 2,384€ ($3,099). **Twelve-day Athens-to-Istanbul** cruise calls at Santorini, Kusadasi (Turkey), Yalta (Ukraine), Sochi, Sevastopol (Russia), Odessa (Ukraine), Constanta (Romania), and Nessebur (Bulgaria). July 2 and September 14. **Rates:** from 2,538€ ($3,299). **Fourteen-day Istanbul-to-Venice** cruise calls at Kusadasi (Turkey), Rhodes, Delos, Mykonos, Santorini, Athens, Positano, Taormina (Italy), Kotor (Yugoslavia), and Dubrovnik (Croatia). July 14, September 26. **Rates:** from 2,999€ ($3,899). **Fourteen-day Venice-to-Istanbul** cruise calls at Dubrovnik (Croatia), Kotor (Yugoslavia), Taormina, Sorrento (Italy), Athens, Santorini, Delos, Mykonos, Rhodes, and Kusadasi (Turkey). October 10. **Rates:** from 2,768€ ($3,599).

REGATTA **Ten-day Athens-to-Istanbul** cruise calls at Dubrovnik (Croatia), Corfu, Katakolon, Santorini, Delos, Mykonos, Rhodes, and Kusadasi (Turkey). April 13. **Rates:** from 1,884€ ($2,449). **Fourteen-day Istanbul-to-Venice** cruise calls at Kusadasi (Turkey), Rhodes, Delos, Mykonos, Santorini, Athens, Positano, Taormina (Italy), Kotor (Yugoslavia), and Dubrovnik (Croatia). April 23. **Rates:** from 1,968€ ($2,559).

PRINCESS CRUISES
24844 Ave. Rockefeller, Santa Clarita, CA 91355. ✆ 800/PRINCESS. www.princess.com.

Premium U.S. operator Princess hasn't completely shed its "Love Boat" past. Captain Stubing still makes appearances on behalf of the line now and then, but it's grown up into a multi-destination, multi-megaship line that blends California-style casual with elegance and sophistication. The line, which became part of the Carnival Corp. family in 2003 and is now a sister line to Carnival Cruise Lines, Holland America, Costa, and others, has grown quickly: It took on three ships within a 4-month period in 2004, and in 2006 it will add its second 3,100-passenger vessel, *Crown Princess.*

The line's Grand-class ships, which are the inspiration for *Crown Princess* and her sisters, are fixtures in Europe during the summers. *Star Princess* (built in 2002; 2,600 passengers; 109,000 GRTs) sails in northern Europe and the Baltic region, but both *Grand Princess* (built in 1998; 2,600 passengers; 109,000 GRTs) and *Golden Princess* (built in 2001; 2,600 passengers; 109,000 GRTs) will ply Mediterranean and Greek waters. In 2006, Princess will offer an expanded Mediterranean season with a nearly 25% capacity increase, including four additional sailings of the line's Greek islands cruises.

All of these ships are recognizable because the stern (the rear of the ship) is straight up and down, and a horizontal bar stretches across the top, like a giant cruise ship sports-car spoiler. The bar is actually where Princess's Skywalker Nightclub is located. It's the highest perch on the ship, affording views all around (and down!). The Grand-class ships have other features—as well they should, since they'll be the largest cruise ships in Greece in 2006. (They once were the largest cruise ships in the world.) Want balconies? At least 710 cabins have them. You can choose between eating at a fixed time each night a la traditional cruise-ship dining, or dining at a different time and table every night. Throw in a plethora of show lounges, bars, and pools, and you've got ships that can keep you busy for a week, never mind the destination.

ITINERARIES & RATES

GRAND PRINCESS   **Twelve-day Rome-to-Venice** cruise calls at Naples (Italy), Santorini, Rhodes, Kusadasi (Turkey), Mykonos, Athens, Katakolon, Corfu, and Dubrovnik (Croatia). May 4. **Twelve-day Venice-to-Rome** cruise calls at Venice (Italy), Dubrovnik (Croatia), Corfu, Katakolon, Athens, Mykonos, Kusadasi (Turkey), Rhodes, Santorini, Naples (Italy). June 3, August 20. **Twelve-day Rome-to-Venice** cruise calls at Monte Carlo (Monaco), Florence and Naples (Italy), Santorini, Kusadasi (Turkey), Mykonos, Athens, Katakolon, Corfu, and Venice (Italy). July 15, September 1. **Twelve-day Barcelona-to-Venice** cruise calls at Marseille (France), Rome, Naples (Italy), Mykonos, Istanbul, Kusadasi (Turkey), and Athens. May 16 and 28, June 9 and 21, July 27, August 8, September 13 and 25, October 7. **Rates** for the above cruises start at 2,200€ ($2,860).

GOLDEN PRINCESS   **Twelve-day Venice-to-Rome** cruise calls at Venice (Italy), Dubrovnik (Croatia), Corfu, Katakolon, Athens, Mykonos, Kusadasi (Turkey), Rhodes, Santorini, and Naples (Italy). May 22, June 15, October 5 and 29. **Twelve-day Rome-to-Venice** cruise calls at Monte Carlo (Monaco), Florence and Naples (Italy), Santorini, Kusadasi (Turkey), Mykonos, Athens, Katakolon, Corfu, and Venice (Italy). June 3, September 23, October 17. **Twelve-day round-trip Rome** cruise calls at Naples, Athens, Kusadasi, Istanbul (Turkey), Mykonos, Port Said (Egypt), and Alexandria (Egypt). November 10. **Rates** for the above cruises start at 2,200€ ($2,860).

RADISSON SEVEN SEAS CRUISES

600 Corporate Dr., Suite 410, Fort Lauderdale, FL 33334. ✆ 800/477-7500. www.rssc.com.

In 1992, Radisson Hotels Worldwide decided to translate its hospitality experience to the cruise industry, offering to manage and market upscale ships for their international owners (though the "Radisson" is gradually being phased out in favor of just "Seven Seas Cruises"). The line has gradually downsized over the past few years—2006 is the last year it will manage *Paul Gauguin* in the Tahitian Islands, and in 2005 it lost its charter for *Radisson Diamond*—but it's left with a core fleet of three similar, small-to-midsize vessels: *Seven Seas Voyager* (built in 2003; 700 passengers; 50,000 GRTs), *Seven Seas Mariner* (built in 2001; 700 passengers; 50,000 GRTs), and *Seven Seas Navigator* (built in 1999; 490 passengers; 33,000 GRTs). The ships all offer itineraries geared toward affluent travelers, with excellent cuisine in an open-seating arrangement, service, and many amenities. A no-tipping policy is employed aboard all their ships.

The line assumes that most of its passengers want to entertain themselves, so organized activities are limited, though they do include lectures by well-known authors, producers, and oceanographers, among others. On-board games and dance lessons are offered.

Seven Seas Voyager is an all-suite, all-balcony luxury vessel. It's both larger and faster than the earlier Radisson ships. Decor is muted and sophisticated. The ship's size means it's easy to get around to the different restaurants and bars. The four restaurants onboard (five if you count the Pool Grill) include a dinner theater with music where the chefs are onstage, and Signatures, operated by Le Cordon Bleu of Paris. Another draw is the cabin configurations: walk-in closets, big bathrooms, lots of space to spread out, and a balcony with every cabin.

Seven Seas Navigator will be sailing to Greece after spending its last three summers cruising in Bermuda. *Navigator* is a smaller, cozier sister to *Voyager*. All of its cabins have ocean views, and 90% of them have balconies. As on *Voyager,* the word on interior design is soft and neutral tones. Tans, reds, and soft blues make up the palette.

ITINERARIES & RATES

SEVEN SEAS NAVIGATOR   **Seven-day Venice-to-Piraeus** cruise calls at Venice (Italy), Dubrovnik (Croatia), Katakolon, Santorini, Mykonos, and Kusadasi (Turkey). August 26. **Rates:** from 3,382€ ($4,396). **Seven-day Piraeus-to-Istanbul** cruise calls at Nafplion, Santorini, Kusadasi (Turkey), Rhodes, Mykonos, and Istanbul. September 2. **Rates:** from 3,382€ ($4,396). **Seven-day Istanbul-to-Piraeus** calls at Istanbul, Mykonos, Rhodes, Kusadasi (Turkey), Santorini, and Nafplion. September 9. **Rates:** from 3,382€ ($4,396). **Seven-day Piraeus-to-Venice** voyage calls at Mykonos, Santorini, Katakolon, Dubrovnik (Croatia), and Venice (Italy). September 16. **Rates:** from 3,382€ ($4,396). **Seven-day voyage from Venice to Piraeus** calls at Venice (Italy), Dubrovnik (Croatia), Katakolon, Santorini, Mykonos, and Kusadasi. October 7. **Rates:** from 3,170€ ($4,121). **Seven-day Piraeus-to-Rome** cruise calls at Santorini, Kusadasi (Turkey), Rhodes, Taormina, and Sorrento (Italy). October 14. **Rates:** from 3,170€ ($4,121). All rates include economy air.

SEVEN SEAS VOYAGER   **Seven-day Rome-to-Piraeus** voyage calls at Sorrento and Taormina (Italy), Rhodes, Kusadasi (Turkey), and Santorini. September 23. **Rates:** from 4,058€ ($5,276), including economy air.

ROYAL CARIBBEAN INTERNATIONAL

1050 Caribbean Way, Miami, FL 33132. (C) **866/562-7625.** www.royalcaribbean.com.

Heard about those megaships carrying the rock-climbing walls? Those are the vessels of Royal Caribbean International, which has made its unusual on-board features—ice-skating rinks and self-leveling billiards tables, for example—a benchmark for other companies in the cruise-vacation business. Royal Caribbean sells a big-ship, American-style experience that's reasonably priced and designed to please everyone—except, perhaps, those turned off by crowds. And they do it very well: The line's ships are consistent and well run.

The line is known for offering a wealth of on-board activities, although in Europe the ports are more the focus than in, say, the Caribbean.

The company's vessel in Greece, *Brilliance of the Seas* (built in 2002; 2,100 passengers; 90,090 GRTs), is, by Royal Caribbean International standards, on the diminutive side. The line's Voyager-class ships, for instance, are 138,000 GRTs and hold a staggering 3,114 passengers. For their part, *Brilliance of the Seas,* and her slightly older sister ship, *Radiance of the Seas,* come with a whole set of cruise industry firsts: General Electric gas turbine engines, which protect the environment; a pair of self-leveling pool tables in the Bombay Billiards Club, and the extensive use of glass—nearly 1.2 hectares (3 acres) of exterior glass, in fact. More than 70% of the ships outside staterooms have balconies.

Splendour of the Seas (built in 1996; 1,804 passengers; 70,000 GRTs) has an indoor-outdoor pool in its Solarium, plus an 18-hole miniature golf course and one of the line's ubiquitous rock-climbing walls.

ITINERARIES & RATES

BRILLIANCE OF THE SEAS **Twelve-day round-trip Barcelona** cruise calls at Villefranche (France), Livorno (Italy), Mykonos, Kusadasi (Turkey), Santorini, Athens, and Naples (Italy). May 11, June 4 and 28, July 22, August 15. **Rates:** from 1,382€ ($1,799). **Twelve-day Barcelona-to-Athens** cruise calls at Villefranche (France); Livorno, Rome, Naples, and Venice (Italy); Dubrovnik (Croatia); Santorini; and Kusadasi (Turkey). October 2. **Rates:** from 1,382€ ($1,799). **Fourteen-day Athens-to-Barcelona** cruise calls at Santorini, Kusadasi (Turkey), Mykonos, Dubrovnik (Croatia), Venice, Naples, Rome, and Livorno (Italy). October 14. **Rates:** from 1,461€ ($1,899).

SPLENDOUR OF THE SEAS **Seven-day round-trip Venice** cruises call at Athens, Mykonos, Dubrovnik (Croatia). May 28, June 11 and 25, July 9 and 23, August 6 and 20, September 3 and 17, October 1 and 15. **Rates:** from 692€ to 922€ ($899–$1,199). **Seven-day round-trip Venice** cruises call at Athens, Kusadasi (Turkey), and Corfu. May 21; June 4; July 2, 18, and 30; August 13 and 27; September 10 and 24; October 8 and 22. **Rates:** from 615€ to 730€ ($799–$949).

SEABOURN CRUISE LINE

6100 Blue Lagoon Dr., Suite 400, Miami, FL 33126. ✆ 800/929-9391. www.seabourn.com.

Seabourn excels in many areas, including food, service, itineraries, and its refined environment. That said, the Seabourn cruise experience is not for everyone. These cruises are pricey, and the customers who can afford them are often very discriminating, though the atmosphere is probably a tad more laid-back and casual than it used to be. Still, these ships aren't for the Carnival crowd (even though Carnival Corporation owns the line).

Discretion is key on these ships, and the sophisticated environment and decor prove it. Like the passengers, the staff and crew are well mannered. Although the ambience aboard the ships can be casual during the day, it becomes decidedly more formal in the evening. Men wear dinner jackets, and everyone dresses up for formal nights.

The line enhances its cruises with guest lecturers, celebrities such as Walter Cronkite or Art Linkletter. Nighttime entertainment is low-key, though cabaret nights with themes like 1950s rock 'n' roll can get the audience going.

All three ships, *Seabourn Spirit* (built in 1989; 204 passengers; 10,000 GRTs), *Seabourn Legend* (built in 1992; 204 passengers; 10,000 GRTs), and *Seabourn Pride* (built in 1988; 204 passengers; 10,000 GRTs) will stop in Greece this summer, although *Spirit* will be there the most.

All cabins on the *Seabourn Spirit* and *Seabourn Pride* are outside suites, and each has a 1.5m-wide (5-ft.) picture window. Each cabin's fully stocked bar is complimentary. Owner's suites are very plush and offer private verandas; the ships were built before private balconies were a must-have amenity, but many cabins do have French balconies with doors you can open to let in the ocean breezes (but which are too narrow to sit on).

The ships come equipped with a floating marina that, when lowered, provides a teak-decked platform for watersports. (Sunfish, kayaks, snorkeling gear, high-speed banana boats, and water skis are available for passenger use.) There's also a mesh net that becomes a saltwater swimming pool.

ITINERARIES & RATES

SEABOURN SPIRIT   Twelve-day Alexandria (Egypt)-to–Rome cruise calls at Rhodes, Bodrum, and Kusadasi (Turkey); Mykonos, Athens, and Santorini; Messina (Taormina), Sicily, Amalfi, and Capri (Italy). May 1. **Rates:** from 5,258€ to 15,212€ ($6,835–$19,776). **Seven-day Rome-to-Athens** cruise calls at Sorrento and Taormina (Italy), Katakolon, Itea, and Nafplion. May 13, June 10, October 7. **Rates:** from 3,374€ ($4,386). **Seven-day Athens-to-Istanbul** cruise calls at Mylos, Mykonos, Patmos, Bodrum, and Kusadasi (Turkey). May 20, June 17, October 14. **Rates:** from 3,374€ ($4,386). **Seven-day Istanbul-to-Venice** cruise calls at Nafplion, Santorini, Corinth Canal, Itea, Corfu, and Korcula (Croatia). May 27. **Rates:** from 3,374€ ($4,386). **Seven-day Istanbul-to-Venice** cruise calls at Nafplion, Santorini, Corinth Canal, Itea, Corfu, and Korcula (Croatia). June 24, August 26, September 23. **Rates:** from 3,615€ ($4,699). **Seven-day Rome-to-Athens** cruise calls at Sorrento, Taormina (Italy), Katakolon, Itea, and Nafplion. July 8, August 12, September 9. **Rates:** from 3,615€ ($4,699). **Seven-day Athens-to-Istanbul** cruise calls at Mylos, Mykonos, Patmos, Bodrum, and Kusadasi (Turkey). July 15, August 19, September 16. **Rates:** from 3,615€ ($4,699). **Seven-day Istanbul-to-Piraeus** cruise calls at Canakkale, Dikili, Kusadasi (Turkey), Mykonos, Mylos, and Nafplion. October 21. **Rates:** from 3,075€ ($3,998). **Seven-day Piraeus-to-Alexandria** cruise calls at Santorini, Aghios Nikolaos, Rhodes, Antalya (Turkey), and Paphos (Cyprus). October 28. **Rates:** from 3,075€ ($3,998). **Fourteen-day Istanbul-to-Venice** cruise calls at Yalta (Ukraine), Sevastopol (Russia), Odessa (Ukraine), Nesebur (Bulgaria), and Istanbul (Turkey), before calling at Nafplion, Santorini, Corinth Canal, Itea, Corfu, and Korcula (Croatia). July 22. **Rates:** from 6,153€ ($7,999).

SEABOURN PRIDE   **Fourteen-day Monte Carlo-to-Istanbul** cruise calls at Ajaccio (Corsica), Valletta, Gozo (Malta), Tripoli (Libya), Aghios Nikolaos, Rhodes, Santorini, and Kusadasi (Turkey). April 18. **Rates:** from 5,332€ ($6,932). **Eighteen-day Istanbul-to-Lisbon (Portugal)** cruise calls at Athens, Delphi, Corinth Canal, Sarande (Albania), Rovinj (Croatia), Venice, Kefalonia, and Palmero (Italy), and Palma de Mallorca (Spain). May 2. **Rates:** from 6,115€ ($7,949).

SEABOURN LEGEND   **Fourteen-day round-trip Monte Carlo** calls at Sousse (Tunisia), Valletta, Gozo (Malta), Santorini, Mylos, Corinth Canal, Delphi, Taormina, Amalfi (Italy), and Porto Azzuro (Elba). July 22. **Rates:** from 6,153€ ($7,999).

SEADREAM YACHT CLUB

2601 S. Bayshore Dr., Penthouse 1B, Coconut Grove, FL 33133. ℂ 800/707-4911. www.seadreamyachtclub.com.

The owner and the operator of SeaDream Yacht Club both have luxury-line pedigrees: Seabourn Cruise Line founder Atle Brynestad and former Seabourn president Larry Pimentel. For the past 5 years, the two have been carrying on the Seabourn tradition of luxury and elegance, albeit on a smaller, more casual yachtlike scale. SeaDream in 2001 purchased the *Sea Goddess I* and *Sea Goddess II* from Seabourn, and after renovations renamed them **SeaDream I** and **SeaDream II** (built 1984; 116 passengers; 4,260 GRTs). The company defines itself not as a cruise line but an ultra-luxury yacht company whose vessels journey to smaller, less charted destinations. Guests are offered an unstructured, casually elegant vacation with no shortage of fun diversions. Toys carried aboard include jet skis and mountain bikes. You can choose to dine outdoors or indoors; there are enough tables to accommodate all the passengers in one outdoor lunch seating. And although none of the cabins have private balconies, Pimentel often urges guests to treat the teak decks as one large veranda where you can sprawl on bed-sized Balinese loungers and congregate for a drink at the Top of the Yacht Bar.

ITINERARIES & RATES

SEADREAM I **Seven-day Venice-to-Athens** voyage visits Hvar, Dubrovnik (Croatia), Corfu, Itea, Mykonos, and Santorini. July 1. **Seven-day Istanbul-to-Athens** cruise calls at Canakkale, Kusadasi (Turkey), Patmos, Santorini, Mykonos, and Hydra. July 15. **Seven-day Dubrovnik-to-Athens** cruise calls at Corfu, Galaxidi, Nafplion, Mykonos, Iraklion, and Santorini. August 5. **Seven-day Athens-to-Istanbul** cruise calls at Hydra, Mykonos, Santorini, Patmos, Kusadasi, and Canakkale (Turkey). August 19. **Seven-day Athens-to-Dubrovnik** voyage calls at Mykonos, Corinth Canal, Zakintos, Katakolon, Corfu, and Korcula (Croatia). August 26. **Seven-day Dubrovnik-to-Athens** cruise visits Korcula (Croatia), Corfu, Katakolon, Zakintos, Corinth Canal, and Mykonos. September 23. **Seven-day Athens-to-Antalya (Turkey)** voyage visits Mykonos, Kusadasi, Bodrum (Turkey), Santorini, Iraklion, and Rhodes. September 30. **Rates:** from 2,999€ to 3,076€ ($3,899–$3,999).

SEADREAM II **Seven-day Venice-to-Athens** cruise calls at Hvar, Dubrovnik (Croatia), Corfu, Itea, Mykonos, and Santorini. June 10. **Seven-day Athens-to-Rome** cruise calls at Hydra, Itea, Fiskardo, Taormina, Sorrento, and Capri (Italy). June 17, September 9. **Seven-day Rome-to-Athens** voyage calls at Capri, Sorrento, Taormina (Italy), Katakolon, and Galaxidi. July 15, September 2. **Rates:** for the cruises above from 2,999€ ($3,899). **Twelve-day Athens-to-Genoa** cruise to Kusadasi, Bodrum (Turkey), Santorini, Mykonos, and Corfu; and to Messina, Lipari, Capri, Porto Ercole, and Portofino (Italy). July 22. **Rates:** from 3,922€ ($5,099).

SILVERSEA CRUISES

110 E. Broward Blvd., Fort Lauderdale, FL 33301. ℂ 800/722-9055. www.silversea.com.

The luxurious sister ships *Silver Cloud* and *Silver Wind* (both built in 1994; 296 passengers; 16,800 GRTs), *Silver Shadow* (built in 2000; 388 passengers; 28,250 GRTs), and *Silver Whisper* (built in 2001, 382 passengers; 28,258 GRTs) carry their guests in true splendor and elegance. Passengers are generally experienced cruisers, not necessarily American, and are well traveled. Most are in the over-50 group. These ships are not for kids.

On *Silver Cloud* and *Silver Wind,* accommodations are outside suites with writing tables, sofas, walk-in closets, marble bathrooms, and all the amenities you'd expect of a top-of-the-line ship. Throughout, both vessels allot more space to each passenger than most other ships. There's also more crew, with the large staff at your service, ready to cater to your every desire on a 24-hour basis.

The newer *Silver Shadow* and *Silver Whisper* carry on the fine tradition in a slightly larger format. The all-suite vessels also feature verandas, poolside dining venues, a larger spa facility, a computer center, a cigar lounge designed by noted cigar purveyor Davidoff, and other niceties. The line emphasizes its Italian heritage through a brand campaign both on and off the ship.

Activities include bridge and other games, aerobics, dance lessons, wine tastings, and lectures (including a *National Geographic Traveler* series), as well as such cruise staples as bingo and quiz shows. Nighttime entertainment venues include showrooms for resident musicians and local talent, a piano bar, a small casino, and rooms for dancing.

The ships offer five-star cuisine; guests can dine when, where, and with whom they choose. In the evening, the elegant buffet restaurant is open for a single-seating dinner with a fixed menu whose theme depends on the day and ranges from Japanese to seafood to Provençal.

ITINERARIES & RATES

SILVER WIND **Nine-day Port Said (Egypt)-to-Athens** voyage calls at Beirut (Lebanon), Tartus (Syria), Rhodes, Kusadasi (Turkey), and Nafplion. February 28. **Rates:** from 4,073€ ($5,295). **Nine-day Istanbul-to-Venice** voyage calls at Dikili (Turkey), Volos, Delos, Mykonos, Santorini, Dubrovnik, Hvar (Croatia), and Rovinjo (Croatia). July 23. **Rates:** from 5,458€ ($7,095). **Nine-day Istanbul-to-Athens** cruise calls at Nessebur (Bulgaria), Constanta (Romania), Odessa (Ukraine), Sebastopol (Russia), Yalta (Ukraine), Kusadasi (Turkey), Santorini, and Athens. October 1. **Rates:** from 4,458€ ($5,795). **Seven-day Athens-to-Rome** cruise calls at Santorini, Drnah (Libya), Tripoli (Libya), Valletta (Malta), and Amalfi (Italy). October 10. **Rates:** from 3,535€ ($4,595).

SILVER WHISPER **Seven-day Rome-to-Venice** cruise calls at Taormina (Italy), Kefalonia, Corfu, Dubrovnik (Croatia), and Venice (Italy). June 5. **Rates:** from 3,996€ ($5,195). **Seven-day Venice-to-Athens** voyage calls at Venice (Italy), Split (Croatia), Kotor (Montenegro), Santorini, and Kusadasi (Turkey). June 13. **Rates:** from 3,996€ ($5,195). **Seven-day Athens-to-Venice** voyage calls at Kusadasi (Turkey), Santorini, Kotor (Montenegro), Split (Croatia), and Venice (Italy). June 19. **Rates:** from 3,996€ ($5,195).

STAR CLIPPERS

4101 Salzedo St., Coral Gables, FL 33146. ℂ 800/442-0551. www.starclippers.com.

Star Flyer (built in 1991; 170 passengers; 3,025 GRTs), the vessel this three-ship line operates in Greece, is a replica of the big 19th-century clipper sailing ships (or barkentines) that once circled the globe. Its tall square rigs carry enormous sails and are glorious to look at, and a particular thrill for history buffs.

And on this ship, the sails are more than window dressing. The *Star Flyer* was constructed using original drawings and specifications of a leading 19th-century naval architect, but updated with modern touches so that today it is among the tallest and fastest clipper ships ever built—it has reached speeds of more than 19 knots.

The atmosphere onboard is akin to being on a private yacht rather than a mainstream cruise ship. It's casual in an L.L. Bean sort of way, and friendly. Passengers generally fall into the 30-to-60 age range.

Cabins are pleasant and decorated with wood accents. There is one owner's suite. The public rooms include a writing room, an open-seating dining room, and an Edwardian-style library with a Belle Epoque fireplace and bookshelf-lined walls. There are two swimming pools.

Local entertainment is sometimes brought aboard, and a resident pianist and a makeshift disco offer music in the Tropical Bar. Movies are shown in passenger cabins.

Activities on the ship tend toward the nautical, such as visiting the bridge, observing the crew handle the sails, and participating in knot-tying classes.

It should be noted that despite stabilizers, movement on this vessel may be troublesome to travelers who get seasick.

ITINERARIES & RATES

STAR FLYER   **Five-day round-trip Athens** cruise calls at Delos, Mykonos, Santorini, Bodrum (Turkey), and Sifnos. May 1, October 7. **Rates:** from 927€ to 3,530€ ($1,205–$2,715). **Seven-day round-trip Athens** cruise calls at Rhodes, Bodrum and Dalyan River (Turkey), Santorini, and Hydra. May 6 and 20; June 17; July 1, 15, and 29; August 12 and 26; September 23. **Rates:** from 1,442€ to 3,073€ ($1,875–$3,995). **Seven-day round-trip Athens** voyage calls at Kusadasi (Turkey), Samos, Delos, Mykonos, and Sifnos. May 13; June 10 and 24; July 8 and 22; August 5 and 19; September 2 and 30. **Rates:** from 1,442€ to 3,073€ ($1,875–$3,995) per person. **Seven-day Athens-to-Istanbul** cruise calls at Delos, Mykonos, Patmos, Bodrum, Kusadasi, and Dikili (Turkey). May 27, September 9. **Rates:** from 1,442€ to 3,073€ ($1,875–$3,995). **Seven-day Istanbul-to-Athens** cruise calls at Dikili, Kusadasi, Bodrum (Turkey), Patmos, Delos, and Mykonos. June 3, September 16. **Rates:** from 1,442€ to 3,073€ ($1,875–$3,995.)

TRAVEL DYNAMICS INTERNATIONAL

132 E. 70th St., New York, NY 10021. ✆ 800/257-5767. www.traveldynamicsinternational.com.

This operator of small yachts offers a number of interesting itineraries that include Greek ports. The journeys, which are available mainly in late summer and fall, are tailored to be unique, visiting some of the smaller and lesser-known ports. Top-notch onboard educational programs complement the itineraries. This line won't attract the budget-minded passenger, or the folks who want to laze around. Itineraries are fast-paced and educational. Each day has several components: a museum in the morning and an archaeological site in the afternoon, for example.

Callisto (rebuilt 2000; 34 passengers; 435 GRTs) is a cozy little yacht. All the cabins have picture windows or portholes. There's a lot of blue-and-white in the design, but it's all very tasteful. The blue-and-white striped cushions on the deck chairs match the Greek flag flying from the ship.

The larger *Corinthian II* (built in 1992; 114 passengers; 4,200 GRTs) is the newest addition to Travel Dynamics' fleet. Luxe touches include marble bathrooms, minifridges, and private balconies. An outdoor bar and cafe accommodates alfresco diners. The ship also has a gym, salon, sun deck with hot tub, and Internet cafe.

ITINERARIES & RATES

CALLISTO: **Nine-day Thessaloniki-to-Zea Marina cruisetour** includes hotel stay at Thessaloniki and calls at Kavalla, Samothraki, Hios, Kusadasi (Turkey), Rhodes, Sitia, Iraklion, Monemvassia, and Leonidion. June 3, June 8, October 12, October 21. **Rates:** Start at 5,373€ ($6,995). **Nine-day roundtrip Rhodes cruisetour** includes hotel stay in Rhodes and calls at Simi; Datca, Ekincik, Kekova, and Antalya (Turkey); Kastellorizo; and Fethiye (Turkey). October 26, November 2, 9. **Rates:** Start at 4,605€ ($5,995).

CORINTHIAN II: **Ten-day roundtrip Athens** cruise calls at Canakkale (Turkey), Nafplion, Valletta (Malta), Trapani, Naples, and Messina (Italy), Corfu, Ithaca. June 4. **Rates:** Start at 5,911€ ($7,695). **Eleven-day roundtrip Athens** cruisetour calls at Thessaloniki, Kavalla, Izmir and Kusadasi (Turkey), Patmos, Rhodes, Kali Limenes, Nafplion, and includes a hotel stay in Athens. June 14. **Rates:** Start at 5,757€ ($7,495). **Eleven-day Athens-to-Anzio** cruisetour includes a hotel stay in Athens, and calls at Nafplion, Santorini, Rhodes, Iraklion, Katakolon, and Messina and Sorrento (Italy). June 20. **Rates:** Start at 5,296€ ($6,895). **Ten-day Istanbul-to-Naples** cruise calls at Canakkale (Turkey), Delos, Mykonos, Rethymnon, Preveza, Syracuse (Italy), Tunis (Tunisia), Trapani (Italy). September 7. **Rates:** Start at 5,988€ ($7,795). **Twelve-day Fiumicino-to-Thessaloniki** cruisetour includes hotel stay in Fiumicino (Italy) and calls at Trapani (Italy), Tunis (Tunisia), Porto Empedocle and Syracuse (Italy), Iraklion, Santorini, Kusadasi (Turkey), Samothraki. September 15. **Rates:** Start at 5,373€ ($6,995). **Fourteen-day Thessaloniki-to-Athens cruisetour** includes a hotel stay in Thessaloniki and calls at Canakkale, Gulluk, Antalya, Tasucu, and Iskenderun (Turkey), Alexandria and Marsa Matruh (Egypt). September 25, October 17. **Rates:** Start at 6,679€ ($8,695). **Ten–day Athens-to-Thessaloniki** cruise calls at Syracuse (Italy), Valletta (Malta), Khoms and Derna (Libya), Kali Limenes, Santorini, Litochoro. October 9. **Rates:** Start at 5,757€ ($7,495).

WINDSTAR

300 Elliott Ave. W., Seattle, WA 98119. ℭ 800/258-7245. www.windstarcruises.com.

Although they look like sailing ships of yore, *Wind Spirit* (built in 1988; 144 passengers; 5,350 GRTs) and *Wind Star* (built in 1987; 144 passengers; 5,350 GRTs) and their bigger sister *Wind Surf* (built in 2000; 308 passengers; 30,745 GRTs) are more like floating luxury resorts with the flair of sailing ships. These vessels feature top-notch service and extraordinary cuisine. Million-dollar computers operate the sails, and stabilizers allow for a smooth ride.

Windstar deploys its two smaller vessels, *Wind Spirit* and *Wind Star,* in the Greek islands. Casual, low-key elegance is the watchword. There's no set regime and no dress code above "resort casual." Most of the passengers are well heeled; the ships appeal to all ages except children. (There are no dedicated kids' facilities onboard the ships.)

None of the roomy outside cabins have balconies, but they have large portholes. The top-level owner's cabins are slightly bigger. Refurbishments completed a few years ago added flatscreen TVs and DVD players; new mattresses, bedding, carpet, and curtains to the cabins; an expanded gym; and an updated spa.

A watersports platform at the stern allows for a variety of activities when the ships are docked. Entertainment is low-key and sometimes includes local entertainers brought aboard at ports of call. Most of the on-board time revolves around the sun deck, plunge pool, and outdoor bar. The ships also have small casinos.

Holland America Line, which in turn is part of Carnival Corporation, owns Windstar.

ITINERARIES & RATES

WIND SPIRIT & WIND STAR Seven-day Athens-to-Istanbul cruises call in Mykonos, Santorini, Rhodes, Bodrum, and Kusadasi (Turkey). *Wind Spirit:* May 20; June 10 and 24; July 8 and 22; August 5 and 19; September 2, 16, and 30; October 14. *Wind Star:* May 20; June 3 and 17; July 1; September 9 and 23; October 7. **Rates:** from 2,301€ ($2,991). **Seven-day Istanbul-to-Athens** cruises call at Kusadasi (Turkey), Rhodes, Bodrum (Turkey), Santorini, and Mykonos. *Wind Spirit:* June 3 and 17; July 1; September 23; October 7 and 21. *Wind Star:* May 27; June 10 and 24; September 16 and 30; October 14. **Rates:** from 2,307€ ($2,999). **Seven-day Istanbul-to-Athens** cruise calls in Canakkale and Izmir (Turkey), Patmos, Kos, Ayios Nikolaos, and Naxos. *Wind Spirit:* July 15 and 29; August 12 and 26; September 9. *Wind Star:* July 8. **Rates:** from 2,310€ ($3,003).

8 Ships Visiting Greece on Longer Mediterranean Itineraries

The following lines and ships visit Greece as part of longer itineraries.

Celebrity Cruises   Celebrity, a decently priced yet upscale U.S. operator, offers eastern Mediterranean itineraries that, for the most part, operate on *Galaxy* (built 1996; 1,890 passengers; 77,713 GRTs). *Galaxy's* 11-day round-trip Rome cruises call at Mykonos, Rhodes, Santorini, Istanbul and Kusadasi (Turkey), Athens, and Naples (Italy). May 22; June 12; July 3 and 24; August 14; September 4 and 25. Rates from 1,038€ to 1,538€ ($1,350–$2,000). A 14-day round-trip Rome cruise calls at Mykonos, Rhodes, Santorini, Istanbul (Turkey), Constanta (Romania), Odessa (Ukraine), Kusadasi (Turkey), Athens, and Naples (Italy). October 16. Rates from 1,577€ ($2,050). *Galaxy* also makes calls in Santorini and Mykonos during a 10-day round-trip Rome cruise that's offered June 2 and 23; July 14; August 4 and 25; September 15. And *Millennium* (built in 2000; 1,950 passengers; 91,000 GRTs) operates 12-day cruises between Barcelona and Venice throughout the summer that call at Athens and Santorini.

1050 Caribbean Way, Miami, FL 33132. ℂ 800/327-6700. www.celebrity.com.

Clipper Cruise Lines   This line offers expedition-style cruising with a fleet of four small vessels. The emphasis is on education. Instead of entertainers, for example, it brings naturalists and historians onboard. It operates two cruises on its *Clipper Adventurer* (built in 1975; 122 passengers; 4,364 GRTs) that sail to Greece, Libya, and Tunisia: an 11-day Piraeus-to-Valletta (Malta) trip that departs March 31 and calls at Mykonos, Santorini, and Iraklion, as well as Cyrene, Benghazi, Al Khums, Tripoli (Libya), Tunis, and Sousse (Tunisia). The same itinerary in reverse departs April 11. *Clipper Adventurer* remains in Greece to do an 11-day Solar Eclipse cruise that will sail from Rome to Athens on March 21 and call at Naples, Palmero (Italy), Athens, Mykonos, Rhodes Iraklion, and Santorini. The ship will drop anchor between Rhodes and Iraklion to view the eclipse.

11969 Westline Industrial Dr., St. Louis, MO 63146. ℂ 800/325-0010. www.clippercruise.com.

Fred Olsen Cruise Lines   British operator Fred Olsen's *Black Watch* (built in 1972; 761 passengers; 28,492 GRTs) is scheduled to operate one 21-day cruise from Southampton (U.K.) on May 5 that includes a call in Corfu. Rates from 3,066€ ($3,985). The line is scheduled to take possession of a fourth ship, a sister ship to *Black Watch,* that will be named *Boudicca.* The vessel will operate out of Dover and Southampton, and will sail a 24-day voyage May 24 that will call at Piraeus, Mykonos, and Santorini in Greece; and at Spain, Turkey, Cyprus, Egypt, and Libya.

5412 Lyndale Ave. S., Minneapolis, MN 55419. ℂ 612/822-4640. www.fredolsencruises.com.

Holland America Line   Holland America, a premium-level line that offers traditional, elegant cruises, sails to Greece on 10-day itineraries aboard the line's newest ship, *Noordam* (built in 2006; 1,848 passengers; 85,000 GRTs). The ship will operate round-trip from Rome and call at Kerkira, Corfu, Katakolon, and Santorini, as well as at Kusadasi (Turkey), Italy, and Malta. May 3 and 11; June 20; July 10 and 30; August 19; September 8. Rates start at 1,422€ ($1,849). It also operates a handful of cruises on the *Prinsendam* (built in 1987, formerly *Seabourn Sun;* 793 passengers; 38,000 GRTs) that stop in Greece, including a 16-day cruise from Rome to Istanbul on August 30 that calls at Kerkira, Corfu, Katakolon, and Athens; and a 16-night Istanbul-to-Athens cruise on September 15 that calls at Rhodes, Iraklion, and Athens. Rates start at 1,422€ ($1,849). The *Rotterdam* (built 1997; 1,316 passengers; 59,652 GRTs), meanwhile, finishes cruises in Piraeus on its April 20, May 14, and October 10 cruises. It embarks from Piraeus on its sailings May 2 and 26, September 28, and October 22.

300 Elliott Ave. W., Seattle, WA 98119. ✆ 877/SAIL-HAL. www.hollandamerica.com.

Orient Lines   This line combines upscale cruises with land tours to create in-depth travel experiences. In 2004, the line downsized by transferring *Crown Odyssey* (built in 1988; 1,026 passengers; 34,250 GRTs) to NCL and now is only using its original ship, *Marco Polo*, formerly *Alexandr Pushkin* (built in 1965; 800 passengers; 22,080 GRTs). The ship embarks passengers on a rolling basis; that is, some climb aboard for a 10-day cruise, while others will embark and stay on for a 21-day voyage. Cruises that start May 4, September 18, and October 16 include calls at Mykonos and Athens. Cruises starting April 27, September 11, and October 9 (as well as the longest versions of the April 11 and August 31 cruises) include calls at Santorini and Athens.

7665 Corporate Center Dr., Miami, FL 33126. ✆ 800/333-7300. www.orientlines.com.

Peter Deilmann EuropAmerica Cruises   This German company, which operates river ships in Europe as well as oceangoing voyages, offers Eastern Mediterranean sailings on its elegant flagship *Deutschland* (built in 1998; 505 passengers; 22,400 GRTs). Three of its cruises embark and debark in Piraeus, but for the most part, they sail elsewhere throughout the Mediterranean: An October 4 sailing from Málaga (Spain) offers an overnight in Piraeus and a call in Iraklion (Crete); an October 17 round-trip includes an overnight in Piraeus; and an October 27 cruise departs from Piraeus.

1800 Diagonal Rd., Suite 170, Alexandria, VA 22314. ✆ 800/348-8287. www.deilmann-cruises.com.

P&O Cruises   British operator P&O stops at ports in Greece with three of its ships on long (2-week-plus) itineraries. *Aurora* (built 2000; 1,874 passengers; 76,000 GRTs) operates more extensive itineraries. The ship stops in Kefalonia, Korcula, and Corfu on 16-day cruises from Gibraltar on April 10 and May 10. A 16-day cruise from Gibraltar on August 4 calls at Corfu, Korcula, and Katakolon; and a 16-day cruise from Málaga (Spain) on October 31 calls at Athens, Dikili, Istanbul (Turkey), and Mytilene. An 18-day cruise from Málaga on November 28 calls at Rhodes, Ephesus, Athens, and Cagliari. *Oriana* (built 1995; 2,016 passengers; 69,153 GRTs) operates a 16-day cruise on July 21 and August 18 from Gibraltar that calls at Zakintos and Corfu; a 17-day cruise from Malaga October 2 calls at Kefalonia, Corfu, and Katakolon.

Richmond House, Terminus Terrace, Southampton, SO14 3PN, England. ✆ 44-845-355-5333. In the U.S., contact Princess Tours, 2815 Second Ave., Suite 400, Seattle, WA 98121-1299. ✆ 206/728-4202. www.pocruises.com.

Swan Hellenic   As mentioned above, this British firm takes smaller ships to more unusual ports of call. Shore excursions, included in the price, focus on the history and culture of the destinations. The line's sole ship is *Minerva II* (built in 2001; 684 passengers; 30,277 GRTs). A 14-day cruise on April 22 stops in Larnaca (Cyprus), Athens, Piraeus, Nafplion, Gythion, Souda Bay, Delos, Istanbul, Canakkale, Kusadasi, and Kas Tasucu (Turkey). A 14-day cruise on May 6 calls at Thessaloniki, Skopelos, Athens, Piraeus, Delos, Monemvassia, Santorini, Iraklion, Rhodes, Istanbul, Bodrum, Kusadasi, and Kos (Turkey). A 14-day cruise on June 3 stops in Istanbul (Turkey); Rhodes and Ayios Nikolaos; Catania, Rome, and Civitavecchia (Italy); Valetta and Palermo (Malta); Ajaccio (France); and Mahon (Spain). June 3. Fares include shore excursions, tips, transfers, and airfare from London.

631 Commack Rd., Commack, NY 11725. ℭ **877/219-4239**. www.swanhellenic.com.

9 Best Shore Excursions in the Ports of Call: Greece

Shore excursions are designed to help you make the most of your limited time in port by transporting you to sites of historical or cultural value, or of natural or artistic beauty. The tours are usually booked on the first day of your cruise; are sold on a first-come, first-served basis; and are nonrefundable. Some lines allow bookings in advance, and some—but not many—include shore excursions in their cruise fares.

Generally, shore excursions that take you well beyond the port area are the ones most worth taking. You'll get professional commentary and avoid hassles with local transportation. In ports where the attractions are all within walking distance of the pier, however, you may be best off touring on your own. In other cases, it may be more enjoyable to take a taxi to an attraction and skip the crowded bus tours (for instance, in Rhodes).

Cruise lines tend to set shore excursion pricing and options closer to the sail-date. We've included 2005 prices here to give you a general idea of how much each shore tour will cost. (The 2006 rates will be determined, among other things, by the strength or weakness of the U.S. dollar.) Shore excursions are a revenue-generating area for the cruise lines, and the tours may be heavily promoted aboard the ship. They aren't always offered at bargain prices.

When touring in Greece, remember to wear comfortable walking shoes and bring a hat, sunscreen, and bottled water to ward off the effects of the hot sun. Most lines offer bottled water for a fee as you disembark.

Also, keep in mind that some churches and other religious sites require modest attire, which means shoulders and knees should be covered.

Below are selected shore-excursion offerings at the major cruise ports. Keep in mind that not all the tours will be offered by every line, and prices will vary. The tour may also show up on different lines with a few variations and a different name. For more information on many of these ports, consult the relevant chapters in this book.

CORFU (KERKIRA)
See chapter 12 for complete sightseeing information.

ACHILLEION PALACE & PALEOKASTRITSA (4–5 hr., 34€/$44): Achilleion Palace was originally built for Austrian empress Elizabeth. (Ownership of the palace was transferred to Kaiser Wilhelm II after the empress was assassinated.) After viewing the statues of Achilles, continue on to the hilltop town of Paleokastritsa, punctuated with olive, lemon, and cypress trees. Visit the 13th-century Monastery of the Virgin Mary. If you have time, use the opportunity to swim in Paleokastritsa. Stop in old Corfu town and visit St. Spyridon Church, named for the patron saint of Corfu; or stroll the narrow streets there.

IRAKLION & AYIOS NIKOLAOS (CRETE)

See chapter 7 for complete sightseeing information.

KNOSSOS & IRAKLION MUSEUM (4 hr., 43€/$56): Travel by motorcoach from Iraklion to Knossos, once the capital of the prehistoric Minoan civilization; it is thought to be the basis for the original mythological Minotaur's labyrinth. Visit the excavation of the palace of King Minos. Return to Iraklion for a museum tour or free time.

ARCADI & OLD RETHYMNON TOWN (5 hr., 42€/$54): Head out to the Monastery of Arcadi, on a rocky plateau just south of Rethymnon. The site, home to a set of buildings constructed like forts, has become a memorial to freedom from Turkish occupation. Rethymnon boasts 16th-century buildings and an archaeological museum. You can stroll the streets and its municipal gardens on your own after a 45-minute guided walking tour of the town.

ITEA (DELPHI)

DELPHI MYTHOLOGY (4 hr., 65€/$85): Delphi is located on the slope of Mount Parnassus. Visit the Sanctuary of Apollo to see the Temple of Apollo where Pythia the Oracle lived, the theater, the treasury buildings, and the Sacred Way. Visit the Archaeological Museum. A short stop at Castalian Spring is usually included.

KATAKOLON (OLYMPIA)

EXCURSION TO OLYMPIA (4 hr., 44€/$57): Visit the site of the original Olympic Games, held from 776 B.C. to A.D. 393. See the Temple of Hera, in front of which burns the Olympic Flame; the Temple of Zeus, which once housed the gold-and-ivory statue of Zeus that was one of the Seven Wonders of the Ancient World; and the original stadium and bouleuterion, where Olympic competitors swore an oath to conform to the rules of the games. Visit the famous Archaeological Museum of Olympia to see the marble statue of the Temple of Zeus and the statue of Hermes. Depending on the tour, a short stop in the town of Olympia is included.

MYKONOS & DELOS

See chapter 8 for complete sightseeing information.

DELOS: BIRTHPLACE OF APOLLO (3½–4½ hr., 42€–45€/$54–$59): Travel by small boat from Mykonos harbor to Delos for a 2-hour guided walking tour of the tiny island that was once the religious and commercial hub of the Aegean but now is home only to ancient ruins and their caretakers. View the Agora; the Sacred Way, which leads to the Sanctuary of Apollo; and the Terrace of the Lions, where marble beasts from the 7th century B.C. guard the now-dry Sacred Lake. View the remains of the Maritime Quarter with its harbors, water houses, and villas (including the House of Cleopatra). Don't miss the renowned mosaic floors in the House of the Masks and the House of Dionysus. Also visit the Archaeological Museum, if it's open.

MYKONOS ISLAND TOUR (3 hr., 34€/$44): The sites around Mykonos include the 16th-century Panagia Tourliani Monastery, with a marble fountain and a carved wooden Florentine screen in the church, and Kalafati Beach. You'll also get a guided tour of Mykonos's famous town.

A DAY AT THE BEACH (3–6 hr., 45€–99€/$59–$129): A sun bed, umbrella, and welcome cocktail will be waiting for you when you arrive at one of Mykonos's hotels on the beach of Platis Yialos. You'll have access to the hotel's pool and facilities and get a 10% discount on beach activities such as water-skiing and WaveRunners. The full-day version of this tour includes a buffet lunch and beverage.

NAFPLION

See *Frommer's Greece* for complete sightseeing information.

PALAMIDI CASTLE & MYCENAE (4 hr., 52€/$67): Visit this area rich with the remains of the ancient Mycenaean civilization, which spread after the fall of Knossos in Crete. At Mycenae, you walk through the Lion Gate to view the acropolis ruins, which call to mind descriptions from Homer's *Iliad*. Visit Palamidi Castle, which was built by Venetians and seized by the Turks. The path up consists of nearly a thousand steps (buses can drive up to the gate).

EPIDAURUS & PALAMIDI CASTLE (4 hr., 48€/$62): See the countryside as you travel to Epidaurus, the town dedicated to Asklepios, god of healing, where Greeks used to visit to take advantage of ancient spas and baths. Visit the 4th-century-B.C. theater with its remarkable acoustics. On the way back, stop by Palamidi Castle, located on a hill above Nafplion.

PATMOS

See chapter 9 for complete sightseeing information.

THE MONASTERY OF ST. JOHN & CAVE OF THE APOCALYPSE (2½–4 hr., 59€/$77): Depart the Port of Skala and travel by bus to the village of Hora and the 900-year-old Monastery of St. John. Visit the main church and view the ecclesiastical treasures in the museum. Continue on by bus to the nearby Cave of the Apocalypse to see the silver niches in the wall that mark the pillow and ledge used as a desk by the author of the Book of Revelation, and to see the crack made by the Voice of God. Longer tours may include a visit to the 300-year-old Simandris House, which boasts a rich collection of antiques, and a stop for a wine tasting at a local taverna.

PIRAEUS/ATHENS

See chapter 5 for complete sightseeing information.

ATHENS SIGHTSEEING & ACROPOLIS (4½–5 hr., 38€–43€/$49–$56): Includes a guided tour of the Acropolis, Athens's most prominent historical and architectural site; a drive past other Athens highlights, including Constitution Square, the Parliament, the Temple of Zeus, Hadrian's Arch, and Olympic Stadium. You will have enough time left for souvenir shopping. A full-day city tour (8½–9 hr., 83€/$108) includes a visit to the National Archeological Museum and sometimes a stop at the Temple of Poseidon, located high on Cape Sounion (the most southern tip of the European landmass), overlooking the Aegean Sea.

ATHENS, THE ACROPOLIS & THE CORINTH CANAL (9 hr., 84€/$109): Visit the Acropolis and, by bus, pass other sights in Athens. Views from the bus include Hadrian's Arch, Lord Byron's estate, and the Temple of Olympian Zeus, to name a few. Then take the highway from Athens to the Corinth Canal (about 96km/60 miles), which is cut right out of the rock. Board a boat in Isthmia and cruise the canal. Lunch is included. Another tour that swaps the town of Corinth for the Acropolis (6½ hr., 61€/$79) allows you to visit the ancient town of Corinth, once a focal point of Greece and a rival of Athens.

RHODES

See chapter 9 for complete sightseeing information.

LINDOS ACROPOLIS (4–4½ hr., 35€–38€/$46–$49): Travel by bus through the scenic countryside to Lindos, an important city in ancient times. At Lindos, view the medieval walls, which were constructed by the Knights of St. John in the 14th century. Walk or take a donkey up to the ancient acropolis. The ruins are a backdrop for great views—and, of course, souvenir shops on the way. (Unfortunately, this site can get extremely crowded, especially during July and Aug.) The trip may include a walking tour of Old Town Rhodes (or a drive through the area), a stop at a workshop selling Rhodian ceramics, and/or a visit to Mount Smith to view the remains of ancient Rhodes, the Temple of Apollo, and Diagoras Stadium.

MOUNT PHILERIMOS & RHODES (4½ hr., 39€/$51): A walking tour of Rhodes's old medieval town, including the Palace of the Grand Masters, is coupled with a visit to Mount Philerimos, a plateau high above sea level that offers astounding views. At its top is the 15th-century Church of Our Lady, built over a Greek temple dedicated to Athena and containing Christian catacombs. On your way to Philerimos, you'll pass the area where the Colossus of Rhodes, one of the Seven Wonders of the World, once stood in Handaraki Harbor.

RHODES BY 4WD (5 hr., 153€/$199): Hop in your four-wheel-drive—yes, you get to drive—and follow the leader throughout the island of Rhodes. Drive through Rhodes to Mount Smith for the views over the old town. You'll visit the stadium; a monastery; the Valley of the Butterflies (where the trees exude a resin that attracts moths by the thousands during the summers); and the Seven Springs area, where you'll stop for snacks and a glass of ouzo.

SANTORINI (THIRA)

See chapter 8 for complete sightseeing information.

AKROTIRI EXCAVATIONS & SANTORINI ISLAND WITH WINE TASTING (3–3½ hr., 45€/$59): Visit Akrotiri, an excavation site that dates back to the 2nd millennium B.C. See pottery, two- and three-story houses, and a variety of rooms, all 3,600 years old. Stop at a winery to taste some of the local wines, made with assyrtiko grapes. Visit Fira, perched on the caldera rim, and then stroll through the town. Take a cable-car ride or mule back down the slope to your ship.

VILLAGE OF OIA & SANTORINI ISLAND WITH WINE TASTING (3½–4 hr., 45€/$59). Another whitewashed hilltop town is Oia, which has small cobblestone streets to explore; pop in at shops and cafes. Stop at a winery to taste local wines made with assyrtiko grapes. The tour ends in Fira; take a cable car down to the water for your return to the ship.

VOLOS

See *Frommer's Greece* for complete sightseeing information.

THE MONASTERIES OF THE METEORA (9 hr., 27€/$165): Visit the Meteora, where incredible granite rocks soaring hundreds of feet in the air served as a refuge for medieval monks. Originally, the only way to get to the site was via net baskets operated by rope pulley, but now a road leads close to the base of the site, and many steps have been cut into the stone. You'll visit monastic buildings that contain Byzantine artifacts, icons, and wall paintings, and enjoy sweeping views of the low plains and neighboring monasteries. Shopping time is offered in Kalambaka, and lunch at a local hotel is included. *Note:* Women are required to wear skirts and cover their shoulders; men are required to wear pants or long shorts.

VOLOS & MOUNT PELION (3 hr., 54€/$70): Visit the Volos Archaeological Museum, which houses a collection of ancient treasures. Also visit Makrinitsa village, located on the slopes of Mount Pelion. The narrow cobblestone streets are lined with small shops selling candied fruit, herbs, spices, and the like. The village square offers a stunning view of the surrounding countryside. Free time to shop is included. In addition, some tours visit Portoria, a resort village located high above sea level, offering stunning views of the Aegean below.

10 Best Shore Excursions in the Ports of Call: Turkey

The following Turkish ports of call are commonly visited on Greek itineraries.

ISTANBUL

HIGHLIGHTS OF ISTANBUL (7–9 hr., 118€/$154): Includes the Hippodrome, once the largest chariot race grounds of the Byzantine empire; Sultan Ahmet Mosque, also known as the Blue Mosque for its 21,000 blue Iznik tiles; the famous St. Sophia, once the largest church of the Christian world; the underground cistern, a reservoir held up by more than 300 Corinthian columns; and Topkapi Palace, the official residence of the Ottoman Sultans and home to treasures that include Spoonmaker's Diamond, one of the biggest diamonds in the world. Also visit the Grand Bazaar, with its 4,000 shops. Some tours bring you back to the ship for lunch, while others include lunch in a first-class restaurant. Abbreviated tours of the above are available.

BEYLERBEYI PALACE (2½ hr., 22€/$29): Visit Istanbul's grandest seaside mansion, built by Sultan Abdulaziz on the Asian side of the Bosporus in 1865. The tour includes the palace's harem, men's quarters, and grand central hall.

A NIGHT AT THE KERVANSARAY (3½ hr., 45€/$59): In a city nightclub, enjoy traditional Turkish cuisine and different types of entertainment: belly dancing, folk dancing, and traditional singing. Available only if you're in town for the evening or overnight.

CHORA MUSEUM, EYUP & SPICE MARKET (4 hr., 25€/$32): Start with a visit to the Chora Museum near the city's old Byzantine walls, which features mosaics and frescoes depicting biblical scenes. Continue on to Eyup, Istanbul's historic district, known for its baths and royal Ottoman tombs. This tour takes you to the Mausoleum of Abu Ayyub Ansari and Eyup Mosque. At the end of the excursion you'll hit the famous spice market, where you can browse for all kinds of exotic items, from birds to jewelry to spices and herbs.

KUSADASI

EPHESUS (3–4 hr.; 34€–35€/$44–$46): Visit one of the best-preserved ancient cities in the world. Your guide will take you down the city's actual marble streets to the baths, theater, and incredible library building, and along the way you'll pass columns, mosaics, monuments, and ruins. The tour may include a shop presentation of Turkish carpets (with an emphasis on getting you to buy).

EPHESUS, ST. JOHN'S BASILICA & VIRGIN MARY SHRINE (4–4½ hr., 45€/$56): This tour combines a visit to Ephesus with the House of the Virgin Mary, a humble chapel located in the valley of Bulbuldagi. Located here is the site where the Virgin Mary is believed to have spent her last days. The site was officially sanctioned for pilgrimage in 1892. The tour includes a visit to St. John's Basilica, another holy pilgrimage site. It is believed to be the site where St. John wrote the fourth book of the New Testament. A church at the site, which is now in ruins, was built by Justinian over a 2nd-century tomb believed to contain St. John the Apostle. This tour may also be offered as a full-day excursion, including lunch at a local restaurant and a visit to the Museum of Ephesus.

EPHESUS & TERRACE HOUSES (3½–4½ hr.; 68€)–72€/$89–$94): You'll see the Ephesus highlights on this tour: the Celsus Library facade, Amphitheater, and Hadrian's Temple. Included are the "Terrace Houses," a newly excavated area opposite Hadrian's Temple. The houses were once inhabited by Ephesus's rich and are decorated with mosaics and frescoes. The area can only be accessed by special permission, such as part of a shore excursion group.

THREE ANCIENT CITIES (6–8 hr., 61€/$79): This tour takes in the ruins that surround the region of Ephesus, including Priene, known for its Temple of Athena, funded by Alexander the Great; Didyma, known for its Temple of Apollo; and Miletus, which includes a stadium built by the Greeks and expanded by the Romans to hold 15,000 spectators. A light lunch at a restaurant in Didyma is included.

EPHESUS, PRIENE & DIDYMA (8 hr., 58€/$75): Includes the above, minus Miletus, but plus Ephesus and lunch in Didim.

5

Athens

by Sherry Marker

Athens is the city that Greeks love to hate, complaining that it's too expensive, too crowded, too polluted. Some 40% of the country lives here. The city bursts at the seams with five million inhabitants, a rumored 15,000 taxis—but try to find one that's empty—and streets so congested that you'll suspect that each of the five million Athenians has a car.

Even though you've probably come here to see the "glory that was Greece," perhaps best symbolized by the Parthenon and the superb statues and vases in the National Archaeological Museum, allow yourself time to make haste slowly in Athens. Your best moments may be spent sitting at a small cafe, sipping a tiny cup of the sweet sludge that the Greeks call coffee; or getting hopelessly lost in the Plaka, but finding yourself in the shady courtyard of an old church. With a little advance planning, you can find a good hotel here, eat well in convivial restaurants, enjoy local customs (the afternoon siesta or the leisurely evening stroll)—and leave Athens planning to return, as the Greeks say, *tou chronou* (next year). Before you leave, take in the new "Archaeological Park," the pedestrianized walkways that stretch from Hadrian's Gate past the Acropolis to an ancient agora and a fascinating cemetery.

1 Essentials

ARRIVING

BY PLANE   The new **Athens International Airport Eleftherios Venizelos** (© **210/353-0000;** www.aia.gr), 27km (17 miles) northeast of Athens at Spata, opened in 2001. The good news: This is a large, modern facility, with ample restrooms, interesting shops, and acceptable restaurants. The bad news: It's a serious slog from Athens (allow an hour by bus or taxi). A taxi into central Athens usually costs around 15€ to 25€ ($20–$33), depending on the time of day and traffic. Bus service to Syntagma Square or to Piraeus costs about 4€ ($5.20). Officially, there's one bus to Syntagma and one to Piraeus every 20 minutes. Bus, metro, and taxi stations are signposted at the airport. The Metro link into Athens is now up and running all the way; the airport Metro stop is by the airport's Sofitel hotel. Trains run from 5am to 1am, and there is talk of initiating 24-hour service (one way 9€ ($12), round trip 10€ ($13)). If you don't have much to carry, the Metro is now a cheap and efficient option for reaching central Athens, especially since buses run erratically and taxis are costly.

Tip: Don't rely on the airport's website and official publications for accurate, up-to-date information.

Athens at a Glance

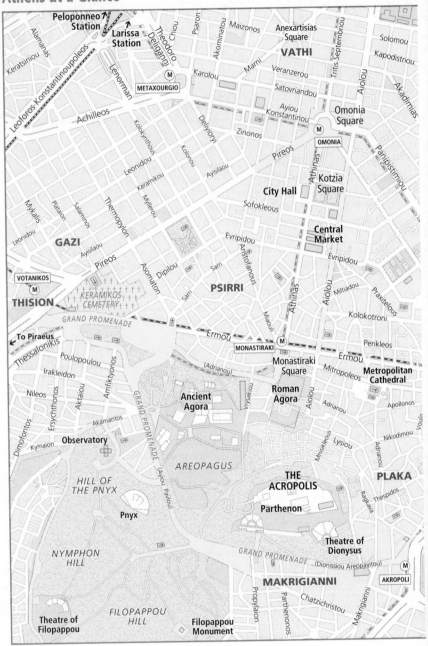

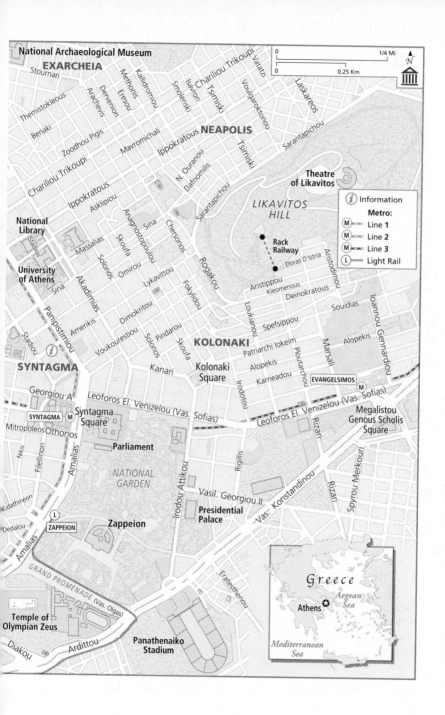

Tips Taxi Savvy

If you decide to take a taxi, ask an airline official or a policeman what the fare should be, and let the taxi driver know you've been told the official rate before you begin your journey. If you're taking a taxi to the airport, have the desk clerk at your hotel order it for you well in advance. Many taxi drivers refuse to go to the airport, fearing that they'll have a long wait before they get a return fare.

When planning your carry-on luggage for the Athens airport, keep in mind that you may have quite a trek from your arrival point to the baggage-claim area. Tourist information, currency exchange, a post office, baggage storage (left luggage), and car rentals are available at the Arrivals level of the Main Terminal. ATMs, telephones, toilets, and luggage carts (1€/$1.30) are available at the baggage-claim area. You can call for a porter from one of several free phones. *Note:* Porters' fees are highly negotiable.

There have been frequent complaints that adequate information on arrivals, departures, cancellations, delays, and gate changes is not always posted on the flight information screens. Nonetheless, it is important to check these screens and ask at the information desks, as there are currently no flight announcements. Arrive at your gate as early as possible; gates are sometimes changed at the last minute, necessitating a considerable scramble to reach the new gate in time.

BY TRAIN   There are two train stations in central Athens; both are just off Dilyianni, about 2km (1 mile) northwest of Omonia Square. Trains from the west, including Eurail connections via Patra, arrive at **Stathmos Peloponnissou (Peloponnese Station),** about 2km (1 mile) northwest of Omonia Square. Trains from the north arrive 3 blocks north at **Stathmos Larissis (Larissa Station),** on the opposite side of the tracks from the Peloponnese Station. If you are making connections from one station to the other, allow 10 to 15 minutes for the walk. Both stations have currency-exchange offices usually open daily from 8am to 9:15pm. They also have baggage-storage offices charging 4€ ($5.20) per bag per day, open daily from 6:30am to 9:30pm. The cafe and waiting room are often closed. A **taxi** into the center of town should cost about 5€ ($6.50). For information on schedules and fares, contact the **Greek Railroad Company (OSE; © 210/512-4913** or 210/529-7777; www.ose.gr).

BY BOAT   Piraeus, the main harbor of Athens's main seaport, 11km (7 miles) southwest of central Athens, is a 15-minute Metro ride from Monastiraki and Omonia squares. The subway runs from about 5am to midnight and costs 1€ ($1.30). The far-slower bus no. 040 runs from Piraeus to central Athens (with a stop at Filellinon off Syntagma Sq.) every 15 minutes between 5am and 1am, and hourly from 1am to 5am, for .70€ ($.91).

You might prefer to take a **taxi** to avoid what can be a long hike from your boat to the bus stop or subway terminal. Be prepared for some serious bargaining. The normal fare on the meter from Piraeus to Syntagma should be about 8€ to 15€ ($10–$20), but many drivers simply offer a flat fare, which can be as much as 20€ ($26). Pay it if you're desperate, or walk to a nearby street, hail another taxi, and insist that the meter be turned on.

If you travel to Piraeus by one of the hydrofoils called Flying Dolphins, you'll probably arrive at **Zea Marina** harbor, about a dozen blocks south across the peninsula from the main harbor. Getting a taxi from Zea Marina into Athens can involve a wait of an hour or more—and drivers usually drive a hard (and exorbitant) bargain. To avoid both the wait and the big fare, walk up the hill from the hydrofoil station and catch bus no. 905 for 1€ ($1.30); it connects Zea to the Piraeus subway station, where you can complete your journey into Athens. You must buy a ticket at the small ticket stand near the bus stop or at a newsstand before boarding the bus. *Warning:* If you arrive late at night, you might not be able to do this, as both the newsstand and the ticket stand may be closed.

VISITOR INFORMATION

TOURIST OFFICE   In 2003, the **Greek National Tourism Organization (GNTO),** also known as the **Hellenic Tourism Organization (EOT),** closed its main office just off Syntagma Square at 2 Amerikis. The new main office is at 7 Tsochas, Ambelokipi (© **210/870-0000;** www.gnto.gr), well out of central Athens. The office is open Monday to Friday 8am to 3pm, and is closed on weekends. At press time, it was unclear whether the office in central Athens at 26 Amalias would remain open.

WEBSITES   Sites include **www.greece.gr, www.culture.gr, www.phantis.com,** and **www.ellada.com** for Athens and Greece in general; **http://city.net** (Athens information); **www.athensnews.gr** (*The Athens News,* Greece's English-language newspaper); **www.eKathimerini.com** (an insert of translations from the Greek press sold with the *International Herald Tribune*); **www.all-hotels.gr/intro.asp** (information on hotels); **www.dilos.com** (travel information, including discounted hotel prices); **www.gtp.gr** (information on ferry service); **www.greekislands.gr** (information on the islands); **www.greektravel.com** (a helpful site on all aspects of Greece run by American Matt Barrett); **www.ancientgreece.com** and **www.perseus.tufts.edu** (excellent resources on ancient Greece); and **www.greekbooks.com, www.book. culture.gr, www.nbc.gr,** and **www.greekbooks.gr** (useful sites for information on books on many aspects of Greece).

CITY LAYOUT

If you, like the Greek mathematician Euclid, find it easy to imagine geometric forms, it will help to think of central Athens as an almost perfect equilateral triangle, with its

---

Tips   Hotels Near the Airport

If you have an early flight out of Spata, you might consider spending the night at Hotel Avra (© **22940/22-780**), 30 to 45 minutes by taxi from the airport on the waterfront in the nearby port of Rafina. The Avra was completely remodeled in 2003-04 and has a decent restaurant (sometimes with live music). Even better, you can stroll to one of Rafina's many harborside restaurants and watch the fishing boats and ferries come and go as you enjoy very fresh seafood. Doubles cost from 100€ ($130). If you want to be at the airport itself, with considerable creature comforts, the charmless but convenient and efficient 345-room Sofitel Athens Airport hotel (© **210/681-0882;** www.sofitel.com), with its own restaurants, fitness club, and swimming pool, is the logical place to stay if you have a very early flight or if you get in very late. Prices are from 140€ to 340€ ($182–$442) double.

Tips **Trying to Catch a Connection**

A word about making air connections after an island trip: It is unwise—even foolhardy—to allow anything less than 24 hours between your return to Piraeus by island boat and your departure by air, as rough seas can make for significant delays.

---

points at **Syntagma (Constitution) Square, Omonia (Harmony) Square,** and **Monastiraki (Little Monastery) Square** near the **Acropolis.** In government jargon, the area bounded by Syntagma, Omonia, and Monastiraki squares is defined as the commercial center, from which cars are banned (in theory, if not in practice) except for several cross streets. Most Greeks consider Omonia the city center, but visitors usually get their bearings from Syntagma, where the House of Parliament is.

Few Athenians were enchanted with Omonia's "face-lift" in honor of the Olympics, which took 27 months of work and cost 2 million euros. The result: It is now possible, somewhat safely, to walk across Omonia Square. On lots of cement. The promised trees did not appear. Omonia and Syntagma squares are connected by the parallel **Stadiou** Street and **Panepistimiou** Street, also called **Eleftherios Venizelos.** West from Syntagma Square, ancient **Ermou** Street and broader **Mitropoleos** Street lead slightly downhill to **Monastiraki Square.** Here you'll find the **flea market,** the **Ancient Agora (Market)** below the Acropolis, and the **Plaka,** the oldest neighborhood, with many street names and a scattering of monuments from antiquity. A special bonus: **Adrianou,** the main drag in Plaka, which once teemed with traffic, is now open for walkers only. From Monastiraki Square, **Athinas** Street leads north past the modern market (Central Market) to Omonia Square. Bustling with shoppers in the daytime, Athinas Street is less savory at night, when prostitutes and drug dealers hang out here.

In general, finding your way around Athens is easy, except in the Plaka, at the foot of the Acropolis. This labyrinth of narrow, winding streets can challenge even the best navigators. Don't panic: The area is small enough that you can't go far astray, and its side streets, with small houses and neighborhood churches, are so charming that you won't mind being lost. One excellent map may help: the Greek Archaeological Service's **Historical Map of Athens,** which includes the Plaka and the city center and shows the major archaeological sites. The map costs about 4€ ($5.20) and is sold at many bookstores, museums, ancient sites, and newspaper kiosks.

If you want to see what's happening in the most happening districts of Athens, head to **Psirri,** between Athinas and Ermou, which until a few years ago would not have merited any mention. Now, you'll find some of Athens's newest and most popular restaurants, cafes, and galleries here. Young entrepreneurs are drawn to Psirri by relatively low rents. The area can still be rather deserted at night (see above).

Near Psirri, two more districts are being revitalized: **Gazi,** formerly known only for its once noxious gasworks, but now the home of the Athens Municipal Technopolis Center gallery and a growing number of boutique hotels, restaurants, and cafes. **Rouf,** known for its warehouses and the fruit and vegetable market, is now dotted with artists' ateliers, galleries, cafes, and restaurants.

GETTING AROUND

By Public Transportation   For most visitors, the new Metro system will suffice. If you must use buses, here's the scoop:

The **blue-and-white buses** run regular routes in Athens and its suburbs every 15 minutes daily from 5am to midnight. The **orange electric trolley buses** serve areas in the city center daily from 5am to midnight. The **green buses** run between the city center and Piraeus every 20 minutes daily from 6am to midnight, then hourly to 6am. Tickets cost .70€ ($.91) and must be bought in advance, usually in packs of 10, from any news kiosk or special bus-ticket kiosks at the main stations. When you board, validate your ticket in the automatic machine. *Tip:* Hold onto your validated ticket. Uniformed and plainclothes inspectors periodically check tickets and can levy a basic fine of 5€ ($6.50) or a more punitive fine of 20€ ($26), on the spot.

The major bus stations in Athens include the suburban bus terminal at Areos Park; Long Distance Bus Terminal A, 100 Kiffissou (reached by bus no. 051 from Zinonos and Menandrou, off Omonia Sq.); and Long Distance Bus Terminal B, 260 Liossion (reached by bus no. 024 from Amalias, Syntagma Sq.). Note that the system is still in flux, and the numbers of buses serving these routes may have changed by the time you visit Athens.

The first station on the new Metro (subway), opened at Syntagma Square in January 2000. Athens's original subway system, which ran from the port of Piraeus to the northern suburb of Kifissia, is now linked with two new lines of ambitious Metro expansion. You may want to stop at the Syntagma station, or at the GNTO, to get a map of the Metro and learn what stations have opened by the time you visit. To travel on the Metro, buy your ticket at the station, validate it in the machines as you enter, and hang onto your ticket until you get off (if you don't, you may be fined). Tickets on the old line cost .60€ ($.78); tickets on the new line cost .75€ ($.98); a day pass costs 3€ ($3.90)—but don't be surprised if these prices have gone up by the time you arrive in Athens. Metro and bus tickets are not yet interchangeable, but may be soon.

Even if you do not use the Metro to get around Athens, you may take it from Omonia or Monastiraki to Piraeus to catch a boat to the islands. (We recommend taking in the spectacular view of the Acropolis as the subway comes aboveground by the Agora.) If you're not carrying much luggage, the harbor in Piraeus is a 5-minute walk (head left) from the station.

By Taxi   Supposedly there are 17,000 taxis in Athens, but finding an empty one is a challenge. Especially if you have travel connections to make, it's a good idea to pay the 2€ ($2.60) surcharge and reserve a radio taxi. The minimum fare in a taxi is 2€ ($2.60).

Tips   Ride the Metro & View Artifacts

Allow a little extra time when you catch the Metro in central Athens. Two stations—**Syntagma Square** and **Acropolis**—handsomely display finds from the subway excavations in what amount to Athens's newest small museums. For more on the Athens Metro, go to **www.ametro.gr**.

> **Tips   A Taxi Warning**
>
> There are more and more unlicensed cab drivers in Athens and Piraeus. Usually, these pirate cabbies do not drive the standard gray Athens taxi; however, they use a gray car that you might mistake for an Athens cab. It's always a good idea to make sure your cab driver has a meter and a photo ID. Many of the unlicensed cab drivers are uninsured and unfamiliar with the metropolitan area.

When you get into a taxi, check to see that the meter is turned on and set on "1" rather than "2." It should be set on "2" (double fare) only from midnight to 5am or if you take a taxi outside the city limits. If you plan to do this, try to negotiate a flat rate in advance. Unless your cab is caught in very heavy traffic, a trip to the center of town from the airport between 5am and midnight shouldn't cost more than 15€ to 25€ ($20–$33). Don't be surprised if your driver picks up other passengers en route. He'll work out everyone's share; the worst that will happen is you'll get less of a break than you would if you spoke Greek. Most Greek passengers round up the fare—for example, from 2.90€ to 3€ ($3.77–$3.90)—and some give a bit more for a tip.

There are about 15 radio taxi companies, including **Athina** (✆ 210/921-7942), **Express** (✆ 210/993-4812), **Kosmos** (✆ 210/645-7000), **Parthenon** (✆ 210/581-4711), and **Piraeus** (✆ 210/418-2333). If you're making travel connections or traveling during rush hours, the service will be well worth the 3€ ($3.90) surcharge.

If you suspect you've been overcharged, ask for help at your hotel or other destination before you pay the fare.

Your driver may have difficulty understanding your pronunciation of your destination. If you are taking a taxi from your hotel, ask a staff member to tell the driver your destination or write down the address for you to show to the driver. Also, carry a business card from your hotel; you can show it to the driver when you return. Most restaurants will call a taxi at no charge.

By Foot   Most of tourist Athens is in the city center, allowing you to sightsee on foot. The pedestrian zones in sections of the Plaka, the commercial center, and Kolonaki make strolling, window-shopping, and sightseeing infinitely more pleasant than on other, traffic-clogged streets. *Tip:* As in many busy cities, a red traffic light or stop sign is no guarantee that cars will stop for pedestrians. Look both ways before crossing.

By Car   Parking is so difficult and traffic so heavy in Athens that you should use a car only for trips outside the city. Consider that on any day trip (to Sounion or Daphni, for example), you'll spend at least several hours leaving and reentering central Athens.

Car-rental agencies in the Syntagma Square area include **Avis,** 48 Amalias (✆ 800/331-1084 in the U.S. or 210/322-4951); **Auto Europe,** 29 Hatzihristou, right off Syngrou (✆ 800/223-5555 in the U.S. or 210/924-2206); and **Budget,** 8 Syngrou (✆ 800/527-0700 in the U.S. or 210/921-4711). You almost always get the best deal if you arrange the rental before leaving home. You will usually get the worst possible deal if you arrive in Athens and want a car for only 1 day. *Warning:* Be sure to take full insurance and ask if the price you are quoted includes everything. Often the quoted price doesn't include all taxes, drop-off fee, gasoline charges, and so on. Be particularly vigilant if you intend to collect or return your car at an airport: Many companies charge—but do not mention it when you reserve your car—a hefty fee for this.

FAST FACTS: **Athens**

ATMs Automatic teller machines are increasingly common at banks throughout Athens. The **National Bank of Greece** operates a 24-hour ATM in Syntagma Square.

Banks Banks are generally open Monday through Thursday from 8am to 2pm and Friday from 8am to 1:30pm. In summer, the exchange office at the **National Bank of Greece** in Syntagma Square (② **210/334-0015**) is open Monday through Thursday from 3:30 to 6:30pm, Friday from 3 to 6:30pm, Saturday from 9am to 3pm, and Sunday from 9am to 1pm. Other centrally located banks include **Citibank,** in Syntagma Square (② **210/322-7471**); **Bank of America,** 39 Panepistimiou (② **210/324-4975**); and **Barclays Bank,** 15 Voukourestiou (② **210/364-4311**). All banks are closed on the long list of Greek holidays. (See "When to Go," in chapter 2.) Most banks exchange currency at the rate set daily by the government. This rate is often more favorable than that offered at unofficial exchange bureaus. Still, a little comparison-shopping is worthwhile. Some hotels offer better-than-official rates, though only for cash, as do some stores, usually when you are making an expensive purchase.

Business Hours Even Greeks get confused by their complicated and changeable business hours. In winter, Athens's shops are generally open Monday and Wednesday from 9am to 5pm; Tuesday, Thursday, and Friday from 10am to 7pm; and Saturday from 8:30am to 3:30pm. In summer, shops are generally open Monday, Wednesday, and Saturday from 8am to 3pm; and Tuesday, Thursday, and Friday from 8am to 2pm and 5:30 to 10pm.

Most food stores are open Monday and Wednesday from 9am to 4:30pm; Tuesday from 9am to 6pm; Thursday from 9:30am to 6:30pm; Friday from 9:30am to 7pm; and Saturday from 8:30am to 4:30pm.

Many shops geared to tourists stay open late into the night—but only if the shop owner thinks that business will be good. In other words, the shop that was open late yesterday may close early today.

Dentists & Doctors Embassies (see below) may have lists of dentists and doctors. Some English-speaking physicians advertise in the daily *Athens News.*

Drugstores See "Pharmacies," below.

Embassies & Consulates Locations are: **Australia,** 37 Leoforos Dimitriou Soutsou (② 210/645-0404-5); **Canada,** 4 Ioannou Yenadiou (② 210/727-3400 or 210/725-4011); **Ireland,** 7 Vas. Konstantinou (② 210/723-2771); **New Zealand,** Xenias 24, Ambelokipi (② 210/771-0112); **South Africa,** 60 Kifissias, Maroussi (② 210/680-6645); **United Kingdom,** 1 Ploutarchou (② 210/723-6211); **United States,** 91 Leoforos Vas. Sofias (② 210/721-2951; emergency number 210/729-4301). Be sure to phone ahead before you go to any embassy; most keep limited hours and are usually closed on their own country's holidays as well as Greek ones.

Emergencies In an emergency, dial ② **100** for the **police** and ② **171** for the **tourist police.** Dial ② **199** to report a **fire** and ② **166** for an **ambulance** and the **hospital.** If you need an English-speaking doctor or dentist, call your embassy for advice; or try **SOS Doctor** (② 210/331-0310 or 210/331-0311). There are two medical hot lines for foreigners: ② **210/721-2951** (day) and 210/729-4301 (night) for U.S. citizens; and ② **210/723-6211** (day) and 210/723-7727 (night) for British citizens. The English-language *Athens News* (published Fri) lists some American- and British-trained doctors and hospitals offering emergency services. Most of the larger hotels can call a doctor for you in an emergency, and embassies will sometimes recommend local doctors.

KAT, the emergency hospital in Kifissia (② **210/801-4411** to -4419), and **Asklepion Voulas,** the emergency hospital in Voula (② **210/895-3416** to -3418), both have emergency rooms open 24 hours a day. **Evangelismos,** a respected centrally located hospital below the Kolonaki district on 9 Vas. Sophias (② **210/ 722-0101**), usually has English-speaking staff on duty. If you need medical attention fast, don't waste time trying to call these hospitals: Just go. Their doors are open and they will see to you as soon as possible.

In addition, every major hospital takes its turn each day being on emergency duty. A recorded message in Greek at ② **210/106** tells you which hospital is open for emergency services and gives the telephone number.

Eyeglasses If anything happens to your glasses, **Artemiadis** has two branches (4 Hermou, Syntagma, ② **210/323-8555;** and 3 Stadiou, in the Kalliga Arcade, Syntagma, ② **210/324-7043**) as well as an e-mail address, info@ARTEMIADIS.GR. Artemiadis offers next-day, sometimes even same-day, replacement service. **Optical,** 2 Patriarchou Ioakim, Kolonaki (② **210/724-3564**), also offers next- or same-day service. Both stores sell sunglasses and have English-speaking staff.

Hospitals Except for emergencies, hospital admittance is gained through a physician. See "Dentists & Doctors," above.

Information See "Visitor Information," earlier in this chapter.

Internet Access Internet cafes, where you can check and send e-mail, are proliferating in Athens almost as fast as cellular telephones. For a current list of Athenian cybercafes, check out **www.netcafeguide.com.**

As a general rule, most cybercafes charge about 5€ ($6.50) an hour. The very efficient **Sofokleous.com Internet C@fe,** 5 Stadiou, a block off Syntagma Square (②/fax **210/324-8105**), is open daily from 10am to 10pm. **Astor Internet Cafés,** 17 Patission, a block off Omonia Square (② **210/523-8546**), is open Monday through Saturday from 10am to 10pm, and Sunday from 10am to 4pm. Across from the National Archaeological Museum is **Central Music Coffee Shop,** 28 Octobriou, also called Patission (② **210/883-3418**), with daily hours from 9am to 11pm. In Plaka, **Plaka Internet World** (② **210/331-6056**), 29 Pandrossou, offers air-conditioned chat rooms and an Acropolis view!

Laundry & Dry Cleaning The **self-service launderette** at 10 Angelou Yeronda, in Filomouson Square, off Kidathineon, Plaka, is open daily from 8:30am to 7pm; it charges 7€ ($9.10) per load, including wash, dry, and soap. **National Dry Cleaners and Laundry Service,** 17 Apollonos (② **210/323-2226**), next to the Hermes Hotel, is open Monday and Wednesday from 7am to 4pm, and Tuesday, Thursday, and Friday from 7am to 8pm. Laundry costs 5€ ($6.50) per kilo (2.2 lb.). Hotel chambermaids will often do laundry as well. Dry cleaning in Athens is reasonable, at about 4€ ($5.20) for a pair of slacks. Next-day service is usually possible.

Lost & Found   If you lose something on the street or on public transportation, it is probably gone for good, just as it would be in any large American city. If you wish, contact the police's **Lost and Found,** 173 Leoforos Alexandras (𝄇 **210/642-1616**), open Monday through Saturday from 9am to 3pm. Lost passports and other documents may be returned by the police to the appropriate embassy, so check there as well. It's an excellent idea to travel with photocopies of your important documents, including passport, prescriptions, tickets, phone numbers, and addresses.

Luggage Storage & Lockers   If you're coming back to stay, many hotels will store excess luggage while you travel. There are storage facilities at Athens International Airport, at the Metro station in Piraeus, and at both of Athens's train stations.

Newspapers & Magazines   The *Athens News* is published every Friday in English, with a weekend section listing events of interest; it's available at kiosks everywhere. Most central Athens newsstands also carry the *International Herald Tribune,* which has an English-language insert of highlights from the Greek daily *Kathimerini* and *USA Today.* Local weeklies include the *Hellenic Times,* with entertainment listings; and *Athinorama* (in Greek), which has comprehensive listings of events. *Athens Best Of* (monthly) and *Now in Athens,* published every other month, have information on restaurants, shopping, museums, and galleries, and are available free in major hotels and sometimes from the Greek National Tourism Organization.

Pharmacies   *Pharmakia,* identified by green crosses, are scattered throughout Athens. Hours are usually Monday through Friday from 8am to 2pm. In the evenings and on weekends, most are closed, but each posts a notice listing the names and addresses of pharmacies that are open or will open in an emergency. Newspapers such as the *Athens News* list the pharmacies open outside regular hours.

Police   In an **emergency,** dial 𝄇 **100.** For help dealing with a troublesome taxi driver, hotel staff, restaurant staff, or shop owner, stand your ground and call the **tourist police** at 𝄇 **171.**

Post Offices   The main post offices in central Athens are at 100 Eolou, just south of Omonia Square; and in Syntagma Square, at the corner of Mitropoleos. They are open Monday through Friday from 7:30am to 8pm, Saturday from 7:30am to 2pm, and Sunday from 9am to 1pm.

All of the post offices accept parcels, but the **Parcel Post Office,** 4 Stadiou inside the arcade (𝄇 **210/322-8940**), is open Monday through Friday from 7:30am to 8pm. It usually sells twine and cardboard shipping boxes in four sizes. Parcels must remain open for inspection before you seal them at the post office.

You can receive correspondence in Athens c/o **American Express,** 2 Ermou, 10225 Athens, Greece (𝄇 **210/324-4975**), near the southwest corner of Syntagma Square, open Monday through Friday from 8:30am to 4pm and

Saturday from 8:30am to 1:30pm. If you have an American Express card or trav-eler's checks, the service is free; otherwise, each article costs 2€ ($2.60).

Radio & Television   Generally, English-language radio—BBC and Voice of America—is available only via shortwave radio. CNN and various European channels such as STAR are available on cable TV. The NET channel has daily news summaries in English, usually at 6pm. Most foreign-language films shown on Greek TV are not dubbed, but feature the original soundtracks with Greek subtitles. All current-release foreign-language films shown in Greek cinemas have the original soundtracks with Greek subtitles.

Restrooms   There are public restrooms in the underground station beneath Omonia and Syntagma squares and beneath Kolonaki Square, but you'll prob-ably prefer a hotel or restaurant restroom. (Toilet paper is often not available, so carry tissue with you. Do not flush paper down the commode; use the recep-tacle provided.)

Safety   Athens is among the safest capitals in Europe, and there are few reports of violent crimes. **Pickpocketing,** however, is not uncommon, especially in the Plaka and Omonia Square areas, on the Metro and buses, and in Piraeus. Unfortunately, it is a good idea to be wary of Gypsy children. We advise trav-elers to avoid the side streets of Omonia and Piraeus at night. As always, leave your passport and valuables in a security box at the hotel. Carry a photocopy of your passport, not the original.

Taxes   A VAT (value-added tax) of between 4% and 18% is added onto every-thing you buy. Some shops will attempt to cheat you by quoting one price and then, when you hand over your credit card, they will add on a hefty VAT charge. Be wary. In theory, if you are not a member of a Common Market/E.U. country, you can get a refund on major purchases at the Athens airport when you leave Greece. In practice, you would have to arrive at the airport a day before your flight to get to the head of the line, do the paperwork, get a refund, and catch your flight.

Telephone, Telegram & Fax   Many of the city's public phones now accept only phone cards, available at newsstands and the **Telecommunications Organization of Greece (OTE)** offices in several denominations, currently starting at 3€ ($3.90). Most OTE offices now sell cellphones and phone cards at very reason-able prices; if you are in Greece for a month, you may find this a good option. Some kiosks still have metered phones; you pay what the meter records. North Americans can phone home directly by contacting **AT&T** (℃ **00/800-1311**), **MCI** (℃ **00/800-1211**), or **Sprint** (℃ **00/800-1411**); calls can be collect or billed to your own phone charge card. You can send a telegram or fax from OTE offices. The OTE office at 15 Stadiou, near Syntagma, is open 24 hours a day. The Omonia Square OTE, at 50 Athinas, and the Victoria Square OTE, at 85 Patission, are open Monday through Friday from 7am to 9pm, Saturday from 9am to 3pm, and Sunday from 9am to 2pm. Outside Athens, most OTEs are closed on weekends.

Tipping   Athenian restaurants include a service charge in the bill, but many vis-itors add a 10% tip. Most Greeks do not give a percentage tip to taxi drivers, but often round up the fare; for example, you would round up a fare of 2.80€ ($3.65) to 3€ ($3.90).

Tips A Warning About ATMs

It is *not* a good idea to rely exclusively on ATMs in Athens, since the machines here are often out of service when you need them most, particularly on holidays or during bank strikes.

If your PIN includes letters, be sure that you know their numerical equivalent, as Greek ATMs do not have letters.

2 Where to Stay

Almost all Greek hotels are clean and comfortable; few are charming, elegant, or memorable. Most, in fact, are monotonous, with one guest room a bit larger, another a bit smaller—but very few have individual touches to warm the traveler's heart. We can give you an idea of the individual virtues of the hotels we recommend, but we do urge you to keep in mind that, in the absence of truly distinguishing characteristics, the old cliché is true: **Location** is the most important factor in choosing your hotel. When a hotel is truly distinctive in other ways as well, we will draw it to your attention.

A few suggestions: In summer, we strongly advise that you reserve ahead of time. If shower and tub facilities are important to you, be sure to have a look at the bathroom: Many Greek tubs are tiny, and the showers are hand-held. Don't assume that just because a hotel says it has air-conditioning, the air-conditioning works, and be sure there's adequately functioning central heating in winter. Also, decent reading lamps are almost unknown—consider bringing a traveler's flashlight that clips onto your book.

Although many guidebooks do, we do not recommend staying at any of the luxury hotels on Syngrou Avenue. The Metropolitan, Leda Marriott, and Athenaeum-Intercontinental have all the creature comforts, but Syngrou Avenue is ugly, noisy, and away from everything you'll want to see in Athens. In short, the Syngrou hotels are good if you're here for a conference and never leave your hotel.

The **Syntagma Square** area and the **Plaka/Monastiraki** district are the most convenient locations for sightseeing. If you have only a few days in Athens, you should seriously consider staying here. **Makriyanni** and the **Embassy district** are also good choices, as well as the area near the National Archaeological Museum, which has some good budget hotels. We've enjoyed staying in **Kolonaki,** the upscale Athenian neighborhood on the slopes of Mount Likavitos, although we didn't always look forward to the uphill walk back to the hotel. We have friends who always stay in the **Koukaki** district, near Filopappos Hill and off the non-Acropolis side of Dionissiou Areopagitou. They love the quiet residential streets in a real Greek neighborhood. If you do stay there, you'll do some extra walking to get to much of what you want to see—although you'll be only steps from pedestrianized Dionyssiou Areopayitou and the Herodes Atticus theater on the slopes of the Acropolis. Trail-blazers may want to take in one of the new hotels such as Iridanos or the Fresh Hotel in Gazi, the neighborhood of the former gasworks, well on its way to becoming cutting-edge chic.

THE PLAKA
EXPENSIVE

Electra Palace ★★   The Electra, just a few blocks southwest of Syntagma Square on a relatively quiet side street, is the most modern and stylish Plaka hotel. The rooms on the fifth, sixth, and seventh floors are smaller than those on lower floors, but a top-floor

Athens Accommodations & Dining

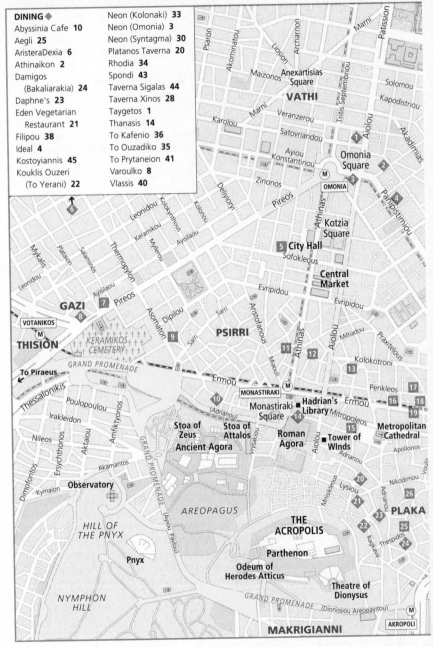

DINING ◆
Abyssinia Cafe **10**
Aegli **25**
AristeraDexia **6**
Athinaikon **2**
Damigos
 (Bakaliarakia) **24**
Daphne's **23**
Eden Vegetarian
 Restaurant **21**
Filipou **38**
Ideal **4**
Kostoyiannis **45**
Kouklis Ouzeri
 (To Yerani) **22**
Neon (Kolonaki) **33**
Neon (Omonia) **3**
Neon (Syntagma) **30**
Platanos Taverna **20**
Rhodia **34**
Spondi **43**
Taverna Sigalas **44**
Taverna Xinos **28**
Taygetos **1**
Thanasis **14**
To Kafenio **36**
To Ouzadiko **35**
To Prytaneion **41**
Varoulko **8**
Vlassis **40**

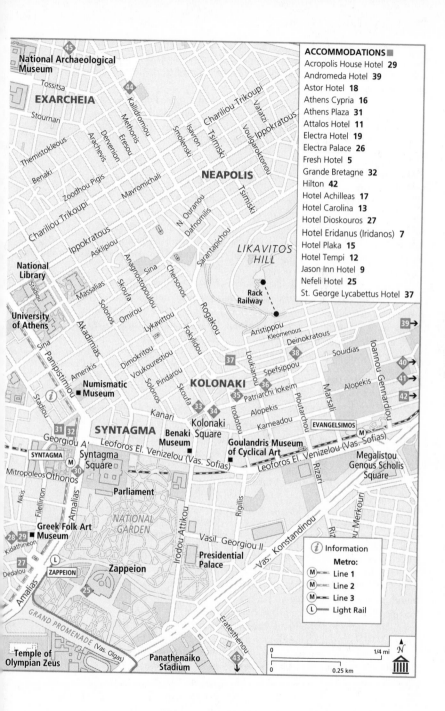

National Archaeological Museum

Tossitsa

EXARCHEIA

Stournari

Themistokleous

Benaki

Kallidromiou

Methonis

Dervenion

Eresou

Arachevis

Zoodhou Pigis

Charilou Trikoupi

Ippokratous

Asklipiou

Isavron

Smolenski

Tsimiski

Chariliou Trikoupi

Vatatzi

Ippokratous

Voulgaroktonou

NEAPOLIS

N. Ouranou

Dafnomilis

Tsimiski

Mavromichali

Anagnostopoulou

Sina

Chersonos

Sarantapichou

National Library

Massalias

Skoufa

Solonos

Omirou

Lykavittou

Fokylidou

Rogakou

LIKAVITOS HILL

Rack Railway

Aristippou

Kleomenous

Deinokratous

University of Athens

Sina

Akadimias

Panipistimiou

Amerikis

Dimokritou

Voukourestiou

Pindarou

Souidias

Ioannou Gennadiou

Numismatic Museum

Solonos

Skoufa

KOLONAKI

Patriarchi Iokeim

Alopekis

Marsali

Kanari

Kolonaki Square

Irodotou

Alopekis

Ploutarchou

Karneadou

EVANGELSIMOS

SYNTAGMA

Georgiou A'

Leoforos El. Venizelou (Vas. Sofias)

SYNTAGMA

Benaki Museum

Goulandris Museum of Cyclical Art

Leoforos El. Venizelou (Vas. Sofias)

Megalistou Genous Scholis Square

Mitropoleos

Othonos

Syntagma Square

Parliament

NATIONAL GARDEN

Nikis

Filellinon

Amalias

Rigillis

Vasil. Georgiou II

Greek Folk Art Museum

Kidathineon

Dedalou

ZAPPEION

Zappeion

Presidential Palace

Irodou Attikou

Vas. Konstandinou

Rizari

Merkouri

Amalias

GRAND PROMENADE (Vas. Olgas)

Temple of Olympian Zeus

Panathenaiko Stadium

Eratesthenou

(i) Information

Metro:
M▬ Line 1
M▬ Line 2
M▬ Line 3
L▬ Light Rail

0 — 1/4 mi
0 — 0.25 km

N

139

room is where you want to be, both for the terrific view of the Acropolis and to escape traffic noise. (Ask for a top-floor unit when you make your reservation. Your request will be honored "subject to availability.") Guest rooms here are hardly drop-dead elegant, but they are pleasant and decorated in soft pastels. Don't miss the rooftop pool. If you're too tired to go out for dinner, the hotel restaurant is quite decent

18 Nikodimou, Plaka, 10557 Athens. © 210/324-1401 or 210/324-1407. Fax 210/324-1975. 106 units. 150€–250€ ($195–$325) double. Rates include breakfast buffet. AE, DC, MC, V. The Electra is about 2 blocks down on the left as you walk along Ermou with Syntagma Sq. behind you. **Amenities:** Restaurant; bar; rooftop pool. *In room:* A/C, TV, minibar, hair dryer.

MODERATE

Acropolis House Hotel ✦   This small hotel in a handsomely restored 150-year-old villa retains many of its original classical architectural details. It offers a central location—just off Kidathineon in the heart of the Plaka, a 5-minute walk from Syntagma Square—and the charm of being on a quiet pedestrian side street. Room nos. 401 and 402 have good views and can be requested (but not guaranteed) when making a reservation. The newer wing, only 60 years old, isn't architecturally special; each unit's spartan bathroom is across the hall

If the Acropolis House is full, try **Adonis Hotel,** on the same street at 3 Kodrou (© **210/324-9737**); it's architecturally undistinguished and somewhat haphazard, but it does have an appealing location and a rooftop garden cafe with a view of the Acropolis. A few steps away, **Kouros Hotel,** 11 Kodrou (© **210/322-7431**), is very basic and can be noisy.

6–8 Kodrou, 10558 Athens. © 210/322-2344. Fax 210/324-4143. 25 units, 15 w/bathroom. 70€ ($91) double without bathroom, 75€ ($98) double with bathroom. 10€ ($13) surcharge for A/C. Rates include continental breakfast. V. Walk 2 blocks out of Syntagma Sq. on Mitropoleos and turn left on Voulis, which becomes Kodrou. **Amenities:** Washing machine (small fee; free after 4-day stay); book swap. *In room:* A/C.

Hotel Plaka ✦✦   This hotel is popular with Greeks, who prefer its modern conveniences to the old-fashioned charms of most other hotels in the Plaka area. It has a terrific location just off Syntagma Square. Most guest rooms have balconies; those on the fifth and sixth floors in the rear, where it's usually quieter, have views of the Plaka and the Acropolis (also visible from the roof-garden snack bar). Friends who stayed here recently were not charmed by the service, but they enjoyed the location, the rooftop bar, and the blue-and-white color scheme.

Mitropoleos and 7 Kapnikareas, 10556 Athens. © 210/322-2096. Fax 210/322-2412. www.plakahotel.gr. 67 units (38 with shower only). 145€–160€ ($189–$208) double. Rates include breakfast. AE, MC, V. Follow Mitropoleos out of Syntagma Sq. past cathedral and turn left onto Kapnikareas. **Amenities:** Bar; roof garden. *In room:* A/C, TV, minibar, hair dryer.

Nefeli Hotel ✦   The charming little Nefeli (Cloud) was completely redecorated in 1999. The guest rooms—most with air-conditioning—are small (as are the bathrooms) and nicely spare, with real character, unlike so many Athenian hotels. We also found the breakfast room congenial and the staff, particularly manager Tasos Kanellopoulos, courteous and helpful. Recent guests have reported considerable nighttime street noise from pedestrianized Angelikes Hatzimihali beside this once-quiet hotel. Evidently, the authorities are turning a blind eye to motorcyclists and revelers.

16 Iperidou, 10558 Athens. © 210/322-8044. Fax 210/322-5800. 18 units (13 with shower only). 85€ ($111) double. Rates include continental breakfast. AE, V. **Amenities:** Breakfast room. *In room:* A/C, TV.

INEXPENSIVE

Hotel Dioskouros (aka Dioskouros Guest House)   This is as good a deal as you'll get in the Plaka. Student friends who stayed here found the staff very helpful and the small garden enjoyable. They didn't mind the cramped (mostly dormitory-style) rooms, Plaka noise, or lack of air-conditioning and ceiling fans. Ah, to be young again! If it's full, try the nearby **Student's Inn,** 16 Kidathineon, where the facilities, prices, and noise are about the same.

6 Pittakou, Plaka, 10558 Athens. ✆ **210/324-8165.** Fax 210/321-0907. 12 units, none with bathroom. 25€–35€ ($33–$46) double. No credit cards.

MONASTIRAKI
MODERATE

Attalos Hotel ⊛   The six-story Attalos is well situated for visitors wanting to take in the frenzied daytime street life of the nearby Central Market, and the Psirri district's exuberant nighttime scene at the cafes and restaurants. Forty of the plain yet pleasant rooms have balconies and 12 have Acropolis views. The roof garden offers fine views of the city and the Acropolis. The Attalos (whose staff is very helpful) often gives Frommer's readers a 10% discount. *Caution:* Drug dealing and prostitution are not unknown on Athinas Street.

29 Athinas, 10554 Athens. ✆ **210/391-2801.** Fax 210/324-3124. www.attalos.gr. 80 units. 80€–100€ ($104–$130) double. Rates include buffet breakfast. AE, MC, V. From Monastiraki Sq., walk about 1½ blocks north on Athinas. **Amenities:** Luggage storage; nonsmoking rooms. *In room:* A/C, TV, hair dryer (most rooms), lock boxes.

Jason Inn Hotel ⊛ *(Value)*   On a dull street, but just a few blocks from the Agora, the Plaka, and the Psirri district, this renovated hotel offers attractive, comfortable rooms with double-paned windows for extra quiet. If you don't mind walking a few extra blocks to Syntagma, this is currently one of the best values in Athens, with an eager-to-help staff. If the Jason Inn is full, the staff may be able to find you a room in one of their other hotels: the similarly priced **Adrian Hotel,** on busy Hadrian in the Plaka; or the slightly less expensive **King Jason** or **Jason** hotels, both a few blocks from Omonia Square.

12 Ayion Assomaton, 10553 Athens. ✆ **210/325-1106.** Fax 210/523-4786. www.douros-hotels.com. 57 units. 90€–120€ ($117–$156) double. Rates include American buffet breakfast. AE, MC, V. From Monastiraki Sq., head west on Ermou, turn right at Thisio Metro station, pass small belowground church, and bear left. **Amenities:** Breakfast room; bar. *In room:* A/C, TV, minibar.

INEXPENSIVE

Hotel Tempi ⊛   If you believe that location is everything for a hotel, consider the three-story Tempi, which faces the flower market by the Church of Ayia Irini on a basically pedestrian-only street. The Tempi has very simply furnished rooms (bed, table, chair), the mattresses are overdue for replacement, and plumbing here can be a problem—hot water is intermittent, and the toilets can smell. But you can see the Acropolis from 10 of its balconied rooms (if you lean). This hotel is very popular with students and other spartan travelers able to ignore the Tempi's drawbacks and focus on its location, rates, and handy communal kitchen facilities.

29 Eolou, 10551 Athens. ✆ **210/321-3175.** Fax 210/325-4179. 24 units, 8 with bathroom. 60€ ($78) double without bathroom, 70€ ($91) double w/bathroom. AE, MC, V. From Syntagma Sq., take Ermou to Eolou.

GAZI
EXPENSIVE

Hotel Eridanus (Iridanos) ⊛   Another new boutique hotel arrives in Athens, this one with colors that alternate between the shockingly bright and the deeply soothing. The well-known fish restaurant Varoulko next door is associated with the hotel. Some rooms have Acropolis views. The walk from here to Omonia or Syntagma takes about 10 minutes. Probably not the place to stay on your first trip to Athens, when you may wish to be closer to the center and in a neighborhood not in the process of being gentrified.

78 Piraeus, 10551 Athens. ⓒ **210/520-5360**. www.eridanus.gr. 38 units. 200€–250€ ($260–$325) double. AE, MC, V **Amenities:** Restaurant; breakfast room; bar. *In room:* A/C, TV, minibar, Internet. From Syntagma Sq., take the Archaeological Park walkway to Piraeus Ave.

OMONIA
MODERATE/EXPENSIVE

Fresh Hotel ★   Trendy young Athenians flock to the in-house bar, Orange. Once an undistinguished hotel from the late 1970s, the redone rooms are now bold and bright with minimalist furnishings. The location is one of Athens's liveliest, what with the nearby Athens Central Market that opens before dawn, and the Omonia Square nightlife that ends after breakfast.

26 Sofokleus, 10564 Athens. ⓒ **210/524-8511**. www.freshhotel.gr. 133 units. 125€–200€ ($163–$260) double. From Omonia Sq., head south along Athinas until you reach Sofokleus. From Monastiraki Sq., head north along Athinas until you reach Sofokleus.

SYNTAGMA
VERY EXPENSIVE

Athens Plaza ★★   The Athens Plaza, managed by the Grecotel group, reopened its glitzy doors in March 1998 after a complete remodeling, and we were pretty excited to stay here shortly thereafter. Acres of marble adorn the lobby, and there's almost as much in some bathrooms, which have their own phones and hair dryers. Many of the guest rooms are larger than most living rooms, and many have balconies overlooking Syntagma Square. That said, the service, although perfectly professional, lacks the personal touch.

Syntagma Sq., 10564 Athens. ⓒ **210/325-5301**. Fax 210/323-5856 www.grecotel.gr. 207 units. 300€–400€ ($390–$520) double. AE, DC, MC, V. **Amenities:** 2 restaurants; 2 bars; health club and spa with Jacuzzi; concierge; tour desk; car-rental desk; courtesy car or airport pickup arranged; business center; 24-hr. room service; same-day laundry/dry-cleaning services; nonsmoking rooms; 1 room for those w/limited mobility. *In room:* AC, TV, dataport, minibar, hair dryer, iron, safe.

Grande Bretagne ★★★   The legendary Grande Bretagne, one of Athens's most distinguished 19th-century buildings, is back after a $70-million renovation. The changes preserved the exquisite Beaux Arts lobby, made dingy rooms grand once more, and added indoor and outdoor swimming pools. From Winston Churchill to Sting, the guests who stay here expect the highest level of attention. The Grande Bretagne prides itself on its service; you are unlikely to be disappointed. Ask for a room with a balcony overlooking Syntagma Square, the Parliament building, and the Acropolis.

Syntagma Sq., 10564 Athens. ⓒ **210/333-000**. Fax 210/333-0160. www.grandebretagne.gr. 328 units. 350€–800€ ($455–$1,040) double. AE, DC, MC, V. **Amenities:** 2 restaurants; 2 bars; 2 pools (indoors and outdoors); health club and spa with Jacuzzi; concierge; tour desk; car-rental desk; courtesy car or airport pickup arranged; business center; 24-hr. room service; same-day laundry/dry-cleaning services; nonsmoking rooms; 1 room for those w/limited mobility. *In room:* AC, TV, dataport, minibar, hair dryer, iron, safe.

EXPENSIVE

Electra Hotel ★ *(Value)*   If Ermou remains a pedestrian street, the Electra can boast a location that is quiet and central—steps from Syntagma Square. Most of the guest rooms have comfortable armchairs, large windows, and modern bathrooms with hair dryers. Take a look at your room before you accept it: Although most are large, some are quite tiny. The front desk is sometimes understaffed but the service is generally acceptable, although it can be brusque when groups are checking in and out.

5 Ermou, 10563 Athens. ☎ 210/322-3223. Fax 210/322-0310. electrahotels@ath.forthnet.gr. 110 units. 150€–200€ ($195–$260) double. Rates include buffet breakfast. AE, DC, MC, V. The Electra is about 2 blocks down on the left as you walk along Ermou with Syntagma Sq. behind you. **Amenities:** Restaurant; bar. *In room:* A/C, TV, minibar, hair dryer.

MODERATE

Astor Hotel
We've never been very impressed with this hotel, which does a heavy business in tour groups and has service that is impersonal at best. That said, a well-traveled journalist tells me that he always stays here when in Athens because of the central location (Karayioryi Servias runs into Syntagma Sq.), bright rooms (some with Acropolis views), and efficient (if not pleasant) front desk staff. He sometimes succeeds in bargaining down the room price.

16 Karayioryi Servias, 10562 Athens. ☎ **210/335-1000.** Fax 210/325-5115. www.astorhotel.gr. 131 units. 100€–150€ ($130–$195) double. Rates include buffet breakfast. AE, V. **Amenities:** Restaurant; bar. *In room:* A/C, TV.

Athens Cypria ★★
In a convenient central location on a (usually) quiet street, the renovated Cypria overlooks the Acropolis from unit nos. 603 to 607. With bright white halls and rooms, cheerful floral bedspreads and curtains, and freshly tiled bathrooms with new fixtures, the Cypria is a welcome addition to the city's moderately priced hotels. The breakfast buffet offers hot and cold dishes from 7 to 10am. The hotel can be infuriatingly slow in responding to faxed reservation requests.

5 Diomias, 10562 Athens. ☎ **210/323-8034.** Fax 210/324-8792. 71 units. 115€–135€ ($150–$176) double. Reductions possible off season. Rates include buffet breakfast. AE, MC, V. Take Karayioryi Servias out of Syntagma Sq; Diomias is on the left, after Lekka. **Amenities:** Breakfast room; bar; snack bar; luggage storage. *In room:* A/C, TV, minibar, hair dryer.

Hotel Achilleas
The Achilleas (Achilles), on a relatively quiet side street steps from Syntagma Square, underwent a total renovation in 2001. The good-sized guest rooms are now bright and cheerful, and the beds have new mattresses. Some rear rooms have small balconies; several on the fifth floor can be used as interconnecting family suites. The very central location of Hotel Achilleas and its fair prices make it a good choice. If you want a room with a safe or a hair dryer, ask at the main desk upon check-in.

21 Lekka, 10562 Athens. ☎ **210/323-3197.** Fax 210/322-2412. www.achilleashotel.gr. 34 units. 150€ ($195) double. Rates include breakfast. AE, DC, MC, V. Take Karayioryi Servias out of Syntagma Sq. for 2 blocks and turn right onto Lekka. **Amenities:** Breakfast room; snack bar. *In room:* A/C, TV, minibar. Hair dryer, safe in some.

INEXPENSIVE

Hotel Carolina ★★
The friendly, family-owned and -operated Carolina, on the outskirts of Plaka, is a brisk 5-minute walk from Syntagma and has always been popular with students. In the last few years, the Carolina has undertaken extensive remodeling and now attracts a wide range of frugal travelers. Double-glazed windows and air-conditioning make the guest rooms especially comfortable. Many rooms have large balconies, and several (such as no. 308) with four or five beds are popular with families and students. The congenial atmosphere may be a bit too noisy for some.

55 Kolokotroni, 10560 Athens. ☎ 210/324-3551. Fax 210/324-3350. hotelcarolina@galaxynet.gr. 31 units. 75€–100€ ($91–$130) double. Breakfast is negotiable 5€ ($6.50). MC, V. Take Stadiou out of Syntagma Sq. to Kolokotroni (on left). **Amenities:** Breakfast room; bar. *In room:* A/C, TV.

KOLONAKI
VERY EXPENSIVE

St. George Lycabettus Hotel ★★ As yet, the distinctive, classy St. George does not get many tour groups, which contributes to its tranquil tone. The rooftop pool is a real plus, as are the two excellent restaurants (much-favored by wealthy Greeks for private events). Floors have differing decorative motifs, from baroque to modern Italian. Most rooms look toward Mount Likavitos; some have views of the Acropolis. Others overlook a small park or have interior views. The hotel is just steps from chic Kolonaki restaurants and shops. The surrounding street traffic, however, keeps it from being an oasis of calm.

2 Kleomenous, 10675 Athens. ℂ 210/729-0711. Fax 210/721-0439. www.sglycabettus.gr. 167 units. 175€–300€ ($228–$390) double. Compulsory breakfast 20€ ($26). AE, DC, MC, V. From Kolonaki Sq., take Patriarchou Ioachim to Loukianou and follow Loukianou uphill to Kleomenous. Turn left on Kleomenous; the hotel overlooks Dexamini Park. **Amenities:** 2 restaurants; 2 bars; pool; concierge; business center; 24-hr. room service; same-day laundry/dry-cleaning services; nonsmoking rooms. *In room:* A/C, TV, minibar, hair dryer.

EMBASSY DISTRICT
VERY EXPENSIVE

Andromeda Hotel ★★★ The city's only boutique hotel is easily the most charming in Athens, with a staff that makes you feel as if this is your home away from home. The very quiet hotel overlooks the garden of the American ambassador's home. Guest rooms are large and elegantly decorated, with furniture and paintings you'd be happy to live with. Marvelous breakfasts and snacks are served (at present there is no on-site restaurant). The only drawbacks: The Andromeda is a serious hike (20–30 min.) or a 10-minute taxi ride to Syntagma; and there are few restaurants in this residential neighborhood, although the superb Vlassis is just around the corner.

22 Timoleontos Vassou (off Plateia Mavili), 11521 Athens. ℂ **210/643-7302.** Fax 210/646-6361. www.andromeda hotels.gr. 42 units. 435€–580€ ($566–$754) double. Rates include breakfast. Special rates sometimes available. AE, DC, MC, V. **Amenities:** Restaurant; breakfast room; bar. *In room:* A/C, TV, minibar, hair dryer, wall safe, Internet access.

Hilton ★★★ When the Hilton opened in 1963, it was the tallest building on the horizon—and the most modern hotel in town. In 2001, it closed for a long-overdue renovation, and 3 years and 96 million euros later, it reopened. Everything that was tired is now spanking-new and fresh. As before, small shops, a salon, and cafes and restaurants surround the glitzy lobby. The guest rooms (looking toward either the hills outside Athens or the Acropolis) have large marble bathrooms and are decorated in the generic but comfortable international Hilton style, with some Greek touches. The Plaza Executive floor of rooms and suites offers a separate business center and a higher level of service. Facilities include a large outdoor pool, conference rooms, and a handy ATM in the lobby. The Hilton often runs promotions, so ask about special rates before booking.

46 Leoforos Vas. Sofias, 11528 Athens. ℂ **800/445-8667** in the U.S., or 210/728-1000. Fax 210/728-1111. www. hilton.com. 275€–437€ ($358–$568) double. AE, DC, MC, V. **Amenities:** 4 restaurants; 3 bars; outdoor freshwater pool; health club and spa with Jacuzzi; game room; concierge; tour desk; car-rental desk; airport pickup arranged; business center; secretarial services; shopping arcade; salon; 24-hr. room service; babysitting; same-day laundry/dry-cleaning services; nonsmoking rooms; partly handicapped accessible. *In room:* A/C, TV, dataport, minibar, hair dryer, safe.

KOUKAKI & MAKRIYANNI (NEAR THE ACROPOLIS)
With all the Makriyanni/Koukaki hotels, you'll do some extra walking to get to most places you'll want to visit.

Acropolis View Hotel **1**
Austria Hotel **2**
Divani-Palace Acropolis **3**
Marble House Pension **4**

VERY EXPENSIVE

Divani-Palace Acropolis ★★   Just 3 blocks south of the Acropolis, in a quiet residential neighborhood, the Divani Palace Acropolis does a brisk tour business but also welcomes independent travelers. The blandly decorated guest rooms are large and comfortable, and some of the large bathrooms even have two wash basins. The cavernous marble-and-glass lobby contains copies of classical sculpture; a section of Athens's 5th-century-B.C. defense wall is preserved behind glass in the basement by the gift shop. The breakfast buffet is extensive. (There's a handy SPAR supermarket a block away at 4 Parthenos, as well as a shop at 7 Parthenos that sells English-language newspapers.) The same hotel group operates **Divani Caravel Hotel,** near the National Art Gallery and the Hilton at 2 Leoforos Vas. Alexandrou (✆ **210/725-3725**).

19–25 Parthenonos, Makriyanni, 11742 Athens. ✆ **210/922-2945.** Fax 210/921-4993. www.divanis.gr/hotels. 253 units. 200€–350€ ($260–$455) double. Breakfast buffet included. AE, DC, MC, V. From Syntagma Sq., take Amalias to Dionissiou Areopagitou; turn left onto Parthenos. The hotel is on your left after 3 blocks. **Amenities:** Restaurant; 2 bars; pool; concierge; business center; 24-hr. room service. *In room:* A/C, TV, dataport, minibar, hair dryer, safe.

MODERATE

Acropolis View Hotel ★   This nicely maintained hotel is on a pleasant residential side street off Rovertou Galli, not far from the Herodes Atticus theater. The usually quiet neighborhood, at the base of Filopappos Hill (itself a pleasant area to explore) is a 10- to 15-minute walk from the heart of the Plaka. Many of the small but pleasant guest rooms are freshly painted each year. All units have good bathrooms as well as balconies. Some, such as room no. 405, overlook Filopappos Hill, while others, such as room no. 407, face the Acropolis.

Rovertou Galli and 10 Webster, 11742 Athens. ℭ **210/921-7303.** Fax 210/923-0705. 32 units. 125€ ($163) double. Rates include buffet breakfast. Substantial reductions Nov–Apr 1. AE, MC, V. From Syntagma Sq. take Amalias to Dionysiou Areopagitou; head west past Herodes Atticus theater to Rovertou Galli. Webster (Gouemster on some maps) is the little street intersecting Rovertou Galli between Propilion and Garabaldi. **Amenities:** Breakfast room; bar. *In room:* A/C, TV, minibar.

Austria Hotel ℛ This very well-maintained hotel at the base of wooded Filopappos Hill is operated by a Greek-Austrian family who can point you to local sites (including a convenient neighborhood laundry!). The Austria's guest rooms and bathrooms are rather spartan (the linoleum floors aren't enchanting) but are more than acceptable—and the very efficient staff is a real plus. You can sun yourself or sit under an awning on the rooftop and enjoy a great view over Athens and out to sea. (I could see the island of Aegina.)

7 Mousson, Filopappou, 11742 Athens. ℭ **210/923-5151.** Fax 210/924-7350. www.austriahotel.com. 36 units (11 with shower only). 125€ ($163) double. Rates include breakfast. AE, DC, MC, V. Follow Dionysiou Areopagitou around the south side of the Acropolis to where it meets Roverto Galli; take Garibaldi around the base of Filopappou Hill until you reach Mousson. **Amenities:** Breakfast room; rooftop terrace. *In room:* A/C, TV.

INEXPENSIVE

Marble House Pension ℛℛ Named for its marble facade, which is usually covered with bougainvillea, this small hotel, whose front rooms offer balconies overlooking quiet Zinni Street, is famous among budget travelers (including many teachers) for its friendly staff. Over the last several years, the pension has been remodeled and redecorated, gaining new bathrooms and guest room furniture (including small fridges). Two units have kitchenettes. If you're spending more than a few days in Athens and don't mind being outside the center (and a partly uphill 25-min. walk to the hotel), this is a homey base.

35 A. Zinni, Koukaki, 11741 Athens. ℭ **210/923-4058.** Fax 210/922-6461. 16 units, 12 with bathroom. 50€ ($65) double without bathroom; 60€ ($78) double w/bathroom. 9€ ($12) supplement for A/C. Monthly rates available off season. No credit cards. From Syntagma Sq. take Amalias to Syngrou; turn right onto Zinni; the hotel is in the cul-de-sac beside the small church. **Amenities:** 2 rooms for those w/limited mobility. *In room:* A/C (9 units), TV, minibar.

3 Where to Dine

Since June 2000, Greek restaurants have been required by law to display a menu with prices either in the window or in another prominent place. Most restaurants have menus in Greek and English, but many don't keep their printed (or handwritten) menus up-to-date. If the menu is not in English, a restaurant employee can almost always either translate or rattle off suggestions for you in English. The same suggestions may be repeated to you at different restaurants, as staff tend to suggest what most tourists request. In Athens, that means moussaka (baked eggplant casserole with ground meat), souvlaki (chunks of beef, chicken, pork, or lamb grilled on a skewer), *pastitsio* (baked pasta with ground meat and a béchamel sauce), or *dolmadakia* (grape leaves stuffed with rice and ground meat). Although these dishes can be delicious—you may have eaten them outside Greece and are looking forward to enjoying the real thing here—you may end up cherishing your memories and regretting your meal. All too often, restaurants catering to tourists tend to serve profoundly dull moussaka and unpleasantly chewy *souvlaki*. We hope that the places we suggest do better.

Over the last decade, an increasing number of Athenian restaurants have begun to experiment with a "nouvelle Greek" cuisine. This involves elements of *paradisiako* (traditional) cooking, but with a lighter hand on the olive oil and an adventurous combination of familiar ingredients. Our reviews draw attention to these restaurants.

Since November 2002, restaurants have been required by law to offer nonsmoking seating. You may or may not find this law enforced.

THE PLAKA

Some of the most charming old restaurants in Athens are in the Plaka—as are some of the worst tourist traps. In general, it's a good idea to avoid places with floor shows; many charge outrageous amounts (and levy surcharges not always openly stated on menus) for drinks and food. If you get burned, stand your ground, phone the **tourist police** (② 171), and pay nothing before they arrive. Often the mere threat of calling the tourist police has the miraculous effect of causing a bill to be lowered.

EXPENSIVE

Daphne's ★★★ ELEGANT GREEK/NOUVELLE   Frescoes adorn the walls of this neoclassical 1830s former home, which includes a shady garden courtyard displaying bits of ancient marble found on-site. Diners from around the world sit at Daphne's tables. The courtyard makes it a real oasis in Athens, especially when summer nights are hot. The food here—recommended by the *New York Times, Travel and Leisure,* and just about everywhere else—gives you all the old favorites with new distinction (try the zesty eggplant salad), and combines familiar ingredients in innovative ways (delicious hot pepper and feta cheese dip). We could cheerfully eat the hors d'oeuvres all night. We have also enjoyed the *stifado* (stew) of rabbit in *mavrodaphne* (sweet wine) sauce and the tasty prawns with toasted almonds. Many nights, live music plays in the background. The staff is attentive, encouraging, endearing, and beyond excellent.

4 Lysikratous. ②/fax 210/322-7971. Main courses 16€–30€ ($21–$39), with some fish priced by the kilo. Reservations recommended. AE, DC, MC, V. Daily 7pm–1am. Closed Dec 20–Jan 15.

MODERATE

Eden Vegetarian Restaurant ★ VEGETARIAN   You can find vegetarian dishes at almost every Greek restaurant, but if you want to experience organically grown products, soy (rather than eggplant) moussaka, mushroom pie with a whole-wheat crust, freshly squeezed juices, and salads with bean sprouts, join the young Athenians

---

Tips A Note on Credit Cards

One of my most humiliating travel moments happened a number of years ago when I was taking Athenian friends out to dinner—and planning to pay with a credit card. The restaurant took only cash, and my friends ended up having to take me to dinner. Much has changed in Athens since then, but one thing that has not changed is that many Athenian restaurants still do not accept credit cards. Consider yourself warned.

and Europeans who patronize the Eden. The prices are reasonable, if not cheap, and the decor is engaging, with 1920s-style prints and mirrors and wrought-iron lamps.

12 Lissiou ©/fax **210/324-8858.** Main courses 8€–15€ ($10–$20). AE, MC, V. Daily noon–midnight. Closed Tues and usually closed Aug. From Syntagma Sq., head south on Filellinon or Nikis to Kidathineon, which intersects Adrianou; turn right on Adrianou and take Mnissikleos up 2 blocks toward Acropolis to Lissiou.

Platanos Taverna ★★ TRADITIONAL GREEK   This taverna on a quiet pedestrian square has tables outdoors in good weather beneath a spreading plane tree (*platanos* means plane tree). Inside, where locals usually congregate to escape the summer sun at midday and where tourists gather in the evening, you can enjoy the old paintings and photos on the walls. The Platanos has been serving good *spitiko fageto* (home cooking) since 1932 and has managed to keep steady customers happy while enchanting visitors. If artichokes or spinach with lamb are on the menu, you're in luck: They're delicious. There's a wide choice of bottled wines from many regions of Greece, although the house wine is tasty. Plan to come here and relax, not rush, through a meal.

4 Dioyenous © **210/322-0666.** Fax 210/322-8624. Main courses 7€–15€ ($9–$20). No credit cards. Mon–Sat noon–4:30pm and 8pm–midnight; Sun in Mar, Apr, May, Sept, and Oct noon–4:30pm. From Syntagma Sq., head south on Filellinon or Nikis to Kidathineon. Turn right on Adrianou, and take Mnissikleos up 1 block toward the Acropolis; turn right onto Dioyenous.

Taverna Xinos ★ TRADITIONAL GREEK   Despite the forgivable spelling lapse, Xinos's business card says it best: "In the heart of old Athens there is still a flace where the traditional Greek way of cooking is upheld." In summer, sit at tables in the courtyard; in winter, warm yourself by the coal-burning stove and admire the frescoes. While the strolling musicians may not be as good as the Three Tenors, they do sing wonderful Greek golden oldies, accompanying themselves on the guitar and bouzouki. (If you're serenaded, you may want to give the musicians a tip. If you want to hear the theme from "Never on Sunday," ask for "Ena Zorbas.") Most evenings, tourists predominate until after 10pm, when locals begin to arrive—as they have since Xinos opened in 1935.

4 Geronta. © **210/322-1065.** Main courses 6€–15€ ($7.80–$20). No credit cards. Daily 8pm to any time from 11pm–1am; sometimes closed Sun. Usually closed part of July and Aug. From Syntagma Sq., head south on Filellinon or Nikis to Kidathineon; turn right on Geronta and look for the xɪɴᴏs sign in the cul-de-sac.

INEXPENSIVE
Damigos (The Bakaliarakia) ★★★ GREEK/SEAFOOD   This basement taverna, with enormous wine barrels in the back room and an ancient column supporting the roof in the front room, has been serving delicious deep-fried codfish and eggplant, as well as chops and stews, since 1865. The wine comes from the family vineyards. There are few pleasures greater than sipping retsina—if you wish, you can buy a bottle to take away—while you watch the cook turn out unending meals in his absurdly small kitchen. Don't miss the delicious *skordalia* (garlic sauce), equally good with cod, eggplant, bread—well, you get the idea.

41 Kidathineon. © **210/322-5084.** Main courses 6€–10€ ($7.80–$13). No credit cards. Daily 7pm to any time from 11pm–1am. Usually closed June–Sept. From Syntagma Sq., head south on Filellinon or Nikis to Kidathineon; Damigos is downstairs on the left just before Adrianou.

Kouklis Ouzeri (To Yerani) ★ GREEK/MEZEDES   Besides Kouklis Ouzeri and To Yerani, Greeks call this popular old favorite with its winding staircase to the second floor the "Skolario" because of the nearby school. Sit down at one of the small tables and a waiter will present a large tray with about a dozen plates of *mezedes*—appetizer portions of fried fish, beans, grilled eggplant, taramosalata, cucumber-and-tomato salad, olives, fried cheese, sausages, and other seasonal specialties. Choose the ones that appeal to you. If you manage not to order all 12, you'll have a tasty and inexpensive meal, washed down with the house *krasi* (wine). No prices are posted, but the waiter will help you if you ask. Now if only the staff could be a bit more patient when foreigners are trying to decide what to order. . . .

14 Tripodon. ℂ **210/324-7605**. Appetizers 5€–15€ ($6.50–$20). No credit cards. Daily 11am–2am. From Syntagma Sq., head south on Filellinon or Nikis to Kidathineon; take Kidathineon across Adrianou to Thespidos and climb toward Acropolis; Tripodon is 1st st. on right after Adrianou.

MONASTIRAKI
INEXPENSIVE

Taverna Sigalas GREEK This longtime Plaka taverna, housed in a vintage 1879 commercial building with a newer outdoor pavilion, boasts that it has been run by the same family for a century and is open 365 days a year. Huge old retsina kegs stand piled against the back walls; dozens of black-and-white photos of Greek movie stars are everywhere. After 8pm, Greek muzak plays. At all hours, both Greeks and tourists wolf down large portions of stews, moussaka, grilled meatballs, baked tomatoes, and gyros, washing it all down with the house red and white retsinas.

2 Plateia Monastiraki. ℂ **210/321-3036**. Main courses 6€–15€ ($7.80–$20). No credit cards. Daily 7am–2am. Sigalas is across Monastiraki Sq. from the Metro station.

Thanasis 🎄 GREEK/SOUVLAKI Thanasis serves terrific souvlaki and pita—and exceptionally good french fries—both to go and at its outdoor and indoor tables. As always, prices are higher if you sit down to eat. On weekends, it often takes the strength and determination of an Olympic athlete to get through the door and place an order here. It's worth the effort: This is both a great budget choice and a great place to take in the local scene, which often includes a fair sprinkling of Gypsies.

69 Mitropoleos (just off the northeast corner of Monastiraki Sq.). ℂ **210/324-4705**. Main courses 4€–10€ ($5.20–$13). No credit cards. Daily 9am–2am.

MODERATE

Abyssinia Cafe 🎄 GREEK This small cafe in a ramshackle building sports a nicely restored interior featuring lots of gleaming dark wood and polished copper. It faces lopsided Abyssinia Square off Ifaistou, where furniture restorers ply their trade and antiques shops sell everything from gramophones to hubcaps. You can sit indoors or out with a coffee, but it's tempting to snack on Cheese Abyssinia (feta scrambled with spices and garlic), mussels and rice pilaf, or *keftedes* (meatballs). Everything is reasonably priced here, but it's easy to run up quite a tab, because everything is so good.

Plateia Abyssinia, Monastiraki. ℂ **210/321-7047**. Appetizers and main courses 5€–15€ ($6.50–$20). No credit cards. Tues–Sun 10:30am–2pm (often open evenings as well). Usually closed for a week at Christmas and Easter; sometimes closed part of Jan and Feb and mid-July to mid-Aug. Abyssinia Sq. is just off Ifaistou (Hephaistos) across from Ancient Agora's entrance on Adrianou.

SYNTAGMA
EXPENSIVE

Aegli 🎄🎄 INTERNATIONAL For years, the bistro in the Zappeion Gardens was a popular meeting spot; when it closed in the 1970s, it was sorely missed. Now it is back, along with a cinema and fine restaurant. Once more, chic Athenian families head here, to the cool of the Zappeion Gardens, for the frequently changing menu of chef

Quick Bites in Syntagma

In general, Syntagma Square is not known for good food, but the area has a number of places at which to get a snack. **Apollonion Bakery,** 10 Nikis, and **Elleniki Gonia,** 10 Karayioryi Servias, make sandwiches to order and sell croissants, both stuffed and plain. **Ariston** is a small chain of *zaharoplastia* (confectioners) with a branch at the corner of Karayioryi Servias and Voulis (just off Syntagma Sq.); it sells snacks as well as pastries.

For the quintessentially Greek, *loukoumades* (round donut-center–like pastries that are deep-fried, then drenched with honey and topped with powdered sugar and cinnamon), try **Doris,** 30 Praxitelous, a continuation of Lekka, a few blocks from Syntagma Square. If you're still hungry, Doris serves hearty stews and pasta dishes for absurdly low prices Monday through Saturday until 3:30pm. If you're nearer Omonia Square when you feel the need for loukoumades or a soothing dish of rice pudding, try **Aigina** ✸, 46 Panepistimiou.

Everest is another chain worth trying; there's one a block north of Kolonaki Square at Tsakalof and Iraklitou. Also in Kolonaki Square, **To Kotopolo** serves succulent grilled chicken to take out or eat in. In the Plaka, **K. Kotsolis Pastry Shop,** 112 Adrianou, serves excellent coffee and sweets; it's an oasis of old-fashioned charm in the midst of the souvenir shops. **Oraia Ellada (Beautiful Greece)** cafe at the Center of Hellenic Tradition, opening onto both 36 Pandrossou and 59 Mitropoleos near the flea market, has a spectacular view of the Acropolis. You can revive yourself here with a cappuccino and pastries.

Jean-Louis Kapsalis. Some of his specialties have included foie gras, oysters, tenderloin with ginger and coffee sauce, profiteroles, fresh sorbets, strawberry soup, and delicious yogurt crème brûlée. Tables indoors or outdoors by the trees offer places to relax with coffee. In the evening, take in a movie at the open-air cinema here before dinner, or have a drink and a snack at one of the nearby cafes. In short, this is a wonderful spot at which to wile away an afternoon or evening—and a definite destination for a special occasion.

Zappeion Gardens (adjacent to the National Gardens fronting Vas. Amalias Blvd.). ℃ 210/336-9363. Main courses 18€–30€ ($23–$39). Reservations recommended. Daily 10am–midnight. Sometimes closed in Aug.

INEXPENSIVE

Neon ✸ *(Value* GREEK/INTERNATIONAL   If you're tired of practicing your restaurant Greek, the Neon restaurants are good places to eat, since they are mostly self-service. You'll find lots of tourists here, as well as Athenians in a rush to get a bite, and a fair number of elderly Greeks who come here for a bit of companionship. This centrally located member of the chain is very convenient, although not as pleasant as the original on Omonia Square. There is also a very handy Neon a block north of Kolonaki Square at Tsakalof and Iraklitou. You're sure to find something to your taste—maybe a Mexican omelet, spaghetti Bolognese, the salad bar, or sweets ranging from Black Forest cake to tiramisu.

3 Mitropoleos (on the southwest corner of Syntagma Sq.). ℃ 210/322-8155. Snacks 5€–8€ ($6.50–$10); sandwiches 5€–10€ ($6.50–$13); main courses 5€–15€ ($6.50–$20). No credit cards. Daily 9am–midnight.

KOLONAKI
MODERATE

Filipou ✦ TRADITIONAL GREEK   This longtime Athenian favorite almost never disappoints. The traditional dishes such as stuffed cabbage, stuffed vine leaves, vegetable stews, and fresh salads are consistently good. In the heart of Kolonaki, near the very fashionable St. George Lykabettus Hotel, this is a place to head for when you want good *spitiko* (home cooking) in the company of the Greeks and resident expatriates who prize the food.

19 Xenokratous. ☎ 210/721-6390. Main courses 6€–20€ ($7.80–$26). No credit cards. Mon–Fri 8:30pm–midnight; Sat lunch; closed Sun. From Kolonaki Sq., take Patriarch Ioakim to Ploutarchou, turn left on Ploutarchou, and then turn right onto Xenokratous.

Rhodia ✦ TRADITIONAL GREEK   This respected taverna is located in a handsome old Kolonaki house. In good weather, tables are set up in its small garden—although the interior, with its tile floor and old prints, is equally charming. The Rhodia is a favorite of visiting archaeologists from the nearby British and American Schools of Classical Studies, as well as of Kolonaki residents. It may not sound like just what you've always hoped to have for dinner, but the octopus in mustard sauce is terrific, as are the veal and *dolmades* (stuffed grape leaves) in egg-lemon sauce. The house wine is excellent, as is the halva, which manages to be both creamy and crunchy.

44 Aristipou. ☎ 210/722-9883. Main courses 8€–18€ ($10–$23). No credit cards. Mon–Sat 8pm–2am. From Kolonaki Sq., take Patriarkou Ioakim uphill to Loukianou; turn left on Loukianou, climb steeply uphill to Aristipou, and turn right.

To Kafeneio ✦✦ GREEK/INTERNATIONAL   This is hardly a typical *kafeneio* (coffee shop/cafe). If you relax, you can easily run up a substantial tab of 50€ ($65) for lunch or dinner for two, but you can also eat more modestly yet equally elegantly. If you have something light, like the artichokes *a la polita,* leeks in crème fraîche, or onion pie (one, not all three!), washed down with draft beer or the house wine, you can finish with profiteroles and not put too big a dent in your budget. I've always found this an especially congenial spot when I'm eating alone (perhaps because I love people-watching and profiteroles).

26 Loukianou. ☎ 210/722-9056. Reservations recommended. Main courses 8€–25€ ($10–$33). No credit cards. Mon–Sat 11am–midnight or later. Closed Sun and most of Aug. From Kolonaki Sq., follow Patriarkou Ioakim several blocks uphill to Loukianou, and turn right.

To Ouzadiko ✦✦ GREEK/MEZEDES   This ouzo bar offers at least 40 kinds of ouzo and as many *mezedes,* including fluffy *keftedes* (meatballs) that make all others taste leaden. To Ouzadiko is very popular with Athenians young and old who come to see and be seen while having a snack or a full meal, often after concerts and plays. A serious foodie friend of mine comes here especially for the wide variety of *horta* (greens), which she says are the best she's ever tasted. If you see someone at a nearby table eating something you want and aren't sure what it is, ask your waiter and it will appear for you—sometimes after a bit of a wait, as the staff here is often seriously overworked.

25–29 Karneadou (in the Lemos International Shopping Center), Kolonaki. ☎ 210/729-5484. Reservations recommended. Most *mezedes* and main courses 8€–20€ ($10–$26). No credit cards. Tues–Sat 1pm–12:30am. Closed Aug. From Kolonaki Sq. take Kapsali across Irodotou into Karneadou. The Lemos Center is the mini-skyscraper on your left.

To Prytaneion ❀ GREEK/INTERNATIONAL   The trendy bare stone walls here are decorated with movie posters and illuminated by baby spotlights. Waiters with cellphones serve customers with cellphones tempting plates of some of Athens's most expensive and eclectic *mezedes,* including beef carpaccio, smoked salmon, bruschetta, and shrimp in fresh cream, as well as grilled veggies and that international favorite, the hamburger. This place is so drop-dead chic that it's a pleasant surprise to learn that it functioned as a neighborhood hangout during the earthquake of 1999 and during the snow storm that shut down Athens in 2001.

7 Milioni, Kolonaki. ℭ 210/364-3353. www.prytaneion.gr. Reservations recommended. *Mezedes* and snacks 8€–30€ ($10–$39). No credit cards. Mon–Sat 10am–2am. From Kolonaki Sq., head downhill a block or 2 until you hit Milioni on your right. To Prytaneion is on your left.

INEXPENSIVE

Neon GREEK/INTERNATIONAL   The Kolonaki Neon serves the same food as the Syntagma and Omonia branches, but the reasonable prices are especially welcome in this pricey neighborhood. Tsakalof is a shady pedestrian arcade, and the Neon has tables inside and outdoors.

6 Tsakalof, Kolonaki Sq. ℭ 210/364-6873. Snacks 5€–8€ ($6.50–$10); sandwiches 5€–10€ ($6.50–$13); main courses 5€–15€ ($6.50–$20). No credit cards. Daily 9am–midnight.

OMONIA SQUARE & UNIVERSITY AREA (NEAR EXARCHIA SQUARE/ARCHAEOLOGICAL MUSEUM)

MODERATE

Athinaikon ❀❀ GREEK/OUZERIE   Not many tourists come to this favorite haunt of lawyers and businesspeople who work in the Omonia Square area. You can stick to appetizers (technically, this *is* an ouzeri) or have a full meal. Appetizers include delicious *loukanika* (sausages) and *keftedes* (meatballs); pass up the more expensive grilled shrimp and the seafood paella. The adventurous can try *ameletita* (lamb's testicles). Whatever you have, you'll enjoy taking in the old photos on the walls, the handsome tiled floor, the marble-topped tables and bentwood chairs, and the regular customers, who combine serious eating with animated conversation.

2 Themistokleous. ℭ 210/383-8485. Appetizers and main courses 5€–16€ ($6.50–$21). No credit cards. Mon–Sat 11am–midnight. Closed Sun and usually in Aug. From Omonia Sq., take Panepistimou a block to Themistokleous; the Athinaikon is almost immediately on your right.

Ideal ❀ GREEK TRADITIONAL   The oldest restaurant in the heart of Athens, today's Ideal has an Art Deco decor and lots of old favorites, from egg-lemon soup to stuffed peppers, from pork with celery to lamb with spinach. Ideal is a favorite of businesspeople, and the service is usually brisk, especially at lunchtime. Not the place for a quiet or romantic rendezvous, but definitely the place for good, hearty Greek cooking.

46 Panepistimiou. ℭ 210/330-3000. Reservations recommended. Main courses 8€–15€ ($10–$20). AE, DC, MC, V. Mon–Sat noon–midnight. From Omonia or Syntagma, take Panepistimiou (the Ideal is just outside Omonia Sq.).

INEXPENSIVE

Neon *(Value)* GREEK/INTERNATIONAL   In a handsome 1920s building, the Neon serves up cafeteria-style food, including cooked-to-order pasta, omelets, and grills, as well as salads and sweets. Equally good for a meal or a snack, the Omonia Neon proves that fast food doesn't have to be junk food. Prices here are a bit lower than those at the Syntagma and Kolonaki branches.

1 Dorou, Omonia Sq. ☎ **210/522-9939.** Snacks 5€–8€ ($6.50–$10); sandwiches 5€–10€ ($6.50–$13); main courses 5€–15€ ($6.50–$20). No credit cards. Daily 9am–midnight.

Taygetos ✭ (*Value*) GREEK/SOUVLAKI   This is a great place to stop for a quick meal on your way to/from the National Archaeological Museum. The service is swift and the souvlaki and fried potatoes are excellent, as are the chicken and the grilled lamb. The menu sometimes features delicious *kokoretsi* (grilled entrails). The Ellinikon Restaurant next door is also a good value.

4 Satovriandou. ☎ **210/523-5352.** Grilled lamb and chicken priced by the kilo. No credit cards. Mon–Sat 9am–1am. From Omonia Sq. take Patision toward National Museum; Satovriandou is 3rd major turning on your left.

HERE & THERE & WORTH THE JOURNEY

AristeraDexia ✭ GREEK/INTERNATIONAL   Gazi, the district once best known as the home of Athens's gasworks, is following in Psirri's fashionable footsteps. AristeraDexia, with its glass catwalk over the wine cellar, open kitchen, and endless small tables packed with hipsters with cellphones, is one of Athens's hot spots. As for the food, it draws on traditional Greek flavors and ingredients, but combines them in unusual ways. The always-changing menu has included crayfish dressed with lavender and squid in egg-lemon sauce. Some simpler—and cheaper—dishes, such as grilled stuffed sardines, have been added.

3 Andronkou, Gazi. ☎ **210/342-2380.** Reservations recommended. Main courses 15€–30€ ($20–$39); fish priced by the kilo. AE, V. Mon–Sat 9pm–1am.

Kostoyiannis ✭✭ TRADITIONAL GREEK   Kostoyiannis has been doing everything right since the 1950s, serving a wide range of fresh seafood, grills, sweetbreads, and their signature *stifados* (rabbit or veal stews). Arriving here is a joy, as you walk past a display of what can be cooked to perfection for you. Inside the bustling restaurant, contented diners tuck into their choices. There's an indoor room and a garden. This is one of the nicest places in town to spend a leisurely evening watching more and more people arrive as concerts and theater performances let out across Athens.

37 Zaimi, Pedion Areos, behind the National Archaeological Museum. ☎ **210/822-0624.** Reservations recommended. Main courses 15€–25€ ($20–$33); fish and shellfish by the kilo. No credit cards. Mon–Sat 8pm–midnight. Closed Sun and late July-Aug.

Spondi ✭✭✭ INTERNATIONAL   *Athinorama,* the weekly review of the Athenian scene, has chosen Spondi several years running as the best place in town. The menu features light dishes—the fresh fish, especially the salmon, is superb—as well as dishes that you will find either delightful or a bit cloying (roast pork with myzithra cheese and a fig and yogurt sauce). The setting, a handsome 19th-century town house with a courtyard, is lovely; the wine list, extensive; the service, excellent; and the desserts, divine. You'll probably want to take a cab here.

5 Pyrronos, Pangrati. ☎ **210/752-0658.** Reservations recommended. Main courses 20€–35€ ($26–$46). No credit cards. Mon–Sat 8pm–1am. Pyrronos runs between Empedokleous and Dikearchou, behind the Olympic Stadium.

Varoulko ✭✭✭ INTERNATIONAL   After years in an unlikely location on a Piraeus side street, chef-owner Lefteris Lazarou has moved into central Athens what many already considered the greater Athens area's finest seafood restaurant. I had one of the best meals of my life here—smoked eel; artichokes with fish roe; crayfish with sun-dried tomatoes; monkfish livers with soy sauce, honey, and balsamic vinegar— and the best sea bass and monkfish I have ever eaten. Sweetbreads, goat stew, and tripe soup have joined seafood on the menu—and the new location on Piraios has a drop-dead view of the Acropolis.

80 Piraios, Athens. © 210/522-8400. www.varoulko.gr. Reservations necessary (several days in advance). Dinner for 2 from about 120€ ($156); fish priced by the kilo. No credit cards. Mon–Sat about 8pm–midnight. Closed Sun and most of June–Sept, when it often relocates outdoors at the Peace and Friendship Stadium. From Syntagma, follow the Archaeological Walkway to Piraios. This is not a short walk and you may prefer to take a taxi.

Vlassis ★★★ TRADITIONAL GREEK   Greeks call this kind of food *paradisiako* (traditional), but paradisiacal is just as good a description. This very reasonably priced food is fit for the gods: delicious fluffy vegetable croquettes, a unique eggplant salad, and hauntingly tender lamb in egg-lemon sauce. Vlassis is so popular with Athenians that it doesn't need even a discreet sign announcing its presence in a small apartment building on hard-to-find Paster. Each time I eat here, I seem to be the only obvious foreigner. Figure the price of a taxi (no more than 10€/$13) into your meal tab; you may feel so giddy with delight after eating that you won't mind the half-hour walk back to Syntagma.

8 Paster (off Plateia Mavili). © 210/646-3060. 8€–20€ ($10–$26). Reservations recommended. No credit cards. Mon–Sat 8pm–1am. Closed much of June–Sept. From Syntagma Sq., take Vasilissis Sophias to Plateia Mavili, and follow D. Tsoustou out of Plateia Mavili to Chatzikosta; Paster is the cul-de-sac on the left after you turn right onto Chatzikosta.

4 Seeing the Sights

THE TREASURES OF ANTIQUITY

At press time, ticket prices for many monuments and museums were in flux. Our prices are based on those available at press time and on "guesstimates" offered by some museums. As there is—surprise!—no fixed policy on cheaper tickets for students and seniors, be sure to ask about a discounted ticket if you fall into either category. Often these discounts apply only to members of Common Market countries. Also, ask for the handy information brochure available at most sites and museums; ticket sellers do not always hand it over unless reminded.

The Acropolis ★★★   The Acropolis is one of a handful of places in the world that is so well known, you may be anxious when you finally get here. Will it be as beautiful as its photographs? Will it be, ever so slightly, a disappointment? Rest assured: The Acropolis does not disappoint—but it *is* infuriatingly crowded. What you want here is time—time to watch the Parthenon's columns appear first beige, then golden, then rose, then stark white in changing light; time to stand on the Belvedere and take in the view over Athens (and listen to the muted conversations floating up from the Plaka); time to think of all those who have been here before you.

When you climb the Acropolis—the heights above the city—you know that you're on your way to see Greece's most famous temple, the **Parthenon.** What you may not know is that people lived on the Acropolis as early as 5,000 B.C. The Acropolis's sheer

---

⌒ *Tips* **Museum Hours Update**

If you visit Greece during the summer, check to see when sites and museums are open. According to the tourist office, they should be open from 8am to 7:30pm, but some may close earlier in the day or even be closed 1 day a week.

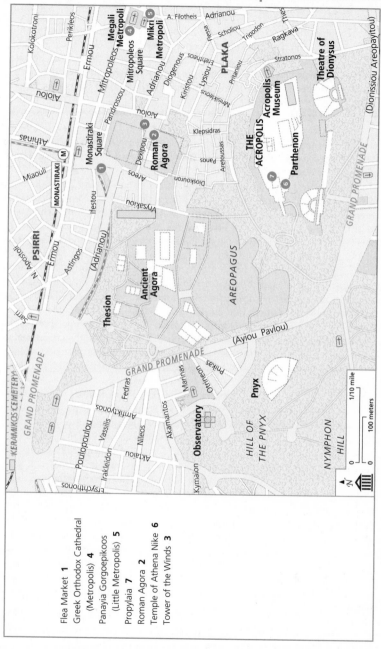

Flea Market **1**

Greek Orthodox Cathedral
(Metropolis) **4**

Panayia Gorgoepikoos
(Little Metropolis) **5**

Propylaia **7**

Roman Agora **2**

Temple of Athena Nike **6**

Tower of the Winds **3**

Warning

At press time, the monuments of the Acropolis were undergoing extensive renovations. The Temple of Nike had been entirely dismantled for restoration. Scaffolding encased the Proplyaia and the Parthenon. The descriptions below will explain what you should see when the renovations are complete. The climb up to the Acropolis is steep; if you don't want to walk, ask if the planned elevator has been installed yet.

---

sides made it a superb natural defense, just the place to avoid enemies and to be able to see invaders coming across the sea or the plains of Attica. And it helped that in antiquity there was a spring here.

In classical times, when Athens's population had grown to around 250,000, people moved down from the Acropolis, which had become the city's most important religious center. The city's **civic and business center**—the **Agora**—and its **cultural center,** with several theaters and concert halls, bracketed the Acropolis. When you peer over the sides of the Acropolis at the houses in the Plaka, and the remains of the Ancient Agora and the theater of Dionysos, you'll see the layout of the ancient city. Syntagma and Omonia squares, the heart of today's Athens, were well out of the ancient city center.

Even the Acropolis's superb heights couldn't protect it from the Persian assault of 480 B.C., when invaders burned and destroyed most of its monuments. Look for the immense column drums built into the Acropolis's walls. They are from the destroyed Parthenon. When the Athenian statesman Pericles ordered the Acropolis rebuilt, he had these drums built into the walls lest Athenians forget what had happened, and so that they would remember that they had rebuilt what they had lost. Pericles's rebuilding program began about 448 B.C.; the new Parthenon was dedicated 10 years later, but work on other monuments continued for a century.

You'll enter the Acropolis through **Beulé Gate,** built by the Romans and named for the French archaeologist who discovered it in 1852. You'll then pass through the **Propylaia,** the monumental 5th-century-B.C. entrance. It's characteristic of the Roman mania for building that they found it necessary to build an entrance to an entrance!

Just above the Propylaia is the elegant little **Temple of Athena Nike (Athena of Victory)**; this beautifully proportioned Ionic temple was built in 424 B.C. and heavily restored in the 1930s. To the left of the Parthenon is the **Erechtheion,** which the Athenians honored as the tomb of Erechtheus, a legendary king of Athens. A hole in the ceiling and floor of the northern porch indicates where Poseidon's trident struck to make a spring gush forth during his contest with Athena to have the city named in his or her honor. Athena countered with an olive tree; the olive tree planted beside the Erechtheion reminds visitors of her victory—as, of course, does Athens's name.

Give yourself time to enjoy the delicate carving on the Erechtheion, and be sure to see the original **Caryatids** in the Acropolis Museum. The Caryatids presently holding up the porch of the Erechtheion are the casts put there when the originals were moved to prevent further erosion by Athens's acid *nefos* (smog).

The **Parthenon** is dedicated to Athena Parthenos (Athena the Virgin, patron goddess of Athens) and is, of course, the most important religious shrine here. Visitors are not allowed inside, both to protect the monument and to allow restoration work to proceed safely. If you're disappointed, keep in mind that in antiquity only priests and honored visitors were allowed in to see the monumental—about 11m-tall (36-ft.)—statue of Athena designed by the great Phidias, who supervised Pericles's building program. Nothing of the huge gold-and-ivory statue remains, but there's a small Roman copy in the National Archaeological Museum—and horrific renditions on souvenirs ranging from T-shirts to ouzo bottles. Admittedly, the gold-and-ivory statue was not understated; the 2nd-century-A.D. traveler Pausanias, one of the first guidebook writers, recorded that the statue stood "upright in an ankle-length tunic with a head of Medusa carved in ivory on her breast. She has a Victory about 2.5m (8 ft.) high, and a spear in her hand and a shield at her feet, with a snake beside the shield, possibly representing Erechtheus."

Look over the edge of the Acropolis toward the **Temple of Hephaistos** (now called the **Theseion**) in the Ancient Agora, and then at the Parthenon, and notice how much lighter and more graceful the Parthenon appears. Scholars tell us that this is because Ictinus, the Parthenon's architect, was something of a magician of optical illusions. The columns and stairs—the very floor—of the Parthenon all appear straight, because all are minutely curved. Each exterior column is slightly thicker in the middle (a device known as *entasis*), which makes the entire column appear straight. That's why the Parthenon, with 17 columns on each side and eight at each end (creating an exterior colonnade of 46 relatively slender columns), looks so graceful, while the Temple of Hephaistos, with only six columns at each end and 13 along each side, seems squat and stolid.

The other reason the Parthenon looks so airy is that it is, quite literally, open to the elements. In 1687, the Venetians, in an attempt to capture the Acropolis from the Turks, blew the Parthenon's entire roof (and much of its interior) to smithereens. A shell fired from nearby Mouseion Hill struck the Parthenon—where the Turks were storing gunpowder and munitions—and caused appalling damage to the building and its sculptures.

A Britisher, Lord Elgin, carted off most of the remaining sculptures to London in the early 19th century. Those surviving sculptures—known as the **Elgin Marbles**—are on display in the British Museum, causing ongoing pain to generations of Greeks, who continue to press for their return. Things heated up again in the summer of 1988, when English historian William St. Clair's book *Lord Elgin and the Marbles* received a fair amount of publicity. According to St. Clair, the British Museum "over-cleaned" the marbles in the 1930s, removing not only the outer patina, but many sculptural details. The museum countered that the damage wasn't that bad—and that the marbles would remain in London.

The Parthenon originally had sculptures on both of its pediments, as well as a frieze running around the entire temple. The frieze was made of alternating **triglyphs** (panels with three incised grooves) and **metopes** (sculptured panels). The east pediment showed scenes from the birth of Athena, while the west pediment showed Athena and Poseidon's

---

(*Tips* **The August Full Moon**

For the past few years, 55 ancient sites throughout Greece—including, of course, the Acropolis—were open to the public on the night of the August full moon. The Culture Ministry plans to do this every August—and to stage free concerts at some of the moonlit sites.

---

contest for possession of Athens. The long frieze showed the battle of the Athenians against the Amazons, scenes from the Trojan War, and struggles of the Olympian gods against giants and centaurs. The message of most of this sculpture was the triumph of knowledge and civilization—that is, Athens—over the forces of darkness and barbarians. An interior frieze showed scenes from the Panathenaic Festival held each August, when citizens paraded through the streets with a new tunic for the statue of Athena. Only a few fragments of these sculptures remain in place, and you will have to decide for yourself whether it's a good or a bad thing that Lord Elgin removed so much before the smog became endemic in Athens and ate away much of what he left here.

If you're lucky enough to visit the Acropolis on a smog-free and sunny day, you'll see the gold and cream tones of the Parthenon's handsome Pentelic marble at their most subtle. It may come as something of a shock to realize that in antiquity, the Parthenon—like most other monuments here—was painted gay colors that have since faded, revealing the natural marble. If the day is a clear one, you'll get a superb view of Athens from the Belvedere at the Acropolis's east end.

Near the Belvedere, the **Acropolis Archaeological Museum** hugs the ground to detract as little as possible from the ancient monuments. Inside, you'll see four of the six original Caryatids from the Erechtheion (one disappeared during the Ottoman occupation and one is in the British Museum). Other delights include statues of smiling *korai* (maidens) and *kouroi* (young men). Don't miss the graceful 5th-century relief called the **Mourning Athena,** the athletic **Calfbearer,** and the three-headed figure of the **Tryphon,** whose tripartite body ends in a snaky tail. You can see clear traces of the ancient paint that decorated much of the Tryphon's ancient sculptures. (At some point, this museum will close and its contents will move to the new Acropolis Museum, which is being built to house the "Parthenon" [Elgin] marbles, should they be returned to Greece.)

Almost all of what you've seen comes from Athens's heyday in the mid–5th-century B.C., when Pericles rebuilt what the Persians destroyed. In the following centuries, every invader who came built monuments, most of which were resolutely destroyed by the next wave of invaders. If you had been here a century ago, you would have seen the remains of mosques and churches, plus a Frankish bell tower. The great archaeologist Heinrich Schliemann, discoverer of Troy and excavator of Mycenae, was so offended by the bell tower that he paid to have it torn down.

If you'd like to know more about the Acropolis and its history, as well as the Elgin Marbles controversy, you can check to see whether the **Center for Acropolis Studies,** on Makriyanni just southeast of the Acropolis (© **210/923-9381**), is open (9am–2:30pm; free admission). The center closes intermittently. It houses artifacts, reconstructions, photographs, drawings, plaster casts of the Elgin Marbles—and hopes, one day, to house the "Parthenon" marbles (see above).

If you find the Acropolis too crowded, you can usually get a peaceful view of its monuments from one of three nearby hills (all signposted from the Acropolis): the **Hill of the Pnyx,** where the Athenian Assembly met; **Hill of the Areopagus,** where the Athenian Upper House met; and **Hill of Filopappos** (also known as the Hill of the Muses), named after the 2nd-century-A.D. philhellene Filopappos, whose funeral monument tops the hill.

Dionysiou Areopagitou. © **210/321-0219.** Admission 12€ ($16) adults. Free Sun. Ticket, valid for 1 week, includes admission to the Acropolis, Acropolis Museum, Ancient Agora, Theater of Dionysos, Karameikos Cemetery, Roman Forum, Tower of the Winds, and Temple of Olympian Zeus. Individual tickets may be bought (6€/$7.80) at the other sites. Acropolis hours are summer daily 8am–7pm; winter daily 8:30am–6pm or as early as 2:30pm. The Acropolis Museum usually closes at least ½ hr. earlier than the Acropolis. Ticket booth, small post office, and snack bar are located slightly below the Acropolis entrance. From Syntagma Sq., take Amalias into Dionysiou Areopayitou, and follow the marble path up to the Acropolis. Metro: Acropolis.

Ancient Agora ★★   The Agora was Athens's commercial and civic center. People used these buildings for a wide range of political, educational, philosophical, theatrical, and athletic purposes—which may be why it now seems such a jumble of ancient buildings, inscriptions, and fragments of sculpture. This is a nice place to wander, enjoy the views up toward the Acropolis, and take in the herb garden and flowers planted around the 5th-century-B.C. Temple of Hephaistos and Athena (the Theseion).

Find a shady spot by the temple, sit a while, and imagine the Agora teeming with merchants, legislators, and philosophers—but very few women. Women did not regularly go into public places. Athens's best-known philosopher, **Socrates,** often strolled here with his disciples, including **Plato,** in the shade of the Stoa of Zeus Eleutherios. In 399 B.C., Socrates, accused of "introducing strange gods and corrupting youth," was sentenced to death. He drank his cup of hemlock in a prison at the southwest corner of the Agora—where excavators centuries later found small clay cups, just the right size for a fatal drink. **St. Paul** also spoke in the Agora; he irritated many Athenians because he rebuked them as superstitious when he saw an inscription here to the "Unknown God."

The one monument you can't miss in the Ancient Agora is the 2nd-century-B.C. **Stoa of Attalos,** built by King Attalos of Pergamon in Asia Minor, and completely reconstructed by American archaeologists in the 1950s. (You may be grateful that they included an excellent modern restroom in the stoa.) The museum on the stoa's ground floor contains finds from 5,000 years of Athenian history, including sculpture and pottery, a voting machine, and a child's potty seat, all labeled in English. The stoa is open Tuesday through Sunday from 8:30am to 2:45pm.

As you leave the stoa, take a moment to look at the charming little 11th-century Byzantine **Church of the Holy Apostles,** also restored by the Americans. The church is almost always closed, but its delicate proportions are a relief after the somewhat too-new, too-flawless, heartless facade of the Stoa of Attalos.

Below the Acropolis at the edge of Monastiraki. (Entrance is on Adrianou, near Ayiou Philippou Sq., east of Monastiraki Sq. and on Ayiou Apostoli, the rd. leading down into Plaka from the Acropolis.) ✆ 210/321-0185. Admission (includes museum) 4€ ($5.20), or free with purchase of 12€ ($16) Acropolis ticket. Agora hours are summer daily 8am–7pm; winter daily 8:30am–6pm, although it may close then as early as 2:30pm. Metro: Monastiraki.

Kerameikos Cemetery ★   Ancient Athens's most famous cemetery, located just outside the city walls, is a lovely spot. Many handsome monuments from the 4th century B.C. and later still line the Street of the Tombs, which has relatively few visitors. You can sit quietly and imagine **Pericles** putting the final touches on his **Funeral Oration** for the Athenian soldiers killed during the first year of fighting in the Peloponnesian War. Athens, Pericles said, was the "school of Hellas" and a "pattern to others rather than an imitator of any." Offering comfort to the families of the fallen, he urged the widows to remember that the greatest glory belonged to the woman who was "least talked of among men either for good or for bad"—which must have caused a few snickers in the audience, since Pericles's own mistress, Aspasia, was the subject of considerable gossip.

Ancient Greek words very often hide familiar English words, and that's true of Kerameikos. The name honors the hero Keramos, who was something of a patron saint of potters, giving his name both to the ceramics made here and to the district itself. The Kerameikos was a major crossroads in antiquity, rather like today's Omonia Square, where major roads from outside Athens intersected before continuing into the city. You can see remains of the massive **Dipylon Gate,** where most roads converged, and the **Sacred Gate,** where marchers in the Panathenaic Festival gathered before heading through the Ancient Agora and climbing to the Parthenon. What you can't see are the remains of **Plato's Academy,** which was located in this district but thus far has eluded archaeologists.

The **Oberlaender Museum,** known for its collection of finds from the Kerameikos, including terra-cotta figureines, vases, and funerary sculptures (several lions and a sphinx among them), is usually open when the site is. Be sure to ask if the handsome, classical statue of a youth known as the Kerameikos Kouros, found here by German archaeologists in 2000, is on view. If you like cemeteries, be sure to visit Athens's enormous **First Cemetery,** near Athens Stadium; it has acres of monuments, many as elaborate as anything you'll see at the Kerameikos.

148 Ermou. ✆ 210/346-3553. Admission 2€ ($2.60), or free with purchase of 12€ ($16) Acropolis ticket. The cemetery is usually open summer Tues–Sun 8am–7pm; winter Tues–Sun 8:30am–6pm, when it may close as early as 2:30pm. Walk west from Monastiraki Sq. on Ermou past Thisio Metro station; cemetery is on the right. Metro: Monastiraki or Thisio.

Roman Agora (Forum) ✦   One of the nicest things about the Roman Agora is that if you don't want to inspect it closely, you can take it in from one of the Plaka cafes and restaurants on its periphery.

In addition to building a number of monuments on the Acropolis and in the Ancient Agora, Roman leaders, beginning with Julius Caesar, built their own agora, or forum, an extension of the Greek agora. Archaeologists want to explore the area between the Greek and Roman agoras; Plaka merchants and fans of the district do not want more digging. At present, the Roman Agora is a pleasant mélange of monuments from different eras, including a mosque built here after the Byzantine Empire was conquered by Mehmet II in 1453.

The Roman Agora's most endearing monument is the octagonal **Tower of the Winds,** with its relief sculptures of eight gods of the winds, including Boreas blowing on a shell. Like so many monuments in Athens—the Parthenon itself had a church inside it for centuries—the Tower of the Winds has had a varied history. Built by a 1st-century-B.C. astronomer as a combination sundial and water-powered clock, it became a home for whirling dervishes in the 18th century. When Lord Byron visited Athens, he lodged near the tower, spending much of his time writing lovesick poetry to the beautiful "Maid of Athens."

You can usually find the remains of the Roman latrine near Tower of the Winds by following the sound of giggles to people taking pictures of each other in the seated position. The less-well-preserved remains of the enormous and once-famous **library of Emperor Hadrian** go largely unnoticed. Draw your own conclusions.

Enter from corner of Pelopida and Eolou. Admission 2€ ($2.60) or free with 12€ ($16) Acropolis ticket. Roman Agora (Forum) hours usually summer Tues–Sun 8am–7pm; winter Tues–Sun 8:30am–6pm, although in winter may close as early as 2:30pm. Metro: Acropolis.

Theater of Dionysos & Odeion of Herodes Atticus ✦   This theater of Dionysos was built in the 4th century B.C. to replace and enlarge the earlier theater in which the plays of the great Athenian dramatists were first performed. The new theater seated some 17,000 spectators in 64 rows of seats, 20 of which survive. Most spectators sat on limestone seats—and probably envied the 67 grandees who got to sit in the front row on thronelike seats of handsome Pentelic marble. The most elegant throne belonged to the priest of Dionysos (god of wine, revels, and theater); carved satyrs and bunches of grapes appropriately ornament the priest's throne.

Herodes Atticus, a wealthy 2nd-century-A.D. philhellene, built the Odeion—also known as the Odeum or Irodio (Music Hall). It is one of an astonishing number of monuments funded by him. If you think it looks suspiciously well preserved, you're right: It was reconstructed in the 19th century.

Although your 2€ ($2.60) entrance ticket for the Theater of Dionysos in theory allows you entrance to the Odeion, this is misleading. The Odeion is open only for performances—when, obviously, you cannot wander around freely. The best ways to see the Odeion are by looking down from the Acropolis or, better yet, by attending one of the performances staged here during the Athens Festival each summer. If you do this, bring a cushion: Marble seats are as hard as you'd expect, and the cushions provided are lousy.

Dionissiou Areopagitou, on the south slope of the Acropolis. ℂ 210/322-4625. Admission 2€ ($2.60) for both monuments; free with purchase of 12€ ($16) Acropolis ticket. Theater of Dionysos: summer Tues–Sun 8am–7pm; winter Tues–Sun 8:30am–6pm, although it may close as early as 2:30pm. Odeion open during performances and sometimes on performance day. Metro: Acropolis.

THE TOP MUSEUMS

Benaki Museum ★★   This stunning private collection of about 20,000 small and large works of art includes treasures from the Neolithic era to the 20th century. The folk art collection (including magnificent costumes and icons) is superb, as are the two entire rooms from 18th-century Northern Greek mansions, ancient Greek bronzes, gold cups, Fayum portraits, and rare early Christian textiles. The new wing that opened in 2003 doubled the exhibition space of the original 20th-century neoclassical town house belonging to the wealthy Benaki family. The new galleries will house special exhibitions. The museum shop is excellent. The cafe offers a spectacular view over Athens, as well as a 25€ ($33) buffet dinner Thursday. This is a very pleasant place to spend several hours—as many lucky Athenians do, as often as possible. After you visit the Benaki, take in its new branch, Benaki Museum of Islamic Art (ℂ 210/325-1311).

1 Koumbari (at Leoforos Vasilissis Sofias, Kolonaki, 5 blocks east of Syntagma Sq.). ℂ 210/367-1000. www.benaki.gr. Admission 6€ ($7.80); free Thurs. Mon, Wed, Fri, Sat 9am–5pm; Thurs 9am–midnight; Sun 9am–3pm; closed Tues. Metro: Syntagma or Evangelismos.

Byzantine and Christian Museum ★★   If you love icons (paintings, usually of saints and usually on wood) or want to find out about them, this is the place to go. As its name makes clear, this museum is devoted to the art and history of the Byzantine era (roughly 4th–15th centuries A.D.). You'll find selections from Greece's most important collection of icons and religious art, along with sculptures, altars, mosaics, religious vestments, Bibles, and a small-scale reconstruction of an early Christian basilica. The museum originally occupied the beautiful 19th-century Florentine-style villa overlooking the new galleries now used for special exhibits. Allow at least an hour for your visit; two are better if a special exhibit is featured. And three is even better. The small museum shop sells books, CDs of Byzantine music, and icon reproductions.

22 Vasilissis Sofias Ave. ℂ 210/723-1570 or 210/721-1027. Admission 4€ ($5.20). Tues–Sun 8:30am–3pm. From Syntagma Sq., walk along Queen Sophias about 15 min. Museum is on your right. If you get to the Hilton Hotel, you've gone too far. Metro: Syntagma or Evangelismos

Greek Folk Art Museum ★★   This endearing small museum showcases dazzling embroideries and costumes from all over the country. Seek out the small room with zany frescoes of gods and heroes done by the eccentric artist Theofilos Hadjimichael, who painted in the early part of the 20th century. We stop by here every time we're in Athens, always finding something new, always looking forward to our next visit—and always glad we weren't born Greek women 100 years ago, when we would have spent endless hours embroidering, crocheting, and weaving. Much of what is on display was made by young women for their *proikas* (dowries) in the days when a bride was supposed to arrive at the altar with enough embroidered linen, rugs, and blankets to last a lifetime. The museum shop is small but good.

17 Kidathineon, Plaka. ✆ 210/322-9031. Admission 2€ ($2.60). Tues–Sun 10am–2pm. Metro: Syntagma or Acropolis.

National Archaeological Museum ★★★   Almost all of this enormous and enormously popular museum's galleries have reopened after extensive renovations and reinstallation of the collection. Try to be at the door when it opens, so you can see the exhibits and not just the backs of other visitors. Early arrival, except in high summer, should give you at least an hour before most tour groups arrive; alternatively, get here an hour before closing or at lunchtime, when the tour groups may not be as dense. If you can, come more than once, so your experience here will be a pleasure rather than an endurance contest. *Tip:* Be sure to get the brochure on the collection when you buy your ticket; it has a handy and largely accurate description of the exhibits.

The **Mycenaean Collection** includes gold masks, cups, dishes, and jewelry unearthed from the site of Mycenae by Heinrich Schliemann in 1876. Many of these objects are small, delicate, and very hard to see when the museum is crowded. Don't miss the stunning **burial mask** that Schliemann misnamed the "Mask of Agamemnon." Archaeologists are sure that the mask is not Agamemnon's, but belonged to an earlier, unknown monarch. Also not to be missed are the stunning **Vaphio cups,** showing mighty bulls, unearthed in a tomb at a seemingly insignificant site in the Peloponnese. If little Vaphio could produce these riches, what remains to be found in future excavations?

The museum also has a stunning collection of **Cycladic figurines,** named after the island chain. Although these figurines are among the earliest known Greek sculptures (about 2,000 B.C.), you'll be struck by how modern the idols' faces look compared to those wrought by Modigliani. One figure, a musician with a lyre, seems to be concentrating on his music, cheerfully oblivious to his onlookers. If you are fond of these Cycladic sculptures, be sure to take in the superb collection at the N. P. Goulandris Foundation Museum of Cycladic Art (see below).

With the reopening of the museum's second floor, the renowned collection of Greek vases is once more on view. In addition, you'll see frescoes from the island of Thira (Santorini). Fortunately, an astonishing number of these beautiful frescoes survived the island's cataclysmic volcanic eruption (ca. 1450 B.C.). Plans to return some of the frescoes to Santorini are in the works.

44 Patission. ✆ 210/821-7724. Fax 210/821-3573. Admission 6€ ($7.80) or 12€ ($16) with admission to the Acropolis. Hours Mon 12:30–5pm; Tues–Fri 8am–5pm; Sat–Sun and holidays 8:30am–3pm. (Sometimes open to 7pm, but you can't count on this.) The museum is ⅓ mile (10 min. on foot) north of Omonia Sq. on the road named Leoforos 28 Octobriou, but usually called Patission. Metro: Omonia or Biktoria.

N. P. Goulandris Foundation Museum of Cycladic Art ★★   Come here to see the largest collection of Modigliani-like Cycladic art outside the National Archaeological

Museum. This handsome museum—the astonishing collection of Nicolas and Aikaterini Goulandris—opened its doors in 1986 and displays more than 200 stone and pottery vessels and figurines from the 3rd millennium B.C. This museum is as satisfying as the National Museum is overwhelming. It helps that the Goulandris does not get the same huge crowds, and it also helps that the galleries here are small and well lit, with labels throughout in Greek and English. The collection of Greek vases is small and exquisite—the ideal place to find out if you prefer black or red figure vases. The museum's elegant little shop has a wide selection of books on ancient art, as well as reproductions of items from the collection, including a pert Cycladic pig.

When you've seen all you want to (and have perhaps refreshed yourself at the basement snack bar), walk through the courtyard into the museum's newest acquisition, the elegant 19th-century **Stathatos Mansion.** The mansion, with some of its original furnishings, provides a glimpse of how wealthy Athenians lived a hundred years ago.

4 Neophytou Douka. ✆ 210/722-8321. www.cycladic-m.gr. Admission 4€ ($5.20). Mon and Wed–Fri 10am–4pm; Sat 10am–3pm. Metro: Syntagma.

ORGANIZED TOURS

Many independent travelers (ourselves included) turn up their noses at organized tours. Nonetheless, such a tour can be an efficient and easy way to get an overview of an unfamiliar city. We're impressed by the number of people we know who confess that they are very glad they took one of these tours, which helped them get oriented and figure out which sights they wanted to see more thoroughly. Most of the tour guides pass stiff tests to get their licenses.

The best-known Athens-based tour groups are **CHAT Tours,** 4 Stadiou (✆ **210/322-3137** or 210/322-3886); and **Key Tours,** 4 Kalliroïs (✆ **210/923-3166;** www.keytours.gr). Each offers half- and full-day tours of the city, "Athens by Night" tours, and day excursions from Athens. Expect to pay about 50€ ($65) for a half-day tour, 80€ ($104) for a full-day tour, and around 100€ ($130) for "Athens by Night" (including dinner and sometimes a folk-dance performance at the Dora Stratou Theater). To take any of these tours, you must book and pay in advance. At that time, you will be told when you will be picked up at your hotel, or where you should meet the tour.

If you want to hire a private guide, speak to the concierge at your hotel, or contact the **Association of Official Guides,** 9a Apollonas (✆ **210/322-9705**). Expect to pay from 100€ ($130) for a 5-hour tour.

5 The Shopping Scene

The museums in Athens have excellent shops, with everything from reproductions and books to postcards and T-shirts, herbs and scented soaps. And, most of the museums have cafes where you can rest between bouts of museum crawling and shopping.

If you want to pick up retro clothes or old copper, try the **flea market,** a daily spectacle between the Plaka and Monastiraki Square. It's most lively on Sunday, but you can find the usual touristy trinkets, copies of ancient artifacts, jewelry, sandals, and various handmade goods, including embroideries, any day. Keep in mind that not everything sold as an antique is genuine, and that it's illegal to take antiquities and icons more than 100 years old out of the country without a hard-to-obtain export license.

Martinos, 50 Pandrossou, Monastiraki (✆ **210/321-2414**), has Venetian glass, woodcarvings (usually including some handsome chests and furniture), old jewelry, coins—and sometimes swords. In the Plaka–Monastiraki area, several shops with nicer-than-usual arts and crafts at fair prices include **Stavros Melissinos,** the "poet-sandalmaker of Athens," after 50 years on Pandrossou, now in his new location at 12 Agias Theklas, still in Monastiraki, (℗ **210/321-9247**); **Iphanta,** a weaving workshop, 6 Selleu (℗ **210/322-3628**); **Emanuel Masmanidis's Gold Rose Jewelry shop,** 85 Pandrossou (℗ **210/321-5662**); and the **Center of Hellenic Tradition,** 59 Mitropoleos and 36 Pandrossou (℗ **210/321-3023**), which sells arts and crafts. At the **Hellenic Folk-Art Gallery,** 6 Ipatias and Apollonos, Plaka (℗ **210/324-0017**), a portion of the proceeds from everything sold (including handsome woven and embroidered carpets) goes to the National Welfare Organization, which encourages traditional crafts.

On your way to Athens' museums, you can ogle the window displays at **LALAoUNIS,** 6 Panepistimiou (℗ **210/362-1371**), and at **Zolotas,** 8 Pandrossou (Plaka; ℗ **210/322-1212**), Greece's two finest jewelers.

To window-shop for elegant clothes, luxury house goods, and designer chocolates along with the beautiful people, head up to **Kolonaki** (preferably on a Sat), and join the throngs strolling along the pedestrianized streets that run in and out of Patriarchou Ioakeim.

6 Athens After Dark

Greeks enjoy their nightlife so much that they take an afternoon nap to rest up for it. The evening often begins with a leisurely *volta* (stroll); you'll see this in most neighborhoods, including the main drags through the Plaka and Kolonaki Square. Most Greeks don't think of dinner until at least 9pm in winter, 10pm in summer. Around midnight, the party may move on to a club for music and dancing.

Check the *Athens News* (published Fri) or the daily *Kathimerini* insert in the *International Herald Tribune* for listings of current cultural and entertainment events, including films, lectures, theater, music, and dance. The weekly *Hellenic Times* and monthly *Now in Athens* list nightspots, restaurants, movies, theater, and much more.

THE PERFORMING ARTS

FESTIVALS

HELLENIC FESTIVAL   Early June through September, the Hellenic Festival (also known as the **Athens or Greek Festival**) features famous Greek and foreign artists from Elton John to Placido Domingo performing on the slopes of the Acropolis. You may catch an opera, concert, drama, or ballet here—and, usually, see the Acropolis illuminated over your shoulder at the same time. To enjoy the performance to the fullest, bring a cushion to sit on (the cushions available are often minimal). For schedules and ticket info, contact the **Hellenic Festival Box Office** (see above). You will have better luck if you come here in person rather than try to reach the office by phone.

LYCABETTUS (LIKAVITOS) FESTIVAL   The Pet Shop Boys, Buena Vista Social Club, and other pop musicians make appearances here at the outdoor amphitheater near the top of Likavitos during the summer. For information on music and special events, check with the **Hellenic Festival Box Office** (see above) or **Likavitos Theater** (℗ **210/722-7209**). Tickets may also be available at **Ticket House,** Panepistimiou 42 (℗ **210/618-9300** or 210/360-8366).

MUSIC, DANCE & THEATRE

The **Megaron Mousikis Concert Hall,** 89 Leoforos Vas. Sofias (℗ **210/729-0391** or 210/728-2333), hosts a wide range of classical music programs that include quartets,

---

Tips **Ticket Information for the Athens (Hellenic) & Lycabettus Festivals**

Tickets for the Athens and Lycabettus festivals are available at the **Hellenic Festival Box Office,** 39 Panepistimiou (in the arcade; ✆ **210/928-2900**). Hours are Monday through Friday 8:30am to 4pm, Saturday 9am to 2:30pm. "Hellenic Festival" is the umbrella term for a number of summer festivals, including the Athens and Epidaurus festivals. (For years, the Hellenic Festival was known as the Athens Festival and you may still see references to it as such.) Advance booking for most events in the Hellenic festival starts 3 weeks before each performance; 10 days before each event for the Lycabettus Festival. Ticket reservation and telephone booking (as above) are also possible by credit card (MasterCard or Visa), with the exact date and performance, number and category of tickets, and number and expiration date of the credit card. Tickets (if available) also go on sale at the box offices at each theater 2 hours before each performance. Events at the Odeion of Herodes Atticus on the slopes of the Acropolis are usually sold out by the day of the performance; for information, call ✆ **210/323-2771.**

Additional information is available at www.hellenicfestival.gr, www.cultureguide.gr, and www.greektourism.com.

---

operas in concert, symphonies, and recitals. On performance nights, the box office is open Monday through Friday from 10am to 6pm, Saturday from 10am to 2pm, and Sunday from 6 to 10:30pm. Tickets are also sold Monday through Friday from 10am to 5pm in the Megaron's convenient downtown kiosk in the Spiromillios Arcade, 4 Stadiou. Ticket prices run from 5€ ($6.50) to as much as 100€ ($130), depending on the performance. The Megaron has a limited summer season but is in full swing the rest of the year.

The **Greek National Opera** performs at **Olympia Theater,** 59 Akadimias at Mavromihali (✆ **210/361-2461**). The summer months are usually off season.

Pallas Theater, 1 Voukourestiou (✆ **210/322-8275**), hosts many jazz and rock concerts, as well as some classical performances. Prices vary from performance to performance, but you can get a cheap ticket from about 10€ ($13).

The **Hellenic American Union,** 22 Massalias between Kolonaki and Omonia squares (✆ **210/362-9886**), often hosts performances of English-language theater and American-style music (tickets 10€/$13 and up). If you arrive early, check out the art shows or photo exhibitions in the adjacent gallery.

The **Athens Center,** 48 Archimidous (✆ **210/701-8603**), often stages free performances of ancient Greek and contemporary international plays in June and July.

Since 1953, **Dora Stratou Folk Dance Theater** has been giving performances of traditional Greek folk dances on Filopappos Hill. At present, performances take place May through September, Tuesday through Sunday at 9:30pm, with additional performances at 8:15pm on Wednesday and Sunday. There are no performances on Monday. You can buy tickets at the **box office,** 8 Scholio, Plaka, from 8am to 2pm (✆ **210/924-4395** or 210/921-4650 after 5:30pm; www.grdance.org). Prices range from 12€ to 25€ ($16–$33). Tickets are also available at the theater before the performances. The program changes every 2 or 3 weeks.

Seen from Pnyx hill, **sound-and-light** shows illuminate (sorry) Athens's history by telling the story of the Acropolis. As lights pick out monuments on the Acropolis and the music swells, the narrator tells of the Persian attack, the Periclean days of glory, the invidious Turkish occupation—you get the idea. Shows are held April through October. The 45-minute performances in English are given at 9pm on Monday, Wednesday, Thursday, Saturday, and Sunday. Tickets (10€/$13) can be purchased at the **Hellenic Festival Box Office,** 39 Panepistimiou (© **210/928-2900**), or at the entrance to the sound-and-light show (© **210/922-6210**). You'll hear the narrative best if you don't sit too close to the very loud public-address system.

CLUBS & BARS

Your best bet here is to have a local friend; failing that, ask someone at your hotel for a recommendation. The listings in the weekly *Athinorama* (Greek) or in publications such as the English-language *Athens News,* the *Kathimerini* insert in the *Herald Tribune,* and hotel handouts such as *Best Of Athens* and *Welcome to Athens,* can be very helpful. If you ask a taxi driver, he's likely to take you to either his cousin George's joint or the place that gives him drinks for bringing you. Be especially wary of heading out of the city to the places that spring up each summer on the airport road; these spots are usually overpriced and often unsavory.

Wherever you go, you're likely to face a cover charge of at least 20€ ($26). Thereafter, each drink will probably cost between 15€ and 20€ ($20–$26). Many clubs plop a bottle on your table that's labeled (but doesn't necessarily contain) Johnny Walker Red or Black, and then they try very hard to charge you at least 100€ ($130) whether you drink it or not. It's best to go to these clubs with someone *trustworthy* who knows the scene. If you hear something you like, **Metropolis** (© **210/380-8549**) in Omonia Square has a wide choice of CDs and tapes of Greek music.

Polis, 7 Pezmatzoglou (© **210/324-9587** to -8), a short ride from Syntagma Square, is usually open from mid-morning to well after midnight, offering everything from recorded classical to live jazz and pop (both Greek and American). Since it's open most of the day, Polis draws regulars who hang out to read the newspaper, write letters—and, of course, talk on cellphones.

For Greek pop music, try **Zoom,** 37 Kidathineon, in the heart of the Plaka (© **210/322-5920**). Performers—often with current hit albums—have been showered with carnations here by adoring fans. The minimum order is 25€ ($33). Almost next door, **Brettos,** 41 Kidathineon (© **210/323-2110**), plays some pop and some traditional music in a very charming old-fashioned bar. If you want to check out the local rock and blues scenes along with small doses of metal, Athenian popsters play at longtime favorite **Memphis,** 5 Ventiri, near the Hilton east of Syntagma Square (© **210/722-4104**); it's open Tuesday through Friday from 10:30pm to 2:30am.

REMBETIKA & BOUZOUKIA

Visitors interested in authentic *rembetika* (music of the urban poor and dispossessed) and *bouzoukia* (traditional and pop music featuring the *bouzouki,* a kind of guitar, today almost always loudly amplified) should consult your hotel concierge or check the listings in *Athinorama,* the weekly *Hellenic Times,* or *Kathimerini. Rembetika* performances usually don't start until nearly midnight, and though there's rarely a cover, drinks can cost as much as 20€ ($26). Many clubs close during the summer.

> ### *Tips* Open in August
>
> A great many popular after-dark spots close in August, when much of Athens flees the summer heat to the country. Some places that stay open include a number of bars, cafes, ouzeries, and tavernas on the pedestrian Iraklion Walkway near the Theseion. Stavlos, the restaurant, bar, and disco popular with all ages, remains open on August weekends. Nearby, Berlin Club, which caters to a young crowd and specializes in rock 'n' roll, is open most nights. Ambibagio features genuine Greek music. The sweet shop Aistisis has great views of the Acropolis and stays open as late as the nearby bars.

One of the more central places for *rembetika* is **Stoa Athanaton,** 19 Sofokleous, in the Central Meat Market (© **210/321-4362**), which serves good food and has live music from 3 to 6pm and after midnight. It's closed Sunday. **Taximi,** 29 Isavron, Exarchia (© **210/363-9919**), is consistently popular. Drinks cost 12€ ($16). It's closed Sunday and during July and August. Open Wednesday through Monday, **Frangosyriani,** 57 Arachovis, Exarchia (© **210/360-0693**), specializes in the music of *rembetika* legend Markos Vamvakaris. The downscale, smoke-filled **Rebetiki Istoria,** in a neoclassical building at 181 Ippokratous (© **210/642-4967**), features old-style *rembetika,* played to a mixed crowd of older regulars and younger students and intellectuals. The music usually starts at 11pm, but arrive earlier to get a seat. The legendary Maryo I Thessaloniki (Maryo from Thessaloniki), described as the Bessie Smith of Greece, sometimes sings *rembetika* at **Perivoli t'Ouranou,** 19 Lysikratous (© **210/323-5517** or 210/322-2048), in Plaka. Expect to pay at least 10€ ($13) per drink in these places, most of which have a cover from 25€ ($33).

JAZZ

A number of clubs and cafes specialize in jazz, but they also offer everything from Indian sitar music to rock to punk. The very popular—and very well-thought of— **Half Note Jazz Club,** 17 Trivonianou, Mets (© **210/921-3310**), schedules performers who play everything from medieval music to jazz; set times vary from 8 to 11pm and later. **Café Asante,** 78 Damareos (© **210/756-0102**), in Pangrati, has music most nights from 11pm. At the **House of Art,** Sahtouri and 4 Sari (© **210/321-7678**), and at **Pinakothiki,** 5 Ayias Theklas (© **210/324-7741**), both in newly fashionable Psirri, you can often hear jazz from 11pm. You'll pay the same here as at the *rembetika* clubs—from 10€ ($13) per drink and a cover of at least 25€ ($33).

GAY & LESBIAN BARS

The gay and lesbian scene in Athens is fairly low-key. In Greece, the weekly publications *Athinorama* and *Time Out* often list gay bars, discos, and special events in the nightlife section. Get-togethers are sometimes advertised in the English-language press, such as the weekly *Athens News.* Information is also available from the Greek national gay and lesbian organization (**EOK;** © **210/253-7333;** www.eok.gr). Look for the Greek publication **Deon Magazine** (© **210/953-6479;** www.deon.gr) or surf the Web to www.gaygreece.gr.

Gay and lesbian travelers will not encounter difficulties at any Athenian hotel, but one with a largely gay and lesbian clientele is 41-room **Hotel Rio Athens** (www.hotel-rio.gr), at 13 Odysseos off Karaiskaki Square. The owners list themselves in gay guides as "bisexual"; the hotel is in a nicely restored neoclassical building.

Similarly, almost all Athenian bars, dance joints, and restaurants are user-friendly for gay and lesbian travelers. We list phone numbers at places where the phone is sometimes answered. **Alekos Island,** 41 Sarri, and **Bee,** 6 Miaouli (𝄖 210/321-2624), are both popular gay bars in Psirri. **Fou Club,** 8 Keleou near Omonia Square (𝄖 210/346-6800), is a good place to dance. Cafes popular with many gay and lesbian Greeks are **Café de Capo,** 1 Tsakalof in Kolonaki (𝄖 210/243-3902), open daily from 9am to 1am; and **Kirki Café,** 31 Apostolou Pavlou near Thission, open Wednesday to Sunday 11am to 2am.

Porta, 10 Phalirou (𝄖 210/924-3858), and **Fairytale,** 25 Kolleti (𝄖 210/330-1763), are well-established lesbian bars.

Koukles, 2 Zan Moreas, Koukaki (𝄖 210/924-8989) (closed Monday and Tuesday) and **Lambda,** 15 Lembesi near Syntagma Square (𝄖 210/922-4202), sometimes have drag shows. Lambda is perhaps the best known gay hangout in Athens.

ESPECIALLY FOR KIDS

The **National Garden** off Syntagma Square has a small zoo, duck ponds, a playground, and lots of room to run around. It's open from sunrise to sunset. The impressive, privately operated **Attica Zoological Park** 🌟🌟 𝄖 **210/663-4724,** in Spata, is home to more than 2,000 birds (320 species), a butterfly garden, and a small farm; the zoo is open daily from 10am to 7pm and charges 8€ ($10) (4€/$5.20 for children).

The ride up **Mount Likavitos** on the cable car is often a hit with kids. It usually operates every 20 minutes in summer (2€/$2.60). The cafe on top sells ice cream.

The multimedia, interactive **Hellenic Cosmos** was founded in 1998 by the Foundation for the Hellenic World, 254 Pireos, Tavros (𝄖 **210/342-2292;** www.fhw.gr/cosmos/; open Mon, Tues, and Thurs 9am–6pm, Wed and Fri 9am–9pm, Sat and Sun 11am–3pm). Kids may also like the more sedate **Museum of Greek Popular Musical Instruments,** 1–3 Dioyenous (𝄖 **210/325-0198;** open Tues and Thurs–Sun. 10am-2pm, Wed noon-6pm.) Admission is free.

6

The Saronic Gulf Islands

by Sherry Marker

The islands of the Saronic Gulf, which lies between Attica and the Peloponnese, are so close to Athens that each summer they are inundated by Athenians—all of whom, of course, are seeking to avoid the crowds of Athens. These islands are especially packed on summer weekends, as well as whenever there is a serious heat wave in Athens. In addition, the Saronic Gulf islands are popular destinations for travelers with limited time but who are determined not to go home without seeing at least one Greek island. Book well in advance; reservations in summer are invariably a necessity, especially on weekends. The website **www.saronicnet.com** is a useful resource for all the islands.

The easiest island to visit is **Aegina,** a mere 30km (17 nautical miles) from Piraeus. The main attractions here are the graceful Doric **Temple of Aphaia,** one of the best-preserved Greek temples; several good beaches; and verdant pine and pistachio groves. That's the good news. The bad news is that Aegina is so close to the metropolitan sprawl of Athens and Piraeus that it's not easy here to get a clear idea of why the Greek islands are so beloved as refuges from urban life. Aegina has become a bedroom suburb for Athens, with many of its 10,000 inhabitants commuting to work by boat. That said, Aegina town still has its pleasures; and both the Temple of Aphaia and deserted medieval town of **Paleohora** are terrific.

Poros is hardly an island at all; only a narrow (370m/1,214-ft.) inlet separates it from the Peloponnese. There are several good beaches, and the landscape is wooded, gentle, and rolling, like the landscape of the adjacent mainland. In spring, the citrus groves of Limonodassos are in bloom. Poros is popular with young Athenians (in part because the Naval Cadets' Training School here means that there are lots of young men eager to party) and with tour groups. On summer nights, the waterfront is either very lively or hideously crowded, depending on your point of view.

Hydra (Idra), with its bare hills, superb natural harbor, and elegant stone mansions, is the most strikingly beautiful of the Saronic Gulf islands. One of the first Greek islands to be "discovered" by artists, writers, and *bon vivants,* Hydra, like Mykonos, is not the place to experience traditional village life. The island has been declared a national monument from which cars have been banished. Its relative quiet is gradually being infiltrated by motorcycles. A major drawback: Few of the beaches are good for swimming, although you can swim from the rocks. Despite the hydrofoils that link Hydra with other islands and the mainland, the island maintains a resolute individuality.

Spetses has always been popular with wealthy Athenians, who built handsome villas here. The several good beaches are home to large hotels that house tour groups. If you like islands that are wooded, you'll love Spetses, although summer forest fires the last few years have destroyed some of Spetses's pine groves. This gentle, forested island is very unlike the images of most Greek islands shown on countless tourist posters that depict the Cycladic isles with their bare, austere landscapes and simple whitewashed houses.

STRATEGIES FOR SEEING THE ISLANDS

If possible, avoid June through August—unless you have a hotel reservation and think that you'd enjoy the hustle and bustle of high season. Also, mid-July through August, boats leaving Piraeus for the islands are heavily booked—often overbooked. It is sometimes possible to get a deck passage without a reservation, but even that can be difficult when as many as 100,000 Athenians leave Piraeus on a summer weekend. Most ships will not allow passengers to board without a ticket.

If you go to an island on a **day trip,** remember that, unlike the more sturdy ferryboats, hydrofoils cannot travel when the sea is rough. You may find yourself an unwilling overnight island visitor, grateful to be given the still-warm bed in a private home surrendered by a family member to make some money. We speak from experience. There are frequent **hydrofoils** from Piraeus to all these islands. For more information, see "Getting There," below. The schedules and carriers change with irritating regularity, however, so it's a good idea to get up-to-date information from the **Greek National Tourism Organization (EOT,** aka GNTO), at 7 Tsochas, Ambelokipi (© 210/870-0000; www.gnto.gr), well out of central Athens. The office is officially open Monday through Friday 8am to 3pm and is closed weekends. At press time it was unclear whether the EOT office at 26 Amalias, in central Athens, would remain open. (Go there in person to get reliable information.) Unfortunately, some hydrofoils leave from the Piraeus Main Harbor while others leave from Marina Zea Harbor—and some leave from both harbors!

Greek Island Hopping, published annually by Thomas Cook, is, by its own admission, out of date by the time it sees print. That said, it's a very useful volume for finding out where (if not when) you can travel among the Greek islands.

1 Aegina

30km (17 nautical miles) SW of Piraeus

Triangular Aegina (Egina), the largest of the Saronic Gulf islands, is still the most-visited island of Greece, due to its proximity to Athens. In fact, many of the 10,000 who live here commute daily to Athens. If you have only one day for one island, you

---

Tips Booking Your Return Trip

With virtually all of the hydrofoils and ferries that serve the Saronic Gulf islands, it is impossible to book a round-trip. As soon as you arrive at your island destination, head for the ticket office and book your return ticket. If you do not do this, you may end up spending longer than you planned—or wished—on one or more of the islands. At press time, both Minoan Flying Dolphins and Ceres Flying Dolphins had been absorbed by Hellas Flying Dolphins (www.dolphins.gr), but there may be more ownership and name changes by the time you arrive.

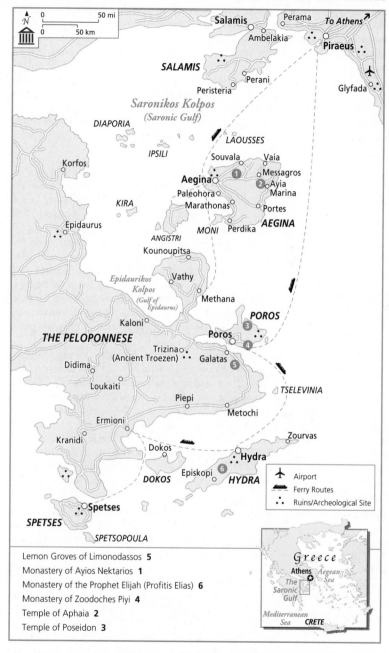

The Saronic Gulf Islands

Salamis
Perama
To Athens
Ambelakia
Piraeus

SALAMIS
Perani
Glyfada
Peristeria

Saronikos Kolpos
(Saronic Gulf)

DIAPORIA

IPSILI
Souvala
Vaia
LAOUSSES

Korfos
Aegina
①
Messagros
② Ayia
Marina
Paleohora
Marathonas
Portes

KIRA
MONI
Perdika
AEGINA

Epidaurus

ANGISTRI

Kounoupitsa

Epidaurikos
Kolpos
(Gulf of
Epidaurus)
Vathy

Methana

Kaloni
POROS
③

THE PELOPONNESE
Poros
④

Trizina
(Ancient Troezen)
Galatas
⑤

Didima

Loukaiti
Piepi

Ermioni
Metochi

Kranidi
TSELEVINIA

Dokos
Zourvas

DOKOS
Episkopi
⑥
HYDRA
Hydra

Spetses

SPETSES

SPETSOPOULA

✈ Airport
⛴ Ferry Routes
∴ Ruins/Archeological Site

0   50 mi
0   50 km
N

Greece
Athens
Aegean
Sea
The
Saronic
Gulf
Mediterranean
Sea   **CRETE**

Lemon Groves of Limonodassos **5**
Monastery of Ayios Nektarios **1**
Monastery of the Prophet Elijah (Profitis Elias) **6**
Monastery of Zoodoches Piyi **4**
Temple of Aphaia **2**
Temple of Poseidon **3**

may decide on a trip here to see the famous Doric **Temple of Aphaia.** Most ships arrive and depart from the main port and capital of **Aegina town** on the west coast, though a few stop at the resort town of **Souvala** on the north coast and at the port of **Ayia Marina** on the east coast. Ayia Marina is about as charmless as it's possible to be, but this port is your best choice if your principal destination is the Temple of Aphaia.

Despite massive tourism and the rapid development devouring much farmland, the area still has its share of almond, olive, and especially **pistachio** orchards. In fact, the island has an endemic water problem simply because of the water necessary for the pistachio groves. Wherever you buy pistachios in Greece, the vendor may assure you that they are from Aegina to indicate their superior quality.

ESSENTIALS

GETTING THERE   **Car ferries** and **excursion boats** to Aegina usually leave from Piraeus's Main Harbor; confusingly, **hydrofoils** leave both from the Main Harbor and from Marina Zea Harbor. Hydrofoil service is at least twice as fast as ferries and at least 40% more expensive (except to Aegina, for which the charge is only about 10% more). The sleek little hydrofoils are outfitted like broad aircraft with airline seats, toilets, and a minimum of luggage facilities. (The fore sections offer better views, but they're also bumpier.) The newer Super Cats are bigger, faster, and more comfortable, with food and beverage service. Reservations are recommended on weekends. Often, in order to continue to another Saronic Gulf island by hydrofoil, you must return to Piraeus and change to another hydrofoil. Some ferries go from Aegina to the other Saronic Gulf islands. As we mentioned above, schedules—and even carriers—can change, so double-check information you get from anyone other than the Greek National Tourism Organization (see above).

Daily service to the Saronic Gulf islands is offered by **Hellas Flying Dolphins** (© **210/419-9200** or 210/419-9000; www.dolphins.gr), 2 Aetolikou and Akti Kondyli, Piraeus, serving Hydra, Poros, and Spetses. **Saronic Dolphins** (© **210/422-4980**), 2 Gounari, Piraeus, makes the run to Aegina and Salamis. **Saronikos Ferries** (© **21041/99-200**) takes passengers and cars to Aegina, Poros, and Spetses; cars are not allowed to disembark on Hydra. A ferry from Perama also goes to Salamis; to get to the embarkation point, take the Metro to the end of the line in Piraeus and then the shuttle bus to the ferry in Perama. You can usually visit any one of the Saronics for about 40€ ($52) round-trip. Several cruises offer day trips to Hydra, Poros, and Aegina; for details, see chapter 4, "Cruising the Greek Islands," and below under "By Organized Tour."

By Organized Tour   A good way to see the Saronic Gulf is via a three-island day cruise, which can be booked through a travel agent such as **Viking Star Cruises** (© **210/898-0729** or 210/898-0829); or through your hotel desk. **Epirotiki Lines** (© **210/429-1000**) provides transportation to and from your hotel in Athens to Flisvos Marina, where its *Hermes* departs daily around 8:30am for **Hydra** (swimming and shopping), **Poros** (lunch and sightseeing), and **Aegina** (Temple of Aphaia or swimming); it returns to Athens about 7:30pm. Lunch is served onboard. For about 120€ ($156), you get a good tour and an introduction to travel aboard a cruise ship.

Ferry and excursion-boat tickets can usually be purchased at the pier. However, do not count on getting a ticket on summer weekends. For information on schedules for most Argo-Saronic ferries, call © **210/412-4585** or 210/459-3123; the **Piraeus Port Authority** at © **210/451-1456**; or the **Port Police** at © **210/451-1311.**

Tips **Culture Calls**

If you visit the islands of the Saronic Gulf in July and August, keep an eye out for posters announcing exhibitions at local museums and galleries. Many Athens galleries close for parts of July and August, and some have shows on the islands. The **Athens Center,** 48 Archimidous (© **210/701-2268;** www.athnescenter.gr), sometimes stages plays on Spetses and Hydra. The center offers a Modern Greek Language Summer Program on Spetses in June and July.

VISITOR INFORMATION **Aegina Tourist Office** (© **22970/22-220**) is in Aegina Town Hall. There's a string of travel agencies at the harbor, including the usually efficient **Aegina Island Holidays,** 47 Demokratias (© **22970/26-439;** fax 22970/26-430). To learn a little about Aegina's history, look for Anne Yannoulis's *Aegina* (Lycabettus Press), usually on sale at **Kalezis Boatokshop** on the harbor (© **22970/25-956**), which stocks foreign newspapers. Check the website **www. aeginagreece.com** for info in English.

GETTING AROUND A left turn as you disembark takes you east to the **bus station** on Plateia Ethatneyersias. There's good service to most of the island, with trips every hour in summer to the Temple of Aphaia and Ayia Marina (2€/$2.60); tickets must be purchased before boarding. **Taxis** are available nearby; the fare to the temple should be about 12€ ($16). You can sometimes negotiate a decent rate for a round-trip by taxi with an hour's wait at the temple. **Bicycles** and **mopeds** can be rented at the opposite end of the waterfront, near the beach. *Tip:* Prices can be exorbitant. An ordinary bike should cost about 10€ ($13) per day; mopeds, from 25€ ($33).

FAST FACTS The **National Bank of Greece** is one of four waterfront banks with currency-exchange service and ATMs; some travel agents, including **Aegina Island Holidays** (© **22970/23-333**), often exchange money both during and after normal bank hours, usually at less favorable rates. The island **clinic** (© **22970/22-251**) is on the northeast edge of town; for **first aid,** dial © **22970/22-222.** The **police** (© **22970/22-391**) and the **tourist police** (© **22970/23-333**) share a building on Leonardou Lada, about 200m (656 ft.) inland from the port. The **port authority** (© **22970/22-328**) is on the waterfront. The **post office** is in Plateia Ethatneyersias, around the corner from the hydrofoil pier. The **telephone office (OTE)** is 5 blocks inland from the port, on Aiakou. There are several Internet cafes, including **Prestige** and **Nesant,** on and just off the waterfront.

WHAT TO SEE & DO
EXPLORING AEGINA TOWN

Before you head out, try to pick up the useful pamphlet *Essential Aegina,* often available from travel agents, hotels, and the tourist police. Aegina town's neoclassical buildings date from its brief stint as the first capital of newly independent Greece (1826–28). Most people's first impression of this harbor town, though, is that of fishing boats and the small cargo vessels that ply back and forth to the mainland. Have a snack at one of the little restaurants in the **fish market** (follow your nose!) just off the harbor. This is where the men who catch your snacks of octopus and fried sprats come to eat their catches. The food is usually much better here than the food at the harborfront places catering to tourists.

If you take a horse-drawn carriage (15€–25€/$20–$33) or wander the streets back from the port, you'll easily spot neoclassical buildings, including restored **Markelos Tower,** where the first Greek parliament met. Fans of Nikos Kazantzakis may want to take a cab to **Livadi,** just north of town, to see the house where he lived when he wrote *Zorba the Greek.* North of the harbor, behind the town beach, and sometimes visible from boats entering the harbor, is the lone worn Doric column that marks the site of the **Temple of Apollo,** open Tuesday through Sunday from 8:30am to 3pm; admission is 2€ ($2.60). The view here is nice, the ruins very ruined.

About 4.8km (3 miles) out of Aegina town, the ruins of **Paleohora,** capital of the island from the 9th to the 19th centuries, sprawl over a steep hillside. This is a wonderful spot to explore (be sure to wear sturdy shoes and a sun hat). You'll see ruined houses and a number of carefully preserved churches. You can walk here from town or take the bus to Ayia Marina, which makes a stop for Paleohora.

SEEING THE TEMPLE OF APHAIA ★★

The **Temple of Aphaia,** set on a pine-covered hill 12km (7½ miles) east of Aegina town (© **22970/32-398**), is one of the best-preserved and most handsome Greek temples. No one really knows who Aphaia was, although it seems that she was a very old, even prehistoric, goddess who eventually became associated both with the huntress goddess Artemis and with Athena, the goddess of wisdom. According to some legends, Aphaia lived on Crete, where King Minos, usually preoccupied with his labyrinth and Minotaur, fell in love with her. When she fled Crete, he pursued her, and she finally threw herself into the sea off Aegina to escape him. At some point in the late 6th or early 5th centuries B.C., this temple was built, on the site of earlier shrines, to honor Aphaia.

Thanks to the work of restorers, 25 of the original 32 Doric columns still stand. The pedimental sculpture, showing scenes from the Trojan War, was carted off in 1812 by King Ludwig of Bavaria. Whatever you think about the removal of art treasures from their original homes, Ludwig probably did us a favor by taking it to the Glyptothek in Munich: While he was doing this, locals were busily burning much of the temple to make lime and hacking up other bits to use in building their homes. Admission to the site is 4€ ($5.20); it's open Monday through Friday from 8:30am to 7pm, Saturday and Sunday from 8:30am to 3pm. Allow at least 4 hours for your visit if you come here by the hourly bus from Aegina town; by taxi, you might spend only 2 hours.

WHERE TO STAY

Places to check out in Aegina town include two small hotels in restored buildings, **Stone House** (© **22970/23-970**), and **Hotel Brown** (© **22970/22-271**). Both charge 80€ to 100€ ($104–$130) double or studio.

Eginitiko Archontiko ★★ This mansion near the cathedral, only a couple of hundred feet from the harbor, was built in 1820 and renovated in 1988 with some loss of original detail, although a few lovely painted ceilings remain. The small guest rooms are traditionally furnished, comfortable, and quiet (although here, as elsewhere in Greece, motorcycle noise can be irritating). The pleasant downstairs lobby retains much 19th-century charm, while the garden is a very welcome sanctuary. The owners care about this handsome building and make guests comfortable. (They may even tell you that Greece's first president, Ioannis Kapodistrias, once stayed here.)

Ag. Nikolaou and 1 Eakou, 18010 Aegina. ℂ **22970/24-968.** Fax 22970/24-156. 12 units. 85€ ($111) double. AE, MC, V. Closed Nov–Mar. **Amenities:** Breakfast room; communal kitchen. *In room:* A/C.

Hotel Apollo ✦   Ayia Marina, with lots of resort hotels, is not our cup of tea. That said, friends with small children who stayed at this beach hotel were pleased with the large bathrooms and bedrooms and with the balconies overlooking the sea. If you come for a long stay, ask about renting a fridge for your room.

Ayia Marina, 18010 Aegina. ℂ **22970/32-271.** Fax 22970/32-688. 107 units. 110€–170€ ($143–$221) double. Compulsory breakfast buffet 8€ ($10); lunch or dinner 20€ ($26); weekly meal plans available. AE, DC, MC, V. Closed Nov–Mar. **Amenities:** Restaurant; bar; fresh and saltwater pools; tennis. *In room:* A/C, TV, minibar, hair dryer.

House of Peace (Spiti tis Irinis) ✦   This place is popular with young travelers, who appreciate its e-mail facilities and travel information, garden, and kitchen. The guest rooms—in double-occupancy bungalows—have high ceilings. Some units overlook the very lovely garden. Children under 12 are not accepted as guests, but everyone else is made more than welcome.

Plateia Ethatneyersias, 18010 Aegina. ℂ **22970/28-726.** Fax 22970/28-818. the_house_of_peace_@yahoo.com. 12 units, 6 with bathroom. 65€–80€ ($85–$104) double. No credit cards. Closed Nov–Mar. **Amenities:** Breakfast room. *In room:* Kitchenette in some units.

WHERE TO DINE

Keep in mind that fish is priced by the kilo at most restaurants. The price varies from catch to catch, so it's a good idea to ask before you order.

Estiatorion Economou ✦ GREEK   A reader suggested this portside taverna with a dark-blue canopy about midway along the waterfront. We recommend the lemony fish soup and grilled fish. Meat dishes are served as well. Grilled local lobster is sometimes available; expect to pay as much as 60€ ($78) per kilo.

Demokratias. ℂ **22970/25-113.** Main courses 8€–20€ ($10–$26); seafood priced by the kilo. AE, MC, V. Daily 9am–midnight.

Maridaki ✦ GREEK   This lively portside spot offers a wide selection of fish, grilled octopus, and the usual taverna fare of souvlaki and moussaka. The *mezedes* here are usually very good, and you can make an entire meal of them if you wish. Come on a quiet evening and you will have the sense of going back in time to an earlier Greece.

Demokratias. ℂ **22970/25-869.** Main courses 8€–20€ ($10–$26); seafood priced by the kilo. No credit cards. Daily 8am–midnight.

Mezedopoleio To Steki ✦✦ SEAFOOD   Locals and Athenians head to this little place by the fish market for its delicious *mezedes,* including succulent grilled octopus. You can make a meal of *mezedes* here. If you eat as the Greeks do, wash it all down with ouzo.

45 Pan Irioti. ℂ **22970/23-910.** *Mezedes* 6€–15€ ($7.80–$20). No credit cards. Daily 8am–midnight.

Taverna Vatsoulia ✦✦ GREEK   This local favorite for dinner is about a 10-minute walk out of town on the road to the Temple of Aphaia. Call ahead to make sure it's open. The menu includes delectable chops, fresh vegetables (including croquettes), and a tasty rabbit stew with onions. Though you can order fish, this is a down-home taverna not catering to tourists who want to sample island fish. Live music is sometimes presented in the flower-scented garden.

Ayii Assomati. (℅ **22970/22-711**. Main courses 7€–18€ ($9.10–$23). No credit cards. Wed and Sat–Sun 6pm–1am. Sometimes closed Mon or Thurs.

AEGINA AFTER DARK

At sunset, the harbor scene gets livelier as everyone comes out for an evening *volta* (stroll). **Perdikiotika,** in another one of Aegina's handsome 19th-century houses, occasionally offers live music. Kanella's **Piano Restaurant** usually features live pop music, heavy on the amplified *bouzouki.* **N.O.A.,** a portside ouzeri, offers a more traditional scene, as does **Avli.** On summer weekends, **En Egina, Kyvrenio,** and **Mousiki Skini** always present live music and occasional traditional *rembetika* music—sometimes all night! The scene in Ayia Marina is sure to be lively, if a bit sordid. (Some holidaymakers attempt to set records for the amount of beer and retsina they consume.) For more sedentary entertainment, the two outdoor cinemas are **Akroyiali** and **Olympia.**

2 Poros

55km (31 nautical miles) SW of Piraeus

Poros shares the gentle, rolling landscape of the adjacent Peloponnesian coastline, and has several good beaches, some decent tavernas, and a lively summer nightlife. If that sounds like lukewarm praise, we're afraid it is: Poros does not have enough island atmosphere to make us want to return often—and, in July and August, the island virtually sinks under the weight of package-tour groups.

As someone once said, "Geography is destiny." Poros (the word means "straits" or "ford") is separated from the Peloponnese by a narrow channel only 370m (1,214 ft.) wide. Technically, Poros is separated by a narrow canal into two islands: little **Sferia,** where Poros town is, and larger **Kalavria,** where everything else is. Poros is so easy to reach from the mainland that weekending Athenians and many tourists flock here each summer. In fact, a car ferry across the straits from Galatas to Poros town leaves almost every 20 minutes in summer—which means there are a *lot* of cars here.

If you wish, you can use Poros as a base for visiting the nearby attractions on the mainland, including Epidaurus, ancient Troezen (modern Trizina), and the lemon groves of Limonodassos. In a long day trip, you can visit Nafplion (Nafplio), Mycenae, and Tiryns.

ESSENTIALS

GETTING THERE Most **hydrofoils** to Poros, Hydra, and Spetses leave from Zea Marina in Piraeus; some leave from the main harbor at Piraeus. Most people take ferries or hydrofoils from Piraeus or the other Saronic Gulf islands, but some cross the narrow (540m/1,771-ft.) strait from Galatas by car ferry, which costs 2€ ($2.60) and takes only a few minutes. For information, call **Hellas Flying Dolphins** in Athens (℅ **210/419-9200** or 210/419-9000; www.dolphins.gr); or **Marinos Tours** (℅ **22980/ 22-297**) in Poros (the local hydrofoil agent). Reservations are recommended on weekends.

The other Saronic Gulf islands are all easy to reach from Poros. In addition, in summer Marinos Tours offers a weekly **round-trip hydrofoil excursion** to Tinos (3½ hr. each way) for 80€ ($104), and to Mykonos via Hydra (4 hr. each way) for 110€

($143). The one-way fare to Mykonos is 75€ ($98). These official prices are often cheaper if business is slow.

VISITOR INFORMATION   The waterfront hotels are generally too noisy for all except heavy sleepers, so if you want to stay in town, we suggest you check with **Marinos Tours** (✆ 22980/22-297; fax 22980/22-980), the local agent for **Hellas Flying Dolphins** who also handles several hundred rooms and apartments, as well as many island hotels. We've had good reports of **Saronic Gulf Travel** (✆ 22980/24-555; fax 22980/24-802), which offers an excellent free map of the island. To learn more about Poros, look for Niki Stavrolakes's enduring classic, *Poros* (Lycabettus Press), for sale on the island. The website **www.poros.com** has information in Greek and English.

GETTING AROUND   You can walk anywhere in Poros town. The island's **bus** can take you to the beaches or to the **Monastery of the Zoodhochou Pigis** and the remains of the **Temple of Poseidon;** the conductor will charge you according to your destination. The **taxi station** is near the hydrofoil dock, or you can call for one at ✆ **22980/23-003;** the fare to or from the Askeli beach should cost about 6€ ($7.80). **Kostas Bikes** (✆ **22980/23-565**), opposite the Galas ferry pier, rents bicycles for about 8€ ($10) per day, and mopeds from about 15€ ($20) per day. (Motorcycle and moped agents are required to, but do not always, ask for proof that you are licensed to drive such vehicles.)

FAST FACTS   The **National Bank of Greece** is one of a handful of waterfront banks with an ATM where you can also exchange money. The **police** (✆ **22980/ 22-256**) and **tourist police** (✆ **22980/22-462**) are on the paralia (harbor). The **port authority** (✆ **22980/22-274**) is on the harborfront. For **first aid,** call ✆ **22980/ 22-600.** The **post office** and **telephone office (OTE)** are also on the waterfront; their hours are Monday through Friday from 8am to 2pm. In summer, in addition to normal weekday hours, the OTE is open Sunday 8am to 1pm and 5 to 10pm. **Coconuts Internet Café** (✆ **22980/35-407**) and **Kentrou Typou** (also a newsagent with foreign newspapers) are both on the harborfront and offer Internet service for about 8€ ($10) per hour.

WHAT TO SEE & DO
ATTRACTIONS IN POROS TOWN

As you make the crossing to the island, you'll see the streets of Poros town, the capital, climbing a hill topped with a clock tower. Poros town is itself an island, joined to the rest of Poros by a causeway. (In short, the island of Poros is made up of two linked islands.) The narrow streets along the harbor are usually crowded with visitors inching their ways up and down past the restaurants, cafes, and shops. At night, the adjacent hills are, indeed, alive with the sound of music; the "Greek" music is usually heavily amplified pop.

Poros town has a **Naval Cadets' Training School**—which means that a lot of young men are looking for company here. Anyone wishing to avoid their attention can visit the small **Archaeological Museum** (✆ **22980/23-276**), with finds from ancient Troezen. It's usually open Monday through Sunday from 9am to 3pm; admission is free.

EXPLORING THE ISLAND

By car or moped, it's easy to make a circuit of the island in half a day. What remains of the 6th-century-B.C. **Temple of Poseidon** lies scattered beneath pine trees on the low plateau of Palatia, east of Poros town. The site is usually open dawn to dusk; admission is free. The ruins are scant, largely because the inhabitants of the nearby island of Hydra plundered the temple and hauled away most of the marble to build their harborside Monastery of the Virgin.

The Temple of Poseidon was the scene of a famous moment in Greek history in 322 B.C. when Demosthenes, the Athenian 4th-century orator and statesman, fled here for sanctuary from Athens's Macedonian enemies. When his enemies tracked him down, the great speechwriter asked for time to write a last letter—and then bit off his pen nib, which contained poison. Even in his death agonies, Demosthenes had the presence of mind to leave the temple, lest his death defile the sanctuary. It seems fitting that Demosthenes, who lived by his pen, died by the same instrument.

Those who enjoy monasteries can continue on the road that winds through the island's interior to the 18th-century **Monastery of the Zoodhochou Pigis (Monastery of the Life-Giving Spring),** south of Poros town. There are usually no monks in residence, but the caretaker should let you in from about 9am to 2pm and from 4 to 7pm. It's appropriate to leave a small donation in the offerings box. There's a little taverna nearby.

Poros's beaches are not enchanting. The beach northwest of town, **Neorio,** is often polluted; the better beaches are found southeast of town at **Askeli** and **Kanali** and to the north at **Vagonia.**

OFF THE ISLAND: A FESTIVAL, ANCIENT TROEZEN & LEMON GROVES

If you're in Poros in mid-June, you might want to catch the ferry across to Galatas and take in the annual **Flower Festival,** with its floral displays and parades of floats and marching bands. (Lots of posters in Poros town advertise the festival.)

From Galatas, you can catch a bus the 8km (5 miles) west to **Trizina** (ancient Troezen), birthplace of the great Athenian hero Theseus. It's also where his wife, Phaedra, tragically fell in love with her stepson, Hippolytus. When the dust settled, both she and Hippolytus were dead and Theseus was bereft. There are the remains of a temple to Asklepius here—but again, these ruins are very ruined.

About 4km (2½ miles) south of Galatas near the beach of Aliki, you'll find the olfactory wonder of **Limonodassos (Lemon Grove),** where more than 25,000 lemon trees fill the air with their fragrance each spring. Alas, many were harmed in a harsh storm in March 1998, and in yet another storm in 2002. Some trees survived, and more were planted. Several cafes nearby serve freshly squeezed lemonade. When the trees aren't in bloom, there's not much point in visiting here, as several readers have irately brought to our attention!

WHERE TO STAY

Hotel Sirena _Kids_   If you're talking creature comforts, and/or are traveling with children, the Sirena, on the beach east of town beyond Askeli, is a good choice. The Sirena is very popular with tour groups; if you want to stay here, you must make a reservation well in advance—and be prepared to be one of the few guests not with a group. Just about all the spacious rooms in this six-story building have excellent views. There are both salt- and freshwater pools near the private beach, and the restaurant is perfectly okay.

Monastiri, Askeli, 18020 Poros, Trizinias. © **22980/22-741.** Fax 22980/22-744. 120 units. 175€–200€ ($228–$260) double. MC. Closed Nov–Mar. **Amenities:** Restaurant; bar; 2 pools; tennis. _In room:_ A/C, TV, minibar, hair dryer.

Sto Roloi ⭐⭐   This small hotel has genuine charm: It's a 2-century-old town house near the island's famous *roloi* (clock tower). The owner rents the building as 2 suites: A garden apartment and a terrace apartment. A separate garden studio is also available. Many of the original details of the building (tiles, woodwork) have been preserved, and a serious attempt has been made to furnish Sto Roloi with appropriate island furniture (rather than the flashy modern furnishings often used in upmarket island hotels). This would be a very good place to spend a week; you can take advantage of the substantial price reduction for a week's stay, watch performances at Epidaurus, tour the eastern Peloponnese, or simply relax. The owners will arrange caïque excursions for guests and will help watersports enthusiasts hook up with Passage Watersports.

13 Karra, 18020 Poros, Trizinias. ℂ 22980/25-808. www.storoloi-poros.gr. 3 units. 75€ ($98) studio, 100€ ($130) garden apt., 135€ ($175) terrace apt. No credit cards. **Amenities:** Breakfast room; bar. *In room:* Kitchen.

WHERE TO DINE

If you're willing to give up your view of the harbor, head into town, a bit uphill, and try one of the restaurants near the church of Ayios Yeorgios, such as **Platanos, Dimitris,** or **Kipos.** As is often the case, these places tend to draw a more Greek crowd than the harborside spots. Fish is priced by the kilo at most restaurants; ask for prices before you order.

Caravella Restaurant GREEK   This portside taverna prides itself on serving organic home-grown vegetables and local (not frozen) fish. Specialties include traditional dishes such as snails, veal *stifado,* moussaka, souvlaki, and stuffed eggplant, as well as seafood and lobster.

Paralia, Poros town. ℂ 22980/23-666. Main courses 6€–18€ ($7.80–$23). AE, MC, V. Daily 11am–1am.

Taverna Grill Oasis ⭐ GREEK   This taverna has been here since the mid-1960s. Its harborside location with indoor and outdoor tables, the excellent fresh fish, and a cheerful staff make it live up to its name as a pleasant oasis for lunch or dinner. One not-so-traditional item on the menu: pasta with lobster.

Paralia, Poros town. ℂ 22980/22-955. Main courses 6€–19€ ($7.80–$25); seafood priced by the kilo. No credit cards. Daily 11am–midnight.

POROS AFTER DARK

There's plenty of evening entertainment in Poros town, including strolls up and down the harborside while people-watching. If you want to dance, **Lithatos, Maskes,** and **Korali,** in town, and **Poseidon,** about a kilometer south of town, are popular discos.

3 Hydra (Idra)

65km (35 nautical miles) S of Piraeus

Hydra is one of a handful of places in Greece that seemingly can't be spoiled. Even in summer, when the waterfront teems with day-trippers, many side streets remain quiet. If you can, arrive here in the evening, when most of the day visitors have left.

With the exception of a handful of municipal vehicles, there are no cars on Hydra. You'll probably run into at least one example of a popular form of local transportation: the donkey. When you see Hydra's splendid 18th- and 19th-century stone *archontika* (mansions) along the waterfront and on the steep streets above, you won't be surprised to learn that the entire island has been declared a national treasure by both the Greek government and the Council of Europe. You'll probably find Hydra town so charming that you'll forgive its one serious flaw: no beach. Do as the Hydriots do, and swim from the rocks at Spilia, just beyond the main harbor.

Whatever you do, be sure to go out on the deck of your ship as you arrive, so you can see Hydra's bleak mountain hills suddenly reveal a perfect horseshoe harbor. This truly is a place where arrival is half the fun.

ESSENTIALS

GETTING THERE   Several **ferries** and **excursion boats** make the 4-hour voyage between Piraeus and Hydra daily; there's also connecting service to several ports on the Peloponnese peninsula as well as with the other Saronic Gulf islands. **Hydrofoils** to Poros, Hydra, and Spetses leave from Zea Marina in Piraeus. For schedules and information, call **Hellas Flying Dolphins** (② 210/419-9200 or 210/419-9000; www. dolphins.gr); **Piraeus Port Authority** (② 210/451-1311); or **Hydra Port Authority** (② 22980/52-279). Reservations are a necessity on summer and on holiday weekends.

VISITOR INFORMATION   The free publications *Holidays in Hydra* and *This Summer in Hydra* are widely available and contain much useful information, including maps and lists of rooms to rent; shops and restaurants pay to appear in these publications. **Saitis Tours** (② 22980/52-184), in the middle of the harborfront, can exchange money, provide information on rooms and villas, book excursions, and help you make long-distance calls or send faxes. For those wanting to pursue Hydra's history, we recommend Catherine Vanderpool's *Hydra* (Lycabettus Press), on sale on the island. The island's English-language website is **www.hydra-island.gr**.

GETTING AROUND   Walking is the only means of getting around on the island itself, unless you bring or rent a donkey or a bicycle. **Caïques** provide water-taxi service to the island's beaches (Molos, Avlaki, Bisti, and Limioniza are the best) and to the little offshore islands of Dokos, Kivotos, and Petasi, as well as to secluded restaurants in the evening; rates run from 5€ to 25€ ($6.50–$33), depending on destination, time of day, and whether or not business is slow.

FAST FACTS   The **National Bank of Greece** and **Commercial Bank** are on the harbor; both have ATMs. Travel agents at the harbor will exchange money from about 9am to 8pm, usually at less favorable rates. The small **health clinic** is signposted at the harbor; cases requiring complicated treatment are taken by boat or helicopter to the mainland. The **tourist police** (② 22980/52-205) are on the second floor at 9 Votsi (signposted at the harbor). The **port authority** (② 22980/52-184) is on the harborside. The **post office** is just off the harborfront on Ikonomou, the street between the two banks. The **telephone office (OTE),** across from the police station on Votsi, is open Monday through Saturday from 7:30am to 10pm, Sunday from 8am to 1pm and 5 to 10pm. For **Internet access,** try HydraNet (② 22980/54-150), signposted by the OTE.

WHAT TO SEE & DO
ATTRACTIONS IN HYDRA TOWN

In the 18th and 19th centuries, ships from Hydra transported cargo around the world and made Hydra very rich indeed. Like ship captains on the American island of Nantucket, Hydra's ship captains demonstrated their wealth by building the fanciest houses money could buy. The captains' lasting legacy: the handsome stone *archontika* (mansions) that give Hydra town its distinctive character.

One archontiko that you can hardly miss is the **Tombazi mansion,** which dominates the hill that stands directly across the harbor from the main ferry quay. This is now a branch of the School of Fine Arts, with a hostel for students, and you can usually get a peek inside. Call the mansion (℗ **22980/52-291**) or **Athens Polytechnic** (℗ **210/619-2119**) for information about the program or exhibits.

The nearby **Ikonomou-Miriklis mansion** (also called the **Voulgaris**) is not open to the public, but the hilltop **Koundouriotis mansion,** built by an Albanian family who contributed generously to the cause of independence, is now a house museum. The mansion, with period furnishings and costumes, is usually open from April until October, Tuesday to Sunday 10am to 4pm. If you wander the side streets on this side of the harbor, you will see many more handsome houses, some of which are being restored so that they can once again be private homes, while others are being converted into stylish hotels.

Hydra's waterfront is a mixed bag, with a number of ho-hum shops selling nothing of distinction—and a handful of very nice boutiques and jewelry shops, especially in the area below the Tombazi mansion. **Hermes Art Shop** (℗ **22980/ 52-689**) has a wide array of jewelry, some good antique reproductions, and a few interesting textiles. **Domna Needlepoint** (℗ **22980/52-959**) offers engaging needlepoint rugs and cushion covers, with Greek motifs of dolphins, birds, and flowers. **Vangelis Rafalias's Pharmacy** is a lovely place to stop in, even if you don't need anything, just to see the jars of remedies from the 19th century.

> **Festivals in Hydra**
>
> On a mid-June weekend, Hydra celebrates **Miaoulia,** honoring Hydriot Admiral Miaoulis, who set much of the Turkish fleet on fire by ramming it with explosives-filled fireboats. In early July, Hydra has an annual **puppet festival** that, in recent years, has drawn puppeteers from countries as far away as Togo and Brazil. As these two festivals are not on set dates, get additional information from the **Hydra tourist police** (℗ **22980/52-205**) or check out **www.hydra-island.gr**.

When you've finished with the waterfront, walk uphill on Iconomou (it's steep) to see a number of quite interesting shops. **Meltemi** (℗ **22980/54-138**) sells original jewelry (including drop-dead earrings) and ceramics. Although the shop is small, just about everything here is borderline irresistible—especially the winsome blue ceramic fish. The owners, Vangelis and Zoe, speak English. Across from Meltemi, **Emporium** (no phone) shows and sells works by Hydriot and other artists. If you want to take home a painting or a wood or ceramic model of an island boat, try here.

Like many islands, Hydra boasts that it has 365 churches, one for every day of the year. The most impressive, the mid-18th-century **Monastery of the Assumption of the Virgin Mary,** is by the clock tower on the harborfront. This is the monastery built of the marble blocks hacked out of the (until then) well-preserved Temple of Poseidon on the nearby island of Poros. The buildings here no longer function as a monastery, and the cells are now municipal offices. The church itself has rather undistinguished 19th-century frescoes, but the elaborate 18th-century marble iconostasis (altar screen) is terrific. Like the marble from Poros, this altar screen was "borrowed" from another church and brought here. Seeing it is well worth the suggested donation.

EXPLORING THE ISLAND: A MONASTERY, A CONVENT & BEACHES

If you want to take a vigorous uphill walk (with no shade), head up Miaouli past Kala Pigadia (Good Wells), still the town's best local source of water. A walk of about an hour will bring you to the **Convent of Ayia Efpraxia** and **Monastery of the Prophet Elijah (Profitis Elias).** Both have superb views, both are still active, and the nuns sell their hand-woven fabrics. (*Note:* Both nuns and monks observe the midday siesta 1–5pm. Dress appropriately—no shorts or tank tops.)

The only real **beach** on the island is at **Mandraki,** a 20-minute walk east of town, where a large hotel has been built. Just outside town, you can swim off the rocks at **Spilia** or **Kamini.** Farther west along a donkey trail is **Kastello,** with the small fort that gives it its name, and another rocky beach with less crowded swimming. Still farther west is the pretty pine-lined cove of **Molos.** The donkey path continues west to the cultivated plateau, **Episkopi,** from which a faint trail leads on west to **Bisti** and **Ayios Nikolaos** for more secluded swimming. (Most of these beaches are best reached by water taxi from the main harbor.)

One fairly good beach on the south coast, **Limnioniza,** can be reached if you have strong legs, sturdy shoes, and a good map from Ayia Triada, though it's much easier to take a water taxi here and to Molos, Avlaki, and Bisti. The island of **Dokos,** northwest off the tip of Hydra, an hour's boat ride from town, has a good beach and excellent diving conditions—it was here that Jacques Cousteau found a sunken ship with cargo still aboard, believed to be 3,000 years old. You may want to take a picnic with you, as the taverna here keeps unpredictable hours.

WHERE TO STAY

In addition to the following choices, you might try the 19-unit **Hotel Greco,** Kouloura (© **22980/53-200;** fax 22980/53-511), a former fishing-net factory in a quiet neighborhood; or the recently redecorated (in traditional island style) **Hotel Leto** (© **22980/53-385**), just off the harbor.

Hotel Angelica ☆ This pension, in a lovingly restored traditional Hydriot home, stands on a quiet street 10 minutes away from the port and out of the usual tourist hubbub. The rooms are simple, with touches of local decor in the prints and furnishings. Most—many with balconies—overlook the quiet garden courtyard, where breakfast is served. You can request, but will not be guaranteed, one of the rooms with a rooftop terrace (room nos. 6, 8, 9, and 10).

42 Miaouli, 18040 Hydra. © **22980/53-202.** Fax 22980/53-542. www.angelica.gr. 15 units. 90€ ($117) double. MC, V. Closed Nov–Mar. **Amenities:** Breakfast room. *In room:* A/C.

Hotel Bratsera ☆ The Bratsera keeps turning up on everyone's list of the best hotels in Greece, which says a lot about the state of hotels in Greece. True, this small hotel, in a nicely restored 1860 sponge factory a short stroll from the harbor, is one of Hydra's nicest. The restaurant is touted as one of the best in the Saronic Gulf islands; it's certainly one of the most expensive! Each unit is unique, many with antique four-poster beds, all distinctively decorated in Hydriot style. The small pool with wisteria-covered trellises is very welcoming; meals are sometimes served poolside in fair weather. The hotel restaurant offers such slightly offbeat treats as fisherman's linguine. So, what's the problem? For one thing, we've had reports that room-service trays left in the hall after breakfast were still not collected by dinner time, and we know that messages left for guests aren't always delivered. And surely a fisherman's linguine should be topped with more than a solitary shrimp and one forlorn crayfish! That said, many readers report having a lovely stay here.

Tombazi, 18040 Hydra. (C) **22980/53-971.** Fax 22980/53-626. www.greekhotel.com. 23 units. 125€–280€ ($163–$364) double. Rates include breakfast. AE, DC, MC, V. Closed mid-Jan to mid-Feb. **Amenities:** Restaurant; bar; pool. *In room:* A/C, minibar, hair dryer.

Hotel Hydra *Value*   This is one of the best bargains in town if you don't mind the steep walk up to the beautifully restored two-story, gray-stone mansion on the western cliff, to the right as you get off the ferry. The carpeted guest rooms have high ceilings and are simply furnished; many have balconies overlooking the town and harbor.

8 Voulgari, 18040 Hydra. (C) **22980/52-102.** Fax 22980/53-330. hydrahotel@aig.forthnet.gr. 12 units, 8 with bathroom. 60€ ($78) double without bathroom; 80€–90€ ($104–$117) double with bathroom. MC, V. Open year-round. **Amenities:** Breakfast room. *In room:* TV.

Hotel Miranda *★★*   Once, when we were trapped for the night on Hydra by bad weather, we were lucky enough to get the last guest room at the Miranda. The unit was small, with a tiny bathroom and no real view—so it's a tribute to this hotel that we have wonderful memories of that visit. Most of the guest rooms here are good-size, with nice views of the lovely garden courtyard and town. The handsome 1820 captain's mansion is decorated throughout with Oriental rugs, antique cabinets, worn wooden chests, marble tables, contemporary paintings, and period naval engravings. There's even a small art gallery—in short, this is a very classy place.

Miaouli, 18040 Hydra. (C) **22980/52-230.** Fax 22980/53-510. www.miranda-hotel.com. 14 units. 120€–180€ ($156–$234) double. Compulsory breakfast 8€ ($10). AE, V. Closed Nov–Mar. **Amenities:** Breakfast room. *In room:* A/C, TV, minibar.

Hotel Orloff *★*   This restored mansion, just a short walk from the port, was built in the 18th century by a Russian philhellene, Count Orloff. Today it's a comfortable small hotel, distinctively decorated with antique furnishings. The very nice basement lounge has a bar. Breakfast is excellent.

9 Rafalia, 18040 Hydra. (C) **22980/52-564.** Fax 22980/53-532. www.orloff.gr. 10 units. 120€–170€ ($156–$221). Rates include buffet breakfast. AE, MC, V. Closed Nov–Mar. **Amenities:** Dining room; bar. *In room:* A/C.

Hydroussa   If you don't need a swimming pool, the Hydroussa is almost as charming as the Bratsera, and less expensive. Ask about the midweek discounts. Many of the spare but pleasant guest rooms have fine views over the town and harbor. Some even have good reading lamps—a real plus in Greece!

18040 Hydra. (C) **22980/52-217.** Fax 22980/52-161. 40 units. 85€–130€ ($111–$169) double. AE, V. Closed Nov–Mar. **Amenities:** Breakfast room. *In room:* A/C.

WHERE TO DINE

The harborside eateries are predictably expensive and not very good, although the views are so nice that you may not care. A number of cafes also lie along the waterfront, including **To Roloi (The Clock),** by the clock tower. Just off the harbor, **Ambrosia Cafe** serves vegetarian fare and good breakfasts. The cost of fish, priced by the kilo at most restaurants, varies from catch to catch, so it's a good idea to ask the price before you order.

Bratsera *★* GREEK/INTERNATIONAL   This restaurant in the Hotel Bratsera just off the harbor generally gets rave reviews, although we've heard complaints of terribly slow service and small portions. The indoor dining area is charming, but in good weather you'll probably want to sit outdoors under the wisteria-covered trellis beside the pool. The menu includes pastas, fresh seafood, grilled meats, and even a few Chinese specialties. (See also the Hotel Bratsera under "Where to Stay," above.)

Tombazi. ✆ **22980/52-794.** Reservations recommended in summer and on weekends. Main courses 15€–45€ ($20–$59). AE, DC, MC, V. Daily 8am–11pm.

Marina's Taverna ⍟ GREEK   Several readers report that they have enjoyed both the food and the spectacular sunset at this seaside taverna, appropriately nicknamed "Iliovasilema" ("Sunset"). Perched on the rocks west of the swimming area at Kamini, it's a 10€ ($13) water-taxi ride from town. The menu is basic, but the food is fresh and carefully prepared by Marina; her *klefltiko* (pork pie), an island specialty, is renowned.

Vlihos. ✆ **22980/52-496.** Main courses 8€–15€ ($10–$20). No credit cards. Daily noon–11pm.

Moita ⍟⍟ GREEK   Friends who visited Hydra kept seeing cards and flyers advertising Moita, so they headed up from the clock tower, turned left toward the OTE, and found the place that calls itself a "gourmet restaurant, cafe, and deli." Our friends left wanting to return, after a delicious meal of fresh grilled fish, pasta, and salads served under a spreading bougainvillea. We agree—and look forward to eggs Benedict for brunch (weekends only in high season, when most people head to the beach by brunch-time). Ask about the special fixed-price weeknight menu with two courses and two glasses of wine. No wonder this place gets e-mail reservation requests from satisfied returning guests en route from London and Berlin!

Off Miaouli. ✆ **22980/52-020.** Snacks and main courses 8€–25€ ($10–$33). No credit cards. Daily 11am–4pm and 8pm–midnight or longer in season.

To Steki GREEK   This small taverna, a few blocks up from the quay end of the harbor, has simple food and reasonable prices. The walls inside have framed murals showing a rather idealized traditional island life. The daily specials, such as moussaka and stuffed tomatoes, come with salad, vegetables, and dessert. The fish soup is memorable.

Miaouli. ✆ **22980/53-517.** Main courses 6€–18€ ($7.80–$23); daily specials 8€–15€ ($10–$20); seafood priced by the kilo. No credit cards. Daily noon–3pm and 7–11pm.

HYDRA AFTER DARK

Hydra has a very energetic nightlife, with restaurants, bars, and discos all going full steam ahead in summer. **Veranda** (up from the west end of the harbor, near the Hotel Hydra) is a wonderful place to escape the full frenzy of the Hydra harbor scene, sip a glass of wine, and watch the sunset.

Many of the discos are low-key and open from June to September. **Heaven** (✆ **22980/52-716**), which has grand views, is up the hill on the west side of town. **Hydronetta** tends to play more Western than Greek music—although the music at all these places is so loud that it's hard to be sure.

Portside, there are plenty of bars. **The Pirate** (✆ **22980/52-711**), near the clock tower, is the best known, although nearby **To Roloi** is probably a quieter place for a nightcap. Friends report enjoying drinks at the **Amalour,** just off the harbor, where they were surrounded by hip, black-clad 20- and 30-somethings. There's still a few local haunts left around the harbor; you'll be able to recognize them.

4 Spetses

98km (53 nautical miles) SW of Piraeus; 3km (2 nautical miles) from Ermioni

Despite a series of dreadful fires, Spetses's pine groves still make it the greenest of the Saronic Gulf islands. In fact, this island was called *Pityoussa* (Pine-Tree Island) in antiquity. Although the architecture here is less impressive than on Hydra, the island has some handsome *archontika* (mansions) built by wealthy 18th- and 19th-century sea captains. The island has long been popular with wealthy Athenians.

Many Spetses homes have handsome pebble mosaic courtyards; if you're lucky, you'll catch a glimpse of some when garden gates are open. One real plus for visitors here: Cars are not allowed to circulate freely in Spetses town, which would make for a good deal of tranquillity if motorcycles were not increasingly endemic.

In recent years, Spetses has become very popular with foreign tourists, especially the British. Some are pilgrims to see the island where John Fowles set his cult novel *The Magus,* but more are with tour groups. Consequently, sometimes you can hear as much English as Greek spoken in cafes and restaurants. As always, if you come here off season, you're bound to have a more relaxed experience and get a better sense of island life—even though some restaurants, shops, and small hotels will be closed.

ESSENTIALS

GETTING THERE   Several **ferries** and **excursion boats** make the 5-hour voyage from Piraeus daily, connecting with the other Saronic Gulf islands; contact the **Piraeus Port Authority** (© 210/451-1311) for schedules. (*Note:* Cars are not allowed on the island without express permission.) Several **hydrofoils** leave Piraeus's Zea Marina daily, most connecting with the other Saronic Gulf islands; express service takes 90 minutes. Contact **Hellas Flying Dolphins** (© 210/419-9200 or 210/419-9000; www.dolphins.gr) for schedules. Reservations are recommended on weekends.

There is less-frequent service from Spetses to the island of Kithatira and various ports on the Peloponnese; again, check with Hellas Flying Dolphins.

VISITOR INFORMATION   The island's main travel agencies are **Alasia Travel** (© 22980/74-098) and **Spetses & Takis Travel** (© 22980/72-215). We recommend Andrew Thatomas's *Spetses* (Lycabettus Press), usually on sale on the island, if you want to pursue Spetses's history.

GETTING AROUND   The island's limited public transportation consists of two municipal **buses** and a handful of **taxis. Mopeds** can be rented everywhere, beginning at 15€ ($20). **Bikes** are also widely available, and the terrain along the road around the island makes them sufficient means of transportation; three-speed bikes cost about 7€ ($9.10) per day, while newer 21-speed models go for about 10€ ($13). **Horse-drawn carriages** can take you from the busy port into the quieter back streets, where most of the island's handsome old mansions are located. Take your time choosing a driver; some are friendly and informative, others are surly. Fares are highly negotiable.

The best way to get to the various beaches around the island, as well as to the beach Kosta, on the Peloponnese, is **water taxi.** Locals call it a *venzina* (gasoline); each little boat holds about 8 to 10 people. A tour around the island costs about 30€ ($39); shorter trips, such as from Dapia to the Old Harbor, cost about 12€ ($16). Schedules are posted on the pier. You can also hire a water taxi to take you anywhere on the island, to another island, or to the mainland. Again, prices are highly negotiable.

FAST FACTS   The **National Bank of Greece** is one of several banks on the harbor with an ATM. Most travel agencies (9am–8pm) will also exchange money, usually at less favorable rates than banks. The local health **clinic** (✆ **22980/72-201**) is inland from the east side of the port. The **police** (✆ **22980/73-100**) and **tourist police** (✆ **22980/73-744**) are to the left off the Dapia pier, where the hydrofoils dock, on Boattassi. The **port authority** (✆ **22980/72-245**) is on the harborfront. The **post office** is on Boattassi near the police station; it's open from 8am to 2pm Monday to Friday. The **telephone office (OTE)**, open Monday to Friday from 7:30am to 3pm, is to the right off the Dapia pier, behind Hotel Soleil. **Internet access** is available at Delphina Net-Café on the harborfront.

WHAT TO SEE & DO
EXPLORING SPETSES TOWN (KASTELLI)

Spetses town (aka Kastelli) meanders along the harbor and inland in a lazy fashion, with most of its neoclassical mansions partly hidden from envious eyes by high walls and greenery. Much of the town's street life takes place on the **Dapia,** the square where the ferries and hydrofoils now arrive. The Old Harbor, **Baltiza,** largely silted up, lies just east of town, before the popular swimming spots at **Ayia Marina.**

If you sit at a cafe on the Dapia, you'll eventually see pretty much everyone in town passing by. The handsome black-and-white pebble mosaic commemorates the moment during the War of Independence when the first flag with the motto "Freedom or Death" was raised. Thanks to its large fleet, Spetses played an important part in the War of Independence, routing the Turks in the Straits of Spetses on September 8, 1822. The victory is commemorated every year on the weekend closest to **September 8** with celebrations, church services, and the burning of a ship that symbolizes the defeated Turkish fleet.

As you stroll along the waterfront, you'll notice the monumental bronze statue of a woman, her left arm shielding her eyes as she looks out to sea. The statue honors one of the greatest heroes of the War of Independence, **Laskarina Bouboulina,** the daughter of a naval captain from Hydra. Bouboulina financed the warship *Agamemnon,* oversaw its construction, served as its captain, and was responsible for several naval victories. She was said to be able to drink any man under the table, and strait-laced citizens sniped that she was so ugly, the only way she could keep a lover was with a gun. You can see where Bouboulina lived when she was ashore by visiting **Laskarina Bouboulina House** (✆ **22980/72-077**) in Pefkakia, just off the port. It keeps flexible hours (posted on the house) but is usually open mornings and afternoons from Easter until October. An English-speaking guide often gives a half-hour tour. Admission is 4€ ($5.20). You can even see Bouboulina's bones, along with archaeological finds and mementos of the War of Independence, at **Spetses Mexis Museum,** in the handsome stone Mexis mansion (signposted on the waterfront). Hours are Tuesday to Sunday 9:30am to 2:30pm; admission is 3€ ($3.90).

Hotel Posidonion figures in Spetses's history. It was built in 1911 as one of Greece's first "European-style" hotels by the island's greatest benefactor, Sotiris Anaryiros. He also built Anaryiros College, now famous because John Fowles taught there. Just outside of town, the hotel is closed most of the year except during August, when it hosts the Anaryiria festival of art exhibits.

The harborfront has the usual tourist shops, but take a look at **Pityoussa** (no phone), which carries decorative folk paintings, ceramics, and interesting gift items;

it's near the OTE, behind Hotel Soleil. **Astrolavos-Spetses Gallery** (℃ **22980/75-228**) sometimes has special events for children in the summer, as well as exhibits by well-known Greek artists.

If you head east away from the Dapia, you'll come to the picturesque **Paleo Limani** (aka the Baltiza or **Old Harbor**), where many wealthy yacht owners moor their boats. **Cathedral of Ayios Nikolaos (St. Nicholas)** is the oldest church in town; it has a lovely bell tower on which the island raised its first Greek flag. A pebble mosaic shows the event, as do a number of similar pebble mosaics in Spetses town. While you're at the Old Harbor, have a look at the boatyards, where you can usually see *kaikia* (caïques) being made with tools little different from those used when Bouboulina's mighty *Agamemnon* was built here.

BEACHES

Ayia Marina, signposted and about a 30-minute walk east of Spetses town, is the best town beach. It has a number of tavernas, cafes, and discos. On the south side of the island, **Ayii Anaryiri** has one of the best sandy beaches anywhere in the Saronic Gulf, a perfect C-shaped cove lined with trees, bars, and tavernas. (We prefer Taverna Tassos.) The best way to get here is by water taxi. Whichever beach you pick, go early, as both can be seriously crowded by midday.

Some prefer the beach at **Ayia Paraskevi,** which is smaller and more private because it's so closely bordered by pine trees. Located here are a cantina and **Villa Yasemia,** residence of The Magus himself. West over some rocks is the island's official nudist beach. **Zogeria** is on the northwest coast, with a few places to eat and some pretty rocky coves for swimming. West of Spetses town, **Paradise beach** is crowded, littered, and to be avoided.

WHERE TO STAY

Finding a good, quiet, centrally located room in spread-out Spetses is not easy. If you are planning a lengthy stay, check out **Hotel Nissia** (℃ **22980/75-000;** www.nissia.gr), open all year. It has 40 rooms and flats clustered to simulate traditional residences around a pool. Doubles cost from 120€ ($156). The hotel is a 5-minute walk from the center of Spetses town. Another centrally located possibility: **Zoe's Club** (℃ **22980/74-447;** www.zoesclub.gr), in a nicely restored 19th-century building with a modern addition. Zoe's good-size apartments come with one to three bedrooms. Units cost from 125€ ($163).

Hotel Faros *(Value* Though there's no *faros* (lighthouse) nearby, this older hotel shares the busy central square with a Taverna Faros, a Faros Pizzeria, and other establishments whose tables and chairs curb the flow of vehicular traffic. Try for the top floor, where the simple, comfortable, twin-bedded rooms are quietest, with balcony views of the island.

Plateia Kentriki (Central Sq.), 18050 Spetses. ℃ **22980/72-613.** Fax 22980/74-728. 50 units. 75€ ($98) double. No credit cards. **Amenities:** Breakfast room.

Hotel Posidonion *(★★* The landmark Poseidon (as we would spell it) is a grand and gracious hotel that was built in 1911 and, under new management, was completely renovated in the early 1990s. This Belle Epoque classic boasts two grand pianos in its lobby and the statue of Bouboulina guarding the plaza in front. The spacious, high-ceilinged guest rooms are sparsely but elegantly furnished; the old-fashioned bathrooms have large tubs. The view over the harbor from the tall front windows is superb.

Dapia, 18050 Spetses. ☎ **22980/72-208** or 22980/72-006. Fax 22980/72-208. 55 units. 85€–120€ ($111–$156) double; 140€ ($182) double with sea view. Rates include breakfast. AE, DC, MC, V. **Amenities:** Restaurant; bar. *In room:* A/C, TV.

Orloff Resort ★★ This glitzy resort, built in 1975 and totally renovated in 2004, occupies the land and some of the buildings of the 1865 Orloff estate. It's a kilometer out of town by the beach, and has its own pool as well as great extras such as tennis and an exercise room. The restaurant is good, too. This would be a great place to spend a relaxing week on Spetses. It's popular with Greek families, many of whom return year after year.

18050 Spetses. ☎ **22980/75-444.** www.orloffresort.com. 22 units. 90€–190€ ($117–$247) double; 160€–290€ ($208–$377) maisonette for 4; 190€–335€ ($247–$435) suite for 4. Rates include breakfast. DC, MC, V. **Amenities:** Restaurant; bar; pool; tennis. *In room:* A/C, TV, minibar, safe.

Star Hotel ★ *Value* This blue-shuttered, five-story hotel—the best in its price range—is flanked by a pebble mosaic, making it off-limits to vehicles. All guest rooms have balconies, the front ones with views of the harbor. Each large bathroom has a tub, shower, and bidet. Breakfast is available a la carte in the large lobby.

Plateia Dapia, 18050 Spetses. ☎ **22980/72-214** or 22980/72-728. Fax 22980/72-872. 37 units. 85€ ($111) double. No credit cards. **Amenities:** Breakfast room.

WHERE TO DINE

Spetses's restaurants can be packed with Athenians on weekend evenings, so you may want to eat unfashionably early—about 9pm—to avoid the Greek crush. The island's considerable popularity with tour groups seems to have led to a decline in the quality of restaurant fare. Let us know if you find someplace particularly good. If the price of your fish is not on the menu, ask for it; fish is often priced by the kilo.

For standard Greek taverna food, including a number of vegetable dishes, try the rooftop taverna **Lirakis,** Dapia, over the Lirakis supermarket (☎ **22980/72-188**), with a nice view of the harbor. **To Kafeneio,** a long-established coffeehouse and ouzo joint on the harborfront, is a good place in which to sit and watch the passing scene, as is **To Byzantino. Orloff,** on the road to the Old Harbor, has a wide variety of *mezedes.*

Spetses has some of the best **bakeries** in the Saronic Gulf; all serve an island specialty called *amygdalota,* small cone-shaped almond cakes flavored with rosewater and covered with powdered sugar.

The Bakery Restaurant GREEK/CONTINENTAL This restaurant is on the deck above one of the island's more popular patisseries. There are a few ready-made dishes, but most of your choices are prepared when you order them. The chef obviously understands foreign palates and offers smoked trout salad, grilled steak, and roasted lamb with peas, in addition to the usual Greek dishes.

Dapia. No phone. Main courses 8€–20€ ($10–$26). MC, V. Daily 6:30pm–midnight.

Exedra Taverna ★ GREEK/SEAFOOD This traditional taverna on the Old Harbor, where yachts from all over Europe moor, is also known by locals as Sioras or Giorgos. This is a good place to try fish Spetsiota (a broiled fish-and-tomato casserole). The freshly cooked zucchini, eggplant, and other seasonal vegetables are also excellent. If you can't find a table for supper, try the nearby **Taverna Liyeri,** also known for good seafood.

Paleo Limani. ✆ **22980/73-497.** Main courses 8€–18€ ($10–$23); fish priced by the kilo. No credit cards. Daily noon–3pm and 7pm–midnight. Closed Feb–Nov.

Lazaros Taverna ★ GREEK   This traditional place is decorated with potted ivy, family photos, and big kegs of homemade retsina lining the walls. It's popular with locals (always a good sign) who come here for the good, fresh, reasonably priced food. The small menu features grilled meats and daily specials, such as goat in lemon sauce.

Dapia. No phone. Main courses 5€–14€ ($6.50–$18). No credit cards. Daily 6:30pm–midnight. Closed mid-Nov to mid-Mar. Inland and uphill about 400m (1,312 ft.) from the water.

SPETSES AFTER DARK

There's plenty of nightlife on Spetses, with bars, discos, and *bouzouki* clubs from the Dapia to the Old Harbor to Ayia Marina, and even to the more remote beaches. For bars, try **Bracciera, Socrates, Tsitsiano,** or **Remezzo** in the heart of Dapia.

As for discos, there's **Figaro,** with a seaside patio and international funk until midnight, when the music switches to Greek and the dancing follows step—often till dawn. **Delfina Disco** is opposite the Dapia town beach on the road to the Old Harbor. **Disco Fever,** with its flashing lights, draws the British crowd, while **Naos,** which looks more like a castle than a temple, features techno music. **Fox** often has live Greek music and dancing; obvious tourists are encouraged to join the dancing—information that may help you decide whether or not to come here!

7

Crete

by John S. Bowman

Few travelers need to be sold on the glories of the Minoan culture of Crete. But Crete also offers cities layered with 4,000 years of continuous inhabitation, including the vibrant heritage of centuries-old Orthodox Christianity and the distinctive imprint left by almost 700 years of Venetian and Turkish rule. Not to mention endless beaches and magnificent mountains, intriguing caves and resonant gorges, and countless villages and sites that provide unexpected and unforgettable experiences. Per square mile, Crete must be one of the most "loaded" places in the world—loaded, that is, in the diversity of history, archaeological sites, natural attractions, tourist amenities, and more. In a world where more and more travelers have "been there, done that,"

Crete remains an endlessly fascinating and satisfying destination.

An elaborate service industry has developed to please the thousands of foreigners who visit Crete each year. Facilities now exist to suit everyone's taste, ranging from luxury resorts to guest rooms in villages that have hardly changed over several centuries. You can spend a delightful day in a remote mountain town where you're treated to fresh goat cheese and olives, then be back at your hotel within an hour, enjoying a cool drink on the beach.

Crete isn't always and everywhere a gentle Mediterranean idyll—its terrain can be raw, its sites austere, its tone brusque. But for those looking for a distinctive destination, Crete will be rewarding.

STRATEGIES FOR SEEING THE ISLAND

If possible, go in June or September, even late May or early October, unless you seek a sun-drenched beach: Crete has become an island on overload in July and August, when it's very hot. The overnight ferry from Piraeus is still the purist's way to go, but the hour-long flight by plane from Piraeus gives you more time for activities. The island offers enough things to do to fill up a week, if not a lifetime of visits. By flying, you can actually see the major sites in 2 packed days. To make things easier, you can fly into Iraklion and out of Chania, or vice versa.

We recommend the following destinations if you have 5 to 7 days. This mix of activities even allows you time to collapse on a beach at the end of the day. Iraklion is a must, with its archaeological museum and nearby Knossos. An excursion to Phaestos, its associated sites, and the caves at Matala can easily occupy most of day 2. If you don't have to see that second Minoan palace, we recommend you move on to Chania or Rethymnon—each or both can fill another day of strolling. Choose your path: The old road that winds through the mountains and villages has its charms, while the coastal expressway offers impressive vistas and a "tunnel" of flowering oleanders. The walk through the famed Samaria Gorge requires 1 long day for the total

Crete

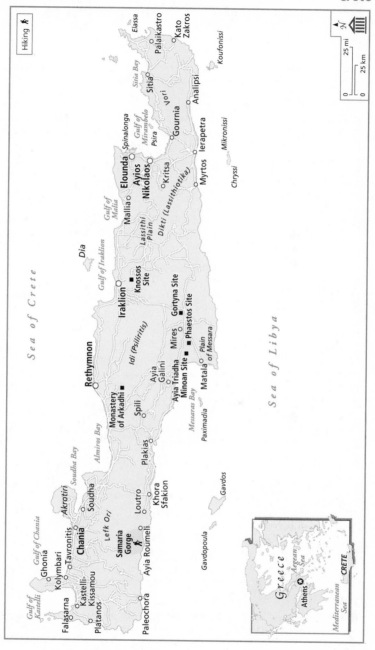

excursion. Those seeking less strenuous activity might prefer a trip eastward to Ayios Nikolaos and its nearby attractions. None of these trips require a car, as public transportation or tour groups are so frequent. However, you might want to rent a car (although not for use in the cities or towns) so you can leave the overdeveloped tourist trail and explore countless villages, spectacular scenery, beaches at the ends of the roads, and lesser-known archaeological, historical, and cultural sites.

A LOOK AT THE PAST

Crete's diversity and distinction begin with its history, a past that has left far more remains than the Minoan sites many people first associate with the island. After being settled by humans around 6500 B.C., Crete passed through the late Neolithic and early Bronze ages, sharing the broader eastern Mediterranean culture.

Sometime around 3000 B.C., new immigrants arrived; by about 2500 B.C., there began to emerge a fairly distinctive culture called Early Minoan. By about 2000 B.C., the Minoans were moving into a far more ambitious phase, the Middle Minoan—the civilization that gave rise to the palaces and superb works of art that now attract many visitors to Crete every year.

Mycenaean Greeks appear to have taken over the palaces about 1500 B.C., and by about 1200 B.C., this Minoan-Mycenaean civilization had pretty much gone under. For several centuries, Crete was a relatively marginal player in the great era of Greek classical civilization.

When the Romans conquered the island in 67 B.C., they revived Knossos and other centers as imperial colonies. Early converts to Christianity, the Cretans slipped into the shadows of the Byzantine world, but the island was pulled back into the light in 1204, when Venetians broke up the Byzantine Empire and took over Crete. The Venetians made the island a major colonial outpost, revived trade and agriculture, and eventually built quite elaborate structures.

By the late 1500s, the Turks were conquering the Venetians' eastern Mediterranean possessions, and in 1669 they captured the last major stronghold on Crete, the city of Candia—now Iraklion. Cretans suffered considerably under the Turks, and although some of Greece finally threw off the Turkish yoke in the late 1820s, Crete was left behind. A series of rebellions marked the rest of the 19th century, resulting in a partly independent Crete.

Finally, in 1913, Crete was for the first time formally joined to Greece. Crete had yet another cameo role in history when the Germans invaded it in 1941 with gliders and parachute troops; the ensuing occupation was another low point. Since 1945, Crete has advanced amazingly in the economic sphere, powered by its agricultural products—particularly olives, grapes, melons, and tomatoes—as well as by its tourist industry. Not all Cretans are pleased by the development, but all would agree that, for better or for worse, Crete owes much to its history.

Tips Museum Hours Update

If you visit Greece during the summer, check to see when sites and museums are open. According to the tourist office, they should be open from 8am to 7:30pm, but some may close earlier in the day or even be closed one day a week.

1 Iraklion (Heraklion)

Iraklion is the gateway to Knossos, one of the most important Minoan palace sites. The museum here is home to the world's only comprehensive collection of Minoan artifacts. Beyond that, the town has magnificent fortified walls and several other testaments of the Venetians' time of power. Iraklion is also big enough (Greece's sixth-largest city) and confident enough to have its own identity as a busy modern city. It often gets bad press because it bustles with traffic and commerce and construction—the very things most travelers want to escape. At any rate, give Iraklion a chance. Follow the advice below, and you just may come to like it.

ESSENTIALS

GETTING THERE   By Plane   Aside from the many who now fly from European cities directly to Crete on charter/package tour flights, most visitors will take the 40-minute flight from Athens to Iraklion or Chania on **Olympic Airways** (✆ 210/926-9111; www.olympic-airways.gr). The cost is 204€ ($265) round-trip. Olympic offers a few direct flights a week between Iraklion and Rhodes, and in high season the airline offers service between Athens and Sitia (in eastern Crete). Otherwise, flights between Crete and other points in Greece (such as Santorini, Mykonos, Thessaloniki) go through Athens. Reservations are a necessity in high season.

    Aegean Airlines, which flies from Athens to Iraklion and Chania, is now an alternative to Olympic. Its fares are somewhat cheaper—and its flights are less frequent. For information, ask your travel agent, go online (www.aegeanair.com), or contact Aegean's Athens offices (✆ 210/998-8300).

    Iraklion's airport is about 5km (3 miles) east of the city, along the coast. Major car rental companies have desks at the airport. A taxi to Iraklion costs about 10€ ($13); the public bus, 2€ ($2.60). To get back to the airport, you have the same two choices—taxi or public bus no. 1. You can take either form of transport from Plateia Eleftheria (Liberty Sq.) or from other points along the way. Inquire in advance at your hotel about the closest stop.

By Boat   Throughout the year, there is at least one ship per day (and as many as two or three in high season) from Piraeus to Iraklion, and other ships to Chania and Rethymnon. All trips take about 10 hours. Less frequent ships link Crete to Rhodes (and Karpathos, Kassos, and Khalki, the islands between the two); to Santorini and some of the other Cycladic islands en route to or from Piraeus; and even to Thessaloniki and various Greek ports en route. In high season, occasional ships from Italy, Cyprus, and Israel put into Iraklion. And now hydrofoils link Iraklion with several Cycladic islands (Santorini, Ios, Paros, Naxos, and Mykonos). **Hellas Flying Dolphins** run daily in high season, four times weekly other times; check online (www.dolphins.gr) or contact their Athens office (✆ 210/419-9100). For information on all ships, inquire at a travel agency, search online (www.gtp.gr), or contact **Paleologos Agency** (www.ferries.gr).

    If you have arrived at Iraklion's harbor by ship, you'll most likely want to take a taxi up into the town, as it's a steep climb. Depending on where you want to go, the fare ranges from 3€ to 10€ ($3.90–$13). Or you can take a bus from the depot.

By Bus   Visitors also come to Iraklion by public bus. Where you arrive depends on where you've come from. Those arriving from points to the west, east, or southeast—Chania or Rethymnon, for instance, or Ayios Nikolaos or Sitia to the east—end up along the harbor. To get into the center of town, you must walk, take a taxi, or hop a public bus. The bus starts its route at the terminal where buses from the east and southeast stop; directly across the boulevard is the station for the Rethymnon-Chania buses. Visitors arriving from the south—Phaestos, Matala, and other towns—will end up at Chania Gate on the southwest edge of town; walking will not appeal to most people, but you can take a public bus or taxi.

VISITOR INFORMATION   The **National Tourist Office** is at 1 Xanthoudidou, opposite the Archaeological Museum (© **2810/228-225;** fax 2810/226-020). Its hours are Monday through Friday 8am to 2:30pm. You'd do better to contact one of the more reliable travel agencies in Iraklion: **Adamis Tours,** 23 25th Avgusto (© **2810/346-202;** www.adamistourscrete.gr); **Creta Travel Bureau,** 20–22 Epimenidou (© **2810/227-002;** fax 2810/223-749); or **Arabatzoglou Travel,** 54 25th Avgusto (© **2810/226-697;** fax 2810/222-184). For those interested in renting an apartment or villa on Crete, see the agencies listed in chapter 2 under "Landing the Best Room."

GETTING AROUND   By Bus   You can see much of Crete by using the public bus system. The buses are cheap, relatively frequent, and connect to all but the most isolated locales. The downside: Remote destinations often have schedules that cater to locals, not tourists. The long-distance bus system is operated by **KTEL,** which serves all of Greece. Ask your travel agent or call © **2810/221-765** to find out more about KTEL buses to Rethymnon-Chania and points west. For buses to Ayios Nikolaos, Sitia, Ierapetra, and points east, call © **2810/245-019.** For buses to Phaestos and other points south, call © **2810/255-965.**

By Car & Moped   A car gives you maximum flexibility in seeing the island. Rental agencies are available at all the main centers of Crete, including the airports. In Iraklion, we recommend the locally owned **Motor Club,** 18 Plateia Agglon at the bottom of 25th Avgusto, overlooking the harbor (© **2810/222-408;** www.motorclub.gr); or **Hertz,** 34 25th Avgusto (© **2810/341-734**). If a moped or motorcycle looks tempting, be *very* sure you can control such a vehicle in chaotic urban traffic and on dangerous mountain roads (with few shoulders but lots of potholes and gravel). Try the Motor Club, above, for rentals.

By Taxi   Taxis are reasonable if two or three people share a trip to a site; no place on Crete is more than a day's round-trip from Iraklion. Ask a travel agent to find you a driver who speaks at least rudimentary English; he can then serve as your guide as well. We can recommend **Antonis Gratsas,** who offers a 4-hour tour of the city for about 100€ ($130); he is best reached (while on Crete) via his mobile phone (© **69440-796237**).

By Boat   Several excursion boats take day trips to offshore islands or to isolated beaches as well as to Santorini; inquire at a travel agency.

FAST FACTS   The official **American Express** agency is Adamis Travel Bureau, 23 25th Avgusto (© **2810/346-202;** fax 2810/224-717). There are numerous **banks** and **ATMs** (as well as several currency-exchange machines) throughout the center of Iraklion, with many along 25th Avgusto. The **British Consul** is at 16 Papa Alexandrou, opposite the Archaeological Museum (© **2810/224-012**); there is no American consulate in Iraklion. **Venizelou Hospital** (© **2810/237-502**) is on Knossos Road. For general **first-aid** information, call © **2810/222-222.** For Internet access, try the Konsova Internet Café, 25 Dikeossinas (© **2810/288-143**) or try Cyberpoint Café, 117 Paraskiyopoulou

Iraklion

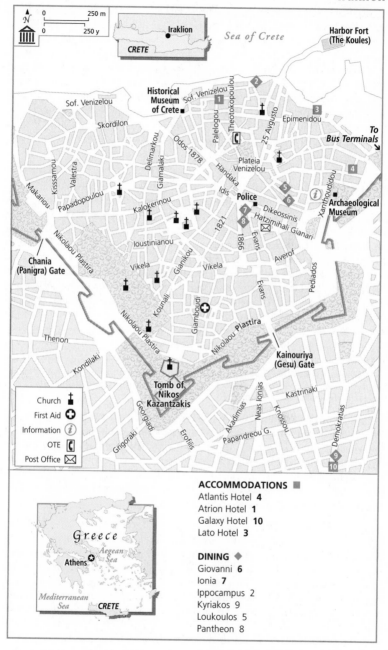

ACCOMMODATIONS ■
Atlantis Hotel **4**
Atrion Hotel **1**
Galaxy Hotel **10**
Lato Hotel **3**

DINING ◆
Giovanni **6**
Ionia **7**
Ippocampus **2**
Kyriakos **9**
Loukoulos **5**
Pantheon **8**

(www.cyberpoint.gr). Both open mid-morning and close at midnight. The access fee at both is 5€ ($6.50) per hour.

The most convenient place to do **laundry** is at 25 Merebellou (behind the Archaeological Museum); its hours are Monday through Saturday from 9am to 9pm. You can leave **luggage** at the airport for 3€ ($3.90) per piece per day; most hotels will hold luggage for brief periods. The **tourist police** are at 10 Dikiosenis, on the main street linking 25th Avgusto to Plateia Eleftheria (© **2810/283-190**); they are open daily from 7am to 11pm. The main **post office** (© **2810/289-995**) is on Plateia Daskaloyiannis and is open daily from 7:30am to 8pm. The **telephone office (OTE)**, 10 Minotaurou (far side of El Greco Park), is open daily from 6am to 11pm.

WHAT TO SEE & DO
ATTRACTIONS

The Archaeological Museum ★★★   This—the world's premier collection of art and artifacts from the Minoan civilization—amazes most visitors who are surprised by the variety of objects, styles, and techniques of the treasures inside. Many of the most spectacular objects are from Knossos; the rest, from other sites on the island. Among the most prized objects are **snake goddesses** from Knossos, the **Phaestos Disc** (with its still undeciphered inscription), the **bee pendant** from Mallia, **carved vases** from Ayia Triadha and Kato Zakros, and objects depicting young men leaping over the horns of charging bulls. Upstairs you'll find the **original frescoes from Knossos** and other sites, their restored sections clearly visible (the frescoes now at Knossos are copies of these). Most displays have decent labels in English, but you may want to invest in one of the guidebooks for sale in the lobby. You will need at least 1 hour for a quick walk-through. To avoid the tour groups in high season, plan to visit very early, late in the day, or on Sunday.

1 Xanthoudidou. © 2810/226-092. Admission 10€ ($13) adults, 6€ ($7.80) students with official ID and E.U. citizens 65 and over. Apr to mid-Oct Tues–Sun 8am–8pm, Mon 12:30–8pm; mid-Oct to Mar, closes daily at 5pm. Far corner of Plateia Eleftheria. Parking in immediate area impossible.

Harbor Fort (The Koules) (Kids   You may feel as if you're walking through a Hollywood set—but this is the real thing! The harbor fort, built on the site of a series of earlier forts, went up between 1523 and 1540, and although greatly restored, it is essentially the Venetian original. Both its exterior and interior are impressive in their dimensions, workmanship, and details: thick walls, spacious chambers, great ramparts, cannon balls, and Lion of St. Mark plaques. It's well worth an hour's visit.

At breakwater on old harbor. © 2810/288-484. Admission 4€ ($5.20). Daily 9am–1pm and 4–7pm.

Historical Museum of Crete ★   This museum picks up where the Archaeological Museum leaves off, displaying artifacts and art from the early Christian era up to the present. You get some sense of the role the Cretans' long struggle for independence still plays in their identity. On display are traditional Cretan **folk arts;** the re-created study of **Nikos Kazantzakis,** Crete's great modern writer; and at least one work attributed to the painter **El Greco,** another of the island's admired sons. Even if you take only an hour for this museum, it will reward you with surprising insights about the island.

7 Lysimakos Kalokorinou (facing coast road 450m/1,500 ft. west of harbor). © 2810/283-219. www.historical-museum.gr. Admission 4€ ($5.20) adults, 2€ ($2.60) students. Mar–Oct Mon–Fri 9am–5pm, Sat 9am–2pm; reduced hours in winter.

The Palace of Knossos ★★★ *(Kids)*   This is undeniably one of the great archaeological sites of the world, yet until Arthur Evans began excavating here in 1900, little was known about the ancient people who inhabited it. Using every possible clue and remnant, Evans rebuilt large parts of the palace—walls, floors, stairs, windows, and columns. Visitors must now stay on a walkway, but you still get a good sense of the structure's labyrinthine nature. You are looking at the remains of two major palaces plus several restorations made from about 2000 B.C. to 1250 B.C. This was not a palace in the modern sense of a royal residence, but a combination of that and the Minoans' chief religious-ceremonial center as well as their administrative headquarters and royal workshops. Take the time for a guided tour here; it's worth the expense (your hotel or a travel agency can arrange it). On your own, you'll need at least 2 hours for a cursory walk-through. The latter part of the day and Sunday tend to be less crowded.

Knossos Rd., 5km (3 miles) south of Iraklion. ② 2810/231-940. Admission 6€ ($7.80), 4€ ($5.20) students with official ID and E.U. citizens 65 or over. Apr to mid-Oct daily 8am–8pm; mid-Oct to Mar Mon–Fri 8am–5pm, Sat–Sun 8:30am–3pm. Free parking down slope on left 90m (295 ft.) before main entrance.

Venetian Walls & Tomb of Nikos Kazantzakis ★   These great walls and bastions were part of the fortress-city the Venetians called Candia. Two of the great city gates have survived fairly well: the Pantocrator or Panigra Gate, better known now as the Chania Gate (dating from about 1570), at the western edge; and the Gate of Gesu, or Kainouryia Gate (about 1587), at the southern edge. Walk around the outer perimeter of the walls to get a feel for their sheer massiveness. They were built by the forced labor of Cretans.

Amid the Venetian structures stands the grave of Nikos Kazantzakis (1883–1947), a native of Iraklion and author of *Zorba the Greek* and *The Last Temptation of Christ*. Here, from Kazantzakis's tomb at the Martinengo Bastion at the southern corner, is one of the best views to the south. Mount Iouktas appears in profile as the head of a man—some say the head of the buried god Zeus. A special visit here requires 1 hour, 2 if you want to examine the gate and a segment of the wall.

The tomb is on the Martinengo Bastion, at the southwestern corner of the walls, along Plastira. Free admission. Sunrise–sunset.

A STROLL AROUND IRAKLION

Start your stroll at **Fountain Square** (also known as Lions Sq., officially Plateia Venizelou), after trying a plate of *bougatsa* at one of the two cafes serving this local pastry. Armenian Greeks introduced this cheese- or cream-filled delicacy to Crete. Francesco Morosini, Crete's Venetian governor, installed the **fountain** ★ here in 1628. Note the now fading but still elegant relief carvings around the basin. Across from the fountain is the **Basilica of St. Mark,** restored to its original 14th-century Italian style and used for exhibitions and concerts. And since the city of Iraklion acquired the painting at an auction in 2004, St. Mark's is now the home of native son El Greco's "The Baptism of Christ."

Proceeding south 50m (164 ft.) to the crossroads, you'll see the **market street** (officially from 1866), which is increasingly overtaken by tourist shops but is still a must-see with its purveyors of fresh fruits and vegetables, meats, and wines.

At the far end of the market street, look for **Kornarou Square,** with its lovely Turkish fountain; beside it is the **Venetian Bembo Fountain** (1588). The modern statue at the far side of the square commemorates the hero and heroine of Vincenzo Kornarou's Renaissance epic poem *Erotokritos,* a Cretan-Greek classic.

Turning right onto Vikela, proceed (always bearing right) until you come to the imposing, if not artistically notable, 19th-century **Cathedral of Ayios Menas,** dedicated to the patron saint of Iraklion. Below and to the left, the medieval **Church of Ayios Menas** boasts old woodcarvings and icons.

At the far corner of the cathedral (to the northeast) is the 15th-century **Church of St. Katherine.** During the 16th and 17th centuries, this church hosted the Mount Sinai Monastery School, where Domenico Theotokopoulou is alleged to have studied before moving on to Venice and Spain. There he became known as **El Greco.** The church houses a small museum of icons, frescoes, and woodcarvings. It's open Monday through Saturday from 10am to 1pm; and Tuesday, Thursday, and Friday from 4 to 6pm. Admission is 5€ ($6.50).

Take Ayii Dheka, the narrow street that leads directly away from the facade of St. Katherine's, and you'll arrive at **Leoforos Kalokerinou,** the main shopping street for locals. Turn right onto it and proceed up to the crossroads of the market and 25 Avgusto. Turn left to go back down past Fountain Square and, on the right, you'll see the reconstructed **Venetian Loggia,** originally dating from the early 1600s. Prominent Venetians once met here to conduct business affairs; it now houses city government offices.

A little farther down 25th Avgusto, also on the right, is the **Church of Ayios Titos,** dedicated to the patron saint of Crete (Titus of the Bible), who introduced Christianity to Crete. Head down to the **harbor,** with a side visit to the **Koules** (Venetian fort), if you have time (see above), then pass on the right the two sets of great **Venetian arsenali**—where ships were built and repaired. (The sea at that time came in this far.) Climbing the stairs just past the arsenali, turn left onto Bofort and curve up beneath the **Archaeological Museum** to **Plateia Eleftheria (Liberty Sq.),** where you can reward yourself with a refreshing drink at one of the many cafes on the far side.

SHOPPING

Costas Papadopoulos, the proprietor of **Daedalou Galerie,** 11 Daedalou (between Fountain Sq. and Plateia Eleftheria; ℂ **2810/346-353**), has been offering his tasteful selection of traditional Cretan-Greek arts and crafts for several decades—icons, jewelry, porcelain, silverware, pistols, and more. Some of it is truly old, and he'll tell you when it isn't.

Eleni Kastrinoyanni-Cretan Folk Art, 3 Ikarou (opposite the Archaeological Museum; ℂ **2810/226-186**), is the premier store in Iraklion for some of the finest in embroidery, weavings, ceramics, and jewelry. The work is new but reflects traditional Cretan folk methods and motifs. Get out your credit card and go for something you'll enjoy for years to come. It's closed October through February.

For one of Crete's finest selections of antique and old Cretan textiles (rugs, spreads, coverlets, and more), along with some unusual pieces of jewelry, try **Grimm's Handicrafts of Crete,** 96 25th Avgusto (opposite the Venetian Loggia; ℂ **2810/282-547**). The finest objects are not cheap, but you get exactly what you pay for here; even the newer textiles can be stunning.

Stores that sell local agricultural products are springing up all over Crete. Crete's olive oil—among the finest in the world—stands side by side with honey, wines and spirits, raisins, olives, herbs, and spices. One store is as good as the other.

WHERE TO STAY

In recent years, mass tourism created a demand here for beach hotels, yet a range of hotels still exists. You still need reservations in high season.

INSIDE THE CITY

Our search for a good hotel here includes the criterion of quiet. Iraklion lies under the flight patterns of some commercial planes and the occasional Greek Air Force jet fighter. The noise factor probably adds up to less than 40 minutes every 24 hours, so the sounds of scooters and motorcycles outside your hotel at night will probably be more annoying. The city plans to add a runway out into the sea or build an airport far inland, but it will take some years for this to happen. Closed windows and air-conditioning promise the best defenses.

EXPENSIVE

Atlantis Hotel ⭐⭐ *Value*   The Atlantis is probably the best value if you want to be in the middle of things. Greece has more luxurious hotels, but few can beat the Atlantis's urban attractions: a central location, modern facilities, and views over a busy harbor. This superior Class A hotel is in the heart of Iraklion yet removed from city noise (especially if you use the air-conditioning). The staff is friendly and helpful, and although the Atlantis is popular with conference groups—it has major conference facilities—individuals get personal attention. Guest rooms, although neither plush nor especially large, are comfortable. You can swim in the pool, send e-mail via your laptop, and then within minutes be out enjoying a fine meal or visiting a museum.

2 Iyias, 71202 Iraklion. ℂ **2810/229-103.** www.theatlantishotel.gr. 162 units. High season 158€ ($205) double; low season 130€ ($157) double. Rates include breakfast. Reduction possible for longer stays. Special rates for business travelers and half-board (breakfast and dinner). AE, DC, MC, V. Private parking arranged. Behind the Archaeological Museum. **Amenities:** Restaurant; 2 bars; small indoor pool; rooftop garden; tennis court across street; Jacuzzi; bike rental; children's playground (across street); video rentals; concierge; tour desk; car rental desk; airport pickup by arrangement; secretarial service; salon; 24-hr. room service; massage; babysitting; laundry service; dry cleaning; non-smoking rooms. *In room:* A/C, TV, minibar, fridge, hair dryer, safe.

Galaxy Hotel ⭐   With a reputation as one of the fancier hotels on Crete, the Galaxy is classy once you get past its rather forbidding gray exterior. The public areas are striking, airport modern, and the Galaxy boasts (for now, at least) the largest indoor swimming pool in Iraklion. Guest rooms are stylish—international modern—but don't expect American-style size. Ask for an interior unit since you lose nothing in a view and gain in quiet. The hotel also offers several expensive suites. Although a reader reported a less-than-gracious tone from desk staff, we have always found them courteous in handling requests for services. The Galaxy appeals most to travelers who prefer a familiar international ambience to folksiness. Although its restaurant serves the standard Greek/international menu, the pastry shop and ice-cream parlor attract locals, who consider the fare delicious.

67 Leoforos Demokratias, 71306 Iraklion. ℂ **2810/238-812.** www.galaxy-hotel.gr. 137 units, some with shower, some with tub. High season 150€ ($195) double; low season 120€ ($156) double. AE, DC, MC, V. Parking on street. Frequent bus to town center within yards of entrance. About ½ mile out main road to Knossos. **Amenities:** Restaurant; pastry shop; bar; indoor pool; sauna; concierge; 24-hr. room service; laundry service; dry cleaning; executive-level rooms; nonsmoking rooms. *In room:* A/C, TV, minibar, hair dryer.

MODERATE

Atrion Hotel   Nothing spectacular here, but we have liked this hotel for many years for its location. Its 2003 renovation opened up the public areas and spruced up the rooms. It's in a quiet, seemingly remote corner that is in fact only a 10-minute walk to the center of town, and an even shorter walk to the coast road and the harbor. True, the adjacent streets are not that attractive, but they are perfectly safe; once inside the hotel, you can enjoy your oasis of comfort and peace. This hotel has well-appointed public areas—a lounge, a refreshing patio garden—and pleasant, good-size guest rooms.

9 Chronaki (behind the Historical Museum). 71202 Iraklion. © **2810/229-225.** Fax 2810/223-292. www.atrion.gr. 74 units, some with tub, some with shower. High season 105€ ($137) double; low season 90€ ($117) double. Rates include buffet breakfast. Reductions for children. AE, MC, V. Parking on street. Public bus within 200m (656 ft.). **Amenities:** Cafeteria; bar/restaurant; babysitting; laundry service; nonsmoking rooms. *In room:* A/C, TV, minibar.

Lato Boutique Hotel *(Value)* Long one of our favorites in all of Greece, the Lato has now jumped to the head of the line when it comes to providing value, a discreetly stylish environment, and warm hospitality. Nothing pretentious, but its latest renovations enlarged the hotel, refurbished the public areas, and completely transformed the rooms' decor and furnishings (including fire and smoke detectors and high-security door locks). A few rooms are a bit small, five are handsome suites, but all are perfectly adequate—and all have state-of-the-art bathrooms. The tasty buffet breakfast is satisfying. Another major plus: its location, which is convenient to the town's center and offers rooms with harbor views. Parking can be a problem but the accommodating staff will take over, just as they are always ready to help you make the most of your stay in Iraklion.

15 Epimenidou, 71202 Iraklion. © **2810/228-103.** Fax 2810/240-350. www.lato.gr. 58 units, some with shower only. High season 130€–175€ ($169–$228) double; low season 120€–165€ ($156–$215) double. Rates include buffet breakfast. 10% discount for Internet reservations. 50% discount for children 6–12. AE, DC, MC, V. Parking on street. **Amenities:** Restaurant/breakfast room; bar; fax and Internet facilities; concierge; car rental service; room service 8am–11pm; laundry service; dry cleaning; nonsmoking rooms. *In room:* A/C, TV, minibar, hair dryer, safe.

INEXPENSIVE

Poseidon *(Value)* If there were a contest among Frommer's Greece guidebook loyalists for the all-time favorite place to stay, the Poseidon would win, hands down. And it's not just because of good value for the money. Longtime owner/host John Polychronides establishes a homey atmosphere, a tone maintained by the desk staff (fluent in English), who are always ready to provide useful information and support for your stay on Crete. In 2004, the hotel was renovated by installing an elevator and, in each unit, air-conditioning, a TV, and a fridge. Yes, the street is not especially attractive—but that's true of most of Iraklion's hotels, and few can match the fresh breezes and an unobstructed view over the port. All rooms have balconies, and the sound-insulated windows keep out most of the exterior noise. Rooms are on the small side and showers are basic, but everything is clean and functional. Frequent buses and cheap taxi fares let you come and go into Iraklion center, a 20-minute walk away. While not for those demanding luxury, this is a pleasant alternative to in-town hotels.

54 Poseidonos, Poros, 71202 Iraklion. © **2810/222-545.** www.hotelposeidon.gr. 26 units, all with shower only. High season 85€ ($111) double; low season 72€ ($94) double. Rates include continental breakfast. A 10% discount for e-mail reservations, 5% discount for stays over 2 nights. AE, MC, V. Parking all around. Frequent public buses 180m (590 ft.) at top of street. About 2.5km (1½ miles) from Plateia Eleftheria, off the main road to the east. *In room:* A/C (7€/$9.10 daily surcharge), TV, fridge.

OUTSIDE THE CITY

Stay on the coast if you want to avoid city noise. We assume that you want to be fairly close to Iraklion. If you just want to stay near a remote beach on Crete, such accommodations are described elsewhere. Although the hotels below can be reached by public bus, a car or taxi will save you valuable time.

EXPENSIVE

Candia Maris ⭐   The grandest of the resort hotels on the western edge of Iraklion, the deluxe-class Candia Maris offers just about everything from special "Cretan nights" with traditional music and dancing to a squash court. Although the beach on the west coast is not always as pleasant as that on the east, it's perfectly clean. And although you have to pass through a rather dreary edge of Iraklion to get here, this area is close to town. The exterior and layout are a bit severe, but the rooms are good-size and cheerful, the bathrooms up to date. (If it looks like a brick-factory owner's idea of a hotel, it's because the owner is just that.) Since you won't spend much time looking at the building's exterior, don't let it deter you from trying this first-class resort hotel. It was one of the first hotels in Greece to offer accessibility for those with limited mobility.

Amoudara, Gazi, 71303 Iraklion. 𝒸 **2810/377-000.** Fax 2810/250-669. www.maris.gr. 258 units. High season 135€–150€ ($176–$195) double in hotel, 160€–185€ ($208–$241) seafront bungalow; low season 75€–90€ ($98–$117) double in hotel, 85€–95€ ($111–$124) bungalow. Rates include buffet breakfast. Reductions for extra person in room and for children; half-board plan (including breakfast and dinner) available for additional 24€ ($31). AE, DC, MC, V. Public bus every half-hour to Iraklion. On beach about 6km (4 miles) west of Iraklion center. **Amenities:** 4 restaurants; 4 bars; 6 pools (2 outdoor, 4 indoor) plus children's pool; tennis courts; squash court; minigolf; volleyball; basketball; bowling; billiards; health club and spa; watersports; bike rental; children's program; game room; concierge; tour arrangements; car rental desk; airport transport arrangements; conference facilities; salon; room service 7am–noon; babysitting; laundry service; dry cleaning; Internet access; rooms for those w/limited mobility. In room: A/C, TV, minibar, fridge, hair dryer.

MODERATE

Xenia-Helios ⭐ (Kids)   We single out the Xenia-Helios because here you can save a bit of money and feel you're contributing to the future of young Greeks. It's one of three such hotels run by the Greek Ministry of Tourism to train young people for careers in the hotel world. (Another is outside Athens, the other outside Thessaloniki.) The physical accommodations may not be quite as glitzy as some of the other beach resorts, but they're certainly first class and the service is especially friendly. The beach here is especially lovely, and children will enjoy Water City, the waterpark just a mile or so east of the hotel.

Kokkini Hani, 71500 Iraklion. 𝒸 **2810/761-502.** Fax 2810/418-363. 108 units. High season 85€ ($111) double; low season 65€ ($85) double. Rates include half-board plan. AE, MC, V. Closed Oct–May. Buses every half-hour to Iraklion or points east. About 13km (8 miles) east of Iraklion. **Amenities:** Restaurant; bar; pool; tennis courts; watersports equipment; conference facilities; hair salon. In room: A/C.

WHERE TO DINE

Avoid eating a meal at either Fountain Square or Liberty Square (Plateia Eleftheria) unless you want the experience—the food at those areas' establishments is, to put it mildly, nothing special. Save these spots for a coffee or beer break.

EXPENSIVE

Kyriakos ⭐ GREEK   In recent years, this restaurant has gained the reputation of offering some of the finest cooking in Iraklion. The menu is essentially traditional Greek, but its specialties include artichokes with potatoes and lettuce, lamb fricassee, and aubergines stuffed with feta. Snails are another delicacy, and if that doesn't tempt you, come back at Christmas for the turkey. The wine choices are appropriately fine and expensive. Two people should expect to drop between 50€ and 75€ ($65–$98) for the full works here, but think what you'd pay at home for such a meal. Its location might disappoint some; it's on a busy boulevard on the edge of town and lacks Cretan "atmosphere." It's a bit stodgy, but if you're serious about what's on your plate, coming here is an occasion.

53 Leoforos Demokratias (about ½ mile from center on the road to Knossos). ℂ 2810/224-649. Reservations recommended for dinner in high season. Appetizers 4€–8€ ($5.20–$10); main courses 6€–28€ ($7.80–$36). AE, DC, MC, V. Daily noon–5pm and 7pm–1am. Closed Sun June 2–July 10. Frequent public bus service.

Loukoulos ✿ ITALIAN/GREEK   Here's another restaurant that has gained a stylish reputation, but with a setting the opposite of the Kyriakos (see above). It's in the very heart of the city on a back street, crammed into a tiny patio with fanciful umbrellas shading the tables. The chairs are comfortable, the table settings lovely, and the selection of *mezedes* (appetizers) varied. The creative Italian menu features lots of pasta dishes, such as a delicious rigatoni with a broccoli-and-Roquefort cream sauce. Treat yourself at least once to Iraklion's "in" place.

5 Korai (1 street behind Daedalou). ℂ 2810/224-435. Reservations recommended for dinner in high season. Main courses 6€–20€ ($7.80–$26); fixed-price lunch about 16€ ($21). AE, DC, V. Mon–Sat noon–1am; Sun 6:30pm–midnight.

MODERATE

Giovanni GREEK   A taverna with some pretensions to chic, this appeals to a slightly younger, more casual set than its neighbor, Loukoulos (see above). Its name may be Italian, but its fare is traditional Greek. House specialties include shrimp in tomato sauce with cheese, baked eggplant with tomato sauce, and *kokhoretsi* (a sort of oversize sausage made from lamb innards; much better than it may sound)—all quite tasty.

12 Korai (1 street behind Daedalou). ℂ 2810/246-338. Main courses 5€–18€ ($6.50–$23). AE, MC, V. Mon–Sat 12:30pm–2am; Sun 5pm–1:30am.

Pantheon *Moments* GREEK   Anyone who spends more than a few days in Iraklion should take at least one meal in "Dirty Alley," where this restaurant is a longtime favorite. Although it lost its rough-hewn atmosphere long ago, Dirty Alley still seems a foreign locale. The menu at Pantheon (much the same as the menus at the other Dirty Alley places) offers taverna standards—meat stews; chunks of meat, chicken, or fish in tasty sauces; and vegetables such as okra, zucchini, or stuffed tomatoes. These places are not especially cheap—the proprietors know to charge for the atmosphere— but the food's tasty. And if you sit in the Pantheon, on the corner of the market street, you'll get a choice view of the scene outside.

2 Theodosaki ("Dirty Alley," connecting the market street and Evans). ℂ 2810/241-652. Main courses 5€–14€ ($6.50–$18). No credit cards. Mon–Sat 11am–11pm.

INEXPENSIVE

Ionia GREEK   Undistinguished as it now appears, this is in some respects the Nestor of Iraklion's restaurants. Founded in 1923, Ionia has served generations of Cretans as well as all the early archaeologists. Although it's greatly reduced in size, the food is as good as ever, and the staff encourages foreigners to step over to the kitchen area and select from the warming pans. You may find more refined food and fancier service elsewhere on Crete, but you won't taste heartier dishes than the Ionia's green beans in olive oil or lamb joints in sauce. We recommend a visit to what is clearly a fading tradition.

3 Evans (just to the left of the market street). ℂ 2810/282-313. Main courses 4€–10€ ($5.20–$13). MC, V. Mon–Fri 8am–10:30pm; Sat 8am–4pm.

Ippocampus SEAFOOD/GREEK   This is an institution among locals, who line up for a typical Cretan meal of appetizers. The zucchini slices, dipped in batter and deep-fried, are fabulous. A plate of tomatoes and cukes, another of sliced fried potatoes, small fish, perhaps fried squid—that's it. You can assemble a whole meal for as little as 12€ ($16)—but go early. Ippocampus is down along the coast road. You can sit indoors or on the sidewalk, a bargain either way.

3 Mitsotaki (off to left of traffic circle as you come down 25 Avgusto). ✆ 2810/282-081. Main courses 2.50€–8€ ($3.25–$10). No credit cards. Mon–Fri 1–3:30pm and 7pm–midnight.

IRAKLION AFTER DARK

To spend an evening the way most Iraklians do, stroll and then sit in a cafe and watch others stroll by. The prime locations for the latter have been Plateia Eleftheria (Liberty Sq.) or Fountain Square, but the packed-in atmosphere of these places—and some overly aggressive waiters—has considerably reduced their charm.

For far more atmosphere, go to **Marina Cafe** at the old harbor (directly across from the restored Venetian arsenalil). For as little as 2€ ($2.60) for a coffee or as much as 6€ ($7.80) for an alcoholic drink, you can enjoy the breeze as you contemplate the illuminated Venetian fort, which looks much like a stage set.

An alternative is **Four Lions Roof-Garden Cafe** (✆ 2810/222-333); enter through an interior staircase in the shopping arcade on Fountain Square. It attracts younger Iraklians, but travelers are welcome. The background music is usually Greek. You get to sit above the crowded crossroads and, with no cover or minimum, enjoy anything from a coffee (2€/$2.60) or ice cream (from 3€/$3.90) to an alcoholic drink (from 3€/$3.90).

There is no end to the number of **bars** and **discos** featuring rock 'n' roll or Greek popular music, although they come and go from year to year to reflect the latest fads. **Disco Athina,** 9 Ikarou, just outside the wall on the way to the airport, is an old favorite with the young; or try the **Veneto Bar** and **Club Itan,** both on Epimenidou.

Most Class A hotels now host a **Cretan Night,** when performers dance and play **traditional music.** For more of the same, take a taxi to either **Aposperides,** out on the road toward Knossos, or **Sordina,** about 5km (3 miles) to the southwest of town.

Iraklion's **arts festival** (though hardly competitive with the major festivals of Europe) brings in world-class performers (ballet companies, pianists, and others), but mostly featured are ancient and medieval-Renaissance Greek dramas, Greek-themed dance, or traditional and modern Greek music. Many performances take place outdoors in one of three venues: on the roof of the **Koules** (the Venetian fort in the harbor), **Kazantzakis Garden Theater,** or **Hadzidaksis Theater.** Ticket prices vary from year to year and for individual events but are well below what you'd pay at such cultural events elsewhere. Maybe you didn't come to Crete expecting to hear Vivaldi, but why not enjoy it while you're here? The festival begins in late June and ends in mid-September.

SIDE TRIPS FROM IRAKLION

Travel agencies arrange excursions setting out from Iraklion to virtually every point of interest on Crete, such as **Samaria Gorge** in the far southwest (p. 213). In that sense, Iraklion can be used as the home base for all your touring on Crete. If you have only one extra day on Crete, we recommend the following trip.

GORTYNA, PHAESTOS, AYIA TRIADHA & MATALA ✮✮

If you have an interest in history and archaeology, and you've already seen Knossos and Iraklion's museum, this is the trip to make. The distance isn't that great—a round-trip of about 165km (100 miles)—but you'd need a full day to take it all in. A taxi or guided tour is advisable if you haven't rented a car. Bus schedules won't allow you to fit in all the stops. (You can, of course, stay at one of the hotels on the south coast, but they're usually booked long in advance of high season.)

The road south takes you up and across the **mountainous spine** of central Crete. At about the 25th mile, you'll leave behind the **Sea of Crete** (to the north) and see the **Libyan Sea** to the south. You then descend onto the **Messara,** the largest plain on Crete (about 32km/20 miles×5km/3 miles) and a major agricultural center. At about 45km (28 miles), you'll see on your right the **remains of Gortyna;** many more remnants lie scattered in the fields off to the left. Gortyna (or Gortyn or Gortys) first emerged as a center of the Dorian Greeks who moved to Crete after the end of the Minoan civilization. By 500 B.C., they had advanced enough to inscribe a code of law into stone. The stones were found in the late 19th century and reassembled here, where you can see this unique—and to scholars, invaluable—document testifying to the legal and social arrangements of this society.

Then, after the Romans took over Crete (67 B.C.), Gortyna enjoyed yet another period of glory when it served as the capital of Roman Crete and Cyrenaica (Libya). Roman structures—temples, a stadium, and more—litter the fields to the left. On the right, along with the **Code of Gortyna** ✮, you'll see a small **Hellenistic Odeon,** or theater, as well as the remains of the **Basilica of Ayios Titos** (admission 4€/$5.20; daily 8am–7pm high season; reduced hours off season). Paul commissioned Titos (Titus) to lead the first Christians on Crete. The church, begun in the 6th century, was later greatly enlarged.

Proceed down the road another 15km (10 miles), turn left at the sign, and ascend to the ridge where the **palace of Phaestos** ✮✮ sits in all its splendor. (Admission is 5€/$6.50; daily 8am–7pm high season; reduced hours off season.) Scholars consider this the second-most powerful Minoan center; many visitors appreciate its attractive setting on a prow of land that seems to float between the plain and the sky. Italians began to excavate Phaestos soon after Evans began at Knossos, but they decided to leave the remains much as they found them. The **ceremonial staircase** is as awesome as it must have been to the ancients, while the **great court** remains one of the most resonant public spaces anywhere.

Leaving Phaestos, continue down the main road 4km (2½ miles) and turn left onto a side road. Park here and make your way to pay your respects to a Minoan minipalace complex known as **Ayia Triadha.** To this day, scholars aren't certain exactly what it was—something between a satellite of Phaestos and a semi-independent palace. Several of the most impressive artifacts in the Iraklion Museum, including the painted sarcophagus (on the second floor), were found here.

Back on the road, follow the signs to **Kamilari** and then **Pitsidia.** Now you've earned your rest and swim, and at no ordinary place: the nearby **beach at Matala** ✮. It's a small cove enclosed by bluffs of age-old packed earth. Explorers found **chambers,** some complete with bunk beds, that probably date back to the Romans (most likely no earlier than A.D. 500). Cretans used them as summer homes, the German soldiers used them as storerooms during World War II, and hippies took over them in the late 1960s. You can visit them during the day; otherwise, they are off limits. Matala has become one more overcrowded beach in peak season, so after a dip and some refreshment, make your way back to Iraklion (straight up via **Mires,** so you avoid the turnoff back to Ayia Triadha and Phaestos).

2 Chania (Hania/Xania/Canea) ★★

150km (95 miles) W of Iraklion

Until the 1980s, Chania was one of the best-kept secrets of the Mediterranean: a delightful town nestled between mountains and sea, a labyrinth of atmospheric streets and structures from its Venetian-Turkish era. Since then, tourists have flocked here, and there's hardly a square inch of the Old Town, which fans back from the harbor, that's not dedicated to satisfying them. Chania was heavily bombed during World War II; ironically, some of its atmosphere is due to still-unreconstructed buildings that are now used as shops and restaurants.

What's amazing is how much of Chania's charm has persisted since the Venetians and Turks effectively stamped the old town in their own images between 1210 and 1898. Visit any time except July and August; whenever you come, dare to strike out on your own and see the old Chania.

ESSENTIALS

GETTING THERE By Plane Olympic Airways offers at least three flights daily to and from Athens in high season. (Flight time is about 40 min.) Flights to Chania from other points in Greece go through Athens. **Aegean Airlines** offers a few weekly flights to and from Athens. See "Getting There" in the section on Iraklion, above, for contact information. The airport is located 15km (10 miles) out of town on the Akrotiri. Public buses meet all flights except the last one at night, but almost everyone takes a taxi (about 12€/$16).

By Boat One ship makes the 10-hour trip daily between Piraeus and Chania, usually leaving early in the evening. This boat arrives at and departs from Soudha, a 20-minute bus ride from the stop outside the municipal market. Many travel agents around town sell tickets. In high season, if you're traveling with a car, make reservations in advance. **Hellas Flying Dolphins** hydrofoil service runs once daily between Chania and Piraeus. Check online (www.dolphins.gr), contact their Athens office (© 210/419-9100), or check with the **Paleologos Agency** (www.ferries.gr).

By Bus Buses run almost hourly from early in the morning until about 10:30pm, depending on the season, connecting Chania to Rethymnon and Iraklion. There are less frequent, and often inconveniently timed, buses between destinations in western Crete. The main **bus station** to points all over Crete is at 25 Kidonias (© 28210/93-306).

VISITOR INFORMATION The official Tourist Information office is at 40 Kriari, off 1866 Square (© 28210/92-943). Local merchants also sponsor an office (© 28210/20-369; skel@chania-cci.gr) on Akti Tombazi, at the back of the Mosque of Djamissis, the domed building on the harbor's east side. The hours at these offices have been unpredictable, and although the staff try, they cannot provide detailed information. Better to turn to private travel agencies. We recommend **Lissos Travel,** Plateia 1866 (© 28210/93-917; fax 28210/95-930); or **Crete Travel** in the nearby village of Monoho (© 28250-32-690; www.cretetravel.com). A useful source of

A Taxi Tip

To get a taxi driver who is accustomed to dealing with English-speakers, call **Andreas** at ✆ **28210/50-821;** you can also try ✆ **69450/365-799** (his mobile phone number). With Andreas, you get an informative guide as well as a driver.

insider's information is **The Bazaar,** 46 Daskaloyiannis, on the main street down to the new harbor (to the right of the Municipal Market). This shop sells used foreign-language books and assorted "stuff." Owned and staffed by non-Greeks, it maintains a listing of all kinds of helpful services.

GETTING AROUND   You can walk to most tourist destinations in Chania. There are public buses to nearby points and to all the major destinations in western Crete. If you want to explore the countryside or more remote parts of western Crete, we recommend that you rent a car to make the best use of your time.

FAST FACTS   **Banks** in the new city have ATMs. For the **tourist police,** dial ✆ **171.** The **hospital** (✆ **28210/27-231**) is on Venizelou in the Halepa quarter. Access the **Internet** at Vranas Studios Cafe, behind the cathedral and at the corner of Aghion Deka. Or go to one of the two locations of Cafe Santé (on the second floor at the far west corner of the old harbor; and at Hotel Manos at 24 Zambeliou). **Speedy Laundry,** 17 Kordiki, on the corner of Koroneou, a block west of Plateia 1866 (✆ **28210/88-411**), promises wash and dry in 90 minutes and will pick up and deliver for free. For **luggage storage,** try the KTEL bus station on Kidonias. The **post office** is on Tzanakaki (leading away from the municipal market); hours are Monday through Friday from 8am to 8pm, Saturday from 8am to noon. Beside it is the **telephone office (OTE),** open daily from 7:30am to 11:30pm.

WHAT TO SEE & DO

In summer, several small **excursion ships** offer 3- to 5-hour trips to the waters and islets off Chania. These trips depart from the old and new harbors and include stops for swimming at one or another of the islets; some provide free snorkeling gear. On the glass-bottomed *Evangelos,* you can see underwater life. The cost is about 20€ ($26) adults, free for children under 12.

Archaeological Museum ☆   Even short-term visitors should stop here, if only for a half-hour's walk-through. The museum, housed in the 16th-century Venetian Catholic Church of St. Francis, was carefully restored in the early 1980s and gives a fascinating glimpse of the different cultures that have played out on Crete, from the Neolithic through the Minoan and on to the Roman and early Christian. You'll come away with a sense of how typical people of these periods lived, as opposed to the elite classes featured in so many museums.

30 Halidon. ✆ **28210/90-334.** www.culture.gr. Admission 5€ ($6.50). Mon 12:30–7pm; Tues–Sat 8am–7pm; Sun 8am–2:30pm. No parking.

A WALK AROUND OLD CHANIA

Start at **Plateia Santrivani,** the large clearing at the far curve of the old harbor. Head along the east side to see the prominent domed **Mosque of Djamissis** (or of Hassan Pasha), erected soon after the Turks conquered Chania in 1645. Proceeding around the **waterfront** toward the **new harbor,** you'll come to what remains of the great

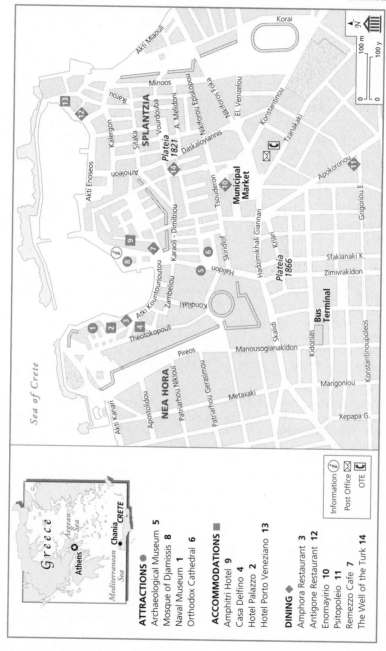

Chania

ATTRACTIONS ●
Archaeological Museum **5**
Mosque of Djamissis **8**
Naval Museum **1**
Orthodox Cathedral **6**

ACCOMMODATIONS ■
Amphitri Hotel **9**
Casa Delfino **4**
Hotel Palazzo **2**
Hotel Porto Veneziano **13**

DINING ◆
Amphora Restaurant **3**
Antigone Restaurant **12**
Enomayirio **10**
Psitopoleio **11**
Remezzo Cafe **7**
The Well of the Turk **14**

Information ⓘ
Post Office ⊠
OTE ☎

207

arsenali, where the Venetians made and repaired ships; exhibitions are sometimes held inside. Go to the far end of this inner harbor and walk along the breakwater to the 19th-century lighthouse. Turn inland at the near end of the arsenali onto Arnoleon, then proceed up Daskaloyiannis, and on the left you'll come to **Plateia 1821** and the **Orthodox Church of St. Nicholas.** Begun as a Venetian Catholic monastery, it was converted by the Turks into a mosque—thus its campanile and minaret! The square is a pleasant place to sit and have a cool drink. Go next to Tsouderon, where you turn right and (passing another minaret) arrive at the back steps of the great **municipal market** (ca. 1911)—definitely worth wandering through.

If you exit at the opposite end of your entrance, you'll emerge at the edge of the **new town.** Go right along Hadzimikhali Giannari until you come to the top of **Halidon,** the main tourist-shopping street. The stylish **Municipal Art Gallery,** at no. 98, sits at the top right side (hours posted). As you continue to make your way, you'll pass on the right the famous **Skridlof,** with its leather workers; the **Orthodox Cathedral** or the Church of the Three Martyrs, from the 1860s; and on the left the **Archaeological Museum** (see above).

As you come back to the edge of Plateia Santrivani, turn left one street before the harbor onto **Zambeliou.** Proceed along this street; you can then turn left onto any of the side streets and explore the **old quarter** (now, alas, overwhelmed by modern tourist enterprises). If you turn up at Kondilaki, follow the signs at the right alley for the **synagogue.** Built in the 17th century and destroyed in World War II, it has now been beautifully restored and is well worth a visit. (Check www.etz-hayyim-hania.org to learn about the history and activities of the synagogue.) Continue along Zambeliou, but take a slight detour to Moskhou to view **Renieri Gate** from 1608. On Zambeliou again, you'll ascend a bit until you come to **Theotokopouli;** turn right here to enjoy the architecture and shops of this Venetian-style street as you make your way down to the sea.

At the end of the street, on the right, the recently restored **Church of San Salvatore** was converted into a fine little museum of Byzantine and post-Byzantine art (© 28210/96-046). After the museum, you'll be just outside the harbor; turn right and pass below the walls of the **Firkas,** the name given to the fort that was a focal point in Crete's struggle for independence at the turn of the 20th century. If you're into naval history, the **Naval Museum** (© 28210/26-437) here has some interesting displays and artifacts (daily 10am–4pm; admission 5€/$6.50); or you can take a seat for welcome refreshment at **Cafe Meltemi,** on the slope before the museum entrance.

SHOPPING

Jewelers, leather-goods shops, and souvenir stores are everywhere—but it's hard to find that very special item that's both tasteful and distinctively Cretan. Below we point out things you will not find anywhere else. Unless otherwise noted, the following shops are open daily.

Carmela, at 7 Anghelou, the narrow street across from the Naval Museum's entrance (© 28210/90-487), has some of the finest ceramics, jewelry, and works of art in Crete—all original, but inspired by ancient works of art and even employing some of the old techniques.

Step into **Cretan Rugs and Blankets,** 3 Anghelou (© 28210/98-571), to experience a realm not found anywhere else on Crete. It's an old Venetian structure filled with gorgeously colored rugs, blankets, and kilims. Prices range from 100€ to 2,000€ ($130–$2,600). Or visit **Roka Carpets,** 61 Zambeliou (© 28210/74-736), where you can watch a traditional weaver at his trade. The carpets come in patterns, colors, and sizes to suit every taste; prices start at 15€ ($20). These are not artsy textiles, but traditional Cretan weaving.

Although **Khalki,** 75 Zambeliou, near the far end of the street (© **28210/75-379**), is one of many little shops that sell ceramics along with other trinkets and souvenirs, it's worth seeking out. It carries the work of several local and Greek ceramicists who draw on traditional motifs and colors. For a more sophisticated selection of Greek handicrafts, try **Mitos** at 44 Halidon (opposite the Orthodox Cathedral). For a varied selection by amateur Cretan artisans, visit the **Local Artistic Handicrafts Association** (© **28210/ 41-885**), located just where the new harbor turns the corner into the old harbor.

Finally, for a truly different souvenir or gift, try **Orphanos,** 24 Tsopuderon (by the stairs at the rear of the public market), with its unexpected collection of dolls and marionettes.

WHERE TO STAY
EXPENSIVE

Casa Delfino ★★   When did you last have the chance to stay in a 17th-century Venetian mansion, with fresh orange juice for breakfast? Its quiet neighborhood (also dating from the 1600s) is conveniently located a block from the harbor. The owners transformed the stately house into stylish independent suites and studios, whose taste-fully decorated rooms are among the most elegant you will find on Crete. All have mod-ern bathrooms (nine with Jacuzzi), and three have kitchenettes. One potential drawback: Several rooms have beds on a second level—little more than sleeping lofts—that require you to go up and down stairs to get to the bathroom. (You can request other rooms.) Casa Delfino provides a wide range of services, from airport transport to tour arrange-ments. The reception desk has a casual air that might not appeal to everyone.

8 Theofanous, 73100 Chania, Crete. © 28210/87-400. Fax 28210/96-500. www.casadelfino.com. 21 units. High sea-son 190€–290€ ($247–$377) double; low season 150€–230€ ($195–$299) double. AE, MC, V. Free parking nearby. Open year-round (with central heating). **Amenities:** Courtyard breakfast area; small bar; Jacuzzi; tour desk; car rental desk; courtesy car or airport pickup arranged; conference facilities for 24; 24-hr. room service; babysitting; laundry service; dry cleaning. *In room:* A/C, TV, kitchenette, minibar, hair dryer, safe.

Creta Paradise Beach Resort Hotel ★★ (Kids)   This luxurious resort is a perfect place to take in the sun on a beach, or to take a tour of western Crete. The full-service resort offers minigolf, volleyball, water polo, billiards, table tennis, and lessons in shooting and archery. Guests can take part in weekly "theme nights" that feature Greek music and dancing. Families with young children will take delight in the small petting zoo as well as a very active children's program. Guest rooms are a bit severe for Americans accustomed to upholstered luxury (don't expect overstuffed beds), but everything is tasteful and comfortable, and bathrooms are up to date. The only down-side: The hotel sometimes draws large international conferences with its high-tech facilities. Beautifully landscaped in the style of a Mediterranean villa, the resort lives up to its image. A special treat: Turtles come onto the hotel's beach to lay their eggs from May to June; these hatch in late August.

Gerani Beach, P.O. Box 89, 73100 Hania (14km/9 miles) west of Chania on coast road. © 28210/61-315. Fax 28210/ 61-134. www.cretaparadise.gr. 230 units. High season 205€–250€ ($267–$325) double; low season 110€–150€ ($143–$195) double. Rates include buffet breakfast. Considerably lower rates for tour groups include half-board plan (breakfast and dinner). AE, DC, MC, V. Ample parking. Taxi or bus to Chania. **Amenities:** Restaurant; poolside taverna; 2 bars; 2 pools; 2 children's pools; tennis court; fully equipped gym w/sauna; aerobics; extensive watersports equipment rentals; children's program; game room (or video arcade); concierge; tour desk; car rental desk; airport pickup arranged; secretarial services; shopping arcade; salon; 24-hr. room service; babysitting; laundry service; dry cleaning; nonsmoking rooms. *In room:* A/C, TV, minibar, fridge on request, hair dryer, safe.

MODERATE

Doma ★★   Long regarded as one of the most distinctive hotels on Crete, the neo-classical, turn-of-the-century Doma was once a fine mansion, former home of the British consulate. Authentic Cretan heirlooms and historical pictures decorate its public areas. Bedrooms and bathrooms are not especially large but are perfectly adequate. The four suites are roomier. All the rooms are plainly decorated—even a bit severe, with muted wall colors and rather old-fashioned furniture. Front rooms have great views of the sea but also the sounds of passing traffic, even though the hotel is far from the noisy town center The third-story dining room offers fresh breezes and a superb view of Old Chania; breakfast here includes several homemade delights, while the evening dinner features Cretan specialties. Among the third floor's special features is a museum-quality display of headdresses from all over the world. (An elevator provides access for those who can't take stairs.) The Doma is not for those seeking luxury, but it appeals to travelers who appreciate a discreet old-world atmosphere.

24 Venizelou, 73100 Chania, Crete. ✆ **28210/51-772.** Fax 28210/41-578. www.hotel-doma.gr. 25 units, all with private bathroom (22 with shower only). 120€ ($156) double; 180€–260€ ($234–$338) suite. Rates include buffet breakfast. Special rates for more than 2 persons in suite; reduced rates for longer stays. AE, MC, V. Closed Nov–Mar. Free parking on nearby streets. Bus to Halepa or Chania center; can be reached by taxi or on foot. 3km (2 miles) from the town center along the coastal road to the airport. **Amenities:** Restaurant; bar; concierge; tours and car rentals arranged; airport pickup arranged; laundry service; dry cleaning; nonsmoking room. *In room:* A/C, TV, hair dryer.

Halepa Hotel   Like the better-known Doma, this hotel is a converted neoclassical mansion. Buffered from the street by its front garden, the Halepa and its neighborhood are quiet. At this restful oasis, classical music often wafts through the air. The bedrooms are furnished in the standard Greek hotel style—which is to say, no particular style—but they are fair sized, and the bathrooms are modern. The owners—Greek-Americans—can take care of your every need, from laundry to car rental. A sun roof offers a spectacular view of Chania and the bay. *Tip:* Ask for a room in the main, or traditional, mansion—otherwise you must settle for a room (albeit quiet and comfortable) in the rather nondescript new wing.

164 Eleftherios Venizelou, 73133 Chania, Crete. ✆ **28210/28-440.** Fax 28210/28-439. www.halepa.com. 49 units, some with tub, some with shower. High season 115€ ($150) double, 140€–180€ ($182–$234) suite for 2; low season 90€ ($117) double, 165€ ($215) suite for 2. Rates include buffet breakfast. AE, DC, MC, V. Parking nearby. Open year-round with central heating. Frequent public buses to Chania (a 20-min. walk along the coast). On the street in Halepa just after the right turn to the airport. **Amenities:** Breakfast room; bar; concierge; tours and car rentals arranged; airport pickup arranged; babysitting; laundry service; dry cleaning. *In room:* A/C, TV, minibar, hair dryer.

Hotel Porto Veneziano ★   Thanks to the owner/manager "on the scene," this hotel combines the best of old-fashioned Greek hospitality with good, modern service. As a member of the Best Western chain, it has to maintain certain standards. The tasteful bedrooms (standard international style) are relatively large; the bathrooms are modern. Many rooms have a fine view of the harbor. (Be warned—that can also mean harbor noise early in the morning!) Six suites offer even more space. Located at the far end of the so-called Old Harbor (follow the walkway from the main harbor all the way around to the east, or right), this hotel offers proximity to the town center with a sense that you're in old Chania. There are many restaurants within a few yards of the hotel. Refreshments from the hotel's own Cafe Veneto may be enjoyed in the garden or at the front overlooking the harbor. The desk personnel are genuinely hospitable and will make tour arrangements.

Akti Enosseos, 73100 Chania, Crete. ✆ **28210/27-100.** Fax 28210/27-105. www.greekhotel.com. 57 units, all with private bathroom (51 with shower only). High season 130€ ($169) double; low season 110€ ($143) double. Rates include buffet breakfast. AE, DC, MC, V. Free parking nearby. Within walking distance of everything. **Amenities:** Breakfast room; cafe-bar; concierge; tours and car rentals arranged; airport pickup arranged; room service 7am–noon; babysitting; laundry service; dry cleaning. *In room:* A/C, TV, minibar, hair dryer.

INEXPENSIVE

Hotel Palazzo   This Venetian town house, now a handsome little hotel, delivers the feeling of old Crete without skimping on amenities. A fridge in every room, a TV in the bar, and a roof garden with a spectacular view of the mountains and sea, make this a comfortable hotel. Nothing fancy about the rooms (furnishings are traditional Cretan rustic, knotty-pine style), but they are good-size; those at the front have balconies. The location is generally quiet, and if occasionally the still night air is broken by rowdy youths (true of all Greek cities), that seems a small price to pay for staying on Theotokopouli—the closest you may come to living on a Venetian canal. The owners speak English and will graciously help you with all your needs—including laundry service, car rentals, and tours.

54 Theotokopouli, 73100 Chania, Crete. ✆ **28210/93-227.** Fax 28210/93-229. 11 units, some with shower, some with tub. High season 85€ ($111) double; low season 60€ ($78) double. Rates include breakfast. MC, V. Ample parking 100m (328 ft.) away. Closed Nov–Mar (but will open for special groups). Within easy walking distance of all of Chania. Around the corner from the west arm of harbor. **Amenities:** Bar; car rentals arranged; laundry service. *In room:* TV, fridge.

WHERE TO DINE
EXPENSIVE

Nykterida ★★ GREEK   Many would nominate this as one of the finest restaurants in all of Crete, especially for its setting, high on a point with spectacular nighttime views of Chania and Soudha Bay. The cuisine is traditional Cretan-Greek, but many of the dishes have an extra something. For an appetizer, try the *kalazounia* (cheese pie speckled with spinach) or the special *dolmades* (squash blossoms stuffed with spiced rice and served with yogurt). Any of the main courses will be well done, from the basic steak filet to the chicken with okra. Complimentary *tsoukoudia* (a potent Cretan liquor) is served at the end of the meal. Traditional Cretan music is played on Monday, Thursday, and Friday evenings until the end of October.

Korakies, Crete. ✆ **28210/64-215.** www.nykterida.gr. Reservations recommended for parties of 7 or more. Main courses 5€–18€ ($6.50–$23). MC, V. Mon–Sat 6pm–1am. Parking on-site. Open year-round. Taxi or car required. About 6.4km (4 miles) from town on road to airport; left turn opposite NAMFI Officers Club.

MODERATE

Amphora Restaurant GREEK   This is a favorite when it comes to balancing price with quality, choice with taste, location with location. As with any Greek restaurant, if you order the lobster or steak, you'll pay a hefty price. But you can assemble a delicious meal here at modest prices. To start, try the aubergine croquettes and the specialty of the house, a lemony fish soup. The restaurant belongs to the Amphora Hotel (Category A), and although its tables and location suggest a basic harbor taverna, its food and friendly service make it first class.

49 Akti Koundouriotou. ✆ **28210/93-224.** Fax 28210/93-226. Main courses 5€–15€ ($6.50–$20); fixed-price meals 10€–23€ ($13–$30). AE, MC, V. Daily 11:30am–midnight. Closed Oct–Apr. Near the far right, western, curve of the harbor.

Antigone Restaurant ★ GREEK/SEAFOOD   One of the many better-than-average restaurants along the new harbor. Start off here with the unusual dip made of limpets and mussels, then move on to a specialty such as stuffed crab or the catch of the day. The ingredients come fresh from the sea. Trust the staff to direct you to whatever is best that day. A colorful interior, fresh flowers on the tables, and a harbor view make this a most pleasant dining experience.

Akti Enoseos. (℃) **28210/45-236.** Main courses 5€–16€ ($6.50–$21). No credit cards. Daily 10am–2am. Park at side of restaurant, or walk from harbor. At farthest corner of new harbor.

The Well of the Turk ⚓ MIDDLE EASTERN/MEDITERRANEAN   At the heart of the old Turkish quarter (Splanzia), in a historic building that contains a well, this restaurant rises above others because of its menu and setting. Diners may choose to sit outside in a quiet street-court. The chef's imaginative touches make the cuisine more than standard Middle Eastern. In addition to tasty kabobs, specialties include meatballs mixed with eggplant, and *laxma bi azeen* (a pita-style bread with a spicy topping). Middle Eastern musicians sometimes play here, and you can settle for a quiet drink at the bar.

1–3 Kalinikou Sarpaki. (℃) **28210/54-547.** Reservations recommended for parties of 7 or more. Main courses 6€–16€ ($7.80–$21). No credit cards. Wed–Mon 7pm–midnight. No parking in immediate area; leave car and walk into old quarter. On a small street off Daskaloyiannis.

INEXPENSIVE

Enomayirio SEAFOOD   Here's a special treat for diners who can handle eating in a cramped, unstylish restaurant smack in the center of Chania's public market. The fish and other seafood come from stalls barely 4.5m (15 ft.) away. All the other ingredients also come straight from the nearby stands. Food doesn't get any fresher nor a dining experience more "immediate." Sit here and watch the world go by.

In the public market, at the "arm" with the fish vendors. Main courses 5€–13€ ($6.50–$17); gigantic platter of mixed fish for 2 is 22€ ($29). No credit cards. Mon–Sat 9am–3:30pm.

Psitopoleio ("The Grill") GREEK   Known to the foreign community of Chania as "The Meatery," this is not for the faint-hearted (or vegetarians!). Its clientele is almost 100% Cretan. We have debated for years whether to include this place but have finally decided that some travelers will appreciate its distinctive ambience. To call its decor "basic" is a major understatement: It is a long, bare space, with the butcher's block at the rear and the grill at the front. Your meat course is literally "butchered" at the former and cooked at the latter. The specialties are lamp chops, pork chops, kidneys, spare ribs, and sausages; french fries that make you forget McDonald's; salads, both the standard Greek and a cabbage version; soup; and tzaziki. House wine, beers, and soft drinks help you wash down the tasty and unforgettable food. Go for it!

48 Apokorono. (℃) **28210/91-354.** Main courses 3€–8€ ($3.90–$10). No credit cards. Daily 7:30pm–1am. No parking nearby. With your back to the municipal market, walk along the main street leading off to the right.

Remezzo Cafe INTERNATIONAL   Sooner or later, we say, "Enough Greek salads!" and want to indulge in a club sandwich or tuna salad. Remezzo, at the very center of the action on the old harbor, is a great choice for breakfasts and light meals (omelets, salads, and so on). It also offers a full range of coffee, alcoholic drinks, and ice-cream desserts. Sitting in one of the heavily cushioned chairs as you sip your drink and observe the lively scene, you'll feel like you have the best seat in the house.

16A Venizelou. (℃) **28210/52-001.** Main courses 4€–10€ ($5.20–$13). No credit cards. Daily 7am–2am. On corner of main sq. at old harbor.

CHANIA AFTER DARK

At night, in addition to seeking out a packed club/bar/disco or walking around the harbor and Old Town, wander instead into Chania's back alleys to see the old Venetian and Turkish remains. Sit in a quayside cafe and enjoy a coffee or a drink, or treat yourself to a ride in a horse-drawn carriage at the harbor. At the other extreme, stroll through the new town; you might be surprised by the modernity and diversity (and prices) of the stores patronized by typical Chaniots.

Clubs come and go from year to year. Some popular spots include **El Mondo** and **Nota Bene,** both on Kondilaki (the street leading away from the center of the old harbor); **Idaeon Andron,** 26 Halidon; and **Ariadne,** on Akti Enoseos (around the corner where the old harbor becomes the new). On Anghelou (up from the Naval Museum) is **Fagotta,** a bar that sometimes offers jazz. **Meltemi,** at the far west corner of the new harbor, is one of the more cosmopolitan cafes, attracting both locals and foreigners, young and old.

Two cafes stand out because of their special locations. You can take a little ferry to **Fortezza,** situated midway along the harbor's outer quay. At **Pallas Roof Garden Cafe-Bar,** on Akti Tobazi (right at the corner where the new harbor meets the old harbor), you can sit high above the harbor, watch the blinking lights, listen to the murmur of the crowds below, and nurse a refreshing drink or ice cream. However, you must climb 44 stairs to get here; as the sign says, IT'S WORTH IT.

A more unusual cafe is **Tzamia-Krystalla,** at 35 Skalidi, the main street heading east out of 1866 Square (© **28210/71-172;** tza-ury@otenet.gr). A welcome addition to the usual tourist scene, it's a combination art gallery/cafe/performance space. The gallery hosts changing exhibits by Greek artists. The cafe serves a standard selection of alcoholic and non-alcoholic drinks (no cover or minimum), and at times offers live music. If you'd prefer to hear traditional Cretan songs, try **Café Lyriaka,** 22 Kalergon (behind the arsenali along the harbor).

The gay community in Chania sometimes hangs out at **Ta Padia Paizei,** on Archoleon, at the far eastern end of the new harbor. The club has no street address but is marked by wheelbarrows with flowers at the door.

Movie houses around town—both outdoor and indoor—usually show foreign movies in their original language. The one in the public gardens is especially enjoyable. Watching a movie on a warm summer night in an outdoor cinema in Greece is one of life's simpler pleasures.

A **summer cultural festival** sometimes features dramas, symphonic music, jazz, dance, and traditional music. These performances take place from July to September at several venues: **Firka** fortress at the far left of the harbor; the **Venetian arsenali** along the old harbor; **East Moat Theater** along Nikiforou Phokas; or **Peace and Friendship Park Theater** on Demokratias, just beyond the public gardens. For details, inquire at one of the tourist information offices when you arrive in town.

A SIDE TRIP FROM CHANIA: SAMARIA GORGE ★★

Everyone with an extra day on Crete—and steady legs and solid walking shoes—should consider hiking through Samaria Gorge. The endeavor involves first getting to the top of the gorge, a trip of about 42km (26 miles) from Chania. Second comes the actual descent and hike through the gorge itself, some 18km (11 miles). Third, a boat takes you from the village of Ayia Roumeli, at the end of the gorge, to Khora Sfakion; from there, it's a bus ride of about 75km (46 miles) back to Chania. (Some boats go westward to Paleochora, approximately the same distance by road from Chania.)

Most visitors do it all in a long day, but you can put up for the night at one of the modest hotels and rooms at Ayia Roumeli, Paleochora (to its west), Souya (to its east), Khora Sfakion (main port to meet buses), and elsewhere along the south coast. We strongly advise you to sign up with one of the many travel agencies in Chania that get people to and from the gorge. This way, you are guaranteed seats on the bus and on the boat.

In recent years, Samaria Gorge has so successfully promoted itself as one of the great natural splendors of Europe that on certain days, it seems that half of the Continent is trekking through it. On the most crowded days, you can find yourself walking single file with several thousand other people. The Gorge is open about mid-April through mid-October (depending on weather conditions); the best chance for a bit of solitude means hiking near the beginning or end of the season. The hike is relatively taxing; and here and there, you will scramble over boulders. Bring water and snacks, and wear sturdy, comfortable shoes. Admission is 6€ ($7.80).

The gorge offers enough opportunities to break away from the crowds. You'll be treated to the fun of crisscrossing the water, not to mention the sights of wildflowers and dramatic geological formations, the sheer height of the gorge's sides, and several unexpected chapels—it will all add up to a worthwhile experience, perhaps as a metaphor of your visit to Crete.

3 Rethymnon (Rethimno)

72km (45 miles) E of Chania; 78km (50 miles) W of Iraklion

Whether visited on a day trip from Chania or Iraklion or used as a base for a stay in western Crete, Rethymnon can be a most pleasant town—provided you pick the right Rethymnon.

The town's defining centuries came under the Venetians in the late Middle Ages and the Renaissance, then under the Turks from the late 17th century to the late 19th century. Its maze of streets and alleys is now lined with shops, its old beachfront is home to restaurants and bars, and its new beach-resort facilities (to the east of the old town) offer a prime, some might say appalling, example of how a small town's modest seacoast can be exploited. Assuming you have not come to see these "developments," we'll help you focus your attention on the old town—the side of Rethymnon that can still work its charm.

ESSENTIALS

GETTING THERE   Rethymnon lacks an airport but is only about 1 hour from the Chania airport and 1½ hours from the Iraklion airport.

By Boat   Rethymnon does have its own ship line, which offers direct daily trips to and from Piraeus (about 10 hr.).

By Car   Many people visit Rethymnon by car, taking the highway from either Iraklion (about 79km/49 miles) or Chania (72km/45 miles). The public parking lot at Plateia Plastira, at the far western edge, just outside the old harbor, is best approached via the coast road from the west.

By Bus   If you don't have your own vehicle, the bus offers frequent service to and from Iraklion and Chania—virtually every half-hour from early in the morning until mid-evening. In high season, buses depart Rethymnon as late as 10pm. The fare has been about 12€ ($16) round-trip. The **KTEL** bus line (© **28310/22-212**) that provides

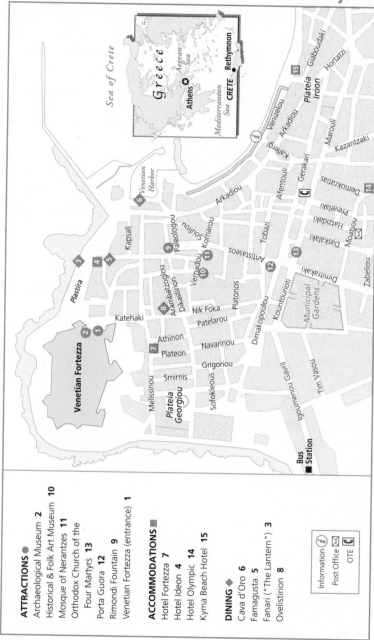

Rethymnon

ATTRACTIONS ●
Archaeological Museum **2**
Historical & Folk Art Museum **10**
Mosque of Nerantzes **11**
Orthodox Church of the
  Four Martyrs **13**
Porta Guora **12**
Rimondi Fountain **9**
Venetian Fortezza (entrance) **1**

ACCOMMODATIONS ■
Hotel Fortezza **7**
Hotel Ideon **4**
Hotel Olympic **14**
Kyma Beach Hotel **15**

DINING ◆
Cava d'Oro **6**
Famagusta **5**
Fanari ("The Lantern") **3**
Ovelistirion **8**

Information ⓘ
Post Office ✉
OTE ☎

Finds For Wine Lovers

Rethymnon's annual wine festival takes place for about 10 days starting near the end of July. It's centered around the public gardens, with music and dancing to accompany the samplings of local wines. The modest affair is a welcome change from larger, more staged festivals elsewhere.

service to and from Chania and Iraklion is located at Akti Kefaloyianithon, at the city's western edge (so allow an extra 10 min. to get there).

VISITOR INFORMATION   The **National Tourism Office** (© 28310/29-148) is on Venizelou, the main avenue that runs along the town beach. In high season, it's open Monday through Friday from 8am to 2:30pm; off season, its hours are unpredictable. Of the numerous private travel agencies in town, one of the oldest is **Creta Travel Bureau,** 3 Venizelou (© 28310/22-915), which can arrange trips to virtually anywhere on the island.

GETTING AROUND   Rethymnon is a walker's town. Bringing a car into the maze of streets and alleys is more trouble than it's worth. The sights you'll want to see are never more than a 20-minute walk from wherever you are. Taxis, meanwhile, are around for anyone who can't endure a short walk—especially in the heat of the day.

To see the countryside of this part of Crete, unless you have unlimited time to use the buses, you'll need to rent a car. Among the many agencies with offices in Rethymnon are **Motor Club** (© 28310/54-253), **Budget** (© 28310/56-910), **Europeo** (© 28310/51-940), and **Hertz** (© 28310/26-286).

FAST FACTS   Several **banks** in both the old town and the new city have ATMs and currency-exchange machines. The **hospital** is at 7–9 Trantallidou in the new town (© 28310/27-491). For **Internet access,** try Caribbean Bar Café (behind Rimondi Fountain) or Alana Taverna (on Salaminas near Hotel Fortezza). The most convenient place to do **laundry** is next to the Youth Hostel, 45 Tombazi; its hours are Monday through Saturday from 8am to 8pm. The **tourist police** (© 28310/28-156) share the same building with the tourist office, along the beach. The **post office** is east of the public gardens at 37 Moatsu (© 28310/22-571); its hours are Monday through Friday from 8am to 8pm, Saturday from 8am to noon. The **telephone office (OTE)** is at 40 Kountourioti; it's open daily from 7:30am to midnight.

WHAT TO SEE & DO
ATTRACTIONS
Archaeological Museum   The exhibits here are not of much interest to any except specialists, and we recommend instead the little Folk Art Museum, described below.

© 28310/29-975. Admission 5€ ($6.50). Daily 8:30am–7pm. On foot, climb Katehaki, a fairly steep road opposite Hotel Fortezza on Melissinou; by car, ascend the adjacent Kheimara.

Historical and Folk Art Museum ⊛   Housed in a centuries-old and architecturally significant Venetian mansion, this small museum displays ceramics, textiles, jewelry, artifacts, implements, clothing, and other vivid reminders of the traditional way of life of most Cretans across the centuries. Well worth a brief visit.

30 Vernadou. © 28310/23-398. Admission 3€ ($3.90) adults, 1€ ($1.30) students, free for children. Mon–Sat 10am–2pm.

The Venetian Fortezza ⚐   Dominating the headland at the western edge of town, this massive fortress is the one site everyone should give at least an hour to visit. Built under the Venetians (but *by* Cretans) from about 1573 to 1580, its huge walls, about 1,130m (1,819 ft.) in perimeter, were designed to deflect the worst cannon fire of its day. In the end, of course, the Turks simply went around it and took the town by avoiding the fort. There's a partially restored mosque inside as well as a Greek Orthodox chapel. It's in this vast area, by the way, that most of the performances of the annual **Rethymnon Renaissance Festival** take place (see below).

A STROLL THROUGH THE OLD TOWN

Rethymnon's attractions are best appreciated by walking through the old town. Start by getting a free map from the tourist office, down along the beachfront.

If you have limited time, first visit the **Fortezza** (see above). Then make your way back along Melissinou to the Catholic church at the corner of Mesologiou. Proceed down Salaminos to Arkadiou; make a left here to the western edge of the **old harbor.** Curving right down to the harbor is an unexpected sight: the wall of restaurants and bars that effectively obliterates the quaint harbor that drew them here in the first place. Making your way through that, you'll emerge at the southeast corner of this curved harbor and come to a square that faces the town's long beach, its broad boulevard lined with even more restaurants and cafes. Turn right up Petikhaki, and at the first crossroads, you'll see the **Venetian Loggia** (ca. 1600)—for many years the town's museum and now a Ministry of Culture gallery that sells officially approved reproductions of ancient Greek works of art. Continue up past it on Paleologou to the next crossroads. On the right is **Rimondi Fountain** (ca. 1623).

Leaving the fountain, head onto Antistaseos toward the 17th-century **Mosque of Nerantzes;** you can climb the minaret Monday to Friday 11am to 7:30pm, Saturday 11am to 3pm (closed in Aug). If you follow Antistaseos to its end, you'll come to **Porta Guora,** the only remnant of the Venetian city walls.

Emerging at that point onto the main east-west road, opposite and to the right are the **municipal gardens.** On your left is the **Orthodox Church of the Four Martyrs,** worth a peek as you walk east along Gerakari. You then come to a large open square that serves as the crossroads between the old town and the new beachfront development.

Turning back into the old town on Arkadiou, you'll see on your left the restored **Mosque of Kara Pasha,** now used as a botanical museum (daily 9am–6pm). Continue along Arkadiou, and in addition to the modern shops, note the surviving remains of the Venetian era—particularly the **facade of no. 154.** From here, you're on your own to explore the narrow streets, go shopping, or head for the waterfront for something cool to drink.

Moments **Rethymnon Renaissance Festival**

Rethymnon's cultural festival offers mostly musical and theatrical events from July to early September. Productions range from ancient Greek dramas to more contemporary artistic endeavors (and now include folk and rock concerts). Most performers are Greek; some are foreigners. The majority of performances are staged in the Fortezza itself—there's nothing quite like listening to 17th-century music or seeing a Renaissance drama in this setting. For details, inquire at the tourist information office.

OUTDOOR PURSUITS

If you're interested in horseback riding, try the **Riding Center,** located southeast of town at Platanias, 39 N. Fokas (© **28310/28-907**). Among the newer diversions offered in Rethymnon are the daily **excursion boats** that take people on day trips for **swimming** on the beach either at **Bali** (to the east) or **Marathi** (on the Akrotiri to the west). The price, which has been about 25€ ($33) for adults, includes a midday meal at a local taverna as well as all the wine you care to drink. You can sign on at the far end of the harbor. **Nias Tours,** 4 Arkadiou (© **28310/23-840**), offers an **evening cruise** that provides a view of Rethymnon glittering in the night.

SHOPPING

Here, as in Chania and Iraklion, you may be overwhelmed by the sheer number of gift shops offering mostly souvenirs. Looking for something different? Try Nikolaos Papalasakis's **Palaiopoleiou,** 40 Souliou, which is crammed with some genuine antiques, old textiles, jewelry, and curiosities such as the stringed instruments made by the proprietor. At **Olive Tree Wood,** 35 Arabatzoglou, the name says it all—the store carries bowls, containers, and implements carved from olive wood.

Haroula Spridaki, 36 Souliou, has a nice selection of Cretan embroidery. **Omodamos,** 3 Souliou, sells imaginative, modern ceramic variations on traditional Greek pottery. And **Talisman,** 32 Arabatzoglou, sells an interesting selection of blown glass, ceramics, plaques, paintings, and other handmade articles.

WHERE TO STAY

There is no shortage of accommodations in and around Rethymnon—but it has become hard to find a place in town that offers location, authentic atmosphere, and a quiet night's sleep. Our choices try to satisfy the last-mentioned criterion first. Note that many places in Rethymnon shut down in winter.

MODERATE

Hotel Fortezza 🐾   Fortezza is one of the more appealing hotels in Rethymnon, as its location isolates it from the noise of the inner town. This is especially true of its inside rooms, which overlook the modest but welcome pool. You're only a few blocks from the inner old town and then another couple of blocks to the town beach and the Venetian Harbor. The Venetian Fortezza rises just across the street. All guest rooms are good-size with modern bathrooms, and most have balconies. Half of the rooms have air-conditioning and phones. This relatively new hotel has become so popular that we recommend making reservations for the high season.

16 Melissinou, 74100 Rethymnon. © **28310/55-551.** Fax 28310/54-073. 54 units. High season 120€ ($156) double; low season 95€ ($124) double. Rates include buffet breakfast. Surcharge for 3rd person sharing room; babies stay free. AE, DC, MC, V. Parking nearby. Public bus service within 100m (328 ft.). On the western edge of town, just below the Venetian Fortezza, which is approached by Melissinou. **Amenities:** Restaurant; bar; pool; TV room; card-playing room; concierge; tour and car rentals arranged; babysitting. *In room:* A/C.

Hotel Ideon   This old favorite boasts a pool with a sunbathing area as well as a conference room that can handle up to 50 people. The friendly desk staff will arrange for everything from laundry service to car rentals. The guest rooms are the standard modern of Greek hotels. We like this place because it offers an increasingly rare combination in a Cretan hotel: It's near the active part of town and near the water (although it doesn't have a beach), yet it's relatively isolated from night noises. A solid choice for sheer convenience.

10 Plateia Plastira, 74100 Rethymnon. ⓒ **28310/28-667.** Fax 28310/28-670. www.hotelideon.gr. 86 units, some with shower, some with tub. High season 75€ ($98) double; low season 55€ ($72) double. Rates include buffet breakfast. Reduced rates for 3rd person in room or for child in parent's room. AE, DC, MC, V. Parking on adjacent street. Closed Nov to mid-Mar. On coast road just west of the Venetian Harbor. **Amenities:** 2 bars; pool; concierge; tours and car rentals arranged; babysitting. *In room:* A/C, fridge, safe.

Kyma Beach Hotel   This is a modern, city hotel—not a resort hotel—designed for people who want to take in Rethymnon and then retire to a beach at the end of the day. It's close to the attractions of old town and to a beach. Its somewhat austere gray exterior might put off some people, but in fact the hotel is relatively well designed. Although its rooms are hardly spacious, they are neatly furnished. Some have sleeping lofts, so if this doesn't appeal to you, speak up. Bathrooms are up-to-date. All rooms have balconies, but insist on a higher floor to escape street noise. The outdoor cafe is a popular watering hole for locals; you won't feel as if you're in a foreigners' compound.

Platai Iroon, 74111 Rethymnon. ⓒ **28310/55-503.** Fax 28310/27-746. 35 units, some with tub, some with shower. High season 85€ ($111) double; low season 65€ ($85) double. Rates include continental breakfast. AE, MC, V. Parking nearby. Public buses nearby. At eastern edge of old town and its beach. **Amenities:** 2 restaurants; 2 bars; concierge; tours and car rentals arranged; babysitting; laundry service; dry cleaning; Internet access. *In room:* A/C, TV, minibar, safe.

Mare Monte Beach Hotel ⭐ *Kids*   Everything about this place is first class, including its beautiful beach. You'll feel like you're living in a remote hideaway, with the sea before you and the mountains behind. Guest rooms are of moderate size with basic Greek hotel furnishings but have fully modern bathrooms. Activities include minigolf, archery, horseback riding by arrangement, and table tennis. Although it lacks the luxury of the grand resorts to the east of Rethymnon, the Mare Monte is a good alternative for those who want to focus their Cretan stay on Rethymnon, Chania, and western Crete, yet prefer to be based well away from a noisy town. The village of Georgioupolis is close enough for an evening stroll.

73007 Georgioupolis, Crete. ⓒ **28250/61-390.** 200 units. High season 95€ ($124) double; low season 70€ ($91) double. Rates include breakfast. DC, MC, V. Parking on-site. Closed Nov–Mar. 25 min. west of Rethymnon, on the main road to Chania. **Amenities:** 2 restaurants; 2 bars; pool; children's pool; 2 night-lit tennis courts; extensive watersports; children's playground; concierge; tours and car rentals arranged; secretarial services; 24-hr. room service; babysitting; laundry and dry cleaning arranged. *In room:* A/C, TV, safe.

INEXPENSIVE

Hotel Olympic   Not for everyone, the Olympic offers fair value for budget travelers. It's about 274m (900 ft.) from the town beach, removed from the main traffic of the town center. Rooms are not especially large and bathrooms are just adequate; all have balconies, if not special views. Ask for an interior room if you want complete quiet.

Corner of Moutsou and Demokratias, 74100 Rethymnon. ⓒ **28310/27-761.** 65 units. High season 75€ ($98) double; low season 60€ ($78) double. Rates include continental breakfast. AE, MC, V. Parking nearby. Public buses nearby. 1 block up from Koundouriotou. **Amenities:** Breakfast room; bar; tours and auto rentals arranged; roof garden. *In room:* A/C.

WHERE TO DINE

For standard but tasty Greek foods, you might consider **Ovelistirion,** at the end of Arambatzoglou, on the square overlooking the Church of the Annunciation. For truly elegant—and expensive—dining in a 700-year-old Venetian mansion, try the new **Veneto** at 4 Epimenidou (a small street halfway between Nerantzes Mosque and the Folk Museum).

EXPENSIVE
Cava d'Oro ✿ GREEK/SEAFOOD   One of the nicest at the Venetian Harbor, this restaurant has a pleasant ambience and food as good as any other's. That appeal is partly based on its air-conditioned dining room—not everyone's idea of being on a Cretan harbor—and its very reputation has made it crowded, especially when tour groups move in. Seafood is its specialty, naturally, and this means the high end of the menu prevails. Not a place to try if all you want are *mezedes*. Save this for a special occasion—and go during the off season or during off-peak hours.

42 Nearchou. ✆ 28310/24-446. Main courses 5€–16€ ($6.50–$21). AE, DC, MC, V. Daily 11am–midnight. Closed Nov–Mar. At the Venetian Harbor.

MODERATE
Famagusta GREEK/INTERNATIONAL   This well-tested, sea-view restaurant is far from the hustle of the harbor yet convenient to the center's attractions. The menu offers Cretan specialties such as breaded, deep-fried zucchini with lightly flavored garlic yogurt or *halumi,* a grilled cheese. Grilled fish and filets are the core of the main courses, but the adventurous chef includes Chinese-style Mandarin beef and that old basic, chili con carne. Eating here makes you feel like you're at an old-fashioned seaside restaurant, not some touristic confection.

6 Plastira Sq., Rethymnon. ✆ 28310/23-881. Main courses 4€–13€ ($5.20–$17). AE, DC, MC, V. Daily 10am–midnight. Closed Christmas through New Year's. Parking lot nearby. Near Ideon Hotel, on coast road just to west of Venetian Harbor.

INEXPENSIVE
Fanari ("The Lantern") ✿Value GREEK   We list this place not because its menu or cooking are exceptional, but because it overlooks the sea and is well removed from the bustle of Rethymnon's center. It offers prompt and pleasant service as well. The old harbor and the old beach strip are now so geared to tourism that an unpretentious taverna like this comes as a relief and a retreat. Take a table at the railing, order a cool drink, and enjoy your meal. You can't go wrong with the standard fare, and fish here can be as tasty as at most of the more expensive locales.

16 Kefaloyianithon. ✆ 28310/54-849. Main courses 3€–12€ ($3.90–$16). Daily special combination plates about 3.50€–10€ ($4.55–$13). No credit cards. Daily 11am–1:30am. Parking lot nearby. On coast road just west of Venetian Harbor, past Hotel Ideon and Famagusta restaurant.

A SIDE TRIP FROM RETHYMNON: MONASTERY OF ARKADHI
The events that took place here can help put modern Cretan history in perspective. The **Monastery of Arkadhi** sits some 23km (15 miles) southeast of Rethymnon and can be reached by public bus. A taxi might be in order if you don't have a car. If you ask the driver to wait an hour, the fare should total about 65€ ($85). What you'll see is a surprisingly Italianate-looking church facade, for although it belongs to the Orthodox priesthood, it was built under Venetian influence in 1587.

Like many monasteries on Crete, Arkadhi provided support for the rebels against Turkish rule. During a major uprising on November 9, 1866, many Cretan insurgents—men, women, and children—took refuge here. Realizing they were doomed to fall to the far larger besieging Turkish force, the abbot, it is claimed, gave the command to blow up the powder storeroom. Whether it was an accident or not is debatable, but hundreds of Cretans and Turks died in the explosion. The event became known throughout the Western world, inspiring writers, revolutionaries, and statesmen of several nations to protest at least with words. To Cretans it became and remains the archetypal incident of their long struggle for "freedom or death." (An ossuary outside the monastery contains the skulls of many who died in the explosion.) Even if you never thought about Cretan history, a brief visit to Arkadhi should go a long way in explaining the Cretans you deal with.

4 Ayios Nikolaos

69km (43 miles) E of Iraklion

Ayios Nikolaos tends to inspire strong reactions, depending on what you're looking for. Until the 1970s, it was a lazy little coastal settlement with no archaeological or historical structures of any interest. Then, the town got "discovered," and the rest is the history of organized tourism in our time.

For about 5 months of the year, Ayios Nikolaos becomes one gigantic resort town, taken over by the package-tour groups who stay in beach hotels along the adjacent coast and come into town to eat, shop, and stroll. During the day, Ayios Nikolaos vibrates with people. At night, it vibrates with music—the center down by the water is one communal nightclub.

Somehow, the town remains a pleasant place to visit, and it serves as a fine base for excursions to the east of Crete. And if you're willing to stay outside the very center, you can take only as much of Ayios Nikolaos as you want—and then retreat to your beach or explore the east end of the island.

ESSENTIALS

GETTING THERE   By Plane   Ayios Nikolaos does not have its own airport but can be reached in 1½ hours by taxi or bus from the Iraklion airport. During the high season, **Olympic Airways** offers a few flights weekly to Sitia, the town to the east of Ayios Nikolaos, but the drive from there to Ayios Nikolaos is a solid 2 hours.

By Boat   Several ships a week each way link Ayios Nikolaos and Piraeus (about 11 hr.). Ships also run from Ayios Nikolaos to Sitia (just east along the coast) and on to Rhodes via the islands of Kassos, Karpathos, and Khalki. In summer, several ships link Ayios Nikolaos to Santorini (4 hr.), and then to Piraeus via several other Cycladic islands. Schedules and even ship lines vary so much from year to year that you may want to wait until you get to Greece to make specific plans.

By Bus   Bus service almost every half-hour of the day each way (in high season) links Ayios Nikolaos to Iraklion; almost as many buses go to and from Sitia. The **KTEL** bus line (℃ **28410/22-234**) has its terminal at Akti Atlantidos by the marina, around the headland.

VISITOR INFORMATION   The **Municipal Information Office** (℃ **28410/22-357**) is one of the most helpful in all of Greece, perhaps because it's staffed by eager young seasonal employees (daily Apr 15–Oct 31, 8am–10pm). In addition to providing maps and brochures, it can help arrange accommodations and excursions. Among the scores of travel agencies, we recommend **Creta Travel Bureau,** at the corner of Paleologou and Katehaki, just opposite Lake Voulismeni (℃ **28410/28-496;** fax 2810/223-749).

GETTING AROUND   The town is so small that you can walk to all points, although taxis are available. The KTEL buses (see above) serve towns, hotels, and other points in eastern Crete. If you want to explore this end of the island on your own, it seems as if car and moped/motorcycle rentals are at every other doorway. We found some of the best rates at **Alfa Rent a Car,** 3 Kap. Nik. Fafouti, the small street between the lake and the harbor road (© **28410/24-312;** fax 28410/25-639). Fotis Aretakis is the man to deal with.

FAST FACTS　　There are several **ATMs** and currency-exchange machines along the streets leading away from the harbor. The **hospital** (© **28410/22-369**) is on the west edge of town, at the junction of Lasithiou and Paleologou. For **Internet access,** head to the **Atlantis Café,** 15 Akti Atlantidos (© **28410/24-876**); it's open daily in high season from 9am to 11pm. The most convenient place to do **laundry** is Xionati Laundromat, 10 Chortatson (a small street leading up from Akti Nearchou, by the bus terminal and beach); it's open Monday through Friday from 8am to 2pm and 5 to 8pm, Saturday from 8am to 4pm. **Luggage storage** is available at the main bus station, at Akti Atlantidos (by the marina). The **tourist police** (© **28410/26-900**) are at 34 Koundoyianni. The **post office** is at 9 28th Octobriou (© **28410/22-276**). In summer, it's open Monday through Saturday from 7:30am to 8pm; in winter, Monday through Saturday from 7:30am to 2pm. The **telephone office (OTE),** 10 Sfakinaki, at the corner of 25th Martiou, is open Monday through Saturday from 7am to midnight, Sunday from 7am to 10pm.

WHAT TO SEE & DO

The focal point in town is the small pool, formally called **Lake Voulismeni,** just inside the harbor. You can sit at its edge while enjoying a meal or a drink. Inevitably, it has given rise to all sorts of tales—that it's bottomless (it's known to be about 65m/213 ft. deep); that it's connected to Santorini, the island about 104km (65 miles) to the north; and that it was the "bath of Athena." Originally it was a freshwater pool, probably fed by a subterranean river that drained water from the mountains inland. A 20th-century channel now mixes the freshwater with seawater.

Archaeological Museum ★　　This is a fine example of one of the relatively new provincial museums that have opened up all over Greece—in an effort both to decentralize the country's rich holdings and to allow local communities to profit from the finds in their regions. It contains a growing collection of Minoan artifacts and art being excavated in eastern Crete. Its prize piece, the eerily modern ceramic **Goddess of Myrtos,** shows a woman clutching a jug; it was found at a Minoan site of this name down on the southeastern coast. The museum is worth at least a brief visit.

74 Paleologou. © **28410/24-943.** Admission 5€ ($6.50). Tues–Sun 8:30am–3pm (reduced hours possible in low season, so call ahead).

SHOPPING

Definitely make time to visit **Ceramica,** 28 Paleologou (© **28410/24-075**). You will see many reproductions of ancient Greek vases and frescoes for sale throughout Greece, but seldom will you have a chance to visit the workshop of one of the masters of this art, Nikolaos Gabriel. His authentic and vivid vases range from 25€ to 200€ ($33–$260). Across the street, at no. 1A, **Xeiropoito** sells handmade rugs.

　　Marieli, 33 28th Octobriou, leading away from the harbor (© **28410/28-813**), carries interesting ceramics, candlesticks, jewelry, and other crafts. **Pegasus,** 5 Sfakianakis, on the corner of Koundourou, the main street up from the harbor (© **28410/24-347**), offers a selection of jewelry, knives, icons, and trinkets—some old, some not. You'll have to trust the owner, Kostas Kounelakis, to tell you which is which.

　　For something truly Greek, what could be better than an icon—a religious painting on a wooden plaque? The tradition is kept alive in Elounda at the studio/store **Petrakis Workshop for Icons,** 22 A. Papendreou, on the left as you come down the

Ayios Nikolaos

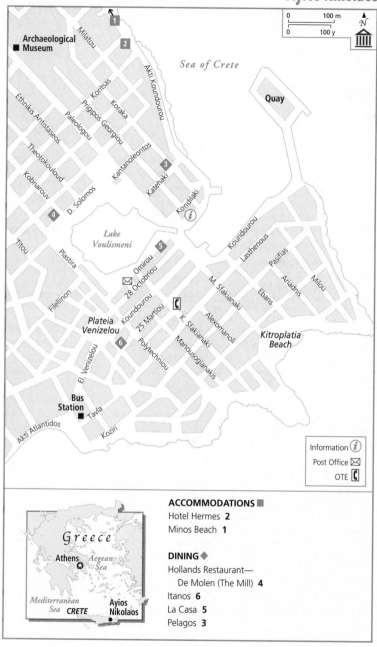

Archaeological Museum

Sea of Crete

Quay

Miliatou
Koritsas
Koraka
Akti Koundourou
Ethniks Antistaseos
Prigipos Georgiou
Paleologou
Theotokouloud
Kobnarouv
D. Solomos
Kantanoleontos
Katehaki
Kondilaki
Titou
Piastira
Filellinon
Lake Voulismeni
Omirou
28 Octobriou
Koundourou
Koundourou
Lasthenous
Pasifias
Ariadnis
Milou
Ebans
M. Sfakianaki
Alexomanoli
K. Sfakianaki
25 Martiou
Polytechniou
Manousogianakis
Plateia Venizelou
El. Venizelou
Kitroplatia Beach
Bus Station
Tavla
Koziri
Akti Atlantidos

0   100 m
0   100 y
N

Information ⓘ
Post Office ✉
OTE ☏

ACCOMMODATIONS ■
Hotel Hermes **2**
Minos Beach **1**

DINING ◆
Hollands Restaurant—
De Molen (The Mill) **4**
Itanos **6**
La Casa **5**
Pelagos **3**

Greece
Athens
Aegean Sea
Mediterranean Sea
CRETE
Ayios Nikolaos

incline from Ayios Nikolaos, just before the town square (© **28410/41-669**). Georgia and Ioannis Petrakis work seriously at maintaining this art. Orthodox churches in North America as well as in Greece buy icons from them. Stop by and watch the artists at their painstaking work—you don't have to be Orthodox to admire or own one. The store also carries local artisans' jewelry, blown glass, and ceramics.

WHERE TO STAY
INSIDE TOWN

Hotel Hermes   This is perhaps the best you can do if you want to stay close to the center of town yet be free from as much of the noise as possible. The Hermes is just far away enough, around the corner from the inner harbor, to escape the nightly din. This won't be in everyone's budget, but it's a compromise between the deluxe beach resorts and the cheaper in-town hotels. Guest rooms are done in the standard style, and most enjoy views over the sea. There's a private terrace (not a beach) on the shore, just across the boulevard. On the roof is a pool, with plenty of space to sunbathe.

If the Hermes is booked, you might try **Hotel Coral,** Akti Koundourou next door to the Hermes on the shore road (© **28410/28-253**). It's under the same management, almost as classy, and slightly cheaper.

Akti Koundourou, Ayios Nikolaos, 72100 Crete. © **28410/28-253.** www.hermes-hotels.gr. 206 units. High season 180€ ($234) double; low season 140€ ($182) double. Rates include half-board plan (breakfast and dinner); cheaper rate for breakfast only; special rate for longer stays. AE, DC, MC, V. Parking on opposite seawall (but beware of spray!). Closed Nov–Mar. On the shore road around from the inner harbor. **Amenities:** 2 restaurants; 2 bars; swimming pool; fitness center and sauna; billiards; video games; conference facilities. *In room:* A/C, TV, fridge, hair dryer.

Minos Beach ★★   We have to admit that we recommend this place out of loyalty to the first of the luxury beach-bungalow resorts in all of Greece. It remains a favorite among many returnees, but we must also admit that the common areas are not as glitzy as those at newer resorts, and that its grounds now look a bit overgrown. As with almost all Greek deluxe hotels, the mattresses seem a bit thin—to Americans, at least. But the hotel does have a civilized air, which is enhanced by the original, modern sculpture of world-famous artists scattered around the grounds. It's a great place to enjoy complete peace and quiet not too far from Ayios Nikolaos. It will appeal to those who like a touch of the "Old World" when they go abroad.

Amoudi, Ayios Nikolaos, 72100 Crete. © **28410/22-345.** Fax 28410/22-548. www.greekhotel.com/crete/agiosnikolaos. 12 units (in main building), 120 bungalows. High season 135€–205€ ($176–$267) double/bungalow; low season 110€–155€ ($143–$202) double/bungalow. Rates are per person and include buffet breakfast. Special rates for children. AE, DC, MC, V. Closed late Oct to late Apr. Frequent public buses to Ayios Nikolaos center or Elounda. A 10-min. walk from center. **Amenities:** 5 restaurants; 2 bars; saltwater pool; night-lit tennis court; health club and sauna; Jacuzzi in some bungalows; watersports equipment rentals; TV room; bike rentals; table tennis; concierge; tours and car rentals arranged; airport transport arranged; conference center; secretarial services; salon; room service 7:30am–9:30pm; babysitting; laundry service; dry cleaning; safe-deposit box at desk. *In room:* A/C, TV, minibar, hair dryer.

OUTSIDE TOWN

Elounda Beach ★★★   This world-class resort consistently appears on all the lists of "best," "top," and "great" hotels and resorts. However, as the saying goes, if you have to ask the price, you can't afford it. It offers more extras than we can list, including a gala dinner every Sunday and open-air movies on Monday. It is truly deluxe. From the prunes at the lavish breakfast buffet to the mini-TV by your bathroom mirror—the management has thought of everything. Guest rooms and bathrooms are appropriately luxuriously appointed. The restaurants serve haute cuisine. And in case you're concerned, the hotel does have its own heliport. Its clientele include the wealthy and well-known from all over the world, but if you go at low season and opt for the least expensive rooms, its rates are not that extreme as expensive hotels go. Definitely a once-in-a-lifetime experience.

72053 Elounda, Crete. ☎ **28410/41-412.** Fax 28410/41-373. www.eloundabeach.gr. 243 units (including 21 suites and bungalows with private swimming pools). High season 245€–395€ ($319–$514) double, 290€–770€ ($377–$1,001) bungalow suite; low season 120€–205€ ($156–$267) double, 150€–325€ ($195–$423) bungalow suite. Rates are per person per day and include breakfast (1 meal supplement costs 40€/$52 extra). AE, DC, MC, V. Closed early Nov to early Apr. Public buses to Ayios Nikolaos or Elounda every hour; Elounda is a 15-min. walk (8km/5 miles) from center of Ayios Nikolaos. **Amenities:** 4 restaurants; 4 bars; pool (and 25 suites w/own pools); 5 night-lit tennis courts; health club, sauna; watersports including scuba diving and sailing; bike rentals; volleyball; table tennis; billiards; children's program; concierge; tours and car rentals arranged; transport from airport arranged (car or helicopter); business center; secretarial services; shopping arcade; salon; 24-hr. room service; massage; babysitting; laundry service; dry cleaning. *In room:* A/C, TV, fridge, hair dryer, safe, Jacuzzi.

Istron Bay ★★   Another beautiful—and quiet—beach resort, this one is nestled against the slope on its own bay. The resort's location, plus its own beach and the tropical-paradise atmosphere, makes the resort a special place. Family-owned, it maintains traditional Cretan hospitality; for example, newcomers are invited to a cocktail party to meet others. The comfortable guest rooms have modern bathrooms and spectacular views. If you can tear yourself away from here, you're well situated to take in all the sights of eastern Crete. The main dining room has a fabulous view to go with its award-winning cuisine; it takes special pride in offering choices based on the "Cretan diet," internationally recognized as especially healthy. The resort offers activities such as scuba diving at an authorized school, nature walks in the spring and autumn, wine tastings, fishing trips, and Greek lessons.

72100 Istro, Crete. ☎ **28410/61-347.** Fax 28410/61-383. www.istronbay.com. 145 units (including 27 bungalows). High season 200€ ($260) double, 295€ ($384) suite or bungalow; low season 155€ ($202) double, 225€ ($293) suite or bungalow. Rates include buffet breakfast. Special rates for extra beds in room, for children, for June, and for half-board plan. AE, DC, MC, V. Closed Nov–Mar. Public buses every hour to Ayios Nikolaos or Sitia. 12km (7 miles) east of Ayios Nikolaos. **Amenities:** 3 restaurants; 2 bars; seawater swimming pool and children's pool; night-lit tennis court; watersports equipment rentals; volleyball; table tennis; billiards; children's program; concierge; tours and car rentals arranged; airport transport arranged; conference facilities; salon; room service 7am–11pm; massage; babysitting; laundry and dry-cleaning service. *In room:* A/C, satellite TV, minibar, hair dryer, safe for rent, bathrobe service (some units).

WHERE TO DINE

Ayios Nikolaos and nearby Elounda have so many restaurants that it's hard to know where to start or stop. When deciding, consider location and atmosphere; those factors have governed our recommendations below.

MODERATE

Hollands Restaurant—De Molen (The Mill) DUTCH/INDONESIAN   Who would go to Crete to eat Indonesian cuisine? Someone looking for a change from the basic Greek menu. Aside from offering a new experience for your palate, this place commands the most dramatic nighttime view of Ayios Nikolaos. Specialties include pork filet in a cream sauce. Vegetarian? Try the crepe with eggplant, mushrooms, carrots, and cabbage, tied up with leeks. We tasted an even more exotic Indonesian dish, *nasi goreng*—a plate heaped with rice, vegetables, and pork in a *satay* (peanut) sauce. It seemed to go with our perch overlooking exotic Ayios Nikolaos.

10 Dionysos Solomos. ☎/fax 28410/25-582. Main courses 5€–14€ ($6.50–$18); combination plates offered. V. Daily 10am–11:30pm. Closed Nov–Mar. A taxi is your only choice if you can't make it up the hill. It's the road at the highest point above the lake.

La Casa GREEK/INTERNATIONAL   With its lakeside location, tasty menu, and friendly Greek-American proprietress, this might be many travelers' first choice in Ayios Nikolaos. You'll enjoy the fine meals Marie Daskaloyiannis cooks up, including such specialties as fried rice with shrimp, lamb with artichokes, and rabbit stifado. Or try the "Greek sampling" plate—moussaka, dolmades, stuffed tomato, meatballs, and whatever other goodies Marie heaps on. There's always a slightly special twist to the food here.

31 28th Octobriou. (C) **28410/26-362.** Main courses 4€–14€ ($5.20–$18). AE, DC, DISC, MC, V. Daily 9am–midnight. No parking in immediate area.

Pelagos 🛦 GREEK/SEAFOOD   Looking for a change from the usual touristy seafront restaurant—something a bit more cosmopolitan? Try Pelagos, in a handsome old house a block up from the hustle and bustle of the harbor. As its name suggests, it specializes in seafood. From squid to lobster (expensive, as it always is in Greece), it's all done with flair. You can sit indoors in a subdued atmosphere or out in the secluded garden; either way you'll be served with style. This restaurant lets you get away from the crowd and share a more intimate meal.

10 Ketahaki. (C) **28410/25-737.** doxan45@hotmail.com. Reservations recommended in high season. Main courses 4€–18€ ($5.20–$23). MC, V. Daily noon–1am. Closed Nov–Feb. Parking on adjacent streets impossible in high season. At corner of Koraka, a block up from the waterfront.

Vritomartes GREEK/SEAFOOD   The 12km (8-mile) trip to get to this Elounda taverna takes a bit of effort, but a seat by the water makes it worthwhile. Besides, buses come and go every hour as well as taxis, and anyone who's come as far as Ayios Nikolaos should get out to Elounda at least once. You can't beat dining at this old favorite—there's been at least a lowly taverna here long before the beautiful people and group tours discovered the area. (Come early or make a reservation.) The specialty, no surprise, is seafood. (You may find the proprietor literally "out to sea," catching that night's fish dinners.) If you settle for the red mullet and a bottle of Cretan white Xerolithia, you can't go wrong. The dining area itself is plain, but this is one experience you won't forget.

Elounda. (C) **28410/41-325.** Reservations recommended for dinner in high season. Main courses 4€–32€ ($5.20–$42); fish platter special for 2 52€ ($68). MC, V. Daily 10am–11pm. Closed Nov–Mar. Parking lot nearby. On the breakwater.

INEXPENSIVE

Itanos GREEK   A now familiar story on Crete: A simple local taverna where you go to experience "authenticity" becomes overrun by tourists, changing the scene. But the fact is, the food and prices haven't changed *that* much. Standard taverna oven dishes are still served—grilled meats; or no-nonsense chicken, lamb, or beef in tasty sauces; and hearty helpings of vegetables. The house wine comes from barrels. During the day, you sit indoors, where you'll experience no-nonsense decor and service. But at night during the hot months, tables appear on the sidewalk, a roof garden opens up on the building across the narrow street, and your fellow travelers take over. Come here if you need a break from the harbor scene and want to feel you're in a place that still exists when all the tourists go home.

1 Kyprou. (C) **28410/25-340.** Reservations not accepted, so come early in high season. Main courses 4€–12€ ($5.20–$16). No credit cards. Daily 10am–midnight. Just off Plateia Venizelos, at top of Koundourou.

SIDE TRIPS FROM AYIOS NIKOLAOS

Almost everyone who spends any time in Ayios Nikolaos makes the two short excursions to Spinalonga and Kritsa. Each can easily be visited in a half-day.

SPINALONGA

Spinalonga is the **fortified islet** in the bay off Elounda. The Venetians built another of their fortresses here in 1579, and it enjoyed the distinction of being their final outpost on Crete, not taken over by the Turks until 1715. When the Cretans took possession in 1903, it was turned into a leper colony, but this ended after World War II. Now Spinalonga is a major tourist attraction. In fact, there's not much to do here except walk around and soak in the atmosphere and ghosts of the past. Boats depart regularly from both Ayios Nikolaos harbor and Elounda as well as from certain hotels.

KRITSA ⚝

Although a walk through Spinalonga can resonate as a historical byway, if you have time to make only one of these short excursions, we advise taking the 12km (8-mile) trip into the hills behind Ayios Nikolaos to the village of Kritsa and its 14th-century **Church of Panagia Kera** ⚝. The church is architecturally interesting, and scholars regard its **frescoes,** dating from the 14th and 15th centuries, as among the jewels of Cretan-Byzantine art. They have been restored, but their power emanates from the original work. Scenes depict the life of Jesus, the life of Mary, and the Second Coming. Guides can be arranged at any travel agency or at the Municipal Information Office in Ayios Nikolaos. After seeing the church, visit the village of Kritsa itself and enjoy the view and the many fine handcrafted goods for sale.

8

The Cyclades

by Sherry Marker

When most people think of the "Isles of Greece," they're thinking of the Cyclades, the rugged (even barren) chain of Aegean islands whose villages of dazzling white houses look from a distance like so many sugar cubes. The Cyclades got their name from the ancient Greek word meaning "to circle," or "surround," because the island chain encircles Delos, the island long sacred to the god Apollo. Today, especially in the summer, it's the visitors who circle these islands, taking advantage of the swift island boats and hydrofoils that link them.

If you were to come up with a few words to describe the best-known Cycladic islands (roughly from north to south), **Tinos** would probably be called the "Lourdes of Greece." Its famous church of the Panagia Evangelistria is Greece's most important pilgrimage destination, especially on the Feast of the Assumption (Aug 15). **Mykonos's** perfect Cycladic architecture and jet-set attractions (you can get a margarita as easily as an ouzo) first made it popular in the 1960s. Although many of the Beautiful People moved on, Mykonos remains a favorite, although expensive, island. Think of **Paros** as the poor man's Mykonos, with excellent windsurfing and

a profusion of restaurants and nightspots less pricey than those on its better-known neighbor. **Naxos** is green and fertile, its hills dotted with dovecotes and a profusion of small Byzantine chapels. The Venetians ruled here and left behind a splendid kastro (castle) in town.

The black-sand beaches and blood-red cliffs of **Santorini (Thira)** are all that remains of this crescent island that was blown apart in antiquity by a volcano that steams and hisses today. Santorini's exceptional physical beauty, dazzling relics, and elegant restaurants and boutiques give it its sophisticated image. Unfortunately, Santorini's charms draw so many day-trippers from cruise ships that the island almost sinks under the weight of tourists each summer. **Folegandros** is the perfect counterbalance to Santorini. As yet, this little island is not overwhelmed with visitors, but a new helipad suggests that the Beautiful People have discovered the great beaches here. The capital—many say it's the most beautiful in all the Cyclades—is largely built into the walls of a medieval castle.

Sifnos, long popular with Athenians, increasingly draws summer visitors to its

---

Ancient Akrotiri **9**

Ancient Thira **10**

Ermoupolis **4**

Kolimbithres Beach **6**

Panayia Ekatondapiliani Cathedral **5**

Panayia Evanyelistria Cathedral **1**

Panayia Paraportiani Church **2**

Paradise Beach **3**

Plaka Beach **8**

The Portara (Temple of Apollo) **7**

Tips **Museum Hours Update**

If you visit Greece during the summer, check to see when sites and museums are open. According to the tourist office, they should be open from 8am to 7:30pm, but some may close earlier in the day or even be closed one day a week.

handsome whitewashed villages, which many consider to have the finest architecture in all the Cyclades. In the spring this is one of the greenest and most fertile of the islands. **Siros,** on the other hand, is as "undiscovered" as a large Cycladic island can be. Its distinguished capital, crowned by the remains of a Venetian city and kastro, also has many handsome neoclassical 19th-century buildings.

These introductory words only hint at what is ahead. If you want to describe the Cyclades in their entirety, you can do worse than string together well-deserved superlatives: Wonderful! Magical! Spectacular! The sea and sky really are bluer here than elsewhere, the islands on the horizon always tantalizing. In short, the Cyclades are very "more-ish"—once you've visited one, you'll want to see another, and then another, and then, yes, yet another.

STRATEGIES FOR SEEING THE ISLANDS

A few practicalities: As you might expect, the Cyclades are crowded and expensive during high season—roughly mid-June to early September—and the season seems to get longer every year. If this doesn't appeal to you (and you don't mind sometimes unpredictable boat service), visit during the off season; the best times are mid-September to October or May to early June. April can still be very cold in these islands. While the restaurant you'd hoped to try may be closed and the chic shops shuttered, you'll be able to enjoy the islands without feeling surrounded by other visitors. Should you visit in winter or spring, keep in mind that many island hotels have minimal heating; make sure that your hotel has genuine heat before you check in. Also, note that most hotels charge a **supplementary fee of 10%** for a stay of fewer than 3 nights.

On most of these islands, the capital town has the name of the island itself. "Hora," or "Chora," meaning "the place," is commonly used for the most important regional town. The capital of Paros, Parikia, is also called Hora, as is Apollonia, the capital of Sifnos.

Although the Cyclades are bound by unmistakable family resemblance, each island is rigorously independent and unique, making this archipelago an island-hopper's paradise. Frequent ferry service makes travel easier—although changes in schedules can keep travelers on their toes (or waiting for transport at unpredictable hours on the harborside). Hydrofoils, in particular, are notoriously irregular, and service is often canceled at the whim of the *meltemi* (severe summer winds). Still, a new fleet of catamarans has greatly facilitated travel between Piraeus and the Cycladic islands of Siros, Paros, Naxos, Mykonos, and Santorini. Service to most islands is highly seasonal, with frequency dropping off significantly between October and April. Between May and September, you can go just about anywhere you want, whenever you want, although winds can upset the most carefully arranged plans.

1 Santorini (Thira)

233km (126 nautical miles) SE of Piraeus

Especially if you arrive by sea, you won't confuse Santorini with any of the other Cyclades. What will confuse you is that the island is also known as Thira. While large ships to Santorini (pop. 7,000) dock at the port of Athinios, many small ships arrive in Skala, a spectacular harbor that's part of the enormous caldera (crater) formed around 1450 B.C. when a volcano blew out the island's center. To this day, some scholars speculate that this destruction gave birth to the myth of the lost continent of Atlantis. In short, this is physically one of the most spectacular islands in the world. Santorini's cliff-faced crescent isle graces tourist brochures and posters in Greek restaurants the world over. Many Greeks joke, somewhat begrudgingly, that there are foreigners who know where Santorini is—but not where Greece is!

The real wonder is that Santorini exceeds all glossy picture-postcard expectations. Like an enormous mandible, Santorini encloses the pure blue waters of its caldera, the core of an ancient volcano. Its two principal towns, **Fira** and **Ia,** perch at the summit of the caldera; as you approach by ship, their whitewashed houses resemble a dusting of new snow on the mountaintop.

Akrotiri is Santorini's principal archaeological wonder: A town destroyed by the volcano eruption here, but miraculously preserved under layers of lava. In 2004, most of Akrotiri closed for extensive preservation work; it's scheduled to reopen in 2006. A small part of the site was open at press time. If it weren't that Akrotiri steals its thunder, the site of **Ancient Thira** would be even more famous. Spectacularly situated atop a high promontory, overlooking a black lava beach, the remains of this Greek, Roman, and Byzantine city are extensive. Ancient Thira is reached after a vertiginous hike or drive up and up and up to the acropolis itself.

Arid Santorini isn't known for the profusion of its agricultural products, but the rocky island soil has long produced a plentiful grape harvest, and the local wines are among the finest in Greece. Be sure to visit one of the island **wineries** for a tasting. And keep an eye out for the tasty, tiny unique Santorini tomatoes and white eggplants—and the unusually large and zesty capers. Most importantly, allow yourself time to see at least one sunset over the caldera; the best views are from the ramparts of the kastro and from the footpath between Fira and Ia.

The best advice we can offer is to avoid visiting during the months of July and August. Santorini experiences an even greater transformation during the peak season than other Cycladic isles. With visitors far in excess of the island's capacity, trash collects in the squares, and crowds make movement through the streets of Fira and Ia next to impossible. *Tip:* Accommodations rates can be marked down by as much as 50% if you travel in May, June, or September.

ESSENTIALS

GETTING THERE   By Plane   Olympic Airways (© 210/966-6666 or 210/936-9111; www.olympic-airways.gr) offers daily flights between Athens and the Santorini airport at Monolithos (which also receives European charters). There are connections with Mykonos five times per week, service three or four times per week to and from Rhodes, and service two or three times per week to and from Iraklion, Crete. For information and reservations, check with the Olympic Airways office in Fira on Ayiou Athanassiou (© 22860/22-493), just southeast of town on the road to Kamari; or in Athens at © 08210/44-444 or 210/966-6666. **Aegean Airlines** (© 210/998-2888 or

210/998-8300 in Athens), with an office at the Monolithos airport (© **22860/28-500**), also has several flights daily between Athens and Santorini. A bus to Fira (3€/$3.90) meets most flights; the schedule is posted at the bus stop, beside the airport entrance. A taxi to Fira costs about 8€ ($10).

By Boat   Ferry service runs to and from Piraeus at least twice daily; the trip takes 9 to 10 hours by car ferry on the Piraeus-Paros-Naxos-Ios-Santorini route, or 4 hours by catamaran if you go via Piraeus-Paros-Santorini. Boats are notoriously late and/or early. In July and August, ferries connect several times a day with **Ios** (1–2 hr.), **Naxos** (3 hr.), **Paros** (2½ hr. by hydrofoil, 4 hr. by car ferry), and **Mykonos** (4–6 hr.); almost daily with **Anafi** (2 hr.) and **Siros** (3 hr. by catamaran, 5–6 hr. by hydrofoil or car ferry); five times a week with **Sikinos** (1 hr.) and **Folegandros** (1½ hr.); and twice weekly with **Sifnos** (3–4 hr.). Service to **Thessaloniki** (17–24 hr.) is offered four to five times per week. There is an almost daily connection by excursion boat with **Iraklion** in Crete, but because this is an open sea route, the trip can be an ordeal in bad weather and is subject to frequent cancellation—better to fly. Confirm ferry schedules with the Athens **GNTO** (**210/870-0000;** www.gnto.gr), the **Piraeus Port Authority** (© **210/451-1456** or 210/459-3223; phone seldom answered), or the **Santorini Port Authority** (© **22860/22-239**).

Almost all ferries dock at **Athinios,** where buses meet each boat and then return directly to Fira (one-way to Fira costs 2€/$2.60); from the Fira dock, buses depart for many other island destinations. Taxis are also available from Athinios, at nearly five times the bus fare. Athinios is charmless; when you come here to catch a ferry, it's a good idea to bring munchies, water, and a good book.

Ferry tickets can be purchased at most travel agencies on the island. In the past, any given travel agency would represent only a selection of the available ferries. A relatively new system now allows any agency to sell tickets for all the boats. The exposed port at **Skala,** directly below Fira, is unsafe for the larger ferries but is often used by small cruise ships, yachts, and excursion vessels. If your boat docks here, head to town either by cable car (4€/$5.20), mule, or donkey (4€/$5.20); or you can tough a 45-minute uphill walk. Be prepared to share the narrow path with the mules. We recommend a mule up and the cable car down. If you suffer from acrophobia, try taking the cable car both ways with your eyes firmly shut.

VISITOR INFORMATION   There's no official government tourist office, but a number of travel agencies can help you. Several travelers have written of good experiences dealing with **Nomikos Travel** (© **22860/23-660** or 22860/23-666), with branches in Karterados and Perissa; **Bellonias Tours** (© **22860/22-469**); **Best of Cyclades Travel** (© **22860/22-622**); and **Kamari Tours** (© **22860/31-390**), all based in Fira. Any of these agencies should be able help you find accommodations, rent a car, get boat tickets, or book a tour. **Nomikos** and **Bellonias** offer bus tours of the island, boat excursions around the caldera, and submarine tours beneath the caldera. Expect to pay about 25€ ($33) to join a bus tour to Akrotiri or Ancient Thira, about the same for a day-trip boat excursion to the caldera islands, and about twice that for the submarine excursion.

GETTING AROUND   **By Bus**   Santorini has reliable bus service. The **central bus station** is just south of the main square in Fira. Schedules are posted here: Most routes are served every hour or half-hour from 7am to 11pm in high season. A conductor on board will collect fares, which range from 1€ to 3€ ($1.30–$3.90). Destinations

include Akrotiri, Athinios (the ferry pier), Ia, Kamari, Monolithos (the airport), Perissa, Perivolas Beach, Vlihada, and Vourvoulos. Excursion buses travel to major attractions; ask a travel agent for details.

By Car Most travel agents can help you rent a car. You might find that a local company such as **Zeus** (© **22860/24-013**) offers better prices than the big names, although the quality might be a bit lower. Of the better-known agencies, try **Budget Rent-A-Car,** at the airport (© **22860/33-290**) or in Fira a block below the small square that the bus station is on (© **22860/22-900**); a small car should cost about 55€ ($72) a day, with unlimited mileage. If you reserve in advance through Budget in the U.S. (© **800/527-0700**), you should be able to beat that price.

If you park in town or in a no-parking area, the police will remove your license plates and you, not the car rental office, will have to find the police station and pay a steep fine to get them back. There's free parking on the port's north side.

By Moped The roads on the island are notoriously treacherous, narrow, and winding; add local drivers who take the roads at high speed, and visiting drivers who aren't sure where they're going, and you'll understand the island's high accident rate. If you're determined to use two-wheeled transportation, expect to pay about 20€ ($26) per day (less during off season).

> ### Tips   Safety First
>
> Use caution when walking around Santorini, especially at night. Keep in mind that many drivers on the roads are newcomers to the island and may not know every twist and turn.

By Taxi   The taxi station is just south of the main square. In high season, book ahead by phone (© 22860/22-555 or 22860/23-951) if you want a taxi for an excursion; be sure that you agree on the price before you set out. For most point-to-point trips (Fira to Ia, for example), the prices are fixed. If you call for a taxi outside Fira, you'll be charged a pickup fee of at least 1.50€ ($1.95); also, you're required to pay the driver's fare from Fira to your pickup point. Bus service shuts down at midnight, so book a taxi in advance if you'll need it late at night.

FAST FACTS   The **American Express** agent is X-Ray Kilo Travel Service (© 22860/22-624; fax 22860/23-600), at the head of the steps to the old port facing the caldera, above Franco's Bar. Its hours are daily from 8:30am to 9pm. The **National Bank** (Mon–Fri 8am–2pm), with an ATM, is a block south of the main square on the right near the taxi station. The **health clinic** (© 22860/22-237) is on the southeast edge of town on Ayiou Athanassiou, immediately below the bus station and the new archaeological museum.

For **Internet access,** try P.C. Club on the main square in Fira, in the Markozannes Tours office (© 22860/25-551). **Penguin Laundry** (© 22860/22-168) is at the edge of Fira on the road to Ia, 200m (656 ft.) north of the main square. The **police** (© 22860/22-649) are several blocks south of the main square, near the post office. For the **port police,** call © 22860/22-239. The **post office** (© 22860/22-238), open Monday through Friday from 8am to 1pm, is south of the bus station. The **telephone office (OTE)** is off Ipapantis, up from the post office; hours are Monday through Saturday from 8am to 3pm.

THE TOP ATTRACTIONS

Tip: If you plan to visit the ancient sites and their associated museums, get the economical 8€ ($10) ticket that's good for the Archaeological Museum, Ancient Akrotiri (if open), Prehistoric Thira, and Ancient Thira.

Ancient Akrotiri ★★★   If even part of Akrotiri is open, go. If the entire site is closed when you want to visit, go elsewhere. Unlike many sites, Akrotiri is *not* visible from the road. In 2004, most of Akrotiri closed to visitors for extensive site preservation; it is scheduled to reopen in 2006.

Since excavations began in 1967, this site has presented the world with a fascinating look at urban life in the Minoan period. Elaborate architecture and vivid frescoes demonstrate the high level of culture that flourished at that time. Akrotiri—sometimes nicknamed the "Minoan Pompeii"—was frozen in time around 1450 B.C. by a cataclysmic eruption of the island's volcano. Most scholars think that this powerful explosion destroyed the prosperous Minoan civilization on Crete. Pots and tools still lie where their owners left them before abandoning the town; the absence of human remains indicates that the residents had ample warning of the town's destruction.

You enter the Akrotiri site along the ancient town's main street, on either side of which are the stores or warehouses of the ancient commercial city. *Pithoi* (large earthen jars) found here contained traces of olive oil, fish, and onion. To get the best sense of the scale and urban nature of this town, go to the triangular plaza, near the exit, where you'll see two-story buildings and a spacious gathering place. Imagine yourself 3,000 years ago leaning over a balcony and spying on the passersby. As you walk along the path through town, look for the descriptive plaques in four languages. A few poor reproductions of the magnificent wall paintings are here; to see the originals, visit the Museum of Prehistoric Thira. As you leave the site, you may notice a cluster of flowers beside one of the ancient walls. This marks the burial spot of Akrotiri's excavator, Professor S. Marinatos, who died in a fall at Akrotiri. Allow at least an hour here.

Akrotiri. © 22860/81-366. Admission 6€ ($7.80). Tues–Sun 8:30am–3pm.

Ancient Thira ★★   A high rocky headland (Mesa Vouna) separates two popular beaches (Kamari and Perissa), and at its top stand the ruins of Ancient Thira. It's an incredible site, where cliffs drop precipitously to the sea on three sides and you'll see dramatic views of Santorini and neighboring islands. This extensive group of ruins is not easy to take in because of the many different periods on view—Roman baths jostle for space beside the remains of Byzantine walls and Hellenistic shops. One main street runs the length of the site, passing first through two agoras. The arc of the theater embraces the town of Kamari, Fira beyond, and the open Aegean.

Dorians lived here as early as the 9th century B.C., though most buildings date from the Hellenistic era when Ptolemaic forces occupied the site. You may not decipher everything, but do take in the view from the large Terrace of the Festivals. This is where naked lads danced to honor Apollo (inadvertently titillating, some of the graffiti suggests, a number of the spectators).

You can reach the site by taxi or, even better, on foot, passing on the way a cave that holds the island's only spring (see "Walking" under "Outdoor Pursuits," below). Excursion buses for the site of Thira leave from the beach at Kamari. You get a ticket and board at Kamari. If you were at Thira and tried to pay on board to get to Kamari, you might be able to do it. Nothing is done the same way two days running in Greece. As someone once said, "The bus is always leaving for the first time in Greece." Allow yourself at least 5 hours to view the site if you walk up there and walk back down.

Kamari. © 22860/31-366. Admission 4€ ($5.20). Tues–Sun 8am–2:30pm; site sometimes open later in summer. On a hilltop 3km (2 miles) south of Kamari by road.

Boutari Winery   Boutari is the island's largest winery, and Greece's best-known wine export. The admission includes a tour, video presentation, and tasting of about six wines, with *mezedes* (light snacks). Three grape varieties grow on Santorini: Asirtiko, Aidani, and Athiri. From these are made the three whites for which the island is known: Nichteri, with its high alcohol content; Kalliste, a wine aged in smoked oak barrels; and Vin Santo, a sweet dessert wine traditionally used for communion in the local churches. Rounding out the tasting are reds and whites from Northern Greece.

(Fun Fact **Akrotiri Trivia**

In 1860, workers quarrying blocks of volcanic ash—for use in building the Suez Canal—discovered ancient remains. Who knows what unnoticed treasures may have been walled into the canal if the workers had not been alert!

Megalohori. ☎ **22860/81-011.** Admission and tasting 6€ ($7.80). Daily 10am–sunset. 1.5km (1 mile) south of Akrotiri village. Just outside Megalohori, on the main road to Perissa.

Museum of Prehistoric Thira ★★   Come here to see frescoes and other finds from Ancient Akrotiri, along with objects imported from ancient Crete and the Northeastern Aegean Islands. Some of the pottery—cups, jugs, and *pithoi*—are delicately painted with motifs familiar to those of the wall paintings (see below). If possible, visit both the museum and the archaeological site at Ancient Akrotiri on the same day. The museum occupies only a small part of its building; anticipate expansion in the future.

☎ **22860/22-217.** Admission 3€ ($3.90). Tues–Sun 8:30am–3pm. Across the street from the bus stop in Fira; entrance is behind the Orthodox Cathedral.

Thira Foundation: The Wall Paintings of Thira ★   This exhibition created copies of the Akrotiri wall paintings, using a sophisticated technique of three-dimensional photographic reproduction that closely approximates the originals. Housed in a former wine storage cave, the displays present some of the paintings in their original architectural context (or as close as they can come in a museum exhibit). The terrace in front of the foundation offers an astonishing view toward Fira and Imerovigli.

Petros Nomikos Conference Center, Fira. ☎ **22860/23-016.** Admission 4€ ($5.20). Recorded tour 3€ ($3.90). On the caldera, 5 min. past the cable car on the way to Firostefani.

EXPLORING THE ISLAND
FIRA

Location, location, location: To put it mildly, Fira has a spectacular location on the edge of the caldera. Just when you think you've grown accustomed to the view down and out to sea and the off-shore islands, you'll catch a glimpse of the caldera from a slightly different angle—and be awed yet again. If you're staying overnight on Santorini, take advantage of the fact that almost all the day-trippers from cruise ships leave in the late afternoon. Try to explore Santorini's capital, Fira, in the early evening, between the departure of the day-trippers and the onslaught of the evening revelers. As you stroll, you may be surprised to discover that Fira has a Roman Catholic cathedral and convent in addition to the predictable Greek Orthodox cathedral, a legacy from the days when the Venetians controlled much of the Aegean. The name Santorini is, in fact, a Latinate corruption of the Greek for "Saint Irene." **Megaron Gyzi Museum** (☎ **22860/22-244**) by the cathedral has church and local memorabilia, including before-and-after photographs of the island at the time of the devastating earthquake of 1956. It is open Monday to Saturday 10:30am to 1pm and 5 to 8pm; Sunday 10:30am to 4:30pm. Admission is 3€ ($3.90).

M. Nomikou Street follows the edge of the caldera, and the evening **volta (stroll)** along this street is one of the most exquisite in the Cyclades: The chanted tones of evening prayer often resound from the Orthodox Cathedral. In contrast, the town supports a wild bar scene that continues throughout the night, banishing all thought or hope—despite fervent prayers—of sleep in high season.

Not surprisingly, Fira is Santorini's busiest and most commercial town. The abundance of **jewelry stores** is matched in the Cyclades only by Mykonos—as are the crowds in July and August. At the north end of Ipapantis (also known as "Gold Street" for its abundance of jewelry stores), you'll find the **cable-car station.** The Austrian-built system, the gift of wealthy ship owner Evangelos Nomikos, can zip you down to the port of Skala in 2 minutes. The cable car makes the trip every 15 minutes from 7:30am to 9pm for 3€ ($3.90), and it's worth every euro, especially on the way up.

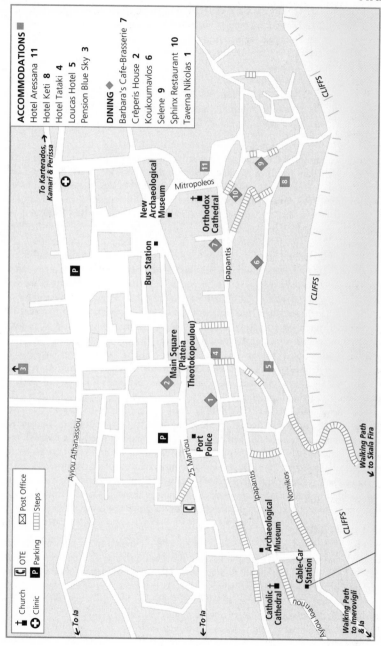

Fira

ACCOMMODATIONS ■

Hotel Aressana **11**
Hotel Keti **8**
Hotel Tataki **4**
Loucas Hotel **5**
Pension Blue Sky **3**

DINING ◆

Barbara's Cafe-Brasserie **7**
Crêperis House **2**
Koukoumavlos **6**
Selene **9**
Sphinx Restaurant **10**
Taverna Nikolas **1**

Legend:
† Church
● Clinic
C OTE
P Parking
⊠ Post Office
▥ Steps

To Karterados,
Kamari & Perissa →

Aylou Athanassiou

To Ia ←

To Ia ←

25 Martiou

Port
Police

New
Archaeological
Museum

Bus Station

Main Square
(Plateia
Theotokopoulou)

Mitropoleos

Orthodox
Cathedral

Ipapantis

Ipapantis

Archaeological
Museum

Nomikos

Ipapantis

Catholic †
Cathedral

Aylou Ioannou

Cable-Car
Station

Walking Path
↙ to Imerovigli
& Ia

Walking Path
↙ to Skala Fira

CLIFFS

CLIFFS

CLIFFS

CLIFFS

Up and to the right of the cable-car station is the small **Archaeological Museum** (© **22860/22-217**), which contains early Cycladic figurines, vases from Ancient Thira, interesting Dionysiac figures, and finds from Ancient Thira. It's open Tuesday through Sunday from 8:30am to 3pm. Admission is 3€ ($3.90) or free with a ticket to the Museum of Prehistoric Thira.

A different way to explore Santorini is the 1-hour submarine tour beneath the caldera's surface. It sinks 25 to 30m (82–98 ft.) below the surface and offers you a glimpse into the submerged volcanic crater. The trip costs 50€ ($65); information is available at most travel agents and at © **22860/28-900.**

IA ⭐

Ia gets most visitors' votes as the most beautiful village on the island. The 1956 earthquake severely damaged it; it remained a virtual ghost town for several decades thereafter. Although only a few buildings survived the earthquake, these exceptions are notable: fine **19th-century mansions** at the top of the town near the castle. Examples of restored neoclassical houses from this period are **Restaurant-Bar 1800** and the **Naval Museum.** Much of the reconstruction continues the ancient Santorini tradition of dwellings excavated from the cliff's face, and the island's most beautiful cliff dwellings can be found here. The village has basically two streets: one with traffic; and the much more pleasant inland pedestrian lane, Nikolaos Nomikou (the other end of the Nomikos street that began in Fira), paved with marble and lined with an increasing number of jewelry shops (as if there weren't enough in Fira), tavernas, and bars.

The battlements of the ruined **kastro** (fortress) at the western end of town are the best place to catch the famous Ia sunset. Below the castle, a long flight of steps leads down to the pebble beach at **Ammoudi,** which is okay for swimming and sunning, and has some excellent fish tavernas (see "Where to Dine," later in this chapter). To the west is the more spacious and sandy **Koloumbos Beach.** To the southeast below Ia is the fishing port of **Armeni,** where ferries sometimes dock and you can catch an excursion boat around the caldera.

The **Naval Museum** ⭐ (© **22860/71-156**) is a great introduction to this town where, until the advent of tourism, most young men found themselves working at sea and sending money home to their families. The museum, housed in a restored neoclassical mansion, was almost completely destroyed during the 1956 earthquake. Workers meticulously rebuilt the mansion using photographs of the original structure. The museum's collection includes ship models, figureheads, naval equipment, and fascinating old photographs. Its official hours are Wednesday through Monday from 12:30 to 4pm and 5 to 8:30pm, although this varies considerably. Admission is 3€ ($3.90).

THE VILLAGES

It's easy to spend all your time in Fira and Ia, with excursions to the ancient sites and beaches, and to neglect Santorini's villages. Easy, but a shame, as there are some very charming villages on the island. As you travel, keep an eye out for the troglodytic **cave houses** hollowed into solidified volcanic ash. At the south end of the island, on the road to Perissa, is the handsome old village of **Emborio.** The town was fortified in the 17th century, and you can see its towers, a graceful marble statue of the muse Polyhymnia in the cemetery, and modern-day homes built into the ruins of the citadel.

Pirgos, a village on a steep hill just above the island's port at Athinios, is a maze of narrow pathways, steps, chapels, and squares. Near the summit of the village is the crumbling Venetian kastro, plus several public squares with excellent views of the surrounding countryside. There is a merciful absence of tourism, and the central square, just off the main road, has the only shops and cafes in town.

The Church of the Panagia at the hamlet of **Gonias Episkopi** ✿ is an astonishingly well-preserved 11th- to 12th-century Byzantine church. As is often the case, the builders pillaged classical buildings. You will see the many fragments they appropriated incorporated into the walls—and two ancient marble altars supporting columns. Among the frescoes, keep an eye out for the figure of a dancing Salome.

As you explore the island and its villages, you may notice large brown circles of intertwined sticks on the ground in many fields. Santorinians twist live grape vines into wreaths that encircle the grapes and protect them from the island's fierce winds.

THE CALDERA ISLETS ✿

These tantalizing **islands** in the caldera are part of the glory of Santorini's seascape, reminders of the larger island that existed before the volcano left today's crescent in the sea. Fortunately, you can visit the islands and get a view of Santorini from there.

Thirassia is a small, inhabited island west across the caldera from Santorini; a cliff-top village of the same name faces the caldera, and is a quiet retreat from Santorini's summer crowds. You can reach the village from the caldera side only by a long flight of steep steps. (Travelers once had to get to Fira and Ia the same way.) Full-day **boat excursions** departing daily from the port of Fira (accessible by cable car, donkey, or on foot) make brief stops at Thirassia, just long enough for you to have a quick lunch in the village; the cost of the excursion—which includes Nea Kameni, Palea Kameni, and Ia—is about 25€ ($33) per person. Another option is local **caïques,** which make the trip in summer from Armeni, the port of Ia; ask for information at any of the Fira travel agents (see "Visitor Information," earlier in this chapter).

The two smoldering dark islands in the middle of the caldera are **Palea Kameni (Old Burnt),** the smaller and more distant one, which appeared in A.D. 157; and **Nea Kameni (New Burnt),** which began to appear sometime in the early 18th century. The day excursion to Thirassia (a far more exciting destination) happens to include these two (unfortunately often litter-strewn) volcanic isles.

OUTDOOR PURSUITS

BEACHES   Santorini's beaches may not be the best in the Cyclades, but the volcanic black sand here is unique in these isles—and gets very hot, very fast. **Kamari,** a little over halfway down the east coast, has the largest beach on the island. It's also the most developed, lined by hotels, restaurants, shops, and clubs. The natural setting is excellent, at the foot of cliffs rising precipitously toward Ancient Thira, but the black-pebbled beach becomes unpleasantly crowded in July and August. **Volcano Diving Center** (✆ **22860/33-177;** www.scubagreece.com), at Kamari, offers guided snorkel swims for around 20€ ($26) and scuba lessons from around 50€ ($65). **Perissa,** to the south, is another crowded beach resort with little to recommend it.

Small beaches lie all along the east coast of the island, the best of which are **Baxedes** and **Koloumbos,** near Ia at the island's north end. Baxedes is accessible by bus from Ia, and offers clean water and several shade trees, while the kilometer of sand at Koloumbos is a 15-minute walk farther down the road. Half of the beach at Koloumbos remains shady for most of the afternoon. **Monolithos,** near the end of the road to the airport, has a small, sheltered beach that tends not to get crowded and is popular with families; a couple of tavernas are located here. **Red beach (Paralia Kokkini),** at the end of the road to Ancient Akrotiri, gets its name from its small red volcanic pebbles.

BICYCLING Although Santorini's roads are in fairly good condition, it's the drivers you need to worry about. A bad combination is local drivers who know the roads with their eyes shut (and sometimes seem to drive that way) and visitors who have no idea where they are. Unfortunately, all too many visitors attempt to emulate speed-demon locals with results that are no fun for cyclists. That said, you can rent high-quality suspension mountain bikes with toe clips, helmet, pump, and repair kit from 10€ ($13) per day. **Moto Chris** (© 22860/23-431) in Fira; and **Moto Piazza** (© 22860/71-055) on the main road in Ia, rent mountain bikes for 12€ ($16) per day. However, at both places the bikes are in sorry shape and receive almost no maintenance.

WALKING The path from **Fira to Ia** (10km/6 miles) follows the edge of the caldera, passes several churches, and climbs two substantial hills along the way. Beginning at Fira, take the pedestrian path on the caldera rim, climbing past the Catholic cathedral to the villages of Firostephani and Imerovigli. In Imerovigli, signs on the path point the way to Ia; you'll be okay so long as you continue north, eventually reaching a dirt path along the caldera rim that parallels the vehicular road. The trail leaves the vicinity of the road with each of the next two ascents, returning to the road in the valleys. The descent into Ia eventually leads to the main pedestrian street in town. Allow yourself at least 2 hours. This walk is especially beautiful around sunset.

In **Imerovigli,** a rocky promontory jutting into the sea is known locally as **Skaros.** From medieval times until the early 1800s, an elaborate building complex here housed all the island's administrative offices. There is little to be seen of the Skaros castle now; it probably fell during a 19th-century earthquake. Skaros's fantastic view of the caldera is especially nice at sunset. The promontory is a tranquil haven from the crowds and bustle of the adjacent towns. The trail there begins from the terrace of a church just below the Blue Note Taverna in Imerovigli; from there it descends steeply to the isthmus connecting Skaros with the mainland. The path wraps around the promontory, after a mile reaching a small chapel with a panoramic view of the caldera. On the way, note the cliffs of glassy black volcanic rock, beautifully reflecting the brilliant sunlight. People used this rock to decorate many of the older buildings in Santorini.

The trail from Kamari to the site of **Ancient Thira** is steep but worth the trouble; it passes the beautiful site of Santorini's only freshwater spring. To reach the trail head from Kamari, take the automobile road (in the direction of Ancient Thira) past the Kamari beach parking, and turn right into the driveway of the hotel opposite Hotel Annetta, to the right of a minimarket. The trail begins behind the hotel. Climbing quickly by means of sharp switchbacks, the trail soon reaches a small chapel with a terrace and olive trees at the mouth of a cave. You can walk into the cave, which echoes with purling water, a surprising and miraculous sound in this arid place. Continuing upward, the trail rejoins the car road after a few more switchbacks, about 300m (984 ft.) from Ancient Thira. The full ascent from Kamari takes about an hour.

SHOPPING

If you're interested in fine **jewelry,** keep in mind that many prices in Fira are higher than in Athens, but the selection here is fantastic. **Porphyra** (© 22860/22-981), in the Fabrica Shopping Center near the cathedral, has impressive work. Santorini's best-known jeweler is probably **Kostas Antoniou** (© 22860/22-633), on Ayiou Ioannou north of the cable-car station. And there are plenty of shops between the two. Generally, the farther north you go, the higher the prices and the less certain the quality.

In Firostephani, **Cava Sigalas Argiris** (© 22860/22-802) stocks all the local **wines,** including their own. Also for sale are locally grown and **prepared foods,** often served as *mezedes*: *fava,* a spread made with chickpeas; *tomatahia,* small pickled tomatoes; and *kapari* (capers). The store is open from 8am to midnight.

The main street in Ia, facing the caldera, has many interesting stores in addition to the inevitable souvenir shops. **Replica** (© 22860/71-916) is a source of contemporary statuary and pottery as well as museum replicas; it will ship purchases to your home at post-office rates. Farther south on the main street is **Nakis** (© 22860/71-813), which specializes in amber jewelry and has a collection of insects in amber.

WHERE TO STAY

Santorini is seriously crowded in July and August; try to make a reservation with a deposit at least 2 months in advance or be prepared to accept potluck (we hear travelers' tales of people sitting miserably in cafes all night). Except in July and August, don't accept lodging offered at the port unless you're exhausted and don't care how meager the room is and how remote the village when you wake up the next morning. In July and August, be very grateful for whatever you get if you show up without a reservation.

The island's unusual **cave houses** have inspired many hotel designers. You may have seen the classic white exteriors in magazine articles about the area. Barrel-vaulted ceilings and perhaps even a bathroom carved into the rock distinguish a typical **cave house.** Built for earthquake resistance and economy, some of the spaces may at first strike you as cramped, dark, and stuffy; like most newcomers, you'll soon see them as part of the island's special charm. The best of them are designed with high ceilings, airy rooms, and good cross-ventilation, and since they are carved into the cliff face, they remain relatively cool throughout the summer.

Many apartments and villas have efficiency kitchens, but the facilities may be minimal. If you plan to do much cooking, check first to see what's in the drawers and cupboards, or you may find yourself frustrated if you try to prepare anything more elaborate than a cup of coffee.

FIRA

In addition to the choices below, you might consider **Pension Blue Sky** (© 22860/24-351 or 22860/25-121; fax 22860/25-120), a modest but comfortable place on the edge of town; or **Hotel Tataki** (© 22860/22-389; fax 22860/23-311; hoteltataki@san. forthnet.gr), a simple hotel with a central location and clean rooms with air-conditioning, fridges, and TVs. Two youth hostels, near Thira's main square—**Thira Youth Hostel** (© 22860/22-387) and **International Youth Hostel** (© 22860/24-472)— usually offer the island's cheapest accommodations, at around 20€ ($26) per person. You don't have to be young to stay at these hostels, but it helps to be young-at-heart and, as always with hostels, relaxed about shared facilities and noise. *Note:* Due to the noise in Fira, consider one of the more remote villages, unless you are in one of the quieter hotels suggested here.

Hotel Aressana ★★   This modern hotel compensates for its lack of a caldera view with a large swimming pool and lots of conveniences. It hosts many weddings and honeymoons. The Aressana is tucked away behind the Orthodox Cathedral, in a relatively quiet location. Most rooms have balconies or terraces; many have the high barrel-vaulted ceilings typical of this island. Unusual in Greece are the nonsmoking rooms. The breakfast room opens onto the pool terrace, as do most of the guest rooms; the elaborate buffet breakfast includes numerous Santorinian specialties. The Aressana also maintains seven nearby apartments facing the caldera, starting at 230€ ($299), which includes use of the hotel pool.

Fira, 84700 Santorini. © **22860/23-900**. Fax 22860/23-902. www.aressana.gr. 55 units, 1 with shower. 210€–250€ ($273–$325) double; 245€–380€ ($319–$494) suite. Rates include full breakfast. AE, DC, MC, V. Closed mid-Nov to Feb. **Amenities:** Snack bar; bar; freshwater pool; room service 7am–noon. *In room:* A/C, TV, minibar.

Hotel Keti *Value*   This tiny, plain hotel offers one of the best bargains on the caldera. All of the rooms have traditional vaulted ceilings and open onto shared terraces over-looking the caldera. The bathrooms, at the back of the rooms, are carved into the cliff face. The rooms are on the small side, and the furnishings are simple. You'll get a greater sense of being on a Greek island here: Laundry sometimes hangs on the ter-race, and local children play on the stairs.

Fira, 84700 Santorini. © **22860/22-324** or 22860/22-380. Fax 22860/25-171. 7 units. 80€ ($104) double. No credit cards. Closed mid-Oct to mid-Apr.

Loucas Hotel *⋒*   The Loucas is one of the first hotels built on the caldera. Its ter-races cascade down the side of the cliff, connected by a giddily steep flight of steps—definitely not for the acrophobic. Amazingly, a pool has been slapped onto the cliff's side. Barrel-vaulted ceilings define the well-maintained guest rooms; many of the bath-rooms are carved into the cliff's rock wall. Most of the rooms overlooking the caldera share terraces, but the thoughtful design provides a surprising degree of privacy. The Renaissance Bar sports a broad terrace above the rooms, with the unexceptional Aris Restaurant immediately below. A travel group's recent report of poor service is worry-ing; let us know if you encounter any difficulties at this long-established hotel.

Fira, 84700 Santorini. © **22860/22-480** or 22860/22-680. Fax 22860/24-882. 16 units. 175€ ($228) double. MC, V. Closed mid-Oct to mid-Apr. **Amenities:** Restaurant; bar; pool. *In room:* A/C, TV.

FIROSTEPHANI

This quieter and less expensive neighborhood is just a 10-minute walk from Fira. The views of the caldera are just as good, if not better.

Tsitouras Collection *⋒*   This top-of-the line luxury hotel will either dazzle or dis-may you: Understatement is conspicuous by its absence here, where antiques and reproductions jostle for space in five themed villas (including "House of Portraits" and "House of Porcelain"). The villa you stay in is all yours, which ensures blissful privacy. Tranquillity is easier to achieve here thanks to the no-television policy. One drawback: There's no pool. We're eager to hear more readers' reports on Tsitouras Collection; thus far, we've had almost as many thumbs-down for the indifferent service as we have had raves for the serious luxury and quiet location (just outside Thira).

Firostefani, 84700 Santorini. © **22860/23-747**. Fax 22860/23-918. tsitoura@otenet.gr. 5 villas (each accommodat-ing at least 4). 600€ ($780) for 2 sharing a villa; 150€ ($195) for each additional guest. MC, V. **Amenities:** Restau-rant; cafe. *In room:* A/C, kitchenette, minibar.

IMEROVIGLI

The next village north along the caldera rim is so named because it is the first place on the island from which you can see the rising sun. The name translates as "day vigil." By virtue of its height, Imerovigli also has the best views on this part of the caldera.

   While everyone else is jostling for a place to see the sunset at Oia, head to Imerovigli and take the path over to the promontory of Skaros, with the picturesque remains of its medieval kastro. Amazingly, this deserted and isolated spot was the island's first capital. It's a blissful place to watch the sunset.

In addition to the places listed below, **Rocabella Traditional Studios** (☏ **22860/ 23-711**), just outside Imerovigli, offers villas clustered around a good-size pool with views out to sea. Studios cost from 210€ ($273), doubles 220€ to 370€ ($286–$481).

Astra Apartments ★★★   Perched on a cliffside, with spectacular views, this is one of the nicest places to stay in all of Greece—in fact, friends who stayed here recently say that this was the highlight of their entire holiday! The Astra Apartments look like a tiny, whitewashed village (with an elegant pool) set in the village of Imerovigli, which is still much less crowded than Fira or Oia. Every detail here is perfect, which is why Astra consistently turns up on *Odyssey* magazine's list of Greece's best hotels. The vibrant blue of the bed coverlets is echoed in the blue paint on the cupboards— and even the lowly mosquito zappers (usually a dull beige in Greece) are the same blue. Nothing is flashy here. Everything is comforting including the transistor radio, flashlight, and welcoming bottles of wine and water. Best of all, although each unit has its own kitchenette, breakfast is served on your private terrace or balcony, and you can order delicious salads and sandwiches from the bar day and night. Manager George Karayiannis is always at the ready to arrange car rentals, recommend a wonderful beach or restaurant—or even help you plan your wedding and honeymoon here. Our only problem when we stayed here: We didn't want to budge from our terrace, especially at sunset, when the view over the offshore islands is dazzling. You may want to go whole hog, as it were, and book one of the new apartments or suites. Several come with private Jacuzzis and pools. You can also indulge yourself at the spa (completed in 2006).

Imerovigli, 84700 Santorini. ☏ **22860/23-641**. Fax 22860/24-765. www.astra-apartments.gr. 85 units. 230€–300€ ($299–$390) standard double apt; 385€–640€ ($501–$832) suite. MC, V. **Amenities:** Bar; pool. *In room:* A/C, TV, minibar, hair dryer, radio.

Chromata ★★   Here you'll get a wonderful view out over the island, an inviting pool, and excellent service. The lovely rooms sport comfortable, stylish chairs and handloomed rugs. If it weren't that its neighbor, Astra, is so special, Chromata would be the place to stay. If Astra is full, you'll be happy here.

Imerovigli, 84700 Santorini. ☏ **22860/24-850**. 17 units. 150€–300€ ($195–$390) double. AE, MC, V. **Amenities:** Bar; pool. *In room:* A/C, TV, minibar.

KARTERADOS

About 2km (1 mile) southeast of Fira, this small village knows the tourist ropes, and has many new hotels and rooms to let. Buses stop at the top of Karterados's main street on their ways to Kamari, Perissa, and Akrotiri. Nevertheless, the location is somewhat inconvenient: not especially close to Fira or to the beach. Karterados beach is a 3km (2-mile) walk from the center of town. Get to Monolithos, a longer beach, by continuing south along the water's edge an additional half-mile.

Pension George ★ *Value*   With a small pool, simple wood furnishings, attractive and reasonably priced rooms, and very helpful owners, the Pension offers good value if you're on a budget. To save even more money, opt for a room without a balcony. George and Helen Halaris will help you arrange car and boat rentals.

P.O. Box 324, Karterados, 84700 Santorini. ☏ **22860/22-351**. www.pensiongeorge.com. 25 units. 50€–80€ ($65–$104) double. No credit cards. Inquire about apts that sleep 2–5. **Amenities:** Breakfast on request; free transportation to airport or harbor. *In room:* A/C, TV (in some), fridge, safety-deposit box.

OIA

Oia was practically a ghost town until it was rebuilt and resettled after the 1956 earth-quake. Now its chic shops (check out **The Art Gallery** and **Art Gallery Oia** on Oia's meandering main drag) and gorgeous sunsets make it an increasingly popular place to stay or to visit—especially for travelers who find Fira too frenetic. If you venture out to either village (local buses run there from Fira, or you can take a taxi), watch for the island's cave dwellings.

Canaves Ia Traditional Houses   Traditional island style—curved white walls carved into the cliffside—defines these spacious two-bedroom apartments. All apart-ments have views of the caldera, and some offer private terraces. In each, a small guest room with a double bed opens onto a living room with barrel-vaulted ceiling. Bath-rooms are extremely compact. There are two complexes within 200m (656 ft.) of each other, each with its own pool and bar; the newer of the two is somewhat more luxu-rious (and more expensive), with marble floors and counters.

Ia, 84702 Santorini. (C) **22860/71-453.** Fax 22860/71-195. canaves@otenet.gr. 32 units. 350€–400€ ($455–$520) double. MC, V. Closed Nov–Apr. **Amenities:** Restaurant; 2 bars; 2 pools. *In room:* A/C, TV, kitchenette, minibar, hair dryer.

Chelidonia ⊛   Many thoughtful details add up to make these among the most appealing traditional apartments in Santorini. Most units are lovingly restored former homes, each with its unique layout—one was even a bakery! Skylights illuminate many rooms from above. Most have truly private terraces, many with small gardens of flowering plants and herbs for cooking. The guest rooms are spacious, the bathrooms luxuriously large, and the interiors simple and very elegant. Slabs of white marble combine with wall extensions to form tables and shelves. All units enjoy the famous Ia view across the caldera toward Imerovigli, Fira, and the southern end of the island. Why anyone would want to make use of the free in-room Internet service is beyond us! The Chelidonia is not a traditional hotel with room service; its apartments have daily maid service, and the staff clearly understands what makes guests feel at home. There's usually a 3-night minimum for stays.

Ia, 84702 Santorini. (C) **22860/71-287.** Fax 22860/71-649. www.chelidonia.com. 10 units. 140€ ($182) studio; 165€ ($215) double. No credit cards. Closed mid-Oct to mid-Apr. *In room:* A/C, kitchenette.

Hotel Finikia (Value)   This small, appealing hotel has a number of rooms with the domed ceilings traditional to Santorini architecture. Some rooms boast local weavings and artifacts. Most units have semiprivate balconies or terraces with views toward the sea—the hotel is on the east slope of the island, so the view is gentle rather than spec-tacular. The pool is good-size and the restaurant/bar is open almost all day. Irene and Theodoris Andreadis are your very helpful and friendly hosts. They have adjacent apartments for rent as well.

Finikia, 84702 Santorini. (C) **22860/71-373,** or 210/654-7944 in winter. Fax 22860/71-118. finikia@otenet.gr. 15 units. From 90€ ($117) double. Rates include breakfast. MC, V. Closed Nov–Mar. **Amenities:** Restaurant; bar; pool. *In room:* A/C, minibar.

Katikies ⊛⊛   If you find a more spectacular pool anywhere on the island, let us know. The main pool—one of four here—runs almost to the side of the caldera. You'll enjoy a world-class endless view. Katikies began as a small hotel, then added suites (some with their own plunge pools), and now has a 7-unit villa (with, of course, its own pool). The hotel's island-style architecture incorporates twists and turns, secluded patios, beamed ceilings, and antiques. If the people in the next room like to sing in the shower, you might hear them, but most people who stay here treasure the tranquillity.

After all, this is a member of the Small Luxury Hotels of the World. The top-of-the-line honeymoon suite has its own Jacuzzi, just in case you can't be bothered going to either outdoor pool. The new White Cave restaurant has only a handful of tables, so be sure to book ahead! Or head to one of Katikies' three other restaurants. A masseur is on call at the small spa on site.

Oia, 84702 Santorini. ℂ 22860/71-401. Fax 22860/71-129. www.katikies.com. 22 units. 290€–400€ ($377–$520) double; prices for suites on request. Rates include breakfast. MC, V. **Amenities:** 4 restaurants; bar; 4 pools; health club and spa; concierge; car rental; laundry service; currency exchange; library and Internet facilities. *In room:* A/C, TV, minibar, hair dryer.

Perivolas Traditional Settlement ★★   You could be forgiven for thinking that this is a pool with a nice little hotel attached: the *Conde Nast Traveler* cover photo of Perivolas's pool meeting the edge of the sky and the lip of the caldera put this place on the jet-setters' map. The 17 houses that make up the hotel offer studios and junior and superior suites. Price differences reflect the sizes of the three categories; each unit has a kitchenette and a terrace. The superior suites have a separate bedroom, whereas the other units are open plan. The architecture—wall niches, skylights, stonework—and some of the furnishings of these greatly enhanced cave dwellings are traditional. Everything is elegant—including the in-house library and Internet service! The hotel cafe is open until 9pm and the bar stays open most nights until midnight. The only downside: Few units have terraces with significant degrees of privacy—but that is true of almost every Santorini hotel.

Ia, 84702 Santorini. ℂ 22860/71-308. Fax 22860/71-309. www.perivolas.gr. 19 units. 450€–600€ ($585–$780) double/suite. Rates include buffet breakfast. No credit cards. Closed mid-Oct to mid-Apr. **Amenities:** Cafe; bar; pool. *In room:* A/C, full kitchen.

Youth Hostel Ia ★ *Value*   This exceptional facility occupies the grounds of a former convent. The one old remaining convent building houses a beautiful long room, now divided into two women's dorms, with a high vaulted ceiling. Most of the buildings surrounding the hostel's bright courtyard were built 10 years ago; the 4-, 6-, and 10-person dorms are large and well ventilated, and the bathrooms are reliably clean. Breakfast is served on a large terrace with fine sea views or in the hostel cafe, where light meals are available throughout the day. Laundry service is available.

Ia, 84702 Santorini. ℂ/fax 22860/71-465. 7 units (dormitories). 20€–30€ ($26–$39) per person. Rates include continental breakfast. No credit cards. Closed Nov–Apr. Near the bus stop. **Amenities:** Breakfast room.

MEGALOHORI

Villa Vedema Hotel ★★   The sleepy village of Megalohori is not where you'd expect to find a luxury hotel, but Santorini is full of surprises. The hotel is a self-contained world, surrounded by a wall like a fortified town. A member of "Small Luxury Hotels of the World," the Vedema is justly proud of its attentive but unobtrusive service—as well it should be, at these prices! The residences are set around several irregular courtyards, much like those found in the village. Each unique apartment comes comfortably and tastefully furnished, and includes a huge marble bathroom. The restaurant is excellent, and the candle-lit wine bar is located in a lovingly restored 300-year-old wine cellar. The principal disadvantage of a stay here is the location: Megalohori is not a particularly convenient base for exploring the island. But then, at these prices, and with this amount of luxury, you won't want to budge!

Megalohori, 84700 Santorini. ℂ 22860/81-796 or 22860/81-797. www.vedema.gr. 42 units. 400€–1,000€ ($520–$1,300) double/suite. Minimum 3-night stay. AE, DC, MC, V. Closed mid-Oct to mid-Apr. **Amenities:** Restaurant; bar; pool; concierge; airport pickup arranged; 24-hr. room service. *In room:* A/C, TV, minibar, hair dryer.

PYRGOS

Zannos Melathron ★★   Relatively uncrowded Pyrgos sits inland between Megalohori and Kamari. This 12-room boutique hotel occupies an 18th-century and a 19th-century building. The beautifully decorated rooms mix antiques with modern pieces, the island views are lovely, the pool is welcoming. If you want nightlife, this is not the place for you; if you want a peaceful retreat and near-perfect service, this may be just the spot for you.

Pyrgos, 84700 Santorini. ☎ **22860/28-220.** www.zannos.gr. 12 units. From 125€ ($163) double. No credit cards. **Amenities:** Restaurant; bar; pool; concierge; airport pickup; 24-hr. room service. *In room:* A/C, TV, minibar, hair dryer.

KAMARI

Tour groups book most of the hotels at Santorini's best and best-known beach resort in the summer. (Below we recommend one that is usually group-free.) You might also try the 42-unit **Hogel Astro,** which offers rooms with balconies, has a freshwater pool, and is off the beach (and away from most of the nightlife noise). Another option is the 27-unit **Matina Hotel** (☎ **22860/31-491;** fax 22860/31-860), which has no views to speak of but is a 2-minute walk from the beach. Doubles at both hotels run from 100€ ($130). If you can't find a room, try the local office of **Kamari Tours** (☎ **22860/31-390** or 22860/31-455), which manages many of the hotels in Kamari and may be able to find you a vacancy.

Rooms Hesperides   This neat, modern pension stands in the middle of a pistachio orchard with excavated Byzantine ruins. Akis Giannakulias, a former ship's captain, owns the place as well as the Akis Hotel across the street. In fact, you have to go to the Akis reception desk to book a room. Each of the simple guest rooms has a balcony with a view of the sea or of Mount Profitis Elias. If you prefer a slightly larger room with fridge and air-conditioning, try the Akis. The 20 rooms here are clean, comfortable, and reasonable—from 65€ ($85) for a double. Breakfast for guests at both hotels is served at the Akis on a sunny terrace.

Kamari, 84700 Santorini. ☎ **22860/31-670.** Fax 22860/31-423. 20 units. 65€–110€ ($85–$143) double. Rates include continental breakfast. AE, MC, V. Closed mid-Oct to mid-Apr. 50m (164 ft.) from the beach, near the Kamari bus stop. **Amenities:** Breakfast room/bar. *In room:* A/C, fridge (in some).

WHERE TO DINE

FIRA

As you might expect, restaurants here range from blah to beatific. The bad ones stint on quality and service, because they know that most tourists are here today and gone tomorrow. The good places cater to the discriminating tourist and to Greek and foreign visitors who come back again and again.

If all you want is breakfast or a light, cheap meal, try **Crêperis House,** Theotokopoulou Square (no phone); or **Barbara's Cafe-Brasserie,** in the Fabrica Shopping Center up from the bus station toward the cathedral (no phone). After 7pm, Barbara's becomes one of the least expensive bars in town.

Note: Many of the restaurants near the cable car fall into the forgettable category. In addition, some of these restaurants have been known to present menus without prices, and then charge exorbitantly for food and wine. If you are given a menu, make sure prices are listed on it.

Koukoumavlos ★★ GREEK   The terrace at Koukoumavlos enjoys the famous caldera view, but unlike most caldera restaurants where a spectacular view has to compensate for mediocre food, here the view is a distraction from the delights of the kitchen. The menu changes often, as the chef tries out new dishes with ingredients not always used in Greece (a wide variety of mushrooms, for example). Many dishes offer creative variations on traditional Greek food, like the shrimp poached in retsina; or the fava served hot in olive oil with grilled zucchini, onions, tomatoes, olives, and toasted almonds. For dessert, try the yogurt panna cotta with pistachios, thyme honey, and sour cherry.

Below the Hotel Atlantis, facing the caldera. © 22860/23-807. Reservations recommended for dinner. Main courses 15€–35€ ($20–$46). AE, MC, V. Daily noon–3pm and 7:30pm–midnight.

Selene ★★★ GREEK   The best restaurant on Santorini—and one of the best in Greece—Selene uses local produce to highlight what owners Evelyn and George Hatziyiannakis call the "creative nature of Greek cuisine." The appetizers, including a delicious sea urchin salad on artichokes and fluffy fava balls with caper sauce, are deservedly famous. Entrees include *brodero* (seafood stew). The baked mackerel with caper leaves and tomato wrapped in a crepe of fava beans will convert even the most dedicated flesh eaters. The local lamb, quail, rabbit, and beef are all excellent. If you eat only one meal on Santorini, eat it here, in a truly distinguished restaurant with distinctive local architecture. In short, everything—location, ambience, view, service—comes together to form the perfect setting (never pretentious or coy, unlike some trendy spots) for the delicious, inventive food. The selection of cheeses from across the Cyclades is impressive. If you want to learn to make some of Selene's selections yourself, check out Selene's cooking school at www.selene.gr.

Fira. © 22860/22-249. Fax 22860/24-395. Reservations recommended. Main courses 17€–25€ ($22–$33). AE, MC, V. Mid-Apr to mid-Oct daily 7pm–midnight. Closed late Oct to early Apr. In the passageway between the Atlantis and Aressana hotels.

Sphinx Restaurant INTERNATIONAL   Antiques, sculpture, and ceramics by local artists fill this restored old mansion that boasts a large outdoor terrace with views of the caldera and the port at Skala Fira. You may not decide that you've come to Santorini to eat ostrich, but the fresh pasta is tasty, as are the fish dishes.

Odos Mitropoleos. © 22860/23-823. Reservations recommended. Main courses 15€–25€ ($20–$33); fish priced by the kilo. AE, DC, MC, V. Daily 11am–3pm and 7pm–1am. Near the Panagia Ypapantis Church.

Taverna Nikolas Value GREEK   This is one of the few restaurants in Fira where locals queue up alongside throngs of travelers for a table—high praise, for a place that has been here forever. There aren't any surprises; you'll get traditional Greek dishes prepared very well. The lamb with greens in egg-lemon sauce is particularly delicious. The dining room is always busy, so arrive early or plan to wait.

Just up from the main sq. in Fira. No phone. Main courses 8€–15€ ($10–$20). No credit cards. Daily noon–midnight.

IA

The best place to eat in Ia is the port of **Ammoudi,** hundreds of feet below the village, huddled between the cliffs and the sea. We recommend two of the fish tavernas there, Katina's and Captain Dimitri's. If you don't want to trek all the way down to the beach, stop along the way at **Kastro** (© 22860/71-045), where you'll still have a fine view and can enjoy Greek dishes, pasta, or fresh fish. To get there, follow the stepped path down from the vicinity of Lontza Castle, hire a donkey (4€/$5.20 one-way), or call a taxi. We recommend the walk down (to build an appetite) and a taxi or donkey up.

Captain Dimitri's ★ SEAFOOD   The cooks here and at Katina's have perfected the art of cooking fish on the charcoal grill. The view is exceptional at both. Even the hours and prices are pretty much the same. Prices for fish—by the kilo—vary; be sure to check the price before you order. That said, two should be able to eat sensibly here for 50€ ($65).

Ammoudi. ℂ **22860/82-210.** No credit cards. Daily 10am–midnight (usually).

Katina's ⭐ SEAFOOD   See the write-up for Captain Dimitri's above. You can't go wrong at either restaurant.

Ammoudi. ℂ **22860/71-280.** No credit cards. Daily 10am–midnight (usually).

Restaurant-Bar 1800 ⭐ CONTINENTAL   For many years recognized as the best place in Ia for a formal dinner, the 1800 has a devoted following among visitors and locals. The restaurant, housed in a splendidly restored neoclassical captain's mansion, has undeniable romantic charm. Curtains billow at some windows and there's often candlelight. After you eat, you can decide whether the owner (an architect and chef) deserves more praise for his skill with the decor or with the cuisine.

Odos Nikolaos Nomikos. ℂ **22860/71-485.** Main courses 15€–30€ ($20–$39). AE, DC, MC, V. Daily 6pm–midnight.

Skala *Value* GREEK   Skala has perfectly fine taverna food, at prices that are less steep than those at many other places here. All the staples of traditional Greek (if not local Santorini) food are reliably good; the management is helpful and friendly. Try the vegetable appetizers and, for your main course, the roasted meats.

Odos Nikolaos Nomikos. ℂ **22860/71-362.** Main courses 8€–15€ ($10–$20). Daily 1pm–midnight. MC.

KAMARI

Camille Stephani ⭐ GREEK/INTERNATIONAL   Even if you're not staying at Kamari, you might like to head out to the beach for a meal at this excellent seaside place. An old standard, the restaurant continues to produce memorable fare. The house specialties include terrific *mezedes* and a tender beef filet with green pepper in Madeira sauce. The outside tables face the water, and a moonlight stroll along the beach is the perfect end to a fine meal.

North end of Kamari beach. ℂ **22860/31-716.** Reservations recommended July–Sept. Main courses 10€–25€ ($13–$33). DC, MC, V. Daily noon–midnight (Fri–Sun in winter). 500m (1,640 ft.) from the bus stop.

SANTORINI AFTER DARK

The height of the tourist season is also the height of the music season in Santorini. If you are here in July, you may want to take in the annual Santorini Jazz Festival (www.jazz festival.gr), which has been bringing several dozen international jazz bands and artists here every summer since 1997. Many performances are on Kamari beach. In August and September, the 2-week **Santorini International Music Festival** (ℂ **22860/23-166**), with international singers and musicians, gives performances of classical music at the Nomikos Centre in Fira. Admission to most events starts at 15€ ($20).

Fira has nightlife aplenty, with some variety. We suggest starting the evening with a drink on the caldera, taking in the spectacular sunset. **Franco's** (ℂ **22860/22-881**) is still the most famous and best place for this magic hour; be prepared to pay 10€ ($13) and up (and up!) per drink. For more reasonable prices, a bit more seclusion, and the same fantastic view, continue through Canava Cafe and below Loucas Hotel to **Renaissance Bar** (ℂ **22860/22-880**). Underneath the square, **Kirathira Bar** plays jazz at a level that permits conversation, and the nearby **Art Café** offers muted music.

Cross the main street and wander around the shopping area to find a number of smaller bars that come alive after 9pm. A bit farther north, the outdoor **Tropical Bar** attracts a louder, rowdier gang. For *bouzoukia,* find **Bar 33. Ellenes** has loud Greek dancing music, starting no earlier than 11pm. Discos come and go, and you need only follow your ears to find them. **Koo Club** is the biggest, while **Enigma** is still popular with travelers interested in good music. **Tithora** is popular with a young, heavy-drinking crowd. There's usually no cover, but drinks start at most places at 10€ ($13).

In Ia, **Zorba's** is a popular cliffside pub. The fine restaurant/bar **1800** is a quiet and sophisticated place to stop in for a drink—and certainly for a meal.

Kamari has its share of bars. **Yellow Donkey Disco** (*©* **22860/31-462**) is popular with younger partiers, while the more sophisticated seek out chic **Valentino's,** near the bus stop.

Greek dancers in traditional costumes often perform a floor show at **Messaria,** at **Canava Roussos Winery** (*©* **22860/31-276**); call first to confirm if there is a show and to make a reservation.

2 Folegandros

181km (98 nautical miles) SE of Piraeus

Tell people that you're off to Folegandros and you're likely to get one of two reactions: from many, quizzical expressions, but from those who know this island, envious glances. Folegandros has one of the most perfect capitals in the islands: Cars and motorcycles are banned in **Hora.** Bliss. More village than town, Hora huddles at the cliff's edge. One small, shaded square spills into the next, with green and blue paving slates outlined in brilliant white. As you prowl the streets, you'll realize that much of Hora is built into the walls of the kastro, a medieval castle. Small houses with overhanging wooden balconies weighed with pots of geraniums line the narrow lanes.

One majestic church, **Kimisis Theotokou,** dominates the skyline of Hora. It's particularly beautiful at night, when it's illuminated. Built at the highest point in town, it stands on the foundations of the ancient Greek town here. Townspeople parade through the village with the church's icon of the Virgin with great ceremony and rejoicing each Easter Sunday. Blessedly, since the town is so compact, and so contained in those castle walls, new development has taken place outside the town, leaving its traditional character intact.

As boats pass the island's forbidding northern coast, precipitous cliffs rise to a height of 250m (820 ft.). As for the main port, Karavostassi, if you don't know about Hora and the island's beguiling interior landscape, you can almost be forgiven for continuing to the next port of call and not getting off here: **Karavostassi** struggles along the harbor and has a grab-bag of small restaurants, a hotel or two, some shops—but, frankly, little appeal (although the small park is nice). Perhaps the port's minimal appeal is why, thus far, relatively few have ventured to experience the island's spare beauty.

The rugged northern slopes of Folegandros offer a contrast to the austere civility of Hora's streets and squares. Here the hills are beribboned with the terraced fields that allow local farmers to grow barley on the island's steep slopes. Rocky coves shelter pristine pebble beaches, and many trails weave their way through the hills, some of them ancient paths paved with marble or carved from bedrock. If you want to explore Folegandros, you can do a good deal by local bus, but you'll also want to walk—and if you do, you'll enjoy the sight of very beautiful terraced hillsides.

ESSENTIALS

GETTING THERE   By Boat   Three ferries a week stop at Folegandros on the Santorini-Folegandros-Sikinos-Ios-Naxos-Paros-Piraeus route; travel times are about 2 to 3 hours to Naxos, 4 hours to Paros (or 1 hr. by hydrofoil), and 10 hours to Piraeus. Information is available at the **Piraeus Port Authority** (② 210/422-6000), which seldom answers the phone; and at the **Piraeus Port Police** (② 210/451-1310). Two ferries per week stop on the Folegandros-Milos-Sifnos-Paros-Mykonos-Tinos-Siros hydrofoil run; it's 2 hours to Sifnos, 3 to 5 hours to Mykonos, 5 to 6 hours to Tinos, and 6 hours to Siros. During the off season, infrequent service and bad weather can easily keep you here longer than you intend. **Folegandros Port Police** are at ② 22860/41-249.

VISITOR INFORMATION Maraki Travel Agency (② 22860/41-273) and **Sottovento Travel** (② 22860/41-444) exchange money, help with travel arrangements, sell maps of the island, and offer Internet facilities. Sottovento also serves as the local Italian consulate. You can buy ferry tickets at a branch of Maraki Travel at the port (② 22860/41-198).

GETTING AROUND By Bus The bus to Hora meets all ferries in peak season and most ferries during the rest of the year; it also makes eight or nine trips a day on the road running along the island's spine between Hora and Ano Meria at the island's northern end. The fare is 1.50€ ($1.95).

By Moped There are two moped-rental outfits on Folegandros: **Jimmy's Motorcycle** (② 22860/41-448) in Karavostassi; and **Moto Rent** (② 22860/41-316) in Hora, near Sottovento Travel.

By Boat Mid-June through August, boat taxis or caïques provide transport to the island's southern beaches. From Karavostassi, boats depart for Katergo and Angali (8€/$10 round-trip); another boat departs from Angali for Ayios Nikolaos, Livadaki, and Ambeli (8€/$10 round-trip). There is also a 7-hour tour of the island's beaches that departs from Karavostassi at least three times weekly in summer, and makes stops at five beaches; the cost is 25€ ($33) per person, including lunch. Reservations can be made at Diaplous or Sottovento Travel (see above); note that tickets must be purchased a day in advance.

FAST FACTS Folegandros has neither bank nor ATM, but you can exchange money at **Maraki Travel** (② 22860/41-273), **Sottovento Travel** (② 22860/41-444), or **Diaplous** (② 22860/41-158). Commissions on money exchange are particularly high in Folegandros, because the banks are off the island. It may be wise to arrive with enough cash for your visit. The **post office** and **telephone office (OTE)** are right off the central square in Hora, open Monday through Friday from 8am to 3pm. The **police station** (② 22860/41-249) is behind the post office and OTE. There's one **taxi** (② 22860/41-048) on the island, but with the frequency of bus service and dearth of places to drive to, you're unlikely to need it.

WHAT TO SEE & DO

Visitors arrive in the unimpressive port of **Karavostassi,** where there's a decent beach and a few hotels and rooms to let. Most will jump aboard the bus that's waiting to chug the 4km (2½ miles) up to Hora.

Hora ⚘ is one of the most beautiful capitals in the Cyclades. The town is centered around five closely connected squares, along and around which you'll find churches, restaurants, and shops. Even from the bus-stop square, the sheer drop of the cliff offers an awesome sight. On the right in the next square, you'll find the **Kastro:** two narrow pedestrian streets connected by tunnel-like walkways, squeezed between the town and the sea cliffs, with remnants of the medieval castle. Above, Kimisis Theotokou Church tempts the energetic to climb the hillside for a closer look and incredible views. The other church to see here is the deserted **Monastery of the Panagia,** north of town, also with lovely views.

Continue west from Hora by foot or bus to reach the village of **Ano Meria.** The widely dispersed, small farms here are barely recognizable as a community, although Ano Meria is the island's second-largest town.

As you rush from island to island, checking in and out of hotels, it's not always easy to feel the rhythm of island life. One great way to do that is to visit Folegandros's small **Folk Museum,** in the village of Ano Meria. Some of the tools and household items have been used for generations, and some are still in use today! The museum (no phone; free admission, but donation appropriate) is open 5 to 8pm weeknights in July and August, and the local bus can drop you a pleasant stroll away. If the museum turns out to be closed, console yourself that this, too, is an insight into the follies of island life!

BEACHES

Swimmers will want to get off the bus to Ano Meria at the first crossroad and walk down to **Angali,** the largest and most crowded fine-sand beach on the island. There are a few tavernas on the beach and rooms to let. **Ayios Nikolaos,** another popular beach where clothing is optional, is a couple of kilometers farther west—a well-used path follows the coast west from Angali, or you can take the boat (5€/$6.50 one-way from Angali). West from Ayios Nikolaos is a series of beaches, the best of which are **Livadaki** and **Ambeli.** You can reach both by boat from Angali (5€/$6.50 one-way) or on foot from the end of the road to Ano Maria (see "Walking," below). The island's best beach, **Katergo** ⚓, is a stretch of fine pebbles at the base of a low cliff on the island's south side, protected from the wind by rocky headlands. It is accessible on foot (about 2km/1¼ miles from Livadi Beach; 3km/2 miles from the port at Karavostassi) or by water: A boat departs from Karavostassi mid-June to August (6€/$7.80 round-trip). At the far northwest end of the island is **Ayios Yeoryios,** a pristine pebble beach in a rocky cove, accessible only on foot (the excursion boats don't often stop here). It's a great walk (see "Walking," below), but the beach is usually too windy for swimming. On a still day, it can be a good place to avoid the crowds. For information on boat taxis to the beaches, inquire at Sottovento Travel or Diaplous (see above).

WALKING

The footpaths through the northern part of the island are for the most part well used and easy to follow. Numerous paths branch off to the southwest from the paved road through Ano Meria; the hills traversed by these trails, between the road and the sea, are particularly beautiful. One easy path leads you from **Ayios Andreas** to the bay at **Ayios Yeoryios.** Take the bus to the next-to-last stop, at the northern end of Ano Meria; it will let you off by the church of Ayios Andreas. At the stop, the sign AG. GEORGIOS 1.5 points to the right. Follow the sign, and continue along a road that quickly becomes a path and descends steeply toward the bay. Follow the main path at each of several intersections; you'll be able to see the bay for the last 20 minutes of the walk. You'll find a small pebble beach at the bay of Ayios Yeoryios, but no fresh water, so be sure to bring plenty. Allow 2 hours for the round-trip.

The walk to **Livadaki beach**(see above), near the lighthouse of Aspropounta on Folegandros's sheltered southwestern coast, begins at the end of the paved portion of the road to Ano Meria. Take the bus to the last stop, which lets you out in front of the Merovigli Taverna; continue on foot about 200m (656 ft.) on the wide dirt road to a sign indicating the trail to Livadaki on the left. From here it's about 40 minutes down to the beach through terraced fields, passing on the way the remote hilltop church of Ayii Anaryiri. The gradually sloping beach itself is well worth the trouble: a stretch of fine pebbles in a glorious rocky cove protected from the wind. Also beginning from the end of the bus line, you can continue a few meters past the turnoff for Livadaki to the signposted trail to **Ambeli Beach,** which is also a 40-minute walk. Ambeli is a lovely, small, intimate beach with nice shade trees. Be sure to bring plenty of water.

WHERE TO STAY

We recommend that you stay in beautiful cliff-top Hora. The island's limited facilities are always fully booked in July and August, so advance reservations are essential. We suggest the two best accommodations on the island. If you surf the Web and find others, accept no substitutes!

Anemomilos Apartments ★★   This is a very congenial place that began to turn up on lists of the "best island retreats" soon after it opened 10 years ago. Anemomilos is spectacularly situated at the edge of a cliff overlooking the sea. You don't have to feel rueful being so far from the sea: There's a fine pool here. Terraces facing the sea grace all but two of the units. Nice wood furniture and tasteful weavings make each apartment attractive. A well-stocked kitchenette means you can actually cook here. If you don't want to make your own breakfast, Cornelia Patelis, who manages the hotel with her husband, Dimitris, makes a delicious sweet breakfast pie with local cheese. The hotel also serves breakfast and snacks throughout the day on the pool terrace. One apartment is accessible for travelers with disabilities. Transport to and from the port, arranged by the hotel, costs about 5€ ($6.50) per person one-way.

Hora, 84011 Folegandros. ℭ **22860/41-309,** or 210/682-7777 in Athens. Fax 22860/41-407, or 210/682-3962 in Athens. 17 units. 100€–175€ ($130–$228) double. V. Closed mid-Oct to Easter. Near the central bus stop. **Amenities:** Breakfast room/bar; pool. *In room:* A/C, kitchenette, fridge.

Castro Hotel ★★   The Castro is a Venetian castle built in 1212; it's the oldest part of Hora, wedged against the cliffs and facing the Aegean 250m (820 ft.) below. Guest rooms are small but comfortable, and seven have phenomenal views. The two most desirable units have balconies surveying the extraordinary view; these don't cost extra and are a great bargain. (Try to reserve room no. 3, 4, 5, 13, 14, 15, or R1.) Even if you opt for a room without the view, you can enjoy it from the shared rooftop terrace. The charming Despo Danassi, whose family has owned this house for five generations, will make you feel at home. And her homemade fig jam is fabulous!

Hora, 84011 Folegandros. ℭ **22860/41-230,** or 210/778-1658 in Athens. Fax 22860/41-230, or 210/778-1658 in Athens. 12 units. 80€–110€ ($104–$143) double. Continental breakfast 10€ ($13). AE, V. Closed Nov–Apr. **Amenities:** Breakfast room.

WHERE TO DINE

Main courses for all the restaurants listed run about 5€ to 15€ ($6.50–$20); hours are generally from 9am to 3pm and 6pm to midnight.

The local specialty, *matsata,* is made with fresh pasta and rabbit or chicken. The best place to sample it is **Mimi's,** in Ano Meria (ℭ **22860/41-377**), where the pasta is made on the premises. Look for two other restaurants in Ano Meria: **Sinandisi** (ℭ **22860/41-208**), also known as Maria's, which has good *matsata* and swordfish (take the bus to the Ayios Andreas stop); and **Barbakosta** (ℭ **22860/41-436**), a tiny room that serves triple duty as bar, taverna, and minimarket (the bus stop has no name, so ask the driver to alert you).

Hora has a number of tavernas, whose tables spill onto and partially fill the central squares. At the bus-stop square, **Pounda** (© 22860/421-063) serves a delicious breakfast of crepes, omelets, yogurt, or coffeecake; lunch and dinner, including vegetarian dishes, are also available. **Silk** (© 22860/41-515), on the *piatsa* (third) square, offers delicious variations on taverna fare, including numerous vegetarian options. **Piatsa** (© 22860/41-274), also on the third square, is a simple taverna with tasty food. **O Kritikos** (© 22860/41-219) is another local favorite, known for its grilled chicken.

3 Sifnos

172km (93 nautical miles) SE of Piraeus

Everyone falls in love with at least one of the Cyclades; we fell in love with Sifnos. Sifnos keeps its riches concealed within a hilly interior. Once you've left the port for the interior, you will see elegantly ornamented dovecotes above cool green hollows, ancient fortified monasteries, and watchtowers that occupy the arid summits of the island's hills. The beautiful slate and marble paths across the island are miracles of care, although many are now covered with concrete and asphalt to accommodate car traffic. The island is a hiker's—even a stroller's—delight. In addition, beaches along the southern coast offer long stretches of fine amber sand; several smaller rocky coves are also excellent for swimming.

The island is sufficiently small that any town can be used as a base for touring; the most beautiful are the **seven settlements** spread across the central hills—notably Apollonia and Artemonas—and **Kastro,** a small medieval fortified town atop a rocky pinnacle on the eastern shore. Bus rides, combined with a few short walks, will take you to the island's top attractions: the ancient acropolis at **Ayios Andreas,** the town of Kastro and its tiny but excellent **archaeological museum,** the southern **beaches,** the once isolated beaches at **Vathi** and **Cheronisso** and, for the ambitious, the walled **Monastery of Profitis Elias** on the summit of the island's highest mountain. While you're on the island, don't miss the **pottery workshops.** Sifnos is renowned for its ceramics, and some of the island's best practitioners are in Kamares and Platis Yialos. It's also famous for its olive oil and excellent cooking. Great olive oil and sublime cooking go together here.

If you feel like splurging, check out the top-of-the-line Elies resort (© 22840/34-000; www.eliesresorts.com), which opened in 2005 on the beach in Vathi and immediately appeared in *Odyssey* magazine's list of the 50 best hotels in Greece. The resort, surrounded by olive groves, is designed to look like a traditional Cycladic village—but has villas with private pools and offers aromatherapy and massage.

ESSENTIALS

GETTING THERE   By Boat   There's one ferry daily from Piraeus (3 hr.), as many as four in high season; contact the **GNTO** in Athens (© 210/327-1300 or 210/331-0562); **Piraeus Port Authority** (© 210/459-3223 or 210/422-6000; phone seldom answered); **Piraeus Port Police** (© 210/451-1310); or **Sifnos Port Authority** (© 22840/33-617) for information. Ferries travel daily to nearby islands such as **Serifos** (30–60 min.), **Kimolos** (30–40 min.), **Milos** (45 min.), and **Kithnos** (1½ hr.). *Note:* In the off season, ferry connections to Sifnos are particularly sparse.

VISITOR INFORMATION   You can book a room, buy ferry tickets, rent a car or motorbike, arrange excursions, and usually leave your luggage at **Aegean Thesaurus Travel and Tourism** ✮✮ on the port (© 22840/32-152; www.thesaurus.gr). Aegean

Thesaurus handles tickets for all hydrofoils and ferries. Check to see if the company, which also has an office on the main square in Apollonia (© **22840/33-151**), has its excellent information packet on Sifnos for 2€ ($2.60).

GETTING AROUND   By Bus   Apollonia's central square, **Plateia Iroon** (which locals call **Stavri**), is the main bus stop for the island. Buses run regularly to and from the port at Kamares, north to Artemonas and Cheronisso, east to Kastro, and south to Faros, Platis Yialos, and Vathi. Pick up a schedule at Aegean Thesaurus Travel (see "Visitor Information," above).

By Car & Moped   Many visitors come to Sifnos for the wonderful hiking and mountain trails. While unnecessary, a car or moped can be rented at **Aegean Thesaurus** (© **22840/33-151**) in Apollonia, or at Kostas Kalogerou's **ProtoMoto** (© **22840/33-791;** www.protomotocar.gr) in Kamares. As always, exercise caution if you decide to rent a car or moped; many drivers, like you, will be unfamiliar with the island roads. The daily rate for an economy car with full insurance is about 50€ ($65); a moped rents for about 22€ ($29).

By Taxi   Apollonia's main square is the island's primary taxi stand. There are about 10 taxis on the island, each privately owned, so you'll have to use the **mobile phone numbers** available at travel agents. Kostas Kalogerou offers reliable service at © **094/ 493-6111.**

FAST FACTS   Visitor services are centered in Apollonia. **National Bank** (© **22840/ 31-317**), with an ATM, is just past Hotel Anthousa on the road to Artemonas (Mon–Thurs 8am–2pm; Fri 8am–1:30pm). The **post office** (© **22840/31-329**), on Plateia Iroon (Stavri to the islanders), the main square, is open in summer Monday through Friday from 8am to 3pm, Saturday and Sunday from 9am to 1:30pm. The **telephone office (OTE),** just down the vehicle road, is open daily year-round from 8am to 3pm, and in summer from 5 to 10pm as well. The **police** (© **22840/31-210**) are just east of the square, and a **first-aid station** is nearby; for **medical emergencies** call © **22840/31-315.**

WHAT TO SEE & DO

The capital town of the island, **Apollonia,** is one of the **seven settlements** which have grown together on these lovely interior hills. It's 5km (3 miles) inland from Kamares; a local bus makes the trip hourly in summer. The town's central square, **Plateia Iroon (Heroes' Square),** is the transportation hub of the island. All vehicle roads converge here, and this is where you'll find the bus stop and taxi stand. Winding pedestrian paths of flagstone and marble slope upward from the square through the beautiful town. **Lakis Kafenion,** an open-air cafe on the square, is the island's principal hangout. Also on Plateia Iroon is the small **Popular and Folk Art Museum;** it's open July 1 to September 15 from 10am to 1pm and 6 to 10pm (admission is 1.50€/$1.95).

Kastro ⚑ is the finest medieval town on Sifnos, built on the dramatic site of an ancient acropolis. Until several decades ago, Kastro was almost entirely deserted; now it has cafes, restaurants, and shops. The 2km (1-mile) walk from Apollonia is easy, except under the midday sun. Start out on the footpath that passes under the main road in front of Hotel Anthousa, and continue through the tiny village of Kato Petali, finishing the walk into Kastro on a paved road. Whitewashed houses, some well preserved and others eroding, adjoin one another in a defensive ring abutting a sheer cliff. Venetian coats of arms are still visible above doorways of older houses. Within the maze of streets are a few tavernas and some beautiful rooms to let. A real gem, the

Archaeological Museum (© **22840/31-022**) here has a good collection of pottery and sculpture found on the island; it's open Tuesday through Saturday from 9am to 2pm, Sunday and holidays from 10am to 2pm. Admission is free.

About 2km (1 mile) south of Apollonia on the road to Vathi is a trail leading to the hilltop church of **Ayios Andreas** and the excavations of an **ancient acropolis.** Broad stone steps begin a long climb to the summit; count on about 20 vigorous minutes to make the ascent. The acropolis ruins are at the top of the hill on your left. These ruins are made up of the outer walls and a block of houses from a Mycenaean fortified town. Excavations haven't been completed and there's no interpretive information at the site, but the location is stirring. It's worth a visit if only for the view.

Well into the 1980s, pottery making flourished on Sifnos. Now, only a handful of potteries remain. The distinctive brown-and-blue glazed Sifnian pottery still being made has become something of a collector's item. If you fall for a piece, buy it—with more and more potteries closing down, you can't be sure you'll find this distinctive ware again.

BEACHES

The central part of **Kamares** cove shelters a sandy beach lined with tamarisk trees and dune grass, but the water here is not so clean because of the harbor-boat traffic.

You'll find a trio of coves with fine-sand beaches at the island's southern end. The most popular of these is **Platis Yialos,** where a slew of hotels, tavernas, and shops have grown up around the beach. More upscale than Kamares, this town attracts the yachting crowd in summer. From here, it's a half-hour walk east through the olive groves and intoxicating oregano and thyme patches over the hill to **Panagia Chrissopiyi,** a double-vaulted whitewashed church on a tiny island. There's good swimming at **Apokofto,** a cove with a long sand beach and several shade trees just beyond the monastery, where rocky headlands protect swimmers from rough water. Nude bathing is permitted at nearby **Fasolou.**

Until 1997, the beach at **Vathi**—one of the best on the island—was accessible only on foot or by boat, but a new automobile road permits regular bus service. The beach does not have the dense development of Kamares and Platis Yialos, but there's every sign that is soon will. You'll find a few tavernas here. The new resort, Elies, opened here in 2005.

The beach at **Cheronisso,** at the island's northern end, is a spectacular spot to watch the sun go down.

WALKING

More and more asphalt roads are appearing on Sifnos, but you'll still be able to do most of your walking on the island's distinctive flagstone and marble paths. You'll probably see village women whitewashing the edges of the paving stones, transforming the monochrome paths into elaborate abstract patterns. Throughout the island, you'll see dovecotes, windmills, and small white chapels in amazingly remote spots.

Sadly, the continuity of these fine paths has been interrupted—even destroyed—in many places by the construction of new roads and houses.

Our favorite walk on the island leads from **Apollonia to Profitis Elias,** passing through a valley of extraordinary beauty to the summit of the island's highest mountain, with a short detour to the church and ruined monastery at Skafis. Pick up a walking map at one of the local travel agencies. The 12th-century walled monastery of Profitis Elias is a formidable citadel, its interior courtyard lined with the monks' cells.

The lovely chapel has a fine marble iconostasis. If you continue straight where the summit path branches right, walk through the next intersection. You'll soon reach the church of Skafis, situated within the ruins of an old monastery and overlooking a small valley shaded by olive trees. Look for the remains of paintings on the walls of the ruined monastery, in what must have been a tiny chapel. Allow about 4 hours for the round-trip to Profitis Elias, with an additional half-hour for the detour to Skafis.

SHOPPING

Famed in antiquity for its riches, then for its ceramics, Sifnos now places its artistic pride in its pottery. Sifnian ceramics are exported throughout Greece; they're in wide use because of their durability and charming folk designs. In Kamares, **Antonis Kalogerou** (✆ 22840/31-651) sells folk paintings of island life and the typical pottery of Sifnos, which is manufactured in his showroom from the deep gray or red clay mined in the inland hill region. In Platis Yialos, **Simos and John Apostolidis** (✆ 22840/71-258) have a ceramics workshop. For those in search of distinctive jewelry rather than ceramics, Spyros Koralis's **Ble** (✆ 22840/33-055) in Apollonia does innovative work in silver and gold. As you stroll the town's winding back streets, you'll find several other contemporary ceramics galleries featuring the excellent work of Greek artisans.

WHERE TO STAY
APOLLONIA

The island's capital and one of its most beautiful villages, Apollonia is our recommendation as a base on Sifnos. Buses depart from the central square to most island towns, and stone-paved paths lead to neighboring villages. Keep in mind that many young Athenians vacation on Sifnos, particularly on summer weekends, when it can be virtually impossible to find a room. If you plan to be in Apollonia or Kamares during the high season, be sure to make reservations by May. If you're here during off season, many of these hotels are closed, although some do remain open year-round.

With advance notice, the efficient **Aegean Thesaurus Travel Agency** (see "Visitor Information," above) can usually place you in a room in a private house with your own bathroom, in a studio with a kitchenette, or in other, more stylish accommodations. A simple double costs from 70€ ($91) in high season. We especially recommend the following three choices, all run by friendly proprietors (none of whom speak English). On the outskirts of Apollonia in Ano Petali, **Eirini Geronti** (✆ 22840/32-316) rents rooms in her house. The view here is good, and the super-clean rooms open onto a terrace shaded by a grape arbor. The rooms offered by **Margarita Kouki** are perched high above town, a 10-minute walk up from Plateia Iroon; the view is fantastic, but this isn't the place to go if you're traveling with heavy bags. In Plati Yialos, **Stella Podola** (✆ 22840/71-261) has lovely rooms, many with their own courtyard or terrace, right on the beach.

Hotel Anthoussa This hotel is above the excellent and popular Yerontopoulos cafe and patisserie, on the right past Heroes' Square. Although street-side rooms offer wonderful views over the hills, they overlook the late-night sweet-tooth crowd and can be recommended only to night owls. Back rooms are quieter and overlook a beautiful bower of bougainvillea.

Apollonia, 84003 Sifnos. ✆ 22840/31-431. 15 units. 70€ ($91) double. MC, V. **Amenities:** Breakfast room. *In room:* A/C, TV.

Hotel Petali ★★ Not far—but all uphill—from Apollonia's main square, on a relatively quiet side street, the Petali has lovely views of the sea beyond the town's many houses. Furnished in Cycladic style, each guest room has a large terrace, handsome and comfortable chairs, good beds, and modern bathrooms. A small restaurant serves delicious Sifnian specialties. Although the Hotel Petali does not accept credit cards, its managing office, Aegean Thesaurus Travel Agency (© **22840/32-152;** www.thesaurus.gr), accepts MasterCard and Visa.

Apollonia, 84003 Sifnos. ©/fax **22840/33-024.** petali@par.forthnet.gr. 11 units. 130€–155€ ($169–$202) double. MC, V. **Amenities:** Restaurant; bar. *In room:* A/C, TV.

Hotel Sifnos ★★ The hospitable owners here have tried hard to make their hotel reflect island taste, using local pottery and weavings in the smallish but cheerful rooms. The hotel restaurant (see "Where to Dine," below) offers good basic meals beneath a broad arbor; it's just as popular with locals as it is with travelers and hotel guests.

Apollonia, 84003 Sifnos. © **22840/31-624.** 9 units. 90€ ($117) double. AE, MC, V. Usually open in winter. **Amenities:** Restaurant; bar. *In room:* A/C, TV.

KASTRO

Aris Rafeletos Apartments These traditional rooms and apartments are distributed throughout the medieval town of Kastro. Most have exposed ceiling beams, stone ceilings and floors, and the long narrow rooms typical of this fortified village. The two smallest units are somewhat dark and musty, but the three apartments are spacious and charming. All apartments have kitchenettes and terraces; three have splendid sea views. The largest apartment is on two levels and can comfortably sleep four. If the antiquity and charm of this hilltop medieval village appeals to you, then these accommodations may be the perfect base for your exploration of the island.

Kastro. ©/fax **22840/31-161.** 6 units. 80€–180€ ($104–$234) apts. No credit cards. The rental office is at the village's north end, about 50m (164 ft.) past the Archaeological Museum. **Amenities:** Breakfast room/bar. *In room:* Kitchenette in some units.

KAMARES

The port of Kamares has the greatest concentration of hotels and pensions on the island, but unfortunately, it has little of the beauty of Sifnos's traditional villages. Two moderately priced hotels that have been here a while are the 14-unit harborside **Hotel Stavros** and the 18-unit **Hotel Stavros,** a 10-minute walk from the beach and harbor (same name, different places!). Information on both is available from Stavros Kalogerou (© **22840/33-383**).

Hotel Boulis This newer hotel, capably managed by Lyn and Antonis Kalogerou (whom readers have praised for their helpfulness), is right on the port's beach. The large, carpeted rooms have balconies or patios, most with beach views; all have fridges and ceiling fans. The hotel has a spacious, cool, marble-floored reception area and a sunny breakfast room.

Kamares, 84003 Sifnos. © **22840/32-122.** Fax 22840/32-381. 45 units. 95€–130€ ($124–$169) double. Rates include breakfast. AE. Closed Oct–Apr. Follow the main street 300m (984 ft.) from the ferry pier, turning left opposite the Boulis Taverna (operated by the same family). The hotel is on your left. **Amenities:** Breakfast room/bar. *In room:* Fridge.

PLATIS YIALOS

A busy beach resort on the island's south coast, Platis Yialos serves as a convenient base for visiting the southern beaches. The town exists for tourism during high season. If Hotel Platis Yialos is full, try little Hotel Philoxenia (© **22840/71-221**), whose rooms have refrigerators; doubles cost from 89€ ($116).

Hotel Platis Yialos 🏖 *Kids*   The island's oldest hotel overlooks the beach on the west side of the cove, set apart from the rest of the town's densely populated beach strip. The hotel's location, on an excellent sand beach that slopes gently into the sea, and its popularity with families, makes this an ideal place to stay if you are traveling with young children; we speak from experience. Originally a government-owned Xenia hotel, its design is functional rather than beautiful. The ground-floor guest rooms, with patios facing the garden and water, are especially desirable; rooms on the upper stories have balconies. A suite contains flagstone floors, beamed ceilings, beds for up to six people, and two bathrooms, one with Jacuzzi; it opens to a small terrace with views of the bay. Frescoes and small paintings by a local artist are displayed throughout the hotel. The Platis Yialos's flagstone sun deck extends from the beach to a dive platform at the end of the cove. A bar and restaurant share the same Aegean views.

Platis Yialos, 84003 Sifnos. ℂ **22840/71-324,** or 2831/022-626 in winter. Fax 22840/71-325, or 2831/055-042 in winter. 29 units. 170€–220€ ($221–$286) double. Rates include breakfast. No credit cards. Closed Oct–Mar. **Amenities:** Restaurant; bar. *In room:* A/C, fridge.

WHERE TO DINE
APOLLONIA
If you want a snack, try **Vegera** or **Sifnos Café-Restaurant,** in Apollonia. Both serve breakfasts and sweets all day—and the island specialty of *revithia* (chickpeas) most Sundays.

To Troulaki 🏖 GREEK   With a pleasant flagstone courtyard and plants, just off Apollonia's main street, this little place serves up delicious island food. *Mastello,* melt-in-the-mouth lamb on vine leaves, has been slowly baked in a (local, of course!) earthenware pot.

Apollonia. ℂ **22840/32-362.** Main courses 6€–12€ ($7.80–$16). No credit cards. Lunch and dinner most days.

ARTEMONAS
To Liotrivi (Manganas) 🏖🏖 GREEK   One of the island's favorite tavernas is in the pretty village of Artemona, just over a mile's walk from Apollonia. Taste for yourself why the Sifnians consider Yannis Yiorgoulis one of their best cooks. Try his delectable *kaparosalata* (minced caper leaves and onion salad), *povithokeftedes* (croquettes of ground chickpeas), or *ambelofasoula* (crisp local black-eyed peas in the pod). The excellent Siphnian specialty of chickpeas *rivithia* is served on Sunday. In short, there're lots of vegetarian delights here, but there's also a very tasty beef filet with potatoes baked in foil.

Artemona. ℂ **22840/31-246.** Main courses 18€–86€ ($23–$112). No credit cards. Daily noon–midnight. From Apollonia, follow the pedestrian street north from Plateia Iroon, past Mama Mia and Hotel Petali; the walk takes a pleasant 10–15 min.

KAMARES
Boulis Taverna GREEK   With an unexceptional location at the top of the town's busy main street, this isn't the place to go for a romantic evening, but it does offer some of the best Greek food in town. The taverna is operated by Andonis Kalogerou of Hotel Boulis, who uses vegetables, cheeses, and meats raised on the organic family farm. The walls of the vast interior room are lined with wooden wine casks. Outside, lamb, chicken, and steak cook on the grill.

At the top of the main street through town. ℂ **22840/31-648.** Main courses 7€–15€ ($9.10–$20). No credit cards. Daily 11am–1am.

Moments A Special Feast

Prophet Elijah's feast day (between July 20 and 22) is one of the most important religious holidays on Sifnos, which has had a monastery dedicated to this saint for at least 800 years. The celebration begins with a mass outing to the monastery of Profitis Elias on the summit of the island's highest mountain, and continues through the night with dancing and feasting.

Kapitain Andreas SEAFOOD   This place, with its sometimes less-than-welcoming host, Andreas, who is both proprietor and fisherman, serves good food and grillls.
On the town beach. (*) 22840/32-356. Main courses 8€–15€ ($10–$20); fish priced by the kilo. No credit cards. Daily 1–5pm and 7:30pm–12:30am.

Poseidonas ★★ GREEK   The first restaurant you pass after disembarking is easily the best place to eat in Kamares: Sophia Patriarke and her daughters are hospitable to strangers and serve tasty grills, truly fresh salads, and fabulous *rivithokeftedes rena* (chickpea croquettes).
(*) 22840/32-362. Fish priced by the kilo. No credit cards. Daily 1–5pm and 7pm–midnight.

PLATIS YIALOS

Sofia Restaurant GREEK   Platis Yialos's best restaurant for Greek taverna fare is popular for its outdoor terrace and large wine list. For many in Apollonia, the casual seaside ambience warrants an evening out.
At the beach's east end. (*) 22840/71-202. Main courses 5€–18€ ($6.50–$23). No credit cards. Daily 9pm–1am.

SIFNOS AFTER DARK

In Apollonia, **Argo Bar** is one of the oldest establishments; it plays European and American pop music with some Greek tunes thrown in. **Isadora** and **Doloma** blast out jazz and rock music. In summer, the large **Dolphin Pub** becomes a lively nightspot; it closes for the season in mid-September. **Aloni,** on the road to Kastro, has traditional *rebetika* music many nights.

In Kamares at sunset, you can seek relative tranquillity near the beach at the picturesque **Old Captain's Bar.** Or join the yacht set drinking Sifnos Sunrises at the rival **Collage Club.** Later, **Mobilize Dance Club** and the more elegant **Follie-Follie,** right on the beach, crank up the volume for dancing.

For classical music, the **Cultural Society of Sifnos** sometimes schedules summer concerts in Artemonas.

4 Paros

168km (91 nautical miles) SE of Piraeus

Paros is accurately known as the "transportation hub" of the Cyclades: Almost all island boats stop here en route to someplace else. As a result, Paros unjustly suffers from the reputation of a place on the way to the place to which you are going. This overlooks the island's attractions, which include its appealing capital, inland villages of great charm, and excellent beaches. At present, Paros is cheaper than either Mykonos or Santorini—in fact, some call it the "poor man's Mykonos"—although rising prices are rapidly outdating that nickname. Comparisons aside, Paros's good beaches and nightlife have made it a very popular destination in its own right—and students of antiquity will be eager to see the island that supplied the famous Parian marble. The marble came from Mount Profitis Elias, the massive peak that dominates the island.

If possible, take a day or two to explore the island and visit its attractions. Paros is large enough that renting a car makes sense. Then, you can make an around-the-island tour that includes a morning visit to **Petaloudes (Valley of the Butterflies),** a visit to Lefkes, a stop for a good lunch in Naoussa, a swim at your beach of choice, and a night back in Parikia, where you can shop and stroll the evening away.

Admittedly, if you come by ship, your first impression will be of the travel agents, the cafes, and the not terribly enticing fast-food joints lining the harborfront. Take a few steps inland, and you'll be struck by the charms of **Parikia,** the lively capital, with its energetic marketplace and fine Byzantine cathedral (one of the three largest and oldest churches in the Greek islands). Although locals call the main shopping street the "agora," we refer to it here as "Market Street."

On the north coast, the fishing village of **Naoussa** has grown into a full-scale resort, and is almost as crowded as Parikia in July and August. The most popular Paros beaches are within easy commuting distance of Naoussa's hotels. The island's west coast has long stretches of fine sand, plus wind conditions that have made this the site of the World Cup windsurfing championship every year since 1993.

Head inland, and you'll find narrow, winding streets and lots of characteristic white sugar-cube Cycladic architecture. Charming **Lefkes,** set within the island's interior hills, has preserved many of its medieval buildings amid a maze of steep narrow streets. You can also walk on the well-preserved Byzantine road that takes off from Lefkes and runs for miles through Paros's gentle countryside.

ESSENTIALS

GETTING THERE   By Plane   Olympic Airways (© **210/966-6666** or 210/936-9111; www.olympic-airways.gr) has at least two flights daily between Paros and Athens; in Parikia, call © **22840/21-900** for flight information.

By Boat   Paros has more connections with more ports than any other island in the Cyclades. The main port, Parikia, has connections at least once daily with Piraeus by ferry (5–6 hr.) and high-speed ferry (3–4 hr.). Confirm schedules with the Athens **GNTO** (© **210/327-1300** or 210/331-0562); **Piraeus Port Authority** (© **210/459-3223** or 210/422-6000; phone seldom answered); or **Piraeus Port Police** (© **210/451-1310**). Daily ferry and hydrofoil service links Parikia with Ios, Mykonos (1½ hr.), Naxos (30 min.), Santorini (2½ hr. by hydrofoil, 4 hr. by car ferry), and Tinos (1½–3 hr.). Several times a week, boats depart for Folegandros (2 hr. by hydrofoil, 4 hr. by

---

Tips   Check Your Calendar

The Feast of the Dormition of the Virgin (Aug 15) is one of the most important religious holidays in Greece—and the most important, after Easter, in Paros. Pilgrims come here from throughout the Cyclades to attend services at the Panagia Ekatondapiliani, which is dedicated to the Virgin. If you come here then, make reservations well in advance, or you will probably find yourself sleeping rough. And on the subject of dates: If you want to visit Paros to see its famous butterflies, remember that they come here in May and June.

car ferry), Sifnos (1 hr. by hydrofoil, 3 hr. by car ferry), and Siros (1–4 hr.). There are daily excursion tours from Parikia or Naoussa (the north coast port) to Mykonos. There's also overnight service to Ikaria and Samos (7–10 hr.) four times a week. (From Samos you can arrange a next-day excursion to Ephesus, Turkey.) In high season, there's hourly caïque service to Andiparos from Parikia and Pounda, a small port 6km (4 miles) south of Parikia, with regular connection by bus. The east coast port of Piso Livadi is the point of departure for travelers heading to the "Little Cyclades." Ferries depart four times weekly for Heraklia, Schinoussa, Koufonissi, and Katapola.

For general ferry information, call **Santorineos Travel** in Parikia (© **22840/24-245**), or try the **port authority** (© **22840/21-240**). Many agents around Mavroyenous Square and along the port sell ferry tickets; schedules are posted along the sidewalk.

VISITOR INFORMATION There is a **visitor information office** on Mavroyenous Square, just behind and to the right of the windmill at the end of the pier. This office is often closed, but there are numerous travel agencies on the seafront, including **Santorineos Travel** (© **22840/24-245;** fax 22840/23-922; santorineos@travelling.gr) and **Paroika Tours** (© **22840/222-470**). The municipality information office in the Paraika town hall can be reached at © **22840/22-078**. The island has a helpful website: **www.parosweb.com**.

GETTING AROUND   By Bus   The **bus station** (© **22840/21-133**) in Parikia is on the waterfront, left from the windmill. There is hourly service between Parikia and Naoussa from 8am to midnight in high season. The other buses from Parikia run hourly from 8am to 9pm in two general directions: south to Aliki or Pounda, and southeast to the beaches at Piso Livadi, Chrissi Akti, and Drios, passing the Marathi Quarries and the town of Lefkes along the way. Schedules are posted at the stations.

By Car & Moped   Paros is large enough that renting a car makes sense. There are many agencies along the waterfront, and except in July and August, you should be able to bargain. **Iria Cars and Bikes** (© **22840/21-232**) and **Santorineos Travel** (© **22840/24-245**) get praise from travelers. Expect to pay from 50€ ($65) per day for a car and from 20€ ($26) per day for a moped.

By Taxi   Taxis can be booked (© **22840/21-500**) or hailed at the windmill taxi stand. Taxi fare to Naoussa with luggage should run about 10€ ($13).

FAST FACTS   The **American Express** agent is Santorineos Travel, on the seafront 100m (328 ft.) south of the pier (© **22840/24-245;** fax 22840/23-922; santorineos@travelling.gr). There are five **banks** in Parikia on Mavroyenous Square, and one in Naoussa; their hours are Monday through Thursday from 8am to 2pm, Friday from 8am to 1:30pm. The private **Medical Center of Paros** (© **22840/24-410**) is to the north of the pier, across from the post office; the public **Parikia Health Clinic** (© **22840/22-500**) is on the central square, down the road from the Ekatondapiliani Cathedral. **Internet access** is available on the Wired Network (www.parosweb.com) at eight locations around the island; you can buy a "smart card" that stores your personal settings and provides access at any of these locations for about 6€ ($7.80) per hour. The main location—often noisy and crowded—is in Parikia at the **Wired Cafe** on Market Street (© **22840/22-003**). **Cyber Cookies** (© **22840/21-610;** mrtigas@pathfinder.gr), just past the square with the ficus tree and Distrato Cafe on the nameless street that runs from the cathedral into Market Street, is much nicer and charges nothing for Internet use when you eat there. In 2004, my 4€ ($5.20) breakfast got me 45 minutes of free Internet access.

Tips   American Students Here?

The Aegean Center for the Fine Arts (www.aegeancenter.org) offers courses in painting, photography, music, creative writing, and other artistic endeavors in a 13-week session here from March to June. You'll see the teen and 20-something students all over Paroika and out on the island.

The **Laundry House** is on the paralia (shore road) near the post office (☎ **22840/24-898**). For the **police,** call ☎ **22840/100** or 22840/23-333. In Marpissa, call ☎ **22840/41-202;** in Naoussa, ☎ **22840/51-202.** The **post office** in Parikia (☎ **22840/21-236**) is left of the windmill on the waterfront road, open Monday through Friday from 7:30am to 2pm, with extended hours in July and August. Parikia's **telephone office (OTE;** ☎ **22840/22-135)** is just to the right of the windmill; its hours are 7:30am to 2pm. (If the front door is closed, go around to the back, as wind direction determines which door is open.) A branch in Naoussa has similar hours.

WHAT TO SEE & DO
THE TOP ATTRACTIONS

Archaeological Museum   The museum's most valued holding is a fragment of the famous Parian Chronicle, an ancient chronology. The Ashmolean Museum at Oxford University has a larger portion of the chronicle, which is carved on Parian marble tablets. Why is this document so important? Because it lists dates for actual and mythical events from Cecrops time (264–263 B.C.). Cecrops was the legendary first king of Athens, whose dates—indeed, existence—cannot be proven. Just to confuse and irritate historians, the chronicle gives information about artists, poets, and playwrights—but doesn't bother to mention many important political leaders or battles. The museum also contains a number of sculptural fragments as well as a splendid running Gorgon and a Winged Victory from the 5th century B.C. There's also part of a marble monument with a frieze of Archilochus, the important 7th-century-B.C. lyric poet known as the inventor of iambic meter and for his ironic detachment. ("What breaks me, young friend, is tasteless desire, lifeless verse, boring dinners.")

Parikia. ☎ **22840/21-231.** Admission 2€ ($2.60). Tues–Sun 8:30am–3pm. Behind the cathedral, opposite the playing fields of the local school. (Excellent toilet facilities.)

Marathi Marble Quarries   The inland road to Lefkes and Marpissa will take you up the side of a mountain to the marble quarries at Marathi, source of the famous Parian marble. Ancient sculptors prized Parian marble for its translucency and fine, soft texture, and they used it for much of their best work, including the *Hermes* of Praxiteles and the *Venus de Milo.* The turnoff to the quarries is signposted, and an odd, rather foolishly monumental path paved with marble leads up the valley toward (but not to) a group of deserted buildings and the ancient quarries. The buildings, to the right of the path, once belonged to a French mining company, which in 1844 quarried the marble for Napoleon's tomb; the company was the last to operate here. The quarry entrances are about 46m (150 ft.) beyond the marble path's end, on the left. The second, very wide quarry on the left has a 3rd-century-B.C. relief of the gods at its entrance, encased in a protective cage. In Roman times, as many as 150,000 slaves labored here, working day and night to the flickering lights of thousands of oil lamps. There isn't much to see today inside the quarries unless you're a spelunker at heart, in which case you'll find it irresistible to explore the deep caverns opened by the miners high above the valley. (Bring a flashlight, wear appropriate clothing, and don't explore alone.)

Marathi. Open site.

Panagia Ekatondapiliani Cathedral ★★   This is a magical spot. According to tradition, the Byzantine cathedral of Panagia Ekatondapiliani (Our Lady of a Hundred Doors) was founded by Saint Helen, the mother of Constantine the Great, the emperor whose conversion to Christianity led to its establishment as the official religion of the Roman Empire. Saint Helen is said to have stopped on Paros en route for the Holy Land, where the faithful believe that she found the True Cross. Her son fulfilled her vow to found a church here, and successive emperors and rulers expanded it—which may in part explain the church's confusing layout, an inevitable result of centuries of renovations and expansions. The work has not stopped: The cathedral was extensively restored in the 1960s, and the large square in front was expanded in 1996 for the church's 1,700th birthday.

A high white wall built as protection from pirates surrounds the cathedral; in the thickness of the wall are rows of monks' cells, which now house a small shop and small ecclesiastical museum. After you step through the outer gate, the noise of the town vanishes, and you enter a garden with lemon trees and flowering shrubs. Ahead is the cathedral, its elegant arched facade a memento both of the Venetian period and of classical times (several of the columns were brought here from ancient temples).

Inside, the cathedral is surprisingly spacious. Almost every visitor instinctively looks up to the massive dome, supported on vaults ornamented with painted six-winged seraphim. Take time to find the handsome icons, including several set in the iconostasis (altar screen), side chapels, and an elegant little 4th-century baptistery, with a baptismal font in the shape of a cross. In the arcade, the museum contains a small but superb collection of 15th- to 19th-century icons, religious vestments, and beautiful objects used in Orthodox Church ceremonies. Everything is labeled in Greek and in English.

The small shop, also in the arcade, features religious books and memorabilia, as well as books on Paros. Panayotis Patellis's *Guide Through Ekatontapiliani* (4€/$5.20) is both useful and charming. When you leave the cathedral precincts, turn left slightly uphill toward the Archaeological Museum for a fine view of the entire cathedral complex with its red-tile roofs.

Parikia. No admission fee for cathedral, although it is customary to leave a small offering. Daily 8am–8pm, but usually closed 2–5pm in winter. Museum ✆ **22840/21-243**. Admission 2€ ($2.60). Daily 10am–2pm and 6–9pm. On Parikia's central sq., opposite and north of the ferry pier.

The Valley of Petaloudes & Convent of Christou stou Dhassous ★   Another name for this oasis of plum, pear, fig, and pomegranate trees is Psychopiani (Soul

---

Finds The Ancient Cemetery

Ask at the Archaeological Museum for directions to Paros's ancient cemetery on the waterfront. Excavations here since the 1980s have revealed much about the island's history between the 11th century B.C. and the Roman period. Many of the graves contained the bones and weapons of warriors, often buried in handsome ceramic jars and marble urns, some of which are on view at the Archaeological Museum.

Softs). The butterflies, actually tiger moths *(Panaxia quadripunctaria poda)*, look like black-and-white-striped arrowheads until they fly up to reveal their bright red under-wings. They have been coming here for at least 300 years because of the freshwater spring, flowering trees, dense foliage, and cool shade; they're usually most numerous in early mornings or evenings in June. Donkey or mule rides from Parikia to the site along a back road cost about 10€ ($13). You can take the Pounda and Aliki bus, which drops you off at the turnoff to the nunnery; you'll have to walk the remaining 2.5km (1½ miles) in to Petaloudes. Be sure to scowl at any visitors who clap and shout to alarm the butterflies and make them fly. A small snack bar serves refreshments; men can wait here, while women visit the nearby Convent of Christou stou Dhassous, which does not welcome male visitors. (Cooling their heels in the courtyard, the men can think of visiting Mount Athos, which is forbidden to female visitors.)

Petaloudes. Admission 3€ ($3.90). Daily 9am–1pm and 4–8pm. Closed Oct–May. Head 4km (2½ miles) south of Parikia on the coast road, turn left at the sign for the nunnery of Christou stou Dhassous, and continue another 2.5km (1½ miles).

BEACHES

The beaches of Paros are small and overcrowded in comparison with those of nearby Naxos, but there is an abundance of sea sand and a few that are truly exceptional. One of the island's best and most famous, picturesque **Kolimbithres** ✦, is an hour's walk or a 10-minute moped ride west from Naoussa. It has smooth giant rocks that divide the gold-sand beach into several tiny coves. Of the few tavernas nearby, we recommend **Dolphin Taverna,** to the south, open from 7am to 2am, for traditional Greek food. North of the beach at Kolimbithres, by the Ayios Ioannis Church, is **Monasteri Beach,** with some nude sunning, and **Monasteri Club,** a bar/restaurant with music and beach service.

About 2.5km (1½ miles) north of Naoussa on an unimproved road is popular **Langeri Beach.** A 10-minute walk farther north will bring you to the nudist beach, with a gay and straight crowd. Before you reach Langeri, the road forks to the right and leads to **Santa Maria beach** ✦, one of the most beautiful on the island. It has particularly clear water and shallow dunes (rare in Greece) of fine sand along the irregular coastline. It also offers some of the best windsurfing on Paros. The nearby **Santa Maria Surf Club** (© 22840/52-490) provides windsurfing gear and lessons for about 20€ ($26) per hour. There's bus service to Santa Maria beach from Naoussa twice a day; caïque day trips from Naoussa are 10€ ($13) round-trip.

Southeast of Naoussa, connected by public bus, is the fishing village of **Ambelas,** which has a good beach and inexpensive tavernas.

Molos, at the tip of a small peninsula, is beautiful and convenient to the attractive inland villages of Marmara and Marpissa, where there are rooms to let, so the beach can sometimes get crowded.

The next major beach, **Chrissi Akti (Golden Beach)** ✦, a kilometer of fine golden sand, is generally considered the best beach on the island. It's also the windiest, although the wind is usually offshore. As a result, this has become the island's primary windsurfing center and has hosted the World Cup championship every year since 1993. Many overnight visitors head south to nearby **Drios,** a pretty village that is fast becoming a resort town, with hotels, luxury villas, and waterside tavernas. Buses run from Drios to Parikia five times daily, hourly in summer. **Aegean Diving School** (© 22840/92-071; www.eurodivers.gr) offers scuba instruction and guided dives here.

The next beach south of Drios, the often uncrowded **Loloantonis,** is about 200m (656 ft.) long and protected from *meltemi* winds by a rocky headland. The beach has a small taverna and a snack shop. If you take the bus, you'll have to walk in 1.5km (1 mile) along a gravel road, signposted from the Drios-Parikia road.

Just south of Aliki, on the south shore of the island, is beautiful, sheltered **Faranga Beach,** a short walk in from the main road.

TOWNS & VILLAGES

Until recently, the fishing village of **Naoussa** remained relatively undisturbed, with simple white houses in a labyrinth of narrow streets, but it's now a growing resort center with increasingly fancy restaurants, trendy bars, boutiques, and galleries. Most of the new building is concentrated along the nearby beaches, so the town itself retains its charm—but for how long? Colorful fishing boats fill the harbor, and fishermen calmly go about their work on the docks, all in the shadow of a half-submerged ruined Venetian minifortress—and, increasingly, tour buses. You can walk to a number of good beaches from town or catch a caïque to the more distant ones.

A handy causeway makes it easy to walk out to the Venetian fortress in the harbor; the remains are absurdly picturesque when illuminated at night. The best night of all to see the fortress is during the **festival** held each **August 23,** when the battle against the pirate Barbarossa is reenacted by torch-lit boats converging on the harbor. Much feasting and dancing follows.

Buses to Parikia leave the main square in Naoussa on the half-hour from 8:30am to 8:30pm, more frequently in July and August. Service to other villages on narrow dirt roads is infrequent (check the schedule at the station). There are daily excursion tours from Naoussa to Mykonos; inquire at any of the travel agencies in Parikia or here at any local travel agency, such as **Nissiotissa Tours** (© **22840/51-480;** fax 22840/51-189).

Hilltop **Lefkes** *⚜* is the medieval capital of the island. Its whitewashed houses with red-tile roofs form a maze around the central square, with its surprising *kafeneion* and imposing neoclassical facade. Lefkes was purposely built in an inaccessible location and with an intentionally confusing pattern of streets to thwart pirates. Test your own powers of navigation by finding **Ayia Triada (Holy Trinity) Church,** whose carved marble towers are visible above the town. The Lefkes Village Hotel is one of the nicest places on the island to stay (see "Where to Stay," below).

OUTDOOR PURSUITS

WALKING   Paros has numerous old stone-paved roads connecting the interior towns, many of which are in good condition and perfect for walking. One of the best-known trails is the **Byzantine Road** between Lefkes and Prodromos, a narrow path paved along much of its 4km (2½-mile) length with marble slabs. Begin in Lefkes, since from here the way is mostly downhill. There isn't an easy way to find the beginning of the Byzantine Road among the labyrinthine streets of Lefkes; we suggest starting at the church square, from which point you can see the flagstone-paved road in a valley at the edge of the town, to the west. Having fixed your bearings, plunge into the maze of streets and spiral your way down and to the right. After a 2-minute descent, you emerge into a ravine, with open fields beyond, and a sign indicates the beginning of the Byzantine Road. It's easy going through terraced fields, a leisurely hour's walk to the Marpissa Road, from which point you can catch the bus back to Parikia. Check the schedule and exact pick-up point beforehand. This also makes a challenging mountain-bike outing.

The Cave of Andiparos

To get away from all the crowds in Parikia, plan a visit to **Andiparos** (opposite Paros). This islet, about 1km (½ mile) off the western coast of Paros, was once connected to it by a natural causeway. Andiparos has begun to attract its own crowds—including jet-setters and movie stars—but this smaller, quieter island still has much to offer. A huge cave filled with fantastic stalactites was discovered on Andiparos during the time of Alexander the Great, and has been a compelling reason to visit ever since.

Excursion caïques leave the port of Parikia regularly (every 30 min. in summer) beginning at 9:45am for the 45-minute ride to the busy little port of Andiparos (2€/$2.60 one-way). A shuttle barge, for vehicles as well as passengers, crosses the channel between the southern port of Pounda and Andiparos continuously from 9am; the fare is 1€ ($1.30) or 5€ ($6.50) with a car; you can take along a bicycle for free. Some caïque excursions include a visit to the cave for about 12€ ($16); they depart from Parikia or Naoussa.

The impressive **cave** is a half-hour walk up from the boat landing or a 2-hour hike from the port of Andiparos; buses travel regularly between Andiparos and the cave (4€/$5.20 round-trip). From the church of Ayios Ioannis, you'll have an excellent view of Folegandros (farthest west), Sikinos, Ios, and part of Paros. Tourists once entered the cave by rope, but today's concrete staircase offers more convenient—if less adventuresome—access. The cave is about 90m (300 ft.) deep, but the farthest reaches are closed to visitors. Through the centuries, visitors have broken off parts of stalactites as souvenirs and left graffiti to commemorate their visits, but the cool, mysterious cavern is still worth exploring. An hour spent in the dark, echo-filled chamber trying to decipher some of the inscriptions offers a unique contrast to all your hours devoted to lying on a sun-drenched beach. You'll be in the company of such distinguished guests as Lord Byron and King Otto of Greece, who each left behind evidence of his visit. The Marquis de Nointel celebrated Christmas Mass here in 1673 with 500 paid attendants; he added explosions for drama.

Caves are very fragile ecosystems. Even one fingerprint can stop a stalactite's growth. Be respectful while you tour.

Andiparos town, with a permanent population of about 700, has several travel agents, a bank with limited hours, a post office, a telephone office (OTE), and an ATM. You'll find a plentiful selection of shops and tavernas along the harborfront, and inland is a fine **kastro,** the remains of the medieval fortified town.

If you decide to spend the night, plenty of places offer what are called "rent rooms"—but remember that here, as on Paros itself, rooms are hard to come by in high season. **Hotel Anaghyros** (© 22840/61-204) and **Hotel Mantalena** (© 22840/61-206; mantalenahotel@par.forthnet.gr) both offer doubles from 90€ ($117) and have rooms with views of the sea and port.

WINDSURFING   The continuous winds on Paros's east coast have made it a favorite destination for windsurfers. Golden beach has hosted the **World Cup** for the past 7 years. The best months are July and August, but serious windsurfers may want to visit earlier or later in the season to avoid the crowds. The free *Paros Windsurfing Guide* is available at most tourist offices in Parikia or Naoussa. On Golden Beach, **Sunwind Surf Center** ✸ (✆ **22840/42-900;** fax 22840/42-901; www.sunwind.gr) charges about 15€ ($20) for 1-hour rental of a board, sail, harness, and wet suit; instruction is an additional 6€ ($7.80) per hour. Reasonable rates for daily or weekly rental are available; Sunwind can assist in booking complete holiday packages as well. In Naoussa, you can rent equipment from **Club Mistral** (✆ **22840/52-010;** fax 22840/51-720), at Porto Paros Hotel near Kolimbithres Beach.

SHOPPING

Market Street in Parikia is the shopping hub of the island, with many interesting alternatives to the ubiquitous souvenir stores. Yvonne von der Decken's shop **Palaio Poleio** ✸ (✆ **22840/21-909**), opposite the Apollon Restaurant, has a fine selection of antique vernacular furniture and household items from the islands and the Greek mainland; it stays open all winter. **Ta Tsila Pou Efere O Notias (The Wood that the South Wind Brings)** ✸ (✆ **22840/24-669**) sells enchanting paintings on wood, some of which are done by Clea Hatzinikolakis, the talented co-owner of Hotel Petres (see "Where to Stay," below); you'll find the shop on the lane on the right just past Hotel Dina. **Audiophile** (✆ **22840/22-357**) has an extensive collection of CDs of Greek and international music, at prices a bit higher than you might pay in Athens.

Several shops that sell local produce, including cheeses, honey, and wine, all merit stars. **Pariana Proionta (Parian Produce)** ✸ (✆ **22840/22-181**), run by the Agricultural Collective, is on Manto Mavroyennis Square; **Topika Proionta (Local Produce)** ✸ (✆ **22840/24-940**) is on Market Street. **Distrato Café** ✸ (✆ **2284024-789**), on the unnamed street that runs from the cathedral to Market Street, has its own shop with organic produce from Paros and elsewhere in Greece. On the harbor, **News Stand** (no phone) sells international newspapers, guide books, maps, and some novels.

Across the island in the old part of Naoussa, **Metaxas Gallery** (✆ **22840/52-667**) holds exhibitions of paintings by local artists, which are sometimes for sale; you can also find locally crafted jewelry here. **Hera,** just down the lane from the **Naoussa Sweet Shop** (✆ **22840/53-566**), sells local pottery, jewelry, carpets from Greece and Turkey, and fine-arts books of local interest. Owner Hera Papamihail is a talented photographer whose prints are available for purchase. The **kiosk** on the main plateia has some international newspapers. **Paria Lexis Bookstore** (✆ **22840/51-121**) offers a selection of travel guides, maps, and novels.

In Lefkes, **Anemi** (✆ **22840/41-182**), by the *kafeneion* on the plateia, has handloomed and embroidered fabrics. In addition, nuns in several of the island's convents often sell crafts. **Market Street** in Parikia is the shopping hub of the island, with many interesting alternatives to the ubiquitous souvenir stores. At **Geteki** (✆ **22840/21-855**), you'll find paintings and sculpture by French artist Jacques Fleureaux, now a full-time resident of Paros. He makes use of local materials (clay and driftwood) and motifs (Cycladic figurines) in his work. Also for sale at Geteki are Afghani rugs and local ceramics by other artists.

WHERE TO STAY

PARIKIA

The port town has three basic hotel zones: **agora, harbor,** and **beach.** The agora is the heart of Parikia, and can get noisy; accommodations in the quiet back streets are most enticing. The harborside near the windmill is a convenient and lively place, but it's often too loud for a good night's rest. The strip of hotels along Livadi beach—north of the windmill, to the left coming from the ferry—have three common features: bland decor, proximity to the crowded town beach, and sea views.

Ignore the room hawkers at the port unless you're absolutely desperate—the rooms offered are usually a considerable distance from town, and many don't meet basic standards of comfort and cleanliness.

Captain Manolis Hotel ⭐   A tempting flower-covered entrance on Market Street by the National Bank leads into a passageway to this small hotel, with its own garden. Rooms have their own balconies, the lobby is perfectly pleasant, and friends who have stayed here praise the staff and say that they were astonished at the tranquillity of this hotel in the heart of Market Street. We were impressed every time we passed through the entrance, because someone was always sweeping and washing it.

Market St., Parikia, 84400 Paros. © **22840/21-244.** Fax 22840/25-264. 14 units. 85€ ($111) double. No credit cards. **Amenities:** Breakfast room. *In room:* A/C, TV, fridge.

Hotel Dina ⭐⭐ *Value*   This is a charming place run by a charming couple. More pension than hotel, it was renovated in 2003. You reach the cozy rooms through a narrow, plant-filled courtyard at the quiet end of Market Street. Dina Patellis has been the friendly proprietor for nearly 3 decades, and her personal touch keeps guests coming back year after year. Her husband wrote the excellent *Guide Through Ekatontapiliani,* available in local bookshops. Three bedrooms overlook Market Street (no. 2 has a balcony). The balcony in room no. 8 looks onto a quintessentially Greek blue-domed church across a narrow lane; the other rooms face a small garden courtyard. As always in Greece, bring ear plugs, in case people talk louder than you'd wish after you've gone to bed.

Market St., Parikia, 84400 Paros. © **22840/21-325** or 22840/21-345. Fax 22840/23-525. 8 units. 60€–75€ ($78–$98) double. No credit cards. The entrance is just off Market St., next to the Apollon Restaurant and across from the Pirate Bar. *In room:* A/C.

SOUTH OF PARIKIA

Hotel Iria ⭐ *Kids*   This new bungalow resort complex (completely renovated in 2003) is just too good to be ignored—and just the place to head for if you are traveling with young children. A playground, a pool—and a beach about 150m (492 ft.) away—make this an irresistible choice for families. The traditional architecture follows a villagelike plan, and while not all rooms have a sea view, the grounds are so beautifully landscaped that you won't feel deprived if your room faces inward. The staff has been praised as helpful.

Parasporos, 84400 Paros. © **22840/24-154.** Fax 22840/21-167. Info@yriahotel.gr. 68 units. 180€–250€ ($234–$325) double. Rates include full buffet breakfast. Lunch or dinner 20€ ($26). AE, DC, MC, V. Closed mid-Nov to Apr. Located 2.5km (1½ miles) south of the port. **Amenities:** Restaurant; bar; freshwater pool; tennis; concierge; car rental; laundry. *In room:* A/C, TV, minibar, hair dryer.

NAOUSSA

If you're unable to find a room, try **Nissiotissa Tours** (© **22840/51-480**), just off the east (left) side of the main square. You might also try the moderately priced **Captain**

Dounas Apartments (© **22840/52-525** or 22840/52-585; in winter 210/894-4047; fax 22840/52-586; dounas@par.forthnet.gr), located on a rocky promontory between Naoussa and Ayii Anaryiri Beach.

Astir of Paros ★★ The most extravagant hotel on the island is built like a self-contained Cycladic village within a luxurious garden, with a private beach, 3-hole golf course, good pool, tennis court, gym, and efficient staff. Double rooms are unexceptional, with simple bed, table, and chair. The spacious suites, however, have more personality, with armchairs, desks, and attempts at fancy window drapes. Four units are equipped for travelers with disabilities. Produce for the two hotel restaurants is grown on a nearby farm, and meals are particularly sumptuous—the breakfast buffet (not included in the room rates) features more than 70 items.

Kolimbithres Beach, 84401 Paros. © **22840/51-976** or 22840/51-707. Fax 22840/51-985. Astir@otenet.gr. 61 units. 200€–240€ ($260–$312) double; 210€–450€ ($273–$585) suite. Rates include continental breakfast. AE, DC, MC, V. Closed Oct 20–Easter. West of Naoussa, off the south end of the beach. **Amenities:** Restaurant; bar; freshwater pool; 3-hole golf course; tennis; health club; concierge; 4 rooms for those w/limited mobility. *In room:* A/C, TV, minibar, hair dryer.

Hotel Petres ★ Clea and Sotiris Hatzinikolakis combine warm hospitality with helpful efficiency to ensure that their guests' needs are met. The large, comfortable rooms, with private terraces or balconies, cluster around the big pool. Throughout, antiques and charming paintings, many done by Clea herself, give the Petres the charm and comfort so sadly lacking in most Greek hotels. The "honeymoon suite" contains Clea's grandmother's marriage bed. The extensive, inventive, and delectable buffet breakfast-brunch served from 9 to 11:30am may well be the highlight of your stay on Paros! Dinner is usually available on request; and most Saturdays in summer there's a barbecue at the poolside grill. The location, facing farm fields and the sea, is blissfully quiet; if you want to get into Naoussa, the hotel offers a frequent, free minibus shuttle. A floodlit tennis court, a state-of-the-art sauna and Jacuzzi, and spa services (massage, shiatsu, reiki, and aromatherapy) will tempt many. In short, the only drawback to the Petres is that its comforts may entice you to put off sightseeing until *aurio* (tomorrow).

Naoussa, 84401 Paros. © **22840/52-467.** Fax 22840/52-759. www.petres.gr. 16 units. 65€–110€ ($85–$143) double. Rates vary depending on location and length of stay and include extensive buffet breakfast. DC, MC, V. Closed Nov–Mar. 3km (5 miles) from town. **Amenities:** Breakfast room/bar; freshwater pool; tennis; Jacuzzi; sauna; airport/port pickup. *In room:* A/C, TV, minibar.

Papadakis Hotel ★ The new Papadakis offers the best views in town—enjoyed from every room as well as from the new pool with Jacuzzi. The large guest rooms were renovated in 1998, with new, dark walnut wardrobes, beds, and desks; some rooms also have sofa beds. The excellent breakfast includes homemade baked goods prepared by owner Argyro Barbarigou, who happens to be an incredible chef—be sure to visit her new venture, the Papadakis fish taverna (see "Where to Dine," below).

Naoussa, 84401 Paros. © **22840/51-269.** Fax 22840/51-269. 19 units. 75€ ($98) double. Breakfast 10€ ($13). No credit cards. A 5-min. walk uphill from the main sq. **Amenities:** Restaurant; bar; freshwater pool; Jacuzzi. *In room:* A/C, TV, minibar.

LEFKES

Lefkes Village Hotel ★★★ This handsome new hotel 10km (6 miles) from Parikia is designed to look like a small island village—admittedly, one with a pool and some rather imposing buildings! It helps that Lefkes is probably the most charming inland village on the island. The spectacular views reach across the countryside to the sea. The pool is so nice that you don't mind not being on the ocean. Guest rooms are light and bright, with good bathrooms; some have balconies. In addition to all the things you'd expect in a tasteful hotel, there's a small Museum of Popular Aegean Culture and a winery. A popular place for wedding receptions and honeymoons.

P.O. Box 71, Lefkes Village, 84400 Paros. ℂ 2284/041-827 or 210/251-6497. Fax 2284/41-0827. www.lefkesvillage. gr. 25 units. 150€–180€ ($195–$234) double. Rates include buffet breakfast. **Amenities:** Restaurant; bar; freshwater pool; Jacuzzi. *In room:* A/C, TV, minibar.

WHERE TO DINE
PARIKIA

We'll be interested in any reports on **Daphne** (ℂ 22840/22-575), just off Market Street on the unnamed street that runs to the cathedral; it's open for lunch and dinner in summer, dinner off season. When we ate here, everything (food, service) was pretentious to a fault, but we've since received good reports on the cuisine. Daphne's sometimes has a nightly special for 18€ ($23). That's good value for a starter, salad, main course, and sweet; unfortunately, since the same special is usually offered several consecutive nights, what you get is not always fresh.

Apollon Garden ⚘ GREEK   THE PLACE TO GO, THE PLACE TO BE SEEN says the business card, and while that may be true, this is also a place with a lovely garden and excellent food. You will find all the Greek standards here—stuffed vegetables in season, grills, stews—and the quality is consistently good.

Market St., Parikia. ℂ 22840/21-875. Main courses 7€–20€ ($9.10–$26). No credit cards. Daily 7pm–midnight. On Market St. just past the HOTEL DINA sign.

Bountaraki ⚘ GREEK   Many small details set this taverna apart from its neighbors: fresh brown bread that's refreshingly flavorful, and simple main courses that aren't overwhelmed by olive oil. There's a small porch in front, facing the quieter southern end of the paralia. As with all the local tavernas, don't bother with the desserts, which are clearly an afterthought.

Paralia (shore road). ℂ 22840/22-297. Main courses 6€–18€ ($7.80–$23). No credit cards. Daily 1–5pm and 7pm–midnight. At the southeast end of the waterfront, just over the bridge.

Distrato ⚘⚘ GREEK/INTERNATIONAL   On the street that runs from the cathedral to Market Street, beneath the spreading branches of a ficus tree, this is as nice a place as any to spend an hour or two, or an entire afternoon. Distrato serves crepes, sandwiches, ice creams, and inventive salads. If you're still hungry when you leave, the shop stocks nicely packaged organic Greek produce. (If there are no tables at Distrato, try **Symposio,** a few steps away, with tasty snacks but no shady tree.)

Paralia. ℂ 22840/22-311. Snacks and main courses 7€–12€ ($9.10–$16). No credit cards. Daily 10am–midnight. Look for the ficus tree as you walk from the cathedral to Market St.

Levantis ⚘ GREEK/INTERNATIONAL   This place gets high praise for its offbeat dishes that combine local produce with international ingredients. Where else on the island will you find Thai dishes alongside stuffed eggplant? Owner-chef George Mavridis likes to cook and likes to talk food, so you can enjoy what you eat while learning about the kitchen. The desserts are well worth saving room for, especially if you're a chocoholic. If you're too full for dessert, you can relax and enjoy the pleasant garden.

Paralia. ℂ 22840/23-613. Main courses 7€–18€ ($9.10–$23). AE, V. Daily 7pm–midnight. On Market St.

Porphyra ✦✦ GREEK/FISH   Locals say Porphyra serves the best fish in town. It's small, and the nondescript, utilitarian service and decor are typical of your average taverna. The difference here is that the owner cultivates the shellfish himself, resulting in an exceptional mussels Saganaki (mussels cooked with tomato, feta, and wine). The tzatziki and other traditional cold appetizers are also very good. The fish is predictably fresh, and offerings vary with the season. The same owners operate the nearby **Art Café;** drinks and snacks are served at the small gallery and cafe, which sometimes features live music.

Paralia. ✆ **22840/22-693.** Main courses 7€–18€ ($9.10–$23); fish priced by the kilo. AE, V. Daily 6:30pm–midnight. Closed Jan–Feb. Between the pier and the post office, just back from the waterfront.

NAOUSSA

Barbarossa Ouzeri ✦ GREEK   This longtime local ouzeri is right on the port. Wind-burned fishermen and gaggles of chic Athenians sit for hours nursing their milky ouzo in water and their miniportions of grilled octopus and olives. If you want more of a meal, this is a fine fish restaurant. If you wonder what language the staff here is speaking, it's often Arabic or Russian—more evidence that the world is indeed becoming a global village.

Naoussa waterfront. ✆ **22840/51-391.** Appetizers 2€–10€ ($2.60–$13). No credit cards. Daily 1pm–1am.

Christo's Taverna ✦ EURO-GREEK   Christo's has been here 25 years and is known for its eclectic menu and Euro-Greek style. A beautiful garden filled with red and pink geraniums serves as a backdrop for dinner. The color of the dark-purple grape clusters dripping through the trellised roof in late summer is unforgettable. Classical music soothes you as you dine on elegantly prepared veal, lamb, or steak.

Archilochus. ✆ **22840/51-442.** Reservations recommended July–Aug. Main courses 8€–18€ ($10–$23). No credit cards. Daily 7:30–11:30pm.

Le Sud ✦ GREEK/INTERNATIONAL   This very ambitious place, which opened in 2003, offers terrine of vegetables, bream with ginger, lamb with lemon and cardamom confit—and blinis. In short, although all the ingredients are fresh and almost all are local, the cuisine is eclectic. Try to reserve one of the handful of tables in the small garden; it's a good idea to call in advance in summer.

✆ **22840/51-547.** Main courses 15€–25€ ($20–$33). No credit cards. Daily 7pm–midnight. About 200m (656 ft.) back from the port.

Mitsi's ✦✦ GREEK/SEAFOOD   This is the sort of seafood taverna you dream about finding and will always remember. We stopped at this little place on the beach beyond the harbor one evening just to have an ouzo and watch the sun set—and left 4 hours later after a number of ouzos and a leisurely dinner of fresh greens, fresh fish, and something tasty that the *patron* called "grandmother's stew." When we sat down, we were the only customers; by the time we left, every table was taken, about half by locals, half by visitors to the island. The retsina wine, which the very engaging owner (Mitsi himself) makes, is terrific.

Harborside. ✆ **22840/51-302.** Main courses 8€–15€ ($10–$20); fish priced by the kilo. No credit cards. Daily 7pm–midnight.

Papadakis ✦ INNOVATIVE GREEK   Fresh fish is one of the specialties here, but be sure not to rush to the main course—the appetizers are admirable. Argyro Barbarigou is a truly imaginative chef, and the tzatziki with dill is delicious and refreshingly different;

> **Tips Beware the *Bomba***
>
> Several places on the strip in Parikia offer very cheap drinks or "buy one, get one free." What you'll get, most likely, is locally brewed alcohol that the locals call *bomba*. This speakeasy brew is made privately and often illegally. And our sources agree that it intoxicates you quickly—and makes you very sick for a long time afterward!

the traditionally prepared *melitzanosalata* is redolent of wood-smoked eggplant. The desserts are worth sampling, especially *kataifi ekmek,* a confection conjured from honey, walnuts, cinnamon, custard, and cream.

Naoussa waterfront. ✆ **22840/51-047.** Reservations recommended. Main courses 8€–30€ ($10–$39). AE, V. Daily 7:30pm–midnight.

Pervolaria ⭐ GREEK   There's something for everyone here. The restaurant is set in a garden, lush with geraniums and grapevines, behind a white stucco house decorated with local ceramics. There's pasta and pizza, and schnitzel a la chef (veal in cream sauce with tomatoes and basil). If you want to eat Greek, order the souvlaki and varied appetizers' special.

✆ **22840/51-598.** Main courses 6€–15€ ($7.80–$20). AE, V. Daily 7pm–midnight. About 100m (328 ft.) back from the port.

PAROS AFTER DARK

Just behind the windmill in Parikia is a local landmark, **Port Cafe,** a basic *kafenio* lit by bare incandescent bulbs and filled day and night with tourists waiting for a ferry, bus, taxi, or fellow traveler. The cafe serves coffee, pastry, and drinks; it's a good place for casual conversation.

Pebbles Bar ⭐ on the paralia plays classical music at sunset; it's a very congenial place, as popular with locals as it is with visitors.

If you're not in the mood to party, Parikia offers more elegant alternatives. **Pirate Bar** ⭐ (✆ **22840/21-114**), a few doors from Hotel Dina in the agora, plays mellow jazz, blues, and classical music. Back on the paralia, **Evinos Bar** has a great view of the harbor—it's above the retaining wall south of the OTE, high enough above the crowds that you can hear the music and enjoy the scenery. **Simple** is another rooftop place. **Alexandros** (✆ **22840/23-133**), in a restored windmill by the harbor, plays music that you can actually hear.

There seems to be little traditional Greek entertainment on Paros, but if you're interested, ask about performances by the local community dance group in Naoussa. They usually perform once each fortnight. You can get information and purchase tickets at **Nissiotissa Tours** in Naoussa (✆ **22840/51-480**).

Bars in Naoussa tend to be more sophisticated and considerably less raucous than those in Parikia. Try **Agnosto** (no phone) for an after-dinner drink. **Music-Dance Naousa** (✆ **22840/52-284**) often performs Greek dances; the group wears costumes and is very good. Look for posters around the island advertising upcoming performances.

5 Naxos

191km (103 nautical miles) SE of Piraeus

Green, fertile, largely self-sufficient Naxos has not needed to go all-out to attract tourists. This wealthy agricultural island exports an abundant harvest of olives, grapes, and potatoes throughout the Aegean, and only recently has begun to import tourists. A new airport and speedier inter-island travel have made it easier for visitors to get here. New hotels have appeared in the port, and more hotels cluster on island beaches.

Thankfully, the island's character hasn't been dominated by the recent development. The inland mountain villages, on the lower slopes of imperious Mount Zas, the highest mountain in all the Cyclades, preserve the rhythms of agrarian life. In Apiranthos, you can taste bread redolent with the smoky aroma of a wood oven, and in Filoti sample local wines beneath a venerable plane tree. The locals maintain a friendly indifference, which could be misconstrued as surliness by visitors who pass through.

The architecture of Naxos is distinct from that of any other Cycladic isle. The Venetians ruled this island from 1207 until the island fell to the Turks in 1566. Some descendants of the Venetians still live here. The influence of **Venetian architecture** is obvious in the Hora's Kastro and in the *piryi* (fortified Venetian towers) that punctuate the hillsides. Also specific to Naxos is the remarkable abundance of small **Byzantine chapels,** many of which contain exceptional frescoes dating from the 9th to the 13th centuries.

Naxos is very well connected to other islands by ferry, so you shouldn't have any trouble getting here at most times of the year. It's possible to catch a bus to a village that interests you, then explore it leisurely on foot; keep in mind that island buses are reliable but infrequent. A bike may be the only transport you need to get to the island's beaches, which happen to be among the best in the Cyclades.

ESSENTIALS

GETTING THERE   By Plane   Olympic Airways (© 210/966-6666 or 210/936-9111; www.olympic-airways.gr) has at least one flight daily between Naxos and Athens. For information and reservations on Naxos, call Olympic (see above); or visit **Naxos Tours,** toward the paralia's south end (© 22850/23-043; naxostours@naxos-island.com), the local representative for Olympic. A bus meets most flights and takes passengers into Naxos town (1€/$1.30).

By Boat   From Piraeus, there is at least one daily ferry (6 hr.) and one daily high-speed ferry (4 hr.). Check schedules at the Athens **GNTO** (© 210/327-1300 or 210/331-0562), **Piraeus Port Authority** (© 210/459-3223 or 210/422-6000; phone seldom answered), **Piraeus Port Police** (© 210/451-1310), or **Naxos Port Authority** (© 22850/22-300). There is at least once-daily ferry connection with Ios, Mykonos (1–2 hr.), Paros (30–60 min.), and Santorini (2–4 hr.). There is ferry connection several times weekly with Siros (1½–2½ hr. by high-speed ferry or hydrofoil), Tinos (2–4 hr.), and Samos (7 hr. to Vathi); and somewhat less frequently with Sifnos (1½ hr. by hydrofoil) and with Folegandros (3 hr.). For ferry tickets, try **Zas Travel** (© 22850/23-330), on the paralia opposite the ferry pier.

VISITOR INFORMATION   The privately operated **Naxos Tourist Information Center** (© 22850/25-201; fax 22850/25-200), across the plaza from the ferry pier, is the most reliable source of information and help. (Don't confuse it with the small office on the pier itself, which is often closed.) The center provides ferry information, books charter flights between various European airports and Athens, books accommodations, books cars and mopeds, arranges excursions, sells maps, exchanges money, holds luggage, assists with phone calls, provides 2-hour laundry service, and offers a **24-hour emergency number** (© 22850/24-525) for travelers on Naxos who need immediate assistance.

Naxos has an excellent website, **www.naxos-island.com**, with maps, bus schedules, hotel listings, and a photo tour of the island.

You will want to find a good map as soon as possible, as Hora (Naxos town) is old, large, and complex, with a permanent population of more than 3,000. The free *Summer Naxos* magazine has the best map of the city. The *Harms-Verlag Naxos* is the best map of the island, but it's pricey at 7€ ($9.10).

GETTING AROUND   By Bus   The bus station is in the center of the port plaza at the harbor's north end. Ask at the nearby KTEL office, across the plaza to the left, for specific schedules. Regular bus service is offered throughout most of the island two or three times a day, more frequently to major destinations. Bus schedules are posted at the station, and free schedules are sometimes available. In summer, there's service every 30 minutes to the nearby south-coast beaches at Ayios Prokopios and Ayia Anna. A popular day trip is to Apollonas, near the northern tip. In summer, the competition for seats on this route can be fierce, so get to the station well ahead of time. In addition to the public buses, excursion buses can be booked through travel agents. A day trip of the island usually costs about 20€ ($26).

By Bicycle & Moped   Moto Naxos (© 22850/23-420), on Protodikiou Square south of the paralia, has the best mountain bikes as well as mopeds for rent. A basic bike is about 6€ ($7.80) per day; aluminum-frame mountain bikes range from 8€ to 12€ ($10–$16) per day. For a moped, expect to pay from 20€ ($26) per day. Naxos has some major inclines that require a strong motor and good brakes, so a large bike (80cc or greater) is recommended.

By Car   It's a good idea to inquire first about car rental at the Naxos Tourist Information Center, which usually has the best deals. Car is the ideal mode of transport on this large island, and most travel agencies in Naxos town rent them, including **AutoTour** (© 22850/25-480), **Auto Naxos** (© 22850/23-420), and **Palladium** (© 22850/26-2000).

By Taxi   The taxi station (© 22850/22-444) is at the port. A taxi trip within Naxos town shouldn't cost more than 4€ ($5.20). The fare to Ayia Anna is about 8€ ($10); to Apiranthos, 18€ ($23).

FAST FACTS   Commercial Bank, on the paralia, has an ATM. It and other banks are open Monday through Thursday from 8am to 2pm, Friday from 8am to 1:30pm. Naxos has a good 24-hour **health center** (© 22850/23-333) just outside Hora on the left off Papavasiliou, the main street off the port. **Holiday Laundry,** on Periferiakos Road, Grotta area (© 22850/23-988), offers drop-off service; or you can leave your laundry with most hotels and some tourist offices. The **police** (© 22850/22-100) are beyond Protodikiou Square, by the Galaxy Hotel. The **telephone office (OTE)** is at the port's south end; summer hours are daily from 7:30am to 2pm. The **post office** is south of the OTE by the basketball court; it's opposite the court on the left, on the second floor (Mon–Fri 8am–2pm).

WHAT TO SEE & DO
THE TOP ATTRACTIONS

Kastro/Archaeological Museum/Venetian Museum ★★ The archaeological museum is located in the heart of the exquisite Venetian kastro, the medieval citadel that dominates the town. The kastro (castle) is Hora's greatest treasure, and you should allow yourself several hours to explore it. Built in the 13th century by Marco Sanudo, nephew of the doge of Venice, it was the domain of the Catholic aristocracy. By walking up from the seafront in Hora, you'll soon reach the outer wall of the castle, which has three entryways. The most remarkable of these is the north entry, known as the **Trani Porta (Strong Gate),** a narrow marble arched threshold marking the transition to the kastro's medieval world. Look for the incision on the right column of the arch, which marks the length of a Venetian yard, and was used to measure the cloth brought here for the ladies of the Venetian court. At the center of the kastro is the 16th-century **Catholic cathedral,** with its brilliant marble facade; it contains an icon of the Virgin that is thought to be older than the church itself. To the right behind the cathedral is the French School of Commerce and the former **Ursuline Convent and School,** where young ladies of the Venetian aristocracy were educated.

The French School has housed schools run by several religious orders, and among its more famous students was the Cretan writer Nikos Kazantzakis, who studied here in 1896. It now houses the **Archaeological Museum** ★. There have been many archaeological finds on Naxos, and this museum has a great diversity of objects from different periods. One of the highlights is the group of white marble Cycladic figurines, the earliest example of sculpture in Greece. The other prize of this museum is its collection of late-Mycenaean-period (1400 B.C.–1100 B.C.) artifacts found near Grotta, including vessels with the octopus motif that still appears in local art. The museum occupies long vaulted chambers in the walls of the kastro, with a great view from its terrace and balconies to the hills of Naxos. There is little in the way of interpretive information, and almost all of it is in Greek; serious museum-goers will appreciate the descriptive booklet available at the ticket desk for 5€ ($6.50).

The **Domus Venetian Museum,** located at the kastro's north entry, is a typical kastro house, home of the Della-Rocca family, recently opened to the public. The 40-minute tour, offered in English and Greek, is a wonderful chance to get an inside look at one of the surviving great Venetian homes and to learn about the island's Catholic aristocracy and the kastro. You'll probably want to spend half a day exploring these three sights.

Be sure to find out whether any concerts are being given in the Venetian Museum's garden while you are on Naxos. You can ask at the museum or at the Naxos Tourist Information Center; or keep an eye out for posters. If there is a concert, you may get to spend a pleasant evening listening to Greek music, a string quartet, or some jazz. Whatever you hear, the setting could not be nicer.

Hora. Archaeological Museum: ✆ **22850/22-725.** Admission 4€ ($5.20). Tues–Sun 8am–2:30pm. Venetian Museum: ✆ **22850/22-387.** Admission and tour 6€ ($7.80). Daily 10am–3pm and 6–10pm.

Mitropolis Site Museum This innovative new museum, located in the square facing Naxos town's Mitropolis Cathedral, preserves the open space of the square while providing access to the excavated archaeological site below. Excavations undertaken from 1982 to 1985 revealed a history of continuous occupation from Mycenaean times to the present, with significant remains of a classical shrine to the founders of the city buried beneath the remains of the Roman city. The museum, a single subterranean room circled by a suspended walkway, is sited inconspicuously beneath the surface of the square. You'll probably want to spend half an hour here.

Hora. ⓒ **22850/24-151.** Free admission. Tues–Sun 8am–2:30pm. Turn in from the paralia at Zas Travel and continue about 100m (328 ft.) until you see the Mitropolis Cathedral Sq. on your right.

The Portara   Naxos harbor is dominated by the picturesque silhouette of the Portara (Great Door) on the islet of Palatia, which is accessible by a causeway off the harbor's northern tip. The massive door is all that remains of an obviously enormous Temple of Apollo. In fact, this 6th-century-B.C. temple was intended to be so huge that it was never finished. People once thought the temple honored Dionysos, the island's patron, and it is associated in the popular imagination with his rescue of Ariadne after she was abandoned on Naxos by the ungrateful Theseus. Most scholars think that the temple was in fact dedicated to Apollo, in part because of a brief reference in the Delian Hymns and in part because it directly faces Delos, Apollo's birthplace. Over the centuries, most of the temple was carted away to build other monuments and buildings, including Naxos's Venetian kastro. Fortunately, the massive posts and lintel of the Portara were too heavy for the Venetians to handle. Each of the four surviving blocks in the gates weighs about 20 tons.

Note: When the midday sun is blazing, the causeway by the Portara is not a place to linger. But at sunset, **Palatia,** the small cafe/ouzeri at the end of the causeway, below the Portara, is a superb spot from which to watch the sky.

Hora. Open site.

Sangri & the Temple of Demeter   Until about 10 years ago, the temple, built in the 6th century B.C., was in a state of complete ruin; it had been partially dismantled in the 6th century A.D. to build a chapel on the site, and what was left was plundered repeatedly over the years. Then, it was discovered that virtually all the pieces of the original temple were on the site, either buried or integrated into the chapel. A long process of reconstruction began. Most of the work has been completed, and it's possible to see the basic form of the temple—one of the few known square-plan temples.

Temple of Demeter at Ano Sangri. Free admission. Depart from Hora on the road to Filoti, and after about 10km (6 miles), turn onto the signposted road to Ano Sangri and the Temple of Demeter. From here it's another 3.5km (2 miles) to the temple, primarily on dirt roads (major turns are signposted).

BYZANTINE CHURCHES

The remarkable number of small Byzantine chapels on Naxos mostly date from the 9th to the 15th centuries, many in or near some of the island's loveliest villages (see below). The prosperity of Naxos during this period of Byzantine and Venetian rule meant that sponsorship existed for elaborate frescoes, many of which can still be seen on the interior walls of the chapels. Restoration has revealed multiple layers of frescoes and, whenever possible, the more recent ones have been removed intact during the process of revealing the initial paintings. Several frescoes removed in this way from the churches of Naxos can be seen at the Byzantine Museum in Athens. Anyone with a particular interest in Byzantine churches (of which we mention only a few) would enjoy Paul Hetherington's *The Greek Islands: Guide to the Byzantine and Medieval Buildings and their Art.*

Just south of Moni, near the middle of the island, is the important 6th-century monastery of **Panagia Drossiani (Our Lady of Refreshment)** ✦, which contains some of the finest—and oldest, dating from the 7th century—frescoes on Naxos. Locals believe the icon of the Virgin ended a severe drought on the island shortly after the frescoes were painted. The church is all that survives of what we are told was an extensive monastery; what an appealing place to have led a contemplative life! Visits are allowed at all hours during the day; when the door is locked, ring the church bell to summon the caretaker (remember to dress appropriately). To get here, drive about 1km (½ mile) south from Moni and look for the low, gray, rounded form of the church on your left.

About 8km (5 miles) from Hora along the road to Sangri, you'll see a sign on the left for the 8th-century Byzantine cathedral of **Ayios Mamas,** which fell into disrepair during the Venetian occupation but has recently been partly restored. The **view** alone from this charming church *vaut le voyage!* Sangri (the Greek contraction of Sainte Croix) today is made up of three villages, and includes the ruins of a medieval castle. The church of Ayios Nikolaos, which dates to the 13th century, has well-preserved frescoes, with a lovely figure of the personified River Jordan. To view them, ask around to find out which villager has the keys.

About 1km (½ mile) west of Sangri, on the road to Halki, is **Kaloritsa Chapel** ✦, a cave inside the hilltop ruins of a Byzantine chapel. The earliest of the frescoes you can see here date from the 10th century. The chapel is accessible only on foot.

You can spend a week seeing the Byzantine churches of Naxos; or you can see a handful in a day. Getting to each one involves at least some walking. In order to see the interiors, allow time to find the caretaker. The churches are kept locked, due to increasing theft, although the caretaker often makes an early-morning or early-evening visit.

THE VILLAGES

There are many small villages within the folds of Naxos's hills. Many of the nicest are in lush **Tragaea Valley** ✦ at the center of the island. Each village is unique, and you can easily spend several days exploring them. The bus between Hora and Apollonas makes stops at each of the villages mentioned below, but you'll have considerably more freedom if you rent a car.

Halki, 16km (10 miles) from Hora, has a lovely central square shaded by a magnificent plane tree. The 19th-century neoclassical homes of this town lend the streets a certain grandeur. The fine 11th-century white church with the red-tiled roof, **Panagia Protothronos (Our Lady Before the Throne),** is sometimes open in the morning. Turn right to reach the **Frankopoulos (Grazia) Tower.** The name is Frankish, but it was originally Byzantine; a marble crest on the tower indicates 1742, when it was renovated by the Venetians. Climb the steps for an excellent view of Filoti, one of the island's largest inland villages.

The brilliant white houses of **Filoti,** 2km (1 mile) up the road from Halki, elegantly drape the lower slopes of **Mount Zas,** the highest peak in the Cyclades. The center of town life is the main square, shaded like Halki's square by a massive plane tree. The *kafenion* at the center of the square and two tavernas within 50m (164 ft.) are all authentic and welcoming. In the town's center, the church of **Kimisis tis Theotokou (Assumption of the Mother of God)** has a lovely marble iconostasis and a Venetian tower.

Apiranthos ✦, 10km (6 miles) beyond Filoti, the most enchanting of the mountain villages, is remarkable in that its buildings, streets, and even domestic walls are built of the brilliant white Naxos marble. The people of Apiranthos were originally from Crete; they fled their homes during a time of Turkish oppression. Be sure to visit **Taverna Lefteris,** the excellent cafe/restaurant just off the main square (see "Where to Dine," below).

Tips **Remember the Repellent**

Note that both Ayios Prokopios and Ayia Anna have mosquito problems in the summer, due to several stagnant ponds behind the beaches that serve as breeding grounds.

Apollonas, at the northern tip of the island, is a small fishing village on the verge of becoming a rather depressing resort. It has a sand cove, a pebbled beach, plenty of places to eat, rooms to let, and a few hotels. From the town, you can drive or take the path that leads about 1km (½ mile) south to the famous **kouros** (a monumental statue of a nude young man). The kouros, about 10m tall (33 ft.), was begun in the 7th century B.C. and abandoned probably because of the fissures exacerbated by time and the elements. Some archaeologists believe the statue was meant for the nearby temple of Apollo, but the kouros's beard suggests that it's Dionysos. Naxos's other kouros is in the village of **Flerio,** about 7km east of Naxos town. The 8m (26-ft.) kouros lies abandoned in a lovely garden yet is still admired by visitors. Both kouroi sites are open to the public and free; in Flerio you can sip refreshments (including the local *kitron,* a lemon liqueur) served at the cafe run by the family that owns the garden. When you visit the National Museum in Athens, you can view a number of successfully completed kouroi statues.

BEACHES

Naxos has the longest and some of the best beaches in the Cyclades, although you wouldn't know it from crowded **Ayios Yioryios** beach just south of Hora. The next beach south, **Ayios Prokopios,** around the headland of Stellida, is a fine-sand beach that is less crowded at its northern end. **Ayia Anna,** the next cove south, is much smaller, with a small port for the colorful caïques that transport beachgoers from the main harbor. Both Ayios Prokopios and Ayia Anna are accessible by public bus in the summer.

South of Ayia Anna, you'll find **Plaka beach**★, the best on the island, a 5km (3-mile) stretch of almost uninhabited shoreline; reach it by walking south from Ayia Anna. Farther south, 16km (10 miles) from Hora, are **Micri Vigla,** known for its windsurfing center; and 7km-long (4½-mile) **Kastraki Beach,** with waters rated the cleanest in the Aegean several years ago. Both remain relatively uncrowded, even in peak season. Farther still, 21km (13 miles) from Hora, **Pyrgaki,** the last stop on the coastal bus route, offers excellent swimming in the large protected bay.

SHOPPING

Hora is a fine place for shopping, both for value and variety. **Zoom** (© 22850/23-675), on the waterfront, is the place to head for books and magazines. To the right and up from the entrance to the Old Market is **Techni** ★ (© 22850/24-767), which has two shops within 20m (66 ft.) of each other. The first shop contains a good array of silver jewelry at fair prices; farther along the street, the second and more interesting of the two features textiles, many handwoven (including some antiques) by island women.

On the paralia next to Grotta Tours is tiny **Galini** (© 22850/24-785), with a collection of local ceramics. Continue south along the paralia to the OTE, turn left on the main inland street, Papavasiliou, and proceed up the left side of the street until your nose leads you into **Tirokomika Proïonda Naxou** ★ (© 22850/22-230). This delightful old store is filled with excellent local cheeses (*kephalotiri,* a superb sharp cheese, and milder *graviera*), barrels of olives, local wines, honey, spices, and dried comestibles. It's a good place to pick up a bottle of *kitron,* the island's famous sweet citron liqueur.

In the kastro itself, **Antico Veneziano** ★ (© **22850/26-206**) has just that— antiques from the island's Venetian period—as well as glassware, woodcarvings, and old weavings from throughout Greece. This is a lovely place to browse; it's in a handsome Venetian-period house.

In the interior of Naxos, on the stretch of road between Sangri and Halki, you'll see a sign pointing toward **Damalas Pottery Workshop** (© **22850/32-890**); 200m (656 ft.) farther along the one-lane road lies the small workshop, operated by a father-and-son team. The father learned his trade on Sifnos, an island renowned for its pottery, and now father and son produce a variety of forms, some of them specific to Naxos.

WHERE TO STAY

Hora's broad paralia is too busy for quiet accommodations, so we recommend hotels in nearby areas, all within a 10-minute walk of the port: Bourgo, the old section of town just above the harbor below the kastro; Grotta, a development of newer houses north and up from the port, behind the town; and Ayios Yioryios, a beach resort just south (right from the harbor) of town.

BOURGO

Apollon   What more appropriate spot to stay, on an island famous for its marble, than in a former marble workshop—one that has taken advantage of its quiet location and been transformed into a small, tasteful hotel? The tidy rooms have balconies (always a big plus) and are simply but tastefully furnished, with twin beds, a table, and chair. Although there is no garden to speak of, there are plants everywhere. In short, Apollon offers welcoming lodging in Naxos town—just behind the imposing Orthodox Cathedral.

Fontana, Hora, 84300 Naxos. © **22850/22-468**. 12 units. 90€–110€ ($117–$143) double. Rates include breakfast. No credit cards. Closed Nov–Mar. **Amenities:** Breakfast room/bar. *In room:* A/C.

Chateau Zevgoli ★   This small hotel, easily the most attractive in Naxos, lies at the foot of the 13th-century kastro walls. The gracious owner, Despina Kitini, decorated the charming lobby and dining area with antiques and family heirlooms. All guest rooms open onto a central atrium with a lush garden. The units are small but distinctively furnished with dark wood and drapes. Room no. 8, for example, features a canopy bed and a private terrace. Several rooms have views of the harbor. Ms. Kitini also rents four apartments in her house, also within the kastro walls and only 100m (328 ft.) from the hotel. These share a large, central sitting room; throughout are

---

(*Tips*   **Walking Tours**

If you're going to spend some time on the island, we recommend buying a copy of Christian Ucke's excellent guide, *Walking Tours on Naxos.* You can take an island bus to reach most of the start and finish points for the walks. It's available for 15€ ($20) at **Naxos Tourist Information Center** on the paralia. As with all off-the-beaten-track walks, be equipped with water, a hat, good shoes, sunblock, a map, a compass—and a good sense of direction.

handsome stone walls and floors. The honeymoon suite has a balcony overlooking the town and the sea. Ms. Kitini also sometimes has studios for rent in town, often at excellent long-term rates.

Bourgo, Hora, 84300 Naxos. ✆ **22850/22-993** or 22850/26-123. Fax 22850/25-200. www.greekhotel.net/cyclades/naxos/chora/zevgoli. 14 units. 90€–110€ ($117–$143) double. Hotel rates include breakfast. AE, MC, V. Closed Nov–Mar. **Amenities:** Breakfast room/bar. *In room:* A/C.

Hotel Anixis　　This simple hotel near the kastro's Venetian tower offers comfortable accommodations in a desirable old neighborhood of Hora. Located on a narrow pedestrian street, the entrance leads you through a small walled garden to a terrace overlooking town and sea. The rooms on the top floor have the best views of the sea, and six of them have their own small balconies. The breakfast terrace enjoys a splendid sea view. If you make advance arrangements, the helpful manager, Dimitris Sideris, will meet you at the port and drive you to the base of the hill—you'll still have to walk the last 100m (328 ft.) up to the hotel!

Bourgo, Hora, 84300 Naxos. ✆ **22850/22-932,** or 22850/22-782 in winter. Fax 22850/22-112. 19 units. 80€ ($104) double. Continental breakfast 6€ ($7.80). V. Closed Oct–Mar. From the bus station, take the nearest major street (with traffic) off the port and turn right through the lancet archway into the Old Market area; follow the stenciled blue arrows to the hotel. **Amenities:** Breakfast room/bar. *In room:* A/C.

AYIOS YIORYIOS

If the following choices are booked, you can try the unexciting but reliable **Galaxy Hotel,** 75m (246 ft.) from the beach at Ayios Yioryios (✆ **22850/22-422** or 22850/22-423; fax 22850/22-889). Some rooms have balconies or terraces facing the water.

Hotels Galini and Sofia ✮　　The hotels Galini and Sofia share the same building, the same friendly management, and the same sea views. In fact, they represent the curious phenomenon of one hotel with two names. There are some differences: The Sofia's guest rooms are decorated in bright pastels, while those in the Galini are a more conservative white. All but two unfortunate units on the interior courtyard have balconies with excellent sea views; the views from room nos. 11 and 14 are especially good. Transportation is provided to and from the port if you make arrangements in advance. There's a small playground for children.

Ayios Yioryios, Hora, 84300 Naxos. ✆ **22850/22-516** or 22850/22-114. Fax 22850/22-677. www.naxos-island.com/hotels/galini. 30 units. 90€ ($117) double. Breakfast 6€ ($7.80). AE, V. Closed Nov–Mar. **Amenities:** Breakfast room/bar; pool. *In room:* A/C, TV.

OUT ON THE ISLAND

We recommend planting yourself in or near Hora and discovering its charms at your own pace. If you do want to head out on the island, check **Orkos Village Hotel** ✮ (✆ **22850/75-321;** www.orkos-naxos.com), a 28-unit apartment complex (mostly bungalows) constructed to suggest a small Cycladic village. Many units have sleeping lofts; all have fully equipped kitchenettes and balconies. Run by a Norwegian, the hotel has a small library, its own excellent restaurant, and a location only 100m (328 ft.) from the beach. No wonder many guests return here year after year. Doubles cost from 90€ ($117); reductions for long stays.

WHERE TO DINE
HORA

The Bakery, on the paralia (✆ **22850/22-613**), sells baked goods at fair prices. Farther north, across from the bus station, **Bikini** (✆ **22850/24-701**) is a good place for breakfast and crepes. **Meltemi** (© **22850/22-654**) and **Apolafsis** (© **22850/22-178**) on the waterfront both offer all the Greek staples; Apolafsis also features live music many nights in summer.

Nikos GREEK   This is one of the most popular restaurants in town. The owner, Nikos Katsayannis, is a fisherman, and the range of seafood available will amaze you. Those not in the mood for fish can try the *eksohiko*, fresh lamb and vegetables with fragrant spices wrapped in crisp filo (pastry leaves). The wine list is quite long, with lots of local and Cyclades choices. The ice-cream desserts are delightful.

Paralia, above Commercial Bank. © **22850/23-153**. Main courses 6€–14€ ($7.80–$18); fish priced by the kilo. MC, V. Daily 8am–1am.

The Old Inn ⭐ INTERNATIONAL   Dieter Ranizewski, who operated for many years the popular Faros Restaurant on the paralia, now runs this place. The courtyard offers a green haven from the noise and crowds of the paralia. The restaurant, once a small monastery, inhabits several buildings surrounding a courtyard. The wine cellar is situated in a former chapel. Another vaulted room houses an eclectic collection of old objects from the island and from Dieter's native Berlin. The Germanic menu (this is one of relatively few places in the Cyclades where you can get jellied or smoked pork) offers an alternative to standard taverna fare. The food is simple, hearty, and abundant.

© **22850/26-093**. Main courses 8€–20€ ($10–$26). AE, DC, MC, V. Daily 6pm–2am. 100m (328 ft.) in from the port.

Taverna To Kastro GREEK   Just outside the kastro's south gate, you'll find small Braduna Square, which is packed with tables on summer evenings. There's an excellent view toward the bay and St. George's beach, and at dusk a pacifying calm pervades the place. The specialty here is rabbit stewed in red wine with onions, spiced with pepper and a suggestion of cinnamon. The local wines are light and delicious.

Braduna Sq. © **22850/22-005**. Main courses 6€–15€ ($7.80–$20). No credit cards. Daily 7pm–2am.

APIRANTHOS

Taverna Lefteris ⭐ GREEK   Find your way to Apiranthos, perhaps the most beautiful town in Naxos, where you'll experience one of the island's best restaurants. The small menu features the staples of Greek cooking, prepared in a way that shows you how good this food can be. The dishes highlight the freshest of vegetables and meats, prepared with admirable subtlety; the hearty homemade bread is delicious. A cozy marble-floored room faces the street, and in back is a flagstone terrace shaded by two massive trees. The homemade sweets are an exception to the rule that you should avoid dessert in tavernas—the trip here is worth making for the sweets alone.

Apiranthos. © **22850/61-333**. Main courses 6€–10€ ($7.80–$13). No credit cards. Daily 11am–11pm.

NAXOS AFTER DARK

Naxos certainly doesn't compare with Mykonos or Santorini for wild nightlife, but it has a lively and varied scene. **Portara,** just below its namesake at the far end of the harbor, is an excellent place to enjoy the sunset. Next, you can join the evening **volta** (stroll) along the paralia. **Fragile** (© **22850/25-336**), through the arch in the entrance to the Old Town, is one of the older bars in town and worth a stop. Up in the kastro, **Notos** offers a sedate evening with mellow jazz.

Day and Night, opposite the OTE, plays a good blend of music that becomes more purely Greek in the early morning. At the end of the waterfront past the National Bank, you'll find **Veggera** (© **22850/23-567**), which doesn't open until 9pm and doesn't get warmed up until much later. Its neighbor, **Cream** (no phone) tries to break existing island records for high decibel levels. **Naxos By Night,** on the way to the beach from Protodikiou Square, showcases *bouzouki* music and dancing. **Super Island** (no phone) gives it stiff competition.

6 Mykonos (Mikonos)

177km (96 nautical miles) SE of Piraeus

If you haven't been to Mykonos (pop. 15,000) for a number of years, you'll probably wander around muttering "ruined" when you arrive. But once you're away from the shops, bars, and restaurants along the harbor, many of the twisting back streets seem familiar. You might even admit that it's not half bad to have such a wide choice of restaurants, shops, and bars. If this is your first visit, you'll find lots to enjoy—especially if you avoid July and August, when it seems that every one of the island's 800,000 annual visitors is here.

What makes this small (about 16km/10 miles long), arid island so popular? At least initially, it was the exceptionally handsome Cycladic architecture—and the willingness of many homeowners to rent their houses to visitors. First came the jet-setters, artists, and expatriates (including many sophisticated gay visitors), as well as the mainland Greeks who opened many of the chic shops and restaurants. This wave of visitors was followed by a curious mixture of jet-set wannabes and backpackers. Now, with cruise ships lined up in the harbor all summer and as many as 10 flights each day from Athens, it's easier to say who doesn't come to Mykonos than who does. During high season, the overcrowding is truly overwhelming. The best way to avoid the crowds is to get up early, visit the beaches before noon, and explore the streets of Hora in the late afternoon, when almost everyone in town wakes up and heads for the beach. Mykonos is one of the only islands in the Aegean where scuba diving is permitted; several dive centers rent equipment and offer instruction.

It's **very** important not to arrive here without reservations in the high season, unless you enjoy sleeping outdoors and don't mind being moved from your sleeping spot by the police, who are not always charmed to find foreigners alfresco.

If you come here in September or October, you'll find a quieter Mykonos, with a pleasant buzz of activity, and streets and restaurants that are less clogged. Unlike many of the islands, Mykonos remains active year-round. In winter it hosts numerous cultural events, including a small film festival. Many who are scared off by the summer crowds find a different, tranquil Mykonos during this off season, demonstrating Hora's deserved reputation as one of the most beautiful towns in the Cyclades.

ESSENTIALS

GETTING THERE   By Plane   Olympic Airways (© 210/966-6666 or 210/ 936-9111; www.olympic-airways.gr) has several flights daily (once daily in off season) between Mykonos and Athens, and one flight daily from Mykonos to Iraklion (Crete) and Santorini. Book flights in advance and reconfirm with Olympic in Athens or on Mykonos (© 22890/22-490 or 22890/22-237). The Mykonos office is near the south bus station; it's open Monday through Friday from 8am to 3:30pm. Travel agencies on the port sell Olympic tickets as well. **Aegean Airlines** (© 210/998-8300 or 210/998-2888; www.aegeanair.com) has initiated service to Mykonos, daily in summer.

By Boat   Mykonos now has two ports: the old port in Mykonos town, and the new port north of Mykonos town at Tourlos. Check before you travel to find out which

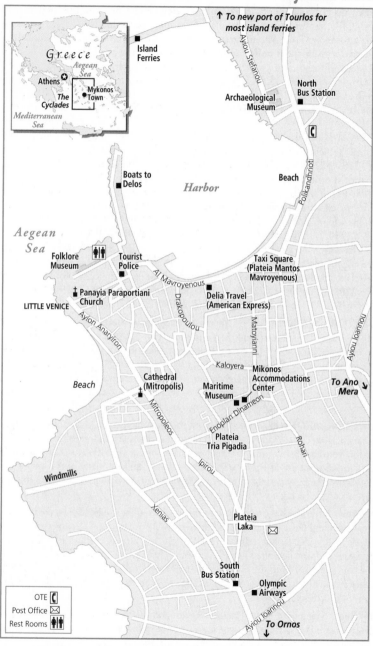

Mykonos Town

To new port of Tourlos for most island ferries ↑

Island Ferries

Greece

Aegean Sea

Athens

The Cyclades

Mykonos Town

Mediterranean Sea

Archaeological Museum

North Bus Station

C

Harbor

Boats to Delos

Beach

Polikandhrioti

Aegean Sea

Folklore Museum

Tourist Police

Ayiou Stefanou

Taxi Square (Plateia Mantos Mavroyenous)

Al Mavroyenous

Drakopoulou

Delia Travel (American Express)

Panayia Paraportiani Church

LITTLE VENICE

Ayion Anaryiron

Matoyianni

Kaloyera

Mikonos Accommodations Center

To Ano Mera ↘

Beach

Cathedral (Mitropolis)

Maritime Museum

Enoplan Dinameon

Ayiou Ioannou

Mitropoleos

Plateia Tria Pigadia

Rohari

Ipirou

Windmills

Xenias

Plateia Laka

✉

South Bus Station

Olympic ■ Airways

Ayiou Ioannou

To Ornos ↓

OTE C
Post Office ✉
Rest Rooms 👫

283

port your boat will use. From Piraeus, **Ventouris Lines** (© 210/482-5815 or 210/482-8001) has departures at least once daily, usually at 8am, with a second on summer afternoons. From Rafina, **Strintzis Lines** has daily ferry service; schedules can be checked with the **port police** (© 22890/22-218). There are daily ferry connections between Mykonos and Andros, Paros, Syros, and Tinos; five to seven trips a week to Ios; four a week to Iraklio, Crete; several a week to Kos and Rhodes; and two a week to Ikaria, Samos, Skiathos, Skyros, and Thessaloniki. **Hellas Flying Dolphins** offers service from **Piraeus** (© 210/419-9100 or 210/419-9000; www.dolphins.gr) in summer.

On Mykonos, your best bet for getting up-to-date lists of sailings is to check at individual agencies. Or you can check with the **port authority** by National Bank (© 22890/22-218), **tourist police** at the north end of the harbor (© 22890/22-482), or **tourist office,** also on the harbor (© 22890/23-990; fax 22890/22-229).

Hydrofoil service to Crete, Ios, Paros, and Santorini is often irregular. For information, check at **Piraeus Port Authority** (© 210/451-1311 or 210/422-6000; phone seldom answered); **Piraeus Port Police** (© 210/451-1310); Rafina Port Police (© 22940/23-300), or Mykonos Port Police (© 22890/22-218).

Warning: Check each travel agency's current schedule, because most ferry tickets are not interchangeable. Reputable agencies on the main square in Mykonos (Hora) town include **Sunspots Travel** (© 22890/24-196; fax 22890/23-790); **Delia Travel** (© 22890/22-490; fax 22890/24-440); **Sea & Sky Travel** (© 22890/22-853; fax 22890/24-753); and **Veronis Agency** (© 22890/22-687; fax 22890/23-763).

VISITOR INFORMATION **Mykonos Accommodations Center,** at the corner of Enoplon Dhinameon and Malamatenias (© 22890/23-160; www.mykonos-accommodation.com), helps visitors find accommodations. It also functions as a tourist information center. **Windmills Travel** ★ (© 22890/23-877; www.windmills.gr) has an office at Fabrica Square where you can get general information, book accommodations, arrange excursions, and rent a car or moped. Look for the free *Mykonos Summertime* magazine, available in cafes, shops, and hotels throughout the island.

GETTING AROUND One of the best things to happen to Mykonos was the government decree that made Hora an architectural landmark and prohibited motorized traffic from its streets. You will see a few small delivery vehicles, but the only ways to get around town are to walk—or to ride a bike or donkey! Many of the town's large hotels ring the busy peripheral road, and a good transportation system serves much of the rest of the island.

By Bus Mykonos has one of the best bus systems in the Greek islands; the buses run frequently and on schedule. Depending on your destination, a ticket costs about .50€ to 4€ ($.65–$5.20). There are two bus stations in Hora: one near the archaeological museum and one near the Olympic Airways office (follow the helpful blue signs). At the tourist office, find out from which station the bus you want leaves, or look for schedules in hotels. Bus information in English is sometimes available from the **KTEL** office (© 22890/23-360).

By Boat Caïques to Super Paradise, Agrari, and Elia depart from Platis Yialos every morning, weather permitting; there is also service from Ornos in high season (July and Aug) only. Caïque service is highly seasonal, with almost continuous service in high season and no caïques October through May. Excursion boats to Delos depart Tuesday through Sunday between 8:30am and 1pm, from the west side of the harbor near the tourist office. (For more information, see a travel agent; guided tours are available.)

By Car & Moped   Rental cars are available from about 50€ ($65) per day, including insurance, in high season; most agencies are near one of the two bus stops in town. **Windmills Travel** (see "Visitor Information" above) can arrange a car rental for you and get good prices. The largest concentration of moped shops is just beyond the south bus station. Expect to pay about 15€ to 30€ ($20–$39) per day, depending on the moped's engine size. Take great care when driving: Island roads can be treacherous.

Warning: If you park in town or in a no-parking area, the police will remove your license plates. You—not the rental office—will have to find the police station and pay a steep fine to get them back.

By Taxi   There are two types of taxis in Mykonos: standard **car taxis** for destinations outside town, and tiny, cart-towing **scooters** that buzz through the narrow streets of Hora. The latter are seen primarily at the port, where they wait to bring new arrivals to their lodgings in town—a good idea, since most in-town hotels are a challenge to find. Getting a car taxi in Hora is easy: Walk to Taxi (Mavro) Square, near the statue, and join the line. A notice board gives rates for various destinations. You can also call **Mykonos Radio Taxi** (✆ **22890/22-400**).

FAST FACTS   **Commercial Bank** and **National Bank of Greece** are on the harbor a couple blocks west of Taxi Square; both are open Monday through Friday from 8am to 2pm. ATMs are available throughout town. **Mykonos Health Center** (✆ **22890/23-994** or 22890/23-996) handles routine medical complaints; serious cases are usually airlifted to the mainland. The **tourist police** (✆ **22890/22-482**) are on the west side of the port near the ferries to Delos; the local **police** (✆ **22890/22-235**) are behind the grammar school, near Plateia Laka. The **post office** (✆ **22890/22-238**) is next to the police station; it's open Monday through Friday from 7:30am to 2pm. The **telephone office (OTE)** is on the north side of the harbor beyond the Hotel Leto (✆ **22890/22-499**), open Monday through Friday 7:30am to 3pm. **Internet access** is expensive here: Mykonos Cyber Café, 26 M. Axioti, on the road between the south bus station and the windmills (✆ **22890/27-684**), is open daily 9am to 10pm and charges 16€ ($21) per hour or 5€ ($6.50) for 15 minutes. Angelo's Internet Café, on the same road (✆ **22890/24-106**), may have lower rates.

WHAT TO SEE & DO
BEACHES

The beaches on the island's **south shore** have the best sand, views, and wind protection. However, these days they are so popular that you'll have to negotiate a forest of beach umbrellas to find your square meter of sand. A few (**Paradise, Super Paradise**) are known as party beaches, and guarantee throbbing music and loud revelry until late at night. Others (**Platis Yialos, Psarou, Ornos**) are quieter and more popular with families. With all the south-coast beaches, keep in mind that most people begin to arrive in the early afternoon, and you can avoid the worst of the crowds by going in the morning. The **north-coast beaches** are less developed but just as beautiful. Since the buses and caïques don't yet make the trip, you'll have to rent a car or scooter; you'll be more than compensated for the trouble by the quiet and the lack of commercial development.

For those who can't wait to hit the beach, the closest to Mykonos town is **Megali Ammos (Big Sand),** about a 10-minute walk south—it's very crowded and not particularly scenic. To the north, the beach nearest town is 2km (1 mile) away at **Tourlos;**

however, since this is now where many ships dock at the new harbor, it's not a place for a relaxing swim. **Ornos** is popular with families; it's about 2.5km (1½ miles) south of town, and has a fine-sand beach in a sheltered bay with extensive hotel development along the shore. Buses to Ornos run hourly from the south station between 8am and 11pm.

Platis Yialos is the best first stop: Although the beach is unexceptional and likely to be extremely crowded, from here you can catch a caïque to the more distant beaches of Paradise, Super Paradise, Agrari, and Elia. The bus runs every 15 minutes from 8am to 8pm, then every 30 minutes until midnight. Nearby **Psarou** is less overwhelmed by resort hotels and has a lovely pale-sand beach that also gets crowded. Its watersports facilities include **Diving Center Psarou,** water-skiing, and windsurfing. **Paranga,** farther east, can be reached easily on foot via an inland path from Platis Yialos; this small cove is popular for nude sunbathing and doesn't get too crowded.

Reach **Paradise** ⟨, the island's most famous beach, on foot from Platis Yialos (about 2km/1 mile), by bus, or by caïque. This was the island's original nude beach, and it still attracts many nudists. A stand of small trees provides some shade, and the beach is well protected from the predominant north winds. Several bars line the waterfront and pump out loud music day and night.

Super Paradise (Plindri) is in a rocky cove just around the headland from Paradise; it's somewhat less developed than its neighbor, but no less crowded. You can get to the beach on foot, by bus, and by caïque; if you go by car or moped, be very careful on the extremely steep and narrow access road. The left side of the beach is a nonstop party in summer, with loud music and dancing, while the right side is mostly nude and gay, with the exclusive Coco Club providing a relaxed ambience for its chic clientele. Farther east across the little peninsula is **Agrari,** a lovely cove sheltered by lush foliage, with a good little taverna and a beach that welcomes bathers in all modes of dress and undress.

Elia, a 45-minute caïque ride from Platis Yialos and the last regular stop, is a sand-and-pebble beach with crowds nearly as overwhelming as at Paradise and minimal shade. Nevertheless, this beautiful beach is one of the longest on the island. Popular with gay travelers, it's also accessible by bus. The next major beach is **Kalo Livadi (Good Pasture).** Located in a farming valley, this long, beautiful beach is about as quiet as a beach on Mykonos gets. There's bus service from Mykonos town's north station. Adjacent to the beach are a taverna and a few villas and hotels on the hills.

The last resort area on the southern coast accessible by bus from the north station is **Kalafatis** ⟨. This fishing village was once the port of the ancient citadel of

---

Beach Notes

Activity on the beaches is highly seasonal, and all the information offered here pertains only to the months of June through September. The prevailing winds on Mykonos (and throughout the Cyclades) blow from the north, which is why the southern beaches are the most protected and calm. The exception to this rule is a southern wind that occurs periodically during the summer, making the northern beaches more desirable for sunning and swimming. In Mykonos town, this southern wind is heralded by particularly hot temperatures and perfect calm in the harbor. On such days, those in the know will avoid Paradise, Super Paradise, and Elia, heading instead to the northern beaches of Ayios Sostis and Panormos—or simply choose another activity for the day.

Mykonos, which dominated the little peninsula to the west. A line of trees separates the beach from the rows of buildings that have grown up along the road. This is one of the longest beaches on Mykonos, and its days of being uncrowded are, alas, over. Adjacent to Kalafatis in a tiny cove is lovely **Ayia Anna,** a short stretch of sand with a score of umbrellas. Several kilometers farther east, accessible by a fairly good road from Kalafatis, is **Lia,** which has fine sand, clear water, bamboo windbreaks, and a small taverna.

Most of the north coast beaches are too windy to be of interest to anyone other than windsurfers—the long fine-sand beach at **Ftelia** would be one of the best on the island if it didn't receive the unbroken force of the north wind. There are, however, two well-sheltered northern beaches, and because you can only reach them by car or moped, they're much less crowded than the southern beaches. Head east from Mykonos town on the road to Ano Mera, turning left after 1.5km (1 mile) on the road to Ayios Sostis and Panormos. At **Panormos,** you'll find a cove with 100m (328 ft.) of fine sand backed by low dunes. Another 1km (¾ mile) down the road is **Ayios Sostis** ★, a lovely small beach just below a village. There isn't any parking, so it's best to leave your vehicle along the main road and walk 200m (656 ft.) down through the village. An excellent small taverna just up from the beach operates without electricity, so it's open only during daylight hours. Both Panormos and Ayios Sostis have few amenities—no beach umbrellas, bars, or snack shops—but they do offer a break from the crowds.

Beaches to avoid on Mykonos because of pollution, noise, and crowds include **Tourlos** and **Korfos Bay.**

With so many sun-worshippers on Mykonos, local merchants have figured out that they can charge pretty steep prices for suntan lotions and sunscreens. You might want to bring some with you. If you want to try a Greek brand, the oddly named Carrot Milk is excellent.

DIVING

Mykonos is known throughout the Aegean as one of *the* places for diving. Scuba diving on many islands is prohibited to protect undersea archaeological treasures from plunder. Here the best month is September, when the water temperature is typically 75°F (24°C) and visibility is 30m (98 ft.). Certified divers can rent equipment and participate in guided dives; first-time divers can rent snorkeling gear or take an introductory beach dive. The best established dive center is **Mykonos Diving Centre,** at Paradise beach (🖉/fax **22890/24-808**), which offers 5-day PADI certification courses in English from about 500€ ($650), including equipment. **Psarou Diving Center** in Mykonos town (🖉 **22890/24-808**) has also been around for a long time. As always, before you sign up for lessons, be sure that all instructors are PADI certified. The **Union of Diving Centers in Athens** (🖉 **210/411-8909**) usually has up-to-date information. In general, certified divers can join guided dives from 50€ ($65) per dive; beginners can take a 2-hour class and beach dive from 60€ ($78). There's a nearby wreck at a depth of 20 to 35m (65–114 ft.); wreck dives run from 60€ ($78).

ATTRACTIONS

Getting lost in the labyrinthine alleys of Hora is an essential element of every Mykonian holiday. Searching for the right bar, a good place to eat, or your hotel is sure to be twice as difficult as you'd expected and twice as enjoyable. Despite its intense commercialism and seething crowds in high season, Hora is still the quintessential Cycladic town and is worth a visit to the island in itself.

The best way to see the town is to venture inland from the port and wander. Keep in mind that the town is bounded on two sides by the bay, and on the other two by the busy vehicular District Road, and that all paths funnel eventually into one of the main squares: **Plateia Mantos Mavroyenous,** on the port (called **Taxi Square** because it's the main taxi stand); **Plateia Tria Pigadia;** and **Plateia Laka,** near the south bus station.

Hora also has the remains of a small **Venetian kastro** (fortress) and the island's most famous church, **Panagia Paraportiani (Our Lady of the Postern Gate),** a thickly whitewashed asymmetrical edifice made up of four small chapels. Beyond the Panagia Paraportiani is the **Alefkandra** quarter, better known as **Little Venice** 👫👫, for its cluster of homes built overhanging the sea. Many buildings here have been converted into fashionable bars prized for their sunset views; you can sip a margarita and listen to Mozart most nights at the Montparnasse or kastro bar. (See "Mykonos After Dark," later in this chapter.)

Another nearby watering spot is the famous **Tria Pigadia (Three Wells)** 👫👫. Local legend says that if a virgin drinks from all three, she is sure to find a husband, but it's probably not a good idea to test this hypothesis by drinking the brackish well water. After your visit, you may want to take in the famous **windmills of Kato Myli** and enjoy the views back toward Little Venice.

Save time to visit the island's clutch of pleasant small museums. **The Archaeological Museum** (© 22890/22-325), near the harbor, displays finds from Delos; it's open Wednesday to Monday 9am to 3:30pm. Admission is 3€ ($3.90); free on Sunday. **Nautical Museum of the Aegean** (© 22890/22-700), across from the park on Enoplon Dinameon Street, has just what you'd expect, including handsome ship models. It's open Tuesday to Sunday 10:30am to 1pm and 6 to 9pm; admission is 3€ ($3.90). Also on Enoplon Dinameon Street, **Lena's House** (© 22890/22-591) re-creates the home of a middle-class 19th-century Mykonos family. It's usually open daily Easter through October; free admission. **Museum of Folklore** (© 22890/25-591), in a 19th-century sea captain's mansion near the quay, displays examples of local crafts and furnishings. On show is a 19th-century island kitchen. It's open Monday to Saturday 4 to 8pm, Sunday 5 to 8pm; admission is free.

When you've spent some time in Hora, you may want to visit **Ano Mera,** 7km (4 miles) east of Hora near the center of the island, a quick bus ride from the north station. Ano Mera is the island's only other real town and we especially recommend this trip for those interested in religious sites—the **Monastery of Panagia Tourliani** southeast of town dates from the 18th century and has a marble bell tower with intricate folk carvings. Inside the church are a huge Italian baroque iconostasis (altar screen) with icons of the Cretan school; an 18th-century marble baptismal font; and a small museum containing liturgical vestments, needlework, and woodcarvings. One kilometer ([b]1/2 mile) southeast is the 12th-century **Monastery of Paleokastro,** in one of the island's greenest spots. Ano Mera also has the island's most traditional atmosphere; a fresh-produce market on the main square sells excellent local cheeses. This is the island's place of choice for Sunday brunch.

SHOPPING

Mykonos has a lot of shops, many selling overpriced souvenirs, clothing, and jewelry to cruise-ship day-trippers. That said, there is also a number of serious shops here, selling serious wares—at serious prices. The finest jewelry shop is **LALAoUNIS** 👌, 14 Polykandrioti (© 22890/22-444), associated with the famous LALAoUNIS museum

> **Tips Finding an Address**
>
> Although some shops hand out maps of Mykonos town, you'll probably do bet-
> ter finding restaurants, hotels, and attractions by asking people to point you in
> the right direction—and saying *efcharisto* (thank you) when they do. Don't
> panic at how to pronounce *efcharisto*; think of it as a name and say "F. Harry
> Stowe." Most streets do not have their names posted. Also, maps leave off lots
> of small, twisting, streets—and Mykonos has almost nothing but small, twist-
> ing, streets! The map published by **Stamatis Bozinakis,** sold at most kiosks for
> 2€ ($2.60), is quite decent. The useful **Mykonos Sky Map** is free at some hotels
> and shops.

and shops in Athens. It has superb reproductions of ancient and Byzantine jewelry as
well as original designs. When you leave LALAoUNIS, have a look at **Yiannis Galan-
tis** (© 22890/22-255), which sells clothing designed by the owner. If you can't afford
LALAoUNIS, you might check out one of the island's oldest jewelry shops, the **Gold
Store,** right on the waterfront (© **22890/22-397**). **Delos Dolphins,** Matoyanni at Enoplon Dimameon (© **22890/22-765**), specializes in copies of museum pieces; **Vildiridis,**
12 Matoyianni (© **22890/23-245**), also has jewelry based on ancient designs.

Mykonos has lots of art galleries, including some based in Athens that move here for
the summer season. **Scala Gallery** ⭐, 48 Matoyianni (© **22890/23-407;** fax 22890/
26-993; www.scalagallery.gr), is one of the best galleries in town. All the artists represented are from Greece, many of them quite well known. There is a selection of jewelry,
plus an interesting collection of recent works by Yorgos Kypris, an Athenian sculptor and
ceramic artist. Nearby on Panahrandou is **Scala II Gallery** (© **22890/26-993**), where
the overflow from the Scala Gallery is sold at reduced prices. In addition, manager **Dimitris Roussounelos** (©/fax **22890/26-993;** scala@otenet.gr) of Scala Gallery manages a
number of studios and apartments in Hora, so you might find lodgings as well as art at
Scala!

There was a time when Mykonos was world-famous for its vegetable-dyed handloomed weavings, especially those of the legendary Kuria Vienoula. Today, **Nikoletta**
(© **22890/27-503**) is one of the few shops where you can still see the island's traditional loomed goods. Eleni Kontiza's tiny shop **Hand Made** (© **22890/27-512**), on
a lane between Plateia Tria Pigadia and Plateia Laka, has a good selection of handwoven scarves, rugs, and tablecloths from around Greece.

The best bookstore on Mykonos is **To Vivlio** ⭐ (© **22890/27-737**), on Zouganeli,
one street over from Matoyianni. It carries a good selection of books in English,
including many works of Greek writers in translation, plus some art and architecture
books and a few travel guides.

Works of culinary art can be found at **Skaropoulos** (© **22890/24-983**), 1.5km (1
mile) out of Hora on the road to Ano Mera, featuring the Mykonian specialties of Nikos
and Frantzeska Koukas. Nikos's grandfather started making confections here in 1921,
winning prizes and earning a personal commendation from Winston Churchill. Try
their famed *amygdalota* (an almond sweet) or the almond biscuits (Churchill's favorite).
You can also find Skaropoulos sweets at **Pantopoleion,** 24 Kaloyerou (© **22890/
22-078**), along with Greek organic foods and natural cosmetics; the shop is in a beautifully restored 300-year-old Mykonian house.

When you finish your shopping, treat yourself to another almond biscuit (or two or three) from **Efthemios,** 4 Florou Zouganeli (© **22890/22-281**), just off the harborfront, where biscuits have been made since the 1950s.

If you're on Mykonos, probably one reason is the travel posters and postcards you've seen of the sun setting behind funky whitewashed buildings with wooden balconies overhanging the sea. That's the district called Little Venice. Almost every other building is now a bar where you can watch the sunset—or you can sit by the three windmills and get a spectacular view of Little Venice itself at sunset. Either way, if you're in luck, you'll be able to combine listening to Mozart with sipping a drink (how about a margarita?), as the sun turns the sea rose red.

WHERE TO STAY

In summer, reserve a room 1 to 3 months in advance (or more), if possible. Ferry arrivals are often met by a throng of people hawking rooms, some in small hotels, others in private homes. If you don't have a hotel reservation, one of these rooms may be very welcome. Otherwise, book as early as you can. Many hotels are fully booked all summer by tour groups or regular patrons. Keep in mind that Mykonos is an easier, more pleasant place to visit in the late spring or early fall. Off-season hotel rates are sometimes half the quoted high-season rate. Also note that many small hotels, restaurants, and shops close in winter, especially if business is slow.

Mykonos Accommodations Center (MAC), 10 Enoplon Dinameon (© **22890/ 23-160** or 22890/23-408; fax 22890/24-137; www.mykonos-accommodation.com), is a very helpful service, especially if you are looking for hard-to-find inexpensive lodgings. The service is free when you book a hotel stay of 3 nights or longer. If you plan a shorter stay, ask about the fee, which is sometimes a percentage of the tab and sometimes a flat fee.

IN HORA

Belvedere Hotel ✿   The spiffy Belvedere, in part occupying a handsomely restored 1850s town house on the main road into town, has stunning views over the town and harbor, a few minutes' walk away. Rooms are nicely, if not distinctively, furnished. Stay here if you want many of the creature comforts of Mykonos's beach resorts, but prefer to be within walking distance of Hora. The in-house **Remvi** restaurant has a cellar holding 5,000 bottles of wine. The food is excellent (and pricey); there's also a sushi bar. In season, the hotel often offers massage, salon, and barber service. Off season, look for excellent specials; after a 4-night stay, this might be a free jeep for a day or a fifth night free.

Hora, 84600 Mykonos. © **22890/25-122.** Fax 22890/25-126. www.belvederehotel.com. 48 units. 225€–350€ ($293–$455) double. Rates include American buffet breakfast. Considerable off-season reductions. AE, MC, V. School of Fine Arts district. **Amenities:** 2 restaurants; bar; pool; fitness center; Jacuzzi; sauna. *In room:* A/C, TV, dataport (in 10 units), minibar, hair dryer.

Cavo Tagoo ✿✿   This elegant hotel set into a cliff with spectacular views over Mykonos town is hard to resist—and consistently makes it onto *Odyssey* magazine's list of 10 best Greek hotels. Cavo Tagoo's island-style architecture has won awards, and its gleaming marble floors, nicely crafted wooden furniture, queen- and king-size beds, and local-style weavings are a genuine pleasure. Hora's harbor is only a 15-minute walk away, although you may find it hard to budge: A saltwater pool and a good restaurant are located right here at the hotel.

Hora, 84600 Mykonos. (© **22890/23-692** to -694. Fax 22890/24-923. www.cavotagoo.com. 72 units. 225€–420€ ($293–$546) double. Rates include buffet breakfast. AE, MC, V. Closed Nov–Mar. **Amenities:** Restaurant; bar; salt-water pool. *In room:* A/C, TV, minibar, hair dryer.

Matina Hotel ⚬ This small hotel set in a large garden is surprisingly quiet, given its central location. If you want to avoid the large, isolated hotels and enjoy the comings and goings in a Hora neighborhood, this may be the place for you. Rooms are a bit on the small side, but have modern facilities and are comfortable. Several readers describe the owner as "very helpful," and we agree.

3 Fournakion, Hora, 84600 Mykonos. (© **22890/22-387.** Fax 22890/24-501. 19 units. 110€ ($143) double. AE, MC, V. Closed Nov–Mar. **Amenities:** Breakfast room; garden.

Philippi Hotel Each room in this homey little hotel in the heart of Mykonos town is different, so you might want to have a look at several before choosing yours. The owner tends a lush garden that often provides flowers for her son's restaurant, the elegant Philippi (see "Where to Dine," below), which can be reached through the garden.

25 Kaloyera, Hora, 84600 Mykonos. (© **22890/22-294.** Fax 22890/24-680. 13 units. 90€ ($117) double. No credit cards. **Amenities:** Restaurant; breakfast room.

OUT ON THE ISLAND

Although most visitors prefer to stay in Hora and commute to the beaches, there are hotels on or near many of the more popular island beaches.

The beaches at Paradise and Super Paradise have private studios and simple pensions, but rooms are almost impossible to get, and prices more than double in July and August. Contact **Mykonos Accommodations Center** (© **22890/23-160**) or, for Super Paradise, **GATS Travel** (© **22890/22-404**), for information on the properties they represent. The tavernas at each beach may also have suggestions.

AT KALAFATI The sprawling **Aphrodite Hotel** (© **22890/71-367**) has a large pool, two restaurants, and 150 rooms. It's a good value in May, June, and October, when a double costs about 100€ ($130). The hotel is popular with tour groups and Greek families.

AT ORNOS BAY ⚬⚬ Elegant **Kivotos Club Hotel** ⚬⚬, Ornos Bay, 84600 Mykonos (© **22890/25-795;** fax 22890/22-844; www.kivotosclubhotel.gr), is a small luxury hotel about 3km (2 miles) outside Mykonos town. Most of the 45 individually decorated units overlook the Bay of Ormos, but if you don't want to walk that far for a swim, head for the saltwater or freshwater pool, the Jacuzzi and sauna, or the pool with an underwater sound system piping in music! Kivotos Clubhouse is small enough to be intimate and tranquil; the service (including frozen towels for poolside guests on hot days) gets raves from guests. If you're ever tempted to leave (and you may not be), the hotel minibus will whisk you into town. You can easily dine at the several restaurants on-site. The hotel also has a traditional sailing ship, at the ready for spur-of-the moment sails. In short, it's no surprise that this popular honeymoon destination appears often on *Odyssey* magazine's annual list of the best hotels in Greece. Doubles cost 375€ to 525€ ($488–$683); suites are priced from 650€ to 1,000€ ($845–$1,300). The enormous **Santa Marina,** also at Ornos Bay (© **22890/23-200;** fax 22890/23-412; info@santa-marina.gr), has 90 suites and villas in 20 landscaped acres overlooking the bay. If you don't want to swim in the sea, two pools and spa facilities are available at the hotel, which has its own restaurant as well. Suites with private pool are available from 1,500€ ($1,950). If you wish, you can arrive here by helicopter and land on the hotel pad.

Doubles cost from 395€ to 600€ ($514–$780); suites and villas from 625€ to 2,400€ ($813–$3,120). The more modest 25-unit **Best Western Dionysos Hotel** (℗ **22890/ 23-313**) is steps from the beach and has a pool, restaurant, bar, and air-conditioned rooms with fridges and TV; doubles cost from 190€ ($247). The even more modest 42-unit **Hotel Yiannaki** (℗ **22890/23-393**) is about 200m (656 ft.) away from the beach and has its own pool and restaurant; doubles begin at 125€ ($163). The nicest units have sea views and balconies.

Families traveling with children will find staying at one of the Ornos Bay hotels especially appealing. The beach is excellent and slopes into shallow, calm water. Furthermore, this is not one of Mykonos's all-night party beaches. If your hotel does not have watersports facilities, several of the local tavernas have surfboards and pedal boats to rent, as well as umbrellas. One minus: the beach is close to the airport, so you will hear planes come and go.

AT PLATI YIALOS   The large and comfortable rooms of the 82-unit **Hotel Petassos Bay,** Plati Yialos, 84600 Mykonos (℗ **22890/23-737;** fax 22890/24-101), all have air-conditioning and minibars. Doubles go for about 150€ ($195). Each has a balcony overlooking the relatively secluded beach, which is less than 36m (132 ft.) away. The hotel has a good-size pool, sun deck, Jacuzzi, gym, and sauna. It offers free round-trip transportation to and from the harbor or airport, safety-deposit boxes, and laundry service. The new seaside restaurant has a great view and serves a big buffet breakfast (a smaller continental breakfast is included in the room rate).

AT AYIOS IOANNIS   **Mykonos Grand** is a 100-room luxury resort a few kilometers out of Hora in Ayios Ioannis, 84600 Mykonos (℗ **22890/25-555;** www.mykonos grand.gr). With its own beach and many amenities—pools, tennis, squash, Jacuzzis, a spa—this is a very sybaritic place. The Mykonos Grand regularly appears on *Odyssey* magazine's list of the 50 best hotels in Greece and is popular with Greeks, Europeans, and Americans. Doubles start at 225€ ($293).

AT AYIOS STEPHANOS   This popular resort, about 4km (2½ miles) north of Hora, has a number of hotels; the 38-unit **Princess of Mykonos,** Ayios Stephanos beach, 84600 Mykonos (℗ **22890/23-806;** fax 22890/23-031), is the most elegant. The Princess has bungalows, a gym, a pool, and an excellent beach; doubles cost from 180€ ($234). **Hotel Artemis,** Ayios Stephanos, 84600 Mykonos (℗ **22890/22-345**), near the beach and bus stop, offers 23 units from 115€ ($150), breakfast included. Small **Hotel Mina,** Ayios Stephanos, 84600 Mykonos (℗ **22890/23-024**), uphill behind the Artemis, has 15 doubles that go for 80€ ($104). All these hotels are usually closed November to March.

AT PSARROU BEACH   **Grecotel Mykonos Blu** ✸✸, Psarrou Beach, 84600 Mykonos (℗ **22890/27-900;** fax 22890/27-783; www.grecotel.gr), is another of the island's serious luxury hotels with award-winning Cyclades-inspired architecture. Like Cavo Tagoo and Kivotos, this place is popular with wealthy Greeks, honeymooners, and jet-setters. The private beach, large pool, and in-house Poets of the Aegean restaurant allow guests to be just as lazy as they wish (although there is a fitness club and spa for the energetic). Doubles run from 250€ to 450€ ($325–$585).

WHERE TO DINE
Camares Cafe (℗ **22890/28-570**), on Mavroyenous (Taxi) Square, has light meals and a fine view of the harbor from its terrace. It's open 24 hours and, for Mykonos, is very reasonably priced. As is usual on the islands, most of the harborside tavernas are

expensive and mediocre, although **Kounelas** ⟨★⟩ on the harbor (no phone; no credit cards) is still a good value for fresh fish—as attested to by the presence of locals dining here.

You'll find plenty of fish on the menu at most Mykonos restaurants; not all of it is local, still less is fresh. If the menu offers squid from the Far East or shrimp from Africa, consider a more local entree.

Restaurants come and go here, so check with other travelers or locals as to what's just opened and is getting good reviews. And let us know if you find something you like!

Antonini's GREEK   Antonini's is one of the oldest of Mykonos's restaurants. It serves consistently decent stews, chops, and *mezedes*. Locals eat here, although in summer they tend to leave the place to tourists.

Plateia Manto, Hora. ℂ **22890/22-319.** Main courses 9€–18€ ($12–$23). No credit cards. Summer daily noon–3pm and 7pm–1am. Usually closed Nov–Mar.

Edem Restaurant ⟨★⟩ GREEK/CONTINENTAL   This is one of the oldest restaurants in Hora, with a reputation for good food built over 30 years. Tables are clustered around a courtyard pool—diners have been known to make a splash upon arrival with a preprandial swim—and the sunny courtyard is a pleasant place to enjoy a leisurely dinner even if you aren't dressed for the water. Edem is known especially for its variety of lamb dishes and fresh fish—but the eclectic menu includes steak, pasta, and a variety of traditional Greek and Continental dishes. The service is good and the produce as fresh as you'll see on Mykonos.

Above Panachra Church, Hora. ℂ **22890/23-355.** Reservations recommended July–Aug. Main courses 8€–30€ ($10–$39); fish priced by the kilo. AE, DC, MC, V. Daily 6pm–1am. In off season, sometimes open for lunch. Walk up Matoyianni, turn left on Kaloyera, and follow the signs up and to the left.

El Greco/Yorgos GREEK/CONTINENTAL   Put aside your suspicions of a place called El Greco and be prepared to enjoy traditional recipes collected from various regions of Greece. The eclectic menu includes traditional dishes; from Kerkira, for example, *bourdeto* is a monkfish-and-shellfish stew in tomato-and-wine sauce. Many concoctions feature such local produce as mushrooms with Mykonian cheese. This place is doing something right: It's been here since the 1960s.

Plateia Tria Pigadia, Hora. ℂ **22890/22-074.** Main courses 9€–30€ ($12–$39); fish priced by the kilo. AE, DC, MC, V. Daily 7pm–1am.

La Maison de Catherine ⟨★⟩ GREEK/FRENCH   This is a very pleasant place to spend the evening. Enjoy a seafood souffle or a seafood pasta, or choose grilled or roasted lamb. The candlelit dining room is so elegant that you won't mind being indoors. In addition to a wide variety of entrees, there is a range of excellent desserts.

Ayios Gerasimos, Hora. ℂ **22890/22-169.** Reservations recommended July–Aug. Main courses 12€–25€ ($16–$33). AE, DC, MC, V. Daily 7pm–1am.

Maria's Garden ⟨★⟩ GREEK   This is another longtime favorite, with a lovely garden often animated by live music and outbreaks of dancing. The vegetable dishes are always fresh and tasty, the lamb succulent, and the seafood enticing. In short, this is a place where ambience and cuisine come together to create a very successful restaurant. There's often a good-value set menu for around 25€ ($33).

30 Kaloyera, Hora. ℂ **22890/27-565.** Reservations recommended July–Aug. Main courses 15€–30€ ($20–$39). DC, V. Daily 7pm–1am.

Philippi ⭐ GREEK/CONTINENTAL One of the island's most romantic dining experiences, Philippi is in a quiet garden. Old Greek favorites share space on the menu with French dishes and a more than usually impressive wine list. What this restaurant provides in abundance is *atmosphere,* and that's what has made it a perennial favorite.

Just off Matoyianni and Kaloyera behind the eponymous hotel, Hora. ℂ 22890/22-294. Reservations recommended July–Aug. Main courses 10€–25€ ($13–$33). AE, MC, V. Daily 7pm–1am.

Sea Satin Market ⭐ GREEK/SEAFOOD Below the windmills, beyond the small beach adjacent to Little Venice, the paralia ends in a rocky headland facing the open sea. This is the remarkable location of one of Hora's most charming restaurants. Set apart from the clamor of the town, it's one of the quietest spots in the area. On a still summer night just after sunset, the atmosphere is all you could hope for on a Greek island. At the front of the restaurant, the kitchen activity is on view along with the day's catch sizzling on the grill. You can make a modest meal on *mezedes* here, or let it rip with grilled bon filet. A couple of readers have recently mentioned "nonchalant" and "slow" service; let us know what you think.

Near the Mitropolis Cathedral, Hora. ℂ 22890/24-676. Main courses 8€–35€ ($10–$46). No credit cards. Daily 6:30pm–12:30am.

Sesame Kitchen GREEK/CONTINENTAL This small, health-conscious taverna, which serves some vegetarian specialties, is next to the Naval Museum. Fresh spinach, vegetable, cheese, and chicken pies are baked daily. A large variety of salads, brown rice, and soy dishes are offered, as well as a vegetable moussaka and stir-fried veggies. Lightly grilled and seasoned meat dishes are available.

Plateia Tria Pigadia, Hora. ℂ 22890/24-710. Main courses 8€–18€ ($10–$23). AE, V. Daily 7pm–midnight.

MYKONOS AFTER DARK

Mykonos has the liveliest, most abundant, and most varied nightlife in the Aegean. It's a bar hopper's paradise, and you'll enjoy wandering through the maze of streets looking for the right spot—and looking at everyone else looking. Our suggestions include a few durable favorites and some new places that were popular last year. We've given phone numbers where available; if you dial one of these places and get no reply, don't assume the place is closed: Business might be brisk.

Be forewarned: Drinks in Mykonos often cost more than they do in London or New York.

Watching the sunset is a popular sport at the sophisticated bars in Little Venice. **Kastro** (ℂ 22890/23-072), near the Paraportiani Church, is famous for classical music and frozen daiquiris. This is a great spot to watch or join handsome young men flirting with each other. If you find it too crowded or tame, sashay along to **Le Caprice,** which also has a seaside perch; or try **Porta** (ℂ 22890/27-807), a popular gay cruising spot. **Montparnasse** (ℂ 22890/23-719), on the same lane, is cozier, with classical music and Toulouse-Lautrec posters. **Veranda** (ℂ 22890/23-290), in an old mansion overlooking the water with a good view of the windmills, is as relaxing as its name implies. **Galeraki** (ℂ 22890/27-118) has a wide variety of exotic cocktails (and customers); the in-house art gallery gives this popular spot its name, "Little Gallery."

The decibel level is considerably higher along the harbor, where **Pierro's** (ℂ 22890/22-177), popular with gay visitors, rocks all night long to American and European music. Adjacent **Icarus** is best known for its drag shows. The **Anchor** plays blues, jazz, and classic rock for its 30-something clients, as does **Argo. Stavros Irish Bar** and **Scandinavian**

Bar-Disco draw customers from Ireland, Scandinavia and, quite possibly, as far away as Antarctica. If you'd like to sample Greek music and dancing, try **Thalami** (© **22890/ 23-291**), a small club underneath the town hall. If you'd like to relax at a movie, head for **Cinemanto** (© **22890/27-190**), which shows films nightly around 9pm. Many films are American; most Greek films have English subtitles.

How much are you going to spend going out on the town for a drink or two in Mykonos? As little as 10€ ($13)—and after that, the sky really is the limit!

If you're visiting between July and September, find out what's happening at **Anemo Theatre** (© **22890/23-944**), an outdoor venue for the performing arts in a garden in Rohari, just above town. A wide variety of concerts, performances, and talks are usually planned.

7 Delos ★★★

The small island of **Delos,** just 3km (2 miles) offshore from Mykonos, was considered by the ancient Greeks to be the holiest of sanctuaries, the sacred center around which the other Cyclades circled. Delos is known locally as the "brightest" island in the Cyclades, a tradition that seems to indicate both its continued significance as a sacred place and the fact that this is one place where you'll need sunglasses. It is unquestionably one of the most remarkable archaeological preserves in the world, displaying ample evidence of its former grandeur. Always a place set apart, Delos had rules different from those of neighboring islands; in ancient times, people were not allowed to die or be born on this sacred island. Today, they are not allowed to spend the night, and the site can be visited only between the hours of 8:30am and 3pm, and not at all on Monday.

We recommend visiting Delos as early as possible in the day, especially in summer, when the crowds and heat become overwhelming by early afternoon. Sturdy shoes and water are necessary; a hat, sunblock, and food are also advised. There is a cafe near the museum, but the prices are high, the quality poor, and the service even worse.

ESSENTIALS

GETTING THERE   If you want to go to Delos, head there at the first opportunity: The island can be visited only by sea—and many days the sea is too rough for boats to put in there. The site is open from 8:30am to 3pm and is always closed on Monday. Most people visit on excursion boats from nearby Mykonos, although there are excursions from other neighboring islands, and Delos is a prominent stop for cruise ships and yachts. Spending the night is not allowed. From Mykonos, organized guided and unguided excursions leave about four times a day Tuesday through Sunday at the harbor's west end. The trip takes about 40 minutes and costs about 15€ ($20) round-trip for transportation alone (departure from Mykonos around 8:30am; return to Mykonos around 3pm). **Yiannakis Tours** (© **22890/22-089**) offers guided tours for about 30€ ($39) that depart at 9 or 10am and return at 12:30 or 2pm.

EXPLORING THE SITE

Entrance to the site costs 6€ ($7.80), unless this was included in the price of your excursion. At the ticket kiosk, you'll see a number of site plans and picture guides for sale; we recommend *Delos & Mykonos: A Guide to the History and Archaeology,* by Konstantinos Tsakos (Hesperos Editions), a reliable guide to the site and the museum. Because the excavations at Delos have been conducted by the French School, many signs are in French, and a thorough English-language map and guide are especially useful.

To the left (north) of the new jetty where your boat will dock is the **Sacred Harbor,** now too silted for use, where pilgrims, merchants, and sailors from throughout the Mediterranean used to land. The commercial importance of the island in ancient times was due to the protection its harbor offered in the shelter of surrounding islands, the best anywhere between mainland Greece and its colonies and trading partners in Asia Minor.

If you're not on a tour and have the energy, you should definitely head up to **Mount Kinthos** ✿, the highest point on the island. It offers an overview of the site and a fine view of most of the Cyclades: the neighboring island of Rinia with Siros beyond it to the west, Tinos to the north, Mykonos to the northeast, Naxos and Paros to the south. From the summit, with the islands of the Cyclades sprawled on all sides, close up and low to the horizon, you get the sense that this is indeed the center of the archipelago. On your way down, don't miss the remarkable **Grotto of Hercules,** a small temple built into a natural crevice in the mountainside—the roof is formed of massive granite slabs held up by their own enormous weight. The grotto commands a fine view of the harbor and much of the archaeological site.

South (to the right) of the Sacred Harbor is the fascinating **Maritime quarter,** a residential area with the remains of houses from the Hellenistic and Roman eras, when the island reached its peak in wealth and prestige. Reminiscent of Pompeii, the outlines of the ancient city are remarkably preserved. Several houses contain brilliant **mosaics** ✿, and in most houses the cistern and sewer systems can be seen. Among the numerous small dwellings are several palaces, built around a central court and connected to the street by a narrow passage. The mosaics in the palace courtyards are particularly dazzling, and include such famous images as Dionysos riding a panther in the **House of the Masks,** and a similar depiction in the **House of Dionysos.** Farther to the south is the massive **Theater,** which seated 5,500 people and was the site of choral competitions during the Delian Festivals, an event held every 4 years that included athletic competitions in addition to musical contests. Behind the theater is a fine arched **cistern,** which was the water supply for the city. If you visit here in spring, the wildflowers are especially beautiful, and the chorus of frogs that live in and around the cisterns will be at its peak.

Adjacent to the Sacred Harbor is the **Agora of the Competialists,** built in the 2nd century B.C. when the island was a bustling free port under Rome. Roman citizens, mostly former slaves, worshipped the *lares competales,* who were minor "crossroad" deities associated with the Greek god Hermes, patron of travelers and commerce. From the far left corner of the Agora of the Competialists, the **Sacred Way**—once lined with statues and votive monuments—leads north toward the Sanctuary of Apollo. By retracing the steps of ancient pilgrims along it, you will pass the scant remains of several temples (most of the stone from the site was taken away for buildings on neighboring islands, especially Mykonos and Tinos). At the far end of the Sacred Way was the **Propylaea,** a monumental marble gateway that led into the sanctuary. In ancient times, the sanctuary was crowded with temples, altars, statues, and votive offerings.

The **museum** contains finds from the various excavations on the island. It displays fine statuary, reliefs, masks, and jewelry, and is well worth a visit. Admission to the museum is included in the site's entrance fee.

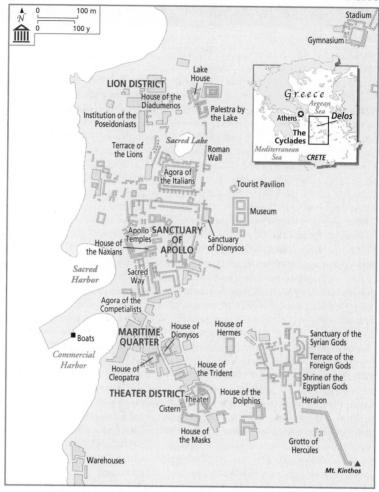

North of the Tourist Pavilion on the left is the **Sacred Lake,** where the oracular swans once swam. The lake is now little more than a dusty indentation most of the year, surrounded by a low wall. Beyond it is the famous **Avenue of the Lions** , made of Naxian marble and erected in the 7th century B.C. There were originally at least nine lions. One was taken away to Venice in the 17th century and now stands before the arsenali there. The whereabouts of the others lost in antiquity remains a mystery; the five survivors are now in the museum for restoration, while replicas line the Avenue. Beyond the lake to the northeast is the large square courtyard of the gymnasium and the long narrow stadium, where the athletic competitions of the Delian Games were held.

8 Tinos

161km (87 nautical miles) SE of Piraeus

Tinos is the most important destination in all of Greece for religious pilgrims, yet it remains one of the least commercialized islands of the Cyclades—and a joy to visit for that reason. **Panagia Evangelistria (Our Lady of Good Tidings)**—sometimes called the "Lourdes of Greece"—draws thousands of pilgrims seeking the healing and comforting assistance of the miraculous icon enshrined here. Some of these pilgrims are Catholics: Many of the Cyclades were under Venetian rule for centuries, and several, including Tinos, still have a considerable Catholic population. A number of fine old Venetian mansions (locally known as *pallada,* the word also used for the harborfront), are located on the streets off the harbor. Important Catholic churches in Tinos town include the harborfront churches of St. Anthony and St. Nicolas; outside town, the Church of the Virgin Mary Vrisiotissa near the village of Ag. Romanos on the main Hora-Pirgos road is an important Catholic pilgrimage shrine.

From well out to sea, Panagia Evangelistria—illuminated at night—is visible atop a hill overlooking Tinos town. (Locals call the hill "Hora.") Almost any day of the year you can see people, particularly elderly women, crawling from the port on hands and knees up Megalocharis, the long, steep street that leads to the red-carpeted steps that are the final approach to the cathedral. Adjacent pedestrian-only Evangelistria is a market street, as well as a pilgrimage route for those who choose to walk it. The street is lined with stalls selling vials of holy water, incense, candles (up to 2m/7 ft. long), and mass-produced icons, as well as hand-painted icons. Also along the street are jewelry and handicraft shops, one or two cafes, groceries, and old-fashioned dry-goods stores.

Don't even think about arriving on Tinos without a reservation around **August 15** (Feast of the Assumption of the Virgin), when thousands of pilgrims travel here to celebrate the occasion. **March 25** (Feast of the Annunciation) is the second-most important feast day here, but it draws fewer pilgrims because it is less easy to travel by sea in March. Pilgrims also come here on July 23 (the anniversary of St. Pelagia's vision of the icon) and on January 30 (the anniversary of the finding of the icon). *Note:* Remember that Tinos *is a pilgrimage place:* It is considered very disrespectful to wear shorts, short skirts, halters, or sleeveless shirts in the precincts of the Evangelistria (or any other church, for that matter). Photographing the pilgrims, especially those approaching the shrine on hands and knees, is not appreciated.

The inland villages of Tinos are some of the most beautiful in the Cyclades. Many of the most picturesque are nestled into the slopes of **Exobourgo,** the rocky pinnacle visible from the port, connected by a network of walking paths that make this island a hiker's paradise. In these villages and dotting the countryside, you'll see the ornately decorated medieval *peristerionades* **(dovecotes)** for which the island is famous, as well as elaborately carved marble lintels, door jambs, and fan windows on village houses. According to one tradition (popular on virtually every one of the Cyclades), there are 365 churches scattered across the island, one for every day of the year; others boast that the island has 1,000 churches. The island's beaches aren't worthy of superlatives, but they are plentiful and uncrowded throughout the summer. All this may change if an airport is built here—all the more reason to visit Tinos now.

ESSENTIALS

GETTING THERE   Several ferries travel to Tinos daily from Piraeus (5 hr.). Catamaran (1½ hr.) and ferry services (4 hr.) are available daily in summer from Rafina.

Check schedules at the Athens **GNTO** (☎ **210/331-0562**); **Piraeus Port Authority** (☎ **210/459-3223** or 210/422-6000; phone seldom answered); or **Rafina Port Authority** (☎ **22940/22-300**). Several times a day, boats connect Tinos with nearby Mykonos (15–40 min.). Boats to Siros (20–50 min.) and hydrofoils to Santorini (4–6 hr.), Paros (1½ hr.), and Naxos (2 hr.) run regularly in summer and less frequently during winter. There is a daily boat to Siros; Tinos has more winter connections than most Cycladic isles due to its religious tourism, which continues throughout the year. In summer, a day excursion to Delos and Mykonos usually departs from the old pier in Tinos harbor at 10am Tuesday through Sunday, returning to Tinos at 7pm; the fare is 25€ ($33) adult and 9€ ($12) children under 11.

There are three ports in Tinos harbor. Be sure to find out from which pier your ship will depart. Most ferries, the small catamarans (Seajet, Flying Cat, and Jet One), as well as the excursion boat to Delos/Mykonos, dock at the old pier in the town center; some use the new pier to the north, on the side of town in the direction of Kionia. **Tinos Port Authority** (not guaranteed to be helpful) can be reached at ☎ **22830/22-348.**

VISITOR INFORMATION   For information on accommodations, car rentals, island tours, and Tinos in general, head to **Windmills Travel** ★★★ (☎ **22830/23-398;** fax 22830/23-327; www.windmills.gr), on the harbor by the new port, next to St. Anthony's Catholic church. The office has a large painting of a windmill's round, spoked pinwheel on its exterior. Sharon Turner is the friendly, amazingly helpful, and efficient manager, with unparalleled knowledge of Tinos and its neighboring islands. She also runs a terrific book exchange out of her office. What's more, Turner can get you substantial discounts on island accommodations, transportation, and tours.

GETTING AROUND   By Bus   The **bus station** (☎ **22830/22-440**) is on the harbor, opposite the National Bank of Greece. Schedules are usually posted or available here. (You can also ask about bus times at Windmills Travel.) There are frequent daily buses to most island villages.

By Car & Moped   Again, inquire at Windmills Travel. Rental agencies in Tinos town include two just off the harbor on Trion Ierarchon, the street where taxis hang out: **Vidalis** (☎ **22830/23-995**) and **Dimitris Rental** (☎ **22830/23-585**) next door. Both have car rentals from 25€ ($33) and moped rentals from 12€ ($16).

By Taxi Taxis hang out on Trion Ierarchon, which runs uphill from the harbor just before Palamaris supermarket and Hotel Tinion.

FAST FACTS There are several **banks** on the harbor, open Monday through Thursday from 8am to 2pm and Friday from 8am to 1:30pm; all have ATMs. The **first-aid center** can be reached at ℭ **22830/22-210.** There's a drop-off **laundry** service (ℭ **22830/32-765**) behind the Lito Hotel—but be forewarned that it can be slow, up to 3 days in peak season. For **luggage storage,** try Windmills Travel (ℭ **22830/ 23-398**). The **police** (ℭ **22830/22-348**) are located just past the new pier, past Lito Hotel and Windmills Travel. The **post office** (ℭ **22830/22-247**), open Monday through Friday from 7:30am to 2pm, is at the harbor's south end next to Tinion Hotel. The **telephone office (OTE),** open Monday through Friday from 7:30am to 12:30pm, is on the main street leading to the church of Panagia Evangelistria, about halfway up on the right (ℭ **22830/22-399**).

WHAT TO SEE & DO

Archaeological Museum Just below the cathedral precinct on Leoforos Megalo-haris is a small museum that, if you are pressed for time, you might pass. The limited collection includes handsome geometric pots and a sundial from the 2nd century A.D. found at the Sanctuary of Poseidon and Amphitrite at Kionia.

Leo. Megaloharis. Admission 3€ ($3.90). Tues–Sun 8:30am–3pm. (No toilet facilities.)

Panagia Evangelistria Cathedral and Museums ★★ Each year, the **Church of Panagia Evangelistria (Our Lady of Good Tidings)** draws thousands of pilgrims seeking the aid of the church's miraculous icon. According to local lore, one night in 1822, a nun named Pelagia dreamed the Virgin told her where to find a miraculous icon. Initially afraid no one would believe her, Pelagia finally went to the bishop and told her story. The bishop, convinced of her piety, ordered excavations to begin. Before long, the remains first of a Byzantine church and then of the icon itself were unearthed. As is the case with many of the most holy icons, this one is believed to be the work of Saint Luke.

It took the community 2 years to build the church, which is made of marble from Paros and Tinos. It has a tall, slender bell tower and handsome black-and-white pebble mosaics in the exterior courtyard.

At the end of Evangelistria Street, a broad flight of marble stairs leads you up to the church. Inside, hundreds of gold and silver hanging lamps illuminate the icon of the Virgin, to the left of the entrance. The icon is almost entirely hidden by votive offerings of gold, silver, diamonds, and precious gems dedicated by the faithful. Even those who do not make a lavish gift customarily make a small offering and light a candle.

Beneath the church is the crypt where the icon was found, surrounded by smaller chapels. The crypt is often crowded with Greek parents and children dressed in white, waiting to be baptized with water from the font. Others come to fill vials with holy water from the spring. Hundreds of small objects in silver and gold hang from the roof—sometimes a hand or a foot, a child's crib, a house, a car, a donkey, or even a barrel. Each one has a story to tell, a tale of thanks for a prayer answered.

Keep in mind that to enter the church, men must wear long pants and shirts with sleeves, and women must wear dresses or skirts and blouses with sleeves. If there is a church service while you are here, you will hear the beautiful, resonant chanting that typifies a Greek Orthodox service—but remember that it's not appropriate to explore the church during a service. There is usually a service in the early morning and others periodically throughout the day.

Within the high walls that surround the church are various museums and galleries, each of which is worth a quick visit: a gallery of 14th- to 19th-century religious art, a gallery of more modern Tinian artists, and a sculpture museum. Admission is sometimes charged at these places.

Hora, Tinos. Free admission. Cathedral: daily 8am–7pm (off-season hours vary). Galleries: Sat–Sun (some weekdays during July and Aug) 8am–8pm (off season usually noon–6pm).

EXPLORING THE ISLAND

If it's a clear day, one of your first sights of Tinos from the ferry will be the odd mountain with a bare summit that looks bizarrely like a twisted fist. This is **Exobourgo** ★★ , a mountain eminence crowned by the remains of a Venetian kastro (castle) about 15km (9 miles) outside of Hora. Sheer rock walls surround the fortress on three sides; the only path to the summit starts behind a Catholic church at the base of the rock, on the road between Mesi and Koumaros. As you make the 15-minute ascent, you'll pass several lines of fortification—the entire hill is riddled with walls and hollowed with chambers. As you might expect, the view over the Cyclades is superb from the summit (565m/1,854 ft.). The fortress itself has long been in ruins—and was never as imposing as, for example, the massive Venetian fortress at Nafplion in the Peloponnese. The Turks defeated the Venetians here in 1714 and drove them from the island.

The towns circling Exobourgo are among the most picturesque on the island; you can visit them by car or on foot (see "Walking," below). **Dio Horia** and **Monastiri** have beautiful village houses. In Dio Horia's main square is a spring where some villagers wash their clothes by hand.

There's a town bus to the nearby **Convent of Kechrovouniou** ★★, one of the largest in Greece—almost a town in its own right. It dates from the 10th century and was the home of Pelagia, the nun whose vision revealed the location of the island's famed icon; you can visit her cell and see a small museum of 18th- and 19th-century icons.

Loutra ★ is an especially attractive village with many *stegasti*, streets in tunnels beneath the projecting second-floor rooms of village houses. An imposing 17th-century Jesuit monastery contains an excellent museum of village life; implements for making olive oil and wine are on display alongside old manuscripts and maps. It's open mid-June to mid-September from 10:30am to 3:30pm.

Volax is in a remote valley known for a bizarre lunar landscape of rotund granite boulders. The villagers constructed a stone amphitheater for theatrical productions there, so be sure to ask **Windmills Travel** (✆/fax **22830/23-398**) for a schedule of performances, most of which occur in August. Volax is also known for its local basket weavers, whose baskets are remarkably durable and attractive; ask for directions to

---

⌐Finds Taverna Special

When you finish climbing Exobourgo, reward yourself with a *froutalia,* a local specialty: a pizza-sized omelet with cheese, sausage, tomatoes, vegetables, and herbs. You can't beat eating it under the grape arbor at the roadside **Taverna Gourni** (✆ **22830-51-274**) in the hamlet of Skalados. If you are traveling with small children, they'll love the play area, with its slides and toys.

their workshops. Be sure to visit the town spring, down a short flight of steps at the bottom of the village. Channels direct the water to the fields, and the basket weavers' reeds soak in multiple stone basins. **Koumaros** is a beautiful small village on the road between Volax and Mesi, both of which have many of the arched passageways known as *stegasti*.

Pirgos ★★, at the western end of the island, is one of Tinos's most beautiful villages, with an enchanting small plateia with trees, a marble fountain, several cafes, and a taverna that is usually open for lunch and dinner in summer, less regularly off season. (If the taverna is closed, **Panormos,** on the sea just beyond Pirgos, has several tavernas, a good beach, and alarming signs of development.) Renowned for its school of fine arts, Pirgos is a center for marble sculpting, and many of the finest sculptors of Greece have trained here. **Dellatos Marble Sculpture School** (© 22830/23-164; www.tinosmarble.com), just outside the village by the police station, offers 1- and 2-week workshops for would-be marble workers. The Museum of Yiannoulis Chalepas and Museum of Panormian Artists occupy adjacent houses, and give visitors a chance not only to see sculpture by local artists, but to step into an island house. After you see the small rooms on the ground floor, you'll be surprised at how large the cool, flag-stoned lower story with the kitchen is. The museums are located near the bus station, on the main lane leading toward the village. Both are open Tuesday through Sunday from 11am to 1:30pm and 5:30 to 6:30pm; admission is 2€ ($2.60).

Although you may be tempted by the sculptures you see on sale in local workshops, even a small marble relief is not easy to slip into a suitcase. In a small hardware shop across from Pirgos's two museums, **Nikolaos Panorios** ★★★ makes and sells whimsical tin funnels, boxes, spoon holders, and dustpans, as well as dovecotes, windmills, and sailing ships. Each item is made of tin salvaged from olive oil and other containers, and every one is unique (some with scenes of Pallas Athena, others with friezes of sunflowers, olive gatherers, fruits, or vegetables). All are delightful; they cost from 10€ ($13). Eugenia and Nikolaos Panoriou are usually in their shop mornings (© 22830/32-263) from about 9am to 1pm.

BEACHES

Tinos is not best known for its beaches, but there's a decent fine-sand beach 3km (2 miles) west of Tinos town at **Kionia.** Another beach lies 2km (1¼ miles) east of town at busy **Ayios Fokas.** From Tinos, there's bus service on the south beach road (usually four times a day) to the resort of **Porto,** 8km (5 miles) to the east. Porto offers several long stretches of uncrowded sand, a few hotel complexes, and numerous tavernas, several at or near the beach. The beach at Ayios Ioannis facing the town of Porto is okay, but you'd be better off walking west across the small headland to a longer, less popular beach, extending from this headland to the church or Ayios Sostis at its western extremity; you can also get here by driving or taking the bus to Ayios Sostis. There are two beaches at **Kolimbithres** on the north side of the island, easily accessed by car, although protection from the *meltemi* winds can be a problem. The second is better, with fine sand in a small rocky cove and two tavernas. There are more beaches around the headland from here—longer, less populous, and more exposed to the wind; you can reach these by a short drive on a poor dirt road beyond the beach mentioned above. The pebble cove at **Livada** is accessible only by a long, rough dirt road, and the north-facing beach receives the worst of the *meltemi* winds. Several beaches on the southwest coast (**Ayios Romanos, Ayios Petros,** and **Isternion**) are accessible by paved road. Just beyond Pirgos, the beach at **Panormou** is in the throes of development as a holiday resort. Finally, a series of hairpin-turn paved and unpaved roads lead down—and when we say "down," we mean "way down"—to beaches at Ayiou Petrou, Kalivia, and Giannaki, west of Tinos town.

WALKING

Tinos is a walker's paradise, with a good network of paths and remote interior regions waiting to be explored. Some of the best walks are in the vicinity of **Exobourgo**—paths connect the cluster of villages circling this craggy fortress, offering great views and many places to stop for refreshment along the way. There isn't a current English-language guide to walks in Tinos, but you can ask for information at **Windmills Travel** (©/fax **22830/23-398**) in Tinos town. The office plans to arrange walking tours in the future, and may be able to offer information about organized or individual walks.

SHOPPING

In Hora, the **flea market** on Evangelistria Street is a pleasant place for a ramble. Pedestrianized Evangelistria parallels Megaloharis, the main street from the harbor up to the cathedral. Shops and stalls lining Evangelistria Street sell icons, incense, candles, medallions, and *tamata* (tin, silver, and gold votives). You'll also find local embroidery, weavings, and the delicious local nougat, as well as *loukoumia* (Turkish delight) from Siros. Weekdays, a **fish market** and a **farmer's market** set up in the square by the docks. Keep an eye out for the rather pink-plumed pelican who hangs out nearby. A **Palamaris** supermarket on the harbor is handy to have nearby, and an even larger Palamaris is just outside Tinos town on the road to Pirgos.

Two fine jewelry shops stand side by side on Evangelistria: **Artemis,** 18 Evangelistria (© **22830/23-781**); and **Harris Prassas Ostria-Tinos,** 20 Evangelistria (© **22830/23-893;** fax 22830/24-568). Both have jewelry in contemporary, Byzantine, and classical styles; silverwork; and religious objects, including reproductions of the miraculous icon. Near the top of the street on the left in a neoclassical building, the small **Evangelismos Biotechni Shop,** the outlet of a local weaving school (© **22830/22-894**), sells reasonably priced table and bed linens, as well as rugs.

Those interested in local produce should head a few steps up and cross over to 16 Megaloharis, the shop of the local **agricultural cooperative,** where pungent capers, creamy cheeses, olive oil, and the fiery local *tsiporo* liqueur are on sale (© **22830/21-184**). If you like capers, stock up; we got ours safely back to Massachusetts and enjoyed them for months.

Several shops along the harbor sell international newspapers, local travel guides, maps, and some novels. The newspapers are on stands outside the shops.

WHERE TO STAY

Unless you have reservations, avoid Tinos during important religious holidays, especially **March 25** (Feast of the Annunciation) and **August 15** (Feast of the Assumption). It is also advisable to have reservations for summer weekends, when Greeks travel here by the hundreds to make a short pilgrimage to the Panagia Evangelistria.

For those planning to stay a week or longer, contact **Windmills Travel** (see "Visitor Information," above), which rents out houses in several villages—a great way to see more of the island and get a taste for village life. The weekly cost is from 100€ ($130) for a one-bedroom house, including car rental.

Oceanis Hotel ✦   This 10-year-old harborfront hotel is not located where the boats dock, so it is quieter than other lodgings by the port. The hotel is often taken over by

Greek groups visiting the island's religious shrines. As an independent traveler, you may feel a bit odd-man-out. The rooms are simply furnished, with good-size bathrooms. The balconies are a real plus. Don't bother with the restaurant. The Oceanis stays open all year and has reliable heat in the winter.

Akti G. Drossou, Hora, 84200 Tinos. ✆ **22830/22-452**. Fax 22830/25-402. 47 units. 80 € ($104) double. No credit cards. From the old harbor, walk south (right) along the paralia until you come to the Oceanis, whose large sign is clearly visible from the harbor. **Amenities:** Restaurant; bar. *In room:* A/C, TV.

Porto Tango ⚐⚐   This is the island's one serious resort hotel, with all the frills—sauna, spa, health club, pool, and more. However, while the hotel overlooks a good beach, the sea is a 10-minute walk away. Many rooms have balconies or terraces; some have both. Rooms in the "green" section have the best views. There are lots of antiques and antique reproductions throughout: chests, glass-globed lamps, and other almost-pseudo French provincial touches. They tend to redecorate every two years or so. A friend who stayed here had high praise for everything except the restaurant, which was perfectly okay but not memorable—and very expensive.

Porto, 84200 Tinos. (✆ **22830/24-411**. Fax 22830/24-416. www.portotango.gr. 61 units. 120€–150€ ($156–$195) double; 250€ ($325) suite. Breakfast buffet included. AE, MC, V. **Amenities:** 2 restaurants; bar; pool; health club; spa. *In room:* A/C, TV, minibar, hair dryer.

Tinos Beach Hotel ⚐ *Kids*   Despite a somewhat impersonal character and fading 1960s elegance, this is the best choice in a beachfront hotel near Hora. It does a brisk business with tour groups. The decent-size rooms all have balconies, most with views of the sea and pool. The suites are especially pleasant—large sitting rooms open onto poolside balconies. The pool is the longest on the island, and there's a separate children's pool as well. Cozy up under an umbrella on the sand-and-cobble beach fronting the hotel. Paddleboats and canoes are available for rent. We have yet to hear anyone praise either the ambience or the service here, but if you want to be on Tinos, near Tinos town but on the beach, this is the place to be.

Kionia, 84200 Tinos. ✆ **22830/22-626** or 22830/22-627. Fax 22830/23-153. www.tinosbeach.gr. 180 units. 130€–160€ ($169–$208) double. Rates include breakfast. Children 7 and under stay free in parent's room. AE, DC, MC, V. Closed Nov–Mar. 4km (2½ miles) west of Tinos town on the coast road. **Amenities:** Restaurant; bar; saltwater pool; children's pool; tennis courts; watersports equipment for rent. *In room:* A/C, TV, minifridge.

WHERE TO DINE

As usual, it's a good idea to avoid most harborfront joints, where food is generally inferior and service can be rushed. Still, we've had perfectly tasty souvlaki while other diners played leisurely games of *tavoli* (backgammon) at **Karkavelas** (✆ **22830/23-122**).

Metaxi Mas ⚐⚐ GREEK   A longtime American resident of Tinos took us here, and we can't wait to return to this family-run restaurant that calls itself a *mezedopoleio* (hors d'oeuvres place). There's a cozy interior dining room with a fireplace for when it's chilly, and tables outside in the pedestrianized lane for good weather. More importantly, the *mezedes* are irresistible: vegetable croquettes, fried sun-dried tomatoes, piquant fried cheeses, succulent octopus, and lots, lots more. If you still want an entree, the cabbage *dolmades* are memorable, and old standbys like veal or goat *stifado* (stew) are very tasty. Did we mention dessert? Try heavenly *galatovouriko* (a cholesterol bomb of milk and butter nestled between the *filo* leaves used in baklava). No wonder we saw several Greek families here whom we'd seen earlier in the day at the Evangelistria Church; Greeks take their food seriously when they travel.

Kontoyioryi, Paralia, Hora. ℂ **22830/24-857**. Main courses 6€–15€ ($7.80–$20). No credit cards. Daily noon–midnight. Off the harbor, in a lane between the old and new harbors. Look for the sign over the door. Sometimes a METAXI MAS banner is strung across the lane.

Palaia Pallada 👌👌 GREEK The same longtime American resident of Tinos who suggested Metaxi Mas also recommended Palaia Pallada. It's a bit more down-home, a bit less inventive, but equally good. Once again, she got it right: There are fewer ruffles and flourishes here, but the food (grills, stews, salads) in this family-run place is excellent, as is the local wine. You can eat indoors or outside in the lane.

Kontoyioryi, Paralia, Hora. ℂ **22830/23-516**. Main courses 5€–12€ ($6.50–$16). No credit cards. Daily noon–midnight. Off the harbor, in a lane between the old and new harbors. Look for the sign over the door, and the sign that overhangs the lane.

Taverna Drosia 👌 GREEK This taverna, perched at the head of a steep valley overlooking the sea, seems a world away from the crowds and traffic of the harbor. From the shaded flagstone terrace, you can watch ships slowly approaching. Siros sits across the water, and your view takes in terraced fields, dovecotes, and an old windmill in the valley. The food is basic taverna fare, though considerably better than average—bread arrives at the table in thick wholesome slabs, salads are sprinkled with succulent capers, and everything is very fresh.

Ktikades. ℂ **22830/41-387**. Main courses 5€–12€ ($6.50–$16). No credit cards. Daily 11am–midnight. 5km (3 miles) from Tinos town.

To Koutouki tis Eleni 👌 GREEK There's usually no menu at this excellent small taverna, known in town simply as Koutouki. Basic ingredients are cooked up into simple meals that remind you how delightful Greek food can be. Local cheese and wine, fresh fish and meats, delicious vegetables—these are the staples that come together so well in this taverna, demonstrating that you don't have to pay a fortune to experience good *paradisiako* (traditional) home cooking.

Paralia, Hora. ℂ **22830/24-857**. Main courses 5€–15€ ($6.50–$20). No credit cards. Daily noon–midnight. From the harbor, turn onto Evangelistria, the market street; take the 1st right up a narrow lane with 3 tavernas. Koutouki is the 1st on the left.

Xynari 👌 GREEK Good food in lovely surroundings in a distinguished 19th-century house are the trademarks of what for years has been considered the town's most upmarket restaurant. This place has been known for grills that make you realize how poorly many places do meat, and for its piquant eggplant dishes. The present owners are new, but initial reports have been good. In warm weather, tables are set up on the balcony. The interior rooms—a little dark wood, some nicely painted walls—are charming. There's often live music on weekends—and the location, just off the harbor on Evangelistria, guarantees great people-watching.

13 Evangelistria, Hora. ℂ **22830/23-665**. Main courses 6€–25€ ($7.80–$33). AE, MC, V. Daily 7pm–midnight.

TINOS AFTER DARK

As we've mentioned, Tinos is a place of pilgrimage, and there's less nightlife here than on many islands. That said, the bars, such as **Sivilla** (no phone listed) and **Koursaros** (ℂ **22830/23-963**), are open until the wee hours. Two sweets shops, **Epilekto** (ℂ **22080/23-787**) and **Meskiles** (fantastic *loukoumades* with ice cream; no phone listed) are also open late and are in the same area, along and just off the Pallada (the waterfront). Several all-night disco joints are walkable distances out of town, but keep a sharp eye out for speeding motorcycles. **Cactus Bar** (ℂ **22830/25-930**) is on the road to Pirgos; and **Paradise Club** (no phone listed) is on the road to Kionia. If you want a late-night (or early-morning) coffee, try **Monopolio** (© 22830/25-770) on the harborfront; instead of a cup, this place brings you a delicious full pot of French filtered coffee.

9 Siros (Syros)

144km (78 nautical miles) SE of Piraeus

Siros offers a rare opportunity to vacation as the Greeks do. Excellent food, a long tradition of the popular music known as *rembetika,* glorious little-known beaches, and the most energetic island capital in the Cyclades are among its pleasures.

The island's capital, **Ermoupolis** is also the administrative capital of the Cyclades. In the 19th century, this was the busiest port in Greece—far busier than Piraeus—and a center of shipbuilding. You'll see several surviving shipyards along the harbor. Signs of the island's former affluence are concentrated in the vicinity of the harbor, where neoclassical mansions abut the rocky waterfront and grandiose public buildings line spacious squares. Although Ermoupolis saw a considerable period of design in the 20th century, recent restoration efforts have brought back much of the glory of the city's heyday; several of the most elaborate mansions have been restored as homes and others have been converted to hotels and guest houses. Other signs of urban revival are a busy calendar of lively public events and some of the best food in the Cyclades.

The north end of the island is a starkly beautiful region of widely dispersed farms, terraced fields, and plentiful walking paths. The island's best beaches are here, accessible only on foot or by boat. You can reach the spectacularly situated Cycladic site at Kastri by trail from here as well. San Mihali and kopanisti cheeses are made here, as well as a delicious thyme honey; all of these can be found in the Ermoupolis open-air market.

The best months to visit Siros are May, June, and September; the worst month is August, when vacationing Greeks fill every hotel room on the island. Getting around this small island by bus is so easy and convenient that you may not need a car or moped.

ESSENTIALS

GETTING THERE By Plane In summer, there's at least one flight daily from Athens. Contact **Olympic Airways** in Athens (© 210/966-6666 or 210/936-9111; www.olympic-airways.gr) or at their office in Ermoupolis, 100m (328 ft.) from the port in the direction of Hotel Hermes (© 22810/88-018 or 22810/82-634).

By Boat Ferries connect Siros at least once daily with Piraeus (2½ hr. by high-speed ferry, 4½ hr. by ferry), Naxos (1½ hr. by high-speed ferry or hydrofoil, 2½ hr. by ferry), Mykonos (30 min. by high-speed ferry, 1½ hr. by ferry), Paros (45 min. by high-speed ferry, 1½ hr. by ferry), Tinos (1 hr.), and Santorini (4–7 hr.). The ferries connect once or twice weekly with Folegandros (5–6 hr.), Sifnos (3 hr.), Iraklion (5–10 hr.), Samos (7–9 hr. to Vathi), and Thessaloniki (12–15 hr.). There are also daily catamarans from Rafina (2 hr.). You'll find numerous ferry-ticket offices at the pier. **Alpha Syros** (© 22810/81-185), opposite the ferry pier, and its sister company **Teamwork Holidays** (© 22810/83-400; teamwork@otenet.gr), sell tickets for all the ferries. Ferry information can be verified with the local **port authority** (© 22810/88-888 or 22810/82-690). Piraeus ferry schedules can be confirmed with the **GNTO** in Athens (© 210/327-1300 or 210/331-0562) or with **Piraeus Port Authority** (© 210/459-3223 or 210/422-6000; phone seldom answered). For Rafina schedules, call **Rafina Port Authority** (© 22940/28-888).

VISITOR INFORMATION   The **Hoteliers Association of Siros** operates an information booth at the pier in summer; it's open daily from 9am to 10pm. Note that the list of hotels they offer is not complete. **Teamwork Holidays** (© 22810/83-400; fax 22810/83-508) on the harbor can book rooms; change money; sell airline tickets; book ferry tickets; and arrange rental cars. In the summer, Teamwork offers around-the-island full-day beach tours by yacht 50 € ($65), as well as a full-day excursion to Mykonos and Delos for 60€ ($78).

GETTING AROUND   By Bus   The **bus stop** in Ermoupolis is at the pier, where the schedule is posted. Buses circle the southern half of Siros hourly in summer between 8am and midnight. There are no buses to the northern part of the island. The off-season schedule is irregular due to the fact that the buses also bring children to and from school.

By Car & Moped   Of the several car rental places along the harbor in the vicinity of the pier, a reliable choice is **Siros Rent A Car** (© 22810/80-409), next to the GNTO office on Dodekanisou, a side street just to the left of the pier. A small car will cost from 55€ ($72) per day, including insurance. A 50cc scooter rents from 25€ ($33) per day.

By Taxi   The taxi stand is on the main square, Plateia Miaoulis (© 2810/86-222).

FAST FACTS   Several **banks** on the harbor have ATMs. The Ermoupolis **hospital** (© 22810/86-666) is the largest in the Cyclades; it's just outside town to the west near Plateia Iroon. For free **luggage storage,** ask at Teamwork Holidays (© 22810/83-400). The **police** (© 22810/82-610) are on the south side of Miaoulis Square. The **port authority** (© 22810/88-888 or 22810/82-690) is on the long pier at the far end of the harbor, beyond Hotel Hermes. The **post office** (© 22810/82-596) is between Miaoulis Square and the harbor on Protopapadaki; it's open Monday through Friday from 7:30am to 2pm. The **telephone office (OTE)** is on the east side of Miaoulis Square (© 22810/87-399); it's open Monday through Saturday from 7:30am to 3pm. Bizanas is an **Internet cafe** on Plateia Miaoulis.

WHAT TO SEE & DO
MUSEUMS
Archaeological Museum   The highlight of this museum's small collection is a room containing finds from the excavations at Halandriani, a prehistoric cemetery in the northern hills of Siros, including several fine Cycladic figurines. You can visit the Bronze Age fortified settlement at Kastri, near Halandriani, where many of the museum's artifacts were found. Since Ermoupolis is the capital of the Cyclades, the archaeological museum has holdings from many of the smaller Cycladic islands, including two beautiful miniature Hellenistic marble heads, a Roman-era sculpture from Amorgos, and a black granite statue originally from Egypt which dates back to 730 B.C.

On the west side of the town hall below the clock tower, Ermoupolis. © 22810/86-900. Admission 3€ ($3.90). Tues–Sun 8:30am–3pm.

Ermoupolis Industrial Museum   Behind the copious cranes and warehouses of the Neorion Shipyard at the southern end of the port, you'll find the Industrial Museum of Ermoupolis, which opened in 2000. It's worth the 20-minute walk from the ferry pier to check out this extensive collection of artifacts from the town's industrial past: weaving machines, metalworking tools and, of course, items related to the town's famed shipyards. Also check out the fine collection of original drawings by the

> ### *Tips* Cyclades Casino
>
> Ermoupolis has the only **casino** (𝄪 **22810/84-400**) in the Cyclades. It's quite an elegant establishment, worth a look even if you aren't interested in gambling. The main entrance is directly opposite the bus station and ferry pier. The management is British, and most of the staff speak perfect English. The entrance fee is 20€ ($26); the minimum bet is 5€ ($6.50). Slot machines take euro coins. There's no cover charge for the restaurant and bar on the back street. The casino is open daily from 8pm to 6am in summer; slot machines are open from 2pm.

architects of Ermoupolis's neoclassical heyday, the interesting photographs and engravings depicting various aspects of island life, and the old maps of Siros and the Cyclades.

Ermoupolis. Just off Plateia Iroon and opposite the hospital. 𝄪 **22810/86-900**. Admission 3€ ($3.90) students; free on Wed. No credit cards. Tues–Sun 10am–2pm and 6–9pm.

EXPLORING ERMOUPOLIS

Ermoupolis is a flourishing city, a city with a life of its own that clearly doesn't rely on tourism. If you arrive on Syros by boat, you'll immediately be aware of the capital's lay of the land: Two hills loom over the waterfront. Originally, the term **Ano Siros** (which means "the area above Siros") was used to describe the peaks of both hills. This is where islanders retreated when threatened by pirate raids. Today, the term Ano Siros describes the taller hill seen to the left of Ermoupolis as you enter the harbor. This was, and still is, the Catholic quarter of the town, founded by the Venetians in the 13th century. Much of the intricate maze of streets from that period remains today. Several Roman Catholic churches stand here; the most important is the **Church of Ayios Yioryios** (Mass Sun 11am). The large buff-colored building on the hilltop is the medieval **Monastery of the Capuchins.** Remnants of castle walls, stone archways, and narrow lanes make this area a delight to explore. Omirou, one of the streets that run uphill, is probably your best bet for an assault on Ano Siro.

The other hill, **Vrondado,** with its blue-domed Greek Orthodox Church of the Resurrection, was built up as the town grew when Greeks from other islands, especially Chios, moved here at the time of the Greek War of Independence in the 1820s. Its narrow streets, marble-paved squares, and dignified mansions lend a certain old-world charm to the bustling inner city. There's a great view of Ermoupolis and the neighboring islands from the terrace outside the **Church of the Resurrection.** This is also the location of the island's two main cemeteries. The Catholic one with the more imposing marble monuments reflects the longstanding prosperity of that community.

The sophisticated neoclassical architecture of Ermoupolis's 19th-century glory days dominates the low-lying areas of the city in the vicinity of the harbor. The central square, **Plateia Miaoulis,** and the elaborately elegant neoclassical **Town Hall** (designed by Ernst Ziller, who designed the Grande Bretagne and Parliament House in Athens) are conspicuous reminders of Ermoupolis's heyday. (To reach Plateia Miaoulis from the port, turn inland on Venizelou, near the bus station.) Plateias this grand are unknown on other Cycladic islands. Ringed by high palm trees and facing the town hall, Plateia Miaoulis is the center of civic life in Ermoupolis. Outdoor theatrical and musical events are often presented here, and every night the square is filled with promenading Ermoupolites.

A couple of blocks northeast of the town hall is the 19th-century **Apollon Theater** ⚜, a smaller version of Milan's La Scala. It's being restored, thanks to funding from the European Union, and there may be performances here by the time you visit. (Contact the **GNTO** at ✆ **22810/86-725** for information and tickets.) Northeast behind it is the imposing Greek Orthodox church of **Ayios Nikolaos,** with a green marble iconostasis by Vitalis, a famed 19th-century marble carver from Tinos. (Vitalis also sculpted the monument to an unknown soldier in the garden near the entrance.) A short stroll beyond the church will bring you to the neighborhood called **Vaporia,** named after the steamships that brought it great prosperity.

BEACHES

Beaches are not the island's strong suit, but there are a number of perfectly adequate places to swim and sun. **Megas Yialos,** as its name states, is the largest beach on the island and the prettiest on the south coast. Its sandy beach is shaded by tamarisk trees and is especially good for families because it's gently shelved. A number of small tavernas offer "rent rooms"; there's also a small hotel.

On the west coast, **Galissas** has one of the best beaches on the island, a crescent of sand bordered by tamarisks. It also has a large campsite (for info, contact www.two hearts-camping.com), so unless you are interested in camping, you may not find Galissas appealing.

Also on the west coast, **Finikas** has a slender beach and a cluster of hotels and restaurants. A few kilometers to the south, **Posidonia** and **Agathopes** have sand beaches and less competition for a place in the sun.

WHERE TO STAY

As you come off the ferry in Ermoupolis, you'll see the kiosk of the **Hoteliers Association of Siros,** which provides a list of island hotels. Note that hotels pay to become members of this association, so not all of the island's best lodgings are represented. In August, when vacationing Greeks pack the island, don't even think of arriving without a reservation.

Hotel Apollonos   This mansion on the water in Vaporia has been meticulously restored and decorated; it's one of the best of the town's period hotels. Those looking for a fully authentic restoration might be disappointed—the furnishings and lighting are contemporary in style—but the overall effect is one of complete harmony between new and old, creating an atmosphere of understated elegance. The best guest rooms are the two facing the water at the back of the house: Both are quite spacious, and one has a loft sleeping area with sitting room below. Bathrooms are large, with tile and

---

Shopping in Ermoupolis

The shops here tend to be functional rather than funky, and there aren't any that stand out. However, just about anything you need can be found somewhere in town. The best street for shopping is **Protopapadaki,** two streets from the port, which is open to car traffic and the location of the post office. The town's **produce market** is on **Hios,** west of the main square. It's open daily, but is particularly lively on Saturday. Don't leave the market without trying two local specialties: *loukoumia,* better known as Turkish delight; and *halvodopita,* a sort of nougat.

---

wood floors. A large common sitting room faces the bay, while a breakfast room faces the street.

8 Apollonos, Ermoupolis, 84100 Siros. © 22810/81-387 or 22810/80-842. Fax 22810/81-681. 3 units. 185€ ($241) double. Rates include breakfast. No credit cards. **Amenities:** Breakfast room/bar. *In room:* A/C.

Hotel Hermes ★ *Value*   The Hermes presents a bright, modern facade to busy Plateia Kanari at the harbor's east end. What you can't see from the street is that many of the deluxe rooms directly face a quiet stretch of rocky coast at the back of the building. The functional, rather dull standard rooms have shower-only bathrooms and views of the street or a back garden. The deluxe rooms in the new wing are worth the extra money for their size, furnishings, and balconies that allow early risers to see the sunrise. The hotel restaurant serves three meals a day, offering quality Greek food at reasonable prices.

Plateia Kanari, Ermoupolis, 84100 Siros. © **22810/83-011** or 22810/83-012. Fax 22810/87-412. 51 units. 85€–100€ ($111–$130) double. Continental breakfast 5€ ($6.50). AE, DC, MC, V. **Amenities:** Restaurant; bar. *In room:* A/C, TV.

Hotel Omiros ★   In 1988, when the work of restoration was begun, this building was in a state of near ruin. Today the Omiros has become one of the most appealing of the neoclassical mansion hotels in Ermoupolis. Rooms are furnished with simple antiques. Some details from the original building have been retained, such as marble hand basins and massive fireplaces. The architectural highlight of the building is the spiral staircase that climbs through a shaft of light to the glass roof. Breakfast, drinks, and light meals are served in a small walled garden. The hotel is on a hill above Miaoulis Square—the climb from the port is steep, so it's best to take a taxi. There is parking, although the route from the port is complex and difficult to follow; call ahead for directions.

43 Omirou, Ermoupolis, 84100 Siros. © **22810/84-910** or 22810/88-756. Fax 22810/86-266. 13 units. 115€ ($150) double. Continental breakfast 10€ ($13). MC, V.

Hotel Vourlis ★★   On a hill overlooking the fashionable Vaporia district, the elegant Hotel Vourlis occupies one of the finest of the city's mansions. Built in 1888, the house has retained its grandeur and charm. The fine details that have sadly been lost in many other restored mansions are here in all their glory. The plaster ceilings in the front rooms are especially resplendent. Most furniture also dates to the 19th century, creating a period setting that incorporates all the comforts you expect from a fine hotel. Bathrooms are spacious, and come with tubs. The two front rooms on the second floor have great sea views. Winter guests will be glad to know that the house is centrally heated. The adjacent five-unit **Ipatia Guesthouse** (© **22810/83-575**) is in a nicely restored town house.

5 Mavrokordatou, Ermoupolis, 84100 Siros. ©/fax **22810/88-440** or 22810/81-682. 8 units. 125€–175€ ($163–$228) double. Continental breakfast 9€ ($12). MC, V. **Amenities:** Breakfast room/bar. *In room:* A/C, TV.

WHERE TO DINE

There are numerous excellent tavernas in and around Ermoupolis. **Boubas Ouzeri** and **Yacht Club of Siros** are both known for ouzo and *mezedes*. In addition to the tavernas mentioned below, try the consistently good **Petrino Taverna** (© **22810/84-427**), around the corner from To Arhontariki; and **Fragosiriani** (© **22810/84-888**), with a great view from its high terrace in Ano Siros (down the street from Taverna Lilis).

Taverna Lilis GREEK/SEAFOOD   Lilis is one of the best of the tavernas in Ano Siros, the quarter cresting the high conical hill behind Ermoupolis. From the outdoor terrace, there's a stellar view of Ermoupolis, the bay, distant Tinos and, even farther out, the shores of Mykonos. The food is better-than-average taverna fare—meats and fish are grilled on a wood fire, and the ingredients are reliably fresh.

Ano Siros. (✆ **22810/88-087.** Reservations recommended in July–Aug. Main courses 8€–18€ ($10–$23). No credit cards. Daily 7pm–midnight. Follow Omirou from the center of Ermoupolis, past the Hotel Omiros, and continue straight up the long flight of steps that leads to Lilis's brightly lit terrace. You can also call a taxi.

To Arhontariki GREEK   This small place fills the narrow street with tables precariously perched on cobblestones and is probably the best of the tavernas in Ermoupolis center. It's easy to find—just plunge into the maze of streets at the corner of Miaoulis Square between Pyramid Pizzeria and Loukas Restaurant, and weave your way left—it's 2 blocks or so in, between Miaoulis and the harbor. The menu is largely composed of specials that change daily. It always includes a few vegetable main courses, which are subtly spiced and delicious.

Ermoupolis. (✆ **22810/81-744.** Main courses 6€–18€ ($7.80–$23). Daily noon–midnight.

To Koutaki Tou Liberi ★ GREEK   Take a taxi to this out-of-the-way place that is definitely worthwhile. There is no menu—the night's offerings are brought out to you on a massive tray, and each dish is explained in turn. The food is often innovative, making slight but significant departures from traditional recipes. The spicing is subtle, and good use is made of the season's best ingredients. The owner is renowned locally for his *bouzouki* playing—late at night, after the last diners have finished their meals, impromptu traditional music sessions sometimes take place. Did we mention the view? It's exquisite.

Kaminia. (✆ **22810/85-580.** Reservations recommended several days in advance in high season. Main courses 8€–18€ ($10–$23). No credit cards. Fri–Sat 9pm–1am. 2km (1¼ miles) from Ermoupolis center.

SIROS AFTER DARK

Siros was among the most fertile grounds for *rembetika;* the famous *rembetika* star Markos Vamvakaris was born here. You can find this special music at **Xanthomalis** (no phone; closed in summer) and at **Lilis** (✆ **22810/28-087**) in Ano Siros, which sometimes have late-night performances on the weekends; reservations are a must.

In Ermoupolis, the waterfront is the best place to be at sunset. Stick your head into any of the many bars to see which is playing music that suits your taste. Contenders include **Kimbara** and **Liquid,** where the phone may ring but is never answered. You can also join in the evening *volta* **(stroll)** around Plateia Miaoulis, take a seat to watch it, or drop in at **Piramatiko.** The outdoor **Pallas Cinema,** east of the main square, has one nightly showing, often in English.

Be sure to pick up a list of events scheduled as part of **Ermoupoleia,** a summer-long arts festival featuring prominent visiting artists; all events are free. The principal venues include Apollon Theater, Miaoulis Square, and Pallas Cinema, where several theatrical, musical, or cinematic events are held each week. Programs are available at the GNTO office, most hotels, and travel agencies throughout town.

9

The Dodecanese

by John S. Bowman

The first thing to note about this Greek archipelago far to the east is that "the Dodecanese"—"the 12 islands"—is in fact 32 islands: 14 inhabited and 18 uninhabited. They have been known collectively as the Dodecanese since 1908, when 12 of them joined forces to resist the revocation of the special status they had long enjoyed under the Ottoman sultans.

The Dodecanese are far from the Greek mainland and mostly hug the coast of Asia Minor. As frontier or borderline territories, their struggles to remain free and Greek have been intense and prolonged. Although they have been recognizably Greek for millennia, only in 1948 were the Dodecanese formally reunited with the Greek nation.

Long accustomed to watching the seas for invaders, these islands now spend their time awaiting the tourists who show up each spring and stay until October. The beginning of the tourist season sets into motion a pattern of activity largely contrived to attract and entertain outsiders. Such is the reality of island life today. As in the past, however, the islanders proudly retain their own character even as they accommodate an onslaught of visitors.

The islands covered in this chapter are selected from "the 12." In high season, you can travel easily from one to the other. The principal islands, south to north, are **Rhodes, Kos,** and **Patmos.** North of Rhodes lies the lesser yet exquisite island of **Simi.** Patmos and Simi are relatively barren in summer, while the interiors of Rhodes and Kos remain fertile and forested. Spectacular historical sights such as ancient ruins and medieval fortresses are concentrated on Patmos, Kos, and Rhodes; so are the tourists. Simi is the not-quite-secret getaway you will not soon forget.

STRATEGIES FOR SEEING THE ISLANDS

In planning a visit to the Dodecanese, keep in mind that Rhodes has the longest tourist season. So, if you're rushing the season in April, begin in Rhodes; if you're stretching the season into October, end up in Rhodes. In general, avoid the Dodecanese late July through August, when they are so glutted with tourists that they nearly sink.

The three islands most worth visiting—both for their own sake and as bases to explore other nearby islands—are **Rhodes, Kos,** and **Patmos.** From the mainland, all are best reached by air. Rhodes and Kos have airports; Patmos is a short jaunt by hydrofoil from Samos, which also has an airport. From Kos and Rhodes, you can get just about anywhere in the eastern Aegean, including nearby **Turkey,** which is worth at least a day's excursion. **Simi** can be reached by ferry from Piraeus but most people will approach it by boat as an excursion from Rhodes.

The Dodecanese

Ancient Lindos **6**
Asklepion **2**
Monastery of St. John
   and the Cave of the Apocalypse **1**
Monolithos Castle **5**
Panormitis Monastery **3**
Petaloudes (Valley of the Butterflies) **4**

PATMOS
Arki
Marathos
Kampos
Skala
Lipsi
Agathonisi
Megalo Horio
Farmakonisi
Partheni
LEROS
Lakki
Ksirokampos
Levitha
Emborios
Arginonta
Telendos
Massouri
Mirties
KALIMNOS
Kalimnos
Psarimos
Lambi
Mastihari
Tigaki
Kos
Ayios Fokas
Asfendiou
Kefalos
Kardamena
KOS
Vathys
Yiali
Loutra
Simi
Pedi
Analipsi
Mandraki
Emborios
SIMI
Astypalea
Astypalea
Avlaki
Nisyros
Sirna
Megalo Horio
Livadia
Tilos
Tria Nissia
Alimia
Halki
Mandriko
RHODES
Embonas
Monolithos
Laerma
Apolakia
Messanagros
Gennadio
Kattavia
Plimiri
Rhodes
Ialisos
Maritsa
Kalithea
Soroni
Fanes
Faliraki
Afandou
Archangelos
Lindos
Saria
Diafani
Olymbos
KARPATHOS
Spoa
Piles
Arkassa
Karpathos
Armathia
Fri
← To Crete
Kassos

Greece
Aegean
Sea
Athens
The
Dodecanese
Mediterranean
Sea
CRETE

Airport ✈
Ferry Routes ---

0   25 mi
0   25 km

N

> *Tips* **Museum Hours Update**
>
> If you visit Greece during the summer, check to see when sites and museums are open. According to the tourist office, they should be open from 8am to 7:30pm, but some may close earlier in the day or even be closed one day a week.

1 Rhodes (Rodos) ★★

250km (135 nautical miles) E of Piraeus

Selecting a divine patron was serious business for an ancient city. Most Greek cities played it safe and chose a mainstream god or goddess, a ranking Olympian: someone like Athena or Apollo or Artemis, or Zeus himself. It's revealing that the people of Rhodes chose **Helios,** the Sun, as their signature god.

Indeed, millennia later the cult of the Sun is alive and well on Rhodes, and no wonder: The island receives on average more than 300 days of sunshine a year. What's more, Rhodes is a destination for sun-worshippers from colder, darker, wetter lands around the globe.

But Rhodes gives visitors more than a mere tan. A location at the intersection of the East and West propelled the island into the thick of both commerce and conflicts. The scars left by its rich and turbulent history have become its treasures. Knights, Turks, Italians—all invaders who wreaked devastation—also left behind fascinating artifacts.

Through it all, Rhodes has remained beautiful. Its beaches are among the cleanest in the Aegean, and its interior is still home to unspoiled mountain villages, rich fertile plains—and beautiful butterflies. Several days in Rhodes will allow you to appreciate its marvels, relax in the sun, and perhaps add a day trip to the idyllic island of Simi or to the coast of Turkey. If Rhodes is your last port of call, it will make a grand finale; if it is your point of departure, you can launch forth happily from here to just about anywhere in the Aegean or Mediterranean.

ESSENTIALS

GETTING THERE **By Plane** In addition to its year-round service between Rhodes and Athens and Thessaloniki, **Olympic Airways** offers summer service between Rhodes and the following Greek locales: Iraklion (Crete), Karpathos, Mykonos, and Santorini. The local Olympic office is at 9 Ierou Lohou (© **22410/24-571** or 22410/24-555). Flights fill quickly, so reserve in advance. **Aegean Airlines** (within Greece © **80111/ 20-000;** www.aegeanair.com), in addition to flights to Rhodes, offers at least high-season flights between Rhodes and Thessaloniki and Iraklion, Crete. Tickets for any flight in or out of Rhodes can be purchased directly from **Triton Holidays,** near Mandraki Harbor, 9 Plastira, Rhodes city (© **22410/21-690;** fax 22410/31-625; www.tritondmc.gr). Triton will either send your tickets to you or have them waiting for you at the airport.

The Rhodes **Paradissi Airport** (© **22410/83-214**) is 13km (8 miles) southwest of the city and is served from 6am to 10:30pm by bus. The bus to the city center (Plateia Rimini) is 3€ ($3.90). A taxi costs 18€ ($23). By the way, some taxi drivers resist taking passengers to hotels in the Old City; note their number and threaten to report them, and they will usually relent.

By Boat Rhodes is a major port with sea links not only to Athens, Crete, and the islands of the Aegean, but also to Cyprus, Turkey, and Israel. Service and schedules

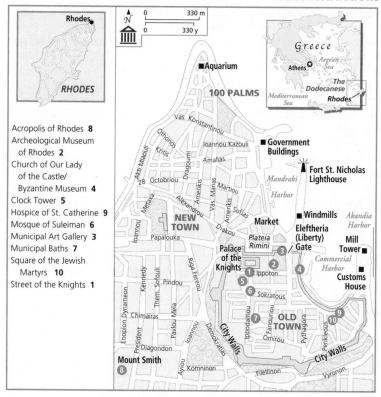

Acropolis of Rhodes **8**
Archeological Museum
  of Rhodes **2**
Church of Our Lady
  of the Castle/
  Byzantine Museum **4**
Clock Tower **5**
Hospice of St. Catherine **9**
Mosque of Suleiman **6**
Municipal Art Gallery **3**
Municipal Baths **7**
Square of the Jewish
  Martyrs **10**
Street of the Knights **1**

are always changing; check with the tourist office or a travel agency for the latest information.

In late spring and summer, daily hydrofoil or catamaran service runs from Mandraki Harbor to Kos, Tilos, Nissiros, and Simi, and less predictable service to many destinations, including Kalimnos, Leros, Patmos, Kastellorizo, and Samos. The advantage of hydrofoils and catamarans is that they make the voyage in half the time, but when the wind blows, the sailings are canceled. Air quality is also poor, especially compared to that on larger open-deck excursion boats or ferries.

Wherever it is you want to go, whether by ferry, hydrofoil, catamaran, or excursion boat, schedules and tickets are available from **Triton Holidays,** 9 Plastira (© **22410/ 21-690;** fax 22410/31-625; www.tritondmc.gr). Although travel agents throughout Rhodes city and island can issue air and sea tickets, we like Triton Holidays' focus on independent travelers.

VISITOR INFORMATION   The staff at the **South Aegean Tourist Office,** at the intersection of Makariou and Papagou (© **22410/23-255;** www.ando.gr/eot), can provide advice and help for all the Dodecanese islands, including Rhodes. Hours are Monday through Friday from 8am to 3pm. During the high season only, you'll find a helpful **Rhodes Municipal Tourist Office** down the hill at Plateia Rimini near the port taxi stand (© **22410/35-945**). It dispenses information on local excursions, buses, ferries, and accommodations, and offers currency exchange as well. Its hours are Monday through Saturday from about 9am to 9pm and Sunday from 9am to 2pm. The above-recommended **Triton Holidays** is also ready, willing, and able to answer any traveler's question, free of obligation, and is sometimes open when the tourist offices are closed.

GETTING AROUND Rhodes is not an island you can see on foot. You need wheels of some sort: public bus, group-shared taxi, rental car, or organized bus tour for around-the-island excursions. The city is a different story. Walking is the best and most pleasurable mode of transport; you'll need a taxi only if you're going to treat yourself to a meal at one of the farther-flung restaurants or if you're decked out for the casino and don't want to walk. Note that wheeled vehicles, except those driven by permanent Old Town residents, are not allowed within the walls. This goes for all taxis, unless you have luggage.

By Bus There's good public bus service throughout the island; the tourist office publishes a schedule of routes and times. Buses to points **east** (except for the eastern coastal road as far as Falilraki) leave from the East Side Bus Station on Plateia Rimini, while buses to points **west,** including the airport, leave from the nearby West Side Bus Station on Averof. Buses for the eastern coastal road as far as Falilraki also leave from the West Side Bus Station. Island fares range from .80€ ($1.05) within the city to 10€ ($13) for the most remote destinations. The city bus system also offers six different tours; details are available from the tourist office.

By Bicycle, Moped & Motorcycle Even where there are strips set aside for bicyclists, it can be risky cycling on Greek highways. You must have a proper license to rent anything motorized. **Bicycle Center,** 39 Griva (✆ **22410/28-315**), rents bikes, mopeds, and motorcycles. The best-looking mountain bikes we've seen are at **Moto Pilot,** 12 Kritis (✆ **22410/32-285**). Starting prices per day are roughly 6€ ($7.80) for a 21-speed; 10€ ($13) for an aluminum mountain bike; from 12€ ($16) for a moped; and 25€ to 35€ ($33–$46) for a motorcycle.

By Taxi In Rhodes city, the largest of many taxi stands is in front of the old town, on the harborfront in Plateia Rimini (✆ **22410/27-666**). There, posted for all to see, are the set fares for one-way trips throughout the island. (A sample fare to Lindos is 35€/$46.) Since many of the cab drivers speak sightseer English, a few friends can be chauffeured and lectured at a reasonable cost. Taxis are metered, but fares should not exceed the minimum on short round-the-city jaunts. For longer trips, negotiate directly with the drivers. Better yet, **Triton Holidays** (see above), will at no extra charge arrange for a private full- or half-day taxi with a driver who not only speaks fluent English, but will also respect your wishes regarding smoking or nonsmoking en route. For **radio taxis,** call ✆ **22410/64-712.** There is a slight additional pickup charge when you call for a taxi.

⌐Tips A Helping Hand

The **Dodecanese Association for People with Special Needs** (✆ **22410/73-109;** mobile 6940/463810) provides free minibus door-to-door service from the port, airport, and hotels—or even if you want to go out for coffee or a swim.

By Car   Apart from the array of international companies—among them **Alamo/ National** (© 22410/73-570), **Avis** (© 22410/82-896), **Europcar** (© 22410/ 21-958), and **Hertz** (© 22410/21-819)—there is a large number of local companies. The latter may offer the lowest rates but have only a handful of cars, so they may be unable to back you up in the event of an accident. Be very certain that you are fully covered, for all minor scrapes as well as major accidents, before signing anything. An established Greek company with roughly 200 cars—reputedly the newest fleet on Rhodes—is **DRIVE Rent-a-Car** (© 22410/68-243). It has an excellent reputation for personal service, as well as low prices from about 50€ ($65) per day. Keep in mind that some of the roads on Rhodes require all-terrain vehicles. Rhodian rental-car companies usually stipulate that their standard vehicles be driven only on fully paved roads.

By Organized Tour & Cruise   Several operators feature nature, archaeology, shopping, and beach tours. In Rhodes city, **Triton Holidays** (see above) is one of the largest and most reliable agencies and specializes in trips designed for independent travelers. Triton offers day and evening cruises, hiking tours, and excursions in Rhodes, as well as in the other Dodecanese islands and in Mamaris in Turkey. We recommend the full-day guided tours, either the one to Lindos (30€/$39); or the "Island Tour" (35€/$46), which takes you to small villages, churches, and monasteries, and includes lunch in the village of **Embonas,** known for its local wines and fresh-grilled meat. There is also a fascinating half-day guided tour to Filerimos Monastery, Valley of the Butterflies, and the ancient city of Kamiros for 30€ ($39). Along Mandraki Harbor, you can find excursion boats that leave for **Lindos** at 9am and return around 6pm, costing 18€ ($23); and daily excursions to **Simi** for 25€ ($33). For an in-depth island experience, Triton Holidays also offers a combination package of car rental and hotel accommodations in four small villages around the island (Kalavarda, Monolithos, Prassonisi, and Asklepion), ranging from 4 to 10 nights.

CITY LAYOUT   Rhodes is not the worst offender in Greece, but it does share the country's widespread aversion to street signs. This means that you need a map marked with every lane, so that you can count your way from one place to another. We recommend the two maps drawn and published by Mario Camerini in 1995, of which the mini-atlas entitled *Map of Rhodes Town* is the best. It's available at kiosks and tourist bookstalls.

Rhodes city (pop. 42,400) is divided into two sections: the Old Town, dating from medieval days, and the New Town. Overlooking the harbor, the **Old Town** ✦ is surrounded by massive walls—4km (2½ miles) around and in certain places nearly 12m (40 ft.) thick—built by the Knights of St. John. The **New Town** embraces the old one and extends south to meet the **Rhodian Riviera,** a strip of luxury resort hotels. At its northern tip is the city beach, in the area called 100 Palms, and famed **Mandraki Harbor,** now used as a mooring for private yachts and tour boats.

Walking away from Mandraki Harbor on Plastira, you'll come to **Cyprus Square,** where many of the New Town hotels are clustered. Veer left and continue to the park where the mighty fortress (the city walls) begins. Down the slope is Plateia Rimini and the Municipal Tourist Office (see "Visitor Information," above).

FAST FACTS   The local **American Express** agent is Rhodos Tours, Ammochostou 29 (© 22410/21-010), in the New Town; it's open Monday through Saturday from 8:30am to 1:30pm and 5 to 8:30pm. The **National Bank of Greece,** on Cyprus Square, exchanges currency Monday through Thursday from 8am to 2pm, Friday from 8am to 1:30pm, and Saturday from 9am to 1pm. There are other currency-exchange offices throughout the Old Town and New Town, often with rates better than those of the banks. For emergency care, call the **hospital** (✆ **22410/80-000**) or, if necessary, an **ambulance** (✆ **166**).

The only **Internet access** in the Old Town has long been **Cosmonet Internet Cafe,** at 45B Evreon Martyron Sq.; it also has an outlet in the New Town, at 17E G. Papaniko-lao (opposite the Rhodes Casino); its hours are daily from 10am to midnight. **Express Laundry,** 5 Kosti Palama, behind Plateia Rimini (✆ **22410/22-514**), is open daily from 8am to 11pm. **Wash-O-Matic** on 33 Platonos (leading off Sokratous) keeps the same hours. **International Pharmacy,** 22 A. Kiakou (✆ **22410/75-331**), is near Thermai Hotel. There are **public toilets** at 2 Papagou and across from 10 Papagou; there is also one just outside the wall at the Marine Gate by the Old Harbor. The **police** (✆ **22410/ 23-849**) in the Old Town can handle any complaints from 10am to midnight. The **tourist police** (✆ **22410/27-423**), on the edge of the Old Town near the port, address tourists' queries, concerns, and grievances. The main **post office** on Mandraki Harbor is open Monday through Friday from 7am to 8pm. A smaller office is on Orfeon in the Old Town, open daily with shorter hours.

WHAT TO SEE & DO IN RHODES CITY

Rhodes is awash in first-rate sights and entertainment. As an international playground and a museum of both antiquity and the medieval era, Rhodes has no serious com-petitors in the Dodecanese and few peers in the eastern Mediterranean. Consequently, in singling out its highlights, we necessarily pass over sights that on lesser islands would be main attractions.

EXPLORING THE OLD TOWN

Best to know one thing from the start about Old Town: It's not laid out on a grid—not even close. There are roughly 200 streets or lanes that simply have no name. Get-ting lost here, however, is an opportunity to explore. Whenever you feel the need to find your bearings, you can ask for **Sokratous,** which is the closest Old Town comes to having a main street.

When you approach the walls of Old Town, you are about to enter the oldest inhab-ited medieval town in Europe. It's a thrill to behold. Although there are many gates, we suggest that you first enter through **Eleftheria (Liberty) Gate,** where you'll come to **Plateia Simi,** containing ruins of the **Temple of Venus,** identified by the votive offer-ings found here, which may date from the 3rd century B.C. The remains of the temple are next to a parking lot (driving is restricted in the Old Town), which rather diminishes the impact of the few stones and columns still standing. Nevertheless, the ruins are a reminder that a great Hellenistic city once stood here and encompassed the entire area now occupied by the city, including the old and new towns. The population of the Hel-lenistic city of Rhodes is thought to have equaled the current population of the whole island (roughly 100,000).

Plateia Simi is also home to the **Municipal Art Gallery of Rhodes,** above the Museum Reproduction Shop (generally Mon–Sat 8am–2pm); admission is 3€ ($3.90). Its impressive collection comprises mostly works by eminent modern Greek artists. The gallery now has a second beautifully restored venue in the Old Town (across from the Mosque of Suleiman) to house its collection of antique and rare maps and engravings (Mon–Fri 8am–2pm). One block farther on is the **Museum of Decorative Arts,** which contains finely made objects and crafts from Rhodes and other islands, most notably

Simi (Tues–Sun 8:30am–3pm). Admission is 2.50€ ($3.25). Continue through the gate until you reach Ippoton, also known as the Street of the Knights. *Note:* If you are ready for serious sightseeing, purchase a ticket for 12€ ($16) that includes admission to the Museum of Decorative Arts, Archaeological Museum, Church of our Lady of the Castle, and Palace of the Knights. It's available at all of the museums.

Street of the Knights ★★ (Ippoton on maps) is one of the best-preserved and most delightful medieval relics in the world. The 600m-long (1,968-ft.) cobble-paved street was constructed over an ancient pathway that led in a straight line from the Acropolis of Rhodes to the port. In the early 16th century, it became the address for most of the inns of each nation, which housed Knights who belonged to the Order of St. John. The inns were used as eating clubs and temporary residences for visiting dignitaries, and their facades reflect the architectural details of their respective countries.

Begin at the lowest point on the hill at **Spanish House,** now used by a bank. Next door is **Inn of the Order of the Tongue of Italy,** built in 1519 (as can be seen on the shield of the order above the door). Then comes the **Palace of the Villiers of the Isle of Adam,** built in 1521, housing the Archaeological Service of the Dodecanese. The **Inn of France,** constructed in 1492, now hosts the French Language Institute. It's one of the most ornate inns, with the shield of three lilies (fleur-de-lis), royal crown, and crown of the Magister d'Aubusson (the cardinal's hat above four crosses) off center, over the middle door. Typical of the late Gothic period, the architectural and decorative elements are all somewhat asymmetrical, lending grace to the squat building. Opposite these inns is one side of the **Hospital of the Knights,** now the **Archaeological Museum,** whose entrance is on Museum Square. The grand and fascinating structure is well worth a visit. (As with so many public buildings in Rhodes, its hours are subject to change, but summer hours are generally Tues–Fri 8am–7pm and Sat–Sun 8:30am–3pm.) Admission is 3€ ($3.90). Across from the Archaeological Museum is the **Byzantine Museum,** housed in the **Church of Our Lady of the Castle** ★ (the Roman Catholic Cathedral of the Knights); it often hosts rotating exhibits of Christian art. Its hours vary but are generally Tuesday through Sunday from 8am to 7pm or later; admission is 3€ ($3.90).

The church farther on the right is **Ayia Triada** (open when it's open), next to the Italian consulate. Above its door are three coats-of-arms: those of France, England, and the pope. Past the arch that spans the street, still on the right, is the **Inn of the Tongue of Provence,** which was partially destroyed in 1856 and is now shorter than it once was. Opposite it on the left is the traditionally Gothic **Inn of the Tongue of Spain,** with vertical columns elongating its facade and a lovely garden in the back.

The culmination of this impressive procession should be **Palace of the Knights** ★★★ (also known as Palace of the Grand Masters), but it was destroyed in a catastrophic accidental explosion in 1856. What you see before you now is a grandiose palace built in the

1930s to accommodate Mussolini's visits and fantasies. Its scale and grandeur are more reflective of a future that failed to materialize than of a vanished past. Today it houses mosaics stolen from Kos by the Italian military as well as a collection of antique furniture. Hours vary, but in summer are Monday from 12:30 to 7pm, Tuesday through Sunday from 8am to 7pm. Admission is 6€ ($7.80).

The **Mosque of Suleiman** and the public baths are two reminders of the Turkish presence in Old Rhodes. Follow Sokratous west away from the harbor or walk a couple of blocks south from the Palace of the Knights, and you can't miss the mosque with its slender, though incomplete, minaret and pink-striped Venetian exterior.

The **Municipal Baths** (what the Greeks call the "Turkish baths") are housed in a 7th-century Byzantine structure and have been considerably upgraded since 2000. They merit a visit by anyone interested in vestiges of Turkish culture that remain in the Old Town, and cost less than the showers in most pensions. The *hamam* (most locals use the Turkish word for "bath") is in Plateia Arionos, between a large old mosque and the Folk Dance Theater. Throughout the day, men and women go in via their separate entrances and disrobe in private shuttered cubicles. A walk across cool marble floors leads you to the bath area—many domed, round chambers sunlit by tiny glass panes in the roof. Through the steam you'll see people seated around large marble basins, chatting while ladling bowls of water over their heads. The baths are open Tuesday through Saturday from 11am to 7pm. Tuesday, Thursday, and Friday, their use costs 3 € ($3.90), but on Wednesday and Saturday the cost is only 2€ ($2.60). Note that Saturday the baths are extremely crowded with locals.

The Old Town was also home to the Jewish community, whose origins date to the days of the ancient Greeks. Little survives in the northeast or Jewish Quarter of the Old Town other than a few homes with Hebrew inscriptions, the Jewish cemetery, and the **Square of the Jewish Martyrs (Plateia ton Martiron Evreon,** also known as Seahorse Sq. because of the seahorse fountain). The square is dedicated to the 1,604 Jews who were rounded up here and sent to their deaths at Auschwitz. On Dosiadou, leading off the square (signed) is a lovely synagogue, where services are held on Friday night; it is usually open daily from 10am to 1pm. A small museum is attached to it (open Apr–Oct, Sun–Fri 10am–4pm; admission free). While at the Square of the Jewish Martyrs, be sure to visit the **Hospice of St. Catherine** ⚐ (Mon–Fri 8am–2pm; free admission). Built in the late 14th century by the Order of the Knights of St. John (Knights Hospitaller) to house and entertain esteemed guests, it apparently lived up to its mission; one such guest, Niccole de Martoni, described it in the 1390s as "beautiful and splendid, with many handsome rooms, containing many and good beds." The description still fits, though only one "good bed" can be seen today. The restored hospice has exceptionally beautiful sea-pebble and mosaic floors, carved and intricately painted wooden ceilings, a grand hall and lavish bedchamber, and engaging exhibits. There's a lot here to excite the eyes and the imagination.

After touring the sites of the Old Town, you might want to walk around the **walls.** The fortification has a series of magnificent gates and towers, and is a remarkable example of a fully intact medieval structure. Much of the structure can be viewed by walking around the outside, but to walk along the top of the walls requires an admission fee of 4€ ($5.20) for adults, 2€ ($2.60) for students. The museum operates a 1-hour tour (6€/$7.80) on Tuesday and Saturday at 3pm, beginning at the Palace of the Knights.

EXPLORING THE NEW TOWN

The New Town is best explored after dark, since it houses most of the bars, discos, and nightclubs, as well as innumerable tavernas. In the heat of the day, its beaches—**Elli beach** and the **municipal beach**—are also popular. What few people make a point of seeking out but also can't miss are landmarks such as **Mandraki Harbor** and the "neo-imperial" architecture (culminating in the Nomarhia or Prefecture) along the harbor, all of which date from the Italian occupation. Other draws are the lovely park and ancient burial site at **Rodini** (2km/1¼ mile south of the city), and the impressive ancient **Acropolis of Rhodes** on Mount Smith.

The remains of the ancient Rhodian acropolis stand high atop the north end of the island above the modern city, with the sea visible on two sides. This is a pleasant site to explore leisurely with a picnic; there's plenty of shade. The restored stadium and small theater are particularly impressive, as are the remains of the Temple of Pythian Apollo. Although just a few pillars and a portion of the architrave still stand, they are provocative and pleasing, giving fodder to the imagination. The open site has no admission fee.

SHOPPING

In Rhodes city, it's the Old Town that is most interesting to shoppers. (But be warned: Most of these shops close at the end of Nov and don't reopen until Mar.) You'll find classic and contemporary **gold and silver jewelry** almost everywhere. The top-of-the-line Greek designer **Ilias LALAoUNIS** has a boutique on Plateia Alexandrou. **Alexandra Gold,** at 18 Sokratous next to the Alexis Restaurant, offers stylish European work, elegant gold and platinum link bracelets, and beautifully set precious gems. For a dazzling collection of authentic antique and reproduction jewelry, as well as ceramics, silver, glass, and everything you'd expect to find in a bazaar, drop in at **Royal Silver,** 15 Apellou (off Sokratous).

For imported **leather goods** and **furs** (the former often from nearby Turkey and the latter from northern Greece), stroll the length of Sokratous. Antiquity buffs should drop by the **Ministry of Culture Museum Reproduction Shop,** on Plateia Simi, which sells excellent reproductions of ancient sculptures, friezes, and tiles. True **antiques**—furniture, carpets, porcelain, and paintings—can be found at **Kalogirou Art,** 30 Panetiou, in a wonderful old building with a pebble-mosaic floor and an exotic banana-tree garden opposite the entrance to the Knights Palace.

Although most of what you find on Rhodes can be found throughout Greece, several products bear a special Rhodian mark. **Rhodian wine** has a fine reputation, and on weekdays you can visit two distinguished island wineries: **C.A.I.R.,** at its new factory 2km (1¼ mile) outside of Rhodes city on the way to Lindos; and **Emery,** in the village of Embonas. Another distinctive product of Rhodes is a rare form of **honey** made by bees committed to thimati (like oregano). To get this you may have to drive to the villages of Siana or Vati and ask if anyone has some to sell. It's mostly sold out of private homes, as locals are in no hurry to give it up. **Olive oil** is another local art, and again the best is sold out of private homes, meaning that you have to make discreet inquiries to discover the current sources.

Rhodes is also famed for handmade **carpets** and **kilims,** an enduring legacy from centuries of Ottoman occupation. Some 40 women around the island currently make carpets in their homes; some monasteries are also in on the act. There's a local carpet factory known as **Kleopatra** at Ayios Anthonias, on the main road to Lindos near

Afandou. In the Old Town, these and other Rhodian handmade carpets and kilims are sold at **Royal Carpet** at 45 Aristotelos and 15 Apellou. At **Pazari,** 1 Aristoteous and Dimokritou, you can watch carpets being made. Finally, there is "Rhodian" **lace** and **embroidery,** much of which, alas, now comes from Hong Kong. Ask for help to learn the difference between what's local and what's imported.

SPORTS & OUTDOOR PURSUITS

Most outdoor activities on Rhodes are beach- and sea-related. For everything from **parasailing** to **jet skis** to **canoes,** you'll find what you need at **Faliraki beach** (see "Sights & Beaches Elsewhere on the Island," later in this chapter), if you can tolerate the crowds.

No license is required for **fishing;** the best grounds are reputed to be off Kamiros Skala, Kalithea, and Lindos. Try hitching a ride with the fishing boats that moor opposite Ayia Katerina's Gate. For sailing and yachting information, call **R Yacht Club** (© **22410/23-287**). Or call **Yacht Agency Rhodes** (© **22410/22-927;** fax 22410/ 23-393), the center for all yachting needs.

If you've always wanted to try scuba diving, both **Waterhoppers Diving Schools** (©/fax **22410/38-146**) and **Dive Med** (© **22410/61-115;** fax 22410/66-584; www.rodos.com/dive-med/index.html) offer 1-day introductory dives for beginners, diving expeditions for experienced divers, and 4- to 5-day courses leading to various certifications.

Other sports are available at **Rhodes Tennis Club** (© **22410/25-705**) in the resort of Elli, or at **Rhodes-Afandu Golf Club** (© **22410/51-225**), 19km (12 miles) south of the port. A centrally located, fully equipped fitness center can be found at the **Fitness Factory** (© **22410/37-667**) at 17 Akti Kanari.

If you want to get some culture as you get in shape, information on traditional **Greek folk-dance lessons** can be obtained from the **Old Town Theater** (© **22410/ 29-085**), where Nelly Dimoglou and her entertaining troupe perform. Or contact the **Traditional Dance Center,** 87 Dekelias, Athens (© **210/251-1080**). Classes run from June to early August, 30 hours per week; each week, dances from a different region are studied. Shorter courses are available.

WHERE TO STAY IN RHODES CITY
IN THE OLD TOWN

Accommodations in the Old Town have an atmosphere of ages past, but character does not always equal charm. There are few really attractive options here, and they are in considerable demand, with all of the attending complications. One is that some hosts will hold you to the letter of your intent—so if you need or wish to cancel a day or more of your stay, they will do their best to extract every last pence. And there is some hedging, which means that the exact room agreed upon may be "unavailable" at the end of the day. Be explicit and keep a paper trail.

Expensive

S. Nikolis Hotel ★★   If you are determined to stay within the walls of the Old Town—an unforgettable experience—and if you are willing and able to pay a premium, this is the place. This one-of-a-kind hotel has the only real finesse and class within the old city walls—but don't confuse this with five-star luxury. Host Sotiris Nikolis is a true artisan with a fine eye. Here, on the site of an ancient Hellenistic agora, he has restored several medieval structures using the original stones and remaining as faithful as possible to the original style. The result is immensely pleasing

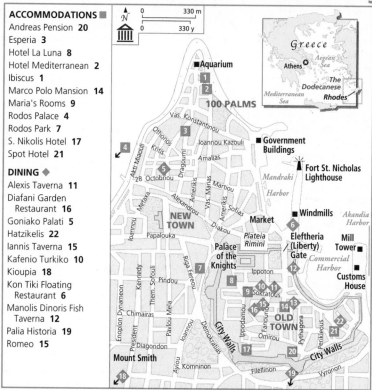

ACCOMMODATIONS ■
Andreas Pension **20**
Esperia **3**
Hotel La Luna **8**
Hotel Mediterranean **2**
Ibiscus **1**
Marco Polo Mansion **14**
Maria's Rooms **9**
Rodos Palace **4**
Rodos Park **7**
S. Nikolis Hotel **17**
Spot Hotel **21**

DINING ◆
Alexis Taverna **11**
Diafani Garden Restaurant **16**
Goniako Palati **5**
Hatzikelis **22**
Iannis Taverna **15**
Kafenio Turkiko **10**
Kioupia **18**
Kon Tiki Floating Restaurant **6**
Manolis Dinoris Fish Taverna **12**
Palia Historia **19**
Romeo **15**

(though not plush). Many of the furnishings are true antiques. Some rooms have sleeping lofts; some suites and studios have Jacuzzis; some studios have very basic kitchenettes. The S. Nikolis also has four studios with completely furnished kitchens and eight less-expensive units in a nearby building. A special business suite comes with two bedrooms, two bathrooms, and a small office area with fax and computer.

In the hotel's enclosed garden are a small fitness center and a computer nook with Internet access. Be sure to check out the adjacent **Ancient Agora Bar and Restaurant** where, in 1990, a 10-ton marble pediment dating from the 2nd century was found beneath the medieval foundations. Note that smoking is not permitted here.

61 Ippodamou, 85100 Rhodes. (✆) **22410/34-561.** www.s-nikolis.gr. 12 units. 80€–200€ ($104–$260) double; 130€–180€ ($169–$234) studio; 200€—3,000€ ($260–$3,900) suite. Rates include breakfast. AE, MC, V. Parking within reasonable distance. Open year-round (but call ahead Nov–Mar). **Amenities:** Restaurant; bar; Jacuzzi in some suites; concierge; tours and car rentals arranged; Internet access. *In room:* A/C, TV, fridge, hair dryer.

Moderate

Marco Polo Mansion ⚐   Come here if you want a history lesson as well as a room with a touch of the exotic. Featured in glossy fashion and travel magazines, the Marco Polo Mansion has captured attention with its timeless style and good taste. As if squeezed from tubes of ancient pigments and weathered in the bleaching sun, the color palate here is all deep blues, mustard, wine, and pitch black. Each guest room is steeped in a history of its own and furnished with antiques and folk art. One was a harem, another a *hamam* (Turkish bath). The "Imperial Room" has six windows, while the "Antika 2" room, lined with kilims, has a view of minarets. The smaller garden rooms, nestled in fragrant greenery, reflect the house's Italian period. Ceiling fans and cross breezes protect you from the heat of the day.

42 A. Fanouriou, 85100 Rhodes. ℂ/fax **22410/25-562**. www.marcopolomansion.web.com. 7 units. 70€–125€ ($91–$163) double. Rates include breakfast. V. No parking in the immediate area. Closed Nov–Mar.

Inexpensive

Andreas Pension   This exceptionally well-run pension offers relief from the cardboard walls and linoleum floors that haunt many of the town's budget choices. Housed in a restored 400-year-old Turkish sultan's house, it offers attractive rooms, some with panoramic views of the town. Others have wooden lofts, which can comfortably sleep a family of four. The bedrooms (with commendably firm beds) were once occupied by the sultan's harem, while the sultan held forth in room no. 11, a spacious corner unit with three windows and extra privacy, perfect for a man for whom every day was a honeymoon! Hosts Dmitri and Josette serve breakfast on a shaded terrace that boasts gorgeous vistas of the town and the harbor, the best views in Old Town. A pet tortoise patrols the full bar, which has a wide-screen TV. Laundry service is provided. Room nos. 10 and 11 have the best views; room nos. 8 and 9 have private terraces.

28D Omirou (located between Omirou 23 and 20, *not* just before 29), 85100 Rhodes. ℂ **22410/34-156**. Fax 22410/74-285. andreasch@otenet.gr. 12 units, 6 with private bathroom. 40€–55€ ($52–$72) double with bathroom. Breakfast 8€ ($10) per person extra. AE, V. No parking in immediate area. Closed Nov–Feb.

Hotel La Luna ⊛   This small, delightful hotel is a block in from taverna-lined, touristy Orfeos, nestled between two churches in a calm residential neighborhood. It features a large shaded garden with a bar and breakfast tables. Looking at the clean, modest rooms, all without toilet or tub, you may wonder why this is a prime spot in Old Town, sought after by diplomats, barons, and movie stars like Ben Kingsley and Helen Mirren. The answer is charm, which the ancient Greek poets knew to be capricious and inscrutable. It also has a lot to do with the private 300-year-old Turkish bath, which more than makes up for the one you don't have in your room. This is a place for visitors who want and respect quiet; blast your radio or make a ruckus, and you'll be asked to leave. Our favorite double is room no. 2 (Sir Ben stayed in room no. 1). Just beyond the encircling walls of La Luna is a fascinating archaeological site encompassing two ancient churches, a traditional Turkish residence and garden, a Byzantine monastery, and more, making this a particularly intriguing corner of Old Town in which to base yourself.

21 Ierokleous, 85100 Rhodes. ℂ/fax **22410/25-856**. www.helios.gr/exr. 7 rooms, none with bathroom. 60€ ($78) double. Rates include breakfast. No credit cards. No parking in immediate area. Closed Nov–Mar. Turn off Orfeos between the halves of Don Kichotis taverna.

Maria's Rooms   This pristine little pension near the Archontiko Restaurant merits very high marks for both price and quality. The accommodations are sparkling white and squeaky clean, and Maria is a warm and welcoming hostess. Even without air-conditioning the rooms are cool, and they are secluded enough from the bustle of the Old Town to be surprisingly quiet.

147-Z Menekleous, 85100 Rhodes. ℂ **22410/22-169**. vasilpyrgos@hotmail.com. 8 units, 3 with bathroom. 38€–53€ ($49–$69) double with private bathroom. No credit cards. No parking in immediate area. Open Easter–Oct.

Spot Hotel   Spotless would be a more suitable name for this small hotel. By Old Town standards, this building is an infant, only 30 years old, but the proprietors have gradually added architectural enhancements that lend Spot an island and medieval atmosphere more in keeping with its location. The garden and terrace sitting areas have also been enlarged. The rooms are simple and tasteful if not especially light. Guests enjoy a large communal fridge, access to a phone for free local calls, free limited use of a PC for e-mail, and free luggage storage. Spot is near the harbor right off Plateia Martiron Hevreon, so breakfast is available at nearby cafes.

21 Perikleous, 85100 Rhodes. ℰ **22410/34-737.** www.islandsinblue.gr. 9 units. 50€–60€ ($65–$78) double. No credit cards. No parking in immediate area. *In room:* A/C in some units.

IN THE NEW TOWN & ENVIRONS

Unlike the Old Town, the New Town doesn't prohibit new construction. You'll find a wild array of options, from boardinghouses to package-tour hotels to luxury resorts. Some are dazzling, but most are dull and so indistinguishable that you may forget which one you're in. Cleanliness, a little comfort, and proximity to beaches and bars are what most travelers expect, so this is what you'll find.

Very Expensive

Rodos Palace ✿✿ *(Kids)*   "Palace" is just the word for Greece's largest five-star hotel (as opposed to beach resort), set amid 121 hectares (30 acres) of gardens just outside Rhodes city and facing the sea. Famed designer Maurice Bailey, who cut his teeth designing the sets for *Quo Vadis* and *Ben-Hur,* did the original decor. Rodos Palace has been the uncontested king of the mountain on Rhodes for the past 40 years, never resting on its laurels, but always making additions and improvements. The tastefully furnished modern-style rooms come in various sizes, but all are relatively large compared to most other Greek hotels. Beyond the usual children's center, this hotel offers what amounts to a resort within a resort designed to provide the ultimate holiday for families with children. The largest of the several pools lies beneath a massive dome constructed by Boeing. The fitness center could stand by itself. It is all but impossible to recount the full array of dining options, entertainment, shopping, and so on offered within this world-class resort.

Leoforos Trianton, Iksia, 85100 Rhodes. ℰ **22410/25-222.** Fax 22410/25-350. www.rodos-palace.com. 785 units, including 20 bungalows, 6 suites, 2 presidential villas. High season 285€–330€ ($371–$429) double, 460€ ($598) and up for suites; low season 230€–270€ ($299–$351) double, 420€ ($546) and up for suites. Rates include breakfast. AE, MC, V. Free parking. Closed Dec–Mar. Frequent public buses. **Amenities:** 6 restaurants; 4 bars; 3 pools, children's pool; golf course nearby; health club and spa w/Jacuzzi and aerobics classes; extensive watersports equipment rentals including scuba classes; bike rental; children's program; game room; concierge; tours and car rentals arranged; airport pickup arranged; conference center; business center; secretarial services; shopping arcade; salon; 24-hr. room service; massage; babysitting; same-day laundry/dry-cleaning services; water polo; horseback riding school. *In room:* A/C, TV, minibar, fridge, hair dryer, safe.

Expensive

Rodos Park ✿   This superb New Town luxury hotel, with gleaming marble and polished wood interiors, enjoys a uniquely convenient yet secluded location. Guests are within a short stroll of the city's attractions: only a few minutes from the Old Town and Mandraki Harbor, yet conveniently close to the New Town shopping and dining areas. Some might regard the rooms as over-decorated in terms of colors and textiles, but they are comfortable and have all the amenities you'd expect to find in a first-class hotel. This is not a beach resort—it's a fine city hotel open year-round. If you want a Jacuzzi in your room, opt for a suite, preferably one with a superb view of the Old

Town walls. If you want to work off surplus calories from the 24-hour room service or the in-house gourmet restaurant, head down to the fitness center, then pamper yourself with a Swedish massage, sauna, or steam bath. A dip in the outdoor pool will offer the perfect finish to your regime.

12 Riga Fereou, 85100 Rhodes. (℃) 800/525-4800 in the U.S., or 22410/89-700. Fax 22410/24-613. www. rodospark.gr. 60 units. High season 420€ ($546) double, 480€ ($624) suite; low season 350€ ($455) double, 415€ ($540) suite. Rates include breakfast. AE, MC, V. Parking nearby. **Amenities:** 3 restaurants; 2 bars; pool; health club; Jacuzzi in suites; concierge; tours and car rental arrangements; conference facilities; fax and computer facilities; 24-hr. room service; babysitting; same-day laundry/dry-cleaning service. *In room:* A/C, TV, minibar, hair dryer.

Moderate

Hotel Mediterranean ★
Directly across from Kos beach and next to Rodos Casino, this location speaks for itself. The Aquarium, a great spot for kids, is also nearby (admission fee 3.50€/$4.55). The year-round hotel's interior, from the common to the private rooms, is grand and elegant, stylish and sophisticated. Doubles have adjoining twin beds, pull-out sofas, and spacious tiled bathrooms. Rates vary according to the view: Of the three, the spectacular sea view far outshines the garden (pool and veranda) or side (city) view. All suites have sea views, sitting areas, and king-size beds. All units have balconies. Rooms for travelers with disabilities are available upon request.

35 Kos beach, 85100 Rhodes. (℃) 22410/22-410. Fax 22410/22-828. www.mediterranean.gr. 241 units. 140€ ($182) double; 155€ ($202) suite. Rates include breakfast. AE, DC, MC, V. Free parking. Frequent public buses. **Amenities:** 2 restaurants; bar; outdoor freshwater pool; night-lit tennis court nearby; watersports equipment rentals; concierge; tours and car rentals arranged; airport pickup arranged; conference facilities; 24-hr. room service; babysitting; same-day laundry/dry-cleaning services; rooms for those w/limited mobility on request. *In room:* A/C, TV, minibar, hair dryer.

Ibiscus ★
The Ibiscus was a well-situated beachfront hotel when it underwent a makeover in 2000 that took it from attractive to striking. The spacious marble entrance hall opens into a stylish cafe bar; you can take your drinks out front to the beach or back onto the poolside garden veranda. The tasteful, spacious, and fully carpeted double rooms have king-size orthopedic beds, large wardrobes, ample desk areas, tile and marble bathrooms, and hair dryers. The suites are especially appealing, with rich wood paneling, parquet floors, and two bedrooms (one with a king-size bed and one with twin beds). Every unit has a balcony, many of which face the sea.

Kos beach, 85100 Rhodes. (℃) 22410/24-421. Fax 22410/27-283. 205 units. 135€ ($175) double; 150€ ($195) suite. Rates include breakfast. AE, DC, MC, V. Free parking. Closed Nov–Mar. Frequent public buses. **Amenities:** Restaurant; bar; dipping pool; concierge; tours and car rentals arranged; shops. *In room:* A/C, TV, minibar, hair dryer.

Inexpensive

Esperia (Value)
This hotel, open year-round, is in a class above its cost. It is rare in Rhodes to find this kind of quality at such reasonable rates. The guest rooms are tasteful and exceptionally clean, each with a large balcony with pleasant views. New double-glazed sliding balcony doors effectively seal the rooms from most of the town's noise. TVs are available on request at a small additional cost. The bar, lounge, and breakfast room are inviting, and the walled outdoor pool and poolside bar are well above average for a modest hotel. The hotel is located near the restaurant district and only a short walk from the beach. Its 19 apartments are for rent only in winter.

7 Griva, 85100 Rhodes. (℃) 22410/23-941. Fax 22410/77-501. 171 units. 80€ ($104) double. Rates include breakfast. AE, DC, MC, V. **Amenities:** Breakfast room; bar; pool. *In room:* A/C, fridge, hair dryer.

WHERE TO DINE IN RHODES CITY
IN THE OLD TOWN

The Old Town is thick with tavernas, restaurants, and fast-food nooks, all doing their best to lure you into places that might be where you want to be. If not, the more brazen their overtures, the more adamant you must be in holding to your course. Don't imagine, however, that all Old Town restaurants are tourist traps. Many Rhodians come to this area for what they consider the island's best food, particularly fish. Don't even think of driving to these places; walk through an entrance to the Old City.

Expensive

Alexis Taverna ✪ GREEK/SEAFOOD   For more than 40 years, this fine restaurant has been the one to beat in Old Town, setting the standard by which the other seafood restaurants are judged. This is the place to abandon restraint. Ask Iannis. He and his brother, Constantine, preserve the traditions established by their grandfather to devise a seafood feast for you, accompanied by the perfect wine from the cellar (which represents vineyards all over Greece). Iannis goes down to the harbor himself each day and chooses the best of the catch. Insisting on quality and freshness, he and Constantine have built their own greenhouse on the outskirts of town to cultivate organic vegetables. Start with a bounteous seafood platter of delicately flavored sea urchins, fresh clams, and tender octopus carpaccio. Try the sargos, a sea-bream-type fish, charcoal-grilled to perfection. The creamy Greek yogurt with homemade green-walnut jam is a perfect ending for a superb culinary experience. Every meal here begins with a chef's consultation and should end with applause. The list of appreciative diners over the years has included Winston Churchill, Jackie Kennedy, presidents, royalty, and innumerable tourists in the know.

18 Sokratous. ✆ **22410/29-347.** Reservations recommended. Individually prepared dinners without wine average 60€ ($78). AE, V. Mon–Sat 10am–4pm and 7pm–1am.

Manolis Dinoris Fish Taverna ✪ GREEK/SEAFOOD   This restaurant, housed in the former stables of the 13th-century Knights of St. John's Inn, provides a unique setting to enjoy delicious and fresh seafood delights. You can order either a la carte or from the set menu of coquille St. Jacques, Greek salad, grilled prawns, swordfish, baklava, coffee, and brandy. In warm weather, the quiet side garden is delightful; in winter, a fire roars in the old stone hearth indoors.

14A Museum Sq. ✆ **22410/25-824.** Main courses 25€–55€ ($33–$72); set menu 60€ ($78). AE, MC, V. Year-round daily noon–midnight.

Moderate

Goniako Palati (Corner Palace) GREEK   The new Goniako Palati may not be a palace, but it is on the corner—a busy corner you overlook once the food arrives. Great canvas awnings cover the seating area, raised well above street level. The extensive taverna menu is basic Greek, fresh and skillfully prepared in a slightly upscale environment at reasonable prices. This is one place local New Towners go for reliable, and then some, taverna fare. The grilled swordfish souvlaki, served with a medley of steamed vegetables, is quite tasty. The *saganaki* (grilled cheese) here is a performance art, and delicious to boot.

110 Griva (corner of Griva and 28 Oktobriou). ✆ **22410/33-167.** Main courses 8€–24€ ($10–$31). AE, MC, V. Year-round daily 9am–midnight.

Hatzikelis ☆ GREEK/SEAFOOD   This delightful fish taverna enjoys a peaceful and pleasant setting in the midst of a small neighborhood park just behind the Church of Our Lady of the Burgh in the Square of the Jewish Martyrs. Although there is an extensive a la carte menu, the special dinners for two are irresistible (even if you must loosen your belt and consume it all on your own). The Fisherman's Plate consists of lobster, shrimp, mussels, octopus, squid, and a liter of wine, while the plates of traditional Rhodian dishes include specialties like pumpkin balls and shrimp saganaki. The portions are challenging, but the quality of the cuisine and the fact that you have until 2am to do your duty increase the odds in your favor. To find Hatzikelis easily without winding your way through the Old Town, enter the walls at Pili Panagias (St. Mary's Gate).

9 Alhadeff. ⓒ **22410/27-215.** Main courses 7€–16€ ($9.10–$21). No credit cards. Year-round daily 11am–2am.

Kon Tiki Floating Restaurant ☆ GREEK/INTERNATIONAL   Still floating after 40 years of serving good food, this was one of Rhodes's first decent restaurants. It's a great place to watch the yachts bobbing alongside while you enjoy well-prepared, creative dishes such as sole *valevska* (filet of sole with shrimp, crab, and mushrooms gratinéed in a béchamel sauce). The saganaki shrimp—prepared with feta cheese, local herbs, and tomato sauce—is an exceptional dish. Count on the chef to offer "fushion" cuisine, which blends Polynesian, international, and Greek techniques and tastes. The restaurant is also open for breakfast and for coffee or a drink at the bar, if that's all you want.

Mandraki Harbor. ⓒ **22410/22-477.** Main courses 7€–24€ ($9.10–$31). AE, MC, V. Year-round daily 8am–midnight.

Romeo ☆ GREEK/SEAFOOD   Though under siege by tourists, many locals gladly frequent the Romeo, as there is a good deal that's authentic within its walls. (For one thing, the walls themselves are roughly 500 years old.) More important, besides the predictable taverna fare, are the number of local dishes on offer. The gracious and helpful waiters will happily explain and discuss the menu with you and accommodate special preferences whenever possible—including vegetarian options. Two house specialties are the mixed fish grill and the stuffed souvlaki. For the grill, you select your own fish from a generous array of fresh deep-sea options—the tender grilled octopus is especially good. The finely cut grilled souvlaki stuffed with melted cheese and tomatoes is a regional dish from the north end of the island. The very reasonably priced dry house wines go quite nicely with each entree. Set back in a quiet enclave, just off and out of the crush of Sokratous, Romeo offers both courtyard and roof-garden seating, as well as tasteful live traditional Greek music and song. If you're keen on a smoke-free environment, the air on the breezy roof garden is particularly fresh.

7–9 Menekleous (off Sokratous). ⓒ **22410/25-186.** Main courses 6€–20€ ($7.80–$26). AE, MC, V. Mid-Mar to mid-Nov daily 10am–1am.

Inexpensive
Diafani Garden Restaurant (value) GREEK   Several locals recommended this family-operated taverna, which cooks up fine traditional Greek fare at bargain prices. You won't find better authentic Greek home cooking than this anywhere in Rhodes, especially at lunch. Sitting under the spreading walnut tree in the vine-shaded courtyard, we enjoyed the splendid *papoutsaki,* braised eggplant slices layered with chopped meat and a thick, cheesy béchamel sauce, delicately flavored with nutmeg and coriander.

3 Plateia Arionos (opposite the Turkish bath). ⓒ **22410/26-053.** Main courses 4€–14€ ($5.20–$18). No credit cards. Year-round daily noon–midnight.

Iannis Taverna ✷ GREEK   For a budget Greek meal, visit chef Iannis's small place on a quiet back lane. The moussaka, stuffed vegetables, and meat dishes are flavorful and well prepared by a man who spent 14 years as a chef in the Greek diners of New York. His Greek plate is the best we found in Rhodes, with an unbelievably large variety of tasty foods. Portions are hearty and cheap, and the friendly service is a welcome relief from service at nearby establishments. The breakfast omelets are a great deal.

41 Platonos. ✆ 22410/36-535. Main courses 3€–12€ ($3.90–$16). No credit cards. Year-round daily 9am–midnight.

Kafenio Turkiko GREEK/SNACKS   Located in a Crusader structure, this is the only authentic place left on touristy Sokratous, otherwise replete with Swatch, Body Shop, Van Cleef, and a multitude of souvenir shops. Each rickety wooden table comes with a backgammon board for idling away the hours while you sip a Greek coffee or juice. The old pictures, mirrors, and bric-a-brac on the walls enhanced our feeling of bygone times.

76 Sokratous. No phone. Drinks/snacks 1€–5€ ($1.30–$6.50). No credit cards. Year-round daily 11am–midnight.

IN THE NEW TOWN & ENVIRONS
Expensive
Kioupia ✷✷ GREEK   Once rated by the *London Guardian* as one of the world's 10 best restaurants, this unique place offers an exquisite gourmet experience. Creative, artistic Michael Koumbiadis, known in Athenian society as "the Colossus of Rhodes," founded Kioupia in 1972. Koumbiadis has uncovered the true harmonies of traditional Greek cuisine, using the best local ingredients and village recipes. In this elegantly decorated, rustic old house, the meal begins with a rinsing of hands in rosewater, and then perhaps a choice of three soups, including the unusual *trahanas*, a Greek wheat-and-cheese soup. Soup is followed by an amazing array of appetizers: sautéed wild mushrooms, pumpkin *beignee* (dumplings), and savory braised red peppers in olive oil, accompanied by home-baked carrot bread and pastrami bread. The main dishes are equally superb—broiled veal stuffed with cheese and sprinkled with pistachio nuts in yogurt sauce; or delectable pork souvlaki with yogurt and paprika sauce on the side. For dessert, try the light crepes filled with sour cherries and covered with chocolate sauce and vanilla crème. Many of the foods are prepared in clay pots in a traditional wood-burning oven, source of the faint woodsy scent permeating the restaurant. The grand fixed-price meal, like the Orthodox liturgy, requires fasting, devotion, and time (roughly 3 hr.).

Tris Village, 11km (7 miles) south of Rhodes Town. ✆ 22410/91-824. Reservations required. Fixed-price meals 25€ ($33) or 50€ ($65) per person; wine and service extra. A la carte available. MC, V. Year-round Mon–Sat 8pm–midnight; Sun noon–3pm.

Moderate
Palia Historia (The Old Story) ✷ GREEK   If you're maxed out on run-of-the-mill Greek taverna fare, this is a good place to come—well worth a taxi ride from wherever you're staying. Most of the clientele is Greek, drawn by the subtle cuisine and lack of tourists. The marinated salmon and capers are worthy of the finest Dublin restaurant, and the broccoli with oil, mustard, and roasted almonds is inspired. As a main course, the shrimps saganaki leave nothing to the imagination. With fish, the dry white Spiropoulos from Mantinia is perfect. For a great finish, go for the banana flambé.

108 Mitropoleos (south in New Town, below modern stadium). ✆ 22410/32-421. Reservations recommended. Main courses 10€–22€ ($13–$29). AE, MC, V. Year-round daily 7pm–midnight.

RHODES CITY AFTER DARK

Rhodes by night brims with energy. Outside of Athens, Rhodes claims one of the most active nighttime scenes in Greece. Granted, some of that energy is grounded in the resort complexes north of the city, but there is enough to go around.

Your own common sense is as good a guide as any in this ever-changing scene. In a city as compact as Rhodes, it's best to follow the lights and noise, and get a little lost. When you decide to call it quits, shout down a taxi to bring you back, if you can remember where you're staying.

As a rule of thumb, the younger set will find the **New Town** livelier than the Old Town. **Cafe scenes** are located on the harbor, behind Academy Square, or on Galias near New Market. The **bar scene** tends to line up along Diakonou. There are at least 100 **nightclubs** on Rhodes, so you're sure to find one to your liking.

Gambling is a popular nighttime activity in Greece. Rhodes for many years housed one of Greece's six legal casinos, a government-operated roulette and blackjack house adjoining the Grand Hotel. In January 1999, however, this was replaced by a much more extensive casino operated by Playboy International. The home of this complex is the once-grand **Hotel Rodon** facing Elli beach.

The **sound-and-light** (*son et lumière*) presentation at Papagou, south of Plateia Rimini (© **22410/21-922**), dramatizes the life of a youth admitted into the monastery in 1522, the year before Rhodes fell to invading Turks. In contrast to Athens's Acropolis show, the dialogue here is more illuminating, though the lighting is unimaginative. Nevertheless, sitting in the lush gardens below the palace on a warm evening can be pleasant, and we heartily recommend the experience to those smitten by the medieval Old Town. Check the posted schedule for English-language performances. Admission is 6€ ($7.80) for adults, 2€ ($2.60) for youths, and free for children under 11.

We also thoroughly recommend the **Traditional Folk Dance Theater,** presented by the Nelly Dimoglou Dance Company, Adronikou, off Plateia Arionos, Old Town (© **22410/20-157**). This internationally acclaimed company is always lively, colorful, and utterly entertaining. Twenty spirited men and women perform dances from many areas of Greece in often embroidered flouncy costumes. The five-man band plays an inspired repertoire. Performances take place May through early October: Monday, Wednesday, and Friday at 9:15pm. Admission is 12€ ($16) for adults.

EXPLORING THE ISLAND

Sun, sand . . . and the rest is history. Nowhere is that more true than on Rhodes, where ruins and beaches lure visitors out of Rhodes city. For the best **beaches,** head to the island's east coast. Visitors also flock to archaeological sites identical to the three original Dorian city-states, all nearly 3,000 years old: **Lindos, Kamiros,** and **Ialisos.** Of these, Lindos was and is preeminent; it is by far the top tourist destination outside of Old Town. So we begin here with Lindos, and explore the island counterclockwise.

LINDOS

Lindos is without question the most picturesque town on the island of Rhodes. Since Lindos has been designated a historic settlement, the Archaeological Society controls development in the village, and the traditional white-stucco homes, shops, and restaurants form the most unified, classically Greek expression in the Dodecanese. Be warned, however, that Lindos is often deluged with tourists, and your first visit may be unforgettable for the wrong reasons. Avoid the crush of mid-July to August, if at all possible.

Frequent public buses leave Plateia Rimini for a fare of 5€ ($6.50); a taxi will cost 35€ ($46) one-way. There are two entrances to the town. The first and northernmost leads down a steep hill to the bus stop and taxi stand, then veers downhill again to the beach. If you're driving, park in the lot above the town. At this square you'll find the friendly, extremely informative **Tourist Information Kiosk** (℃ **22440/31-900;** fax 22410/31-288), where Michalis will help you April through October, daily from 9am to 10pm. Here, too, is the commercial heart of the village, with the Acropolis looming above. The rural **medical clinic** (℃ **22410/31-224**), **post office,** and **telephone office (OTE)** are nearby. The second road into town leads beyond it and into the upper village, blessedly removed from the hordes. This is the better route for people more aesthetically minded. Follow signs to the Acropolis. You'll pass a stand where, for 6€ ($7.80), you can ride a donkey (also known as a Lindian taxi) all the way to the top. Along the way, the sides of your path will be strewn with embroidery and lace for sale, which may or may not be the handiwork of local women. Embroidery from Rhodes was highly coveted in the ancient world. In fact, it is claimed that Alexander the Great wore a grand Rhodian robe into battle at Gaugemila, and in Renaissance Europe the French ladies used to yearn for a bit of Lindos lace. Much of what is for sale in Lindos today, however, is from Hong Kong.

Before you start the final ascent to the acropolis, be sure to inspect the famous **relief carving of a trireme** ✿, or three-banked ship, dating from the 2nd century B.C. At the top, from the fortress ramparts, are glorious views of medieval Lindos below, where most homes date from the 15th century. To the south you can see the lovely beach at St. Paul's Bay—legend claims St. Paul put ashore here—along with Rhodes's less-developed eastern coastline. Across to the southwest rises Mount Krana, where caves, dug out to serve as ancient tombs, are thought to have sheltered cults to Athena well into the Christian period.

The **Acropolis** ✮ (℃ **22410/27-674**) is open Tuesday through Sunday from 8am to 7pm, Monday from 12:30 to 7pm. Admission is 6€ ($7.80) for adults and 3€ ($3.90) for students and children. This is one of three original Dorian acropolises in Rhodes. Within the much-later medieval walls stand the impressive remains of the **Sanctuary of Athena Lindos,** with its large Doric portico from the 4th century B.C. St. John's Knights refortified the Acropolis with monumental turreted walls and built a small church to St. John inside. Today, stones and columns are strewn everywhere as the site undergoes extensive restoration.

On your descent, as you explore the labyrinthine lanes of medieval Lindos, you will come to the exquisite late-14th- or early-15th-century **Byzantine Church of the Panagia** ✿. Still the local parish church (admission 2€/$2.60), its more than 200 iconic frescoes cover every inch of the walls and arched ceilings. Dating from the 18th century, all of the frescoes have been painstakingly restored at great expense and with stunning results. Be sure to spend some time here; many of these icons are sequentially narrative, depicting the Creation, the Nativity, the Christian Passover, and the Last Judgment. And after you've given yourself a stiff neck from looking up, look down at the extraordinary floor, made of sea pebbles.

Adjoining the Church of the Panagia is the **Church Museum** (℃ **22440/32-020**), open April through October daily from 9am to 3pm; admission is 2€ ($2.60). The historical and architectural exhibits and collected ecclesiastical items, including frescoes, icons, texts, chalices, and liturgical embroidery, comprise a surprisingly significant collection. A visit here is useful in guiding you through the medieval town.

Then, of course, there's the inviting **beach** below, lined with cafes and tavernas.

Where to Stay & Dine in Lindos & Environs

In high season, Lindos marks the spot where up to 10,000 day-trippers from Rhodes city converge with 4,000 resident tourists. Since no hotel construction is permitted, almost all of the old homes have been converted into pensions (called "villas" in the brochures) by English charter companies. **Triton Holidays** (✆ **22410/21-690;** www. tritondmc.gr) books six-person villas, including kitchen facilities (reservations are often made a year in advance). In peak season, the local **Tourist Information Kiosk** (✆ **22440/31-900;** fax 22440/31-288) has a list of homes that rent rooms. Plan to pay 45€ ($59) for a double and 60€ to 85€ ($78–$111) for a studio apartment.

Melenos Hotel, in an authentically Lindian-style villa, with hand-painted tiles, local antiques, handcrafted lamps—in short, traditional splendor combined with contemporary comforts and convenience—charges hefty prices (suites in high season run 310€–490€/$403–$637). If you're up for this, check it out at **www.melanoslindos. com** and then contact Michalis Melenos.

You'll have a paralyzing array of restaurants and tavernas to choose from in tiny Lindos. On the beach, the expansive **Triton Restaurant** gets a nod because you can easily change into your swimsuit in the bathroom, essential for nonresidents who want to splash in the gorgeous water across the way. The restaurant is also not as pricey as the others.

Argo Fish Taverna ✦ GREEK/SEAFOOD

Haraki Bay is a quiet fishing hamlet with a gorgeous, crescent-shaped pebbly beach and this excellent seafood taverna. Consider stopping here for a swim and lunch on a day trip to Lindos. We appreciated the freshness of the food, as well as a creative variation on a Greek salad that added mint, dandelion leaves, and other fresh herbs and was served with whole-wheat bread. The lightly battered fried calamari was tasty and a welcome relief from the standard over-battered fare. The mussels, baked with fresh tomatoes and feta cheese, were also right on.

Haraki beach (10km/6 miles north of Lindos). ✆ **22440/51-410.** Reservations recommended. Main courses 13€–55€ ($17–$72). AE, MC, V. Easter–Oct daily noon–1am.

Atrium Palace ✦

Just over 6.4km (4 miles) out of Lindos on the long beach of crystal-clear Kalathos Bay, this luxurious resort hotel features an eclectic architectural design—a neo-Greek, Roman, Crusader, and Italian pastel extravaganza. The rooms are colorful and comfortable—they are especially proud of their wooden floors. The inner atrium is an exotic, tropical garden of pools and waterfalls. The beautifully landscaped outdoor pool complex is a nice alternative to the nearby beach, and the indoor pool, sauna, and fitness club will keep you busy. To fully entertain the whole family on the rainy days that never occur, there are game rooms, a miniclub for young children, and an arcade of shops. Despite the hotel's five-star status, the atmosphere here is relaxed, unpretentious, and friendly, all perhaps due to the Atrium Palace's excellent staff.

Kalathos beach, 85100 Rhodes. ✆ **22440/31-601.** Fax 22440/31-600. 256 units. 95€–160€ ($124–$208) double; 112€–340€ ($146–$442) suite for 2. Rates include breakfast. AE, DC, MC, V. Closed Nov–Mar. *In room:* A/C, TV, minibar.

Ladiko Bungalows Hotel

Anthony Quinn obtained permission to build a retirement home for actors on this pretty little bay on the road to Lindos, 3km (2 miles) south of the swinging beach resort of Faliraki, but never realized his plans. The location *is* exceptional—both quiet and convenient. This friendly family-operated lodge has activities for nature lovers (swimming, fishing, and hiking to nearby ruins and less-frequented beaches) but is just a 20-minute walk to noisy, bustling Faliraki. The outside terrace bar and dining area with a splendid view of Ladiko Bay provide lovely tranquil spots for a drink or a meal. The guest rooms are not exceptional, but are quite comfortable. Fourteen rooms come with fridges.

Faliraki, P.O. Box 236, 85100 Rhodes. ℂ **22410/85-560.** Fax 22410/80-241. 42 units. 55€–85€ ($72–$111) double. Rates include breakfast. MC, V. Closed Nov–Mar. *In room:* A/C.

Lindos Mare ✩   This relatively small and classy cliff-side resort hotel is a prime site at which to drop anchor on the east shore. The rooms are a notch above those of comparable luxury hotels on the coast, and the views of the bay below are glorious. A tram descends from the upper lobby, restaurant, and pool area to the lower levels of attractive Aegean-style bungalows, and continues onward down to the beach area, where you'll find umbrellas and watersports. The hotel is only a 2km (1¼-mile) walk or ride into Lindos, although you might want to stay put in the evenings to enjoy in-house social activities, such as barbecues, folklore evenings, or dancing.

Lindos Bay, 85100 Rhodes. ℂ **22440/31-130.** Fax 22440/31-131. lindmare@otenet.gr. 138 units. 95€ ($124) double, 175€ ($228) junior suite for 2 with half-board plan (breakfast and dinner). AE, DC, MC, V. Closed Nov–Mar. *In room:* TV.

Mavriko ✩ GREEK/FRENCH   We're aren't the only ones for whom Mavriko is the first choice for a memorable meal in Lindos. Other notable fans have included Nelson Rockefeller and Jackie Kennedy. More recently, in July 2000, King Abdullah of Jordan, when visiting Rhodes, had his private yacht sail to Lindos just to eat his supper here at Mavriko. Over the years, the restaurant and expansive shaded terrace have retained their special rustic charm—David Gilmore of Pink Floyd was so furious when they brought in new, modern chairs that Michalis quickly restored and returned the originals.

Brothers Michalis and Dimitri continue a family tradition of fine Greek and French cuisine, such as their oven-baked lamb and fine beef filets, or the perfectly grilled and seasoned fresh red snapper. The Mavrikos also run a great ice-cream parlor, **Geloblu,** serving homemade frozen concoctions and cakes. It's within the labyrinth of the old town near the church.

Main Sq., Lindos. ℂ **22440/31-232.** Reservations recommended. Main courses 6€–14€ ($7.80–$18). V. Year-round daily noon–midnight.

SIGHTS & BEACHES ELSEWHERE ON THE ISLAND

A tour around the island provides you with a chance to view the wonderful variations of Rhodes's scenery. The sights described below, with the exception of Ialisos and Kamiros, are not of significant historical or cultural importance, but if you're tired of lying on the beach, they provide a pleasant diversion. The route outlined below traces the island counterclockwise from Rhodes city, with a number of suggested sorties to the interior. Even a cursory glance at a map of Rhodes will explain the many zigs and zags in this itinerary. Keep in mind that not all roads are equal; all-terrain vehicles are required for some of the detours suggested below.

Ialisos was the staging ground for the four major powers that were to control the island. The ancient ruins and monastery on Mount Filerimos reflect the presence of two of these groups. The Dorians ousted the Phoenicians from Rhodes in the 10th century B.C. (An oracle had predicted that white ravens and fish swimming in wine would be the final signs before the Phoenicians were annihilated. The Dorians, quick to spot opportunity, painted enough birds and threw enough fish into wine jugs that the Phoenicians left without raising their arms.) Most of the Dorians left Ialisos for other parts of the island; many settled in the new city of Rhodes. During the 3rd to

2nd centuries B.C., the Dorians constructed a temple to Athena and Zeus Polios, whose ruins are still visible, below the monastery. Walking south of the site will lead you to a well-preserved 4th-century-B.C. fountain.

When the Knights of St. John invaded the island, they, too, started from Ialisos, a minor town in Byzantine times. They built a small, subterranean chapel decorated with frescoes of Jesus and heroic knights. Their little whitewashed church is built right into the hillside above the Doric temple. Over it, the Italians constructed the **Monastery of Filerimos,** which remains a lovely spot to visit. Finally, Suleiman the Magnificent moved into Ialisos (1522) with his army of 100,000 and used it as a base for his eventual takeover of the island.

In summer, the site of Ialisos is open Monday through Saturday from 8am to 7pm; hours are irregular the rest of the year. Proper dress is required. Admission is 3€ ($3.90). Ancient Ialisos is 6km (3½ miles) inland from Trianda on the island's northwest coast; buses leave from Rhodes frequently for the 14km (8½-mile) ride.

Petaloudes is a popular attraction because of the millions of black-and-white-striped **"butterflies"** (actually a species of moth) that overtake this verdant valley in July and August. When resting quietly on plants or leaves, the moths are well camouflaged. Only the wailing of infants and the Greek rock blaring from portable radios disturbs them. Then the sky is filled with a flurry of red, the moths' underbellies exposed as they try to hide from the summer crush. The setting, with its many ponds, bamboo bridges, and rock displays, is admittedly a bit too precious. Petaloudes is 25km (16 miles) south of Rhodes and inland; it can be reached by bus but is most easily seen on a guided tour. It's open daily from 8:30am to 6:30pm; admission is 3€ ($3.90) from mid-June to late September, and 1€ ($1.30) the rest of the year.

The ruins at **Kamiros** are much more extensive than those at Ialisos, perhaps because this city remained an important outpost after the new Rhodes was completed in 408 B.C. The site is divided into two segments: the upper porch and the lower valley. The porch served as a place of religious practice and provided the height needed for the city's water supply. Climb to the top and you'll see two aqueducts, which assured the Dorians of a year-round supply of water. The small valley contains ruins of homes and streets, as well as the foundations of a large temple. The site is well enough preserved to visualize what life in this ancient Doric city was like more than 2,000 years ago. Think about wearing a swimsuit under your clothes: Across from the site is a good stretch of **beach**, where there are some rooms to let, a few tavernas, and the bus stop. The site is open Tuesday through Sunday from 8:30am to 3pm. Admission is 4€ ($5.20). Kamiros is 34km (21 miles) southwest of Rhodes city, with regular bus service.

Driving south along the western coast from Kamiros, you'll come to the late-15th-century Knights castle of **Kastellos (Kritinias Castle),** dominating the sea below. From here, heading south and then cutting up to the northeast, make your way inland to **Embonas,** the wine capital of the island and home to several tavernas famed for their fresh meat barbecues. This village is on the tour-group circuit, and numerous tavernas offer feasts accompanied by live music and folklore performances. If you then circle the island's highest mountain, **Attaviros** (1,196m/3,986 ft.), you come to the village of **Ayios Issidoros,** where devoted trekkers can ask directions to the summit. (It's a 5-hr., round-trip hike from Ayios Issidoros to the top of Mount Attaviros.) Otherwise, proceed to the picturesque village of **Siana,** nestled on the mountainside. From here, head to **Monolithos,** with its spectacularly sited crusader castle perched on the pinnacle of a coastal mountain.

If, to reach the eastern coast, you now decide to retrace your path back through Siana and Ayios Issidoros, you will eventually reach **Laerma,** where you might consider taking a 5km (3-mile) seasonal road to **Thami Monastery,** the oldest functioning monastery on the island, with beautiful though weather-damaged frescoes. From Laerma, it's another 10km (6 miles) to Lardos and the eastern coastal road, where you can either head straight to **Lindos** (see above) or take another detour to **Asklipio,** with its ruined castle and impressive Byzantine church. The church has a mosaic-pebbled floor and gorgeous cartoon-style frescoes, which depict the 7 days of Creation (check out the octopus) and the life of Jesus.

The **beaches** south of Lindos, from Lardos Bay to Plimmiri (26km/16 miles in all), are among the best on Rhodes, especially the short stretch between Lahania and Plimmiri. At the southernmost tip of the island, for those who seek off-the-beaten-track places, is **Prasonisi (Green Island),** connected to the main island by a narrow sandy isthmus, with waves and world-class windsurfing on one side and calm waters on the other.

From Lindos to Faliraki, there are a number of sandy, sheltered beaches with relatively little development. **Faliraki beach** is the island's most developed beach resort, offering every possible vacation distraction imaginable—from bungee jumping to laser clay shooting. The southern end of the beach is less crowded and frequented by nude bathers.

North of Faliraki, the once-healing thermal waters of **Kalithea,** praised for their therapeutic qualities by Hippokrates, have long since dried up—but this small bay, only 10km (6 miles) from Rhodes city, is still a great place to swim and snorkel. Mussolini built a fabulous Art Deco spa here; the abandoned derelict retains an odd grandeur evoking an era thankfully long gone.

2 Simi (Symi)

11km (7 miles) N of Rhodes

Tiny, rugged Simi is often called "the jewel of the Dodecanese." Arrival by boat affords you a view of pastel-colored neoclassical mansions climbing the steep hills above the broad, horseshoe-shaped harbor. Yialos is Simi's port, and Horio its old capital. The welcome absence of nontraditional buildings is due to an archaeological decree that severely regulates the style and methods of construction and restoration of all old and new buildings. Simi's long and prosperous tradition of shipbuilding, trading, and sponge diving is evident in its gracious mansions and richly ornamented churches. Islanders proudly boast that there are so many churches and monasteries that you can worship in a different sanctuary every day of the year.

During the first half of this century, Simi's economy gradually deteriorated as the shipbuilding industry declined, the maritime business soured, and somebody went and invented a synthetic sponge. Simiots fled their homes to find work on nearby Rhodes or in North America and Australia (a startling 70% eventually returned). Today, the island's picture-perfect traditional-style houses have become a magnet for moneyed Athenians in search of real-estate investments, and Simi is a highly touted "off-the-beaten-path" resort for European tour groups trying to avoid other tour groups. The onslaught of tourists for the most part arrives at 10:30am and departs by 4pm.

In recent years, the **Simi Festival,** running June through September, has put Simi on the cultural map as a serious seasonal contender offering an exciting menu of international music, theater, and cinema. In July, August, and September, there's something happening virtually every night.

By the way, Simi has no natural source of water—all water has to be transported by boat from nearby islands. Day visitors will scarcely be aware of this, but everyone is asked to be careful about using water.

ESSENTIALS

GETTING THERE   Many (if not most) visitors to Simi arrive by boat from Rhodes. Several **excursion boats** arrive daily from Rhodes; two of them (the *Simi I* and *Simi II*) are owned cooperatively and are booked locally in Rhodes through **Triton Holidays** (© 22410/21-690; ww.tritondmc.com). Round-trip tickets are 30€ ($39). The schedules and itineraries for the boats vary, but all leave from Mandraki Harbor and stop at the main port of Simi, Yialos, with an additional stop at Panormitis Monastery or the beach at Pedi, before returning to Rhodes. Currently, there are daily **car ferries** from Piraeus, and two **local ferries** weekly via Tilos, Nissiros, Kos, and Kalimnos. From late spring to summer, **hydrofoils** and a **catamaran** skim the waters daily from Rhodes to Simi, usually making both morning and afternoon runs.

VISITOR INFORMATION   Check out the wonderfully helpful website launched by Simi's delightful and informative independent monthly, *The Symi Visitor* (**www.symivisitor.com**). Through the site's e-mail option, you can request information on accommodations, buses, weather, and more. Or you can address your queries to *The Symi Visitor,* P.O. Box 64, Simi, 85600 Dodecanese. Don't ask them, however, to recommend one hotel over another; explain exactly what you're looking for and they'll provide suggestions. Once you're on Simi, you'll find free copies of the latest *Symi Visitor* at tourist spots.

The resourceful George Kalodoukas of **Kalodoukas Holidays** (© 22410/71-077; fax 22410/71-491), just off the harbor up the steps from the Cafe Helena, can help with everything from booking accommodations (often at reduced rates) to chartering a boat. Once you've arrived on Simi, drop by the office (Mon–Sat 9am–1pm and 5–9pm). In summer, George plans a special outing for every day of the week, from cruises to explorations of the island. Most involve a swim and a healthy meal.

A **tourist information kiosk** on the harbor keeps hours that remain a mystery. Information and a free pamphlet may also be obtained at the **town hall,** located on the town square behind the bridge.

GETTING AROUND   Ferries and excursion boats dock first at hilly **Yialos** on the barren, rocky, northern half of the island. Yialos is the liveliest village on the island and the venue for most overnighters. The clock tower, on the right as you enter the port, is used as a landmark when negotiating the maze of car-free lanes and stairs. Another landmark used in giving directions is the bridge in the center of the harbor.

Simi's main road leads to **Pedi,** a developing beach resort one cove east of Yialos, and a new road rises to **Horio,** the old capital. The island's 4,000 daily visitors most often take an excursion boat that stops at Panormitis Monastery or at Pedi beach. **Buses** leave every hour from 8am until 11pm for Pedi via Horio (.70€/90¢). There is a grand total of four **taxis** on the island—leaving from the taxi stand at the center of the harbor and charging a set fee of 2.50€ ($3.25) to Horio and 3€ ($3.90) to Pedi. **Mopeds** are also available, but due to the limited network of roads, you'll do better relying on public transportation and your own two feet. **Caïques** (converted fishing boats) shuttle people to various beaches: Nimborios, Ayia Marina, Ayios Nikolaos, and Nanou; prices range from 6€ to 9€ ($7.80–$12), depending on distance.

FAST FACTS   For a **doctor,** call © **22410/71-316;** for a dentist, call © **22410/71-272;** for the **police,** © **22410/71-11.** The **post office** (© **22410/71-315**) and **telephone office (OTE)** (© **22410/71-212**) are located about 100m (328 ft.) behind the waterfront; both open Monday through Friday from 7:30am to 3pm. For **Internet access,** try Vapori Bar (vapori@otenet.gr), just in from the harbor at the taxi stand and next to Bella Napoli Restaurant, open most evenings.

WHAT TO SEE & DO

Simi's southwestern portion is hilly and green. Located here is the medieval **Panormitis Monastery,** dedicated to St. Michael, the patron saint of seafaring Greeks. The monastery is popular with Greeks as a place of pilgrimage and of refuge from modern life; young Athenian businessmen speak lovingly of the monks' cells and small apartments that can be rented for rest and renewal. There is also an "alms house" that provides a home for the elderly. Call the **guest office** (© **22410/72-414**) to book accommodations, ranging from 25€ to 60€ ($33–$78) for an apartment or house. All units are self-contained, with their own stove and fridge. The least expensive units have shared outdoor toilets. Most sleep at least four people.

The whitewashed compound has a verdant, shaded setting and a 16th-century gem of a church inside. **Taxiarchis Mishail of Panormitis** boasts icons of St. Michael and St. Gabriel adorned in silver and jewels. The combined folk and ecclesiastical museums are well worth the 2€ ($2.60) entrance fee, which goes to support the "alms house" mentioned above.

The town of **Panormitis Mihailis** is at its most lively and interesting during the annual November 8 festival, but it can be explored year-round via local boats or bus tours from Yialos. The hardy can hike here—it's 10km (6 miles), about 3 hours from town—and then enjoy a refreshing dip in the sheltered harbor and a meal in the taverna. In Yialos, by all means hike the gnarled, chipped stone steps of the **Kali Strate** ("the good steps"). This wide stairway ascends to Horio, a picturesque community that reflects a Greece in many ways long departed. Old women sweep the whitewashed stone paths outside their homes, and occasionally a young boy or very old man can be seen retouching the neon-blue trim over doorways and shutters. Nestled among the immaculately kept homes, which date back to the 18th century, are renovated villas now rented to an increasing number of tourists. And where tourists roam, tavernas, souvenir shops, and *bouzouki* bars soon follow. Commercialization has hit once-pristine Simi, but it remains at a bearable level despite constant pressure to transform the island for the worse.

There's an excellent small **Archaeological Museum** in Horio, housing archaeological and folklore artifacts that the islanders consider important enough for public exhibition. You can't miss the blue arrows that point the way. It's open Tuesday through Saturday from 9am to 2pm. Admission is 2€ ($2.60). The **Maritime Museum** in the port also costs 2€ ($2.60) and is open daily from 11am to 2:30pm.

Crowning Horio is the **Church of the Panagia.** The church is surrounded by a fortified wall and is therefore called the kastro (castle). It's adorned with the most glorious frescoes on the island, which can be viewed only when services are held (Mon–Fri 7–8am; all morning Sun).

Simi is blessed with many beaches, though they are not wide or sandy. Close to Yialos are two: **Nos,** a 15m-long (50-ft.) rocky stretch; and **Nimborios,** a pebble beach.

A bus to **Pedi** followed by a short walk takes you to **St. Nikolaos beach,** with shady trees and a good taverna, or to **St. Marina,** a small beach with little shade but stunning turquoise waters as well as views of the St. Marina islet and its cute church.

Local Industries

One skill still practiced on Simi is **shipbuilding.** If you walk along the water toward Nos beach, you'll probably see boats under construction or repair. It's a treat to watch the men fashion planed boards into graceful boats. Simi was a boat-building center in the days of the Peloponnesian War, when spirited sea battles were waged off its shores.

Sponge fishing is almost a dead industry in Greece. Only a generation ago, 2,000 divers worked waters around the island; today only a handful undertake this dangerous work, and most do so in the waters around Italy and Africa. In the old days divers often went without any apparatus. Working at depths of 50 to 60m (164–197 ft.), many divers were crippled or killed by the turbulent sea and too-rapid depressurization. The few sponges that are still harvested around Simi—and many more imported from Asia or Florida—are sold at shops along the port. Even if they're not from Simi's waters, they make inexpensive and lightweight gifts. For guaranteed-quality merchandise and an informative explanation and demonstration of sponge treatment, we recommend the **Aegean Sponge Center** (© **22410/71-260**), operated by Kyprios and his British wife, Leslie.

The summertime cornucopia of outings provided by Kalodoukas Holidays has already been mentioned; but if you want to set out on your own, be sure to pick up a copy of *Walking on Symi: A Pocket Guide,* a private publication of George Kalodoukas (7€/$9.10). It outlines 25 walks to help you discover and enjoy Simi's historic sites, interior forests, and mountain vistas.

WHERE TO STAY

Many travelers bypass hotels for private apartments or houses. Between April and October, rooms for two with shower and kitchen access go for 30€ to 60€ ($39–$78). More luxurious villa-style houses with daily maid service rent for 80€ to 130€ ($104–$169). To explore this alternative, contact Kalodoukas Holidays or the Simi website (see "Visitor Information," above).

Aliki Hotel ★   This grand Italianate sea captain's mansion, dating from 1895, is the most elegant and exclusive tourist address on Simi. It has the atmosphere of a boutique guesthouse, intimate and charming, and offers tastefully styled accommodations furnished with Italian antiques. Four rooms have balconies. Several units enjoy dramatic waterfront views, and the roof garden provides a spectacular 360-degree vista of the sea, town, and mountains. Because the Aliki has become a chic overnight getaway from bustling Rhodes, reservations are absolutely required.

Akti Gennimata, Yialos, 85600 Simi. © **22410/71-665.** Fax 22410/71-655. 15 units. 105€–125€ ($137–$163) standard double; 120€–135€ ($156–$176) suite. Rates include breakfast. MC, V. Closed mid-Nov to Mar. *In room:* A/C.

Dorian Studios   In a beautiful part of town, only 10m (33 ft.) from the sea, this rustically furnished hotel offers comfortable lodging (orthopedic beds!) and a kitchenette in every room. Some of the studios have vaulted beamed ceilings as well as balconies or terraces overlooking the harbor, where you can enjoy your morning coffee or evening ouzo.

Yialos, 85600 Simi. ✆ **22410/71-181.** 10 units. 45€–60€ ($59–$78) double. MC, V. Closed Nov to mid-Apr. Just up from the Akti Gennimata at the Aliki Hotel. *In room:* A/C in 5 units.

Hotel Nireus 🛪   This beautifully maintained hotel right on the waterfront is gracious and inviting, with its own shaded seafront cafe and restaurant, sunning dock, and swimming area. Its location, amenities, and price make it our personal favorite on Simi—and it has become a popular venue for vacationing Greeks as well. The traditional Simiot-style facade has been preserved, while the spacious guest rooms are contemporary and comfortable. All have fridges, and the beds are perhaps the best we've found in Greece. Ask for one of the 18 units that faces the sea and offers stunning views; if you're fortunate, you might get one with a balcony. All four suites front on the sea.

Akti Gennimata, Yialos, 85600 Simi. ✆ **22410/72-400.** nireus@astronet.gr. 37 units. 85€ ($111) double; 100€ ($130) suite. Rates include breakfast buffet. MC, V. Open Easter–Oct. *In room:* A/C, TV.

Hotel Nirides   If you crave tranquil seclusion, this small cluster of apartments, on a rise overlooking Nimborios Bay and only minutes on foot from the one-taverna-town of Nimborios, may be exactly what you're seeking. It's about 35 minutes from Yialos on foot and appreciably less by land or sea taxi. Each attractive and spotless apartment sleeps four (two in beds and two on couches) and has a bedroom, bathroom, salon, and kitchenette. Seven apartments have balconies, three have terraces, and all face the sea. The Nirides has its own small bar and rents bicycles for excursions to town or beyond. There's a small beach with pristine water just a few minutes down the hill.

Nimborios Bay, 85600 Simi. ✆/fax **22410/71-784.** 11 units. 58€–85€ ($75–$111) double. Rates include breakfast. MC, V. Closed Nov–Mar. *In room:* A/C.

WHERE TO DINE

For traditional home cooking and a respite from the crowds, look for the tiny **Family Taverna Meraklis,** hidden on a back lane behind Alpha Credit Bank and the National Bank (✆ **22410/71-003**).

Hellenikon (The Wine Restaurant of Simi) 🛪 GREEK/MEDITERRANEAN If you have the impression that the Greek culinary imagination spins on a predictable wheel, you need a night at the Hellenikon. In addition to spectacular fare, this diminutive open-air restaurant on the Yialos town square often provides, by virtue of its location, free evening concerts, compliments of the Simi Festival.

The chef's fish soup, which starts with the head of a grouper and finishes with saffron and yogurt, is spectacular, as are the grilled vegetables. In addition to a piquant array of other entrees, you can select one of seven homemade pastas and combine it with any of 19 sauces. The black pasta with shrimp, tomatoes, saffron, and feta is one of our favorites. Meanwhile, host Nikos Psarros is a wine master who has over 140 Greek wines in his cellar, all organic and all from small independent wineries. Every meal here begins with a personal consultation with Nikos in his cellar, where he will help you select an exquisite wine to complement your meal.

Yialos. ✆ **22410/72-455.** psarrosn@otenet.gr. Main courses 9€–16€ ($12–$21). MC, V. May–Oct daily 8pm–midnight.

Mylopetra (The Mill Stone) 🛪 MEDITERRANEAN   Owners Eva and Hans converted this 200-year-old flour mill into an exquisite setting for a gourmet dining experience. Their collection of antique Greek furniture and fabrics graces this most unusual space simply yet elegantly. (Note the 2,000-year-old grave visible through a glass window in the floor; it's made of pebble mosaic and rose marble.) Find an excuse to ascend to the toilet on the upper veranda, where you can get an overall view of the wonderful interior. Guests dine outdoors on the patio or inside by the open kitchen, enjoying a different menu every day. We were especially impressed by the lamb and fish dishes, made with wonderful Simiot hill spices; and the homemade pastas, such as ravioli Larissa, filled with potatoes and homemade cheese and served in sage butter.

Yialos. ℂ 22410/72-333. Fax 22410/72-194. Main courses 14€–33€ ($18–$43). V. May–Oct daily 7pm–midnight.

Muragio Restaurant ★ GREEK/SEAFOOD   This restaurant, which opened in 1995, has become a big hit among locals, who praise the generous main courses and the quality of the food. Try the *bourekakia,* skinned eggplant stuffed with a special cheese sauce and then fried in a batter of eggs and bread crumbs. We were told to order the extremely popular lemon lamb, but instead we chose the saganaki shrimp in tomato sauce and feta cheese, and were delighted.

Yialos. ℂ 22410/72-133. Main courses 6€–26€ ($7.80–$34). V. Year-round daily 11am–midnight.

Nireus Restaurant ★ GREEK   Michalis, the chef of this superior restaurant in the Nireus Hotel on the waterfront, has gained quite a reputation in recent years. Kudos to his *frito misto,* a mixed seafood plate with tiny, naturally sweet Simi shrimp and other local delicacies. We also recommend the savory filet of beef served with a Madeira sauce. They say you can't eat the scenery, but the view from here is delicious all the same.

Yialos. ℂ 22410/72-400. Main courses 5€–17€ ($6.50–$22). MC, V. Easter–Oct daily 11am–11pm.

Taverna Neraida *Value* SEAFOOD   Proving the rule that fish is cheaper far from the port, this homey taverna on the town square has among the best fresh-fish prices on the island, as well as a wonderful range of *mezedes.* Try the black-eyed-pea salad and *skordalia* (garlic sauce). The grilled daily fish is delicious, while the very typical ambience is a treat.

Yialos. ℂ 22410/71-841. Main courses 4€–18€ ($5.20–$23). No credit cards. Year-round daily 11am–midnight.

3 Kos

370km (230 miles) E of Piraeus

Kos has been inhabited for roughly 10,000 years, and has for a significant portion of that time been both an important center of commerce and a line of defense. Its population in ancient times may have reached 100,000, but today it is less than a third of that number. Across the millennia, the unchallenged favorite son of the island has been Hippokrates, the father of Western medicine, who has left his mark not only on Kos but also on the world.

Today, Kos is identified with and at times nearly consumed by tourism, in which perhaps three-quarters of the island's working people are directly engaged. The scale of demand tells you something about Kos's beauty and attractions, which some visitors have done their best to diminish. But the island and its people have endured, and so will you, with a little determination and good advice.

The principal attractions of Kos are its **antiquities**—most notably the Asklepion—and its **beaches.** You can guess which are more swamped in summer. But the taste of most tour groups is thankfully predictable and limited. The congestion can be evaded, if that's your preference.

You'll get the most out of Kos by following the locals. If you're in a village and see no schools or churches, and no old people, chances are you're not in a village at all, but in a resort. Kos has many, especially along its coasts. In Kos town, the same is true of neighborhoods and, by extension, restaurants. Greek food is what Greeks eat, not necessarily what they sell.

Kos town is still quite vital. Since the island is small, you can base yourself in the town, in an authentic neighborhood if possible, and venture out from there.

ESSENTIALS

GETTING THERE   By Plane   Kos is now serviced by both **Olympic Airways** (Kos town office, 22 Vas. Pavlou; ✆ 22420/28-331) and **Aegean Airlines** (✆ 22420/51-654). Although Olympic has experimented with expanded service and may do so again, at present its only direct flights to Kos are from Athens and Rhodes. From **Hippokrates Airport** (✆ 22420/51-229), a bus will take you the 26km (16 miles) to the town center for 3.50€ ($4.55); or you can take a taxi for 14€ ($18).

By Boat   As the transportation hub of the Dodecanese, Kos offers (weather permitting) a full menu of options: car ferries, passenger ferries, hydrofoils (Flying Dolphins), excursion boats, and caïques. Though most schedules and routes are always in flux, the good news is that you can, with more or less patience, make your way to Kos from virtually anywhere in the Aegean. Currently, the only ports linked to Kos with year-round nonstop and at least daily ferry service are Piraeus, Rhodes, Kalimnos, and Bodrum. Leros and Patmos enjoy the same frequency but with a stop or two along the way. The Kos harbor is strewn with travel agents who can assist you; or check current schedules with the Municipal Tourism Office (see below).

VISITOR INFORMATION   The **Municipal Tourism Office** (✆ **22420/24-460;** fax 22420/21-111), on Vas. Yioryiou, facing the harbor near the hydrofoil pier, is your one-stop source of information in Kos. It's open May through October, Monday to Friday from 8am to 8:30pm and Saturday and Sunday from 8am to 3pm; and November through April, Monday to Friday from 8am to 3pm. Hotel and pension owners keep the office informed of what rooms are available in the town and environs; you must, however, book your room directly with the hotel. Be sure to pick up a free map of Kos. For a more extensive and detailed guide to Kos—beaches, archaeological sites, birds, wildflowers, tavernas, and much more—pick up a copy of *Where and How in Kos,* available at most news kiosks for 4€ ($5.20).

GETTING AROUND   By Bus   The **Kos town (DEAS) buses** offer service within roughly 6.4km (4 miles) of the town center, while the **Kos island (KTEL) buses** will get you nearly everywhere else. For the latest schedules, consult the **town bus office,** on the harbor at Akti Kountourioti 7 (✆ **22420/26-276**); or the **island bus station,** at 7 Kleopatras (✆ **22420/22-292**), around the corner from the Olympic Airways office. The majority of DEAS town buses leave from the central bus stop on the south side of the harbor.

By Bicycle   This is a congenial island for cyclists. Most of Kos is quite flat, and the one main road from Kos town to Kefalos has all but emptied the older competing routes of traffic. Since bike trails are provided until well beyond Kos town, you can also avoid the congested east-end beach roads. But don't expect to pedal one-way and then hoist your bike onto a bus, because that won't work here. Rentals are available throughout Kos town and can be arranged through your hotel. Prices range from 4€ to 12€ ($5.20–$16) per day.

By Moped & Motorcycle   It's easy to rent a moped through your hotel or a travel agent. Or, as with bicycles, you can walk toward the harbor and look for an agency.

Rentals range from 16€ to 22€ ($21–$29). You can also call **Motoway,** 9 Vas. Yioryiou 9 (© **22420/20-031**), for mopeds and motorcycles.

By Car   It's unlikely that you'd need to rent a car for more than 1 or 2 days on Kos, even if you wanted to see all its sights and never lift a foot. Numerous companies, including **Avis** (© **22420/24-272**), **Europcar** (© **22420/24-070**), and **Hertz** (© **22420/28-002**), rent cars and all-terrain vehicles. Expect to pay at least 95€ ($124) per day including insurance and fuel. Gas stations are open Monday through Saturday from 7am to 7pm; there are also several stations open (in rotation) in Kos town on Sunday; ask your hotelier or the tourist office for directions.

By Taxi   For a taxi, drop by or call the **harbor taxi stand** beneath the minaret and across from the castle (© **22420/23-333** or 22420/27-777). All Kos drivers are required to know English, but then again, you were once required to know trigonometry.

ORIENTATION   Kos town is built around the harbor from which the town fans out. In the center are an **ancient city** *(polis)* consisting of ruins, an old city limited mostly to pedestrians, and the new city with wide, tree-lined streets. Most of the town's hotels are near the water, either on the road north to Lambi or on the road south and east to Psalidi. If you stand facing the harbor, with the castle on your right, **Lambi** is to your left and **Psalidi** on your right. In general, the neighborhoods to your right are less overrun and defined by tourists. This area, although quite central, is overall more residential and pleasant. The relatively uncontrolled area to your left (except for the occasional calm oasis, like that occupied by the Pension Alexis) has been largely given over to tourism. Knowing this will help you find most of the tourist-oriented services by day and action by night, as well as where to find a bit of calm when you want to call it quits. Most recommended places to stay lie to your left, east of the castle.

FAST FACTS   Of the three banks that exchange currency, **Ionian Bank of Greece,** El. Venizelou, has the most extensive hours: Monday through Friday from 8am to 2pm and 6 to 8pm. The **hospital** is at Hippokratous 32 (© **22420/22-300**). **Del Mare Internet Cafe,** 4a Megalo Alexandrou (© **22420/24-244;** www.cybercafe.gr) is open daily from 9am to 2am. **Happy Wash,** 20 Mitropoleos, across from Ayios Nikolaos (© **22420/23-424**), is open May through October, daily from 8am to 9pm; and November through April, daily from 9am to 1:30pm and 4 to 9pm. The **post office** on Vas. Pavlou (at El. Venizelou) is open Monday through Friday from 7:30am to 2:30pm. Across from the castle, the **tourist police** (© **22420/22-444**) are available 24 hours to address any outstanding need or emergency, even trouble finding a room.

Moments **The Oldest Tree in Europe**

From the Kos Museum, you might want to walk directly across to the **Municipal Fruit Market,** then have a picnic at the foot of the oldest tree in Europe, only a short walk toward the harbor at the entrance bridge to the castle. The bizarre-looking tree standing with extensive support is said to be the **Tree of Hippokrates** ✦, where he once instructed his students in the arts of empirical medicine and its attending moral responsibilities.

WHAT TO SEE & DO
ATTRACTIONS IN KOS TOWN

Dominating the harbor, the **Castle of the Knights** stands in and atop a long line of fortresses defending Kos since ancient times. What you see today was constructed by the Knights of St. John in the 15th century and fell to the Turks in 1522. Satisfying your curiosity is perhaps the only compelling reason to pay the 4€ ($5.20) admission fee. The castle is a hollow shell, with nothing of interest inside that you can't imagine from the outside, except when it serves as a venue for concerts. Best to stand back and admire from a distance this massive reminder of the vigilance that has been a part of life in Kos from prehistory to the present.

At the intersection of Vas. Pavlou and E. Grigoriou stands the **Casa Romana** (© 22420/23-234), a restored 3rd-century Roman villa that straddles what appears to have been an earlier Hellenistic residence. It's open Tuesday through Sunday from 8:30am to 3pm and costs 3€ ($3.90) for adults. If you have no fire in your belly for ruins, this won't ignite one. Nearby, however, to the east and west of the Casa Romana, are a number of interesting open sites, comprising what is in effect a small archaeological park. Entrance is free. To the east lie the remains of a **Hellenistic temple** and the **Altar of Dionysos,** and to the west and south a number of impressive excavations and remains, the jewel of which is the **Roman Odeon,** with 18 intact levels of seats. The other extensive area of ruins is in the agora of the **ancient town** just in from Akti Miaouli. Kos town is strewn with archaeological sites opening like fissures and interrupting the flow of pedestrian traffic. Rarely is anything identified for passersby, so they seem like mere barriers or building sites, which is precisely what they were. The rich architectural tradition of Kos did not cease with the eclipse of antiquity—Kos is adorned with a surprising number of striking and significant structures, sacred and secular, enfolded unselfconsciously into the modern town.

While you're strolling about town, note the **sculptures** by Alexandros Alwyn in the Garden of Hippokrates opposite Dolphins Square, down along the Old Harbor. A painter and sculptor with something of an international reputation, Alwyn long maintained a studio in the village of Evangelistra.

Asklepeion ⭐   Unless you have only beaches on the brain, Asklepeion is reason enough to come to Kos. On an elevated site with grand views of Kos town, the sea, and the Turkish coastline, this is the Mecca of modern Western medicine, where Hippokrates—said to have lived to the age of 104—founded the first medical school in the late 5th century B.C. (In case your mythology is a bit rusty, Asklepius was the Greek god of healing.) For nearly a thousand years after his death, this was a place of healing where physicians were consulted and gods invoked in equal measure. The ruins date from the 4th century B.C. to the 2nd century A.D. Systematic excavation of the site was not begun until 1902. Truth to tell, this is one of those archaeological sites that work best for those who bring something to them—namely some associations, some knowledge, some respect for the history behind the ruins. In this case, a sense of the role of Hippokrates in our own lives.

Located 4km (2½ miles) southwest of Kos town. © 22420/28-763. Admission 4€ ($5.20) adults, 2€ ($2.60) seniors and students, free for children under 17. Oct to mid-June Tues–Sun 8:30am–3pm; mid-June to Sept Tues–Fri 8:30am–7pm, Sat 8:30am–3pm.

Kos Museum   For a town the size of Kos, this is an impressive archaeological museum, built by the Italians in the 1930s to display mostly Hellenistic and Roman sculptures and mosaics uncovered on the island. Although there is nothing startling or enduringly memorable in the collection, a visit reminds visitors of the former greatness of this now quite modest port town. Look in the museum's atrium for the lovely 3rd-century mosaic showing how Hippokrates and Pan once welcomed Asklepius, the god of healing, to this, the birthplace of Western medicine.

Plateia Eleftherias (across from the municipal market). © 22420/28-326. Admission 3€ ($3.90) adults, 2€ ($2.60) seniors and students, free for children under 17. Year-round Tues–Sun 8:30am–3pm.

SHOPPING

Kos town is compact and the central shopping area all but fits in the palm of your hand, so you can explore every lane and see what strikes you. If you've grown attached to the traditional music you've been hearing since your arrival in Greece and want some help in making the right selection, stop by either of the **Ti Amo Music Stores,** 11 El. Venizelou and 4 Ipsilandou, where Giorgos Hatzidimitris will help you find traditional or modern Greek music. At either shop you may sit and listen before making a purchase.

Even if you're unwilling to pack another thing, you won't notice the weight of the unique handmade gold medallions at the jewelry shop of **N. Reissi,** opposite the museum at 1 Plateia Kazouli (© **22420/28-229**). Especially striking are the Kos medallions designed and crafted by Ms. Reissi's father (60€–110€/$78–$143). Handcrafted rings, charms, and earrings are also on display. For unusual ceramic pieces, visit the shop of **Lambis Pittas** at 6 Kanari (leading away from the inner harbor), or his factory at G. Papendreou (on the coast leaving town for the southeast).

Another sort of treasure to bring home is a hand-painted Greek icon. **Panajiotis Katapodis** has been painting icons for over 40 years, both for churches and for individuals. His studio and home are on a lovely hillside little more than a mile west of Kos center at Ayios Nektarios, and visitors are welcome April through October, Monday through Saturday from 9am to 1pm and 4 to 9pm. The way is signposted from just east of the Casa Romana.

BEACHES & OUTDOOR PURSUITS

The beaches of Kos are no secret. Every foot of the 290km (180 miles) of mostly sandy coastline has been discovered. Even so, for some reason, people pack themselves together in tight spaces. You can spot the package-tour sites from afar by their umbrellas, dividing the beach into plots measured in centimeters. **Tingaki** and **Kardamena** epitomize this avoidable phenomenon. Following are a few guidelines to help you in your quest for uncolonized sand.

The beaches 3 to 5km (2–3 miles) east of Kos town are among the least congested on the island, probably because they're pebbled rather than sandy. Even so, the view is splendid and the nearby hot springs worth a good soak. In summer, the water on the northern coast of the island is warmer and shallower than that on the south, though less clear due to stronger winds. If you walk down from the resorts and umbrellas, you'll find some relatively open stretches between **Tingaki** and **Mastihari.** The north side of the island is also best for **windsurfing;** try Tingaki and Marmara, where everything you need can be rented on the beach. A perfect day at the northwestern tip of the island would consist of a swim at **Limnionas Bay** followed by grilled red mullet at Taverna Miltos.

Opposite, on the southern coast, **Kamel beach** and **Magic beach** are less congested than **Paradise beach,** which lies between them. Either can be reached on foot from

Paradise beach, a stop for the Kefalos bus. The southwestern waters are cooler yet calmer than those along the northern shore; and apart from Kardamena and Kefalos Bay, the beaches on this side of the island are less dominated by package tours. Note that practically every sort of watersport, including jet-skiing, can be found at **Kardamena.** The extreme southwestern tip of the island, on the **Kefalos peninsula** near Ayios Theologos, offers remote shoreline ideal for surfing. You can end the day watching the sunset at **Sunset Wave beach,** where you can also enjoy a not-soon-forgotten family-cooked feast at **Agios Theologos Restaurant,** which rents molded plastic surfboards as well.

For yachting and sailing, call the **Yachting Club of Kos** (© **22420/20-055**) or **Istion Sailing Holidays** (© **22420/22-195;** fax 22420/26-777). For diving, contact **Kos Diving Centre,** Plateia Koritsas 5 (© **22420/20-269** or 22420/22-782), **Dolphin Divers** (© **2940/548-149**), or **Waterhoppers** (© **22420/27-815;** mobile 69440/130533).

As already outlined (see "Getting Around," above), the island is especially good for **bicycling,** and rentals are widely available. You can arrange guided horseback excursions through **Marmari Riding Centre** (© **22420/41-783**), which offers 1-hour beach rides and 4-hour mountain trail rides. **Bird-watchers** will be interested in the wild peacocks in the forests at Skala, and the migrating flamingos that frequent the salt-lake preserve just west of Tingaki.

EXPLORING THE HINTERLANDS

The most remote and authentic region of the island is comprised of the forests and mountains stretching roughly from beyond Platani all the way to Plaka in the south. The highest point is Mount Dikeos, reaching nearly 900m (3,000 ft.). The mountain villages of this region were once the true center of the island. Only in the last 30 years or so have they been all but abandoned for the lure of more level, fertile land and, since the 1970s, the cash crop of tourism.

There are many ways to explore this region, which begins little more than a mile beyond the center of Kos town. Trekkers will not find this daunting, and by car or motorbike it's a cinch, but by mountain bike the ups and downs may be a challenge. Regardless of which way you go, the point is to take your time. You could take a bus from Kos to Zia and walk from Zia to Pili, returning then from Pili to Kos town by bus. The 5km (3-mile) walk from Zia to Pili will take you through a number of traditional island villages. Along the way you'll pass the ruins of **old Pili,** a mountaintop castle growing so organically out of the rock that you might miss it. As your reward at day's end, have **dinner in Zia** at **Sunset Taverna,** where at dusk the view of Kos island and the sea is magnificent. Zia also has a ceramics shop and a Greek art shop to occupy you as you wait for your taxi. For those looking to get away from the crowds, an hour's drive from Kos town all the way to the southwest coast leads to **Sunset Wave beach** below Ayios Theologos. There the Vavithis family, including some repatriated from North America, maintain a restaurant that makes for a most enjoyable setting and meal.

VENTURING OFFSHORE

Two interesting offshore options lie within easy reach of Kos. Hop one of the daily ferries from Kardamena and Kefalos to the small island of **Nissiros.** Nissiros, while not too attractive, has at its center an active volcano, which blew the top off the island in 600 B.C. and last erupted in 1873. There are also daily ferries from Kos harbor to **Bodrum, Turkey** (ancient Halikarnassos). Note that you must bring your passport to the boat an hour before sailing so that the captain can draw up the necessary documents for the Turkish port police.

WHERE TO STAY

Plan ahead and make a reservation well in advance. Most places are booked solid in summer and closed tight in winter.

EXPENSIVE

Hotel Kipriotis Village *Kids*   If you want to spend part of your vacation amid loads of fun-seeking Europeans with all the possible holiday facilities, try this luxurious new resort, only 4km (2½ miles) from Kos and right on the beach. Constructed as a village of sorts, the two-story bungalows and apartments surround an attractively designed sports area. The attractive rooms vaguely suggest an Ikea-modern style with a Greek touch. Kids can take part in a full day of supervised activities. If you're here to soak up the sun, you'll never have to leave the premises, but there is public transportation every 15 minutes into Kos town. While this place is classy, it does tend to be booked by groups, so don't expect a cozy atmosphere.

P.O. Box 206, Psalidi beach, 85200 Kos (5km/3 miles south of Kos town). © **22420/27-640.** Fax 22420/23-590. 512 units. 170€ ($221) double; 190€ ($247) bungalow for 2 (including breakfast). AE, MC, V. Closed mid-Oct to mid-Apr. Parking on premises. **Amenities:** 3 restaurants; 4 bars; 2 outdoor pools; 1 heated indoor pool; tennis; health center w/sauna and hydromassage; Turkish bath; solarium; watersports equipment; minigolf, volleyball, basketball, billiards, and table tennis; children's program; tours and car rentals arranged; salon; babysitting; same-day laundry and dry cleaning. *In room:* A/C (July–Aug only), TV, fridge, hair dryer.

MODERATE

Hotel Astron *★*   This is the most attractive hotel directly on the harbor (and some 360m/1,181 ft. from a swimming beach). The entrance and lobby—a mélange of glass, marble, and Minoan columns—are quite striking and suggest an elegance that does not in fact extend to the rooms and suites. All units are, however, tasteful and clean, with firm beds and balconies. The pricier units include extras such as harbor views and Jacuzzis. In the larger and more expensive suites, the extra space is designed to accommodate a third person and is wasted if you intend to use it as a sitting area. The only extra worth the money, in our opinion, is a harbor view, but remember that by night you are facing the action—Kos is no retirement community. In summer, about 65% of the rooms here are allotted to package tours. The 14m-long (46-ft.) pool and the patio behind the hotel are pleasant, although diminished by the adjoining vacant lot.

31 Akti Kountourioti, 85300 Kos. © **22420/23-703.** Fax 22420/22-814. 80 units. 110€ ($143) double; 130€ ($169) suite. Rates include breakfast. AE, MC, V. Open year-round. **Amenities:** Restaurant; bar; swimming pool; children's pool; Jacuzzi; tours and car rentals arranged. *In room:* A/C, TV, fridge.

INEXPENSIVE

Hotel Afendoulis *Value*   Nowhere in Kos do you receive so much for so little. Nestled in a gracious residential neighborhood a few hundred yards from the water and less than 10 minutes on foot from the very center of Kos, Afendoulis offers the magical combination of convenience and calm. The rooms are clean and altogether welcoming, with firm beds. Nearly all units have private balconies, and most have views of the sea. Whatever room you have, you can't go wrong. Note that the hotel has an elevator. This is a long-established family-run place, and the Zikas family—Alexis, Hippokrates, Dionisia, and Kiriaki—spare nothing to create a very special holiday community in which guests enjoy and respect one another. If you are coming to Kos to raise hell, do it elsewhere.

Although this is likely to be many people's non-negotiable first choice in Kos, don't despair if you haven't made a reservation. Alexis Zikas holds several extra rooms, including a two-room apartment, open and unreserved in order to accommodate such emergencies. He also owns a pension several blocks away and can usually accommodate someone who shows up at the last minute.

1 Evrepilou, 85300 Kos. *C* **22420/25-321.** Fax 22420/25-797. 17 units. 40€–55€ ($52–$72). No credit cards. Closed mid-Oct to mid-Apr.

Hotel Yiorgos   This is an inviting, family-run hotel a block from the sea and no more than a 15-minute walk from the center of Kos town. Although the immediate neighborhood is not residential, the hotel enjoys relative quiet year-round. Guest rooms are modest and very clean. All units have balconies, most with pleasant but not spectacular views of either sea or mountains. Individually controlled central heating makes this an exceptionally cozy small hotel at the chilly edges of the tourist season. Convenience, hospitality, and affordability have created a place to which guests happily return.

9 Harmilou, 85300 Kos. *C* **22420/23-297.** Fax 22420/27-710. yiorgos@kos.forthnet.gr. 35 units. 35€–55€ ($46–$72) double. Rates include breakfast. No credit cards. *In room:* Fridge, coffeemaker.

Pension Alexis   Ensconced in a quiet residential neighborhood only a stone's throw from the harbor, Pension Alexis feels like a home because it is one, or was until it opened as a guesthouse. This is a gracious dwelling, with parquet floors and many tasteful architectural touches. The expansive rooms have high ceilings and open onto shared balconies. Most have sweeping views of the harbor and the Castle of the Knights. Individual rooms are separated from the halls by sliding doors, and share three large bathrooms. Room no. 4 is a truly grand corner space with knockout views. What was a great location is now even better with the new Hippokrates Gardens located just across from the pension, closing the one street to cars. In summer, the heart of the pension is the covered veranda facing private gardens, where in the morning guests can enjoy breakfast and at dusk can share stories late into the night.

9 Irodotou, 85300 Kos. *C* **22420/28-798** or 22420/25-594. Fax 22420/25-797. 14 units. 30€–35€ ($39–$46) double. No credit cards. Closed mid-Oct to mid-Apr.

WHERE TO DINE

In Kos, as anywhere else, there's a lot of fast food, fast consumed and fast forgotten. But there's no need to make eating on Kos a Greek tragedy; the key is to eat where the locals do. Along with your meals, you may want to try some of the local wines: dry **Glafkos,** red **Appelis,** or crisp **Theokritos** retsina.

EXPENSIVE

Petrino ⚑ GREEK   When royalty come to Kos, this is where they dine—so why not live the fantasy yourself? Housed in an exquisitely restored, century-old, two-story stone *(petrino)* private residence, this is hands-down the most elegant taverna in Kos, with food to match. In summer, sit outside on the spacious three-level terrace overlooking the ancient agora; but be sure to take a look at the glorious architecture inside, especially upstairs.

Although the menu focuses on Greek specialties, it is vast enough to include lobster, filet mignon, and other Western staples. But don't waste this opportunity to experience Greek traditional cuisine at its best. The stuffed peppers, grilled octopus, and *beki meze* (marinated pork) are perfection. More than 50 carefully selected wines, all

Greek, line the cellar—this is your chance to learn why Greece was once synonymous with wine. The dry red kalliga from Kefalonia is exceptional.

1 Plateia Theologou (abutting agora's east extremity). ⓒ 22420/27-251. Reservations recommended. Main courses 8€–45€ ($10–$59). AE, DC, MC, V. Mid-Dec to Nov daily 5pm–midnight.

MODERATE

Platanos Restaurant ✸ GREEK/INTERNATIONAL   Not only is Platanos in one of Kos's best locations, overlooking the Hippokrates Tree, it is in a gorgeous building, a former Italian officers' club replete with arches and the original tile floor. Try reserving a place on the upstairs balcony with its impressive vista. Among the creatively prepared appetizers is chicken stuffed with dates in a spicy sauce. If you're tired of Greek salads, try the mixed vegetable salad. For a main course, we recommend the souvlaki, a combination of chicken, lamb, and beef; or the duck Dijonnaise, served with a tasty sauce and a selection of seasonable vegetables. A generous selection of choice wines, live music, and gracious service makes for a splendid evening.

Plateia Platanos. ⓒ 22420/28-991. Main courses 13€–26€ ($17–$34). AE, MC, V. Apr–Oct daily noon–11:30pm.

Taverna Mavromatis ✸ GREEK   One of the best choices in town is this 30-year-old vine- and geranium-covered beachside taverna run by the Mavromati brothers. Their food is what you came to Greece for: melt-in-your-mouth saganaki, mint- and garlic-spiced *sousoukakia* (meatballs in red sauce), tender grilled lamb chops, moist beef souvlaki, and perfectly grilled fresh fish. In summer, the taverna spills out along the beach; you'll find yourself sitting only feet from the water watching the sunset and gazing at the nearby Turkish coast. A dinner here can be quite magical, something locals know very well; so arrive early to ensure a spot by the water.

Psalidi beach. ⓒ 22420/22-433. Main courses 4€–15€ ($5.20–$20). AE, MC, V. Year-round Wed–Sun 11am–11pm. A 20-min. walk southeast of the ferry port; or accessible by the local Psalidi Beach bus.

INEXPENSIVE

Arap (Platanio) Taverna GREEK/TURKISH   Like the population of Platinos, the food here is a splendid mix of Greek and Turkish. The spirit of this unpretentious family restaurant is contagious. Whatever you order from the extensive menu, it's impossible for you to choose wrong. Although there are many meat dishes, vegetarians will have a feast. The roasted red peppers stuffed with feta and the zucchini flowers stuffed with rice are splendid, as is the *bourekakia* (a kind of fried pastry roll stuffed with cheese). For a really top-notch meal, put yourself in the hands of the Memis brothers and let them order for you. Afterwards, you can walk across the street for the best homemade ice cream on Kos, an island legend since 1955. This combination is well worth the walk or taxi ride.

Platinos-Kermetes. ⓒ 22420/28-442. Main courses 5€–12€ ($6.50–$16). No credit cards. Apr–Oct daily 10am–midnight. Located 2km (1¼ miles) south of town on the road to the Asklepion.

Olimpiada ⁄Value GREEK   Around the corner from the Olympic Airways office, this is one of the best values in town for simple Greek fare. The food is fresh, flavorful, and inexpensive, and the staff is remarkably courteous and friendly. The vegetable dishes, including okra in tomato sauce, are a treat.

2 Kleopatras. ⓒ 22420/23-031. Main courses 5€–12€ ($6.50–$16). MC, V. Year-round daily 11am–11pm.

Taverna Ampavris ✸ GREEK   This is undoubtedly one of the best tavernas on Kos. It's outside the bustling town center on the way to the Asklepion, down a quiet village lane. In the courtyard of this 130-year-old house, you can feast on local dishes from Kos island. The *salamura* from Kefalos is mouthwatering pork stewed with onions and coriander; the *lahano dolmades* (stuffed cabbage with rice, minced meat, and herbs) is delicate, light, and not at all oily. The *faskebab* (veal stew on rice) is tender and lean, while the vegetable dishes, such as the broad string beans cooked and served cold in garlic and olive-oil dressing, are out of this world. Hats off to Emanuel Scoumbourdis and his family, who operate this fine place.

Ampavris. ☏ 22420/25-696. Main courses 4€–10€ ($5.20–$13). No credit cards. Apr–Oct daily 5:30pm–1am.

Taverna Ampeli ★ GREEK   Due in no small part to the fact that Mom is in the kitchen here, this is as close as you come in Kos to authentic Greek home cooking. Facing the sea and ensconced in its own vineyard, Ampeli is delightful even before you taste the food. The interior is unusually tasteful, with high-beamed ceilings, and the outside setting is even better. The dolmades are the best we've had in Greece. Other excellent specialties are *pliogouri* (gruel), *giouvetsi* (casserole), and *revithokefteves* (meatballs). Even the fried potatoes set a new standard. The house retsina is unusually sweet, almost like a sherry. The house white wine, made from the grapes before your eyes, is dry and light and quite pleasing—the red, however, is less memorable. If you're here on Saturday or midday on Sunday, the Easter-style goat, baked overnight in a low oven, is not to be missed.

Tzitzifies, Zipari village (8km/5 miles from Kos town). ☏ 22420/69-682. Main courses 5€–15€ ($6.50–$20). MC, V. Apr–Oct daily 10am–midnight; Nov–Mar daily 6–11pm. Closed Easter week and 10 days in early Nov. Off the beach road 1km (½ mile) east of Tingaki. Take a bus to Tingaki and walk, or take a taxi.

Taverna Nikolas (Value) GREEK/SEAFOOD   Known on the street as Nick the Fisherman's, this is one taverna in Kos that wasn't designed with tourists in mind. Off season, it's a favorite haunt for locals, with whom you'll have to compete for one of eight tables. In summer, however, seating spills freely onto the street. Although you can order anything from filet mignon to goulash, the point of coming here is the seafood. If the Aegean has it, you'll find it here: grilled octopus, shrimp in vinegar and lemon, calamari stuffed with cheese, and mussels souvlaki, for example. The menu is extensive, so come with an appetite.

21 G. Averof. ☏ 22420/23-098. Main courses 4€–10€ ($5.20–$13); fixed-price dinners 8€–14€ ($10–$18), with a seafood dinner for 2 24€ ($31). No credit cards. Year-round daily noon–midnight.

KOS AFTER DARK

Kos nightlife is no more difficult to find than your own ears. Just go down to the harbor and follow the noise. The **portside cafes** opposite the daily excursion boats to Kalimnos are best in the early morning. **Platanos,** across from the Hippokrates Tree, has live music, often jazz; and just across from Platanos is the beginning of **Bar Street,** which needs no further introduction. The lively **Fashion Club,** Kanari 2 Dolphins Sq., has the most impressive light-and-laser show. On Zouroudi there are two popular discos, **Heaven** and **Calua,** with a swimming pool. If you want to hit the bar scene, try **Hamam** on Akti Kountourioti; **Beach Boys** at 57 Kanari; or **The Blues Brothers** on Dolphins Square. Another option is an old-fashioned outdoor movie theater, Kos style, at **Open Cine Orfeas,** 10 Vasileos Yioryiou. Relatively recent films, often in English, cost 6€ ($7.80).

4 Patmos ✫

302km (187 miles) E of Piraeus

Architects sometimes speak of "charged sites," places where something so powerful happened that its memory must always be preserved. Patmos is such a place. It is where **St. John the Divine** ✫, traditionally identified with the Apostle John, spent several years in exile, dwelling in a cave and composing the Apocalypse, or the Book of Revelation. From that time on, the island has been regarded as hallowed ground, re-consecrated through the centuries by the erection of more than 300 churches, one for every nine residents.

Neither the people of Patmos nor their visitors are expected to spend their days in prayer, but the Patmians expect—and deserve—a heavy dose of respect for their traditions. Patmos is a place for those seeking a "retreat," and by that, we do not mean a religious calling, but a more subdued, civilized alternative to major tourist destinations. Some guidebooks highlight the island's prohibitions on nude bathing and how to get around them—but if this is a priority for you, then you've stumbled onto the wrong island. Go to Patmos, by all means, but don't expect raucous nightlife.

If we were to compose and dedicate a piece to Patmos, it might be a suite for rooster, moped, and bells (church and goat), for these are the sounds that fill the air. But just because Patmos is wonderfully unspoiled, don't imagine that it's "primitive." In fact, in recent years it has developed quite sophisticated tourist facilities—and a following.

ESSENTIALS

GETTING THERE   By Plane   Patmos has no airport, but it is convenient (especially by hydrofoil and catamaran in spring and summer) to three islands which do: Samos, Kos, and Leros. Rather than endure the all-but interminable ferry ride from Piraeus, fly from Athens to one of these, then hop a boat or hydrofoil the rest of the way to Patmos. Samos is your best bet: With the right schedule, you can get from the Athens airport to Patmos in 3 hours via Samos.

By Boat   Patmos, the northernmost of the Dodecanese Islands, is on the daily ferry line from Piraeus to Rhodes—confirm schedules with **Piraeus Port Authority** (© 210/417-2657 or 210/451-1310) or **Rhodes Port Authority** (© 22410/23-693 or 22410/27-695). Patmos has numerous sea links with the larger islands of the Dodecanese, as well as with the islands of the northeast Aegean. Options are limited from late fall to early spring, but Easter through September, sea connections with most of the islands of the eastern Aegean are numerous and convenient. With **Blue Star Line**'s (www.bluestarferries.com) new high-speed ferries, the travel time from Piraeus has been reduced to about 6 hours.

VISITOR INFORMATION   The **tourism office** (© 22470/31-666) in the port town of Skala is directly in front of you as you disembark from your ship; it's open June through August daily from 9am to 10pm. It shares the Italianate "municipal palace" with the post office and the **tourist police** (© 22470/31-303), who take over when the tourism office is closed. The **port police** (© 22470/31-231), in the first building on your left on the main ferry pier, are very helpful for boat schedules and whatever else ails or concerns you; it's open year-round, 24 hours a day. There is also a host of helpful information about Patmos at **www.travelpoint.gr**.

Apollon Tourist and Shipping Agency, on the harbor near the central square (© 22470/31-724; fax 22470/31-819), can book excursion boats and hydrofoils and arrange lodging in hotels, rental houses, and apartments throughout the island. It's open year-round from 8am to noon and 4 to 6pm, with extended summer hours. **Astoria Tourist and Shipping Agency** (℃ **22470/31-205;** fax 22470/31-975) is also helpful. For the "do-it-yourselfer" in you, pick up a free copy of *Patmos Summertime*. *Warning:* The map of the island provided in that publication is grossly inaccurate, as are many other tourist maps of Patmos.

GETTING AROUND   By Moped & Bicycle   Mopeds are definitely the vehicle of choice on the island, provided you have a proper license. At the shops that line the harbor, 1-day rentals start at around 15€ ($20) and go up to 35€ ($46). Michael Michalis at **Australis Motor Rent** (℃ **22470/32-284**), in Skala's new port, operates a first-rate shop and is quite conscientious. Unlike at most dealers, you can rent for less than a full day at a discounted rate. You can also contact **Billis** (℃ **22470/ 32-218**) or **Theo & Georgio's** (℃ **22470/32-066**), both on the harbor in Skala. Bicycles are hard to come by on the island, but Theo & Georgio's has 18-speed mountain bikes for 8€ ($10) per day.

By Car   Two convenient car rental offices, both in Skala, are **Patmos Rent-a-Car,** just behind the police station (℃ **22470/32-203**); and **Avis,** on the new port (℃ **22470/33-095**). Daily rentals in high season start at 45€ ($59). The island does not have that many gas stations, so be sure you watch your gas tank gauge.

By Taxi   The island's main taxi stand is on the pier in Skala Harbor, right before your eyes as you get off the boat. From anywhere on the island, you can request a taxi by calling ℃ **22470/31-225.** As the island is quite small, it's much cheaper to hire a taxi than to rent a car.

By Bus   The entire island has a single bus, whose current schedule is available at the tourist office and is posted at locations around the island. Needless to say, it provides very limited service—to Skala, Hora, Grikos, and Kambos—so it's best to use another method to get around.

ORIENTATION   Patmos lies along a north-south axis; were it not for a narrow central isthmus, it would be two islands, north and south. **Skala,** the island's only town of any size, is situated near that isthmus joining the north island to the south. Above Skala looms the hilltop capital of **Hora,** comprising a mazelike medieval village and the fortified monastery of St. John the Divine. There are really only two other towns on Patmos: **Kambos** to the north and **Grikou** to the south. While Kambos is a real village of roughly 500 inhabitants, Grikou is mostly a resort, a creation of the tourist industry.

Most independent visitors to Patmos, especially first-timers, will choose to stay in Skala (Hora has no hotels) and explore the north and south from there. Patmos is genuinely addicting, an island to which visitors, Greek and foreign, return year after year. So while it makes sense on your first visit to Patmos to be centrally located, you may wish to stay elsewhere during future visits.

Tips **For Your Health**

One essential you need to know about Patmos from the outset is that tap water is not for drinking. *Drink only bottled water.*

FAST FACTS   Commercial Bank of Greece on the harbor and **National Bank of Greece** on the central square offer exchange services and ATMs. Both are open Monday through Thursday from 8am to 2pm and Friday from 8am to 1:30pm. You will also find an ATM where ferries and cruises dock at the main pier. For **dental or medical emergencies,** call ℭ **22470/31-211;** for special **pharmaceutical needs,** call ℭ **22470/31-500.** The **hospital** (ℭ **22470/31-211**) is on the road to Hora. The **post office** on the harbor is open Monday through Friday from 8am to 1:30pm. The **tourist police** (ℭ **22470/31-303**) are directly across from the port.

For **Internet access,** the Internet Cafe at Blue Bay (Blue Bay Hotel) is open April through October, daily from 8am to 8pm. Millennium Internet Cafe (on the lane to Horio, near the OTE office) is open year-round, daily from 9am to 10pm. A short walk down toward the new port will bring you to **Just Like Home** (ℭ **22470/ 33-170**), where a load of laundry costs 15€ ($20). It's open daily until 9pm year-round, and until 10pm in July and August. Cold-water wash and rinse are available, as are hand washing and dry cleaning.

WHAT TO SEE & DO
THE TOP ATTRACTIONS

What Patmos lacks in quantity it makes up for in quality. Apart from its natural beauty and its 300-plus churches, to which we can't possibly provide a detailed guide here, there are several extraordinary sights: the **Monastery of St. John, Cave of the Apocalypse,** and medieval town of **Hora** ☆. The latter is a labyrinthine maze of whitewashed stone homes, shops, and churches in which getting lost is the whole point.

Off season, the opening days and times for the **cave** and the **monastery** are unpredictable, as they are designed to accommodate groups of pilgrims and cruise-ship tours rather than individual visitors. Neither place is public. The cave is enclosed within a convent, and the monastery is just that. It's best to consult the tourist office or one of the travel agents listed above for the open hours on the day of your visit (the times given below are for the peak season May–Aug). To visit both places, appropriate attire is required, which means that women must wear full skirts or dresses and have covered shoulders, while men must wear long pants.

The road to Hora is well marked from Skala; but if you're walking, take the narrow lane to the left just past the central square. Once outside the town, you can mostly avoid the main road by following the uneven stone-paved donkey path, which is the traditional pilgrims' route to the sanctuaries above.

Cave of the Apocalypse ☆

Exiled to Patmos by the Roman emperor Domitian in A.D. 95, St. John the Divine is said to have made his home in this cave, though Patmians insist quite reasonably that he walked every inch of the small island, talking with its people. The cave is said to be the epicenter of his earth-shaking revelation, which he dictated to his disciple and which has come down to present believers as the Book of the Apocalypse, or Revelation, the last book of the Christian Bible. The cave is now encased within a sanctuary, which is in turn encircled by a convent. A stirring brochure written by Archimandrite Koutsanellos, Superior of the Cave, provides an excellent description of the religious significance of each niche in the rocks, as well as the many icons in the cave. Other guides are available in local tourist shops. The best preparation, of course, is to bone up on the Book of Revelation.

On the road to Hora. ℭ **22470/31-234.** Free admission. May–Aug Sun 8am–1pm and 2–6pm; Mon 8am–1:30pm; Tues–Wed 8am–1:30pm and 2–6pm; Thurs–Sat 8am–1:30pm. Otherwise, hours vary (as described above).

Monastery of St. John ★   Towering over Skala and, for that matter, over the south island, is the medieval Monastery of St. John, which looks far more like a fortress than a house of prayer. Built to withstand pirates, it is certainly up to the task of deterring runaway tourism. The monastery virtually controls the south island, where the mayor wears a hat but the monastic authority wears a miter. In 1088, with a hand-signed document from the Byzantine emperor Alexis I Comnenus ceding the entire island to the future monastery, Blessed Christodoulos arrived on Patmos to establish here what was to become an independent monastic state. The monastery chapel is stunning, as is the adjoining **Chapel of the Theotokos,** whose frescoes date from the 12th century. On display in the treasury is but a fraction of the monastery's exquisite Byzantine treasures, which are second only to those of Mount Athos, a monastic state.

Hora. ℭ 22470/31-234. Free admission to monastery; 4€ ($5.20) to treasury. May–Aug Sun 8am–1pm and 2–6pm; Mon 8am–1:30pm; Tues–Wed 8am–1:30pm and 2–6pm; Thurs–Sat 8am–1:30pm. Otherwise, hours vary (as described above).

OUTDOOR PURSUITS

The principal outdoor activities on Patmos are walking and swimming. The best **beaches** are highlighted below (see "Exploring the Island") and the best **walking trails** are the unmarked donkey paths, which crisscross the island. You won't find jet-skis or surfboards on Patmos, although limited **watersports** are available. Paddleboats and canoes can be rented and water-skiing arranged on Agriolivada beach at Hellen's Place, as well as on the beach at Grikos. Also at Grikos is a **summer club** where you can join in a volleyball game or play tennis (rackets and balls provided). For **snorkeling** and **skin diving,** accompanied if you wish by your own underwater photographer and cameraman, call ℭ **22470/33-059.**

SHOPPING

Patmians are quick to lament and apologize for the fact that just about everything, from gas to toothpaste, is a bit more expensive here. Patmos doesn't even have its own drinking water, and import costs inevitably get passed along to the customer. That said, the price differences are much more evident to the locals than to tourists.

There are several excellent jewelry shops, like **Iphigenia** (ℭ **22470/31-814**) and **Midas** (ℭ **22470/31-800**), on the harbor, though **Filoxenia** (ℭ **22470/31-667**) and **Art Spot** (ℭ **22470/32-243**), both behind the main square in the direction of Hora, have more interesting contemporary designs, often influenced by ancient motifs. The Art Spot also sells ceramics and small sculptures, and is well worth seeking out. Farther down the same lane is **Parousia** (ℭ **22470/32-549**), the best single stop for hand-painted icons and a wide range of books on Byzantine subjects. The proprietor, Mr. Alafakis, is quite learned in the history and craft of icon painting and can tell you a great deal about the icons in his shop and the diverse traditions they represent.

The most fascinating shop on Patmos may be **Selene** (ℭ **22470/31-742**), directly across from the port authority office. The highly selective array of Greek handmade art and crafts here is extraordinary, from ceramics to hand-painted Russian and Greek icons to marionettes, some as tall as 1m (4 ft.). And be sure to notice Selene's structure, also a work of art. Built in 1835, it was once a storage space for sails and later a boat-building workshop. Look down at the shop's extraordinary floor made of hand-made stamped and scored bricks, quite special and traditional to Patmos.

WHERE TO STAY IN SKALA

There are no hotels or pensions in Hora, although you will find many in Skala. Unless you plan to visit Patmos during Greek or Christian Easter or late July through August, you should not have difficulty finding a room upon arrival, though it's always safer to book ahead. Residents offering private accommodations usually meet ferries at the harbor. If you're interested in renting a kitchenette apartment or villa, contact the **Apollon Agency** (© 22470/31-724; fax 22470/31-819).

EXPENSIVE

Porto Scoutari *(Kids)* High on a bluff overlooking Meloï Bay, this new luxury hotel is seductively gracious, with the largest rooms and pool on the island. Ground-level suites are designed with families in mind, while upper-level suites, with four-poster beds and bathtubs, have "honeymoon" written all over them. The decor, a blend of reproduction antiques and contemporary design, is both elegant and comfortable. Each bungalow-style studio has a kitchenette, year-round climate control, and a private balcony. The common areas—breakfast room, lounge, piano bar, and pool—are simultaneously informal and refined. This is the most ambitious "full-service" hotel on the island. If your stay on Patmos is brief, you probably wouldn't want to stay here, only because you're paying for facilities that you might not have time to use.

Scoutari, 85500 Patmos. © 22470/33-123. Fax 22470/33-175. www.portoscoutari.com. 30 units. 110€–165€ ($143–$215) double; 120€–260€ ($156–$338) studio or suite. Rates include full breakfast buffet. MC, V. Open Easter–Oct. Note that this hotel overlooks, but is not in, Meloï Bay—so follow the signs to Kambos, not to Meloï Bay. It's less than 3km (2 miles) from the center of Skala. **Amenities:** Restaurant; pool; Internet and fax facilities; room service; transfers arranged; laundry and dry cleaning arranged. *In room:* A/C, TV, minibar, coffeemaker, hair dryer, safe.

MODERATE

Blue Bay Hotel Two unique features distinguish this hotel (operated by a Greek-Australian couple): First, its stellar location on the southwest side of the harbor offers a rare fusion of convenience and quiet. Second, guests are requested not to smoke anywhere in the hotel except on the private balconies. The bedrooms are spacious, immaculate, and comfortable. Room nos. 114 and 115 share a terrace the size of a tennis court overlooking the sea. The hotel emphasizes service and gracious hospitality. The new Blue Bay Internet Cafe offers Internet access for 2€ ($2.60) per 20 minutes.

Skala, 85500 Patmos. © 22470/31-165. www.blubay.50g.com. 27 units. 115€ ($150) double; 135€ ($176) suite. Breakfast buffet 6€ ($7.80) extra. MC, V. Closed Nov–Mar. **Amenities:** Breakfast room; bar; Internet access. *In room:* A/C.

Romeos Hotel Of Skala's newer lodgings, this one, run by a Greek-American family from Virginia, is especially commodious, with a large pool and a quiet garden. The simply decorated, spotless rooms are built like semi-attached bungalows on a series of tiers, with balconies offering views across the countryside to Mount Kastelli. Large honeymoon suites, with double beds, full bathtubs, and small lounges, are available. One downside is the unsightly lot in front of the property, though it's hardly a factor once you're inside the hotel compound.

Skala (in the back streets behind the OTE), 85500 Patmos. © 22470/31-962. Fax 22470/31-070. romeosh@12net.gr. 60 units. 100€ ($130) double; 120€ ($156) suite. Rates include breakfast. MC, V. Closed Nov–Mar. **Amenities:** Pool. *In room:* A/C, minibar.

Skala Hotel Tranquilly but conveniently situated well off the main harbor road behind a lush garden overflowing with arresting pink bougainvillea, this comfortable hotel has aged like a fine wine and become an established Skala favorite. Attractive features include a large pool with an inviting sun deck and bar, the large breakfast buffet, and personalized service. The three views to choose from are the sea, the western mountains, and the Monastery of St. John—and all are striking. If you want to stay here at Easter or in late July and August, you'll need advance reservations.

Skala, 85500 Patmos. ℂ **22470/31-343**. Fax 22470/31-747. skalahtl@12net.gr. 78 units. 110€ ($143) double. Rates include breakfast. MC, V. Closed Nov–Mar. **Amenities:** Restaurant; 2 bars; pool; conference facilities. *In room:* A/C, TV, minibar.

INEXPENSIVE

Australis Hotel and Apartments ✿   On the approach, you may have misgivings regarding this hotel's location, down a less-than-charming lane off the new port area. Your doubts will vanish when you enter the startlingly lovely hotel compound, a blooming hillside oasis. Once featured in *Garden Design* magazine, the grounds are covered with bougainvillea, fuchsias, dahlias, and roses. The pleasant communal porch, where breakfast is served, offers delightful views of the open harbor. The guest rooms are bright, tasteful, and impeccably clean, with some of the best (firmest) beds we've found in Greece. Within the same compound and enjoying the same floral and sea vistas, Fokas Michellis's four new luxury apartments offer spacious homes away from home for families or groups of four to six people. They are fully equipped with kitchenettes, TVs, and heat for the winter months. In addition to these apartments, Fokas's oldest son, Michael Michellis, has three handsome new studios over his house on the old road to Hora. Each has a well-stocked kitchen and goes for 37€ to 55€ ($48–$72) per day.

Skala (a 5-min. walk from the center), 85500 Patmos. ℂ **22470/31-576**. Fax 22470/32-284. 29 units. 70€ ($91) double; 155€ ($202) apt, depending on size and season. Rates include breakfast. No credit cards. Closed Nov–Mar. *In room:* TV in some, fridge in some.

Castelli Hotel   Guests stay in two white-stucco blocks framed with brown shutters. The large, spotless rooms have white walls, beige tile floors, fridges, and covered balconies. The common lounge and lobby areas are filled with photographs, flower-print sofas, seashells, fresh-cut flowers from the surrounding gardens, and other knickknacks of seaside life. The hotel's striking sea vista can be enjoyed from cushioned wrought-iron chairs on each room's balcony or from a pleasant covered terrace/bar. The price you pay for the view is a mildly challenging 5-minute climb from the harbor.

Skala, 85500 Patmos. ℂ **22470/31-361**. Fax 22470/31-656. 45 units. 78€ ($101) double, year-round. Rates include breakfast. No credit cards. **Amenities:** Bar. *In room:* A/C, fridge.

Villa Knossos   This small white villa off the new port is set within an abundant garden of palms, purple and pink bougainvillea, potted geraniums, and hibiscus. The tasteful, spacious guest rooms have high ceilings (making them cool even in the summer's heat). All rooms have their own fridges, and all but one have private balconies. The two units facing the back garden are the most quiet, while room no. 7 in front has a private veranda. Guests can use a comfortable sitting room.

Skala, 85500 Patmos. ℂ **22470/32-189**. Fax 22470/32-284. 7 units. 42€–65€ ($55–$85) double. No credit cards. Closed Nov–Mar. *In room:* Fridge.

WHERE TO DINE IN SKALA & HORA

The culinary scene in Skala and Hora is fairly unpredictable. While we haven't discovered any true standouts, we have found many restaurants that will not disappoint. In Hora, on the path to the Monastery of St. John, you'll find **Pirgos; Balcony View** facing Skala Harbor; **Patmian House;** and (following signs from the monastery)

Vagelis in Plateia Theofakosta (Central Sq.). Vagelis enjoys lovely views of the south island. In Skala, you will want to browse for yourself, though we've recommended our favorite local haunts below. Alternatively, venture out to the north and south islands, which serve up some of Patmos's most enticing food. In particular, the restaurant at the Petra Apartments Hotel (see "Exploring the Island," below) stands out.

Grigoris Grill GREEK   One of Skala's better-known eateries, this place was formerly the center of Patmian chic. We recommend any of the grilled fish or meat dishes, particularly in the off season, when more time and attention are lavished on the preparation. Well-cooked veal cutlets, tender lamb chops, and the swordfish souvlaki are favorites. Grigoris also offers several vegetarian specials. Both curbside seating and a more removed and quiet roof garden are available.

Opposite Skala car ferry pier. ⓒ 22470/31-515. Main courses 5€–10€ ($6.50–$13). No credit cards. Easter–June and Sept–Oct 6pm–midnight; July–Aug 11am–midnight.

Pantelis Restaurant GREEK   Pantelis is a proven local favorite for no-frills Greek home cooking. The food here is consistently fresh and wholesome—the basics prepared so well that they surprise you. Daily specials augment the standard menu. Portions are generous, so pace yourself; and if you're not yet a convert to the Greek cult of olive oil, order something grilled. The lightly fried calamari, chickpea soup, swordfish kabob, and roasted lamb met all expectations. In winter, the spacious dining hall with very high ceilings makes this a relatively benign environment for nonsmokers.

Skala (1 lane back from the port). ⓒ 22470/31-922. Main courses 4€–13€ ($5.20–$17). No credit cards. Year-round daily 11am–11pm.

PATMOS AFTER DARK

Going to Patmos for nightlife is a little like going to Indiana to ski. The scene here, while not ecclesiastical, just doesn't swing. Clubs tend to open for a few weeks in season, then close like flowers. In Hora at Plateia Agia Lesvias, there's **Kafe 1673,** locally known as **Astivi,** where you can dance to whatever the DJ spins. In Skala, a sturdy standby—never fully "in" and never fully "out"—that survives each year's fads is **Consolato Music Club,** to the left of the quay. Skala also has the **Kahlua Club,** at the far end of the new port; and **Sui Generis,** behind the police station. Two others recommended by visitors are **Pyrgos Bar** and **Kafe Aman.** On a more traditional note, **Aloni Restaurant** in Hora offers Greek music and dance performances in traditional costume a few nights each week in summer. Most clubs charge a modest admission and tend to stay open into the early hours of the morning.

EXPLORING THE ISLAND

Apart from the seductive contours of the Patmian landscape, the myriad seascapes, and the seemingly countless churches, the **beaches** of Patmos draw most visitors beyond the island's core. Don't be tempted to think of the strand between the old and new ports in Skala as a beach. Better and safer to take a shower in your bathroom. Most beaches have tavernas on or very near them, as well as rooms to rent by the day or week. They're too numerous and similar to list here.

THE NORTH ISLAND

The nicest beaches in the north lie along the northeastern coastline from Lambi Bay to Meloï Bay. The northwestern coastline from Merika Bay to Lambi is too rocky, inaccessible, and exposed. The most desirable northern beaches are in the following bays (proceeding up the coast from south to north): **Meloï, Agriolivada,** and **Lambi.**

Meloï has some shade and good snorkeling. **Kambos Bay** is particularly suitable for children and families, offering calm, shallow waters, rental umbrellas, and some tree cover, as well as a lively seaside scene with opportunities for windsurfing, paragliding, sailing, and canoeing. East of Kambos Bay at Livada, it's possible to swim or sometimes to walk across to **Ayiou Yioryiou Isle;** be sure to bring shoes or sandals, or the rocks will do a number on your feet. The stretch of shoreline from **Thermia to Lambi** is gorgeous, with crystalline waters and rocks from which you can safely dive. The drawback here is that access is only by caïque from Skala. Also, avoid the north coast when the *meltemi* (severe north summer winds) are blowing.

Where to Stay & Dine

Aspri GREEK   Poised on a north island headland just minutes by taxi from Skala, this dramatically situated restaurant enjoys splendid views of Meloï Bay, Aspris Bay, and Skala and Hora from its multiple terraces. In addition to the standard taverna fare offered throughout the islands, which Aspris prepares with great skill, the menu has unusual, enticing items such as cuttlefish with Patmian rice. The portions are very generous (for which you will be glad!), and extra attention is paid to presentation in this quite stylish and widely recommended spot.

Geranos Cape. ② 22470/32-240. Main courses 5€–17€ ($6.50–$22). MC, V. June–Sept 7pm–midnight.

Patmos Paradise   Perched high above Kambos Bay, this is one of several upscale hotels on the island. The rooms are spacious and inviting, with private balconies that enjoy spectacular sea vistas, in some cases broken by a power line. This unpretentious place is exceptionally pleasant and quite chic. Down below, Kambos Bay has a modest strand, a handful of shops and tavernas, and rental outlets for windsurfing boards, paddleboats, and canoes. A hotel minibus transports you to and from Skala Harbor when you arrive at or depart from Patmos.

Kambos Bay, 85500 Patmos. ② 22470/32-590. Fax 22470/32-740. 37 units. 80€–165€ ($104–$215) double. Rates include breakfast. MC, V. Easter–Oct. **Amenities:** Large terrace pool; outdoor tennis and indoor squash courts; sauna. *In room:* A/C, minibar.

Taverna Leonida ⭐ GREEK   At least one Patmian in the know claims "the best saganaki in the world" is served here. A taxi driver went further, calling this the "number-one taverna" as he dropped off his passengers on Leonida's pebble beach. The restaurant enjoys a dramatic location; at high tide it's just a few yards from the clear water of Lambi Bay. If the wind is high, the waves come pounding in. The drama continues with the arrival of your flaming *saganaki* (grilled cheese). Your next course should be the fresh catch of the day. But you can also order a steak, and there is a good selection of the standard Greek dishes.

Lambi Bay. ② 22470/31-490. Main courses 5€–8€ ($6.50–$10). No credit cards. Easter–Oct daily noon–11pm.

Taverna Panagos & Sarandin GREEK   Eating here is an experience that goes beyond merely consuming food. Just above Kambos Bay sits the sleepy village of Kambos; and squarely on its pulse, directly across from the village church, sits the cafe-estiatorion-taverna (covering every base) Panagos. In this local hangout for everyone from children to cats to timeless, bent figures in black, the sea vistas are replaced by myriad glimpses into Patmian village life. The food is the same fare villagers eat at home, and the origins of the succulent daily specials are visible on the nearby hillsides: capons in wine, kid in tomato sauce, lamb in lemon sauce, Patmian goat cheese.

Kambos. ② 22470/31-570. Main courses 5€–25€ ($6.50–$33). No credit cards. Year-round daily noon–midnight.

THE SOUTH ISLAND

There are two main beaches at the island's south end, one at **Grikou Bay** and the other at **Psili Ammos.** Grikou Bay, only 4km (2½ miles) from Skala, is the most developed resort on Patmos and home to most of the package-tour groups on the island. Psili Ammos is another story, an extraordinary isolated fine-sand cove bordered by cliffs. Most people arrive by one of the caïques leaving Skala Harbor at 10am, and on arrival (at 10:45am) do battle for the very limited shade offered by some obliging tamarisks. The only way to ensure yourself of a place in the shade is to arrive before 10:30am; the best way to do that is to take a taxi to Diakofti for 12€ ($16) and ask the driver to point the way to Psili Ammos, which is about a 30-minute trek on goat paths (wear real shoes). The caïques returning to Skala leave Psili Ammos around 5pm. At any given time, a range of caïques provide this service. One of these, the *Afroditi,* charges 15€ ($20) round-trip and 8€ ($10) one-way.

Another reason to head south is to dine at Benetos, only a short taxi ride from Skala and known as the finest restaurant on the island.

Where to Stay & Dine

Benetos Restaurant ⚘ MEDITERRANEAN   For fashionable, non-pretentious, fine dining on Patmos, this Tuscan villa at the sea's edge is the place. Where else could you find light jazz filling the air, a fresh arugula salad with shaved Parmesan, shrimp baked in filo, filet mignon, and Bailey's chocolate-chip cheesecake, all accompanied by an exclusively Greek wine list? Nowhere but Benetos, where the owners, Benetos and his American wife Susan Matthaiou, have made it their goal to give Greeks and their visitors "a night out" from what they will find anywhere else on these islands. Their winning recipe begins with the freshest and finest local ingredients, mostly from their own organic garden and from nearby waters. The regular menu is quite focused, striking primarily Greek notes with its appetizers, and the occasional Asian note with its entrees. A handful of daily specials like herb-crusted tuna or house-cured salmon with wasabi sauce are inspired by the day's best crop or catch. With only 12 tables on offer, you must reserve yours several days in advance during high season.

Sapsila. ✆ **22470/33-089.** Reservations necessary in high season. Main courses 6€–18€ ($7.80–$23). No credit cards. June–Sept Tues–Sun 7:30pm–1am.

Joanna Hotel-Apartments   These comfortable, relatively spacious, and fully equipped apartments are just a few minutes on foot from the beach. Each has a balcony. Rooms with air-conditioning cost an extra 4€ ($5.20) per day. The layout and feel of the one-bedroom apartments is better than that of the two-bedroom apartments, which have very limited kitchen space. Room no. 15 has a large private deck with a sea view, but it is usually reserved for friends, clients, and guests staying 2 to 3 weeks—still, there's no harm in asking. A special feature is the attractive air-conditioned lounge with satellite TV and bar.

Grikos, 85500 Patmos. ✆ **22470/31-031.** Fax 22470/32-031, or 210/981-2246 in Athens. 17 units. 60€–75€ ($78–$98) apt for 2 persons. Full hot breakfast 7€ ($9.10) extra. A/C 4€ ($5.20) extra. V. Easter to mid-Oct. **Amenities:** Bar. *In room:* A/C (added charge), fan, kitchenette, fridge.

Petra Hotel and Apartments ⚘ *(Kids)*   Petra Hotel, true to its name, has long been a rock-solid sure thing. Since completing renovations in 2002, it has bolstered its position as one of the best boutique hotels in Greece. The Stergiou family lavishes care on their stylish, spacious apartments. These one-and two-bedroom apartments come with handsome bathrooms. All except one unit have balconies that enjoy splendid views of Grikos Bay. Each is simply and handsomely decorated, with the necessities of home plus local touches. It's a perfect family place, just a 2-minute walk from the beach. It's also ideal for couples, who can enjoy a drink on Petra's elegant, romantic main veranda. The Stergious provide an intimate dining experience as well, with a menu that includes both Greek standards and gourmet offerings. Advance reservations are advised, especially in August.

Grikos, 85500 Patmos. © 22470/31-035. Fax 22470/34-020. Off season ©/fax 210/806-2697 Athens. www.petra hotel.gr. 13 units. 115€–185€ ($150–$241) apt for 2–4 persons. Rates include breakfast. AE, MC, V. Closed Oct–May. **Amenities:** Room service 8am–1am. *In room:* A/C, TV, kitchenette, fridge, Internet connection.

Stamatis Restaurant GREEK   Stamatis, serving consistently reliable taverna fare since 1965, is a landmark in Grikou. On its covered terrace practically at water's edge, diners enjoy drinks and consume prodigious amounts of fresh mullet while watching yachts and windsurfers. This is a very pleasant spot at which the evening can unwind while you enjoy delicious island dishes.

Grikos beach. © 22470/31-302. Main courses 3€–12€ ($3.90–$16). No credit cards. Easter–Oct daily 10am–11pm.

10

The Northeastern Aegean Islands

by John S. Bowman

The four islands covered in this chapter—Samos, Hios, Lesvos (Mitilin), and Limnos—are dispersed along the coast of Turkey, and far removed from the Greek mainland and Greece's other Aegean islands. This remoteness has its advantages: Unlike other areas of Greece, most parts of these islands remain relatively untouched by tourism. The crowds here tend to be concentrated in a few resorts, leaving the vast interior and much of the coast open to exploration. Along the coastline, you'll find some of the finest beaches in the Aegean, and within the interior richly forested valleys, precipitous mountain slopes, and exquisite mountain villages. These agricultural islands produce olives, grapes, and honey in abundance, providing the basis for excellent local cuisine.

The influence of Asia Minor is not as evident as you might expect, given the proximity of the **Turkish coast.** What you may notice is the sizable Greek military presence—large areas of each island are occupied by the military and are strictly off-limits, which shouldn't bother you unless you're hiking or biking in the area. Even though this military presence is a sore point with the Turks, travel between Greece and Turkey remains unrestricted, and relations between the two countries on a personal level seem amicable. Many travelers use the Northeastern Aegean islands as jumping-off points for Turkey: **Samos** is the closest island (only 3km/2 miles at the closest point), with easy access to Ephesus; **Lesvos** is the closest to Ancient Troy; and **Limnos** to Istanbul.

STRATEGIES FOR SEEING THE ISLANDS

Since the distances between islands are substantial, island-hopping by boat can be costly and time-consuming. Add the fact that each island is quite large, and it becomes clear that you're best off choosing one or two islands to explore in depth rather than attempting a grand tour. **Olympic Airlines** flights between the islands are inexpensive, frequent, and fast; **Aegean Airlines** offers daily flights between Athens and Lesvos (Mitilini in their literature) and Chios. If you travel by **ferry,** you'll find that departure times are more reasonable for travel from north to south, whereas traveling in the opposite direction usually involves departures in the middle of the night. The islands are too large and the roads often too rough for mopeds to be a safe option; since the bus routes and schedules are highly restricting, you'll find that if you want to get around it's necessary to rent a car.

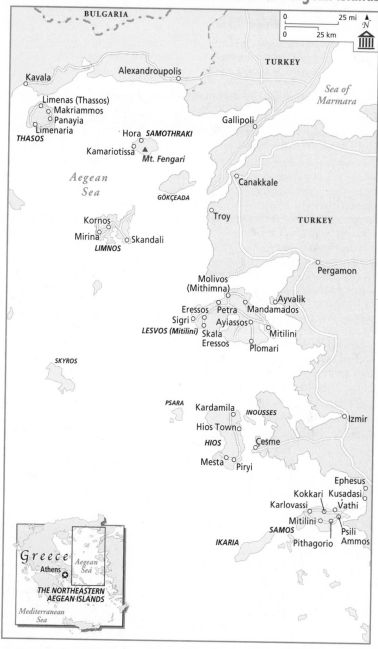

BULGARIA

TURKEY

0   25 mi
0   25 km

N

Kavala

Alexandroupolis

Sea of
Marmara

Limenas (Thassos)
Makriammos
Panayia
Limenaria
THASSOS

Gallipoli

Hora *SAMOTHRAKI*
Kamariotissa
Mt. Fengari

*Aegean
Sea*

Canakkale

GÖKÇEADA

Troy

TURKEY

Kornos
Mirina
Skandali
LIMNOS

Pergamon

Molivos
(Mithimna)

Ayvalik

Eressos Petra Mandamados
Sigri Ayiassos
Skala Mitilini
Eressos
LESVOS (Mitilini)
Plomari

SKYROS

PSARA

Kardamila
INOUSSES

Izmir

Hios Town

HIOS

Çesme

Mesta
Piryi

Ephesus

Kokkari Kusadasi
Karlovassi Vathi
Mitilini
SAMOS
IKARIA Pithagorio
Psili
Ammos

Greece *Aegean
Sea*
Athens

*THE NORTHEASTERN
AEGEAN ISLANDS*

*Mediterranean
Sea*

(**Tips**   **Museum Hours Update**

If you visit Greece during the summer, check to see when sites and museums are open. According to the tourist office, they should be open from 8am to 7:30pm, but some may close earlier in the day or even be closed one day a week.

---

1 Samos

322km (174 nautical miles) NE of Piraeus

The most mountainous and densely forested of the Northeastern Aegean isles, Samos appears wild and mysterious as you approach its north coast by ferry. The hills plunging to the sea are jagged with cypresses, and craggy peaks hide among the clouds. Samos experienced a series of wildfires during the summer of 2000, which briefly brought the island to the attention of the international press—signs of these recent events are still visible but fading.

In recent years, Samos has played host to that highly impersonal form of mass tourism involving "package" groups from Europe. This is mostly confined to the eastern coastal resorts—Vathi, Pithagorio, and Kokkari—all of which have developed a generic waterfront of hotels, cafes, and souvenir shops. The rugged splendor of the island's interior hides the most interesting and beautiful villages. Difficult terrain and a remote location made these villages an apt refuge from pirates in medieval times; in this age, the same qualities have spared them from tourism's worst excesses.

Although Samos has several fine archaeological sites, the island is most noted for its excellent beaches and abundant opportunities for hiking, cycling, and windsurfing. Also, Samos is the best crossover point for those who want to visit **Ephesus,** one of the most important archaeological sites in Asia Minor.

GETTING THERE   Although ferries connect Piraeus to Samos, the trip is long. The best way to get here is to fly.

By Plane   **Olympic Airways** has three flights daily (five in summer) between Athens and Samos. The **Olympic office** (© **22730/27-237**) in Vathi is at the corner of Kanari and Smirnis, 1 block from the bus station. Contact Olympic Airways in Athens at © **210/926-9111,** or check out www.olympic-airways.gr. The Samos airport is 3km (2 miles) from Pithagorio, on the road to Ireon; from the airport you can take a taxi to Vathi (18€/$23) or Pithagorio (12€/$16).

By Boat   The principal port of Samos is **Vathi,** also called Samos; the other two ports are **Karlovassi** and **Pithagorio.** Ferries from the Cyclades usually stop at both Vathi and Karlovassi: Take care not to get off at the wrong port! There are daily boats (sometimes two) from Piraeus to Karlovassi (11–14 hr.) and Vathi (8–14 hr.); in the opposite direction, ferries travel daily or nearly daily from Samos to Mykonos (5½ hr.). Boats to Hios from Vathi via Karlovassi (5 hr.) travel three times per week; there is also a once-weekly Rhodes-Vathi-Lesvos-Alexandroupoli run. Boats (mostly hydrofoils) to the Dodecanese islands depart regularly from Vathi and Pithagorio. If you want to travel one-way to Turkey, there are daily Turkish ferries (Apr 1–Oct 31; less regular off season); a visa is required for all American, British, and Irish citizens who intend to stay for more than 1 day. Be sure to inquire in advance about current visa regulations with a local travel agency. For more information on visas, see "A Side Trip to Turkey: Kusadasi & Ephesus," below. For more information on such tours, contact one of the two major travel agencies in Samos: **Ellinas Tours** (© 22730/89-111; www.ellinas tours.com); or **Rhenia Tours** (© 22730/88-800; www.rhenia.gr). Or check out the website **www.gtp.gr**.

VATHI, KARLOVASSI & THE NORTHERN COAST

Vathi (aka Samos town) on the northeast coast and Karlovassi to the northwest are the two principal ports of Samos and the island's largest towns. Neither is particularly exciting, and we recommend both as convenient bases rather than as destinations in themselves.

Vathi has become a slightly tired resort town but is beautifully situated in a fine natural harbor. An extensive development project in Pithagora Square and along the paralia (beachfront road) now means visitors can walk on a widened pedestrian pathway along the water and take in open-air concerts at the large bandstand. The old town, **Ano Vathi**, rises to the hilltops in steep, narrow streets that hide a few small tavernas and cafes. Karlovassi is somewhat less interesting as a town—although it's adjacent to several of the best beaches on the island, the town is spread out and offers fewer amenities than Vathi. Most tourist facilities are clustered along the water at the west end of town, forming a tiny beach resort with several hotels, restaurants, grocery stores, and souvenir shops. The old town hovers above the lower town on the slopes of a near-vertical pillar of rock; the lovely small chapel of **Ayia Triada** is at the rock's summit.

The **north coast** of the island is wild and steep, with mountains rising abruptly from the water's edge. One of the most interesting areas to explore is the **Platanakia** region, known for its rushing streams, lush valleys, and picturesque mountain villages. A sequence of excellent **beaches** between Kokkari and Karlovassi includes the two finest beaches on the island: **Micro Seitani** and **Megalo Seitani;** you can reach them via a short boat ride or a somewhat long hike to the west of Karlovassi.

ESSENTIALS

VISITOR INFORMATION   There is a local tourist office at 4 28th March (© **22730/28-582**), but it is easier to go directly to private travel agencies for information. Try one of the three major travel agencies in Samos: **Ellinas Tours** (262 Themistoklis Sofouli; © 22730/89-111; www.ellinastours.com); **Rhenia Tours** (15 Themistoklis Sofouli; © 22730/88-800; www.rhenia.gr); and **Samina Tours** (67 Themistoklis Sofouli; © 22730/87-100; www.samina.gr). Here you can make arrangements for accommodations and excursions (including excursions to Turkey, Patmos, and Fourni, as well as tours of Samos), rent cars, and so on. The Diavlos website (www.diavlos.gr) has information on ferries, attractions, and accommodations. Another website with useful information is www.samos-travel.com.

GETTING AROUND   By Bus   There's good public bus service on Samos throughout the year, with significantly expanded summer schedules. The **Vathi bus terminal** (© 22730/27-262) is a block inland from the south end of the port on Kanari. The bus makes the 20-minute trip between Vathi and Pithagorio frequently. Buses also travel to Kokkari, the inland village of Mitilini, Pirgos, Marathokambos, Votsalakia beach, and Karlovassi. Schedules are posted in English at the bus terminal.

By Boat   From Karlovassi there are daily excursion boats to **Megalo Seitani,** the best fine-sand beach on the island. A once-weekly around-the-island tour aboard the *Samos*

Star is a great way to see the island's remarkable coastline, much of it inaccessible by car. The excursion boat departs from Pithagorio at 8:30am (a bus from Vathi departs at 7:30am), currently on Tuesday, and returns to Pithagorio at 5:30pm; the fare is 50€ ($65). Book with one of the travel agencies listed above. Most excursions depart from Pithagorio, although many offer bus service from Vathi an hour prior to departure; for descriptions, see "Pithagorio & the Southern Coast," later in this chapter.

By Car & Moped   **Autoplan** (17 Themistoklis Sofouli; © **22730/23-555**) and **Aramis Rent a Car** (at the pier in Vathi; © **22730/23-253**) offer good prices and selections. The least expensive car in high season is about 50€ ($65), including insurance and 100 free kilometers (62 miles). Mopeds go for 15€ to 25€ ($20–$33) per day. But there are other agencies, so shop around.

By Taxi   The principal taxi stand in Vathi is on Plateia Pithagora, facing the paralia. The fare from Vathi to Pithagorio is 12€ ($16). To book by phone, call © **22730/ 23-777** in Vathi, or 22730/33-300 in Karlovassi.

FAST FACTS   The **banks** in Vathi are on the paralia in the vicinity of Plateia Pithagora and are open Monday through Thursday from 8am to 2pm, Friday from 8am to 1:30pm; most have ATMs. Most travel agents change money, sometimes at bank rates, and they're open later. The island's **hospital** (© **22730/83-100**) is in Vathi. **Internet access** is available at Diavlos Internet Cafe (www.diavlos.gr) on the paralia next to the police station, around the corner from the bus stop. Diavlos is open daily from 9:30am to 11pm; Net access here is a bargain at 2.50€ ($3.25) for 30 minutes. A **self-service laundry** (© **22730/28-833**), behind Aeolis Hotel on the town's market street, is open daily from 8am to 11pm. The **post office** (© **22730/27-304**) is on the same street as the Olympic Airways office, 1 block farther in from the paralia and 2 blocks from the bus station. The **telephone office** (OTE; © **22730/28-499**) is down the street from the Olympic Airways office in the direction of the archaeological museum. The **tourist police** (© **22730/81-000**) are on the paralia, by the turn into the bus station.

ATTRACTIONS

Archaeological Museum ✦   This fine museum is actually two buildings at the south end of the harbor, near the post office. The newest building houses sculpture— the island's best sculptors traveled all over the Hellenistic world to create their art. The most remarkable work is a massive *kouros* (statue of a boy), which stands 5m (16 ft.) tall. The large and varied collection of bronze votives found at the Heraion is also impressive.

Kapetan Yimnasiarhou Kateveni (near park and behind town hall). © **22730/27-469**. Admission 3€ ($3.90), 2€ ($2.60) seniors. Tues–Sun 8:30am–3pm.

Moni Vronta   The 15th-century fortified monastery of Moni Vronta is on a high mountain overlooking the sea and the lovely hilltop village of Vourliotes. Only one monk still lives in the monastery, along with several soldiers who operate a nearby surveillance post. If the gate is locked when you arrive, try knocking; one of the soldiers may be around to let you in. Ask to see the *spileo* (cave), an old chapel in the thickness of the outer wall that holds a collection of ancient objects, some from the time of the monastery's founding. To get there, continue driving uphill about 2km (1 mile) past the village of Vourliotes.

Vourliotes. No phone. Free admission. Daily 8am–5pm. 23km (15 miles) west of Vathi.

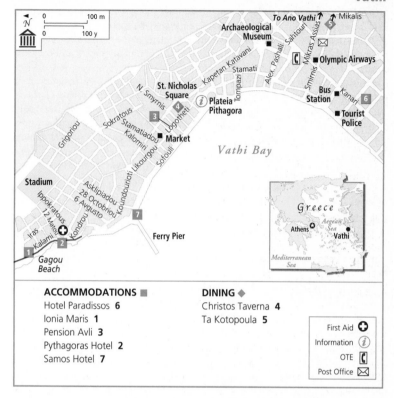

ACCOMMODATIONS ■

Hotel Paradissos **6**
Ionia Maris **1**
Pension Avli **3**
Pythagoras Hotel **2**
Samos Hotel **7**

DINING ◆

Christos Taverna **4**
Ta Kotopoula **5**

First Aid ✚
Information *i*
OTE 📞
Post Office ✉

THREE HILL TOWNS ON THE RUGGED NORTH COAST

Amid the densely wooded valleys, cascading streams, and terraced slopes of Samos's *Platanakia* region, hide many villages that sought to evade the pirates who repeatedly ravaged all settlements visible from the sea. Three of the most picturesque of the surviving hill villages in this region are Manolates, Vourliotes, and Stavrinides.

Manolates is a 4km (2½-mile) drive uphill from the coast road. The village was until recently inaccessible by car, but once the paved road was built, many more visitors have come here to explore the steep, narrow cobblestone streets. There are several tavernas, numerous shops, and two kafenions (where the locals go).

Vourliotes, about 20km (13 miles) west of Vathi, was settled largely by repatriated Greeks from the town of Vourla in Turkey. It's the largest producer of wine in the region, and the local wine is among the best on the island. Walk from the parking lot at the Moni Vronta turnoff to the charming central square. Try **Manolis Taverna** (📞 **22730/93-290**), on the left as you enter the square, which has good *revidokeftedes,* a delicious local dish made with chickpea flour and cheese. Also on the square, across from Manolis, is a small market whose displays seem not to have changed in the past 50 years. Be sure to visit the monastery of **Moni Vronta** (aka Vrontiani), 2km (1 mile) above the town (see "Attractions," above).

Stavrinides, perched on the mountainside high above Ayios Konstandinos, is the least touristic of the Platanakia villages. Here the tavernas and the few shops cater primarily to the villagers. **Taverna Irida** in the first square of the village offers good, simple food. A walking path between Stavrinides and Manolates makes an exceptional outing; the route out from Stavrinides is signposted.

The easiest way to visit these towns is by car. The island buses are an option if you don't mind the steep 4 to 6km (2½–3¾-mile) walk from the coastal road to the villages. An abundance of footpaths connect these villages—ask locally for routes. **Ambelos Tours** (✆ 22730/94-136; fax 22730/94-114) in Ayios Konstandinos, operated by the friendly and extremely knowledgeable Manolis Folas, is a useful resource. Manolis is also a good source for renting traditional houses in the hilltop village of Ano Ayios Konstandinos. Each unit sleeps three, and costs about 35€ ($46) per night.

A SIDE TRIP TO TURKEY: KUSADASI & EPHESUS

In high season, two boats a day make the run between Vathi and Kusadasi, Turkey (a popular, well-developed resort 20 minutes from the magnificent archaeological site at Ephesus). There is one excursion daily from Vathi and two excursions daily from Pithagorio to Turkey. A round-trip ticket to Kusadasi costs about 60€ ($78); the guided tour with entrance fee and transport from the port is an additional 30€ ($39). If you're not returning the same day, you'll need to investigate visa requirements. Visas are granted without difficulty at time of sailing and cost $50 for Americans, 6€ for Irish citizens, 14€ for U.K. citizens, C$50 for Canadians, and A$25 for Australians; New Zealanders don't need a visa. The travel agencies recommended above will help you with arrangements.

BEACHES

The closest decent beach to Vathi is **Gagou,** 2km (1 mile) north of the pier. But the best beaches on Samos are found along the north coast, the most beautiful and rugged part of the island. The busy seaside resort of **Kokkari,** 10km (6 miles) west of Vathi, has several beaches in rock coves as well as the crowded stretch of sand running parallel to the town's main road. To find the smaller cove beaches, head seaward from the main square. Just west of Kokkari is **Tsamadou,** a short walk down from the coast road, which offers sufficient seclusion for nude sunbathing. Continue west past Karlovassi to find **Potami,** an excellent long pebble-and-sand beach with road access.

The two best beaches on the island, **Micro Seitani** ✮ and **Megalo Seitani** ✮, are accessible only by boat or on foot. Boat excursions depart daily from the pier in Karlovassi. To get here on foot, continue past the parking lot for the beach at Potami on a dirt road; walking time to the first beach is 45 minutes. After about 5 minutes of uphill walking, the road splits—turn right, continuing to follow the coast. After another 5 minutes of walking, three obvious paths turn off to the right in close succession. Take the third, marked by a cairn, and follow the well-worn path another half-hour to Micro Seitani, a glorious pebble-and-cobble beach in a rocky cove. On the beach's far side, a ladder scales the cliff to the trail which will take you after an additional 30 minutes of walking to Megalo Seitani, as incredible a stretch of sea sand as any in the Aegean. At the far end of Megalo Seitani are a few houses and a taverna; the near end, at the outlet of a magnificent cliff-walled gorge, is completely undeveloped.

OUTDOOR PURSUITS

BICYCLING   Samos has many dirt roads and trails perfect for mountain biking. The only obstacles are the size of the island, which limits the number of routes available for day trips, and the fact that much of the backcountry is off-limits due to Greek military operations. Bike rentals, information about trails, and guided mountain-bike tours are available in Vathi at **Bike** (© **22730/24-404**), managed by the friendly and knowledgeable Yiannis Sofoulis. The shop is open daily from 8:30am to 2pm and 5 to 9pm; it's behind the old church opposite the port, on the market street. The bikes are high quality and the rental includes helmet, pump, and repair kit; clipless pedals and shoes are also available for an extra charge. The basic aluminum-frame bike is 10€ ($13) per day; the full-suspension bike is 18€ ($23).

WALKING   Some of the best walking on the island is in and around the Platanakia region of Samos's north coast, where well-marked trails connect several lovely hilltop villages. Manolates and Vourliotes (see above) are among the villages on this network of trails. A trail goes from Manolates to the summit of Mount Ambelos, the second-highest peak on Samos at 1,153m (3,780 ft.); the demanding round-trip takes about 5 hours. Those seeking a more "professional" exploration of the truly natural Samos might be interested in the British outfit, **Nature Trek** (www.naturetrek.co.uk), whose trained botanists and ornithologists lead 8-day trips from London that track the island's flora and fauna.

WHERE TO STAY
Vathi

Hotel Paradissos   Despite a central location just off the paralia and a block away from the bus station, the walled garden and pool terrace here seem a world away from the traffic and dust of Vathi. Drinks and simple Greek food are served all day at the poolside bar. The pool invites lingering, with lounge chairs and umbrellas for sunning, and shaded tables for meals or drinks. All guest rooms have balconies, although the views aren't great. Bathrooms are small, but they do have full tubs. Note that although there is air-conditioning in every room, it isn't turned on until sometime in July (unlike the majority of hotels, which will turn on the air-conditioning in June if it's needed—and it usually is).

21 Kanari, Vathi, 83100 Samos. © **22730/23-911**. Fax 22730/28-754. 51 units. 78€ ($101) double. Rates include continental breakfast. MC, V. Closed Nov–Mar. **Amenities:** Restaurant; bar; pool; tours and car rentals arranged; 24-hr. room service. *In room:* A/C, TV, minibar, hair dryer.

Ionia Maris   The Ionia Maris is the best beachfront hotel in Vathi. Gagou's pebble beach is about 2km (1¼ miles) north of Vathi; the hotel is about 91m (300 ft.) back from the water. The large terrace has two pools (one for children), a snack bar, and an abundance of umbrellas. A buffet breakfast and dinner are served daily; full-board rates are available. The somewhat plain rooms are moderate in size, with tile floors and small balconies. Poolside units have oblique views of the sea.

Gagou Beach, Vathi, 83100 Samos. © **22730/28-428** or 22730/28-429. Fax 22730/23-108. 56 units. 85€ ($111) double. Rates include breakfast. MC. Closed Nov–Mar. **Amenities:** 2 rooms for those w/limited mobility. *In room:* A/C, TV.

Pension Avli *Value*   Although you won't find any luxuries here, you will discover the most charming and romantic pension on the island. Abundant bougainvillea fill the arcaded courtyard of this former 18th-century convent. Most rooms have been renovated within the last few years, but there is no denying they are spartan, with minimal furnishings. Each tiny bathroom is encased entirely in a plastic shell, making a shower a surreal experience. This is definitely a place for those with big imaginations and small budgets.

2 Areos, Vathi, 83100 Samos. © **22730/22-939**. 20 units. 40€ ($52) double. No credit cards. Turn in from the paralia at Agrotiki Trapeza (down from Aeolis Hotel), turn left on town's market street, and you'll see the Avli's unassuming sign directly ahead. *In room:* No phone.

Pythagoras Hotel   This plain but comfortable family hotel on a hill overlooking Vathi Bay offers the best views in town from its nine seaside units and from the restaurant terrace. Guest rooms facing the road can be very noisy—book ahead to ensure a unit on the water. Guest rooms and bathrooms are small, clean, and minimally furnished. The neighborhood cafe downstairs serves a good, inexpensive breakfast, light meals, and snacks from 6:45am to midnight. Stelios Michalakis, the friendly manager, will meet you at the port at any time, a generous offer given the frequency of early-morning ferry arrivals.

Kalami, Vathi, 83100 Samos. © 22730/28-422. Fax 22730/28-893. smicha@otenet.gr. 19 units. From 38€ ($49) double. MC, V. On the coast road, 600m (1,968 ft.) north of the pier. *In room:* No phone.

Samos Hotel   For travelers who need a modern hotel on the harbor with all (well, most of) the amenities, this is *the* place in Vathi. Located right along the paralia, the hotel is subject to a certain amount of harbor noise. But the hotel is air-conditioned, making it somewhat insulated, and it was thoroughly renovated in 2001. Rooms—which have ceiling fans in place of air-conditioning units—are nothing special in size or decor, but beds and bathrooms are comfortable; most have balconies overlooking the harbor. Only about a 20-minute walk from Gagou Beach, this is a functional hotel, not for those seeking atmosphere.

11 Themistoklis Sofouli, 83100 Vathi. © 22730/28-377. Fax 22730/28-842. 105 units. High season 60€ ($78) double; low season 50€ ($65) double. Rates include continental breakfast. MC, V. **Amenities:** 2 restaurants; 2 bars; pool; Jacuzzi; game room; concierge; tours and car rentals arranged; conference facilities; 24-hr. room service; roof garden. *In room:* TV, fridge, hair dryer, safe, ceiling fan.

Ayios Konstandinos

This coastal town in the heart of the Platanakia region is a great base for touring the north coast of Samos. Ask Manolis Folas of **Ambelos Tours** (© **22730/94-136;** fax 22730/94-114) about traditional houses for rent: Each unit sleeps three and costs only 35€ ($46) per night.

Dafni Hotel ⭐   The Dafni is the finest small hotel on the island. Artfully incised into the steep hillside in a series of terraces, the hotel commands a fine view of the stream valley leading to Manolates and a wide sweep of sea. The dining room has a large picture window and an outdoor terrace that steps down to the pool and an exquisite view. All rooms are moderate in size and have balconies with the same great view; bathrooms have both shower and tub. This is a good location for walkers, with many trails nearby to Manolates and other hill towns. Make your reservations well in advance, as this hotel is filled through much of the summer by European tour groups. There is free transportation to and from the airport or the port; due to the somewhat remote location, you'll probably want a car during your stay here.

Ayios Konstandinos, 83200 Samos. © **22730/94-003** or 22730/94-493. Fax 22730/94-594. www.daphne-hotel.gr. 35 units. 75€ ($98) double. Rates include breakfast. V. Take the 1st right after turning onto the Manolates rd., 19km (12 miles) from Vathi. Closed Nov–Apr. *In room:* A/C.

WHERE TO DINE
Vathi

The food along the paralia in Vathi is mostly tourist-quality and mediocre; you'll find the best restaurants in the small towns away from the harbor. The local wines on Samos have for a long time been known for their excellence. (As Byron exclaimed, "Fill high the bowl with Samian wine!") Samaina is a good, dry white; Selena, a relatively dry rosé. The Greeks here also like sweet wines, with names like Nectar, Doux, and Anthemis. Almost any restaurant on the island will serve one or all of these choices.

Christos Taverna GREEK   This simple little taverna, under a covered alleyway decorated with odd antiques, is to the left off Plateia Pithagora as you come up from the port. The food is simply prepared and presented; it comes in generous portions and is remarkably good. Try the *revidokeftedes,* a Samian specialty made with cheese fried in chickpea batter.

Plateia Ayiou Nikolaou. ✆ **22730/24-792.** Main courses 4€–10€ ($5.20–$13). No credit cards. Daily 11am–11pm.

Ta Kotopoula GREEK   Ta Kotopoula is located on the outskirts of Vathi, somewhat hard to find but worth the trouble. From the harbor's south end, walk inland past the Olympic Airways office and the post office, bearing right with the road as it climbs toward Ano Vathi. Where the road splits around a large tree, about 700m (2,296 ft.) from the harbor, you'll see the vine-sheltered terrace of this taverna on the left. The food is basic Greek fare, but the ingredients are exceptionally fresh—chicken being the specialty as the name suggests. Local wine is available by the carafe.

Vathi. ✆ **22730/28-415.** Main courses 4€–11€ ($5.20–$14). No credit cards. Daily 11am–11pm.

Ayios Konstandinos

Platanakia Paradisos GREEK   Paradisos is a large garden taverna located at the Manolates turnoff from the coast highway; it has been in the Folas family for nearly 30 years and has been operating as a taverna for more than 100. Mr. Folas, the owner, makes his own wine from the excellent Samian grapes. Mrs. Folas's *tiropita*—freshly baked after 7pm—is made from local goat cheese wrapped in a flaky pastry. Live traditional music is performed Wednesday and Saturday nights in summer.

Ayios Konstandinos. ✆ **22730/94-208.** Main courses 4€–14€ ($5.20–$18). No credit cards. Daily 3–11pm.

VATHI AFTER DARK

The hottest disco in Vathi is **Metropolis,** behind the Paradise Hotel. For *bouzouki,* there's **Zorba's,** out of town on the road to Mitilini. There are various kinds of bars on the lanes just off the port. **Number Nine,** at 9 Kephalopoulou, beyond the jetty on the right, is one of the oldest and best known.

PITHAGORIO & THE SOUTHERN COAST

Pithagorio, south across the island from Vathi, is a charming but overcrowded seaside resort built on the site of an ancient village and harbor. Although this is a convenient base for touring the southern half of Samos, the town exists primarily for the tour groups that pack its streets in the summer. We recommend staying here for a day or two to explore the nearby historic sites, then moving on to the more interesting and authentic villages of the north coast.

ESSENTIALS

GETTING THERE   By Plane   The Samos airport is 3km (2 miles) from Pithagorio; from the airport, you can take a taxi into town for 7€ ($9.10).

By Boat   Ferries from the Cyclades typically don't stop at Pithagorio, so you'll need to take a taxi or bus from Vathi. There is near-daily hydrofoil service between Pithagorio and Patmos (60–90 min.), Lipsi (1½–3 hr.), Leros (1½–3 hr.), Kalymnos (3–6 hr.), and Kos (3–4 hr.); there are also excursion boats to Patmos four times weekly. Check the most current ferry schedules at the **Pithagorio Municipal Tourist Office**

(© **22730/61-389** or 22730/61-022; www.gtp.gr), or at **Pithagorio Port Authority** (© **22730/61-225**).

By Bus Buses depart frequently for the 20-minute trip between Vathi and Pithagorio. Contact the **Vathi bus terminal** (© **22730/27-262**) for current schedules.

VISITOR INFORMATION The **Pithagorio Municipal Tourist Office** (© **22730/ 61-389** or 22730/61-022) is on the main street, Likourgou Logotheti, 1 block up from the paralia; its hours are daily from 8am to 10pm. Here you can get information on ferries, buses, island excursions, accommodations, car rental, and just about anything else. Pick up the handy *Map of Pithagorion,* which lists accommodations, attractions, and other helpful information.

GETTING AROUND **By Bus** The Pithagorio **bus terminal** is in the center of town, at the corner of Polykrates (the road to Vathi) and Likourgou Logotheti. The bus makes the 20-minute trip between Vathi and Pithagorio frequently. There are also four buses daily from Pithagorio to Ireon (near the Heraion archaeological site).

By Boat Summertime **excursion boats** from the Pithagorio harbor go to **Psili Ammos beach** (on the east end of the island) daily, and to the island of **Ikaria** three times weekly. A popular day cruise goes to **Samiopoula,** a small island with a single taverna and a long sandy beach. Boats leave daily at 9:15am and return to Pithagorio at 5pm; the fare of 20€ ($26) includes lunch. Four times each week, the *Samos Star* sails to **Patmos,** departing from Pithagorio at 8am and returning the same day at 4pm; travel time to Patmos is 2 hours, and the fare is 30€ ($39). A Sunday excursion to the tiny isle of **Fourni,** also aboard the *Samos Star,* gives you 6 hours to check out the beaches and sample the island's renowned fish tavernas; the boat leaves Pithagorio at 8:30am and the cost is 25€ ($33) per person. A once-weekly **around-the-island tour** aboard the *Samos Star* offers a great way to see this island's remarkable coastline, much of it inaccessible by road. The excursion boat departs from Pithagorio at 8:30am (a bus from Vathi departs at 7:30am) on Tuesday and returns to Pithagorio at 5:30pm; the fare is 40€ ($52).

By Car & Moped **Aramis Rent a Motorbike-Car** has a branch near the bus station in Pithagorio (© **22730/62-267**). It often has the best prices, but shop around.

By Taxi The taxi stand is on the main street, Likourgou Logotheti, where it meets the harbor. The fare from Vathi to Pithagorio is 12€ ($16). To book by phone, call © **22730/61-450.**

FAST FACTS **National Bank** (© **22730/61-234**), opposite the bus stop, has an ATM. A small **clinic** (© **22730/61-111**) on Plateia Irinis, next to the town hall, is located 1 block in from the beach near the port police. Access the **Internet** at Nefeli (© **22730/61-719**), a cafe on the paralia's north side (left if you're facing the harbor), open from 11am to 2am daily. The rate is 5€ ($6.50) per hour for use of one of the two computers. Alex Stavrides runs a self-service **laundry** off the main street on the road to the old basilica; Metamorphosis Sotiros is open daily from 9am to 9pm, in summer until 11pm. The **post office** is several blocks up from the paralia on the main street, past the bus stop. The **telephone office (OTE)** is on the paralia near the pier (© **22730/61-399**). The **police** (© **22730/61-100**) are a short distance up Polikrates, the main road to Vathi.

ATTRACTIONS

Efpalinion Tunnel ⭐ One of the most impressive engineering accomplishments of the ancient world, this 1,000m (3,280-ft.) tunnel through the mountain above Pithagorio was excavated to transport water from mountain streams to ancient Vathi. The great architect Efpalinos directed two teams of workers digging from each side, and after nearly 15 years they met within a few meters of each other. If you can muster the courage to squeeze through the first 20m (66 ft.)—the tunnel is a mere sliver in the rock for this distance—you'll see that it soon widens considerably, and you can comfortably walk another 100m (328 ft.) into the mountain. Even though a generator supposedly starts up in the event of a power outage, you might be more comfortable carrying a flashlight.

Pithagorio. ℂ **22730/61-400.** Admission 2€ ($2.60) adults, 1€ ($1.30) students and seniors, free for youths under 18. Tues–Sun 8:45am–2:45pm. 3km (2 miles) northwest of Pithagorio; sign posted off the main road to Vathi.

Heraion All that survives of the largest of all Greek temples is its massive foundation, a lone reconstructed column, and some copies of the original statuary. A forest of columns once surrounded this temple, so many that rival Ionian cities were so impressed that they rebuilt many of their ancient temples in similar style. The Temple of Artemis in nearby Ephesus is a direct imitation of the great Samian structure. The Heraion was rebuilt and greatly expanded under Polycrates. It was damaged during numerous invasions and finally destroyed by a series of earthquakes.

Ireon. ℂ **22730/95-277** or 22730/27-469 (the Archaeological Museum in Vathi). Admission 3€ ($3.90) adults, 1.50€ ($1.95) students and seniors, free for youths under 18. Tues–Sun 8am–2:30pm. 9km (5½ miles) southwest of Pithagorio, signposted off the road to Ireon.

BEACHES

In Pithagorio, the local beach stretches from Logotheti Castle at the west side of town several kilometers to Potokaki and the airport. Expect this beach to be packed throughout the summer. Excursion boats depart daily in the summer for **Psili Ammos,** 5km (3 miles) to the east. The daily boats also leave Pithagorio for **Samiopoula,** an island off the south coast with two good beaches.

On the south coast of the island, the most popular beaches are on Marathokambos Bay. The once-tiny village of **Ormos Marathokambos** has several tavernas and a growing number of hotels and pensions. Its rock-and-pebble beach is long and narrow, with windsurfing an option. A couple of kilometers farther west of Ormos Marathokambos is **Votsalakia,** a somewhat nicer beach.

WHERE TO STAY

Rooms in Pithagorio are quickly filled by tour groups, so don't count on finding a place here if you haven't booked well in advance.

Georgios Sandalis Hotel Above Pithagorio, this homey establishment has a front garden bursting with colorful blossoms. The tastefully decorated rooms all have balconies with French doors. Back rooms face quiet hills and another flower garden, while the front units face a busy street and can be noisy. The friendly Sandalises are gracious hosts; they spent many years in Chicago and speak perfect English.

Pithagorio, 83103 Samos. ℂ **22730/61-691.** Fax 22730/61-251. 13 units. 55€ ($72) double. No credit cards. Head north on Polykrates (the road to Vathi); hotel is on your left, about 100m (328 ft.) from the bus station. *In room:* No phone.

Hotel Zorbas *Value* This place is more pension than hotel, but the rooms are comfortable. Seven units have great views of Pithagorio Harbor. The atmosphere is decidedly casual and friendly—the hotel lobby doubles as the Mathios family's living room. The hotel is on a steep hill on the north side of town, a healthy climb from the paralia at the port police station. Rooms facing the sea have spacious balconies with views over the rooftops to fishing boats docked in the harbor, while street-side rooms are a bit noisier and have no views. Breakfast is served on a terrace facing the sea.

Damos, Pithagorio, 83103 Samos. ✆ **22730/61-009.** Fax 22730/61-012. 12 units. 55€ ($72) double. Breakfast 5€ ($6.50). No credit cards.

WHERE TO DINE

Esperides Restaurant INTERNATIONAL   This pleasant restaurant with a walled garden is a few blocks inland from the port, and west of the main street. You'll find uniformed waiters and a dressier crowd here. The Continental and Greek dishes are well presented and will appeal to a wide variety of palates. You run the risk of frozen french fries served with the tasty baked chicken, but the meats and vegetables are fresh.

Pithagorio. ✆ **22730/61-767.** Reservations recommended in summer. Main courses 5€–16€ ($6.50–$21). No credit cards. Daily 6pm–midnight.

I Varka ★ GREEK/SEAFOOD   This ouzeri/taverna is in a stand of salt pines at the south end of the port. Delicious fresh fish, grilled meats, and a surprising variety of *mezedes* (appetizers) are produced in the small kitchen. The grilled octopus, strung up on a line to dry, and the pink *barbounia* (clear gray mullet), cooked to perfection over a charcoal grill, are the true standouts of a meal here. The new cafe pavilion by the water is a cool, breezy location for a drink or dessert.

Paralia, Pithagorio. ✆ **22730/61-088.** Main courses 7€–19€ ($9.10–$25). MC, V. Daily noon–midnight. Closed Nov–Apr.

2 Hios (Chios)

283km (153 nautical miles) NE of Piraeus

"Craggy Hios," as Homer dubbed it, remains very much unspoiled—and that's why we recommend it. The black-pebble beaches on the southeast coast of the island are famous and not neglected, but white-sand beaches on the west coast see only a few hundred people in a year. The majestic mountain setting of **Nea Moni**—an 11th-century Byzantine monastery in the center of the island—and the extraordinary mosaics of its chapel make for an unforgettable visit. The mastic villages on the island's south side are among the finest medieval towns in Greece; the towns get their name from a tree resin used in chewing gum, paints, and perfumes that grows nowhere else in the world.

The paralia of **Hios town** is likely to be your first glimpse of the island, and it isn't a pretty sight—unappealing modern buildings and generic cafes have taken over what must once have been a fine harbor. Thankfully, a few pockets of the original town farther inland have survived earthquakes, wars, and neglect. The kastro, the mosque on the main square, the mansions of Kampos, and the occasional grand gateway (often leading nowhere) are among the signs of a more prosperous and architecturally harmonious past.

ESSENTIALS

GETTING THERE   By Plane   Olympic Airways (✆ **22710/22-414;** www. olympic-airways.gr) has flights four times a day between Athens and Hios. There is a connection once or twice a week with Lesvos (Mitilini) and Thessaloniki. The

Olympic office in Hios town is in the middle of the harborfront (℃ **22710/24-515**). **Aegean Airlines** (℃ **22710/81-051;** www.aegeanair.com) also offers several flights weekly in high season. Contact the **airport** at ℃ **22710/23-998.** If you arrive by plane, count on taking a cab into town at about 10€ ($13) for the 7km (4¼-mile) ride.

By Boat   From Piraeus, one daily car ferry leaves bound for Hios (8–9 hr.); there's also daily connection with Lesvos (3 hr.). There are three ferries weekly to Limnos (9 hr.) and Thessaloniki (16–19 hr.), two ferries weekly to Samos (5 hr.), and one weekly to Siros (5 hr.). Check with **Hios Port Authority** (℃ **22710/44-434**) or www.gtp.gr for current schedules.

VISITOR INFORMATION   The **Tourist Information Office** on 18 Kanari (℃ **22710/44-389**) stocks free brochures, including maps; it's located on the second street from the north end of the harbor, between the harbor and the Central (Plastira) Square. In summer it's open Monday to Friday from 7am to 2:30pm and 6:30 to 9:30pm, Saturday and Sunday from 10am to 1pm; reduced hours off season. Ask here (or at any travel agency) about free guided tours to some of Chios's major sites, sponsored by the island's government (or try ℃ **22710/44-830**).

Another mine of information is **Chios Tours** (℃ **22710/29-444;** www.chios tours.gr), 89 Aegeou, at the paralia's southern end. The office is open Monday through Saturday from 8:30am to 1:30pm and 5:30 to 8:30pm. The staff will assist you with a room search, often at a discount. The free *Hios Summertime* magazine has a lot of useful information, as well as maps. The sites **www.chios.com** and **www.chiosnet.gr** are also helpful.

GETTING AROUND   **By Bus**   All buses depart from one of the two bus stations in Hios town. The **blue buses** (℃ **22710/23-086**), which leave from the blue bus station on the north side of the public garden by Plateia Plastira, serve local destinations like Karfas to the south and Daskalopetra to the north. The **green long-distance KTEL buses** (℃ **22710/27-507**) leave from the green bus station, a block south of the park near the main taxi stand. There are six buses a day to Mesta, eight a day to Piryi, five to Kardamila, and four to Emborio, but only two buses a week to Volissos and to Nea Moni. Fares are .60€ to 4€ ($.80–$5.20).

By Car   Hios is a large island that is fun to explore, so we recommend a car. **Vassi-lakis Rent-A-Car** (℃/fax **22710/29-300**) is at 3 Evyenias Handri (the same street as Hotel Kyma) in Hios. If you're making arrangements from elsewhere, try **Pangosmio Rent a Car** (℃ **2810/811-750**).

By Taxi   Taxis are easily found at the port, though the taxi station is beyond the OTE, on the northeast corner of the central square. You can call ℃ **22710/41-111** or

---

Tips   **A MOST Important Note on Car Rentals on Hios**

Currently, anyone who is not carrying a driver's license from a country in the European Union must have an International Driver's License to rent a car on Hios. If you expect to rent a car during your stay on Hios, get an International Driver's License before leaving your home country. Relatively easy and cheap to obtain, it can be issued through national automobile associations.

22710/43-312 for a cab. Fares from Hios town run about 16€ ($21) to Piryi, 20€ ($26) to Mesta, and 22€ ($29) round-trip to Nea Moni.

By Moped   Hios is too large, and the hills too big, for mopeds—if you don't have the license to rent a genuine motorbike, you're better off with a car.

FAST FACTS   **Commercial Bank (Emboriki Trapeza)** and **Ergo Bank** are located at the harbor's north end near the corner of Kanari. Both have ATMs and are open Monday through Thursday from 8am to 2pm, Friday from 8am to 1:30pm. The English-speaking **dentist** Dr. Freeke (✆ **22710/27-266**) is highly recommended. The **hospital** is 7km (4¼ miles) from the center of Hios town (✆ **22710/44-301**). **Internet access** is available daily from 9am to midnight at Enter Internet Café (✆ **22710/41-058**), 98 Aegeou, at the paralia's south end. One hour online costs 4€ ($5.20). There's a full-service **laundry** around the corner from the post office on Psichari (✆ **22710/44-801**); one load costs 12€ ($16), and the turnaround time is about 24 hours. The **post office** is at the corner of Omirou and Rodokanaki (✆ **22710/44-350**). The **telephone office (OTE)** is across the street from the tourist office on Kanari (✆ **131**). The **tourist police** are headquartered at the harbor's northernmost tip, at Neorion 35 (✆ **22710/44-427**).

ATTRACTIONS

Argenti Museum and Koraï Library ✪   Philip Argenti is the great historian of Hios, a local aristocrat who devoted his life and savings to the recording of island history, costumes, customs, and architecture. The museum consists largely of his personal collection of folk art, costumes, and implements, supplemented with a gallery of family portraits and copies of Eugene Delacroix's *Massacre of Hios,* a masterpiece depicting the Turkish massacre of the local population in 1822. On display in the lobby are numerous old maps of the island. The library is excellent, with much of its collection in English and French. If you're interested in local architecture and village life, ask to see the collection of drawings by Dimitris Pikionis (a renowned 20th-century Greek architect). The drawings of the Kampos mansions and village houses are beautiful, and have yet to be published.

Koraï, Hios town. ✆ **22710/44-246**. Museum admission 2€ ($2.60); free admission to library. Both open Mon–Thurs 8am–2pm; Fri 8am–2pm and 5–7:30pm; Sat 8am–12:30pm.

Nea Moni ✪   The 11th-century monastery of Nea Moni is one of the great architectural and artistic treasures of Greece. The monastery is in a spectacular setting high in the mountains overlooking Hios town. Its grounds are extensive—the monastery was once home to 1,000 monks—but the resident population has dwindled to several elderly nuns. The focus of the rambling complex is the katholikon, or principal church, whose square nave has eight niches supporting the dome. Within these niches are a sequence of extraordinary mosaics, among the finest examples of Byzantine art. Sadly, a seemingly interminable process of restoration often conceals the most beautiful of these behind scaffolding. You can still see the portrayals of the saints in the narthex, and a representation of Christ washing the disciples' feet. The museum contains a collection of gifts to the monastery, including several fine 17th-century icons. Also of interest is the cistern, a cavernous vaulted room with columns (bring a flashlight); and the small Chapel of the Holy Cross at the entrance to the monastery, dedicated to the martyrs of the 1822 massacre by the Turks (the skulls and bones displayed are those of the victims themselves). The long barrel-vaulted refectory is a beautiful space, its curved apse dating from the 11th century.

The bus to Nea Moni is part of an island excursion operated by KTEL, departing from the Hios town bus station Tuesday and Friday at 9am and returning at 4:30pm. The route: Nea Moni to Anavatos to Lithi beach to Armolia and back to Hios town; it costs 20€ ($26) per person. A taxi will cost about 30€ ($39) round-trip from Hios town, including a half-hour at the monastery.

Nea Moni. No phone. Free admission to monastery grounds and katholikon; museum admission 2€ ($2.60) adults, 1€ ($1.30) students and seniors. Monastery grounds and katholikon daily 8am–1pm and 4–8pm; museum Tues–Sun 8am–1pm. 17km (11 miles) west of Hios town.

A DAY TRIP TO THE MASTIC VILLAGES: PIRYI, MESTA & OLIMBI ⚓

The most interesting day trip on Hios is the excursion to the mastic villages in the southern part of the island, which offer one of the best examples of medieval town architecture in all of Greece. Mastic is a gum derived from the resin of the mastic tree, used in candies, paints, perfumes, and medicines. It was a source of great wealth for these towns in the Middle Ages, and it is still produced in small quantities. All the towns were originally fortified, with an outer wall formed by an unbroken line of houses with no doors and few windows facing out. You can see this distinctive plan at all three towns, although in Piryi and Olimbi, the original medieval village has been engulfed by more recent construction.

Piryi is known for a rare technique of geometric decoration, known as *Ksisti.* In the main square, this technique reaches a level of extraordinary virtuosity. The beautiful **Ayioi Apostoli** church and every available surface of every building are banded with horizontal decorations in a remarkable variety of motifs. At the town center is the tower for which the village was named, now mostly in ruins. It was originally the heart of the city's defenses, and a final place of refuge during sieges.

Mesta is the best-preserved medieval village on Hios, a maze of narrow streets and dark covered passages. The town has two fine churches, each unique on the island. **Megas Taxiarchis,** built in the 19th century, is one of the largest churches in Greece, and it was clearly built to impress. The arcaded porch with its fine pebble terrace and bell tower create a solemn and harmonious transition to the cathedral precinct. The other church in town, **Paleos Taxiarchis,** is located a few blocks below the main square. As the name suggests, this is the older of the two, built in the 14th century. The most notable feature here is the carved wooden iconostasis, whose surface is incised with miniature designs of unbelievable intricacy. If either church is closed, you can ask for the gatekeeper in the central square; Despina Flores of **Messaionas Taverna** (© **22710/76-050**) will probably know where he can be found.

Olimbi is the least well known of the three. While not as spectacular as Piryi nor as intact as Mesta, it contains many medieval buildings. It has a central tower similar to that of Piryi, and stone vaults connect the houses.

Piryi is the closest of the three villages to Hios town, at 26km (16 miles); Olimbi and Mesta are within 10km (6 miles) of Piryi. The easiest way to see all three villages is by car. Taxis from Hios to Piryi cost about 16€ ($21). KTEL buses travel from Hios to Piryi eight times a day, and to Mesta five times a day. The bus to Piryi is 3.20€ ($4.15), to Mesta 4.50€ ($5.85).

BEACHES

There's no question that Hios has the best beaches in the Northeastern Aegean. They're cleaner, less crowded, and more plentiful than those of Samos or Lesvos, and would be the envy of any Cycladic isle.

The fine-sand beach of **Karfas,** 7km (4¼ miles) south of Hios town, is the closest decent beach to the town center; it can be reached by a local (blue) bus. The rapid development of tourism in this town ensures, however, that the beach will be crowded.

The most popular beach on the south coast is **Mavra Volia** ("black pebbles") in the town of Emborio. Continue over the rocks to the right from the man-made town beach to find the main beach. Walking on the smooth black rocks feels and sounds like marching through a room filled with marbles. The panorama of the beach, slightly curving coastline, and distant headland is a memorable sight. Buses from Hios town or from Piryi (8km/5 miles away) run regularly to Emborio. A short distance south is the south coast's best beach, **Vroulidia** ⓐ, a 5km (3-mile) drive in from the Emborio road. This white-pebble-and-sand beach in a rocky cove offers great views of the craggy coastline.

The west coast of the island has a number of stunning beaches. **Elinda Cove** shelters a long cobble beach, a 600m (1,968-ft.) drive in from the main road between Lithi and Volissos. Another excellent beach on this road is **Tigani-Makria Ammos,** about 4km (2½ miles) north of Elinda; turn at a sign for the beach and drive in 1.5km (1 mile) to this long white-pebble beach. (There's also a small cove-sheltered cobble beach about 300m/984 ft. before the main beach.) There are three beaches below Volissos, the best of which is Lefkathia, just north of the harbor of Volissos (Limnia).

South of Elinda, the long safe beach at **Lithi Bay** is popular with families. Of the several tavernas there, we recommend **Ta Tria Adelphia (The Three Brothers;** ℰ **22710/73-208).** It's the last taverna you come to as you're walking along the beach.

The beaches of the north coast are less remarkable. **Nagos** (4km/2½ miles north of Kardamila) is a charming town in a small, spring-fed oasis, with a cobble beach and two tavernas on the water. This beach can get very crowded—the secret is to hike to the two small beaches a little to the east. To find them, take the small road behind the white house near the windmill.

WHERE TO STAY
HIOS TOWN

Chios Chandris Hotel   For those who prefer a modern hotel with resort-type facilities within walking distance of the town's attractions, this is the place to be. Completely renovated in 2000, it offers several of the amenities associated with beach resorts. Rooms are of standard size and decor, but there are suites and studios for those who want something a bit roomier; almost all units have views overlooking the port of Chios Town. During the summer you can take your meals or drinks at the poolside cafe. There's no need to oversell this hotel—what recommends it is the fact that after a day of enjoying other places in town or around the island, you can stroll back in about 10 minutes and be in the pool.

Port, 82100 Hios. ℰ **22710/44-401.** Fax 22710/25-768. www.chandris.gr. 139 units. 155€ ($195) double; 165€–225€ ($215–$293) suite or studio. DC, MC, V. Rates include breakfast. Parking adjacent to hotel. **Amenities:** Restaurant; 2 bars; pool; tennis courts nearby; concierge; tours and car rentals arranged; salon; 24-hr. room service; laundry service; dry cleaning. *In room:* A/C, TV, dataport, minibar, hair dryer.

Hotel Kyma ⓐ   Our favorite in-town lodging was built in 1917 as a private villa for shipping magnate John Livanos. (You'll notice the portraits of the lovely Mrs. Livanos on the ceiling in the ground-floor breakfast room.) Though the hotel is of historic interest—the treaty with Turkey was signed here in 1922—most of the original architectural details are gone, and the rooms have been renovated in a modern style. Many units have views of the sea, and a few have big whirlpool baths.

1 Evyenias Handri, 82100 Hios. ☎ **22710/44-500.** Fax 22710/44-600. kyma@chi.forthnet.gr. 59 units. 85€ ($111) double. Rates include breakfast. No credit cards. *In room:* A/C, TV.

KARFAS

Karfas, 7km (4½ miles) south of Hios town around Cape Ayia Eleni, is a resort area exploding with tourist groups in summer. It has a fine-sand beach lined with resort hotels.

Hotel Erytha   Built in 1990, the Erytha currently offers the most luxurious accommodations in the vicinity of Hios town. The spacious double rooms of this sprawling resort are distributed among five beachfront buildings connected by plant-filled terraces. The outdoor breakfast area steps down to the pool terrace, which is just above a tiny cove and private beach. Guest rooms are simply furnished. All have balconies and most face the sea, although a few open onto the terraces between buildings. Bathrooms are moderate in size, and include a tub/shower combo. The 21 studios and apartments in a separate building aren't as well maintained as units in the main hotel. The kitchen facilities in the studios and apartments are minimal: You're better off avoiding them entirely. The air-conditioning operates only in July and August.

Karfas, 82100 Hios. ☎ **22710/32-311.** Fax 22710/32-182. erytha@compulink.gr. 102 units. 190€ ($247) double. Rates include breakfast. AE, DC, MC, V. *In room:* A/C, TV, minibar.

KARDAMILA

Kardamila, on the northeastern coast, is our choice among the resort towns because it's prosperous, self-sufficient, and not at all touristy.

Hotel Kardamila ⚐   This modern resort hotel was built for the guests and business associates of the town's ship owners and officers, and it has its own small cobble beach. The guest rooms are large and plain, with modern bathrooms and balconies overlooking the beach. The gracious Theo Spordilis, formerly with Hotel Kyma, has taken over its management, so you can be sure the service will be good.

Kardamila, 82300 Hios. ☎ **22710/23-353.** Fax 22710/23-354. (Contact Hotel Kyma for reservations.) 32 units. 100€ ($130) double. Rates include breakfast. No credit cards. *In room:* A/C.

VOLISSOS

This small hilltop village is one of the most beautiful on the island. A fine Byzantine castle overlooks the steep streets of the town, which contains numerous cafes and tavernas. Volissos is too far north to be a convenient base for touring the whole island, but if you want to get to know part of it, you couldn't choose a better focus for your explorations.

Volissos Traditional Houses ⚐   The care with which these village houses have been restored is unique on this island, if not in the whole Northeastern Aegean. Stella Tsakiri is a trained visual artist, and the influence of her discerning eye is evident in every detail of the reconstruction. The beamed ceilings, often supported by forked tree limbs—a method of construction described in the *Odyssey*—are finely crafted and quite beautiful. Built into the stone walls are niches, fireplaces, cupboards, and couches. This spirit of inventiveness is also seen in imaginative recycling: A cattle yoke serves as a beam, while salvaged doors and shutters from the village have become mirrors or furniture. The houses and apartments are distributed throughout the village of Volissos, so your neighbors are likely to be locals rather than fellow tourists. Each apartment and house has a small kitchen, a spacious bathroom, and one or two bedrooms. The largest units (on two floors of a house) have two bedrooms, sitting rooms, kitchens, and large terraces.

Volissos, Hios. ✆ **22740/21-421** or 22740/21-413. Fax 22740/21-521. volissos@otenet.gr. 16 units. 45€–82€ ($59–$107) double. No credit cards. *In room:* No phone.

MESTA

The best-preserved medieval fortified village on Hios, Mesta is a good base for touring the mastic villages (see above) and the island's south coast.

Pipidis Traditional Houses ✿ These four homes, built more than 500 years ago, have been restored and opened by the Greek National Tourism Organization as part of its Traditional Settlements program. The houses have a medieval character, with vaulted ceilings and irregularly sculpted stone walls (covered in plaster and whitewash). One unfortunate aspect of these authentic dwellings is the dearth of natural light: If a room has any windows at all, they're small and placed high in the wall. Each house comes equipped with a kitchen, a bathroom, and enough sleeping space for two to six people. The managers are the admirable Pipidis family.

Mesta, Hios. ✆ **22710/76-029.** 4 units. 55€ ($72) double; 70€ ($91) 4 persons. No credit cards. *In room:* No phone.

WHERE TO DINE
HIOS TOWN

Hios Marine Club GREEK This good, simple taverna serves the usual Greek dishes, pasta, grilled meats, and fish. Don't be put off by the ugly yellow-and-white concrete facade. The sign in front reads RESTAURANT-FRESCA PSARIA. It's on the bay at the edge of town, just south of the port, 50m (164 ft.) beyond Hotel Chandris.

1 Nenitousi. ✆ **22710/23-184.** Main courses 4€–15€ ($5.20–$20). MC, V. Daily noon–2am.

Hotzas Taverna GREEK Hotzas is a small taverna that offers simple, well-prepared food. It's the best option in a town not known for its restaurants. The summer dining area is a luxuriant garden with lemon trees and abundant flowers. There's no menu; you choose from a few unsurprising but delicious offerings each night. Many of the dishes are meat-based but some are fish-based—and squid is always available. This place isn't easy to find: Take Kountouriotou in from the harbor, and look for the first right turn after a major road merges at an oblique angle from the right; after this it's another 50m (164 ft.) before the taverna appears on your left.

3 Yioryiou Kondili. ✆ **22710/42-787.** Main courses 4€–15€ ($5.20–$20). No credit cards. Mon–Sat 6–11pm.

LANGADA

Yiorgo Passa's Taverna ✿ GREEK/SEAFOOD Langada is a fishing village with a strip of five or six outdoor fish tavernas lining the harbor. Our favorite of these is Yiorgo Passa's Taverna, the first on the left as you approach the waterfront. Prices are low—fish is traditionally priced per kilo—portions are generous, and the ambience is warm and friendly. *Note:* There are evening dinner cruises to Langada from Hios; check with Chios Tours (see "Visitor Information," earlier) for details.

Langada. ✆ **22710/74-218.** Fish from 45€ ($59) per kilo. No credit cards. Daily 11am–2am. 20km (12 miles) north of Hios town on the Kardamila rd.

MESTA

Messaionas Taverna GREEK You'll find Despina Sirimi's taverna on the main square in Mesta. The menu features a great variety of *mezedes,* many with interesting variations on traditional dishes. The stuffed tomatoes with pine nuts and raisins are delicious, as are the fried dishes like *domatokeftedes* (tomatoes with herbs) or *tiropitakia* (cheese balls). Despina knows the village well, and can direct you to its most distinctive features, such as Paleos Taxiarchis church and its remarkable carved wooden iconostasis.

Mesta. ℂ **22710/76-050.** Main courses 4€–11€ ($5.20–$14). No credit cards. Daily 11am–midnight.

3 Lesvos (Mitilini)

348km (188 nautical miles) NE of Piraeus

Roughly triangular Lesvos—now called Mitilini in many Greek publications—is the third-largest island in Greece, with a population of nearly 120,000. At the tips of the triangle are the three principal towns: **Mitilini, Molivos,** and **Eressos.** Due to its remote location, Eressos is a good destination for a day trip, but not a recommended base for touring the island.

Mitilini and Molivos are about as different as two towns on the same island could possibly be. Mitilini, a tough cousin of Thessaloniki, is a port town low on sophistication or pretension, with little organized tourism and lots of local character. Molivos is a picture-postcard seaside village, a truly beautiful place, but in the summer it exists only for tourism.

Not to be missed are the Archaeological and Theophilos museums in Mitilini; the town of **Mandamados** and its celebrated icon (the east coast road, between Mandamados and Mitilini, is the most scenic on the island); the remarkable, mile-long beach of Eressos; and the labyrinthine streets of Molivos's castle-crowned hill.

Getting around on Lesvos is greatly complicated by the presence of two huge tear-shaped bays in the south coast, which divide the island down its center. East-west distances are far, and since bus service is infrequent, this is one island where you'll definitely need a car.

GETTING THERE   By Plane   The **airport** (ℂ **22510/61-490** or 22510/61-590) is 7km (4 miles) south of Mitilini. There's no bus to the town; a taxi will cost about 5€ ($6.50). **Olympic Airways** (ℂ **22710/22-414** or 210/966-6666; www.olympic-airways.gr) has several flights daily to Mitilini from Athens. There are connections with Thessaloniki daily; with Limnos three times weekly; and with Hios twice weekly. The **Olympic office** in Mitilini (ℂ **22510/28-660**) is at 44 Kavetsou, about 200m (656 ft.) south of Ayia Irinis park. To find it, walk 300m (984 ft.) south from the harbor; then turn right at a large park, just before the World War II monument (a statue of a woman with sword). Take the first right, and the office will be immediately on your left. **Aegean Airlines** (ℂ **210/998-2888** in Athens; www.aegeanair.com), with an office at the Mitilini airport (ℂ **22510/61-120**), also has two flights daily between Athens and Mitilini, and one or two flights daily between Thessaloniki and Mitilini.

By Boat   The principal port of Lesvos is Mitilini, from which almost all the ferries arrive and depart, although there is some ferry traffic through the west coast port of Sigri. There's one ferry daily to Mitilini from Piraeus, stopping at Hios (10–12 hr.); there are also several ferries weekly from Rafina to Sigri (9 hr.). There are daily boats in both directions between Mitilini and Hios (3 hr.), and four ferries weekly from Mitilini to Limnos (6–7 hr.). There are also two ferries weekly between Sigri and Limnos (4½ hr.). Two boats call weekly at Mitilini from Kavala (10 hr.) and Thessaloniki (10–13 hr.), stopping at Limnos on the way. There's also one ferry a week from Siros (9 hr.). Check schedules with a local travel agent, **www.gtp.gr**, **Mitilini Port Authority** (ℂ **22510/28-827**), or **Sigri Port Authority** (ℂ **22530/54-433**).

Once you get to Lesvos, double-check the boat schedule for your departure, as the harbor is extremely busy in the summer and service is often inexplicably irregular.

MITILINI & SOUTHEAST LESVOS

With an ambience more like that of a big mainland city than an island capital, Mitilini isn't to everyone's taste. Your first impression is likely to be one of noise, car exhaust, and crazy taxi drivers. Sadly, recent development has resulted in a generic beachfront; the only signs of a more auspicious past are the cathedral dome and the considerable remains of a hilltop castle. Still, once you leave the paralia, there's little or nothing in the way of amenities for tourists, which can be remarkably refreshing. In the vicinity of Ermou (the market street), Mitilini's crumbling ocher alleys contain a mix of traditional coffeehouses, artisans' studios, ouzeries, stylish jewelry shops, and stores selling antiques and clothing. Although good restaurants are notably absent in the town center, a few authentic tavernas lie on the outskirts of town.

ESSENTIALS

VISITOR INFORMATION   The Greek National Tourism Organization (EOT) has turned its functions over to the **North Aegean Islands Tourism Directorate.** Its office is at 77 Kountourioti, 81100 Mitilini (② **22510/47-958;** fax 22510/27-601). Primarily an administrative center, the office is not especially set up to provide hands-on help for tourists. It's open daily from 8am to 2:30pm, with extended hours in the high season. The **tourist police** (② **22510/22-276**) may also be helpful, but private travel agencies are your best bets for information.

GETTING AROUND   By Bus   There are two bus stations in Mitilini, one for local and the other for round-the-island routes. The **local bus station** (② **22510/ 28-725**) is near the harbor's north end, by the (closed) Folklife Museum and across from the Commercial Bank (Emporiki Trapeza). Local buses on Lesvos are frequent, running every hour from 6am to 9pm most of the year. The destinations covered are all within 12km (7½ miles) of Mitilini, and include Thermi, Moria, and Pamfilla to the north; and Varia, Ayia Marina, and Loutra to the south. The most expensive local fare is 3€ ($3.90). The posted schedule is hard to read, but ticket-sellers can decipher it. You can catch the **round-the-island KTEL buses** (② **22510/28-873**) in Mitilini at the port's south end behind Argo Hotel. There's daily service in summer to Kaloni and Molivos (four times), Mandamados (once), Plomari (four times), and Eressos and Sigri (once).

By Car   Rental prices in Mitilini tend to be high, so be sure to shop around. A good place to start is **Payless Car Rental** (automoto@otenet.gr), with offices at the airport (② **22510/61-665**) and on the port in Mitilini (② **22510/43-555**), near the local (north) bus station. Summer daily rates start at around 65€ ($85) with 100 free kilometers; each kilometer over 100 is an additional .75€ ($1). Assuming an average day's drive is 150km (94 miles), count on paying about 100€ ($130) a day.

By Taxi   Lesvos is a big island. The one-way taxi fare from Mitilini to Molivos is about 35€ ($46); from Mitilini to Eressos or Sigri, about 55€ ($72). The main taxi stand in Mitilini is on Plateia Kyprion Patrioton, a long block inland from the port's southern end; there's a smaller taxi stand at the port's north end, near the local bus station.

FAST FACTS   The **area code** for Mitilini is 22510, for Molivos (Mithimna) and Eressos 22530, and for Plomari 22520. There are **ATMs** at several banks on the port, including the Ioniki Trapeza and Agrotiki Trapeza (both south of the local bus station).

Vostani Hospital (✆ **22510/43-777**) on P. Vostani, southeast of town, will take care of emergencies. **Glaros Laundry** (✆ **22510/27-065**), opposite the tourist police near the ferry pier, is open from 9am to 2pm and 6 to 8pm; the turnaround time is usually 24 hours. The **post office** and the **telephone office (OTE)** are on Plateia Kyprion Patrioton, 1 block inland from the town hall at the south end of the port. The principal **taxi stand** is also on Plateia Kyprion Patrioton. The **tourist police** (✆ **22510/ 22-776**) are located just east of the ferry quay.

ATTRACTIONS

Archaeological Museums of Mitilini   The excellent Mitilini Archaeological Museum was augmented recently by the construction of a large new museum a short distance up the hill toward the kastro. The museums have the same hours, and the price of admission includes both locations. The new museum presents extensive Roman antiquities of Lesvos and some finds from the early Christian basilica of Ayios Andreas in Eressos. The highlight of its collection is a reconstructed Roman house from the 3rd century B.C., whose elaborate mosaic floors depict scenes from comedies of the poet Menander and from classical mythology. All the exhibits are thoughtfully presented, with plenty of explanatory notes in English. Entering the yard of the original archaeological museum, you're greeted by massive marble lions rearing menacingly on their hind legs, perhaps representing the bronze lion sculpted by Hephaestus, which is said to roam the island of Lesvos and serve as its guardian. A rear building houses more marble sculpture and inscribed tablets, while the main museum contains figurines, pottery, gold jewelry, and other finds from Thermi, the Mitilini kastro, and other ancient Lesvos sites.

7 Eftaliou, Myrina. ✆ **22510/28-032**. Admission 3€ ($3.90) adults, 1€ ($1.30) students and seniors. Tues–Sun 8:30am–3pm. A block north of the tourist police station, just inland from the ferry pier.

Kastro   Perched on a steep hill north of the city, the extensive ruins of Mitilini's castle are fun to explore and offer fine views of city and sea from the ramparts. The kastro was founded by Justinian in the 6th century A.D., and was restored and enlarged in 1737 by the Genoese. The Turks also renovated and built extensive additions to the castle during their occupation. In several places you can see fragments of marble columns embedded in the castle walls—these are blocks taken from a 7th-century-B.C. Temple of Apollo by the Genoese. Look for the underground cistern at the north end of the castle precinct: This echoing chamber is a beautiful place, with domed vaults reflected in the pool below. In summer, the castle is sometimes used as a performing-arts center.

8th Noemvriou, Mitilini. ✆ **22510/27-297**. Admission 3€ ($3.90) adults, 1€ ($1.30) students and seniors. Tues–Sun 8am–2:30pm. Just past the new Archaeological Museum, turn right on the path to the kastro.

Theophilos Museum ✮   One of the most interesting sights near Mitilini is this small museum in the former house of folk artist Hatzimichalis Theophilos (1868–1934). Most of Theophilos's works adorned the walls of tavernas and ouzeries, often painted in exchange for food. Theophilos died in poverty, and none of his work would have survived if it weren't for the efforts of art critic Theriade (see below), who commissioned the paintings on display here during the last years of the painter's life. These primitive watercolors depicting ordinary people, daily life, and local landscapes are now widely celebrated, and are also exhibited at the Museum of Folk Art in Athens. Be sure to take in the curious photographs showing the artist dressed as Alexander the Great.

Varia. ✆ **22510/41-644**. Admission 3€ ($3.90). Tues–Sun 9am–1pm and 4:30–8pm. 3km (2 miles) south of Mitilini, on airport rd. next to Theriade Museum.

Moments   Excursion to a Mountain Village

An enjoyable destination for a day trip is the rural hamlet of **Ayiassos,** 23km (14 miles) west of Mitilini. The town, built on the foothills of Mount Olymbos, consists of traditional gray stone houses (with wooden "Turkish" balconies, often covered in flowering vines), narrow cobblestone lanes, and fine small churches. Here local craftspeople still turn out their ceramic wares by hand. Excursion buses can bring you from Mitilini, or you can share a taxi (about 40€/$52 for the ride and a reasonably brief wait).

Theriade Library and Museum of Modern Art   The Theriade Library and Museum of Modern Art is in the home of Stratis Eleftheriadis, a native of Lesvos who emigrated to Paris and became a prominent art critic and publisher. (Theriade is the Gallicized version of his surname.) On display are copies of his published works, including *Minotaure* and *Verve* magazines, as well as his personal collection of works by Picasso, Matisse, Miró, Chagall, and other modern artists.

Varia. (✆ **22510/23-372.** Admission 3€ ($3.90). Tues–Sun 9am–1pm and 5–8pm. 3km (2 miles) south of Mitilini, on airport rd. next to Theophilos Museum.

A SIDE TRIP TO PERGAMUM IN TURKEY

From Mitilini, there's a direct connection to Turkey via its port of Ayvalik, a densely wooded fishing village that makes a refreshing base camp from which to tour the ancient Greek site of Pergamum. The acropolis of Pergamum is sited on a dramatic hilltop, with substantial remains of the town on the surrounding slopes. The complex dates back to at least the 4th century B.C., and there are significant remains from this period through Roman and Byzantine times. It is one of Turkey's most important archaeological sites. All-inclusive 1-day tours to Pergamum—including round-trip boat fare, bus ride to the site, and guided tour—cost about 60€ ($78); inquire at Mitilini travel agencies such as **Aeolic Cruises Travel Agency** (✆ **22510/23-266**), 47A Koutouriotou Sq., on the port in Mitilini. Ships to Turkey usually sail three times a week, more often in high season if the demand is there. No visa is required for a 1-day visit. U.S., British, Irish, Canadians, and Australians need a visa for even an overnight; it costs about 50€ ($65) but is good for 3 months in Turkey. Your visa is issued at the Customs House upon your arrival in Ayvalik.

WHERE TO STAY

Hotel Erato   On a busy street just south of the port, this hotel offers convenience, cleanliness, a friendly and helpful staff, and a noise level marginally below that in many portside hotels. Most of the small bright rooms have balconies facing the street, with a view over the traffic to Mitilini Bay. The four-story hotel was converted from a medical clinic and retains an atmosphere of institutional anonymity; on the positive side, it's very well maintained, and the high-pressure showers and fluffy towels are a bonus. *Note:* If you intend to pay by credit card, do so well in advance of your planned departure.

P. Vostani, Mitilini, 81000 Lesvos. (✆ **22510/41-160.** Fax 22510/47-656. 22 units. 70€ ($91) double. MC, V. Open year-round. *In room:* A/C, TV.

Hotel Sappho   The Sappho, one of the port's better hotels, offers simple accommodations in a renovated building. Nine rooms have balconies facing the port; the rest have no balconies and face a sunny rear courtyard. All units have wall-to-wall carpets, white walls, minimal furnishings, and tiny bathrooms with showers. A breakfast room on the second floor has an outdoor terrace with a fine port view.

Kountourioti, Mitilini, 81000 Lesvos. ℂ **22510/22-888.** Fax 22510/24-522. 29 units. 60€ ($78) double. Continental breakfast 6€ ($7.80). AE, V. *In room:* A/C, TV

Villa 1900   The Villa 1900 is a somewhat upscale pension in a fine old house on the edge of town, about 700m (2,296 ft.) south of the Mitilini port. The best rooms (nos. 3 and 7) are quite spacious, with ornate painted ceilings. However, the smaller ones (nos. 6, 8, and 9) are claustrophobic and overpriced. The remaining two units are plain but adequate, and offer reasonable value for your money. The house is buffered from street noise by a small front garden; a larger garden with abundant fruit trees begins at the back terrace and offers a pleasant shaded retreat. The amiable owners speak no English, but someone is usually on hand to translate.

24 P. Vostani, Mitilini, 81000 Lesvos. ℂ **22510/23-448.** Fax 22510/28-034. 7 units. 75€ ($98) double. No credit cards. 150m (492 ft.) south of the Olympic Airways office, opposite the stadium. *In room:* A/C, fridge, no phone.

WHERE TO DINE

Mitilini has more portside cafes than your average bustling harbor town. A cluster of chairs around the small lighthouse at the point heralds the most scenic (as well as the windiest) of the many small ouzeries that specialize in grilled octopus, squid, shrimp, and local fish. We found that the best restaurants were a short taxi ride outside the city.

Averof 1841 Grill GREEK   This taverna, located midport near the Sappho Hotel, is one of the better grills around, and one of the only restaurants in Mitilini center worth trying. Its beef dishes are particularly good. Try any of the tender souvlaki dishes or the lamb with potatoes.

Port, Mitilini. ℂ **22510/22-180.** Main courses 4€–14€ ($5.20–$18). No credit cards. Daily 7am–5pm and 7–11pm.

O Rembetis GREEK   Kato Halikas is a hilltop village on the outskirts of Mitilini, and although this simple taverna might be hard to find, it's well worth the effort. At the south end of the terrace you can sit beneath the branches of a high sycamore and enjoy a panoramic view of the port. The food isn't sophisticated or surprising, but it's very Greek, and the clientele is primarily local. There's no menu, so listen to the waiter's descriptions or take a look in the kitchen—there's usually fresh fish in addition to the taverna standards. The wind can be brisk on this hilly site, so bring a jacket if the night is cool. The best way to get here is by taxi; the fare is about 3€ ($3.90) each way.

Kato Halikas, Mitilini. ℂ **22510/27-150.** Main courses 4€–14€ ($5.20–$18). No credit cards. Daily 8pm–midnight.

Salavos GREEK   Despite its location on the busy airport road, this small taverna is one of the best in Mitilini. A garden terrace in back offers partial shelter from road noise. The seafood is fresh and delicious; try the calamari stuffed with feta, vegetables, and herbs. The restaurant is very popular with locals, who fill the place on summer nights. As you travel south from Mitilini toward the airport, it's about 3km (2 miles) from town, on the right. Taxi fare is about 3€ ($3.90) each way.

Mitilini. ℂ **22510/22-237.** Main courses 4€–14€ ($5.20–$18). No credit cards. Daily noon–1am.

MITILINI AFTER DARK

In Mitilini, there's plenty of nightlife action at both ends of the harbor. The east side tends to be younger, cheaper, and more informal—**Hott Spot** (63 Koundouriotou) being one such. The more sophisticated places are off the harbor's south end. Outdoor

Park Cinema, on the road immediately below the stadium, and **Pallas,** on Vournazo (by the post office), are both open May through September. Summer brings occasional entertainment to the kastro.

MOLIVOS & NORTHEAST LESVOS

Molivos (aka Mithimna) is at the northern tip of the island's triangle. It's a highly pictur-esque, castle-crowned village where mansions of stone and pink-pastel stucco are capped by red-tile roofs. Balconies and windowsills are decorated with geraniums and roses.

The town has long been popular with package-tour groups, especially during the summer months. Souvenir shops, car rental agencies, and travel agents outnumber local merchants, and the restaurants are geared toward tourists. Despite this, it is a beautiful place to visit and a convenient base for touring the island.

ESSENTIALS

GETTING THERE **By Bus** **KTEL buses** (✆ **22510/28-873**) connect Molivos with Mitilini four times daily in the high season. The Molivos bus stop is just past the Municipal Tourist Office on the road to Mitilini.

By Taxi The one-way taxi fare from Mitilini to Molivos is about 35€ ($46).

VISITOR INFORMATION The **Municipal Tourist Office,** 6 J. Aristarchou on the road heading down to the sea (✆ **22530/71-347**), is housed in a tiny building next to the National Bank. It's open Monday through Friday. **Tsalis Tours,** 2 J. Aristarchou (✆ **22530/71-389;** fax 22530/71-345), can book car rentals, accommo-dations, and excursions. Both the tourist office and Tsalis are open daily in summer from 8:30am to 9:30pm.

GETTING AROUND **By Car** There are numerous rental agencies in Molivos, and rates are comparable to those in Mitilini.

By Boat Boat taxis to neighboring beaches can be arranged at the port or in a travel agency (see Tsalis Tours, above).

By Bus Tickets for day excursions by bus can be bought in any of the local travel agencies. The destinations include Thermi/Ayiassos (40€/$52), Mitilini town (20€/$26), Sigri/Eressos (40€/$52), and Plomari (43€/$56); the excursions are offered once or twice each week in the summer.

FAST FACTS An ATM can be found at the **National Bank,** next to the Municipal Tourist Office on the Mitilini road. The **Internet** can be accessed at Communication and Travel (✆ **22530/71-900**) on the main road to the port. The **police** (✆ **22530/71-222**) are up from the port, on the road to the town cemetery; the **port police** (✆ **22530/71-307**) are, predictably, on the port. The **post office** (✆ **22530/71-246**) is on the path circling up to the castle—turn right (up) past the National Bank.

ATTRACTIONS

Kastro The hilltop Genoese castle is better preserved than Mitilini town, but it's much less extensive and not as interesting to explore. There is, however, a great view from the walls, worth the price of admission in itself. There's a stage in the southwest corner of the courtyard, often used for theatrical performances in the summer. To get here by car, turn uphill at the bus stop and follow signs to the castle parking lot. On foot, the castle is most easily approached from the town, a steep climb no matter which of the many labyrinthine streets you choose.

Molivos. No phone. Admission 3€ ($3.90) adults, 1€ ($1.30) students and seniors. Tues–Sun 8:30am–3pm.

Mandamados Monastery ⭐

Mandamados is a lovely village on a high inland plateau, renowned primarily for the remarkable icon of the Archangel Michael housed in the local monastery. A powerful story is associated with the creation of the icon: It is said that during a certain pirate raid, all but one of the monks were slaughtered. This one survivor, emerging from hiding to find the bloody corpses of his dead companions, responded to the horror of the moment with an extraordinary act. Gathering the blood-soaked earth, he fashioned in it the face of man, an icon in relief of the Archangel Michael. This simple icon, its lips worn away by the kisses of pilgrims, can be found at the center of the iconostasis at the back of the main chapel.

Mandamados. Free admission. Daily 6am–10pm. 24km (15 miles) east of Molivos, 36km (23 miles) northwest of Mitilini.

BEACHES

The long, narrow town beach in Molivos is rocky and crowded near the town, but becomes sandier and less populous as you continue south. The beach in **Petra,** 6km (3¾ miles) south of Molivos, is considerably more pleasant. The beach at **Tsonia,** 30km (19 miles) east of Molivos, is only accessible via a difficult rutted road, and isn't particularly attractive. The best beach on the island is 70km (44 miles) west of Molivos in **Skala Eressos** (see "An Excursion to Western Lesvos," below).

SHOPPING

Molivos is unfortunately dominated by tacky souvenir shops. To find more authentic local wares, you'll have to explore neighboring towns. **Mandamados,** known as a center for pottery, has numerous ceramics studios. **Eleni Lioliou** (✆ 22530/61-170), on the road to the monastery, sells brightly painted bowls, plates, and mugs. **Anna Fonti** (✆ 22530/61-433), on a pedestrian street in the village, produces plates with intricate designs in brilliant turquoise and blue. Also in Mandamados is the diminutive studio of icon painter **Dimitris Hatzanagnostou** (✆ 22530/61-318), who produces large-scale icons for churches and portable icons for purchase.

WHERE TO STAY

Hotel-Bungalows Delphinia ⭐

The best thing about this white-stucco and gray-stone resort is its panoramic setting above the Aegean. A path leads 200m (656 ft.) from the hotel to a fine-sand beach and a recreation complex with saltwater swimming pool, snack bar, and tennis courts (the latter illuminated for night games). The hotel rooms are simple, with small, shower-only bathrooms. The 57 bungalows are more spacious: The living room has a couch that pulls out to provide an extra bed, most bathrooms include a bathtub, and each unit has either a large terrace or a balcony. Breakfast at the hotel is served in a large dining room, while the bungalows include free room service for breakfast only. The second-floor rooms in the bungalows are the most spacious, have the best views, and cost a bit more.

Molivos, 81108 Lesvos. ✆ **22530/71-315** or 22530/71-580. Fax 22530/71-524. 125 units. 75€–95€ ($98–$124) double; 104€–126€ ($135–$164) 2-person bungalow. Rates include buffet breakfast. AE, DC, V. Parking adjacent. 1 mile from town center. **Amenities:** Restaurant, bar; pool; 3 night-lit tennis courts; basketball, volleyball, and table tennis; children's playground; tours and car rentals arranged; fax and photocopying arranged; 24-hr. room service; babysitting; laundry service; dry cleaning. *In room:* A/C, TV, minibar.

Hotel Olive Press

The most charming hotel in town is located on the water in the traditional style. The rooms are on the small side, but they're quiet and very comfortable, with terrazzo floors, handsome furnishings, and bathtubs. Some of the units have windows opening onto great sea views, with waves lapping just beneath. The nice inner courtyard has several gardens. Staff is gracious and friendly. There's neither air-conditioning nor TV in the rooms, so this is a place for those who prefer old-fashioned atmosphere.

Molivos, 81108 Lesvos. ℂ 22530/71-205 or 22530/71-646. Fax 22530/71-647. 50 units. 90€ ($117) double (includes breakfast); 130€ ($169) studio. AE, DC, V. Closed Nov–May.

Sea Horse Pension (Thalassio Alogo) A cluster of recently built Class C hotels is set below the old town, near the beach—among them is this smaller, homier pension. The friendly manager, Stergios, keeps the rooms tidy. All units come with a balcony facing the sea; four also have minimal kitchen facilities. On-site are a restaurant and an in-house travel agency.

Molivos, 81108 Lesvos. ℂ **22530/71-630** or 22530/71-320. Fax 22530/71-374. 16 units. 55€ ($72) double. Continental breakfast 7€ ($9.10). No credit cards. **Amenities:** Restaurant; tour desk. *In room:* A/C, TV, fridge, hair dryer.

WHERE TO DINE

Captain's Table ⭐ SEAFOOD/VEGETARIAN Overlooking the harbor at Molivos, this is many visitors' favorite restaurant in the area. It's run by Melinda, an Australian, and her Greek husband, Theo. Although the emphasis is now on fresh fish, the menu still offers some of Melinda's excellent trademark vegetable dishes. Try *imam bayeldi,* a dish made with eggplant, onions, tomato, and garlic. Then there's the smoked and grilled mackerel—or the fresh mussels with the house white, if that's to your taste. Live *bouzouki* music is played 3 nights a week. Needless to say, the restaurant is crowded in high season.

The Harbor, Molivos. ℂ **22530/71-241.** Main courses 4€–16€ ($5.20–$21). V. Daily 11am–1am.

Octopus SEAFOOD One of the oldest restaurants on the harbor of Molivos, the Octopus has had to serve tasty food in order to survive the tides of fashion. It specializes in grilled fish and meats but offers a selection of other dishes—peppers stuffed with spicy cheese, for instance. Not only can Yannis, the waiter, help you assemble your meal, he can advise you about the island's attractions.

The Harbor, Molivos. ℂ **22530/71-317.** Main courses 4€–16€ ($5.20–$21). No credit cards. Daily 11am–1am.

Tropicana ⭐ CAFE Stroll up into the old town to sip a cappuccino or have a dish of ice cream at this outdoor cafe, which offers soothing classical music and a relaxed ambience. The owner, Hari Procoplou, learned the secrets of ice creamery in Los Angeles.

Molivos. ℂ **22510/71-869.** Snacks/desserts 2.50€–13€ ($3.25–$17). No credit cards. Daily 8am–1am.

MOLIVOS AFTER DARK

Vangelis Bouzouki (no phone) is Molivos's top acoustic *bouzouki* club. It's located west from Molivos on the road to Efthalou, past the Sappho Tours office. After about a 10-minute walk outside of town, you'll see a sign that points to an olive grove. Follow it for another 500m (1,640 ft.) through the orchard until you reach a clearing with gnarled olive trees and a few stray sheep. When you see the circular cement dance floor, surrounded by clumps of cafe tables, you've found the club. Have some ouzo and late-night *mezedes,* and sit back to enjoy the show. Inquire at the tourist offices about summer theatrical performances in the kastro.

AN EXCURSION TO WESTERN LESVOS: ERESSOS & SKALA

Western Lesvos is hilly and barren, with many fine-sand beaches concealed among rocky promontories. Admirers of Sappho's poems (this was her birthplace) and avid beachgoers should be sure to travel the steep and winding 65km (41-mile) road between Molivos and Eressos, on the island's westernmost shore. Excursion buses (30€/$39) make this trip daily from Mitilini; inquire at **Samiotis Tours,** 43 Kountouriotou, Mitilini (ⓒ **22510/42-574).**

Eressos is an attractive small village overlooking the coastal plain. Its port, Skala Eressou, 4km (2½ miles) to the south, has become a full-blown resort popular with Greek families as well as with gay women. This isn't surprising, since the beach here is the best in Lesvos, a wide, dark sandy stretch over a mile long and lined with tamarisks. A stretch of sandy beaches and coves extends from here to Sigri, the next town to the north. Skala Eressou has a small **archaeological museum** (ⓒ **22530/53-332),** near the 5th-century basilica of Ayios Andreas, with local finds from the Archaic, Classical, and Roman periods. It's open Tuesday through Sunday from 7:30am to 3:30pm; admission is free.

4 Limnos (Lemnos)

344km (186 nautical miles) NE of Piraeus

Limnos is decidedly tame in comparison with its Northeastern Aegean neighbors. Here low hills break up the cultivated plains, circled by a rocky but gently sloping coastline. The towns are more functional than beautiful, and the beaches pleasant but not spectacular. This absence of superlatives, combined with its remote location at the edge of Asia Minor, explains the small scale of local tourism and the refreshing simplicity of life even in the principal port of Mirina.

Low on picture-postcard sights but full of small-town charm, **Mirina** is the best base for exploring the island. Several of the town's restaurants and hotels cluster around a small square at the port, in the shadow of the fine Ottoman castle on its lofty promontory. Connecting port and beach is the market street, P. Kida, where you can find preserves made from local black plums, Limnian honey (a favorite of the gods), and the famous Limnian wines. The most noted wines include Kalavaki, a dry white that was Aristotle's favorite, and the sweet Moschato. The two town **beaches**—Romeïkos Yialos and Riha Nera—are slivers of sand extending north as far as the renowned Akti Marina luxury resort. Stop in at the excellent **archaeological museum** on Romeïkos Yialos; it's a good introduction to the rest of the island's archaeological sites.

Due to its remote location, Limnos is one island you'll want to reach by plane—ferry journeys can be painfully long. Once on the island, you'll find that public bus schedules are scarce, and that a rented car or moped is the best option.

ESSENTIALS

GETTING THERE   By Plane   Olympic Airways (ⓒ **210/966-6666** in Athens; www.olympicairlines.gr) has three flights daily between Limnos and Athens; one connection daily with Thessaloniki, Lesvos, and Rhodes; and about two flights a week to and from Chios (but only via Thessaloniki or Athens). The local office (ⓒ **22540/22-214)** is on Garoufalidou, in Mirina. You can either rent a car or take a taxi (about 10€/$13) to get into town.

By Boat   The principal port of Mirina has frequent connections with Northeast Aegean destinations. Ferries depart four times weekly for the port of Kavala in Macedonia (4–5 hr.), and five times weekly for Mitilini town, Lesvos (5–6 hr.). There is twice-weekly service to and from Hios (11 hr.) and Samothrace (1½ hr.). There is also a connection three or four times weekly with Rafina, Attica (10–15 hr.) and Thessaloniki (8 hr.). We recommend avoiding the 21-hour journey from Mirina to Piraeus via Lesvos and Hios—instead, catch a ferry on the Mirina-Ayios Efstratios-Piraeus route (10 hr.), or opt to fly (1 hr.). For current ferry information, contact one of the travel agencies (see "Visitor Information" below).

VISITOR INFORMATION   The Greek National Tourism Organization (EOT) no longer maintains an office in Mirina, so visitors are dependent on private travel agencies. Fortunately there are several helpful ones. **Petrides Travel,** 116 Karatsa (© **22540/22-039;** www.petridestravel.gr), 50m (164 ft.) beyond the main square on the town's market street (P. Kida), offers car rentals, accommodations booking, luggage storage, and island excursions. **Pravlis Travel** (© **22540/22-471**), on the port square, specializes in air tickets and will also book accommodations.

GETTING AROUND   By Bus   In Mirina, the **central bus station** (© **22540/ 22-464**) is 3 blocks up from the main (taxi) square on the right. Except for Moudros and Kondias, most places on the island get service only once a day, usually in the afternoon. Bus excursion tours can be booked through Petrides Travel, and include various combinations of island villages and archaeological sites. The frequency depends upon demand; tours depart at least weekly in the summer. The cost is 10€ ($13) for the half-day tour and 16€ ($21) for the full-day tour.

By Boat   Service to the island's beaches and the grottos at Skala is offered by caïques on the north side of Mirina's harbor. You can buy tickets at most of the town's travel agencies.

By Car   Car rental prices on Limnos tend to be high compared with those of its Northeastern Aegean neighbors. We recommend **Myrina Rent a Car** (© **22540/24-476**), where a basic car costs about 60€ ($78) in peak season, with insurance.

FAST FACTS   Both **National Bank** and **Agrotiki Trapeza,** 100m (328 ft.) past the square in the direction of Romeïkos Yialos, have **ATMs.** There's a drop-off **laundry** service (© **22540/24-392**) on Garoufalidou across from the Olympic Airways office, next to the Hotel Astro; if it's closed, ask at the hotel. Continue a couple of blocks past the laundry service and turn left to find the **hospital** (© **22540/71-201**). The **post office** is on Garoufalidou, 1 block toward Romeïkos Yialos from the square and to the right, just down the street from the Olympic Airways office. **Joy Internet Cafe** is at 14 Garofallidou (© **22540/25-453**). The **taxi station** (© **22540/23-033** or 22540/ 22-348) marks what might conveniently be called a main square, midway along the market street. The **telephone office (OTE)** is on this square, as is the National Bank. The **tourist police** (© **22540/22-221**) are on the port, just down from the port police.

ATTRACTIONS

Archaeological Museum   This unassuming building, originally a Turkish Commandery during the Ottoman occupation, was thoroughly renovated and now houses one of the better archaeological museums in the Aegean islands. The artifacts are very well presented, and the descriptive plaques offer fascinating insights concerning the exhibits. If your appetite for exploration is whetted by the exhibits, bus excursions make it possible to visit three of the island's archaeological sites: Poliochni; the Ifestia (the sanctuary of Hephaestus); and the sanctuary of the Kaviri (see "Getting Around," above).

Mirina. ☎ 22540/22-990. Admission 2€ ($2.60) adults, 1€ ($1.30) students and seniors. Tues–Sun 8am–2:30pm. On Romeïkos Yialos Beach/Esplanade, next to the Castro Hotel.

Kastro   The Ottoman fortress that dominates Mirina from its craggy perch is easily accessible from the town, and the extensive ruins are a delight to explore. The climb from the port is long and exposed, so go in the early morning or wait for the relative cool of late afternoon. The foundations of the walls date to Byzantine times, and rock-carved inscriptions indicate that a temple to Artemis once occupied the site. There are numerous subterranean vaults and caves within the castle walls, so bring a flashlight. The shores of the castle's rocky promontory offer several secluded coves for bathing.

Mirina. Open site. The best access path is reached via a steeply climbing road from the port, between the port police and the police station.

EXPLORING THE ARCHAEOLOGICAL SITES

There isn't much to see at the archaeological sites on Limnos's northern and eastern shores, but they do offer a great follow-up to the fascinating exhibits of Mirina's archaeological museum. **Kavirio,** dramatically situated on a rocky coastal promontory 10km (6 miles) north of the Hephaistia, is the most spectacularly placed of the three sites; only the floor plan remains of the once-extensive temple. The ruins of **Hephaistia,** on the island's northern shore, about 40km (25 miles) from Mirina, were once an ancient city dedicated to Hephaestus, the god of metallurgy, who is said to have inhabited a volcano. Born ugly, Hephaestus was rejected by his father, Zeus, and abandoned on Limnos. On-site is a Greek theater, a Temple of Hephaestus, and the excavation site of a pre-Hellenic necropolis which provided many of the items now housed in the archaeological museum in Mirina. Of less interest is **Poliochni,** about 5km (3 miles) east of Moudros, which is still being excavated and offers little for the imagination. All three sites are open from 9:30am to 3:30pm, and admission is free. Some travel agencies include one or two of these sites as part of a **bus tour** of Limnos (see "Getting Around," above); the only alternative is to rent a car.

WHERE TO STAY

Hotel Ifestos   The Ifestos is in a quiet neighborhood of Mirina, surrounded by greenery. Built in 1991, the hotel facade imitates the wide arcaded porches of the town's older houses. The rooms are plain and clean; all have small balconies or terraces and views over the neighboring gardens. The beach is a 2-minute walk away; the port, a leisurely 15 minutes.

Riha Nera, Mirina, 81400 Limnos. ☎ 22540/24-960. Fax 22540/23-623. 41 units. 78€ ($101) double. Rates include breakfast. MC, V. 2km (1¼ miles) north of the port.

Hotel Lemnos   This hotel on the harbor is attractive, clean, comfortable, and quiet. Less than 100m (328 ft.) from the ferry pier, it's the most convenient option if you're arriving by boat. The owners, Harry Geanopoulos and Bill Stamboulis, spent many years in New Jersey and speak excellent English. They've also patterned their hotel on an American standard: a good night's sleep at a fair price. Breakfast, although not included in the room rate, is available a la carte in the hotel cafe.

Arvanitaki, Mirina, 81400 Limnos. ☎ 22540/22-153. Fax 22540/23-329. 29 units. 75€ ($98) double. No credit cards. *In room:* TV.

Kastro Beach Hotel   The Kastro is the best seafront hotel in Mirina; its neoclassical facade faces the water and the narrow strip of sand called Romeïkos Yialos. The large-scale marble reception room suggests elegance, which is, unfortunately, not continued in the rest of the hotel. The rooms are plain, with wall-to-wall carpeting and more in-room amenities than any of the neighboring hotels along the paralia. All units have balconies, although only a few actually face the sea—so it might be worth paying the bit extra for one of these.

Romeïkos Yialos, Mirina, 81400 Limnos. (℃) **22540/22-772**. www.castrohotel.gr. 76 units. 90€ ($117) double. Rates include breakfast. AE, MC, V. 1km (½ mile) north of the port. *In room:* A/C, TV, minibar.

WHERE TO DINE

Mirina is not known for its restaurants. A host of fast-food places inhabit the paralia along Romeïkos Yialos Beach, but the most attractive options are on the market street or at the port. Fish is about the island's only specialty, so take advantage of it.

Taverna Avra GREEK   Sheltered from the bustle of the port by a luxuriant grape arbor, the Avra is a good, basic taverna with fair prices. There isn't a menu, so choose from the dishes displayed on the steam table. There's nothing surprising about the offerings, except perhaps the scarcity of fish in a taverna meters from the sea.

Mirina. (℃) **22540/22-523**. Main courses 4€–11€ ($5.20–$14). No credit cards. Daily 11:30am–12:30am. Next to the port authority, near the pier.

Taverna O Platanos GREEK   O Platanos is a good, reliable taverna. The "platanos" in question is a handsome mammoth of a plane tree arching above this small square on Mirina's market street, offering abundant shade in the afternoon. The limited menu changes daily; and the standard taverna fare is complemented by a variety of vegetables.

Mirina. (℃) **22540/22-070**. Main courses 4€–13€ ($5.20–$17). No credit cards. Daily 11am–11pm. On the market street, 100m (328 ft.) from the central sq. toward Romeïkos Yialos.

11

The Sporades

by John S. Bowman

With their fragrant pine trees and excellent golden sand beaches, you might think that the Sporades (Scattered) islands had always been tourist magnets. But because these islands lack major archaeological remains and historical associations, visitors traditionally headed elsewhere in Greece.

These days, however, the Sporades are no longer the natural retreats they once were. **Skiathos** is among the more expensive islands in Greece and becomes horrendously crowded in high season—although in spring and fall it can be lovely and relaxing. Even in summer, it's worth a visit by those interested in a beach vacation, good food, and active nightlife. **Skopelos** is nearly as expensive as Skiathos in the high season but isn't

quite as sophisticated. Its beaches are fewer and less impressive, but Skopelos town is among the more attractive ports in Greece, and the island offers some pleasant excursions. These two most popular islands also have fine restaurants, fancy hotels, and an international (heavily British) following.

More remote **Skyros** seems hardly a part of the group, especially as its landscape and architecture are more Cycladic. But it has a few excellent beaches, as well as a colorful local culture, and it remains a good destination for those who want to get away from the crowds. Although space limits do not allow us to describe the fourth of these islands, Alonissos might also be attractive to those seeking a less popular, more natural island.

STRATEGIES FOR SEEING THE ISLANDS

If you have only 1 to 3 days, plan on seeing just one of the Sporades. If you have a bit more time, you will be able to get a ship directly (from various ports, identified below for each island) to any of them—and a plane in the case of Skiathos and Skyros; if time is a factor, we strongly advise flying to Skiathos or Skyros. If you have more time, you can continue around the islands via hydrofoils (known as Flying Dolphins) or ferryboats. (*Note:* The frequency of all connections is cut back considerably Sept–May.)

1 Skiathos

108km (58 nautical miles) from Ayios Konstandinos, which is 166km (103 miles) from Athens

Skiathos remained isolated and agrarian until the early 1970s. Today it's one of Greece's most cosmopolitan islands, a rapid change that has left a few disturbing ripples in its wake. Although the island's inhabitants are eager to please, in high season they are often overextended and rely on imported help. Many of these workers come from Athens and don't care much about providing local flavor. Worse, the sheer numbers of foreigners means that some show little concern for the island's indigenous character. This is a

> **Tips Museum Hours Update**
>
> If you visit Greece during the summer, check to see when sites and museums are open. According to the tourist office, they should be open from 8am to 7:30pm, but some may close earlier in the day or even be closed one day a week.

"package tour" island, and during high season, Skiathos town, also known as Hora, can feel like a shopping mall.

Yet Skiathos town does have its attractions, and at its best seems fairly sophisticated, with the handsome Bourtzi fortress on its harbor, elegant shops, excellent restaurants, and a flashy nightlife. For an even more exotic experience, take one of the horse-drawn carriages around town.

The rest of the island retains much of its natural allure. For most visitors, in fact, the main attractions are the purity of the water and the lovely fine-sand beaches. The island boasts more than 60 beaches, the most famous of which, **Koukounaries,** is considered one of the very best in Greece. If you relish sun, sand, and sea, and don't mind crowds, you'll love it here.

If possible, avoid Skiathos from July 10 to September 10, when the tourist crush is at its worst and the island's population of under 5,000 swells to over 50,000. If you must visit during high season, reserve a room well ahead of time and be prepared for the crush.

ESSENTIALS

GETTING THERE   By Plane   Olympic Airways has service daily (twice daily in Apr and May, five times daily June–Sept) from Athens; contact the Athens office (② 210/966-6666) for information and reservations. At this time, Olympic does not maintain an office in Skiathos town, but can be reached at the nearby **airport** (② 24270/22-049). Public bus service to and from the airport is so infrequent that everyone takes a taxi; expect to pay about 4€ ($5.20) depending on your destination.

By Boat   Skiathos can be reached by either ferryboat (3 hr.) or hydrofoil (1½ hr.) from Volos or Ayios Konstandinos. (Ayios Konstandinos is a 3-hr. bus ride from Athens.) From Kimi on Evvia, there is also hydrofoil service (50 min.) and ferryboat service (4 hr.). In high season, there are frequent hydrofoils daily from Volos and from Ayios Konstandinos, as well as service from Thessaloniki (3 hr.). Hydrofoils also link Skiathos to Skopelos (30–45 min.), Alonissos (60–75 min.), and Skyros (2⅓ hr.).

In Athens, **Alkyon Travel,** 97 Akademias, near Kanigos Square (② 210/383-2545; fax 210/383-3948), can arrange bus transportation from Athens to Ayios Konstandinos as well as hydrofoil or ferry tickets. Alkyon will not accept phone reservations— you must appear in person. The 3-hour bus ride costs about 16€ ($21) one-way.

For hydrofoil schedules and information, contact the **Hellas Flying Dolphins** in Athens (② 210/419-9100; www.dolphins.gr). For ferryboat information, contact the **G.A. Ferries** line in Piraeus (② 210/458-2640) or at their Athens office, 32 Leaforos Amalias (② 210/321-0061; www.gaferries.com). Ferry tickets can be purchased at travel agencies in Athens or on the islands. During high season, we recommend that you purchase your boat tickets in advance through the boat lines. While you may purchase tickets at Alkyon in person, they will not reserve ferryboat or hydrofoil tickets for you in advance, and these often sell out.

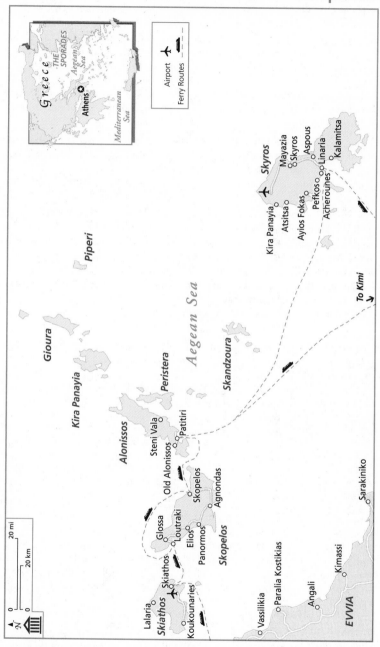

Airport
Ferry Routes

The Sporades

Greece

Athens

Aegean Sea

Mediterranean Sea

THE SPORADES

Skyros
Mayazia
Skyros
Aspous
Linaria
Kalamitsa
Pefkos
Acherounes
Ayios Fokas
Atsitsa
Kira Panayia

To Kimi

Piperi

Gioura

Kira Panayia

Peristera

Skandzoura

Aegean Sea

Alonissos
Steni Vala
Old Alonissos
Pattitiri

Skopelos
Agnondas
Skopelos
Loutraki
Glossa
Elios
Panormos

Sarakiniko

Paralia Kostikias
Kimassi
Angali
Vassilikia

EVVIA

Skiathos
Lalaria
Koukounaries
Skiathos

20 mi
20 km

N

VISITOR INFORMATION   The town maintains an **information booth** at the western corner of the harbor; in summer, at least, it's open daily from about 9am to 8pm. Meanwhile, private travel agencies abound and can help with most of your requests. We highly recommend **Mare Nostrum Holidays,** 21 Papadiamandis (© **24270/21-463;** marenostrum@n-skiathos.gr). It books villas, hotels, and rooms; sells tickets to many around-the-island, hydrofoil, and beach caïque (skiff) trips; books Olympic Airways flights; exchanges currency; and changes traveler's checks without commission. The staff speak excellent English, are exceedingly well informed, and have lots of tips on everything from beaches to restaurants. The office is open daily from 8am to 10pm.

GETTING AROUND   By Bus   Skiathos has public bus service along the south coast of the island from the bus station on the harbor to Koukounaries (2€/$2.60), with stops at the beaches in between. A conductor will ask for your destination and assess the fare after the bus starts moving. Buses run at least six times daily April through November; every hour from 9am to 9pm May through October; every half-hour from 8:30am to 10pm June through September; and every 20 minutes from 8:30am to 2:30pm and 3:30pm to midnight July through August.

By Car & Moped   Reliable car and moped agencies, all on the paralia (shore road), include **Avis** (© **24270/21-458;** avisvolos@otenet.gr), run by the friendly Yannis Theofanidis; **Aivalioti's Rent-A-Car** (© **24270/21-246**); and **Creator** (© **24270/ 22-385**). In high season, expect to pay 55€ to 85€ ($72–$111) per day for a small car. Mopeds start at about 20€ ($26) per day.

By Boat   The north coast beaches, adjacent islands, and historic kastro are most easily reached by caïque; these smaller vessels, which post their beach and island tour schedules on signs, sail frequently from the fishing harbor west of the Bourtzi fortress. An around-the-island tour that includes stops at Lalaria Beach and the kastro will cost about 20€ ($26).

The Flying Dolphins agent, **Skiathos Holidays,** on the paralia, is open from 7am to 9:30pm; in high season there are as many as eight high-speed hydrofoils daily to Skopelos and Alonissos. (We feel the extra cost for the hydrofoils is worth it for traveling among the Sporades islands.) There are also daily excursions to Skyros in high season. Call © **24270/22-018** for up-to-date schedules. Note that even if you have a ticket, you must appear at the agent's ticket office at least 30 minutes before the scheduled sailing to get your ticket confirmed and seat assigned. **Vasilis Nikolaou** (© **24270/22-209**), the travel agent at the corner of the paralia and Papadiamandis, sells tickets for the ferryboats to the other islands.

FAST FACTS   The official **American Express** agent is Mare Nostrum Holidays, 21 Papadiamandis (© **24270/21-463;** marenostrum@n-skiathos.gr); open daily from 8am to 10pm. There are many banks in town, such as the **National Bank of Greece,** Papadiamandis, open Monday through Friday from 8am to 2pm and 7 to 9pm, and Sunday from 9am to noon. The **hospital** (© **24270/22-040**) is on the coast road at the far-west edge of town. For **Internet access,** try Internet Zone Café, 28 Evangelistrias (zonecafe@hotmail.com).

A self-service **laundry** is at 14 Georgios Panora (© **24270/22-341**), 85m (279 ft.) up Papadiamandis, opposite the National Bank; or you can drop off a load at the **Snow White Laundry** (© **24270/24-256**) one street up from the paralia, behind the Credit Bank; both are open daily from about 8am to 2pm and 5 to 11pm. The **police station** (© **24270/21-111**) is about 250m (820 ft.) from the harbor on Papadiamandis, on the left. The **tourist police** booth is about 15m (49 ft.) farther along on the right. The **post office** (✆ **24270/22-011**) is on Papadiamandis, away from the harbor about 160m (525 ft.) and on the right; it's open Monday through Friday from 7:30am to 2pm. The **telephone office (OTE;** ✆ **24270/22-135)** is on Papadiamandis, on the right, some 30m (98 ft.) beyond the post office. It's open Monday through Friday from 7:30am to 10pm, Saturday and Sunday from 9am to 2pm and 5 to 10pm.

WHAT TO SEE & DO

Skiathos is a relatively modern town, built in 1930 on two low-lying hills, then reconstructed after heavy German bombardment during World War II. The handsome **Bourtzi fortress** (originally from the 13th c., but greatly rebuilt across the centuries) jutting into the middle of the harbor is on an islet connected by a broad causeway. Ferries and hydrofoils stop at the port on the right (east) of the fortress, while fishing boats and excursion caïques dock on the left (west). Whitewashed villas with red-tile roofs line both sides of the harbor. The small church of **Ayios Nikolaos** dominates the hill on the east side as does the larger church of **Trion Ierarchon (Three Archbishops)** on the west side.

The main street leading away from the harbor and up through town is named **Papadiamandis,** after the island's best-known son (see description of the Papadiamandis House, below). Here you'll find numerous restaurants, cafes, and stores, plus services such as Mare Nostrum Holidays, the post office, the telephone office, and the tourist police.

On the west flank of the harbor (the left side as you disembark from the ferry) are numerous outdoor cafes and restaurants, excursion caïques (for the north coast beaches, adjacent islands, and around-the-island tours) and, at the far corner, the stepped ramp (above the Oasis Café) leading up to the town's next level. Mounting these broad steps will lead you to **Plateia Trion Ierarchon,** a stone-paved square around the town's most important church. The eastern flank, technically the New Paralia, is home to many tourist services as well as a few recommended hotels and many restaurants. At the far end, the harborfront road branches right along the yacht harbor, an important nightlife area in summer, and left toward the airport and points of interest inland.

The Papadiamandis House   Alexandros Papadiamandis (1851–1911) was born on Skiathos, and after his adult career as a journalist in Athens, he returned in 1908 and died in this very house. His nearly 200 short stories and novellas, mostly about Greek island life, assured him a major reputation in Greece, but his rather idiosyncratic style and vernacular language make his work difficult to translate into foreign languages. His house is less a museum than a shrine containing personal possessions and tools of his writing trade. (A statue of Papadiamandis stands in front of the Bourtzi fortress on the promontory at the corner of the harbor.)

An alley to right of Papadiamandis (main street), 50m (164 ft.) up from harbor. ✆ **24270/23-843**. Admission 2€ ($2.60). Tues–Sun 9:30am–1pm and 5–8pm.

BEACHES

Skiathos is famous for its beaches, and we'll cover the most important ones briefly, proceeding clockwise from the port. The most popular beaches are west of town along 12km (8 miles) of coastal highway. At most of them, you can rent an umbrella and two chairs for about 15€ ($20) per day.

The first, **Megali Ammos,** is the sandy strip below the popular package-tour community of Ftelia. It's so close to town and so packed with the groups it probably won't appeal to most. **Vassilias** and **Achladias** are also crowded and developed; **Tzanerias** and **Nostos** are slight improvements. Farther out on the Kalamaki peninsula, south of the highway, **Kanapitsa** is good for fans of watersports; **Kanapitsa Water-Sport Center** (© **24270/21-298**) has water and jet skis, windsurfing, air chairs, sailing, and speedboat hire. Scuba divers will want to stop at **Dolphin Diving Center** (© **24270/21-599**) at the big Nostos Hotel.

Across the peninsula, **Vromolimnos (Dirty Lake)** is fairly attractive and relatively uncrowded, perhaps because of its unsavory name and the cloudy (but not polluted) water that inspires it. The beach offers water-skiing and windsurfing. **Koulos** and **Ayia Paraskevi** are fairly well regarded. **Platanias,** the next major beach, isn't crowded, perhaps because the big resort hotels here have their own pools and sun decks. Past the next headland, **Troulos** is one of the prettiest beaches, due to its relative isolation, crescent shape, and the islets that guard the small bay. Nearby is **Victoria Leisure Center** (© **24270/49-467**), which has rooms to rent, a pool, shops, and two tennis courts.

The last bus stop is at much ballyhooed **Koukounaries** ⚘, 16km (10 miles) from Skiathos town. The bus chugs uphill past the Pallas Hotel luxury resort, then descends and winds alongside the inland waterway, Lake Strofilias, stopping at the edge of a fragrant pine forest. *Koukounaries* means "pine cones" in Greek, and behind this grove of trees is a half-mile-long stretch of fine gold sand in a half-moon-shaped cove. Tucked into the evergreen fold are some changing rooms, a small snack bar, and the concessionaires for beach chairs, umbrellas, and windsurfers. The beach can be extremely crowded but with an easy mix of families, singles, and topless sunbathers. (There are several hotels near the beach, but because of the intense mosquito activity and ticky-tacky construction, we prefer to stay back in town or along the coast road.)

Ayia Eleni, a short but scenic walk from the Koukounaries bus stop (the end of the line) west across the island's tip, is a broad cove popular for windsurfing, as the wind is a bit rougher than at the south coast beaches but not nearly as gusty as at the north. Across the peninsula, at the far right end of the beach, 15 to 20 minutes of fairly steep grade from the Koukounaries bus stop, is **Banana Beach** (sometimes called Krassa). It's slightly less crowded than Koukounaries, but with the same sand and pine trees. There's a snack bar or two, plus chairs, umbrellas, windsurfers, and jet skis for rent. One stretch of Banana Beach is the island's most fashionable nude beach.

Limonki Xerxes, also called Mandraki, north across the island's tip, a 20-minute walk up the path opposite the Lake Strofilias bus stop, is the cove where Xerxes brought in 10 *triremes* (galleys) to conquer the Hellenic fleet moored at Skiathos during the Persian Wars. It's a pristine and relatively secluded beach for those who crave a quiet spot. **Elia,** east across the little peninsula, is also quite nice. Both beaches have small refreshment kiosks.

Continuing along the northeast coast from Mandraki, you arrive at **Megalos Aselinos,** a windy beach where free camping has taken root. It is linked to the southern coastal highway via the road that leads to the Kounistria monastery (see below). You must continue north when the main road forks off to the right toward the monastery. There's also an official campsite and a fairly good taverna. **Mikros Aselinos,** farther east, is smaller and quieter, and you can reach it via a dirt road that leads off to the left just before the monastery.

Skiathos's north coast is much more rugged and scenic, with steep cliffs, pine forests, rocky hills, and caves. Most of these beaches are accessible only by boat, and of these, one is well worth the effort: **Lalaria** ⚘, on the island's northern tip, is one of Greece's most picturesque beaches. One of its unique qualities is the **Tripia Petra,** perforated rock cliffs that jut into the sea on both sides of the cove. These have been worn through by the wind and the waves to form perfect archways. You can lie on the gleaming white pebbles and admire the neon-blue Aegean and cloudless sky through their rounded openings. The water at Lalaria is an especially vivid shade of aquamarine because of the highly reflective white pebbles and marble and limestone slabs, which coat the sea bottom. The swimming here is excellent, but the undertow can be quite strong; inexperienced swimmers should not venture very far. There are several naturally carved caves in the cliff wall that lines the beach, providing privacy or shade for those who have had too much sun. Lalaria is reached by caïque excursions from the port; the fare is about 20€ ($26) for an around-the-island trip, which usually includes a stop for lunch (not included in the fare) at one of the other beaches along the northwest coast.

Three of the island's most spectacular grottoes—**Skotini, Glazia,** and **Halkini**—are just east of Lalaria. Spilia Skotini is particularly impressive, a fantastic 6m-high (20-ft.) sea cave reached through a narrow crevice in the cliff wall just wide enough for caïques to squeeze through. Seagulls drift above you in the cave's cool darkness, while below, fish swim in the 9m (30-ft.) subsurface area. Erosion has created spectacular scenery and many sandy coves along the north and east coasts, though none are as beautiful or well sheltered from the *meltemi* (high winds) as Lalaria beach.

THE KASTRO & THE MONASTERIES

When you want a change from the beach, we recommend an excursion to the **kastro,** the old fortress capital on the northernmost point of the island, east of Lalaria beach. The kastro was built in a remote and spectacular site in the 16th century, when the island was overrun by the Turks. It was abandoned shortly after the War of Independence, when such fortifications were no longer necessary. Once joined to firm ground by a drawbridge, it can now be reached by cement stairs. The remains of the more than 300 houses and 22 churches have mostly fallen to the sea, but three of the churches, porcelain plates imbedded in their worn stucco facades, still stand, and the original frescoes of one are still visible. From this citadel prospect there are excellent views to the **Kastronisia** islet below and the sparkling Aegean. Kastro can be reached by excursion caïque, by mule or donkey tour (available through most travel agencies), or by car via the road that leads northeast out of town, passing the turnoff to the Moni Evangelistrias (see below), and continuing on to the end near the church of Panagia Kardasi. From here it is a mildly demanding 2km (1-mile) walk.

Moni Evangelistrias ⚓ is the more rewarding of the two monasteries that draw many visitors. Public buses travel here sporadically, but with your own vehicle it can be easily visited in not much more than an hour from Skiathos town. (Driving will also allow you to stop and admire the views.) To get here, take the road out of the northeast end and pass by the turnoff to the airport. After less than a kilometer, take the sharp right turnoff (signed) and climb about 3km (2 miles) to the monastery. Dating from the late 18th century, it has been completely (but authentically) restored; its architecture, icons, and woodcarvings are fascinating.

The other monastery, **Panagia Kounistria,** is approached from the coastal highway along the beaches (described above); just before Troulos Beach, take the right branch of the road (signed ASELINOS) and climb about 4km (2½ miles) to the monastery. The pretty 17th-century structure contains some fine icons (although its most important icon is now displayed in the Tris Ierarches Church in Skiathos town). Nothing spectacular, but a satisfying excursion. Horseback enthusiasts should note that **Pinewood Horse Riding Club** is also located on the road to this monastery.

SHOPPING

Skiathos town has no shortage of shops, many offering standard wares but some with distinctive items. The highlight for Greek crafts and folk art is **Archipelago** (© 24270/ 22-163). Adjacent to the Papadiamandis House, it offers a world-class assemblage of exquisite objects of art and folklore, both old and new, including textiles, jewelry, and sculpture. **Galerie Varsakis** (© 24270/22-255), on Trion Ierarchon Square above the fishing port, also has a virtually museum-quality collection of folk antiques, embroidered bags and linens, rugs from around the world, and other collectibles. Less stylish but full of curiosities is **Gallery Seraina** (© 24270/22-0390), at the first junction of Papadiamandis (opposite the alleyway to the Papadiamandis House); it has a goodly selection of ceramic plates, jewelry, some textiles, and unusual glass lampshades.

WHERE TO STAY

Between July 1 and September 15, it can be very difficult to find accommodations. Try calling ahead from Athens to book a room or, better still, book your accommodations before you leave home. Note that most of the "luxury" hotels were thrown up quickly some years ago, and some have since been managed and maintained poorly—so if you plan an extended stay at a beach resort, we recommend you first check into one of the hotels in town and then look over the possibilities before you commit to an extended rental.

If you crave the restaurant/shopping/nightlife scene, or you've arrived without reservations at one of the resort communities, try setting up base in **Skiathos town.** From here, you can take public buses to the beaches on the south coast or go on caïque excursions to the spectacular north coast or other islands.

Families often prefer to stay in two- to four-bedroom villas outside of town or at hotels overlooking a beach, with only an occasional foray into town.

One of the most pleasant parts of Skiathos town is the quiet neighborhood on the hill above the bay at the western end of the port. Numerous **private rooms** to let can be found on and above the winding stairs/street. Take a walk and look for the signs, or ask a passerby or neighborhood merchant. All over the hillside above the eastern harbor are several unlicensed "hotels," basically rooms to rent. You'll be surprised at which buildings turn out to be lodgings.

By the way, the in-town hotels (Alkyon excepted) cannot provide adjacent parking, but there are possibilities at the harbor's far eastern edge of the harbor.

IN & AROUND SKIATHOS TOWN

In addition to the following options, consider moderately priced **Hotel Athos,** on the "ring road" that skirts Skiathos town (©/fax **24270/22-4777**), which offers ready access to town without the bustle; and **Hotel Meltemi,** on the paralia (© **24270/ 22-493**), a comfortable, modern place on the east side of the harbor (but avoid the front units, which can be noisy). Another choice is 30-unit **Hotel Bourtzi,** 8 Moraitou (© **24270/21-304;** fax 24270/23-243), where doubles go for 150€ ($195). Ask for a unit that faces the back garden.

Hotel Alkyon ✪   This is probably the best place for those who want it all—to be near the harbor of Skiathos town, to enjoy quiet and seclusion, and to return to a hotel with some creature comforts. It's not glitzy or luxurious, but neat and subdued; its rooms are of medium size (and offer taped music), and bathrooms are modern. On-site is a small swimming pool with an adjacent bar. Best of all, the Alkyon is a great place for those who look forward to a shady retreat after time in the sun or exploration of the town.

Far eastern end of paralia, 37002 Skiathos. ☏ **24270/22-981**. Fax 24270/21-643. 89 units. 50€–105€ ($65–$137) double. Rates include buffet breakfast. AE, MC, V. Parking in adjacent area. *In room:* A/C, minibar.

Hotel Australia

If you've come to Skiathos expecting some style, this plain, clean, quiet hotel is not for you. Run by a couple who lived in Australia and speak English quite well, the rooms are sparsely furnished but comfortable, with balconies; bathrooms are small but functional. Guests can share a fridge in the hallway. Definitely for budget travelers—no phones in the room, for example.

Parados Evangelistrias, 37002 Skiathos. ☏ **24270/22-488**. 18 units. 50€ ($65) double; 70€ ($91) studio with kitchen. No credit cards. Turn right off Papadiamandis at the post office, then take the 1st left. *In room:* No phone.

Hotel Morfo

Looking for a slightly "atmospheric" offbeat hotel? Turn right off the main street opposite the National Bank, then left at the plane tree (there's a sign). You'll find this attractive hotel on your left on a quiet back street in the center of town. You enter through a small garden into a festively decorated lobby. The rooms are comfortable and tastefully decorated.

23 Anainiou, 37002 Skiathos. ☏ **24270/21-737**. Fax 24270/23-222. 17 units. 85€ ($111) double. No credit cards. *In room:* A/C, fridge.

Hotel Orsa 🎖

One of the most charming small hotels in town is on the western promontory beyond the fishing harbor. To get here, walk down the port west all the way past the fish stalls, proceed up two flights of steps, and watch for a recessed courtyard on the left, with handsome wrought-iron details. Rooms are standard in size but tastefully decorated; most have windows or balconies overlooking the harbor and the islands beyond. A lovely garden terrace is a perfect place for a tranquil breakfast. For booking, contact **Heliotropio Travel** on the harbor's east end (☏ **24270/22-430;** fax 24270/21-952; helio@skiathos.gr).

Plakes, 37002 Skiathos. ☏ **24270/22-430**. Fax 24270/21-952. helio@n-skiathos.gr. 17 units. 105€ ($137) double. Rates include breakfast. No credit cards.

ON THE BEACH

Atrium Hotel

This is Skiathos's class act when it comes to hotels. Its location (on a pine-clad slope overlooking the sea) plus amenities make the Atrium Hotel a most pleasant place to vacation. A sandy beach is some 100m (328 ft.) below and a beautiful pool sits on a plaza high above the Aegean. The rooms have balconies or terraces that offer views over the sea. The hotel has a popular bar and restaurant; if you like, you can enjoy your meal outdoors on the veranda. We have always found the desk personnel and staff most courteous and helpful. Be aware that both the staff and the guests here observe a certain level of style in dress and conduct.

Platanias (some 8km/5 miles along the coast road southeast of Skiathos town), 37002 Skiathos. ☏ **24270/49-345**. Fax 24270/49-444. www.atriumhotel.gr. 75 units. 150€ ($195) double; 195€ ($254) for family of 4. Rates include buffet breakfast. MC, V. Parking on grounds. **Amenities:** Restaurant; bar; fitness room; watersports gear; car rentals and tours arranged; gift shop; billiards; Ping-Pong. *In room:* A/C, TV, fridge, hair dryer.

Troulos Bay Hotel *(Value)*

Though it's not exactly luxurious, this is our first choice among the beach hotels. It's set on handsomely landscaped grounds on one of the south coast's prettiest little beaches. Like most of Skiathos's hotels, it's used mostly by groups, but individual rooms are often available. The restaurant serves good food at reasonable prices, and the staff is refreshingly attentive and truly helpful. The bedrooms are large, attractive, and comfortably furnished; most have a balcony overlooking the beach and the lovely wooded islets beyond it.

Troulos (9km/6 miles along the coast road southeast of Skiathos, down from the Alpha Supermarket), 37002 Skiathos. ℂ **24270/49-390.** Fax 24270/49-218. troulosbay@skt.forthnet.gr. 43 units. 120€ ($156) double. Rates include breakfast. MC, V. Parking on grounds.

WHERE TO DINE

As in most of Greece's overdeveloped tourist resorts, cafes, fast-food stands, and over-priced restaurants abound, but there are also plenty of good—even excellent—eateries in Skiathos town. Some of the best-regarded restaurants are above the west end of the harbor, around Trion Ierarchon church.

EXPENSIVE

Asprolithos ⭐ GREEK/INTERNATIONAL   An elegant ambience, friendly and attentive service, and superb meals of light, updated taverna fare make this one of our favorite places to dine on Skiathos. You can get a classic moussaka here if you want to play it safe, or try specialties like artichokes and prawns smothered in cheese. The excellent snapper baked in wine with wild greens is served with thick french fries that have obviously never seen a freezer. A handsome stone fireplace dominates the main dining room. You can sit at outside tables and catch the breeze.

Mavroyiali and Korai (up Papadiamandis a block past the high school, then turn right). ℂ **24270/21-016.** Reservations recommended. Main courses 6€–20€ ($7.80–$26). MC, V. Daily 6pm–midnight. Closed late Oct to mid-Mar.

The Windmill Restaurant ⭐⭐ INTERNATIONAL   The town's most special dining experience is at an old windmill visible from the paralia. (You can approach it in several ways, but the signed route begins on the street between the back of the Akti and San Remo hotels at the eastern end of the harbor.) It is quite a climb, but well worth it. You couldn't ask for a more romantic setting than on one of the terraces, where you can enjoy the sunset with your meal. The Scottish couple that took over recently have upgraded the premises, but kept the same imaginative cuisine. Many of the main courses are distinctive, even exotic—roast duck breast, Thai fish cakes, vegetarian specialties. The desserts, too, are unusual, and there are nearly two dozen wines to choose from, including the best from Greece. A three-course meal with house wine will cost a couple some 50€ ($65), but the money is well worth it.

Located on peak east of Ayios Nikolaos church. ℂ **24270/24-550.** www.skiathosinfo.com. Reservations strongly recommended. Main courses 8€–24€ ($10–$31). MC, V. Daily 7–11pm.

MODERATE

Carnayio Taverna TAVERNA/SEAFOOD   One of the better waterfront tavernas is next to Hotel Alkyon. Favorites over the years have been the fish soup, lamb *you-vetsi,* and grilled fish. The garden setting is still special. If you're here late, you might be lucky enough to see a real round of dancing waiters and diners.

Paralia. ℂ **24270/22-868.** Main courses 4€–14€ ($5.20–$18). AE, V. Daily 8pm–1am.

Taverna Limanakia TAVERNA/SEAFOOD   In the style of its next-door neighbor Carnayio, the Limanakia serves some of the best taverna and seafood dishes on the waterfront. We vacillate about which of the two we prefer, but we've always come away feeling satisfied after a meal at this reliable eatery.

Paralia (at far eastern end, past Hotel Alkyon). ℂ **24270/22-835.** Main courses 5€–15€ ($6.50–$20). MC. Daily 6pm–midnight.

Taverna Mesoyia TAVERNA   You'll have to exert yourself a bit to find some of the best authentic traditional food in town. This little taverna is in the midst of the town's most labyrinthine neighborhood, above the western end of the harbor, but there are signs once you approach it. Try an appetizer such as the fried zucchini balls, enjoy the evening specials, or go for fresh fish in season. (As all Greek restaurants are supposed to, this one reveals when something is frozen—as some fish must be at certain times of the year, when they're illegal to catch.) You'll feel as though you're at an old-fashioned neighborhood bistro, not a large tourist attraction.

Grigoriou (follow the signs behind Trion Ierarchon, high above western end of the harbor). ℭ **24270/21-440.** Main courses 6€–13€ ($7.80–$17). No credit cards. Daily 7pm–midnight.

INEXPENSIVE

Kabourelia Ouzeri GREEK€Although it bills itself as an ouzeri—for drinks and snacks—this is really your standard taverna, and one of the most authentic eateries in town. You can have the ouzo and octopus (which you can see drying on the front line!) combo for 5.50€ ($7.15); or make a meal of the rich supply of cheese pies, fried feta, olives, and other piquant *mezedes.*

Paralia (on harbor's western stretch). ℭ **24270/21-112.** Main courses 3€–12€ ($3.90–$16). AE, MC, V. Daily 10am–1am.

SKIATHOS AFTER DARK

The **Aegean Festival** presents nightly performances of ancient Greek tragedies and comedies, traditional music and dance, modern dance and theater, and visiting international troupes. Festival events take place from late June to early October in the outdoor theater at the **Bourtzi Cultural Center,** on the promontory on the harbor. (The center itself, open daily from 10am to 2pm and 5:30 to 10pm, hosts art exhibits in its interior.) Performances begin at 9:30pm and usually cost 15€ ($20); call ℭ **24270/23-717** for information.

Skiathos town has a lively nightlife scene, more concentrated on each end of the port, but many prefer to pass the evening with a **volta** (stroll) along the harbor or around and above the Plateia Trion Ierarchon.

The main concentration of **nightclubs** is in the warren of streets west of Papadiamandis (left as you come up from the harbor). On the street opposite the post office is the **Blue Chips Club.** Farther along Papadiamandis, another turn to the left leads to **Borzoi,** which you may want to check out several times during the evening, as it generally gets livelier toward midnight. Continue past it to find **Banana Bar,** for "surprising dance music," on the right; then **Admiral Benbow Club,** which offers something a bit quieter. Across from Admiral Benbow Club is flashy **Spartacus.** At the next intersection south you'll find **Kirki,** with jazz and blues.

Back across Papadiamandis, just before the post office, along Parados Evangelistrias you can find **Adagio,** a gay establishment that plays classical music and Greek ballads at

---

⸜Moments⸝ A Local Favorite

We think the best-kept secret of Skiathos town is the **little outdoor cafe** at the tip of the promontory with the Bourtzi fortress, a 3-minute stroll from the harbor. Removed from the glitter of the town, you can sit and enjoy a (cheap) drink in the cool of the evening and watch the ships come and go—this is the Aegean lifestyle at its best.

volumes low enough for conversation. Wander back down the main street to find **Kentavros Bar,** on the left beyond the Papadiamandis House, which plays classic rock and jazz.

On the far west end of the harbor, if you want sports with your drinks, try **Oasis Cafe;** if there's a game of any sort going on, it'll be on the tube. Meanwhile, at the far eastern end of the harbor are a few clubs popular with the younger set—among them, **Remezzo** and **Rock 'n' Roll Bar.**

Movie fans might enjoy the open-air showings at **Attikon** (on Papadiamandis, opposite Mare Nostum Holidays), or at **Cinema Paradiso** (up along the "ring road"). Both have two shows nightly, the first around 8:30 pm; tickets are 5€ ($6.50).

2 Skopelos

121km (65 nautical miles) from Ayios Konstandinos, which is 166km (103 miles) from Athens

It was inevitable that handsomely rugged Skopelos would also be developed, but it has happened a bit more wisely and at a slower pace than on Skiathos. Although Skopelos's beaches are neither so numerous nor so pretty, Skopelos town is one of the most attractive ports in Greece, and the island is rich in vegetation, with windswept pines growing down to secluded coves, wide beaches, and terraced cliffs of angled rock slabs. The interior is densely planted with fruit and nut orchards, and Skopelos's unique cuisine makes liberal use of the famous plums and almonds grown here. Like Skiathos, impressive grottoes and bays punctuate the coastline, providing irresistible photo ops. Skopelos is also known for keeping alive *rembetika* music, the Greek version of American "blues," that can be heard in tavernas late in the evening.

ESSENTIALS

GETTING THERE   By Plane   Skopelos cannot be reached directly by plane, but you can fly to nearby Skiathos and take a hydrofoil or ferry to the northern port of Loutraki (below Glossa) or to the more popular Skopelos town.

By Boat   If you're in Athens, take a boat or hydrofoil from Ayios Konstandinos to Skopelos (75 min.). **Alkyon Travel,** 97 Akademias, near Kanigos Square (✆ **210/383-2545**), can arrange the 3-hour bus ride from Athens to Ayios Konstandinos (about 15€/$20) and hydrofoil or ferry tickets.

Coming from Central or Northern Greece, depart for Skopelos from Volos (about 2 hr.). For hydrofoil and ferryboat information, contact **Hellas Flying Dolphins** in Athens (✆ **210/419-9100;** www.dolphins.gr). For other ferryboat information, contact **G.A. Ferries** line in Piraeus (✆ **210/458-2640**) or at their Athens office, 32 Leaforos Amalias (✆ **210/321-0061;** www.gaferries.com).

From Skiathos, the ferry to Skopelos takes 90 minutes if you call at Skopelos town, or 45 minutes if you get off at Glossa/Loutraki; the one-way fare to both is about 8€ ($10). Ferry tickets can be purchased at **Vasilis Nikolaou** (✆ **24270/22-209**), the travel agent at the corner of the Paralia and Papadiamandis. The Hellas Flying Dolphin hydrofoil takes 15 minutes to Glossa/Loutraki (4–5 times daily; 9€/$12), and 45 minutes to Skopelos (6–8 times daily; 10€/$13). From Skiathos, you can also take one of the many daily excursion boats to Skopelos.

It's possible to catch a regular ferry or hydrofoil from Alonissos to Skopelos (seven times daily; 9€/$12); or you can ride one of the excursion boats. Expect to pay a little more on the excursion boats—but if they're not full, you can sometimes negotiate the price.

There are infrequent ferryboat connections from Kimi (on Evvia) to Skopelos. Check with **Skopelos Port Authority** (✆ 24240/22-180) for current schedules, as they change frequently. As stated previously, we think hydrofoils are worth the extra expense for hopping around the Sporades.

In the port of Skopelos town, hydrofoil tickets can be purchased at the Hellas Flying Dolphin agent, **Madro Travel,** immediately opposite the dock (✆ 24240/22-300). It's open all year and also operates as the local Olympic Airways representative, so it can make any arrangements you need.

VISITOR INFORMATION   The **Municipal Tourist Office** of Skopelos is on the waterfront, to the left of the pier as you disembark (✆ 24240/23-231); it's open daily from 9:30am to 10pm in high season. It provides information, changes money, and reserves rooms. If you want to call ahead to book a room, the **Association of Owners of Rental Accommodation** maintains a small office on the harbor (✆ 24240/24-567).

At the travel agency **Skopelorama Holidays,** about 100m (328 ft.) beyond Hotel Eleni on the left (east) end of the port (✆ 24240/23-040; fax 24240/23-243), the friendly staff can help you find a room, exchange money, rent a car, or take an excursion; they know the island inside-out and can provide information on just about anything. It's open daily from 8am to 10pm.

GETTING AROUND   **By Bus**   Skopelos is reasonably well served by public bus; the bus stop in Skopelos town is on the east end of the port. There are four routes. Buses run the main route every half-hour in the high season beginning in Skopelos and making stops at Stafilos, Agnondas, Panormos, the Adrina Beach Hotel, Milia, Elios, Klima, Glossa, and Loutraki. The fare from Skopelos to Glossa is 2€ ($2.60).

By Car & Moped   The most convenient way to see the island is to rent a car or moped at one of the many shops on the port. A four-wheel-drive vehicle at **Motor Tours** (✆ 24240/22-986; motortours@yahoo.gr; enquiries@madrotravel.com) runs around 90€ ($117), including insurance; expect to pay less for a Fiat Panda. A moped should cost about 20€ ($26) per day.

By Taxi   The taxi stand is at the far end of the waterfront. Taxis will provide service to almost any place on the island. Taxis are not metered—negotiate the fare before accepting a ride. A typical fare, from Skopelos to Glossa, runs 30€ ($39).

By Boat   To visit the more isolated beaches, take one of the large excursion boats; these cost about 60€ ($78) including lunch, and should be booked a day in advance in high season. Excursion boats to Glisteri, Gliphoneri, and Sares beaches operate only in peak season (about 12€/$16). From the port of Agnondas, on the south coast, fishing boats go to Limnonari, one of the island's better beaches.

FAST FACTS   There are several **ATMs** at banks around the harbor. The **health center** is on the road leading out of the east end of town (✆ 24240/22-222). Plynthria, a self-service **laundry,** is located (in a basement) just past Adonis Hotel on the upper road at the east end of the harbor (✆ 24240/22-123). It's open Monday through Saturday from 9:30am to 1:30pm and 6 to 8pm. The **police station** (✆ 24240/22-235) is up the narrow road (Parados 1) to the right of the National Bank, along the harbor. For **Internet access,** try Click & Surf (info@skopelosnetcafe.com), just up from the police station. The **post office,** on the port's far east end (take the stepped road leading away from the last kiosk, opposite the bus/taxi station), is open Monday through Friday from 8am to 2:30pm. The **telephone office (OTE)** is at the top of a narrow road leading away from the center of the harbor; it's open Monday through Saturday from 8am to 5pm.

Finds **National Marine Park**

One of the more unusual attractions of a stay on Skopelos could be a day's excursion to the National Marine Park off the adjacent island of Alonissos. There you are guaranteed to see some of the many dolphins that frequent this protected area. The trip includes a stop at the islet of Psathoura, with a chance to dive into a sunken city, and a visit into the Blue Grotto of Alonissos. Any travel agency in Skopelos will be able to arrange such an excursion on one of several licensed ships.

WHAT TO SEE & DO

The ferries from Alonissos, Skyros, and Kimi, and most of the hydrofoils and other boats from Skiathos, dock at both Glossa/Loutraki and Skopelos town. Most boats stop first at **Loutraki,** a homely little port near the northern end of the west coast, with the more attractive town of **Glossa** high above it. Especially if this is your first visit, we suggest you stay onboard for the trip around the island's northern tip and along the east coast to the island's main harbor. You'll understand why the island's name means "cliff" in Greek when your boat pulls around the last headland into a huge and nearly perfect C-shaped harbor, and you get your first glimpse of Skopelos town rising like a steep amphitheater around the port.

Skopelos town (also called Hora) is one of Greece's most treasured towns, on a par with Hydra and Simi. It scales the steep, low hills around the harbor and has the same winding, narrow paths that characterize the more famous Cycladic islands to the south. Scattered on the slopes of the town are just a few of the island's 123 churches, which must be something of a record for such a small locale. The oldest of these is **Ayios Michali,** past the police station. The waterfront is lined with banks, cafes, travel agencies, and the like. Interspersed among these prosaic offerings are truly regal shade trees. Many of the shops and services are up the main street leading away from the center of the paralia. The back streets are amazingly convoluted (and unnamed); it's best that you wander around and get to know a few familiar landmarks.

The **Venetian Kastro,** which overlooks the town from a rise on the western corner, has been whitewashed. It looks too new to have been built over an archaic Temple of Athena, and too serene for the Turks to have deemed it impossible to impregnate during the War of Independence in the early 19th century.

At the far eastern end of town is the **Photographic Center of Skopelos** (*C* **24240/ 24-121**), which during the high season sponsors quite classy photography exhibitions in several locales around town.

SHOPPING

Skopelos has a variety of shops selling Greek and local ceramics, weavings, and jewelry. One of the most stylish is **Armoloi,** in the center of the shops along the harbor (*C* **24240/22-707**). It sells only Greek jewelry, ceramics, weavings, and silver; some of the objects are old. The owners make the most of the handsome ceramics. Another special store is **Ploumisti,** at a corner of an alley about midway along the paralia (*C* **24240/22-059;** kalaph-skp@skt.forthnet.gr). It sells beautiful Greek rugs, blankets, jewelry, pottery, and crafts. Its friendly proprietors, Voula and Kostas Kalafatis, are full of helpful information for visitors, especially about the *rembetika* music scene.

Nick Rodios (© 24240/22-924), whose gallery is between Hotel Eleni and Skopelo-rama Holidays agency, is from a Skopelos family who have made ceramics for three generations. His elegant black vessels, at once classical and modern, are a change from the usual pottery found around Greece.

EXPLORING THE ISLAND

The whole island is sprinkled with monasteries and churches, but five **monasteries** south of town can be visited by following a pleasant path that continues south from the beach hotels. The first, **Evangelistria,** was founded by monks from Mount Athos, but it now serves as a nunnery, and the weavings of its present occupants can be bought at a small shop; it's open daily from 8am to 1pm and 4 to 7pm. The fortified monastery of **Ayia Barbara,** now abandoned, contains 15th-century frescoes. **Metamorphosis,** very nearly abandoned, comes alive on August 6, when the feast of the Metamorphosis is celebrated here. **Ayios Prodromos** is a 30-minute hike farther, but it's the handsomest and contains a particularly beautiful iconostasis. **Taxiarchon,** abandoned and overgrown, is at the summit of Mount Polouki to the southeast, a hike recommended only for the hardiest and most dedicated.

There is basically a single highway on the island, with short spurs at each significant settlement. It runs south from Skopelos town, then cuts north and skirts the west coast northwest, eventually arriving at Glossa; it then runs down to Loutraki. The first spur leads off to the left to **Stafilos,** a popular family beach recommended by locals for a good seafood dinner, which you must order in the morning. About half a kilometer across the headland is **Velanio,** where nude bathing is common.

The next settlement west is **Agnondas,** named for a local athlete who brought home the gold from the 569 B.C. Olympic Games. This small fishing village has become a tourist resort thanks to nearby beaches. **Limnonari,** a 15-minute walk farther west and accessible by caïque in summer, has a good fine-sand beach in a rather homely and shadeless setting.

The road then turns inland again, through a pine forest, coming out at the coast at **Panormos.** With its sheltered pebble beach, this has become the island's best resort with a number of taverns, hotels, and rooms to let, as well as watersports facilities. The road then climbs again toward **Milia** ⌘, which is considered **the island's best beach.** You will have to walk down about half a kilometer from the bus stop, but you'll find a lovely light-gray beach of sand and pebbles, with the island of Dassia opposite and watersports facilities at **Beach Boys Club** (© 24240/23-995).

The next town, **Elios,** was thrown up to shelter the people displaced by the 1965 earthquake. It's become home to many of the locals who operate the resort facilities on the west coast, as well as something of a resort itself.

The main road proceeds on to **Glossa** ⌘, which means "tongue," and that's what the hill on which the town was built looks like from the sea. Most of it was spared during the earthquake, so it remains one of the most Greek and charming towns in the Sporades. Those tempted to stay overnight will find a number of rooms for rent, a good hotel, and a very good taverna.

Most of the coastline here is craggy and has a few hard-to-reach beaches. Among the best places to catch some rays and do a bit of swimming is the small beach below the picturesque monastery of **Ayios Ioannis,** on the coast east from town, which reminds many of Meteora. (Bring food and water.) As for the port of **Loutraki,** it's a winding 3km (2 miles) down; we don't recommend a stay there.

That ends the road tour of Skopelos, but other sites can be reached from Skopelos town by caïque. Along the east coast north of Skopelos is **Glisteri,** a small, pebbled beach with a nearby olive grove offering respite from the sun. It's a good bet when the other beaches are overrun in summer. You can also go by caïque to the grotto at **Tripiti,** for the island's best fishing, or to the little island of **Ayios Yioryios,** which has an abandoned monastery.

The whole of Skopelos's 95 sq. km (38 sq. miles) is prime for **hiking** and **biking,** and the interior is still waiting to be explored. There's also **horseback riding, sailing** (ask at the Skopelos travel agencies), and a number of interesting **excursions** to be taken from and around the island. Both Skopelorama Holidays and Madro Travel (see "Getting There," above) operate a fine series of excursions, such as monasteries by coach, a walking tour of the town, and several cruises. Another possibility is a nature walk led by a longtime English resident, Heather Parsons (www.skopelos-walks.com). One boat excursion that might appeal to some is to the waters around Skopelos that are part of the **National Marine Park;** if you're lucky, you'll spot Mediterranean monk seals, an endangered species protected within the park.

WHERE TO STAY

In high season, Skopelos is nearly as popular as Skiathos. If you need advice, talk to the Skopelorama Holidays agency (see "Visitor Information," above) or to the officials at the town hall. Be sure to look at a room and agree on a price before you accept anything, or you may be unpleasantly surprised. To make matters confusing, there are few street names in the main, older section of Skopelos town, so you'll have to ask for directions in order to find your lodging.

IN SKOPELOS TOWN

Handsome, traditional-style **Hotel Amalia,** along the coast, 500m (1,640 ft.) from the port's center ((*C*) **24240/22-688;** fax 24240/23-217), is largely occupied by groups but should have spare rooms in spring and fall.

Hotel Denise   One of the best hotels in Skopelos thanks to its premier location, clean facilities, and pool, the Hotel Denise stands atop the hill overlooking the town and commands spectacular vistas of the harbor and Aegean. A wide balcony rings each of the hotel's four stories. The guest rooms have hardwood floors and furniture, and most boast views that are among the best in town. The Denise is popular and open only in high season; before hiking up the steep road, call for a pickup and to check for room availability—or better yet, reserve in advance.

Skopelos town 37003. (*C*) **24240/22-678.** Fax 24240/22-769. www.denise.gr. 25 units. 95€ ($124) double. Rates include continental breakfast. Credit cards accepted for deposit only. *In room:* A/C, TV, minibar.

Hotel Drossia *(Value)*   This small hotel next to the Hotel Denise (see above), atop the hill overlooking the town, is a good value. The Drossia is of the same vintage as the Denise, with exceptional views but slightly less expensive and less well-equipped rooms.

Skopelos town 37003. (*C*) **24240/22-490.** 10 units. 60€ ($78) double. No credit cards. Closed Oct.–May.

Hotel Eleni   Hotel Eleni is a modern hotel, set back from the coast and 300m (984 ft.) to the left from the harbor's center. After many years spent operating pizzerias in New York, Charlie Hatzidrosos returned from the Bronx to build this establishment. His daughter now operates the hotel and provides gracious service. All guest rooms have balconies.

Skopelos town 37003 ✆ **24240/22-393**. Fax 2424/022-936. 37 units. 65€ ($85) double. AE, MC, V. *In room:* TV, fridge.

Hotel Prince Stafilos ⭐

Although Hotel Prince Stafilos charges considerably more than other Skopelos hotels, it's well worth it. This is a hotel for those who can afford to spend a civilized vacation on Skopelos. The most handsome hotel on the island—made of the stone and wood associated with the island's traditional homes—it's about a half mile south of town. The friendly owner, Pelopidas Tsitsirgos, is also the architect responsible for the establishment's special charm. The lobby is spacious and attractively decorated with local artifacts. Rooms are larger than those in many Greek hotels and furnished in a more traditional Greek style than standard hotel rooms. The restaurant is quite grand; the swimming pool, large. The hotel provides transportation to and from the town center.

About 1.6km (1 mile) from center, Skopelos town 37003. ✆ **24240/22-775**. Fax 24240/22-825. 65 units. 150€ ($195) double. Rates include large buffet breakfast. AE, MC, V. **Amenities:** Restaurant; 2 bars; pool. *In room:* A/C.

Skopelos Village

Guests here may want to settle in for a while so they can take advantage of this miniresort's amenities. The buildings are tastefully constructed as "traditional island houses." Each bungalow is equipped with kitchen, private bathroom, and one or two bedrooms, and can sleep from two to six persons. Facilities include a breakfast room and snack bar. In the evening, the restaurant offers Greek meals accompanied by Greek music and dance. The hotel provides free transportation to various beaches.

About a half-mile southeast of town center, Skopelos 37003. ✆ **24240/22-517**. Fax 24240/22-958. 36 units. High season bungalow for 2 persons, with a kitchen 195€ ($254), mid-season 145€ ($189). MC, V. **Amenities:** 2 restaurants; pool; tennis nearby; children's playground; 24-hr. room service. *In room:* A/C, TV, minibar.

IN PANORMOS

This pleasant little resort is on a horseshoe-shaped cove along the west coast, about halfway between Skopelos town and Glossa. Here you'll find several cafeteria-style snack bars and minimarkets. We recommend it as a base, especially since one of the best hotels on the island—Adrina Beach Hotel—is just above it. As for restaurants, a particularly lively taverna, **Dihta,** is right along the beachfront.

Panormos Travel Office (✆ **24240/23-380;** fax 24240/23-748) has decent rooms to let; offers phone and fax services; exchanges money; arranges tours (including night squid fishing); and rents cars, motorbikes, and speedboats.

If you can't get a room at the Adrina, try 38-unit **Afroditi Hotel** (✆ **24240/23-150;** fax 24240/23-152), a more modern choice about 100m (328 ft.) across the road from the beach at Panormos.

Adrina Beach Hotel ⭐

This traditional hotel, 500m (1,640 ft.) on the beach beyond Panormos, rates as one of the better ones on the island. The guest rooms are large and tastefully furnished in pastels, each with its own balcony or veranda. In addition to the main building's rooms, eight handsome "maisonettes" are ranked down the steep slope toward the hotel's private beach. The complex has a big saltwater pool with its own bar, a restaurant, a bar, a buffet room, spacious sitting areas indoors and out, a playground, and a minimarket. Conference facilities for 50 to 60 people can be provided.

Panormos, 37003 Skopelos. ✆ **24240/23-371**, or 210/682-6886 in Athens. www.adrina.gr. 52 units. 140€ ($182) double. Rates include buffet breakfast. AE, DC, MC, V. **Amenities:** 2 restaurants; bar; pool; children's playground; minimarket. *In room:* A/C, TV, fridge.

IN GLOSSA

There are approximately 100 rooms to rent in the small town of Glossa. Expect to pay about 40€ ($52) for single or double occupancy. The best way to find a room is to visit one of the tavernas or shops and inquire about vacancies. You can ask George Antoniou at **Pythari Souvenir Shop** (✆ **24240/33-077**) for advice. If you can't find a room in Glossa, you can take a bus or taxi down to Loutraki and check into a pension by the water; or you can head back to Panormos.

WHERE TO DINE
IN SKOPELOS TOWN
Finikas Taverna and Ouzeri 🔆 GREEK   Tucked away in the upper back streets of Skopelos is a picturesque garden taverna/ouzeri dominated by a broadleaf palm. The Finikas offers what might be Skopelos's most romantic setting, thanks to its isolated and lovely garden seating. Among the many fine courses are an excellent ratatouille and pork cooked with prunes and apples, a traditional island specialty.

Upper back street of Skopelos town. ✆ 24240/23-247. Main courses 4€–9€ ($5.20–$12). No credit cards. Daily 7pm–2am.

The Garden Restaurant GREEK   Some locals claim this is the best restaurant in town. Two young brothers operate what most people call simply "The Garden," for its setting and casual atmosphere. The food is tasty and often a bit different. We've enjoyed the mushrooms with garlic (an appetizer), and kalamares with cheese (a main course).

At harbor's far eastern end, 1st left at corner of Amalia Hotel. ✆ 24240/22-349. Reservations recommended in high season. Main courses 5€–16€ ($6.50–$21). MC, V. Daily 11am–midnight. Closed Oct to mid-June.

Platanos Jazz Bar SNACK/BAR FOOD   For everything from breakfast to a late-night drink, try this pub. Breakfast in the summer starts as early as 5 or 6am for ferry passengers, who can enjoy coffee, fruit salad with nuts and yogurt, and fresh-squeezed orange juice, all for about 8€ ($10). Platanos is equally pleasant for evening and late-night drinks. Accompanying your meal will be music from the proprietors' phenomenal collection of jazz records.

Beneath the enormous plane tree just to the left of the ferry dock. ✆ 24240/23-661. Main courses 3€–8€ ($3.90–$10). No credit cards. Daily 5am–3am.

IN GLOSSA
Taverna Agnanti 🔆 TRADITIONAL SKOPELITIAN   Highly praised by numerous international travel magazines (*Time* and Sweden's *Novair,* among them), this is the place to meet, greet, and eat in Glossa. The food is inexpensive, the staff friendly, and the view spectacular. The menu is standard taverna style, but the proprietors make a point of using the finest fresh products and wines. Specialties include herb fritters, fish stifado with prunes, pork with prunes, and almond pie. Traditional music is occasionally played. The Stamataki family runs this and the nearby souvenir shop Pythari.

Glossa. ✆ 24240/33-076. agnanti-rest@agnanti-rest.gr. Main courses 3€–17€ ($3.90–$22). No credit cards. Daily 11am–midnight. About 200m (656 ft.) up from the bus stop.

SKOPELOS AFTER DARK

The nightlife scene on Skopelos isn't nearly as active as on neighboring Skiathos, but there are still plenty of bars, late-night cafes, and discos. Most of the coolest bars are on the far (east) side of town, but you can wander the scene around Platanos Square, beyond and along the paralia. Above Hotel Amalia is indoor **Cocos Club;** continue along the beachfront to find outdoor **Karyatis.** The best place for *bouzouki* music is **Metro.** And for live music try **Anatoli Ouzeri,** above the town with spectacular views.

3 Skyros (Skiros)

47km (25 nautical miles) from Kimi; 182km (113 miles) from Athens

Skyros is an island with good beaches, attractive whitewashed pillbox architecture, picturesque surroundings, low prices—and relatively few tourists. Why? First, it's difficult to get to. In summer, occasional ferries and hydrofoils link Skyros to the other Sporades as well as to ports on the mainland, but these links are either fairly infrequent or involve land transportation to ports that are not on most tourists' itineraries. Second, most visitors to the Sporades seem to prefer the more thickly forested (and thickly touristed) islands. Others of us, however, think Skyros's more meager tourist facilities and the stark contrast between sea, sky, and rugged terrain make it all the more inviting.

Also, many Skyriots have been ambivalent about developing this very traditional island for tourism. Until about 1990, only a handful of hotels existed on the entire island. Since then, Skyros has seen a miniboom in the tourist business, and with the completion of a giant marina, it's set to become yet another tourist hot spot. Don't let this deter you, however; at least for now, Skyros remains an ideal place for a getaway.

ESSENTIALS

GETTING THERE   By Plane   In summer, **Olympic Airways** has about two flights a week between Athens and Skyros. Call the Olympic office in Athens (✆ **210/966-6666**) for information and reservations; the local Olympic representative is **Skyros Travel and Tourism** (✆ **22220/91-123**). A bus meets most flights and goes to Skyros town, Magazia, and sometimes Molos; the fare is 4€ ($5.20). A taxi from the airport is about 10€ ($13), but expect to share a cab.

By Boat   Skyros Shipping Company (www.sne.gr) offers the only ferry service to Skyros; it's operated by a company whose stockholders are all citizens of the island. In summer, it runs twice daily (usually early afternoon and early evening) from Kimi (on the east coast of Evvia) to Skyros, and twice daily (usually early morning and mid-afternoon) from Skyros to Kimi; the trip takes a little over 2 hours. Off season, there's one ferry each way, leaving Skyros early in the morning and Kimi in late afternoon. The fare is 12€ ($16). For information, call the company's office either in Kimi (✆ **22220/22-020**) or Skyros (✆ **22220/91-790**). The Skyros Shipping Company's offices also sell connecting bus tickets to Athens; the fare for the 3½-hour ride is about 15€ ($20). In Athens, **Alkyon Travel,** 97 Akademia, near Kanigos Square (✆ **210/383-2545**), arranges bus transportation to Kimi and sells ferry tickets to the Sporades.

If you're trying to "do" the Sporades and want to make connections at Kimi, the tricky part can be the connection with ferries or hydrofoils from the other Sporades islands. When they don't hold to schedule, it's not uncommon to see the Skyros ferry disappearing on the horizon as your ship pulls into Kimi. You might have to make the best of the 24-hour layover and get a room in Paralia Kimi. (We recommend **Hotel Korali,** at ✆ **22220/22-212;** or the older **Hotel Krineion,** at ✆ **22220/22-287.**)

From Athens, buses to Kimi and Ayios Konstandinos leave the Terminal B (260 Lission) six times a day, though you should depart no later than 1:30pm; the fare for the 3½-hour trip is about 18€ ($23). From Kimi, you must take a local bus to Paralia Kimi. Ask the bus driver if you're uncertain of the connection.

On Skyros, the ferries and hydrofoils dock at **Linaria,** on the opposite side of the island from Skyros town. The island's only public bus will meet the boat and take you over winding, curving roads to Skyros town for 1€ ($1.30). On request, the bus will also stop at Magazia beach, immediately north below the town, next to Xenia Hotel.

VISITOR INFORMATION The largest tourist office is **Skyros Travel and Tourism** (© 22220/91-123; www.skyrostravel.com), next to Skyros Pizza Restaurant in the main market. It's open daily from 8am to 2:30pm and 6:30 to 10:30pm. English-speaking Lefteris Trakos offers assistance with accommodations, currency exchange, Olympic Airways flights (he's the local ticket agent), phone calls, interesting bus and boat tours, and Hellas Flying Dolphin tickets.

GETTING AROUND By Bus The only scheduled service is the Skyros-Linaria shuttle that runs four to five times daily and costs 1€ ($1.30). Skyros Travel (see above) offers a twice-daily beach-excursion bus in high season and day-long island excursions in a small bus with an English-speaking guide (35€/$46); for many, this may be the best way to get an overview of the island.

By Car & Moped A small car rents for about 70€ ($91) per day, including insurance. Mopeds and motorcycles are available near the police station or the taxi station for about 25€ ($33) per day. The island has a relatively well-developed network of roads.

By Taxi Taxis can take you just about any place on the island at the standard Greek rates, but discuss the price before setting off; service between Linaria and Skyros costs about 13€ ($17).

On Foot Skyros is a fine place to hike. The island map, published by Skyros Travel and Tourism, will show you a number of good routes, and it is pretty accurate.

FAST FACTS The most convenient ATM on Skyros is at the **National Bank of Greece** in the main square of Skyros town. (Because Skyros's tourist services are relatively limited, we recommend bringing cash and/or traveler's checks for emergencies.) The **clinic** is near the main square (© **22220/92-222**). The **police station** (© **22220/ 91-274**) is on the street behind the Skyros Travel Center. The **post office** is near the bus square in Skyros town; it's open Monday through Friday from 8am to 2pm. The **telephone office (OTE)** is opposite the police station. It's open Friday only, from 7:30am to 3pm, but there are card phones in town.

WHAT TO SEE & DO

The Faltaits Historical and Folklore Museum

This is one of the best island folk-art museums in Greece. Located in an old house belonging to the Faltaits family, the private collection of Manos Faltaits contains a large and varied selection of plates, embroidery, weaving, woodworking, and clothing, as well as many rare books and photographs, including some of local men in traditional costumes for Carnival. Attached to the museum is a workshop where young artisans make lovely objects using traditional patterns and materials. The proceeds from the sale of workshop items go to the upkeep of the museum. The museum also has a shop, **Argo,** on the main street of town (© **22220/92-158**). It's open daily from 10am to 1pm and 6:30 to 11pm.

Plateia Rupert Brooke. © 22220/91-232. faltaits@otenet.gr. 2€ ($2.60). Summer daily 10am–1pm and 6–9pm. Off season, ring the bell and someone will let you in.

EXPLORING THE ISLAND

All boats dock at **Linaria,** a plain, mostly modern fishing village on the west coast, pleasant enough but not recommended for a stay. Catch the bus waiting on the quay to take you across the narrow middle of the island to the west coast capital, Skyros town, which is built on a rocky bluff overlooking the sea. (The airport is near the northern tip of the island.) **Skyros town,** which is known on the island as Horio or Hora, looks much like a typical Cycladic hill town, with whitewashed houses built on top of one another. The winding streets and paths are too narrow for cars and mopeds, so most of the traffic is by foot and hoof. After you alight at the bus stop square, continue on up toward the center of town and the main tourist services.

Near the market, signs point to the town's **kastro.** The climb takes 15 minutes, but the view is worth it. On the way you'll pass the church of **Ayia Triada,** which contains interesting frescoes; and the monastery of **Ayios Yioryios Skyrianos.** The monastery was founded in 962 and contains a famous black-faced icon of St. George brought from Constantinople during the Iconoclastic controversy. From one side of the citadel, the view is over the rooftops of the town, and from the other the cliff drops precipitously to the sea. According to one myth, King Lykomides pushed Theseus to his death from here.

The terrace at the far (northern) end of the island is **Plateia Rupert Brooke,** where the English poet, who is buried on the southern tip of the island, is honored by a nude statue, "Immortal Poetry." (Brooke died on a hospital ship off Skyros in 1915 while en route to the Dardanelles as an army officer.) The statue is said to have greatly offended the local people when it was installed, but you're more likely to be amused when you see how pranksters have chosen to deface the hapless bronze figure. (The Faltaits Folklore Museum, described above, is near this site, as is the not especially distinguished archaeological museum.)

Local customs and dress are currently better preserved on Skyros than in all but a few locales in Greece. Older men can still be seen in baggy blue pants, black caps, and leather sandals with numerous straps, and older women still wear long head scarves. The **embroidery** you will often see women busily working at is famous for its vibrant colors and interesting motifs—such as people dancing hand-in-hand with flowers twining around their limbs and hoopoes with fanciful crests.

Peek into the doorway of any Skyrian home, and you're likely to see what looks like a room from a dollhouse with a miniature table and chairs, as well as **colorful plates**—loads of them—hanging on the wall. These displays are said to date back to the Byzantine era, when the head clerics from Epirus sent 10 families to Skyros to serve as governors. They were given control of all the land not owned by Mount Athos and the Monastery of St. George. For hundreds of years, these 10 families dominated the affairs of Skyros. With Kalamitsa as a safe harbor, the island prospered, and consulates opened from countries near and far. The merchant ships were soon followed by pirates, with whom the ruling families went into business. The families knew what boats were expected and what they were carrying, and the pirates had the ships and bravado to steal the cargo. The pirates, of course, soon took to plundering the islanders as well, but the aristocrats managed to hold onto much of their wealth.

Greek independence reduced the influence of these ruling families, and during the hard times brought by World War I, they were reduced to trading their possessions to the peasant farmers for food. Chief among these bartered items were sets of dinnerware. Plates from China, Italy, Turkey, Egypt, and other exotic places became a sign of wealth, and Skyrian families made elaborate displays of their newly acquired trophies. Whole walls were covered, and by the 1920s local Skyrian craftsmen began making their own plates for the poorer families who couldn't afford the originals. This, at least, is the story they tell.

Moments **The Famous Carnival of Skyros**

The 21-day Carnival celebration is highlighted by a 4-day period leading up to Lent and the day known throughout Greece as *Kathari Deftera* (Clean Monday). On this day, Skyros residents don traditional costumes and perform dances on the town square. Unleavened bread *(lagana)* is served with *taramosalata* and other meatless specialties. (Traditionally, vegetarian food is eaten for 40 days leading up to Easter.) Much of this is traditional throughout Greece, but Skyros adds its own distinctive element. Culminating on midafternoon of the Sunday before Clean Monday is a series of ritual dances and events performed by a group of weirdly costumed men. Some dress as old shepherds in animal skins with belts of sheep bells and masks made of goatskin. Other men dress as women and flirt outrageously. (Skyros seems to have an age-old association with cross-dressing: It was here that Achilles successfully beat the draft during the Trojan war by dressing as a woman, until shrewd Odysseus tricked him into revealing his true gender.) Other celebrants caricature Europeans. All behave outlandishly, reciting ribald poetry and poking fun at bystanders. This ritual is generally thought to be pagan in origin, and what you see has deep roots. Some of the antic elements might seem similar to parts from ancient Greek comedies, and the word tragedy means "goat song," so the goat-costume ceremonies may go way back also.

Skyros is also the home of a unique breed of **wild pygmy ponies,** often compared to the horses depicted on the frieze of the Parthenon and thought to be similar to Shetland ponies. Most of these rare animals have been moved to the nearby island of Skyropoula, though tame ones can still be seen grazing near town. Ask around and you might be able to find a local who will let you ride one.

Every July 15, the ponies of Skyros are assembled and rated as to their characteristics, and then young boys race some of the ponies around a small track.

BEACHES & OUTDOOR PURSUITS

The island is divided almost evenly by its narrow waist; the northern half is fertile and covered with pine forest, while the southern half is barren and quite rugged. Both halves have their attractions, though the most scenic area of the island is probably to the south toward **Tris Boukes,** where Rupert Brooke is buried. The better beaches, however, are in the north.

To get to the beach at **Magazia,** continue down from Plateia Rupert Brooke. (If your load is heavy, take a taxi to Magazia, as it is a hike.) From Magazia, once the site of the town's storehouses (magazines), it's about a half-mile to **Molos,** a fishing village, though the two villages are quickly becoming indistinguishable because of development. There's windsurfing along this beach and, beyond Molos, windsurfing at fairly isolated beaches with nudist sections.

South of town, the beaches are less enticing until you reach **Aspous,** which has a couple of tavernas and rooms to let. **Ahili,** a bit farther south, is where you'll find the big new **marina,** so it's no longer much of a place for swimming. Farther south, the coast gets increasingly rugged and has no roadway.

If you head back across the narrow waist of the island to **Kalamitsa,** the old safe harbor, 3km (2 miles) south of Linaria, you'll find a good clean beach. Buses run here in summer.

North of Linaria, **Acherounes** is a very pretty beach. Beyond it, **Pefkos,** where marble was once quarried, is better sheltered and has a taverna that's open in summer. The next beach north, **Ayios Fokas,** is probably the best on the island, with a lovely white pebble beach and a taverna open in summer. Locals call it paradise, and like all such places it's very difficult to reach. Most Skyrians will suggest walking, but the hike is long and hilly. To get here from Skyros town, take the bus back to Linaria, tell the driver where you're going, get off at the crossroads with Pefkos, and begin your hike west from there.

North of Ayios Fokas is **Atsitsa,** another beach with pine trees, but it's a bit too rocky. It can be reached by road across the Olymbos mountains in the center of the island, and has a few rooms to let. It is also the location of a **holistic health-and-fitness holiday community;** for information on its activities, contact Skyros Holistic Vacations, 92 Prince of Wales Rd., London NW5 3NE (© **020/7267-4424** in England; www.skyros.com). This same British outfit runs the **Skyros Centre** at the edge of Skyros town; it differs from the one at Atsitsa in that it offers courses and a somewhat more conventional touristic experience. A 15-minute walk farther north from Atsitsa, **Kira Panagia** is a sandy beach that's a bit better.

The northwest of the island is covered in dense pine forests, spreading down to the Aegean. The rocky shore opens onto gentle bays and coves. This area provides wonderful **hiking** for the fit. Take a taxi (25€/$33) to **Atsitsa,** and arrange for it to return in 5 or 6 hours. Explore the ruins of the ancient mining operation at Atsitsa, then head south for about 7km (4½ miles) to **Ayios Fokas,** a small bay with a tiny taverna perched right on the water. Kali Orfanou, the gracious hostess, will provide you with the meal of your trip: fresh fish caught that morning in the waters before you, vegetables plucked from the garden for your salad, and her own feta cheese and wine. Relax, swim in the bay, and then hike back to your taxi. The ambitious may continue south for 11 or 12km (7–8 miles) to the main road and catch the bus or hail a taxi. Note that this part of the road is mainly uphill. In case you tire or can't pry yourself away from the secluded paradise of Ayios Fokas, Kali offers two extremely primitive rooms with the view of your dreams, but without electricity or toilets.

SHOPPING

Skyros is a good place to buy local crafts, especially embroidery and ceramics. **Ergastiri,** on the main street, sells interesting ceramics, Greek shadow puppets, and a great selection of postcards. **Yiannis Nicholau,** whose studio is next to Xenia Hotel, is known for his handmade plates. You can find good hand-carved wooden chests and chairs made from beech (in the old days it was blackberry wood) from **Lefteris Avgoklouris,** former student of the recently departed master, Baboussis, in Skyros town; his studio (© **22220/91-106**) is on Konthili, around the corner from the post office. Another fine carver is **Manolios,** in the main market.

WHERE TO STAY

The whole island has only a few hotels, so most visitors to Skyros take private rooms. The best are in the upper part of Skyros town, away from the bus stop, where women in black dresses accost you with cries of "Room! Room!" A more efficient procedure is to stop at Skyros Travel and Tourism (see "Visitor Information," above). The island of Skyros is somewhat more primitive in its facilities than the other Sporades, so before agreeing to anything, check out the room to ensure that it's what you want.

IN SKYROS TOWN

Hotel Nefeli   One of the best in-town options is furnished in the traditional Skyrian style. The bedrooms and bathrooms are decent in size and well appointed; many units have fine views. The large downstairs lobby is a welcoming space. Reserve in advance, as the Nefeli is one of the favorite choices on Skyros.

Skyros town center, 34007 Skyros. ℰ **22220/91-964**. Fax 22220/92-061. 16 units. 85€ ($111) double. Breakfast 5€ ($6.50) extra. AE, MC, V.

IN MAGAZIA BEACH & MOLOS

Hotel Angela *(Value)*   This is among the most attractive and well-kept abodes in the Molos/Magazia beach area, located near the sprawling Paradise Hotel complex. All rooms are clean and tidy with balconies, but because the hotel is set back about 91m (300 ft.) from the beach, it has only partial sea views. Nevertheless, the facilities and hospitality of the young couple running the Angela make up for its just-off-the-beach location, and it's your best bet for the money.

Molos, 34007 Skyros. ℰ **22220/91-764**. Fax 2222/92-030. anghotel@otenet.gr. 14 units. 85€ ($111) double. No credit cards.

Paradise Hotel   This pleasant lodging is at the north end of Magazia beach, in the town of Molos. The older part of the hotel has 40 rooms; these more basic units run about 50% less. We recommend one of the newer section's 20 rooms, which are better kept and have much better light. The hotel is somewhat removed from the main town, but there is a taverna on the premises and another down the street.

Molos, 34007 Skyros. ℰ **22220/91-220**. Fax 22220/91-443. 60 units. 75€ ($98) double in the new building. Breakfast 4€ ($5.20) extra. No credit cards.

Pension Galeni   The small but delightful Pension Galeni offers modest rooms, all with private bathrooms. We like the front, sea-facing rooms on the top floor for their (currently) unobstructed views. The Galeni overlooks one of the cleanest parts of Magazia beach.

Magazia beach, 34007 Skyros. ℰ **22220/91-379**. 13 units. 58€ ($75) double. No credit cards.

Xenia   With the best location on the beach at Magazia, the Xenia offers some of the nicest (if not cheapest) accommodations on Skyros. The guest rooms have handsome 1950s-style furniture and big bathrooms with tubs, as well as wonderful balconies and sea views. You can get all your meals here if you want. Perhaps the hotel's greatest drawback is the unsightly concrete breakwater that's supposed to protect the beach from erosion.

Magazia Beach, 34007 Skyros. ℰ **22220/92-063**. Fax 22220/92-062. 22 units. 105€ ($137) double. Rates include buffet breakfast. V.

IN ACHEROUNES BEACH

Pegasus Apartments   These fully equipped studios and apartments were built by the resourceful Lefteris Trakos (owner of Skyros Travel). They are at Acherounes, the beach just south of the port of Linaria, on the east coast. One of the pluses of staying here is the chance to see (and ride, if you're under 15) Katerina, a Skyriot pony.

Acherounes Beach, 34007 Skyros. ℰ **22220/91-552**. 8 units. 45€ ($59) studio for 2 persons; 105€ ($137) apt for 3–5 persons. MC, V. *In room:* minibar.

IN YIRISMATA

Skyros Palace Hotel ★ If you want to get away from it all and enjoy upscale amenities to boot, this is the place for you. This out-of-the-way resort—about 1.6km (1 mile) north of Molos, and 3km (2 miles) north of Skyros town—has the most luxurious accommodations on the island. The plainly furnished but comfortable guest rooms come with large balconies. The beach across the road is an especially windy, rocky stretch of coastline, with treacherous waters. Facilities include a lovely (seawater) pool and adjacent bar, some air-conditioned rooms, and a well-planted garden—not to mention a soundproof disco, the island's most sophisticated. A minibus heads into town twice a day.

Yirismata, 34007 Skyros. ⓒ **22220/91-994.** Fax 22220/92-070. 80 units. 110€ ($143) double. Rates include breakfast. AE, DC, MC, V. **Amenities:** 2 restaurants; bar; disco; pool; tennis; basketball court; minibus to town. *In room:* A/C, TV.

WHERE TO DINE

The food in Skyros town is generally pretty good and reasonably priced. **Anemos,** on the main drag (ⓒ **22220/92-155**), is a nice spot for breakfast, with filtered coffee, omelets, and freshly squeezed juice. Nearby **Skyros Pizza Restaurant** (ⓒ **22220/91-684**) serves tasty pies as well as other Greek specialties. For dessert, head to **Zaccharoplasteio** (the Greek word for sweet shop/bakery) in the center of town.

Linaria offers three decent tavernas to choose from—**Almyria, Filippeos,** and **Psariotos.**

Kristina's/Pegasus Restaurant ★ INTERNATIONAL Come here if you need a break from standard Greek fare. Kristina's has been an institution in Skyros town for some years, but in 2000 it moved to the locale of the former Pegasus Restaurant, a neoclassical building (ca. 1890) in the center of town. The Australian proprietor/chef, Kristina, brings a light touch to everything she cooks. Her fricasseed chicken is excellent, her herb bread is tasty, and her desserts, such as cheesecake, are exceptional.

Skyros town. ⓒ **2222/91-123.** Reservations recommended in summer. Main courses 6€–15€ ($7.80–$20). No credit cards. Mon–Sat 7am–4pm and 7pm–1am.

Maryetes Grill GRILL One of the oldest and best places in town, the Maryetes is a second-generation-run grill that's equally popular with locals and travelers. Go for the food, not the dining room, which is as simple as can be. We recommend the grilled chicken and meat. A small sampling of salads is also on the menu.

Skyros town. ⓒ **22220/91-311.** Main courses 5.50€–8€ ($7.15–$10). No credit cards. Daily 1–3pm and 6pm–midnight.

Restaurant Kabanero *Value* GREEK One of the best dining values in town, this perpetually busy eatery serves the usual Greek menu: moussaka, stuffed peppers and tomatoes, fava, a variety of stewed vegetables, and several kinds of meat. The dishes are tasty and the prices somewhat lower than those at most other places in town.

Skyros town. ⓒ **22220/91-240.** Main courses 5€–9€ ($6.50–$12). No credit cards. Daily 1–3pm and 6pm–midnight.

SKYROS AFTER DARK

If you gotta dance, try **Kastro Club** in Linaria; or **Stone,** on the road to Magazia. Linaria's **O Kavos** is another popular hangout. Aside from these, you'll find few evening diversions other than bar-hopping on the main street of Skyros town. **Apocalypsis** draws a younger crowd. **Kalypso** attracts a more refined set of drinkers who appreciate its better-made but pricier cocktails. **Renaissance** is loud and lively. **Rodon** is best for actually listening to music, while **Kata Lathos (By Mistake)** has also gained a following.

12

The Ionian Islands

by John S. Bowman

"The isles of Greece, the isles of Greece"—when Lord Byron tossed his bouquet, he was not under the spell of today's popular Cycladic islands but of the Ionian Islands. Located off Greece's northwest coast, the Ionians offer some of the country's loveliest natural settings, including beaches, a fine selection of hotels and restaurants; a distinctive history and lore; and some unusual architectural and archaeological sites.

The Ionian Islands are rainier, greener, and more temperate than other Greek islands, so the high season lasts a little longer, from late June to early September. The roads are generally in fine condition, even if unavoidably steep and twisting. Accommodations range from luxury resorts to quiet little rooms on remote beaches. The local cuisine and wines offer numerous special treats. Among the best are *sofrito,* a spicy veal dish; *bourdetto,* a spicy fish dish; and wines such as Robola, Liapaditiko, and Theotaki (this last preferred by James Bond).

The Ionian Islands include **Corfu** (Kerkira), **Paxos** (Paxoi), **Levkas** (Lefkas, Lefkada), **Ithaka** (Ithaki), **Kefalonia** (Kefallinia, Cephalonia), and **Zakinthos** (Zakynthos, Zante); the seventh, **Kithira** (Cythera, Cerigo)—off the south coast of the Peloponnese—is linked only as a government administrative unit. There are many more islands in the archipelago along Greece's northwest coast, including several that are sparsely inhabited.

STRATEGIES FOR SEEING THE ISLANDS

In this chapter, we single out **Corfu** and **Kefalonia,** with a side trip to **Ithaka.** With a couple of weeks to spare, you can take a ship or plane to either Corfu in the north or Zakinthos in the south and then make your way by ship to several of the other Ionians (although outside high season, you will have to do considerable backtracking). If you have only a week, you should fly to one island and then use ships to get to a couple of the others. In either case, rent a car to get around the larger islands. If it comes down to visiting only one, Corfu is a prime candidate, but if you want to get off the beaten track, consider Kefalonia or Ithaka. All the Ionians—especially Corfu—are overrun in July and August; aim for June or September, if you can.

A LOOK AT THE PAST   In the fabric of their history, the Ionian Islands can trace certain threads that both tie and distinguish them from the rest of Greece. During the late Bronze Age (1500–1200 B.C.), a Mycenaean culture thrived on at least several of these islands. Although certain names of islands and cities were the same as those used today—Ithaka, for instance—scholars have never been able to agree on exactly which were the sites described in the *Odyssey.*

People from the city-states on the Greek mainland then recolonized the islands, starting in the 8th century B.C. The Peloponnesian War, in fact, can be traced back to

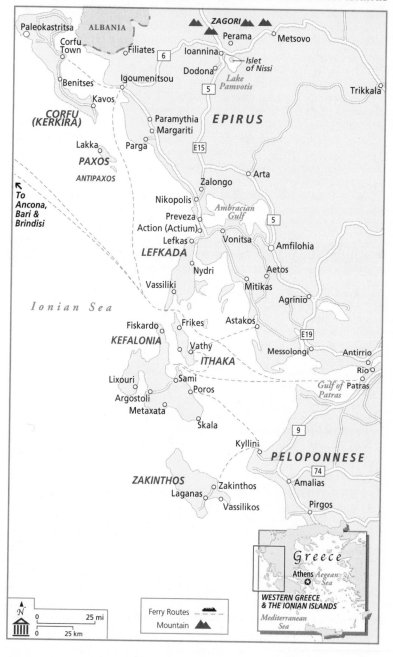

Paleokastritsa

ALBANIA

Corfu Town
Filiates

ZAGORI

Perama

Metsovo

6

Ioannina

Benitses

Igoumenitsou

Dodona

Islet of Nissi

Lake Pamvotis

5

Trikkala

Kavos

CORFU (KERKIRA)

Paramythia
Margariti

EPIRUS

Lakka

Parga

PAXOS

ANTIPAXOS

E15

Zalongo

Arta

To Ancona, Bari & Brindisi

Nikopolis

Ambracian Gulf

Preveza
Action (Actium)
Lefkas

5

Vonitsa

Amfilohia

LEFKADA

Nydri

Aetos

Ionian Sea

Vassiliki

Mitikas

Agrinio

Fiskardo

Frikes

Astakos

KEFALONIA

Vathy

E19

Lixouri

Sami

ITHAKA

Messolongi

Antirrio

Rio

Poros

Gulf of Patras

Patras

Argostoli
Metaxata

Skala

9

Kyllini

PELOPONNESE

ZAKINTHOS

Zakinthos

74

Amalias

Laganas

Vassilikos

Pirgos

Greece

Athens
Aegean Sea

WESTERN GREECE & THE IONIAN ISLANDS

Mediterranean Sea

N

0   25 mi
0   25 km

Ferry Routes
Mountain

a quarrel between Corinth and its colony at Corcyra (Corfu) that led to Athens's interference and eventually the full-scale war. The islands later fell under the rule of the Romans, then the Byzantine empire. They remained prey to warring powers and pirates in this part of the Mediterranean for centuries. By the end of the 14th century, Corfu fell under Venice's control, and the Italian language and culture—including Roman Catholicism—became predominant.

When Napoleon's forces overcame Venice in 1797, the French took over here and held sway until 1815. The Ionian Islands then became a protectorate of the British; although the islands experienced peace and prosperity, they were in fact a colony. When parts of Greece gained true independence from the Turks by 1830—due in part to leadership from Ionians such as Ioannis Capodistrias—many Ionians became restless under the British. In 1864, British prime minister Gladstone allowed the Ionians to unite with Greece.

During World War II, Italians first occupied these islands, but when the Germans took over, the Ionians, especially Corfu, suffered greatly. Since 1945, the waves of tourists have brought considerable prosperity to the Ionian Islands.

1 Corfu (Kerkira)

32km (20 nautical miles) W of mainland; another 558km (342 miles) NW of Athens

There's Corfu the coast, Corfu the town, and Corfu the island, and they don't necessarily appeal to the same vacationers. Corfu the coast lures travelers who want to escape civilization and head for the water—whether an undeveloped little beach with a simple taverna and rooms to rent, or a spectacular resort. Then there's the more cosmopolitan **Corfu town,** with its distinctive Greek, Italian, French, and British elements. Finally, there's a third and little-known Corfu: the interior, with its lush vegetation and gentle slopes, modest villages and farms, and countless olive and fruit trees. (It should be admitted that there's now a fourth Corfu—rather tacky beach resorts crowded with "package tourists" from western Europe who can be extremely raucous. You will probably want to avoid this Corfu.)

Whichever Corfu you choose, it should prove pleasing. It was, after all, this island's ancient inhabitants, the Phaeacians, who made Odysseus so comfortable. Visitors today will find Corfu similarly hospitable.

ESSENTIALS

GETTING THERE **By Plane** **Olympic Airways** provides at least three flights daily from and to Athens, and three flights weekly from and to Thessaloniki. Round-trip fare for each route is about 220€ ($286). The Olympic Airways office in Corfu town (© **26610/38-694**) is at 11 Polila, down from the Ionian Islands Tourism Office, but many agents all over town sell tickets. **Aegean Airlines** also offers occasional flights; in Athens, call © **210/626-1000;** in Corfu, call © **26610/27-100.**

Corfu airport is about 4km (2½ miles) south of the center of Corfu town. Fortunately, the flight patterns of most planes do not bring them over the city. Everyone

---

⌐*Tips* **Kerkira = Corfu**

Kerkira is the modern Greek name for Corfu. Look for it on many schedules, maps, brochures, and other publications.

takes taxis into town; the standard fare should be 8€ ($10) but may fluctuate with destination, amount of luggage, and time of day.

By Boat   Many lines and ships link Corfu to both Greek and foreign ports. Ferries run almost hourly between Corfu and Igoumenitsou, directly across on the mainland (1–2 hr.), and several go weekly to and from Patras (about 7 hr.). At least during high season, there is now a twice-daily hydrofoil express (about 30 min.) between Corfu and Igoumenitsou. Also in high season are daily ships linking Corfu to ports in Italy—Ancona, Bari, Brindisi, Trieste, Venice—or to Piraeus and/or Patras. The schedules and fares vary so much from year to year that it would be misleading to provide details here; work with a travel agent in your homeland or Greece; or check **www.ferries.gr**. The ship lines are: **Adriatica** (📞 210/429-0487 in Piraeus), **ANEK Lines** (📞 210/323-3481 in Athens), **Fragline** (📞 210/821-4171 in Athens), **Hellenic Mediterranean Line,** or **HML** (📞 210/ 422-5341 in Piraeus), **Minoan Lines** (📞 210/414-5700 in Piraeus), **Strintzis Lines** (📞 210/422-5015 in Piraeus), and **Ventouris Line** (📞 210/988-9280 in Piraeus). In high season, the typical one-way cost from Brindisi or Ancona to Corfu is about 200€ ($260) to 250€ ($325) for two people in a double cabin with a standard-size vehicle.

   Note: If you're coming by yacht from a non-E.U. country, Corfu town is one of Greece's official international entry/exit harbors, with Customs and health authorities as well as passport control.

Tips   **Museum Hours Update**

If you visit Greece during the summer, check to see when sites and museums are open. According to the tourist office, they should be open from 8am to 7:30pm, but some may close earlier in the day or even be closed 1 day a week.

By Bus   KTEL offers service from Athens or Thessaloniki; its ferry carries you between Corfu and Igoumenitsou on the mainland opposite. Buses allow you to get on or off at main points along the way, such as Ioannina. The buses are comfortable enough, but be prepared for many hours of winding roads. The **KTEL office** (© 26610/39-627) is located along Leoforos Avramiou, up from the new port.

VISITOR INFORMATION   **Ionian Islands Tourism Directorate** (© 26610/ 37-520) is on the second floor of a modern, unnumbered building at the corner of Rizospaston and Polila in the new town, a block across from the post office. It's open Monday through Friday from 8:30am to 1pm; in July and August, it's also open on Saturday. The office may have brochures with maps of the town and island. Those with an interest in environmentally responsible tourism can check the website of a British organization, Friends of Ionia (www.foi.org.uk).

GETTING AROUND   **By Bus**   The dark-blue public buses service Corfu town, its suburbs, and nearby destinations. The semiprivate green-and-cream KTEL buses offer frequent service to points all over the island—Paleokastritsa, Glifada, Sidari, and more. The **KTEL office** (© 26610/39-627) is located along Leoforos Avramiou, up from the new port.

By Taxi   In and around Corfu town, a taxi is your best bet—sometimes the only way around, such as to and from the harbor and the airport. Although taxi drivers are supposed to use their meters, many don't, so you should agree on the fare before setting out. You may also decide to use a taxi to visit some of the sites outside Corfu town; again, be sure to agree on the fare beforehand.

By Car   You'll find car rental agencies all over Corfu. Even so, in high season it can be very difficult to get a vehicle at the spur of the moment. If you're sure of your plans on Corfu, make arrangements with an established international agency before departing home. Otherwise, try **Greek Skies Travel Agency,** in Corfu town at 20A Kapodistriou (© 26610/33-410; fax 26610/36-161); or **Avanti Rent A Car,** 12A Ethnikis Antistasseos, along the new port (© 26610/42-028).

By Moped   It's easy to rent mopeds, scooters, and motorcycles, but the roads are so curving, narrow, and steep that you should be very experienced before taking on such a vehicle. And insist on a helmet.

FAST FACTS   The official **American Express** agent for Corfu is Greek Skies Travel Agency, 20A Kapodistriou (© 26610/33-410; fax 26610/36-161). There are numerous **banks** in both the old town and new town; you'll find ATMs at most of them. The **British Consul** is at 1 Menekrates (© 26610/30-055), at the south end of the town, near the Menekrates monument. There is no U.S. consulate in Corfu. The **hospital** is on Julius Andreatti, and is signed from around town.

There are two convenient **Internet cafes:** Online Cafe, 28 Kapodistriou, along the Esplanade (cafe_online1@yahoo.com); and Netoikos, on 14 Kalochairetou, behind

Ayios Spiridon Church. Both are open daily from late morning to late evening. You can count on quick, careful, and fair-priced **laundry** or **dry cleaning** at the Peristeri, 42 Ioannis Theotikos (leading from San Rocco Sq. on the way to the KTEL Bus Terminal). It's open Monday through Saturday from 8am to 2pm, with additional hours on Tuesday, Thursday, and Friday from 6 to 8pm. The **police station** (© 26610/ 39-575) is at 19 Leoforos Alexandros (near the post office). The **post office** (© 26610/25-544) is at 26 Leoforos Alexandros. It's open Monday through Friday from 7:30am to 8pm; in July and August, it's also open for a few hours on Saturday. The main **telephone office (OTE)** is at 9 Mantzarou; it's open Monday through Friday from 7am to midnight, to 10pm on Saturday and holidays.

WHAT TO SEE & DO
THE TOP ATTRACTIONS

Archaeological Museum ⭐ Even if you're not a devotee of ancient history or museums, you should take an hour to visit this small museum. On your way to see its master work, you'll pass a **stone lion** dating from around 575 B.C. (found in the nearby Menekrates tomb, along the waterfront by the museum). Go around and behind it to the large room with arguably the finest example of Archaic temple sculpture extant, the **pediment from the Temple of Artemis.** (The temple itself is located just south of Corfu town and dates from about 590 B.C. The remains do not interest most people.) The pediment features the **Gorgon Medusa,** attended by two panther-like animals. You don't have to be an art historian to note how this predates the great classical works such as the Elgin marbles—not only in the naiveté of its sculpture but also in the emphasis on the monstrous, with the humans so much smaller in scale.

Interesting for comparison is the fragment from another Archaic pediment found at Figare, Corfu. In an adjoining room, it shows Dionysos and a youth reclining on a couch. Only a century younger than the Gorgon pediment, here the humans have reduced the animal in size and placed it under the couch.

1 P. Armeni-Vraila (on the corner of Demokratias, the blvd. along the waterfront). © 26610/30-680. Admission 4€ ($5.20); free on Sun. Tues–Sun 8:30am–2:30pm. Wheelchair accessible.

Kalypso Star _Kids_ This glass-bottomed boat takes small groups offshore and provides fascinating views of marine life and undersea formations.

Old port, Corfu town. © 26610/46-525. kalypso2@otenet.gr. Admission 12€ ($16) adults, 6€ ($7.80) children. In high season, trips leave daily on the hour 10am–6pm, plus they make a 10pm night trip. Call for the off-season schedule.

Museum of Asian Art The building itself, an impressive example of neoclassical architecture, was constructed between 1819 and 1824 for several reasons: to serve as the residence of the Lord High Commissioner, the British ruler of the Ionian Islands; to house the headquarters of the Order of St. Michael and St. George; and to provide the assembly room for the Ionian senate. When the British turned the Ionian Islands over to Greece, they gave this building to the king of Greece. As the king seldom spent much time here, it fell into disrepair until after World War II, when it was restored and turned into a museum.

The centerpiece of the museum is the collection of Chinese porcelains, bronzes, and other works from the Shang Dynasty (1500 B.C.) to the Ching Dynasty (19th c.). Go, too, to see the impressive Japanese works: woodblock prints, ceramics, sculpture, watercolors, and _netsuke_ (carved sash fasteners). You may not have come to Greece to appreciate Asian art, but this is one of Corfu's several unexpected delights.

The Palace of St. Michael and St. George, north end of Esplanade. ☎ **26610/38-124.** protocol@hepka.culture.gr. Admission 4€ ($5.20). Tues–Sun 8am–2:30pm.

Old Fort (Paleo Frourio)

Originally a promontory attached to the mainland, now separated by a moat, this area is known for its two peaks, *koryphi* in Greek, which gave the town and the island their modern names. A castle crowns each peak; you can get fine views of Albania to the east and Corfu, town and island, to the west. The promontory itself was for a long time the main town, and it appears as such in many old engravings. The Venetians dug the moat in the 16th century; it successfully held off several attempts by the Turks to conquer this outpost of Christianity. What looks like a Greek temple at the south side is in fact a British church (ca. 1830).

In summer, a **Sound-and-Light** show is held several nights a week (in different foreign languages, so be sure to check the schedule).

The Esplanade (opposite the Liston). Admission 4€ ($5.20) adults, 2€ ($2.60) students and seniors over 60. Tues–Fri 8am–8pm; Sat–Sun and holidays 8:30am–3pm.

Petrakis Line

During high season, this line offers several 1-day excursions a week to destinations including Albania, Kefalonia, and Paxoi. On Kefalonia, you visit Melissani Grotto and Drogarati Cave (see below) but not Argostoli. The excursion to Albania is becoming popular even though it doesn't visit the capital; the fare for a day trip to Albania now costs about 30€ ($39), and there are several other fees for visas, meals, and such.

9 Venizelou, new port, Corfu town. ☎ **26610/31-649.** Fax 26610/38-787. petrakis@hol.gr.

A STROLL AROUND CORFU TOWN

This is definitely a browser's town, where as you're strolling in search of a snack or souvenir, you may serendipitously discover an old church or monument. To orient yourself, start with the **Esplanade area** bounded by the Old Fort (see above) and the sea on one side. The small haven below and to the north of the Old Fort is known as **Mandraki Harbor,** while the shore to the south is home port to the **Corfu Yacht Club.**

Dousmani bisects the Esplanade; at the far side is the circular monument that honors the union of the Ionian Islands with Greece. You might catch a cricket game at the **Plateia,** the northern part of the field. At the far north side of the Esplanade, the Palace of St. Michael and St. George is the home of the **Museum of Asian Art** (see above). If you proceed along the northwest corner of the palace, you'll come out above the coast and can make your way around Arseniou above the *mourayia* (medieval sea walls).

On your way you will pass (on the left, up a flight of stairs) the **Byzantine Museum** in the **Church of Antivouniotissa.** Even if you're not a particular fan of Byzantine art, you should enjoy the small but elegant selection of icons from around Corfu; of particular interest are works by Cretan artists who came to Corfu, some of whom went on to Venice. The museum is open Monday from 12:30 to 7pm, Tuesday through Saturday from 8am to 7pm, and Sunday and holidays from 8:30am to 3pm. Admission is 3€ ($3.90).

Proceed along the coast road and descend to the square at the old port. Above its far side rises the **New Fortress,** and beyond this is the new port. Off to the left of the square is a large gateway, what remains of the 16th-century Porta Spilia. Go through it to get to the Plateia Solomou.

If you go left from Plateia Solomou along Velissariou, look on the right for the green doors of the 300-year-old **synagogue,** with its collection of torah crowns. It's open on Saturday from 9am until early evening. To gain entry during the week, call the Jewish Community Center at ☎ **26610/38-802.**

Continue on to the part of Old Corfu known as **Campiello,** with its stepped streets and narrow alleys. You may feel as if you are in a labyrinth—and you will be—but sooner or later you'll emerge onto one or another busy commercial street that will bring you down to the Esplanade.

Heading south on the Esplanade, you'll see a bandstand and at its far end the **Maitland Rotunda,** which honors Sir Thomas Maitland, the first British lord high commissioner of the Ionian Islands. Past this is the statue of Count Ioannis Kapodistrias (1776–1836), the first president of independent Greece.

Head south along the shore road from this end of the Esplanade, and you'll pass the Corfu Palace Hotel (see below) on your right; then the **Archaeological Museum** (see above), up Vraila on the right. After 2 more blocks, off to the right on the corner of Marasli, you'll see the **Tomb of Menekrates,** a circular tomb of a notable who drowned about 600 B.C. Proceeding to the right here onto Leoforos Alexandros will bring you into the heart of new Corfu town.

Back at the Esplanade, the western side of the north half is lined by a wide tree-shaded strip filled with cafe tables and chairs, then a street reserved for pedestrians, and then arcaded buildings patterned after Paris's Rue de Rivoli. Begun by the French and finished by the British, these arcaded buildings, known as the **Liston,** provide a great backdrop for a cup of coffee or a glass of ginger beer.

At the back of the Liston is **Kapodistriou,** and perpendicular from this extend several streets that lead into the heart of Old Corfu—a mélange of fine shops, old churches, souvenir stands, and other stores in a maze of streets, alleys, and squares that seem like Venice without the water. The broadest and most stylish is **Nikiforio Theotoki.** At the northern end of Kapodistriou, turn left onto Ayios Spiridon and come to the corner of Filellinon and the **Ayios Spiridon Cathedral,** dedicated to Spiridon, the patron saint of Corfu. Locals credit Spiridon, a 4th-century bishop of Cyprus, with saving Corfu from famine, plagues, and a Turkish siege. Inside the church are the saint's embalmed body in a silver casket, as well as precious gold and silver votive offerings and many fine old icons. Four times a year the faithful parade the remains of St. Spiridon through the streets of old Corfu: Palm Sunday, Holy Saturday, August 1, and the first Sunday in November.

Proceeding up Voulgareos behind the southern end of the Liston, you'll come to the back of the **town hall,** built in 1663 as a Venetian loggia; it later served as a theater. Turn into the square it faces and enter what seems like a Roman piazza, with steps and terraces, the Roman Catholic cathedral on the left and, reigning over the top, the restored Catholic archbishop's residence (now the Bank of Greece).

From here, finish your walk by wandering up and down and in and out the various streets of Old Corfu.

SHOPPING

Corfu town has so many shops selling jewelry, leather goods, olive wood objects, and handmade needlework that it is impossible to single out one or another. If you're looking for needlework, the stores along Filarmonikis (off N. Teotoki) may have something that pleases you; prices are generally fair and uniform.

We would never recommend a trip to Corfu *just* for the kumquat liqueur, but this Chinese fruit has been cultivated on the island since the late 1800s and the liqueur makes a unique treat—or gift if it doesn't appeal to you!

Standing out from the many standard souvenir-gift shops, **Antica,** 25 Ayios Spiridon, leading away from the north end of Liston (© **26610/32-401**), offers unusual older jewelry, plates, textiles, brass, and icons. **Gravures,** 64 Ev. Voulgareos, where the street emerges from the old town to join the new town (℃ **26610/41-721**), has a fine selection of engravings and prints of scenes from Corfu, all nicely matted. Originals (taken from old books or magazines) can cost 150€ ($195), reproductions as little as 10€ ($13). The elegant **Terracotta,** 2 Filarmonikis, just off N. Theotoki, the main shopping street (℃/fax **26610/45-260**), sells only contemporary Greek work: jewelry, one-of-a-kind pieces, ceramics, and small sculptures, some by well-known Greek artists and artisans. Nothing is cheap, but everything is classy.

No dearth of ceramics can be found in Corfu, but we like the **Pottery Workshop,** 15km (10 miles) north of Corfu on the right of the road to Paleokastritsa (℃ **26610/ 90-704**), where you get to observe Sofoklis Ikonomides and Sissy Moskidou making and decorating all the pottery on sale here. Whether decorative or functional, something will certainly appeal to your taste. Two kilometers (1¼ miles) farther along the road, on the left, is the **Wood's Nest,** offering a large selection of olive wood objects just slightly cheaper than in town.

WHERE TO STAY

The island of Corfu has an apparently inexhaustible choice of accommodations, but in high season (July and Aug), package groups from Europe will book many rooms. Reservations are recommended if you have specific preferences for that time, especially for Corfu town.

IN TOWN
Very Expensive
Corfu Palace Hotel ★★   This grand hotel combines the most up-to-date features of a Swiss enterprise (which it is) with Greek hospitality: Every comfort goes hand in hand with modern business and conference conveniences, fine service, and elegant decor. The landscaping feels tropical; the lobby and public areas bespeak luxury. The very comfortable guest rooms, while not exceptionally large, are well appointed; the marbled bathrooms are large. Every balconied room enjoys views of the sea. In addition to its splendid surroundings, superb service, and grand meals, the hotel provides restful isolation above the bay even though it is near the city center. The hotel's two restaurants, the Scheria (a grill room on the poolside terrace) and the Panorama (with a view of the bay), serve Greek and international menus; both vie to claim the finest cuisine on Corfu. Guests can use the facilities of the nearby Corfu Tennis Club and Yacht Club and the Corfu Golf Club, 14km (9 miles) away.

2 Leoforos Demokratias, 49100 Corfu. ℃ **26610/39-485** to -487. Fax 26610/31-749. www.corfupalace.com. 115 units. High season 225€–325€ ($293–$423) double; low season 150€–225€ ($195–$293) double. Children up to age 12 stay free in parent's room (without meals). Rates include buffet breakfast; half-board available. AE, DC, MC, V. Free parking. A 5-min. walk from Esplanade. Along Garitsa Bay, just south of center. **Amenities:** 2 restaurants; 3 bars; 3 pools (1 for children); night-lit tennis courts nearby; bicycle rentals; game room; concierge; tours and car rentals arranged; conference facilities; salon; 24-hr. room service; babysitting; laundry service; dry cleaning; newspaper delivery. *In room:* A/C, TV, minibar, hair dryer, safe.

Moderate
If you prefer old-fashioned period hotels to shiny new accommodations, consider **Astron Hotel,** 15 Donzelot (waterfront road down to old harbor), 49100 Corfu (℃ **26610/39-505**). Renovated in 2001, it offers up-to-date bathrooms and other facilities while retaining touches of its original charm.

Arcadion Hotel ⭐   This hotel's total renovation—in fact, more like a total reconstruction—completed in late 2000, makes it as pleasurable as it is convenient. The new rooms have furniture and fabrics in a traditional Corfiot style; bathrooms are up to the highest standards for this class. If you like to be at the center of a city, you can't get much closer than this: When you step out the door, the Esplanade and the Liston are 15m (50 ft.) away and the beach is just a little farther. Admittedly, this also means that on pleasant evenings there will be crowds in front of the hotel, but ask for a room off the front. (All windows are double-glazed for sound control.) Hard to beat for location and comfort. In the evening, you can sit on the new roof garden and enjoy a cool drink with a fabulous view.

44 Kapodistriou, 49100 Corfu. ✆ **26610/30-104.** Fax 26610/45-087. 33 units. High season 140€ ($182) double; low season 80€ ($104) double. Rates include buffet breakfast. AE, MC, V. Public parking lot (fee) nearby. Diagonally across from south end of Liston, facing the Esplanade. **Amenities:** Restaurant; bar; health club; concierge; tours and car rentals arranged; salon; 24-hr. room service; laundry service; dry cleaning. *In room:* A/C, TV, dataport, minibar, hair dryer, safe.

Bella Venezia *Value*   Like the gold-medal winner of the decathlon, this hotel may not win in any single category, but its combined virtues make it the first choice of many. The building is a restored neoclassical mansion, with character if not major distinction. The location is just a bit off center and lacks fine views, but it's quiet and close enough to any place you'd want to walk to; a decent beach is 274m (900 ft.) away. The common areas are not especially stylish but they do have atmosphere. Although not luxurious or large, the guest rooms have some old-world touches; the showers, however, are undeniably cramped. There is no restaurant, but there's a colorful patio-garden for breakfast and an enclosed kiosk for light snacks. Finally, the hotel's rates are below those of similar hotels.

4 N. Zambeli (approached from far south end of Esplanade), 49100 Corfu. ✆ **26610/46-500.** Fax 26610/20-708. belvenht@hol.gr. 32 units. High season 125€ ($163) double; low season 85€ ($111) double. Rates include buffet breakfast. AE, DC, MC, V. Parking on adjacent streets. Within walking distance of old and new towns. *In room:* A/C, TV.

Cavalieri ⭐   If you like your hotels in the discreet old European style, this place is for you. For glitz, look elsewhere. The Cavalieri is in an old building with a small elevator. The main lounge is Italian velvet. Service is low-key, rooms are spare, and bathrooms standard. The restaurant is nothing special. However, because of the hotel's appealing location, advance reservations are required. Ask for one of the front rooms on the upper floors, which boast great views of the Old Fort. Another draw is the rooftop garden, which after 6:30pm offers drinks, sweets, and light meals along with a spectacular view. Even if you don't stay here, it's a grand place to pass an hour in the evening.

4 Kapodistriou, 49100 Corfu. ✆ **26610/39-041.** Fax 26610/39-283. 50 units. High season 190€ ($247) double; low season 100€ ($130) double. Rates include buffet breakfast. AE, DC, MC, V. Parking on adjacent streets. Within easy walking distance of old and new towns. At far south end of Esplanade. **Amenities:** Bar; concierge; tours and car rentals arranged; room service 7am–midnight; laundry service; dry cleaning. *In room:* A/C, TV, minibar, hair dryer.

OUTSIDE TOWN
Expensive
Corfu Holiday Palace ⭐   Formerly the Hilton, this is a grand hotel in the contemporary manner—more like a resort if you consider the range of its facilities. Its lobby sets the tone—spacious and relaxed. The staff is professional yet friendly. Guest rooms are standard Greek-hotel-size, with comfortable beds and state-of-the-art bathrooms. The grounds create a semitropical ambience. In addition to the pools, a lovely private beach below beckons. Kanoni, an island landmark, is nearby. The island's airport is off

in the middle distance—not a major problem unless your windows are open, but we suggest you ask for a room facing the sea and not the airport. Patrons get a 50% discount at Corfu Golf Club (18km/12 miles away). Perhaps the biggest surprise of all: a casino on the premises.

P.O. Box 124, Nausicaa, Kanoni, 49100 Corfu. (✆ **26610/36-540.** Fax 26610/36-551. 266 units. High season 140€–210€ ($182–$273) double; low season 105€–130€ ($137–$169) double. Rates include buffet breakfast. Half-board includes a fixed-price menu. Special packages available for extended stays. AE, DC, MC, V. Free parking on grounds. Hotel offers a shuttle bus; public bus no. 2 stops 200m (656 ft.) away; and taxi is easily summoned. About 5km (3 miles) south of Corfu town. **Amenities:** 2 restaurants; 2 bars; 2 pools; lit tennis courts; health club; watersports equipment; concierge; tours and car rentals arranged; conference facilities; boutiques; salon; babysitting; laundry service; dry cleaning; bowling, billiards, and table tennis; jogging track. *In room:* A/C, TV, minibar, hair dryer.

Inexpensive
Hotel Royal *(Value)* This might be considered an alternative to the nearby Corfu Holiday Palace if your desire is to stay outside Corfu town but you can't afford the Palace. It's a kind of funky place: The architecture is neo-baroque, the interior decor is folksy, and the lobby is filled with traditional works of art. Guest rooms and bathrooms are standard but do not have air-conditioning or TVs. The most spectacular features are the three tiered pools, making this a great place (in high season only) to bring the kids back to after sightseeing. As with the more expensive Palace, the airport is off in the middle distance, but the noise problem exists only during a relatively short part of the day. You can't beat the rates at this big hotel with a family atmosphere.

110 Figareto, Kanoni, 49100 Corfu. (✆ **26610/37-512.** Fax 26610/38-786. 125 units. High season 80€ ($104) double; low season 55€ ($72) double. Rates include continental breakfast. No credit cards. Closed Nov–Mar. Parking on grounds. Public bus no. 2 stops 100m (328 ft.) away, but a taxi may be easier. 3km (2 miles) from Corfu center, a few hundred yd. from Corfu Holiday Palace. **Amenities:** 3 pools; concierge; tours and car rentals arranged.

WHERE TO DINE
IN TOWN
Expensive
If you're in a celebratory mood, you might consider **Chambor,** 71 Guilford (✆ **26610/ 39-031**). It's certainly a cut above your average Greek restaurant, but much of what you pay for are the elaborate settings and presentation.

Venetian Well ✦ MIDDLE EASTERN/INTERNATIONAL/GREEK This remains our top pick in Corfu town. Diners sit at a candlelit table in a rather austere little square with a Venetian wellhead (ca. 1699) and a church opposite. When the weather changes, guests sit in a stately room adorned with a mural. The atmosphere is as discreet as the food is inventive. There is no printed menu—you learn what's available from a chalkboard or from your waiter—and there's no predicting what the kitchen will offer on any given evening. Since the chef uses seasonal vegetables, salads vary from month to month. Main courses may range from standard Greek dishes such as beef *giouvetsi* (cooked in a pot) to chicken prepared with exotic ingredients. The wine list is more extensive than in most Greek restaurants.

Plateia Kremasti. (✆ **26610/44-761.** Reservations recommended in high season. Main courses 10€–22€ ($13–$27). No credit cards. Mon–Sat noon–midnight. On small sq. up from old harbor, behind Greek Orthodox cathedral.

Moderate
If you want to dine along the coast, consider **Antranik,** 19 Arseniou (✆ **26610/ 22-301**), located under the awnings on the sea side of the road leading from north of the Esplanade down to the new port. **Faliraki,** at the corner of Kapodistrias and Arseniou,

below the wall ((C) **26610/30-392**), also has a wonderful location right on the water, although the food is standard Greek fare.

Aegli Garden Restaurant GREEK/CONTINENTAL   The tasty and varied menu of this old favorite attracts both residents and travelers to its several dining areas—indoors, in the arcade, under awnings across from the arcade, or along the pedestrian mall of Kapodistriou. Try the selection of *orektika* with the wine or beer on tap. The staff takes special pride in their Corfiote specialties, several of which are traditional Greek foods with rather spicy sauces: filet of fish, octopus, *pastitsada* (baked veal), *baccala* (salted cod fish), and *sofrito* (veal). If spiciness isn't your thing, try the swordfish or prawns. Everything is done with great care, including a delicious fresh-fruit salad that you can order by itself.

23 Kapodistriou. (C) **26610/31-949**. Fax 26610/45-488. Main courses 6€–15€ ($7.80–$20). AE, DC, MC, V. Daily 9am–1am. In Liston.

Bellissimo GREEK/INTERNTIONAL   This restaurant has lived up to its promise of being a welcome addition to the Corfu scene—unpretentious but serving tasty food. Located on a central and lovely town square, it's run by the hospitable Stergiou family, Corfiots who returned from Canada. They offer a standard Greek menu with some "exotics," including hamburgers and chicken curry. Especially welcome is their modestly priced "Greek sampling plate"—tzatziki, tomatoes-and-cucumber salad, *keftedes* (meatballs), fried potatoes, grilled lamb, and pork souvlaki.

Plateia Lemonia. (C) **26610/41-112**. Main courses 4€–14€ ($5.20–$18). No credit cards. Daily 10:30am–11pm. Just off N. Theotoki.

CORFU TOWN AFTER DARK

Corfu town definitely has a nightlife scene, though many people are content to linger over dinner and then, after a promenade, repair to one of the cafes at the Liston, such as the **Capri, Liston, Europa,** or **Aegli**—all of which have similar selections of light refreshments and drinks. (Treat yourself to the fresh fruit salad at the Aegli!) Others are drawn to the cafes at the north end of the Esplanade, just outside the Liston— **Cafe Bar 92, Magnet,** or **Cool Down.** For a special treat, ascend to the rooftop cafe/bar at **Cavalieri** hotel (see "Where to Stay," above). Another choice is **Lindos Cafe,** overlooking the beach and facilities of the Nautical Club of Corfu. It's approached by steps leading off Leoforos Demokratias, just south and outside the Esplanade. And one of the best-kept secrets of Corfu town is the little **Art Cafe,** to the right and behind the Museum of Asian Art; its garden provides a wonderful, cool, quiet retreat from the hustle and bustle of the rest of the town.

If you enjoy a bit more action, there are several nightspots along the coast to the north, between Corfu town and the beach resort of Gouvia. They include **Ekati,** a typical Greek nightclub; **Esperides,** featuring Greek music; and **Corfu by Night,** definitely touristy. Be prepared to drop money at these places.

The youngest night crawlers find places that go in and out of favor (and business) from year to year. Among the more enduring up around the Esplanade are the relatively sedate **Aktaion,** just to the right of the Old Fort; and **Café Classico,** in an old mansion at 10 Kapodistriou, featuring the latest music. Young people seeking more excitement go down past the new port to a strip of flashy discos—**Apokalypsis, Hippodrome,** and **DNA.** Be aware that these clubs charge a cover (about 10€/$13, including one drink).

In summer, frequent **concerts** by orchestras and bands are held on the Esplanade; most of them are free. Corfu town boasts the oldest band in Greece. The **Sound-and-Light** performances are described in the listing for the Old Fort (see "What to See & Do," earlier in this chapter). September brings **Corfu Festival,** with concerts, ballet, opera, and theater performances by a mix of Greek and international companies. **Carnival** is celebrated on the last Sunday before Lent with a parade and the burning of an effigy representing the spirit of Carnival.

For those who like to gamble, the **casino** at the **Corfu Holiday Palace** (see "Where to Stay," above) is a few miles outside of town. Bets are 5€ ($6.50) minimum and 750€ ($975) maximum. Open nightly, it may not have the glamour of Monte Carlo, but it attracts an international set during the high season.

SIDE TRIPS FROM CORFU TOWN
KANONI, PONDIKONISI & ACHILLEION

Although these sites and destinations are not next door to one another and have little in common, they are grouped here because they all lie south of Corfu town and can easily be visited in half a day's outing. Everyone who comes to Corfu town will want to visit these places, even if you go nowhere else on the island. History buffs will revel in the sites' many associations, and even beach people cannot help but be moved by their scenic charms.

Kanoni is approached south of Corfu town via the village Analepsis; it's well signed. Ascending most of the way, you arrive after about 4km (2½ miles) at the circular terrace (on the right). The area is known as Kanoni (after the cannon once sited here). Make your way to the edge and enjoy a wonderful view. Directly below in the inlet are two islets. If you want to visit one or both, you can take a 10-minute walk down a not-that-difficult path from Kanoni; with a vehicle you must retrace the road back from Kanoni a few hundred yards to a signed turnoff (on the left coming back).

One islet is linked to the land by a causeway; here you'll find the **Monastery of Vlakherna.** To get to the other islet, **Pondikonisi (Mouse Island),** you must go by small boat, which is always available (2€/$2.60). Legend has it that this rocky islet is a Phaeacian ship that turned to stone after taking Odysseus back to Ithaka. The chapel here dates from the 13th century, and its setting among the cypress trees makes it most picturesque. Many Corfiotes make a pilgrimage here in small boats on August 6. It's also the inspiration for the Swiss painter Arnold Boecklin's well-known work *Isle of the Dead,* which in turn inspired Rachmaninoff's music of the same name.

A causeway across the little inlet to Perama on the main body of the island (the Kanoni road is on a peninsula) is for pedestrians only. So to continue on to your next destination, a villa known as **Achilleion,** you must drive back to the edge of Corfu town and then take another road about 8km (5 miles) to the south, signed to Gastouri and the villa of Achilleion. The villa is open daily from 9am to 4pm. Admission is 4€ ($5.20). Bus no. 10, from Plateia San Rocco, runs directly to the Achilleion several times daily.

Empress Elizabeth of Austria built this villa between 1890 and 1891. Her beloved son Rudolf and his lover died mysteriously (most likely a double suicide) at Mayerling in 1889. The empress identified him with Achilles, and so the villa is really a memorial to

---

Taking a Dive

All of the bays and coves that make up Paleokastritsa boast clear, sparkling turquoise waters. **Korfu Diving** offers weeklong courses for beginners, as well as day excursions for advanced divers. Call or fax ℂ/fax **26630/41-604** for details.

Rudolf—thus the many statues and motifs associated with Achilles (including the dolphins, for Achilles's mother was the water nymph Thetis). Approaching the villa from the entrance gate, you will see a slightly Teutonic version of a neoclassical summer palace. Take a walk through at least some of the eclectic rooms. Among the curiosities is the small saddle-seat on which Kaiser Wilhelm II of Germany sat while performing his imperial chores. (He bought the villa in 1907, after Elizabeth was assassinated in 1898.)

The terraced gardens that surround the villa are now lush and tropical. Be sure to go all the way around and out to the back terraces. Here you will see the most famous of the statues Elizabeth commissioned, *The Dying Achilles,* by the German sculptor Herter; also, you cannot miss the 4.5m-tall (15-ft.) Achilles that the Kaiser had inscribed, TO THE GREATEST GREEK FROM THE GREATEST GERMAN, a sentiment removed after World War II. But for a truly impressive sight, step to the edge of the terrace and enjoy a spectacular view of Corfu town and much of the eastern coast to the south.

If you have your own car, you can continue on past the Achilleion and descend to the coast between **Benitses** and **Perama;** the first, to the south, has become a popular beach resort. Proceeding north along the coast from Benitses, you come to Perama (another popular beach resort), where a turnoff onto a promontory brings you to the pedestrian causeway opposite Pondikonisi (see above). The main road brings you back to the edge of Corfu town.

PALEOKASTRITSA

If you can make only one excursion on the island, this is certainly a top competitor with Kanoni and the Achilleion. Go to those places for their fascinating histories, to Paleokastritsa for its natural beauty.

The drive here is northwest out of Corfu town via well-marked roads. Follow the coast for about 8km (5½ miles) to Gouvia, then turn inland. (It is on this next stretch that you pass the **Pottery Workshop** and the **Wood's Nest;** see "Shopping," earlier in this chapter.) The road eventually narrows but is asphalt all the way as you gradually descend to the west coast and **Paleokastritsa** (25km/16 miles). There's no missing it: It's been taken over by hotels and restaurants, although some of the bays and coves that make up Paleokastritsa are less developed than others. Tradition claims it as the site of **Scheria,** the capital of the Phaeacians—so one of these beaches should be where Nausicaa found Odysseus, though no remains have been found to substantiate this.

Continue on past the beaches to climb a narrow, winding road to the **Monastery of the Panagia** at the edge of a promontory. (The monastery is about a mile from the beach, and many prefer to go by foot, as parking is next to impossible once you get there.) Although founded in the 13th century, the monastery has no remains that old. It's worth a brief visit, especially at sunset. The monastery's hours are April through October, daily from 7am to 1pm and 3 to 8pm.

More interesting in some ways, and certainly more challenging, is a visit to the **Angelokastro,** the medieval castle that sits high on a pinnacle overlooking all of Paleokastritsa. Only the most hardy will choose to walk all the way up from the shore, a taxing hour at least. The rest of us will drive back out of Paleokastritsa (2.5km/1½ miles) to a turnoff to the left, signed LAKONES. There commences an endless winding ascent that eventually levels out and provides spectacular views of the coast as the road passes through the villages of Lakones and Krini. (*A word of warning:* Don't attempt to drive this road unless you are comfortable pulling over to the very edge of narrow roads—with sheer drops—to let trucks and buses by, something you will have to do on your way down.) Keep going until the road takes a sharp turn to the right and down, and you'll come to a little parking area. From here, walk up to the castle, only 200m (656 ft.) away but seemingly farther because of the trail's poor condition. What you are rewarded with, though, is one of the most spectacularly sited medieval castles you'll ever visit, some 300m (1,000 ft.) above sea level.

If you've come this far, reward yourself with a meal and the spectacular view at one of the restaurants or cafes on the road outside Lakones: **Bella Vista, Colombo,** or **Casteltron.** At mealtimes in high season, these places are taken over by busloads of tour groups. If you have your own transport, try to eat a bit earlier or later.

On your way back to Corfu town from Paleokastritsa, you can vary your route by heading south through **Ropa Valley,** the agricultural heartland of Corfu. Follow the signs indicating Liapades and Tembloni, but don't bother going into either of these towns. If you have time for a beach stop, consider going over to **Ermones Beach** (the island's only golf club is located above it) or **Glifada Beach.**

WHERE TO STAY & DINE If you want to spend some time at Paleokastritsa, it's good to get away from the main beach. We like the 70-unit **Hotel Odysseus** (© 26630/41-209), high above the largely undeveloped cove before the main beach. A double in high season goes for 65€ ($85); in low season, the rate is 50€ ($65) double. Rates include buffet breakfast, the hotel has a pool. The Odysseus is open May to mid-October. Guests have also recommended its restaurant.

On its own peninsula and both fancier and pricier is the 127-unit **Akrotiri Beach Hotel** (© 26630/41-237), where an air-conditioned double in high season goes for 130€ ($169), in low season 100€ ($130), including buffet breakfast. All rooms have balconies and sea views. In addition to the adjacent natural beaches, it has two pools. It's open May through October.

The restaurants on the main beach in Paleokastritsa strike us as over-touristy. However, if you like to eat where the action is, the best value and most fun at the main beach can be had at the **Apollon Restaurant** in Hotel Apollon-Ermis (© 26630/41-211). Main courses are 5€ to 14€ ($6.50–$18). The Apollon is open mid-April to late October, daily from 11am to 3pm and 7 to 11pm.

We prefer someplace a bit removed, such as **Belvedere Restaurant** (© 26630/41-583), just below Hotel Odysseus, which serves solid Greek dishes at reasonable prices. Main courses range from 4€ to 13€ ($5.20–$17). The restaurant is open mid-April to late October from 9am to midnight.

2 Kefalonia (Cephalonia)

Don't come to Kefalonia for glamour. Come to spend time in a relaxing environment, to enjoy handsome vistas and a lovely countryside. This is a Greek island the way they used to be; it pretty much goes its own way while you travel around and through it. It does have its natural wonders, a few historical buildings and archaeological sites, and many fine beaches. Kefalonia also has a full-service tourist industry, with fine hotels, restaurants, travel agencies, car rental agencies—the whole show. Since Kefalonia was virtually demolished by the earthquake of 1953, most structures on this island are fairly new. It has long been one of the more prosperous and cosmopolitan parts of Greece, thanks to its islanders' tradition of sailing and trading in the world at large. The filming of the 2001 movie *Captain Corelli's Mandolin* also gave a temporary boost to tourism here.

ESSENTIALS

GETTING THERE By Plane From Athens, there are at least three flights daily on **Olympic Airways** (with some flights via Zakinthos). The Argostoli office is at 1 Rokkou Vergoti, the street between the harbor and the square of the Archaeological Museum (*©* **26710/28-808**). **Kefalonia airport** is 8km (5 miles) outside Argostoli. As there is no public bus, everyone goes to Argostoli by taxi, which costs about 10€ ($13).

By Boat As with most Greek islands, it's easier to get to Kefalonia in summer than in the off season, when weather and reduced tourism eliminate the smaller boats. Ferries to Cephalonia are operated by the **Strintzis Line** (*©* **210/823-6011** in Athens; strintzis-ferries@ferries.gr); if you haven't made arrangements with a travel agent, you can buy tickets dockside. Throughout the year, a car-passenger ferry leaves daily from Patras to Sami (about 2½ hr.) There is also at least one car-passenger ferry daily (1½ hr.) from Killini (on the northwest tip of the Peloponnese) to Argostoli and Poros (on the southeastern coast of Kefalonia).

Beyond these more or less dependable services, during the high-season months of July and August there are alternatives—ships to and from Corfu, Ithaka, Levkas, Brindisi (Italy), or other ports—but they do not necessarily hold to the same schedules every year.

VISITOR INFORMATION Argostoli Tourism Office in Argostoli is at the Port Authority Building on Ioannis Metaxa along the harbor (*©* **26710/22-248**). It's open in high season daily from 7:30am to 2:30pm and 5 to 10pm; in low season, Monday through Friday from 8am to 3pm.

GETTING AROUND **By Bus** You can get to almost any point on Kefalonia—even remote beaches, villages, and monasteries—by **KTEL bus** (© **26710/22-276** in Argostoli). Schedules, however, are restrictive and may cut deeply into your preferred arrival at any given destination. KTEL also operates special tours to major destinations around the island. The **KTEL station** is on Leoforos A. Tritsi, at the far end of the harbor road, 200m (656 ft.) past Trapano Bridge.

By Taxi If you don't enjoy driving on twisting mountain roads, taxis are the best alternative. In Argostoli, go up to Vallianou (Central) Square and work out an acceptable fare. A trip to Fiskardo, with the driver waiting a couple of hours, might run to 140€ ($182)—with several passengers splitting the fare, this isn't unreasonable. Everyone uses taxis on Kefalonia. Although drivers are supposed to use their meters, many don't; agree on the fare before you set off.

By Car There are literally dozens of car rental firms, from the well-known international companies to hole-in-the-wall outfits. In Argostoli, we found **Auto Europe,** 3 Lassis (© **26710/24-078**); and **Euro Dollar,** 3A R. Vergoti (© **26710/23-613**), to be reliable. In high season, rental cars are scarce, so don't expect to haggle. A compact will come to at least 60€ ($78) per day (gas extra); better rates are usually offered for rentals of 3 or more days.

By Moped & Motorcycle The roads on Kefalonia are asphalt and in decent condition but are often narrow, lack shoulders, and twist around mountain ravines or wind along the edges of sheer drops to the sea. That said, many travelers choose to get around Kefalonia this way. Every city and town has places that will rent two-seater mopeds and motorcycles for about 20€ to 30€ ($26–$39) per day.

FAST FACTS There are several **banks** with ATMs in the center of Argostoli. The **hospital** (© **26710/22-434**) is on Souidias (the upper road, above the Trapano Bridge). **Internet access** is available at Excelixis Computers, 3 Minoos (© **26710/25-530;** xlixis@otenet.gr). **Express Laundry,** 46B Lassi, the upper road that leads to the airport, is open Monday through Saturday from 9:30am to 9pm. A load costs 3€ ($3.90). Argostoli's **tourist police** (© **26710/22-200**) are on Ioannis Metaxa, on the waterfront across from the port authority. The **post office** is in Argostoli on Lithostrato, opposite no. 18 (© **26710/22-124**); its hours are Monday through Saturday from 7:30am to 2pm. The main **telephone office (OTE)** is at 8 G. Vergoti. It's open daily, April through September from 7am to midnight, and October through March from 7am to 10pm.

WHAT TO SEE & DO

Staying in Kefalonia's capital and largest city, **Argostoli,** allows you to go off on daily excursions to beaches and mountains yet return to the comforts of a city. It has the island's most diverse offering of hotels and restaurants, and it feels urban. For those who find that Argostoli doesn't offer enough in the way of old-world charm or diversions, we point out some of the other "getaway" possibilities on Kefalonia.

Argostoli's appeal does not depend on any archaeological, historical, architectural, or artistic particulars. It's a city for observers—travelers who are content strolling or sitting and observing the passing scene: ships coming and going along the waterfront, locals shopping in the market, children playing in the squares. Head to **Vallianou**

(Central) Square or the waterfront to find a cafe where you can nurse a coffee or ice cream. **Premier Cafe** on the former and **Hotel Olga** on the latter are as nice as any.

If you do nothing else, walk along the waterfront and check out **Trapano Bridge,** a shortcut from Argostoli (which is actually on its own little peninsula) to the main part of the island.

The best nearby **beaches** are just south of the city in **Lassi,** which now has numerous hotels, pensions, cafes, and restaurants much loved by package groups.

Historical and Folklore Museum of the Corgialenos Library ★

We recommend this museum over the nearby, rather dry archaeological museum. Many so-called folklore museums, little more than typical rooms, have sprung up in Greece in recent years, but this is one of the most authentic and satisfying. Meticulously maintained and well-labeled displays showcase traditional clothing, tools, handicrafts, and objects used in daily life across the centuries. Somewhat unexpected are the displays revealing a stylish upper-middle-class life. Most engaging is a large collection of photographs of pre- and post-1953 earthquake Kefalonia. The gift shop has an especially fine selection of items, including handmade lace.

Ilia Zervou. ✆ **26710/28-835.** Admission 3€ ($3.90). Apr–Oct, Mon–Sat 9am–2pm; off season by arrangement. 2 blocks up the hill behind public theater and Archaeological Museum sq.

SHOPPING

Interesting ceramics are for sale at **Hephaestus,** on the waterfront at 21 May; **Alexander's,** on the corner of Plateia Museio (the square 1 block back from the waterfront); and **The Mistral,** 6 Vironis, up the hill opposite the post office, offering the work of the potter/owner.

For a taste of the local cuisine, consider Kefalonia's prized Golden Honey, tart quince preserve, or almond pralines. Another possibility is a bottle of one of Kefalonia's highly praised wines. You can visit **Calliga Vineyard** (selling white Robola and red Calliga Cava) or **Gentilini Vineyard** (with more expensive wines), both near Argostoli; or **Metaxas Wine Estate,** south of Argostoli. The tourist office (see "Visitor Information," above) on the waterfront will tell you how to arrange a tour.

WHERE TO STAY

Accommodations on Kefalonia range from luxury hotels to basic rooms. During peak times, we recommend reservations. **Filoxenos Travel** (✆ **26710/23-055;** info@ filoxenostravel.gr) can help.

EXPENSIVE

White Rocks Hotel & Bungalows ★　This low-key place is where travelers catch up on the reading they've meant to do all year. Although not the most elaborate, it is probably the most elegant hotel on Kefalonia. On arriving, you descend a few steps from the main road to enter an almost tropical setting. The lobby is subdued and stylish, a decor that extends to the hotel's guest rooms, which are modest in size but have first-rate bathrooms. Guests have use of their own small beach as well as a larger one which is open to the public. White Rocks is a couple of miles south of Argostoli just above the two beaches.

Platys Yialos, 28100 Argostoli. ✆ **26710/28-332** or 26710/28-335. Fax 26710/28-755. 102 units, 60 bungalows. High season 185€ ($241) double; low season 130€ ($169) double. Rates are for either rooms or bungalows and include breakfast and dinner. AE, DC, V. Closed Nov–Apr. Private parking. Occasional public buses go from the center of town to and from Yialos, but most people take taxis. At the beach at Lassi, outside Argostoli. **Amenities:**

Restaurant; bar; pool; concierge; tours and car rentals arranged; conference facilities; room service 7am–midnight; laundry service; dry cleaning. *In room:* A/C.

MODERATE

In addition to the following options, you might consider the 60-unit **Hotel Mira-mare**, 2 I. Metaxa, at the far end of the paralia (shore road) (✆ **26710/25-511;** fax 26710/25-512); it's slightly removed from the town's hustle yet within walking distance of any place you'd want to go.

Cephalonia Star   A location along the bay and balconied front rooms with fine views earn this Class C hotel more kudos than many. The white-walled rooms are a bit austere—along the lines of American motel rooms!—but perfectly adequate. Bathrooms are standard issue, but all are clean and well serviced. There's a cafeteria-restaurant on the premises, but except for breakfast, you'll probably want to patronize Argostoli's many fine eateries, all within a few minutes' walk. In August, a mobile amusement park has been known to set up on the quay just opposite, but then August all over Greece is a carnival. Definitely for those who enjoy being on a waterfront.

50 I. Metaxa, 28100 Argostoli. ✆ **26710/23-181.** Fax 26710/23-180. 40 units, some with shower, some with tub. High season 70€ ($91) double; low season 50€ ($65) double. Rates include breakfast. MC, V. Street parking. Along waterfront, across from the port authority. *In room:* A/C, TV.

Hotel Ionian Plaza ⭐   Although it doesn't quite qualify as a grand hotel, this is the class act of "downtown" Argostoli, and it's also a fine deal. The lobby, public areas, and guest rooms share a tasteful, comfortable, natural tone. Individual details in the furnishings and decor convey the sense of visiting a fine mansion rather than a commercial hotel. Guest rooms are larger than most, while bathrooms are modern if not mammoth. Breakfast takes place under the awning, the evening meal at the hotel's own **Il Palazzino** restaurant, indoors and outdoors; the menu has a strong Italian flavor and prices are surprisingly modest. Stay here if you like to be in the heart of a city; the front rooms overlook the Central Square but because no vehicles are allowed there, it's not especially noisy.

Vallianou Sq. (Central Sq.), 28100 Argostoli. ✆ **26710/25-581.** Fax 26710/25-585. 43 units. High season 85€ ($111) double; low season 70€ ($91) double. Rates include buffet breakfast. AE, MC, V. Street parking. *In room:* A/C, TV.

Mouikis Hotel   This is your basic Class C hotel, popular with groups but usually with a few rooms available for individual travelers. Although its rooms don't provide air-conditioning or TVs, its common areas do. The desk has safe-deposit boxes. Bathroom facilities are standard for the class. Definitely for those on a limited budget.

3 Vironis, 28100 Argostoli. ✆ **26710/23-281.** Fax 26710/28-010. www.mouikis.com. 39 units. High season 95€ ($124) double; low season 60€ ($78) double. Rates include buffet breakfast. AE, MC, V. Street parking.

WHERE TO DINE

Try the two local specialties: *kreatopita* (meat pie with rice and a tomato sauce under a crust) and *crasato* (pork cooked in wine). The island's prized wines include the Robola, Muscat, and Mavrodaphne.

EXPENSIVE

Captain's Table GREEK/INTERNATIONAL   Most guests dress up a bit, and there's definitely a touch of celebration to meals at this slightly upscale restaurant. Specialties include the Captain's Soup (fish, lobster, mussels, shrimp, and vegetables), filets of beef, delicate squid, and fried *courgette* (small eggplants). You can get out cheap by ordering from the low end of the menu, but then why eat here? Go early (it can get crowded in high season), order a bottle of wine, and enjoy!

Leoforos Rizopaston. tel] **26710/23-896.** Main courses 5€–17€ ($6.50–$22). MC, V. Daily 6pm–midnight. Just around corner from Central Sq.; identifiable by its boat-model display case.

MODERATE

Consider **Old Plaka Taverna,** 1 I. Metaxa, at the far end of the waterfront ((*C* **26710/ 24-849**), for modest prices and tasty Greek dishes.

La Gondola GREEK/ITALIAN   Everyone should take at least one meal on the main square to experience the "dinner theater," with Argostoli's citizens providing the action. Frankly, all of the restaurants on the square are about the same in quality and menu, but we've enjoyed some special treats at this one. It offers a house wine literally made by the house, and serves a special pizza-dough garlic bread, zesty chicken with lemon sauce, and cannelloni that stands out with its rich texture and distinctive flavor. Staff and diners always seem to enjoy themselves here, so we think you will, too.

Central Sq. (*C* **26710/23-658.** Main courses 4€–12€ ($5.20–$16). AE, MC, V. Daily 6pm–2am.

Patsouras ⭐ GREEK   Patsouras continues to live up to its reputation as the favorite of travelers seeking authentic Greek taverna food and ambience. Dine under the awnings on the terrace across from the waterfront, and try either of the local specialties, *kreatopita* (meat pie) or *crasto* (pork in wine). Such standards as the tzatziki and moussaka had a special zest. Greeks love unpretentious tavernas, and you'll see why if you eat at Patsouras.

32 I. Metaxa. (*C* **26710/22-779.** Main courses 4€–14€ ($5.20–$18). V. Daily noon–midnight. A 5-min. walk from Central Sq. Along the waterfront.

INEXPENSIVE

Portside Restaurant GREEK   This unpretentious taverna is what the Greeks call a *phisteria,* a restaurant specializing in meats and fish cooked on the grill or spit. Run by a native of Argostoli and his Greek-American wife, it offers hearty breakfasts, regular plates with side portions of salads and potatoes, and a full selection of Greek favorites. On special nights outside the high season, the restaurant roasts a suckling pig. It's popular with Greeks as well as foreigners, and you've got a front-row seat for harborside activities.

58 I. Metaxa. (*C* **26710/24-130.** Main courses 4€–12€ ($5.20–$16). MC, V. Apr–Oct daily 10am–midnight. Along the waterfront, opposite the port authority.

ARGOSTOLI AFTER DARK

Free outdoor concerts are occasionally given in the Central Square. At the end of August, a **Choral Music Festival** hosts choirs from all over Greece and Europe. The grand new **Kefalos Public Theater** stages plays, almost always in Greek and seldom in high season. Young people looking for a bit more action can find a number of cafes, bars, and discos on and around the Central Square; they change names from year to year, but **Cinema Music Club, Rumours, Prive, Stavento, Daccapo,** and **Traffic** have been fairly steady. At the beach resort of Lassi, **So Simple Bar** is popular. If your style runs more to British-style pub-crawling, try **Pub Old House,** 57 I. Metaxas, on a corner of tiny streets between the Central Square and the waterfront.

SIDE TRIPS FROM ARGOSTOLI
FISKARDO, ASSOS & MYRTOS BEACH

We'd choose this excursion if we only had 1 day for a trip outside Argostoli. The ending destination is **Fiskardo,** a picturesque port-village, that is the only locale on Kefalonia to have survived the 1953 earthquake. Its charm comes from its many surviving 18th-century structures and its intimate harbor.

You can make a round-trip from Argostoli to Fiskardo in a day on a **KTEL** bus (6€/$7.80). But with a rental car, you can detour to the even more picturesque port and village of **Assos** (another 10km/7 miles along the upper coast road) and then reward yourself with a stop at **Myrtos beach,** one of Greece's great beaches.

Plenty of restaurants dot Fiskardo's harbor. We recommend **Tassia's, Vassos, Nicholas Taverna,** and **Panormos.** The latter two offer rooms as well. For advance arrangements, contact **Fiskardo Travel** (© **26740/41-315;** fax 26710/41-026) or **Aquarius Travel** (©/fax **26740/41-306**). Britons may prefer to deal with the **Greek Islands Club,** which specializes in waterfront apartments and houses. Its main office is at Sunvil House, Old Isleworth, Middlesex TW7 7BJ (gic@vch.co.uk).

SAMI, MELISSANI GROTTO & DROGARATI CAVE

When you arrive in Kefalonia, you may come first to Sami, an unexceptional town on the east coast and the island's principal point of entry before tourism put Argostoli in the lead. Sami is still a busy port. Besides the unusual white cliffs seen from the harbor, travelers are drawn by **two caves** to the north of Sami, both of which can be visited on a half-day excursion from Argostoli.

Spili Melissani, about 5km (3 miles) north of Sami, is well signed. Once you're inside, you will be taken by a guide in a small rowboat around a relatively small, partially exposed, partially enclosed lake, whose most spectacular feature is the play of the sun's rays striking the water, which creates a kaleidoscope of colors. It's open daily from 9am to 6pm. Admission is 6€ ($7.80).

On the road that leads west to Argostoli (4km/2 miles from Sami), there's a well-signed turnoff to **Drogarati Cave.** Known for its unusual stalagmites, its large chamber has been used for concerts (once by Maria Callas). You walk through it on your own; the cave is well illuminated but can be slippery. It's open daily from 9am to 6pm, with an admission of 4€ ($5.20).

ITHAKA

Because of its association with Odysseus, Ithaka might seem to rate the treatment of a major destination. But it is small and not easily approached, and does not offer many tourist or historical attractions. Given its sites linked to the Homeric epic, however, it will appeal to certain travelers, and its rugged terrain and laid-back villages reward those who enjoy driving through unspoiled Greek countryside.

We strongly recommend that you rent a car in Argostoli first. The boat connecting to Ithaka sails not from Argostoli but from Sami, the port on the east coast of Kefalonia; to make a bus connection with that boat, and then to take a taxi from the tiny isolated port where you disembark on Ithaka, costs far too much time. Rather, in your rented car, drive the 40 minutes from Argostoli to Sami; the boat fare for the car is 10€ ($13), for each individual 2€ ($2.60). Once on Ithaka, you can drive to **Vathy,** the main town, in about 10 minutes, and you'll have wheels with which to explore Ithaka and return to Argostoli, all within a day.

Vathy itself is a little port, a miniversion of bigger Greek ports with their bustling tourist-oriented facilities. For help in making any arrangements, try **Polyctor Tours** on the main square (© **26740/33-120**). You might enjoy a cold drink or coffee and admire the bay stretching before you, but otherwise there's not much to do or see here. Instead, drive 16km (10 miles) north to **Moni Katheron;** the 17th-century monastery itself is nothing special, but the bell tower offers a spectacular view over much of Ithaka. For a more ambitious drive, head north via the village of **Anogi,** stopping in its town square to view the little church with centuries-old frescoes and the Venetian bell tower opposite it. Proceed on via Stavros and then down to the northeast coast to **Frikes,** a small fishing village. Finally, take a winding road along the coast to **Kioni,** arranged like an amphitheater around its harbor.

As for the sites associated with the *Odyssey,* what little there is to be seen is questioned by many scholars, but that should not stop you; after all, it's your imagination that makes the Homeric world come alive. From the outskirts of Vathy, you'll see signs for the four principal sites. Three kilometers (1½ miles) northwest of Vathy is the so-called **Cave of the Nymphs,** where Odysseus is said to have hidden the Phaeacians's gifts after he had been brought back (supposedly to the little **Bay of Dexia,** north of the cave). Known locally as Marmarospilia, the small cave is about a half-hour's climb up a slope.

The **Fountain of Arethusa,** where Eumaios is said to have watered his swine, is about 7km (4 miles) south of Vathy; it is known today as the spring of Perapigadi. The **Bay of Ayios Andreas,** below, is claimed to be the spot where Odysseus landed in order to evade Penelope's suitors. To get to the fountain, drive the first 3km (2 miles) by following the signposted road to the south of Vathy as far as it goes; continue on foot another 3km (2 miles) along the path.

About 8km (5 miles) west of Vathy is the site of **Alalkomenai,** claimed by Schliemann among others to be the site of Odysseus's capital; in fact, the remains date from several centuries later than the official dates of the Trojan War. Finally, a road out of Stavros leads down to the **Bay of Polis,** again claimed by some as the port of Odysseus's capital; in the nearby cave of Louizou, an ancient pottery shard was found with the inscription "my vow to Odysseus," but its age suggests that this was the site of a hero-cult.

For lunch, we recommend **Gregory's Taverna,** on the far northeast corner of Vathy's bay (keep driving, with the bay on your left, even after you think the road may give out). Ideally, you will find a table right on the water, where you can look back at Vathy while you enjoy your fresh fish dinner (not cheap, but then fresh fish never is cheap in Greece).

Most visitors will be able to see what they want of Ithaka in a day before setting off to the little ports where the last ferryboat to Kefalonia leaves, usually at 5pm—but ask!

Appendix A:
Greece in Depth

In Greece, you will inevitably lose track of time—and not just what day it is. The timelessness of Greece's mountaintops and beaches, its natural and constructed temples, its glistening waters and slow sunsets bring a cleansing confusion of past and present, a delightful disorientation, even before you have your first glass of *ouzo*. Greece—defined by seas and mountains and a translucent sky—is a land of vistas, a place of spectacles.

That said, it is easy to overlook something you are not prepared to see. One of the oldest and greatest of the Greek philosophers, Heraclitus, known even in his own day as "the obscure," once pointed out that, "Reality likes to hide." So does much of Greece. The aim of this appendix is to excite your imagination and to guide your eyes. Think of this chapter as a collection of trail notes—things to keep in mind and to look for as you make your own way around Greece.

1 A Legacy of Art & Architecture

Whether you dig or dive (being restless mariners, the Greeks lost many of their treasures to the sea) into the Greek past, what you find is mostly things and not words, a rubble of stones and pots. Even after vases are reconstructed and walls are rebuilt, they don't speak to you or tell you their stories. At best, they mumble. Like the Oracle at Dodona, whose voice spoke through the sacred oaks, the past speaks through the ruins of cities and wrecks of ships, but not without professional assistance, in our time via the increasingly accurate stories of archaeologists.

Ancient authors, whose works we still can read, offer another bridge to the prehistoric past; often in their books they described events that were in their remote past. Until recently, Homer's stories of Helen, Achilles, and Odysseus were assumed to be variations of legends and myths—not remembrances of people and events from the historical past handed down from generation to generation. Modern archaeology, however, has

illuminated and certified the accounts of Homer and others.

THE DIGGERS The most notorious instance of modern shovel being led by ancient book is surely that of **Heinrich Schliemann's** discovery of **Troy.** He wasn't entirely alone in thinking that Homer wrote about real times and real places, but he went further than anyone else to prove it. Schliemann was a man with a single obsession: to unearth Homer's Troy. At age 7 he swore to find Troy, and at 48 he stuck his shovel into the mound at **Hissarlik** in northwestern Turkey, where he eventually unearthed Homer's ancient city. To get there he had used the *Iliad* as a divining rod, leading him from text to stone, from poetry to prehistory.

From Troy, Schliemann went on to other Bronze Age sites straight from the pages of Homer. His excavations at **Mycenae, Tiryns,** and **Orchomenos**—the three cities called "golden" by Homer—were characterized by the same bold and impetuous enthusiasm, genius, and miscalculation. By the time of Schliemann's death in 1890, the shape and stature of the Mycenaean world had risen from the pages of Homer to open sight.

What Schliemann was to the Mycenaean world, **Arthur Evans** became to the still earlier and more fantastic world of the Minoans. Evans's initial interest in **Crete** was linguistic, and he went there to test a theory of hieroglyphic interpretation. What he found astounded him and the rest of the world. At **Knossos,** Evans unearthed the all but unknown Minoan civilization, the legendary and splendorous kingdom of Minos. Homer had once again proven himself a man of his word. Indeed, the world of the late Bronze Age—the geographical and cultural contexts of the *Iliad* and the *Odyssey*—as it continues to emerge from excavations in the Peloponnese, on Crete, and throughout the Eastern Mediterranean, looks more and more as Homer described it.

THE SITES The ancient Greeks were convinced that there are portals or openings into the next world, the world beyond this one. They even found a few to their satisfaction, like **Eleusis, Dodona,** and **Delphi.** Entrances to the old world, the world before this one, are still easier to find, especially in Greece. Nowhere is the archaeological "water table" any higher. A little digging almost anywhere uncovers the ancient past.

Evidence of human habitation of mainland Greece dates from as early as 4000 B.C. Several caves in the **Louros River Valley** in Epirus have yielded deposits from the middle and late Paleolithic periods. Hunters and gatherers, however, traveling light, left faint traces behind. By contrast, the settled communities of the Neolithic period, 6,000 to 8,000 years old, left enough evidence behind to be read like a book. This is where the story of ancient Greece begins,

with the first agricultural settlements. The site at **Sesklo,** in Thessaly, has given its name to a thriving, 6th- to 5th-millennium agricultural civilization, which found no need for fortifications, produced fine pottery, and engaged in trade with nearby islands. Most of what you find here are private spaces, modest homes of mud brick on stone foundations.

Only a thousand years later, at the nearby site of **Dimini,** signs that life had changed dramatically were found. Fortification walls, arranged in concentric rings, tell of social division and turbulence. On the hill, a great house, whose plan points towards the later *megara* or palaces of the Mycenaeans, indicates that already there was a human hierarchy, with a few at the top and most at the bottom. Here, in these stones, the focusing of power, the accumulation of wealth, and the organization of society are recognizably underway. From here it is only a matter of time and development to the feudal hilltop citadels and palaces of the Bronze Age—**Mycenae, Athens,** and **Tiryns,** to mention a few—and from there to the city-states and empires of the Archaic and Classical periods.

The first question to ask of any site is, "Why here?" Before people build, they look for a location—and their choice of site is revealing. Is the construction to be open or closed to its surroundings? Porous or defensible? What will it reach for or look to, and on what will it turn its back? Before you concern yourself with whether a temple is of the Doric, Ionic, or Corinthian order, you should remember, for instance, that the word temple (*templum* in Latin, *hiera* in Greek) does not refer to a building but to something sacred, a sacred place or object, to which the building is a secondary response. Buildings only mark or point to temples. Nowhere is this more clear than at

Delphi. Delphi is first of all itself a *templum,* a sanctuary, which accounts for all of the structures located there. While the latter lie in ruins, the power of the place endures. Thus the absence of temple buildings on **Minoan Crete** does not mean that the Minoans were without temples. Their temples, their sacred places or environs, were instead the surrounding mountaintops and caves—notably **Mount Ida** and **Dicteon Cave,** by which and in whose embrace they constructed their palaces, such as **Knossos** and **Phaestos.** The Mycenaeans, in contrast, occupied and fortified the peaks, building mountaintop citadels like **Mycenae** and **Tiryns** for their royalty. Still later, in the city-states of Archaic and Classical Greece, the mountaintops were returned to the gods and goddesses, where they were housed in royal fashion.

The next thing we notice at most every ancient site is the absence of private or domestic structures. We find stones—not brick or wood, but stones. After the Neolithic period, cut stones were mostly reserved for palaces, temples, public buildings, and fortifications. Private homes were made mostly of wood beams and sunbaked brick. For the most part, these vanished quickly, without a trace, like their inhabitants. What endured were the structures of stone, the pillars, as it were, of society.

THE GODS & GODDESSES The ancient Greeks were neither the first nor the last to acknowledge the existence and activity of forces, personal and impersonal, beyond their grasp and control. Wisdom and piety began, then as always, with knowing where to draw the line between what lay within human control and what lay beyond human control. No line, however, could be in more constant flux and dispute. Birth, death, agriculture, war, travel, commerce, weather, health, beauty, art, love—all of the ingredients of life as we know it—were realms where humans and gods had their hands in the same pot. One minute everything seemed to depend upon human initiative and energy; the next minute human effort appeared to count for nothing. The controversial 5th-century philosopher Protagoras, a friend of the playwright Euripides, began his famous theological treatise with the confession that everything about the gods—whether or not they exist and what they may be like—outstrips human understanding, both because the subject is so obscure and because life is so short.

In the Greek imagination, then, the world was full of divine forces. Death, sleep, love, fate, memory, laughter, panic, rage, day, night, justice, victory—all of the timeless, elusive forces confronted by humans—were named and numbered among the gods and goddesses with whom the Greeks shared their universe. Understandably, in such a world, the cities, homes, roads, gardens, mountains, caves, forests, and countrysides of ancient Greece were thick with temples, altars, shrines, and consecrated precincts, where people left their offerings and petitions, hoping to be blessed with or spared the gods' interventions. To make these forces more familiar and approachable, the Greeks (like every other ancient people) imagined their gods to be somehow like themselves. They were male and female, young and old, beautiful and deformed, gracious and withholding, lustful and virginal, sweet and fierce.

Most of the myriad divine forces, named and nameless, familiar and faceless, in the Greek tradition can be found in the pages of the two great poets of archaic Greece, **Hesiod** and **Homer**—but the "plot lines" driving the poets' stories are dominated by one particular family of divinities, the **Olympians,** the household of Zeus and Hera ensconced on a great mountain in the northeast corner of Thessaly. Thanks, in part, to the

Principal Olympian Gods & Goddesses

Greek Name	Latin Name	Description
Zeus	Jupiter	Son of Kronos and Rhea, high god, ruler of Olympus. Thunderous sky god, wielding bolts of lightning. Patron-enforcer of the rites and laws of hospitality.
Hera	Juno	Daughter of Kronos and Rhea, queen of the sky. Sister and wife of Zeus. Patroness of marriage.
Demeter	Ceres	Daughter of Kronos and Rhea, sister of Hera and Zeus. Giver of grain and fecundity. Goddess of the mysteries of Eleusis.
Poseidon	Neptune	Son of Kronos and Rhea, brother of Zeus and Hera. Ruler of the seas. Earth-shaking god of earthquakes.
Hestia	Vesta	Daughter of Kronos and Rhea, sister of Hera and Zeus. Guardian of the hearth fire and of the home.
Hephaestos	Vulcan	Son of Hera, produced by her parthenogenetically. Lord of volcanoes and of fire. Himself a smith, the patron of crafts employing fire (metalworking and pottery).
Ares	Mars	Son of Zeus and Hera. The most hated of the gods. God of war and strife.
Hermes	Mercury	Son of Zeus and an Arcadian mountain nymph. Protector of thresholds and crossroads. Messenger god, patron of commerce and eloquence. Companion-guide of souls en route to the underworld.
Apollo	Phoebus	Son of Zeus and Leto. Patron god of the light of day, and of the creative genius of poetry and music. The god of divination and prophecy.
Artemis	Diana	Daughter of Zeus and Leto. Mistress of animals and of the hunt. Chaste guardian of young girls.
Athena	Minerva	Daughter of Zeus and Metis, born in full armor from the head of Zeus. Patroness of wisdom and of war. Patron goddess of the city-state of Athens.
Dionysos	Dionysus	Son of Zeus and Semele, born from the thigh of his father. God of revel, revelation, wine, and drama.
Aphrodite	Venus	Daughter of Zeus. Born from the bright sea foam off the coast of Cyprus. Fusion of Minoan tree goddess and Near Eastern goddess of love and war. Patroness of love.

stature and notoriety bestowed on them by their poets, these gods and goddesses were not only cast in leading roles in the theaters of Greece but were also made the focal point for the civic cults of most Greek states and, in sum, became household words.

As told by the ancient poets, the "lives of the Olympians" is nothing less than a Greek soap opera. Sometimes generous, courageous, insightful, they are also notoriously petty, quarrelsome, spiteful, vain, frivolous, and insensitive. And how could it be otherwise with the Olympians? Not made to pay the ultimate price of death, they need not know the ultimate cost of life. Fed on *ambrosia* (not mortal) and *nektar* (overcoming death), they cannot go hungry, much less perish. When life is endless, everything is reversible.

THE GREEK THEATER Ancient Greek **tragedy,** a unique art form developed in Athens in the 6th and 5th centuries B.C., was essentially musical. Greek music, the "realm of the Muses," encompassed what we know as poetry, dance, and music. Tragedy represented the fusion of all three—dramatic poetry, music, and dance—in a single art form.

The **Greek theater** was quite literally a "seeing-place," a place of shared spectacle and insight, where—during two annual festivals—the citizens of Athens and their guests assembled in the Theater of Dionysos to see the latest original work of their master playwrights. Here, before the eyes of thousands, the great figures of myth and legend—Agamemnon, Helen, Herakles, and others—appeared in open sight and reenacted the stories that had shaped the Greek imagination. The ultimate spectacle of the Greek theater was and is humanity: humanity denied, deified, bestialized, defiled, and restored, which is why the works of Aeschylus, Sophocles, and Euripides play today with undiminished power and poignancy.

In ancient Greece, every city deserving the name had its theater, many of which even today host **festival productions** of the ancient masterworks. The most eminent of these is held every summer in the stunning theater at **Epidaurus.** There are also performances in the ancient theaters of Dodona, Thasos, and Phillipi, as well as the archaeological site at Eleusis, which has an annual "Aeschylia" in honor of the founder of Greek tragedy. Another summer arts festivals features theatrical performances (notably the Athens or Hellenic Festival) in the striking Odeion of Herodes Atticus on the southwest slope of the Acropolis. The Lycabettus Theater also stages a variety of performances, with a recent emphasis on contemporary and ethnic music. Additionally, the International Festival at Patras, Epirotika Festival in Ioannina, Hippokrateia Festival on Kos, Demetria Festival in Thessaloniki, Aegean Festival on Skiathos, Molyvos Festival on Lesvos, and Lefkada Festival include theatrical performances. In September, the Ithaki Theatre Festivals recognize works by the new generation of playwrights.

2 The Greek People

If you were truly to beware of Greeks bearing gifts, a visit to Greece would call for sleepless vigilance, for the Greeks are among the most spontaneously generous people you are likely ever to meet, provided you do not offend them. And they can be easily offended, for their pride matches their generosity. In a poll taken a few years ago, it was shown, to no one's surprise, that the Greeks' pride in being Greek surpasses the ethnic satisfaction of any other European nation. More specifically, 97% of the Greek population is proud as punch to be Greek; only the Irish come close to this level, at 96%.

Although Greek politics sometimes resembles the sheer chaos of a circus fire, the social fabric remains intact: 99% of the Greek people speak Greek as their first language, and 98% belong to the Greek Orthodox Church. Elsewhere in the world, you'd have to look in a Benedictine monastery to find the same level of homogeneity. The core of Greek society, however, remains the family; and this is unlikely to change anytime soon.

3 A Taste of Greece

Greek food and drink tell a long story. The ancient Athenians are said to have invented the first hors d'oeuvre trolley, and most Greek dinners still start off with *mezedes,* a selection of hot and cold dishes served on small plates and shared from the center of the table. Spit-roasted mutton, goat, and pork were what Patroclus prepared for Achilles's late-night dinner party in the *Iliad,* and you'll still find them featured on Greek menus (though pork, much less boar, has declined in popularity across the millennia and been upstaged by chicken). You'll also find the freshly netted catch of the day, reminiscent of ancient Aegean murals from Santorini or Minoan Crete. Other ancient staples were olives, figs, barley, and almonds—crops still flourishing across the Greek countryside. Take away olive oil from Greek cooks and you might as well cut off their hands.

The distinctive flavor of Greek cuisine may be traced to oregano and lemons: oregano from the hillsides of Greece and lemons first hauled from South Asia at the urging of Empress Theodora. As the first lady of Byzantium, she used her imperial clout to encourage the importing of rice, lemons, and eggplant from India, all of which have helped condition the Greek palate. The soups and stews employing various pastas and tomato-based sauces are a Venetian contribution welcomed by Greek households, which until recently had no ovens. The Italians brought with them a spree of Eastern spices—cinnamon, aniseed, pepper, cloves, and allspice—now well ensconced in the Greek diet. The Turks, too, left their mark with yogurt, the omnipresent kabob, and an inky sweet syrup they call coffee. Finally, a Greek meal is likely to end with a flaky *filo* pastry—first brought from Persia in Byzantine times—soaked in honey, of which the ancient poets sang.

There it is: the history of Greece on a plate.

A DINING PRIMER In past years, the **taverna** usually had simpler food than the **estiatorio,** or restaurant. Over the years, these distinctions have largely blurred. You can usually find the same dishes on the menu at many tavernas and estiatoria: grilled meats, including *souvlaki,* commonly available in lamb, pork, and chicken; *keftedes* (meatballs), usually fried (though on Hios they may turn out to be made of ground chickpeas and equally delicious); the "Greek" salad, featuring tomatoes, olives, and feta cheese; *moussaka* (eggplant casserole, with lots of regional variation, often with minced meat); *yemista* (tomatoes or green peppers filled with rice and sometimes minced meat); and the often bland but filling *pastitsio* (baked pasta).

Many tavernas and restaurants still don't serve desserts, which are often very sweet. Examples include *baklava* (filo soaked in honey, which some Greeks insist is actually Turkish) and *halva* (a sort of nougat, sweeter yet and undeniably Turkish). Those with a serious sweet tooth may want to stop at a **zaharoplastion** (confectioner) or **patisserie,** as French bakeries are fairly common.

Another venue is the **ouzeri**—usually informal though not necessarily inexpensive—which serves ouzo, the clear, anise-flavored national aperitif. Ouzo is especially intoxicating on an empty stomach—which is why ouzeries serve food, usually an assortment of *mezedes,* hearty appetizers eaten with bread: the common *tzatziki* (yogurt with cucumber and garlic), *taramosalata* (fish-roe dip), *skordalia* (hot garlic and beet dip), *melitzanosalata* (eggplant salad), *yigantes* (giant beans in tomato sauce), *dolmades* (stuffed grape leaves), grilled *kalamarakia* (squid), *oktapodi* (octopus), and *loukanika* (sausage).

There is also the **psarotaverna,** which specializes in fish and seafood. Fish is no longer abundant in Greek waters, and trawling with nets is prohibited from mid-May to mid-October, so prices can be exorbitant. Often you'll have to settle for smaller fish, such as *barbounia,* which are delicious if not overcooked. Ask locals to recommend reputable places at which you can choose your own fish dinner—and make sure it isn't switched on you.

Fast food is rapidly becoming common, especially pizza, which can be okay but is rarely good. Many young Greeks seem to subsist on *gyros* (thin slices of meat slowly roasted on a vertical spit, sliced off, and served in pita bread). **Tip:** If the spindle of meat is "skinny" in the morning, you should guess it isn't fresh and pass it by.

A few other warnings: Much of the squid served in Greece is frozen; and many restaurants serve dreadful *keftedes, taramosalata,* and *melitzanasalata* made with more bread than any other ingredient. That's the bad news. The good news is that the bad news leaves you free to order things you may not have had before—grilled green or red peppers or a tasty snack of *kokoretsia* (grilled entrails)—or something you probably have had, such as Greek olives, but never in such variety and pizzazz.

To avoid the ubiquitous favorites-for-foreigners, you might indicate to your waiter that you'd like to have a look at the food display case, often positioned just outside the kitchen, and then point to what you'd like to order. Many restaurants are perfectly happy to let you take a look

in the kitchen itself, but it's not a good idea to do this without checking first. Not surprisingly, you'll get the best value for your money and the tastiest food at establishments serving a predominantly Greek rather than tourist clientele.

When it's not being used as filler, fresh Greek bread is generally tasty, substantial, nutritious, and inexpensive. If you're buying bread at a bakery, ask for *mavro somi* (black bread). It's almost always better than the more bland white stuff. An exception is the white bread in the *koulouria* (pretzel-like rolls covered with sesame seeds); you'll see Greeks buying them from street vendors on their way to work in the morning.

One of the most reliable of snacks is the ubiquitous *tiropita* (cheese pie), usually made with feta, though there are endless variations. On Naxos, the tiropita may look like the usual flaky round pastry but contains the excellent local cheese, *graviera.* In Metsovo, it may resemble cornbread and contain leeks and *metsovella,* a mild local cheese made from sheep's milk. On Alonissos, the tiropita may contain the usual feta but be rolled in a big spiral and deep-fried. A close relative to the tiropita is *spanokopita* (spinach pie), which is also prepared in a variety of ways.

MEALS   Breakfast is not an important meal to the Greeks. In the cities, you'll see people grabbing a *koulouri* (pretzel-like roll) as they hurry to work. Most hotels will serve a continental breakfast of bread or rolls with butter and jam, coffee, usually juice (often fresh), and occasionally yogurt. Better hotels may serve an American buffet

---

⌒Tips   Insider Tip

Most restaurants, even very good restaurants, have no objection to meals made of multiple appetizers or *mezedes,* which is both the most interesting and the most economical way of putting a meal together.

with eggs, bacon, cheese, yogurt, and fresh fruit.

Lunch is typically a heavier meal in Greece than it is in most English-speaking countries, and most Greeks take a siesta afterwards. Keep siesta hours, about 2 to 5pm, in mind when planning your own day, especially in more provincial destinations. (Even in Athens you should be considerate about contacting friends or acquaintances at home during these hours.)

Dinner is often an all-evening affair for Greeks, starting with *mezedes* at 7 or 8pm, and the main meal itself as late as 11pm. (You might consider a snack before joining Greek friends in their long evening meal.)

IN THE GLASS Your drinking glass also has a history. Until classical times, most Greeks drank water at their meals and broke out the wine only for special occasions. Today you'll find both, side by side. The wines for which ancient Greeks were most famous—the wines of Hios and Lesvos—were sweet and thick, almost a sticky paste, requiring serious dilution of up to 20 parts water to 1 part wine, though Alexander the Great is said to have taken his wine "neat" until it killed him. A fine, or not so fine, tokay might today come closest to the legendary wines of the Aegean islands.

Today the most characteristic Greek wine is *retsina,* or resinated wine. It is definitely an acquired taste and possibly an addictive one, as you will find yourself years later longing for Greece and a glass of retsina, all in the same breath. At first gulp, however, it's a bit like drinking your Christmas tree. The ancient Greeks were big on adding herbs and spices to their wine, but they sometimes added pine pitch, mostly to wines they considered otherwise undrinkable. Today, many villages make their own home-brewed retsina (which is traditionally fermented and stored in resin-caulked barrels). If you prefer a more canonized blend, we recommend Kourtaki, available throughout Greece as well as overseas, in case you learn to crave the resinated cask. Otherwise, ask for *krasi*—Greek wine without the resin—of which there are many.

All controlled appellations of origin in Greece (identified by blue banderoles), however, are liqueur wines, such as the mavrodaphne of Kefalonia or the muscat of Limnos. Beyond these, 20 areas throughout Greece boast appellations of origin of superior quality (identified by red banderoles), including dry reds from western Macedonia and Crete; and dry whites from Attica, Patras, Crete, and several islands. Local table wines can be full of surprises. Finally, what might be called the Greek national drink is *ouzo,* an 80- to 100-proof anise-flavored aperitif, served with water or ice, for which you can always substitute a glass of Metaxa brandy, which calls itself "the Greek spirit."

Appendix B:
The Greek Language

1 Making Your Way in Greek

There are many different kinds of Greek—the Greek of conversation in the street, the Greek used at a fashionable dinner party, the Greek used in newspapers, the Greek of a government notice, the Greek used by a novelist or a poet, and more—and they can differ from one another in grammar and in vocabulary much more than the English of, for example, a conversation at the water cooler and that of an editorial in the *New York Times*. Why this is so is a long—and we mean *long*—story. Greek, like English, has a long written history molded by influential works that continue to be read and studied for centuries—in Greek even for millennia—so that, as in English, older words and styles of expression remain available for use even while the spoken language happily evolves on its own.

Also like English, Greek has kept the spelling of its words largely unchanged even though their pronunciation has changed in fundamental ways. In English this spelling lag has extended for some 5 centuries, but in Greek it is 25 centuries old. This makes it easier for us to read Shakespeare and for Greeks to read Herodotus than it might otherwise be, but it also means that Greek children, like English-speaking children, have to learn to spell words that they already know to use in conversation.

Our dilemma is further complicated by the fact that many Greek words and names have entered our language not directly but by way of Latin or French, and so have become familiar to English speakers in forms that owe something to those languages. When these words are directly transliterated from modern Greek (and that means from Greek in its modern pronunciation, not the ancient one that Romans heard), they almost always appear in a form other than the one you may have read about in school. "Perikles" for Pericles or "Delfi" for Delphi are relatively innocent examples; "Thivi" for Thebes or "Omiros" for Homer can give you an idea of the traps often in store for the innocent traveler. The bottom line is that the names of towns, streets, hotels, items on menus, historical figures, archaeological sites—you name it—are likely to have more than one spelling as you come across them in books, on maps, or before your very eyes.

Sometimes the name of a place has simply changed over the centuries. If you think you've just arrived in Santorini but you see a sign welcoming you to Thira, smile, remember you're in Greece, and take heart. (Santorini is the name the Venetians used, and it became common in Europe for that reason. Thira is the original Greek name.) You're where you want to be. This appendix offers a few aids to help you make your way in Greek. First: remember that literacy is virtually universal in Greece. The table below will help you move from Greek signs or directions to a sense of how they should sound. This transliteration of modern Greek is used throughout this book, except in reference to names that have become household words in English, like Athens, Socrates, Olympus, and so on. The good news here is that you won't be confused as long as you have your nose in your book; the bad news is that confusion is probably inevitable as soon as your eyes leave the page. All you have to say is what you are looking for, raising your voice at the end of the word to let your listener know it's a question, and bingo!—someone will help.

Do remember that *óhi,* although it can sound a bit like "okay," in fact means "no," and that *ne,* which can sound like a twangy "nay," means "yes." To complicate matters, some everyday gestures will be different from those you are used to: Greeks nod their heads upward to express an unspoken *óhi* and downward (or downward and to one side) for an unspoken *ne.* When a Greek turns his or her head from side to side at you—and you will see this despite your best efforts—it is a polite way of signaling, "I can't make out what you're saying." And remember: Almost any 40-year-old Greek can read Greek, and most people under 30 can also make out some English. If you find that your attempts at speaking fall on deaf ears, show someone the word for what you want and if you stumble over *efharisto* (thank you) you can place your hand over your heart and bow your head slightly.

ALPHABET		TRANSLITERATED AS	PRONOUNCED AS IN
Α α	álfa	a	*f*ather
Β β	víta	v	*v*iper
Γ γ	gámma	g before α, ο, ω, and consonants	*g*et
		y before αι, ε, ει, η, ι, οι, υ	*y*es
		ng before κ, γ, χ, or ξ	si*ng*er
Δ δ	thélta	th	*th*e (not as the *th*- in "thin")
Ε ε	épsilon	e	s*e*t
Ζ ζ	zíta	z	la*z*y
Η η	íta	i	magaz*i*ne
Θ θ	thíta	th	*th*in (not as the *th*- in "the")
Ι ι	ióta	i	magaz*i*ne
		y before a, o	*y*ard, *y*ore
Κ κ	káppa	k	*k*eep
Λ λ	lámtha	l	*l*eap
Μ μ	mi	m	*m*arry
Ν ν	ni	n	*n*ever
Ξ ξ	ksi	ks	ta*x*i
Ο ο	ómicron	o	b*ou*ght
Π π	pi	p	*p*et
Ρ ρ	ro	r	*r*ound
Σ σ/ς	sígma	s before vowels or θ, κ, π, τ, φ, χ, ψ	*s*ay
		z before β, γ, δ, ζ, λ, μ, ν, ρ	la*z*y

ALPHABET	TRANSLITERATED AS		PRONOUNCED AS IN
Τ τ	taf	t	take
Υ υ	ípsilon	i	magazine
Φ φ	fi	f	fee
Χ χ	chi	h	hero (before e and i sounds; like the ch- in Scottish "loch" otherwise
Ψ ψ	psi	ps	collapse
Ω ω	ómega	o	bought

COMBINATIONS	TRANSLITERATED AS	PRONOUNCED AS IN
αι	e	get
αϊ	ai	aisle
αυ before vowels or β, γ, δ, ζ, λ, μ, ν, ρ	av	Ave Maria
αυ before θ, κ, ξ, π, σ, τ, φ, χ, ψ	af	pilaf
ει	i	magazine
ευ before vowels or β, γ, δ, ζ, λ, μ, ν, ρ	ev	ever
ευ before θ, κ, ξ, π, σ, τ, φ, χ, ψ	ef	left
μπ at beginning of word	b	bane
μπ in middle of word	mb	lumber
ντ at beginning of word	d	dumb
ντ in middle of word	nd	slender
Οι	i	magazine
Οϊ	oi	oil
Ου	ou	soup
τζ	dz	roads
τσ	ts	gets
υι	i	magazine

2 Useful Words & Phrases

When you're asking for or about something and have to rely on single words or short phrases, it's an excellent idea to use "sas parakaló" to introduce or conclude almost anything you say.

Airport	Aerothrómio
Automobile	Aftokínito
Avenue	Leofóros

Bad	Kakós, -kí, -kó*
Bank	Trápeza
The bill, please.	Tón logaryazmó(n), parakaló.
Breakfast	Proinó
Bus	Leoforío
Can you tell me?	Boríte ná moú píte?
Car	Amáxi
Cheap	Ft(h)inó
Church	Ekklissía
Closed	Klistós, stí, stó*
Coast	Aktí
Coffeehouse	Kafenío
Cold	Kríos, -a, -o*
Dinner	Vrathinó
Do you speak English?	Miláte Angliká?
Excuse me.	Signómi(n).
Expensive	Akrivós, -í, -ó*
Farewell!	Stó ka-ló! *(to person leaving)*
Glad to meet you.	Chéro polí.**
Good	Kalós, lí, ló*
Goodbye.	Adío *or* chérete.**
Good health (cheers)!	Stín (i)yá sas *or* Yá-mas!
Good morning *or* Good day.	Kaliméra.
Good evening.	Kalispéra.
Good night.	Kaliníchta.**
Hello!	Yássas *or* chérete!**
Here	Ethó
Hot	Zestós, -stí, -stó*
Hotel	Xenothochío**
How are you?	Tí kánete *or* Pós íst(h)e?
How far?	Pósso makriá?
How long?	Póssi óra *or* Pósso(n) keró?
How much does it cost?	Póso káni?
I am a vegetarian.	Íme hortophágos.
I am from New York.	Íme apó tí(n) Néa(n) Iórki.
I am lost *or* I have lost the way.	Écho chathí *or* Écho chási tón drómo(n).**
I'm sorry.	Singnómi.
I'm sorry, but I don't speak Greek (well).	Lipoúme, allá thén miláo elliniká (kalá).
I don't understand.	Thén katalavéno.

I don't understand, please repeat it.	Thén katalavéno, péste to páli, sás parakaló.
I want to go to the airport.	Thélo ná páo stó aerothrómio.
I want a glass of beer.	Thélo éna potíri bíra.
I would like a room.	Tha íthela ena thomátio.
It's (not) all right.	(Dén) íne en dáxi.
Left (direction)	Aristerá
Ladies' room	Ghinekón
Lunch	Messimerianó
Map	Chártis**
Market (place)	Agorá
Men's room	Andrón
Mr.	Kírios
Mrs.	Kiría
Miss	Despinís
My name is . . .	Onomázome . . .
New	Kenoúryos, -ya, -yo*
No	Óchi**
Old	Paleós, -leá, -leó* (pronounce palyós, -lyá, -lyó)
Open	Anichtós, -chtí, -chtó*
Pâtisserie	Zacharoplastío**
Pharmacy	Pharmakío
Please or You're welcome.	Parakaló.
Please call a taxi (for me).	Parakaló, fonáxte éna taxi (yá ména).
Point out to me, please . . .	Thíkste mou, sas parakaló . . .
Post office	Tachidromío**
Restaurant	Estiatório
Restroom	Tó méros or I toualétta
Right (direction)	Dexiá
Saint	Áyios, ayía, (plural) áyi-i (abbreviated ay)
Shore	Paralía
Square	Plateía
Street	Odós
Show me on the map.	Díxte mou stó(n) chárti.**
Station (bus, train)	Stathmos (leoforíou, trénou)
Stop (bus)	Stási(s) (leoforíou)
Telephone	Tiléfono
Temple (of Athena, Zeus)	Naós (Athinás, Diós)
Thank you (very much).	Efcharistó (polí).**

Today	Símera
Tomorrow	Ávrio
Very nice	Polí oréos, -a, -o*
Very well	Polí kalá *or* En dáxi
What?	Tí?
What time is it?	Tí ôra íne?
What's your name?	Pós onomázest(h)e?
Where is . . . ?	Poú íne . . . ?
Where am I?	Pou íme?
Why?	Yatí?

* Masculine ending -os, feminine ending -a or -i, neuter ending -o.

** Remember, *ch* should be pronounced as in Scottish *loch* or German *ich*, not as in the word *church*.

NUMBERS

0	Midén	18	Dekaoktó	152	Ekatón penínda dío
1	Éna	19	Dekaenyá		
2	Dío	20	Íkossi	200	Diakóssya
3	Tría	21	Íkossi éna	300	Triakóssya
4	Téssera	22	Íkossi dío	400	Tetrakóssya
5	Pénde	30	Triánda	500	Pendakóssya
6	Éxi	40	Saránda	600	Exakóssya
7	Eftá	50	Penínda	700	Eftakóssya
8	Októ	60	Exínda	800	Oktakóssya
9	Enyá	70	Evdomínda	900	Enyakóssya
10	Déka	80	Ogdónda	1,000	Chílya*
11	Éndeka	90	Enenínda	2,000	Dío chilyádes*
12	Dódeka	100	Ekató(n)	3,000	Trís chilyádes*
13	Dekatría	101	Ekatón éna	4,000	Tésseris chilyádes*
14	Dekatéssera	102	Ekatón dío		
15	Dekapénde	150	Ekatón penínda	5,000	Pénde chilyádes*
16	Dekaéxi	151	Ekatón penínda éna		
17	Dekaeftá				

* Remember, ch should be pronounced as in Scottish *loch* or German *ich,* not as in the word *church.*

DAYS OF THE WEEK

Monday	Deftéra	Friday	Paraskeví
Tuesday	Tríti	Saturday	Sávvato
Wednesday	Tetárti	Sunday	Kiriakí
Thursday	Pémpti		

MONTHS OF THE YEAR

January	Ianouários
February	Fevrouários
March	Mártios
April	Aprílios
May	Máios
June	Ioúnios
July	Ioúlios
August	Ávgoustos
September	Septémvrios
October	Októvrios
November	Noémvrios
December	Dekémvrios

MENU TERMS

arní avgolémono   lamb with lemon sauce

arní soúvlas   spit-roasted lamb

arní yiouvétsi   baked lamb with orzo

astakós (ladolémono)   lobster (with oil-and-lemon sauce)

bakaliáro (skordaliá)   cod (with garlic)

barboúnia (skáras)   red mullet (grilled)

briám   vegetable stew

brizóla chiriní   pork steak or chop

brizóla moscharísia   beef or veal steak

choriátiki saláta   "village" salad ("Greek" salad to Americans)

chórta   dandelion salad

dolmádes   stuffed vine leaves

domátes yemistés mé rízi   tomatoes stuffed with rice

eksóhiko   lamb and vegetables wrapped in filo

garídes   shrimp

glóssa (tiganití)   sole (fried)

kalamarákia (tiganitá)   squid (fried)

kalamarákia (yemistá)   squid (stuffed)

kaparosaláta   salad of minced caper leaves and onion

karavídes   crayfish

keftédes   fried meatballs

kokorétsia   grilled entrails

kotópoulo soúvlas   spit-roasted chicken

kotópoulo yemistó   stuffed chicken

kouloúri   pretzel-like roll covered with sesame seeds

loukánika   spiced sausages

loukoumádes   round doughnut center–like pastries deep-fried, then drenched with honey and topped with powdered sugar and cinnamon

melitzanosaláta   eggplant salad

moussaká   meat-and-eggplant casserole

oktapódi   octopus

païdákia   lamb chops

paradisiakó   traditional Greek cooking

pastítsio   baked pasta with meat

piláfi rízi   rice pilaf

piperiá yemistá   stuffed green peppers

revídia   chickpeas

revidokeftédes   croquettes of ground chickpeas

saganáki   grilled cheese

skordaliá   hot garlic-and-beet dip

soupiés yemistés   stuffed cuttlefish

souvláki   lamb (sometimes veal) on the skewer

spanokópita   spinach pie

stifádo   stew, often of rabbit or veal

taramosaláta   fish roe with mayonnaise

tirópita   cheese pie

tsípoura   dorado

tzatzíki   yogurt-cucumber-garlic dip

youvarlákia   boiled meatballs with rice

Appendix C:
Useful Toll-Free Numbers & Websites

AIRLINES

Aer Lingus
℗ 800/474-7424 in the U.S.
℗ 01/836-5000 in Ireland
www.aerlingus.com

Air Canada
℗ 888/247-2262
www.aircanada.ca

Air France
℗ 800/237-2747 in the U.S.
℗ 0820/820-820 in France
www.airfrance.com

Air India
℗ 800/223-7776 in the U.S.
℗ 22/2279-6737 in India
www.airindia.com

Air Malta
℗ 866/357-4155 in the U.S.
℗ 356/2169-0890 in Malta
www.airmalta.com

Air New Zealand
℗ 800/262-1234 in the U.S.
℗ 800/663-5494 in Canada
℗ 0800/737-767 in New Zealand
www.airnewzealand.com

Air Plus Comet
℗ 877/999-7587 in the U.S.
℗ 34/91-3294929 in Spain
www.aircomet.com

Air Portugal
℗ 800/221-7370 in the U.S.
℗ 707/205-700 in Portugal
www.tap-airportugal.pt

Airtran Airlines
℗ 800/247-8726
www.airtran.com

Alitalia
℗ 800/223-5730 in the U.S.
℗ 8488-65641 in Italy
www.alitalia.it

American Airlines
℗ 800/433-7300
www.aa.com

American Trans Air
℗ 800/435-9282
www.ata.com

Austrian Airlines
℗ 800/843-0002 in the U.S.
℗ 43/51789 in Austria
www.aua.com

BMI
No U.S. number
℗ 0870/607-0222 in Britain
www.flybmi.com

British Airways
℗ 800/247-9297
℗ 0845/77-333-77 in Britain
℗ 0345/222-111 in Ireland
www.british-airways.com

Continental Airlines
℗ 800/525-0280
www.continental.com

Delta Air Lines
℗ 800/241-4141
www.delta.com

Czech Airlines
℗ 800/223-2365 in the U.S.
℗ 420/224-81-04-26 in Czech Republic
www.czechairlines.com

Easyjet
No U.S. number
℡ 0870/600-0000 in Britain
www.easyjet.com

Egyptair
℡ 800/334-6787 in the U.S.
℡ 3903-444 in Egypt
www.egyptair.com.eg

El Al
℡ 800/223-6700 in the U.S.
℡ 03/9710000 in Israel
www.elal.co.il

Finnair
℡ 800/950-5000 in the U.S.
℡ 358/09-818-800 in Finland
www.finnair.com

Iberia
℡ 800/772-4642 in the U.S.
℡ 902/400-500 in Spain
www.iberia.com

Icelandair
℡ 800/223-5500 in the U.S.
℡ 354/50-50-100 in Iceland
www.icelandair.is

Jet Blue Airlines
℡ 800/538-2583
www.jetblue.com

KLM/Northwest
℡ 800/447-4747 in the U.S.
℡ 020/4-747-747 in Netherlands
www.klm.nl

Kuwait Airways
℡ 800/458-9248 in the U.S.
℡ 434-5555 in Kuwait
www.kuwait-airways.com

Lot Polish
℡ 800/223-0593 in the U.S.
℡ 0801/300-952 in Poland
www.lot.com

Lufthansa
℡ 800/645-3880 in the U.S.
℡ 49/0 180-5-838426 in Germany
www.lufthansa.com

Malev Hungarian
℡ 800/223-6884 in the U.S.
℡ 06/40-212121 in Hungary
www.hungarianairlines.com

Northwest Airlines
℡ 800/225-2525
www.nwa.com

Olympic Airways
℡ 800/223-1226 in the U.S.
℡ 80/111-44444 in Greece
www.olympic-airways.gr

Pakistan International Airlines
℡ 800/578-6786 in the U.S.
℡ 457-2011 in Pakistan
www.piac.com.pk

Qantas
℡ 800/227-4500 in the U.S.
℡ 612/9691-3636 in Australia
www.qantas.com

Royal Jordanian
℡ 800/223-0470 in the U.S.
℡ 567-8321 in Jordan
www.rja.com.jo

Scandinavian Airlines
℡ 800/221-2350 in the U.S.
℡ 0070/727-727 in Sweden
℡ 70/10-20-00 in Denmark
℡ 815/20-400 in Norway
www.scandinavian.net

Song
℡ 800/359-7664
www.flysong.com

Swiss International Airlines
℡ 877/359-7947 in the U.S.
℡ 0848/85-2000 in Switzerland
www.swiss.com

Tarom Romanian
℡ 212/560-0840 in the U.S.
℡ 4021/2041000 in Romania
www.tarom.ro

Turkish Airlines
℡ 800/874-8875 in the U.S.
℡ 90-212-663-63-00 in Turkey
www.flyturkish.com

United Airlines
© 800/864-8331
www.united.com

US Airways
© 800/428-4322
www.usairways.com

CAR RENTAL AGENCIES

Advantage
© 800/777-5500
www.advantagerentacar.com

Alamo
© 800/522-9696
www.alamo.com

Auto Europe
© 800/223-5555 in continental U.S.
© 888/223-5555 in Canada
www.autoeurope.com

Avis
© 800/331-1084 in continental U.S.
© 800/272-5871 in Canada
www.avis.com

Budget
© 800/527-0700
www.budget.com

Dollar
© 800/800-4000
www.dollar.com

Virgin Atlantic Airways
© 800/862-8621 in continental U.S.
© 0870/380-2007 in Britain
www.virgin-atlantic.com

Hertz
© 800/654-3001 in continental U.S.
© 800/263-0600 in Canada
www.hertz.com

Kemwel Holiday Auto (KHA)
© 800/678-0678
www.kemwel.com

National
© 800/227-7368
www.nationalcar.com

Payless
© 800/PAYLESS (729-5377)
www.paylesscarrental.com

Thrifty
© 800/367-2277
www.thrifty.com

Index

FROMMER'S® COMPLETE TRAVEL GUIDES

Alaska
Alaska Cruises & Ports of Call
American Southwest
Amsterdam
Argentina & Chile
Arizona
Atlanta
Australia
Austria
Bahamas
Barcelona
Beijing
Belgium, Holland & Luxembourg
Bermuda
Boston
Brazil
British Columbia & the Canadian
  Rockies
Brussels & Bruges
Budapest & the Best of Hungary
Calgary
California
Canada
Cancún, Cozumel & the Yucatán
Cape Cod, Nantucket & Martha's
  Vineyard
Caribbean
Caribbean Ports of Call
Carolinas & Georgia
Chicago
China
Colorado
Costa Rica
Cruises & Ports of Call
Cuba
Denmark
Denver, Boulder & Colorado Springs
Edinburgh & Glasgow
England
Europe
Europe by Rail
European Cruises & Ports of Call
Florence, Tuscany & Umbria

Florida
France
Germany
Great Britain
Greece
Greek Islands
Halifax
Hawaii
Hong Kong
Honolulu, Waikiki & Oahu
India
Ireland
Italy
Jamaica
Japan
Kauai
Las Vegas
London
Los Angeles
Madrid
Maine Coast
Maryland & Delaware
Maui
Mexico
Montana & Wyoming
Montréal & Québec City
Munich & the Bavarian Alps
Nashville & Memphis
New England
Newfoundland & Labrador
New Mexico
New Orleans
New York City
New York State
New Zealand
Northern Italy
Norway
Nova Scotia, New Brunswick &
  Prince Edward Island
Oregon
Ottawa
Paris
Peru

Philadelphia & the Amish Country
Portugal
Prague & the Best of the Czech
  Republic
Provence & the Riviera
Puerto Rico
Rome
San Antonio & Austin
San Diego
San Francisco
Santa Fe, Taos & Albuquerque
Scandinavia
Scotland
Seattle
Seville, Granada & the Best of
  Andalusia
Shanghai
Sicily
Singapore & Malaysia
South Africa
South America
South Florida
South Pacific
Southeast Asia
Spain
Sweden
Switzerland
Texas
Thailand
Tokyo
Toronto
Turkey
USA
Utah
Vancouver & Victoria
Vermont, New Hampshire & Maine
Vienna & the Danube Valley
Virgin Islands
Virginia
Walt Disney World® & Orlando
Washington, D.C.
Washington State

FROMMER'S® DOLLAR-A-DAY GUIDES

Australia from $50 a Day
California from $70 a Day
England from $75 a Day
Europe from $85 a Day
Florida from $70 a Day
Hawaii from $80 a Day

Ireland from $80 a Day
Italy from $70 a Day
London from $90 a Day
New York City from $90 a Day
Paris from $90 a Day
San Francisco from $70 a Day

Washington, D.C. from $80 a Day
Portable London from $90 a Day
Portable New York City from $90
  a Day
Portable Paris from $90 a Day

FROMMER'S® PORTABLE GUIDES

Acapulco, Ixtapa & Zihuatanejo
Amsterdam
Aruba
Australia's Great Barrier Reef
Bahamas
Berlin
Big Island of Hawaii
Boston
California Wine Country
Cancún
Cayman Islands
Charleston
Chicago
Disneyland®
Dominican Republic

Dublin
Florence
Frankfurt
Hong Kong
Las Vegas
Las Vegas for Non-Gamblers
London
Los Angeles
Los Cabos & Baja
Maui
Miami
Nantucket & Martha's Vineyard
New Orleans
New York City
Paris

Phoenix & Scottsdale
Portland
Puerto Rico
Puerto Vallarta, Manzanillo &
  Guadalajara
Rio de Janeiro
San Diego
San Francisco
Savannah
Vancouver Island
Venice
Virgin Islands
Washington, D.C.
Whistler

FROMMER'S® NATIONAL PARK GUIDES

Algonquin Provincial Park
Banff & Jasper
Family Vacations in the National
  Parks

Grand Canyon
National Parks of the American West
Rocky Mountain

Yellowstone & Grand Teton
Yosemite & Sequoia/Kings Canyon
Zion & Bryce Canyon

FROMMER'S® MEMORABLE WALKS

Chicago
London

New York
Paris

San Francisco

FROMMER'S® WITH KIDS GUIDES

Chicago
Hawaii
Las Vegas
New York City

Ottawa
San Francisco
Toronto

Vancouver
Walt Disney World® & Orlando
Washington, D.C.

SUZY GERSHMAN'S BORN TO SHOP GUIDES

Born to Shop: France
Born to Shop: Hong Kong, Shanghai
  & Beijing

Born to Shop: Italy
Born to Shop: London

Born to Shop: New York
Born to Shop: Paris

FROMMER'S® IRREVERENT GUIDES

Amsterdam
Boston
Chicago
Las Vegas
London

Los Angeles
Manhattan
New Orleans
Paris
Rome

San Francisco
Seattle & Portland
Vancouver
Walt Disney World®
Washington, D.C.

FROMMER'S® BEST-LOVED DRIVING TOURS

Austria
Britain
California
France

Germany
Ireland
Italy
New England

Northern Italy
Scotland
Spain
Tuscany & Umbria

THE UNOFFICIAL GUIDES®

Beyond Disney
California with Kids
Central Italy
Chicago
Cruises
Disneyland®
England
Florida
Florida with Kids
Inside Disney

Hawaii
Las Vegas
London
Maui
Mexico's Best Beach Resorts
Mini Las Vegas
Mini Mickey
New Orleans
New York City
Paris

San Francisco
Skiing & Snowboarding in the West
South Florida including Miami &
  the Keys
Walt Disney World®
Walt Disney World® for
  Grown-ups
Walt Disney World® with Kids
Washington, D.C.

SPECIAL-INTEREST TITLES

Athens Past & Present
Cities Ranked & Rated
Frommer's Best Day Trips from London
Frommer's Best RV & Tent Campgrounds
  in the U.S.A.
Frommer's Caribbean Hideaways
Frommer's China: The 50 Most Memorable Trips
Frommer's Exploring America by RV
Frommer's Gay & Lesbian Europe

Frommer's NYC Free & Dirt Cheap
Frommer's Road Atlas Europe
Frommer's Road Atlas France
Frommer's Road Atlas Ireland
Frommer's Wonderful Weekends from
  New York City
Retirement Places Rated
Rome Past & Present